Reading Narrative Fiction

Reading Narrative Fiction

SEYMOUR CHATMAN
University of California, Berkeley

With material contributed by
BRIAN ATTEBERY
Idaho State University

Macmillan Publishing Company
New York

Editor: Barbara A. Heinssen
Production Supervisor: Jane O'Neill
Production Manager: Sandra E. Moore
Text Designer: Marilyn Prudente
Cover Designer: Proof Positive
Cover Illustration: Pierre Bonnard, "The Window," 1925, Tate Gallery,
   London/Art Resource

This book was set in 10/12 Garamond Book by Digitype, Inc.
and was printed and bound by Book Press, Inc.
The cover was printed by New England Book Components, Inc.

Acknowledgments appear on pages 631–635, which constitute an extension of the
copyright page.

Macmillan Publishing Company
866 Third Avenue, New York, New York 10022

Macmillan Publishing Company is part of
the Maxwell Communication Group of Companies.

Maxwell Macmillan Canada, Inc.
1200 Eglinton Avenue East
Suite 200
Don Mills, Ontario M3C 3N1

Library of Congress Cataloging-in-Publication Data

Reading narrative fiction / [edited by] Seymour Chatman; with
   material contributed by Brian Attebery.
      p.   cm.
   Includes index.
   ISBN 0-02-322111-9
   1. Short stories.   2. Short story.   3. Narration (Rhetoric)
   I. Chatman, Seymour Benjamin, 1928–   . II. Attebery, Brian, 1951–
PN6120.2.R44   1993
808.3'1 — dc20   92-21747
                    CIP

Printing: 1   2   3   4   5   6   7   Year: 3   4   5   6   7   8   9

For Mariel

Preface

My anthology begins and ends by assuming that we read stories for pleasure: no responsible teacher wants to interfere with that pleasure. It is the pleasure of immersion, of being caught up in a fictional world, a web of events, characters, and settings. But an additional pleasure is that of understanding how authors create that world, weave that web. So I provide detailed explanations, derived from recent studies in narratology, about the important building blocks authors use to create their fictions. I begin by defining narrative, especially in comparison to other kinds of texts, such as description and argument. Later chapters describe, and in some cases redefine, basic notions such as plot, character, setting, theme, irony, narrator, and "point of view."

The sixty short stories I have chosen are worthy of inclusion on their literary merit alone, and some literature classes will elect to use this book without further concern for my technical input. But these stories also furnish a treasure trove of narrative strategies. They can be enjoyed in two stages: first, in their own right as engaging and, in some cases, moving entertainments, and second, as constructed works of art worth analyzing. Space restriction prevents me from including a novel (though Joseph Conrad's "The Secret Sharer" qualifies at least as a novella), but the insights to be acquired about narrative from these short fictions can easily be applied to novels as well.

Many of the terms used to name narrative features — such as "characterization" and "point of view" — are familiar to high school students. But in classroom discussions of actual stories they tend to be used vaguely or not at all. I hope that clearer and more exact definitions — and especially illustrations of how these features operate in short stories — will enable all students, whether in freshman composition courses, sophomore survey courses, or advanced literature courses, to read narratives more sensitively and with a new awareness of how they are constructed. (Terms for narrative features are listed alphabetically in the Glossary on pp. 625–629.)

Each of the nine chapters in the first part of the book discusses one aspect of fiction and offers short stories that employ that aspect in a particularly effective way. One or more of the short stories may be read before or after the discussion; ideally, they would be read *both* before and after. The Further Reading section provides many additional short stories which, aside from their intrinsic merits, serve as challenging targets for narrative analysis.

I have tried to pick short stories that are particularly relevant to our times. Uppermost in my mind was fiction's uncanny power to capture, often more accurately than news accounts, the actual social and psychological diversity of human lives. That overriding thought led me to a large number of short stories by women and by people of color. Further, since English is the native language of many nations and a second language for many other people throughout the world, I have included stories from Ireland, Canada, the Caribbean, Africa, India, and Australia. The book also offers classic short stories, both in English and in translation from foreign languages, that illustrate (however modestly) the history of the genre. One consequence of this diversity was the need to limit the book to a single short story per author. But readers who would like more selections by a particular author will find ample book references in the biographical headnote preceding each selection. To simplify the task of understanding historical, geographical, and other details that American students might find unfamiliar, I have added explanatory footnotes.

Reading short stories and analyzing their structure is a crucial educational exercise. Happily, unlike many exercises, it is pleasurable in itself. However hard-headed our society may be, rare is the individual who dislikes voyages into the worlds of fiction. Even students who haven't read much enjoy watching stories unfold on television and at the movies. They are aware of and are more interested in narrative forms than teachers sometimes think. This anthology tries to show how given narrative techniques — say, "flashback" or "point of view" — work in any narrative medium whatsoever and, consequently, how a student who already understands a bit about their workings in film and television can easily transfer this competence to literature. The benefits of an improved ability to read narrative fiction extend far beyond the simple pleasure of make-believe. These benefits are discussed in the Introduction. The Introduction also outlines the kind of discussion to be found in the following nine chapters and sketches in brief how the various parts of a narrative fit together.

I have designed my book to stimulate oral and written discussion of these short stories. In the first section, each story is followed by a group of questions about its content and form, and each chapter ends with suggestions for writing about the chapter topic and the stories that illustrate it. An appendix entitled "How to Write about Fiction" (pp. 603–624) offers explicit instruction — even concrete "do's" and "don'ts" — for composing critical papers. A sample student journal entry as well as two drafts of a student essay, with instructional commentary, are also provided. I recommend that students read this appendix carefully before submitting their first written exercises.

Though I have not included explicit instruction in writing fiction, the material in the nine chapters and the sixty short stories should inspire those who want to try their hand at the art. If you feel so inclined, go for it; and don't worry too much about being original. Many famous authors have started out by imitating their predecessors. Fitting your own experience to the form and style of a Nadine Gordimer or a William Faulkner short story would be a fascinating exercise and might prove very interesting to read.

I am much indebted to friends who helped with this book. First and foremost is Professor Brian Attebery of Idaho State University. His advice on the selection of short stories, and his work on the appendix and on the questions and suggestions for writing have added incalculably to whatever merits this book might possess. For devoted bibliographical and other help I thank Rebecca Kidd and Kirsten Anderson. I am very grateful to Barbara Heinssen of Macmillan for her steady faith in and support of this project, and to Jane O'Neill and Kathy Pruno for detailed editorial assistance. To my students of the past two years, at Berkeley and at the University of Melbourne, I express my gratitude for patiently reading the text and suggesting ways to improve it. To Cindy Tobisman in particular, a student whose writing appears in the appendix, a hearty thank you. I am also grateful to the following colleagues who read and evaluated early versions of the manuscript: Mary Louise Buley-Meissner, University of Wisconsin-Milwaukee; Donesse Champeau, SUNY at Stony Brook; Paula R. Feldman, University of South Carolina; Bernard L. Kaplan, The University of Delaware; Mary Pinkerton, University of Wisconsin, Whitewater; Paul Wood, Villanova University; and Michael G. Yetman, Purdue University.

Contents

How to Write about Fiction

Glossary

Index

Reading Narrative Fiction

Introduction:
The Pleasures of
Reading Fiction

Have you ever gotten so absorbed in a book or a movie that you lost all sense of what time it was or where you were? Did you have the sensation, even hours later, that you were still in the story, that your room or the theater lobby was less real than the fictional world you had just experienced? How is it that we get so carried away by mere marks on paper or shadows projected on a screen? Where do novels, short stories, and films get their mesmerizing power?

Not everyone enjoys the experience of being rapt, virtually "carried off" by a fiction. But millions do, for why else would they spend so many hours at the movies, watching television, or curled up with a book? What kind of pleasure is it, exactly, that we get from fiction? Pleasure is a highly personal matter, and you probably have your own answer to that question. Fiction offers the pleasure of following gripping actions for their own sake; of encountering unusual characters; of experiencing worlds different from the one we ordinarily inhabit, yet worlds that oddly illuminate our own; of feeling the satisfaction of *closure*, the sense that everything somehow gets resolved, that events and characters, settings and themes all hang together. This sense of closure is important because ordinary life seems so inconclusive or downright messy in comparison. Whether the fiction offers clear-cut heroines and villains or only nondescript characters, whether it ends on a happy or a tragic note or only inconclusively, its appeal remains strong.

Regardless of the source of pleasure, one thing is clear: The ability to understand and to tell stories seems universal. Though I am not an anthropologist, I find it difficult to conceive of a culture without stories. Indeed, most aboriginal cultures have splendidly elaborate mythologies — anthologies of sacred stories — to explain their origin and history. We effortlessly acquire narrative ability at an early age. As very young children, even before we learn to read, we know how to follow plot and character, how to draw inferences from what the story *says* to what it *means*. Watch children as young as three in front of a television set. They understand the stories projected by animated cartoons or puppets. They know who the characters are, what they are like, what they are doing, what it all adds up to. From prior experience with the antics of Roadrunner or Bugs Bunny, they can even predict what these characters might

1

do next. Or given a picture book without words, they can "tell" you the story. They know how to fill in narrative gaps. Show them a drawing of a girl in the kitchen on page 1 and another of her at the amusement park on page 2, and they can tell you that "somewhere in between" she got from her home to the park. They can even draw you a picture of how she did it—for example, sitting next to her father in the car. This capacity to "fill in" is crucial to understanding narratives, and we have had it most of our lives. It is a sophisticated skill for a small child, isn't it? And she learns it on her own, in the same unself-conscious way that she learns to walk and to talk.

As we grow older, we acquire more complex narrative skills. We come to understand such sophisticated plot arrangements as flashbacks and flashforwards (narrative devices that have existed since Homer). We learn to track the separate strands of compound plots. Whatever we may think of soap operas, we effortlessly follow their elaborate intertwinings (figuring out, for example, that though Claude says he loves Janine, he is secretly attracted to Dana, but can't admit it because she's involved with his best friend Tim, who, of course, can hardly reciprocate because he is in jail on a murder charge, although *we* know that he spent the fatal weekend in New York with Gayle, who . . . etc.). We also learn how to understand the behavior of characters more complex than Bugs Bunny.

Our narrative skills are considerable, even if we are not conscious of how or when we acquired them. We bring these skills to bear on stories in any medium—film, television, literature, opera, comic strips, puppet shows, stage plays. When laser-projected holographic movies arrive on the scene, they will surely tell stories, and as we make our way through the spaces that they eerily construct, we shall use these same narrative skills to understand the story that "surrounds" us.

In a very real sense, then, college fiction anthologies, like this one, don't need to teach you what you already know how to do very well. Indeed, many anthologies simply assume your narrative competence and just reprint short stories without further ado. Others, like mine, try to name, define, and explain narrative techniques. There are a number of reasons for studying them. For one thing, they constitute an interesting subject in their own right. Just as someone on the swimming team—already an expert at moving arms and legs in the water—might take a course in physiology to learn the names of the muscles that she uses so well, a student who enjoys reading fiction might study how narrative techniques shape his understanding and therefore his narrative pleasure. For another thing, a knowledge of narrative technique helps one appreciate how authors achieve their effects, for example, the illusion of the passage of time, or the experience of a character's inner life, or the sense that the story means more than first meets the eye. Many students (and moviegoers in general) are interested in learning the technical names by which film illusions are created, such as the editing "dissolve," the "voice-over," the "point-of-view" shot, or "mood music." As I shall try to demonstrate in the following chapters, the techniques of literary narrative are no less interesting and ingenious than those of the cinema.

Even an elementary understanding of narrative technique helps sharpen one's ability to read fictions. It boosts one's confidence about tackling those that are difficult. That at least has been my experience. Stories that seemed totally opaque to me grew clearer as I thought about what it was in their forms that was blocking my comprehension. Was it the language? Was it the arrangement of events in the plot? Was it the motivation of the characters? Was it the identity of the speaker at a given moment (the narrator? a character?)? Was it the theme of the whole story? Learning something about narrative technique may not answer such questions, but it may help you, as it helped me, to identify the source of the difficulty, even if only roughly. Then you can at least focus your energies in the right direction. I have always found it pleasurable—and ego-boosting—to learn to read fictions that are difficult but highly prized by our own or other cultures. My pleasure has increased with a growing appreciation of the *craft* that makes some fictions the magical things they are.

Some people don't want to think about that craft. They say that excessive analysis—learning the author's or filmmaker's "secrets"—spoils the illusion and hence the pleasure of a novel, film, or stage play. But is that really true? Do we really give up the pleasure of driving a sports car by learning how it's assembled? Speaking for myself, I find that analysis only increases my pleasure in the fiction. I look at a good short story the way I look at a well-played football game. True, part of the pleasure is that I have seen my team win, but another is watching *how* they win—the dexterity of the field-goal kicker or the power and drive of the fullback as he plows into the line. As enjoyable as it is to discover the outcome of a story, it is no less pleasant, even exciting, to consider how the author made it all happen, how she made us *care* about those characters and events and themes.

Why do I lump literary fictions together with television dramas and movies? Because there are narrative affinities among novels and stage plays, puppet and mime shows, comic strips, ballets, even some circus acts. Of course, the media differ profoundly. It's no news that books rely solely on print, while movies and television dramas use visual images and sound tracks, But there are important similarities. For example, regardless of the medium, something must *happen* in a narrative fiction—there must be a sequence of events. Further, these events must be performed and experienced by the personages we call characters. And they must happen in certain settings. Whether through printed words, photographed images, or recorded sounds, we experience certain basic narrative elements—plot, character, setting, and theme. Deciding whether the movie version is better or worse than the novel is amusing but usually unprofitable, a bit like ranking apples and oranges. But of one thing we can be sure: Though a novel obviously differs in important ways from a television drama or a movie, they are all narratives. Plots, characters, and settings are common to all, and clearly we use the same narrative skills in reading, watching, and listening to them.

Educational critics sometimes say that lazy viewers prefer movies and television dramas to literature because the images directly show meanings, so viewers need not bother with words. I disagree: We don't have to downgrade movies to appreciate the glories of literature. For one thing, it is obviously untrue that movies ignore language. On the contrary, dialogue is of vital importance in the visual media. (Even silent films needed subtitles.) As to difficulty, the fast-paced or intricate dialogue of some films may actually be harder to follow than the dialogue in a book. A book at least allows for slow reading and rereading, but (unless we watch them on videotape) movies or stage plays give us only one shot at comprehension. Nor does the verbal medium per se make literary narratives hard to comprehend. Young children understand what is read to them, even from books that contain no pictures.

It is true that most movies and television plays are geared to huge mass markets. Because production is so expensive, studios want to ensure that their films will be easily understood by everyone. They tend to simplify their products, to make them overly explicit. We sometimes feel that our intelligence is being insulted. But intellectually challenging movies and television plays do get made. Some of them entail as much craft and ingenuity as go into good short stories and novels. Each medium has created its own classics, and there is no need to deprecate one at the expense of the other. There is no narratively superior medium; we may prefer one medium over the others, but narrative structure underlies them all, and with it, narrative pleasure. This book is about the pleasure of reading short stories, but I would never argue that words on the printed page are intrinsically superior to photographed images and recorded sounds. Reading, in and of itself, it is not a more virtuous activity than watching a movie. It all depends on what you read or watch.

Still, some say that films and television dramas are crowding literature out of the marketplace. If that ultimately happens, it will be a terrible shame, for literary narrative furnishes several unique pleasures. For example, it permits you to create your own visual image of a character or action. If you read *Wuthering Heights* before seeing the movie version, or "Heart of Darkness" before seeing *Apocalypse Now*, you may picture Heathcliff or Kurtz quite differently from the characters played by Laurence Olivier or Marlon Brando.

Another and even more important source of literary pleasure is that of experiencing the inner lives of characters. Because films stick closely to the *appearance* of things, filmmakers usually don't convey all of a characters' thoughts and feelings in words. We may guess what they are thinking in *general* by drawing inferences from their dialogue, facial expressions, gestures, and bodily movements, but we don't come to know these thoughts as exactly as we know the thoughts of characters in novels and short stories. We don't know them *explicitly*, in the precise language that literature can employ. Thoughts can be verbalized on the film or video sound track by such special effects as voice-over, but modern filmmakers seem to find such techniques artificial.[1] They prefer to have actors convey their own feelings through their

---

[1] In earlier periods or in other national cinemas (like the French), voice-over representations of characters' thoughts have been more common. And the pendulum of fashion may swing back for American films as well. Films such as Woody Allen's *Annie Hall* certainly point in that direction.

faces, bodies, and speech. If they want the audience to know precisely what a character is thinking, they tend to put the thought into dialogue — but in that case the thought is no longer hidden or private.

For several years I have taught a course called "Novel Into Film," which attracts more film than literature buffs. Many students come primarily to watch the films, but I am struck each semester by the number who tell me what a revelation the novel was, how it enabled them to "live inside the skins" of characters in ways that the film didn't permit. When we watch a movie adapted from a great novel, such as Charles Dickens's *Great Expectations* or Alice Walker's *The Color Purple*, we may "identify" with one or another character, but we don't have the sense the novel gives us of literally occupying his or her mind. No matter how good a film or television actor may be, he or she cannot communicate, through speech and movements alone, the character's precise thoughts, thoughts that the novel may simply state in so many words. Print remains the more inner-directed medium. At the movies, we remain spectators, but short stories and novels give us deep access to the inner lives of the characters. Even "camera-eye" short stories, such as Ernest Hemingway's "The Killers," which narrate only the externals of action and appearance, allow us, indeed, encourage us, to infer what the characters are thinking and feeling. We have a harder time doing that when we watch a movie. The action happens too quickly, perhaps; the events come at us so rapidly that we have no time to speculate about what is going through the characters' minds. Even if we have a sense of what they must be thinking, that sense can only be hazy, not exact, as in a literary fiction.

I have spent so much time discussing films and television dramas because they are literature's chief competitors for the leisure time we allot to the consumption of fiction. If you have already read a lot of fiction, you don't need to be persuaded of its pleasures. However, if reading fiction has not been your favorite activity, you might look at it from the perspective I am suggesting.

There are other reasons for reading fiction in our electronic age, but let me mention only one. That is the painless way in which it increases one's general literacy. Nobody needs to tell you that an important goal of education is improving the quality and scope of your reading. We hear today a general call for "cultural literacy." Students, it is proclaimed, should seek out a broader education. They should not focus too exclusively on their future professions. In particular, they should learn something about the basic documents of our multicultural society. Cultural literacy will not only improve their chances in the economic sphere, but also enhance the quality of their leisure hours.

This argument seems to me obvious, though worth repeating. However, I hasten to add that the study of literature entails no direct and immediate payoff of the sort offered by a course in, say, accounting. Few jobs depend on an applicant's knowledge of Dickens or Faulkner (unless, of course, the job is teaching literature), but there are more subtle spinoffs. It isn't too farfetched to believe that the more you read, the more you improve your command of the language, and that of two interviewees, an employer will pick the more articulate and better-read one. For all the number-crunching that goes on these days, it is still those who listen and communicate well who are prized and rewarded by our society. I am not saying that accomplished speaking and writing necessarily derive from reading a lot of literature. But clearly *any* reading will help improve one's ability to communicate, and literature provides an especially enjoyable kind of reading. More particularly, the skill of analyzing literary texts is quite like the analytical skills that many professions require. As Professor Mary Louise Buley-Meissner of the University of Wisconsin-Milwaukee has put it: "Learning to change perspectives, to recognize the interrelationships of people and things in complex scenarios, to go beyond summarizing and hypothesizing, to interpret and to draw inferences and even speculations from one's interpretations—these skills acquired from reading literature connect directly with professional training and success."

My task, however, is not to promote literature as a means to a high-paying job. Rather, I am content to echo the argument that literature makes people wiser and richer—not monetarily, but in ways that are no less real. Reading fiction is one of the best—and certainly one of the most enjoyable—routes to an understanding of the astonishing variety of people and events in our world (not to mention other conceivable worlds). Among the stories in this collection, you'll share the meditation of a conservative old man watching his beloved Mississippi wetlands retreat before the relentless "progress" of civilization. You'll occupy the mind of a crazed murderer who can't make the heart of his victim stop pounding. You'll learn something about a mother's ambivalence when told that her troubled daughter may have a future as an entertainer. You'll feel what it is like to go back to elementary school in your thirties because of a glitch in the system. Hopefully these short stories will whet you appetite for other rich experiences awaiting you in the library of fiction.

A wise critic once called literature "equipment for living." Certainly, novels and short stories provide an excellent (and blissfully safe) way to experience life-styles that are radically different from our own. If the English countryside of the eighteenth century interests you, read Henry Fielding's *Tom Jones*. If you want to know about life at sea in the age of the great sailing ships, you can't find better introductions than the fiction of Herman Melville or Joseph Conrad. If you are curious about what it is like to be a compulsive gambler, no psychiatric treatise can match Dostoevsky's novel *The Gambler*. (Indeed, Sigmund Freud was so convinced of the power of great fiction to shed light on the human psyche that he peppered his books with citations from novels.)

Can you think of anything more exciting than trading your own identity—for a little while, of course, and with no danger of losing it—for someone else's? Or imaginatively journeying through worlds remote from the safe and familiar? Reading narrative fiction is a delightful way to have such experiences.

1 What Is a Narrative? Some Basic Terms

To understand how narratives work we need some terminology. Literary terms are numerous and sometimes used in vague and even contradictory senses. I will try to keep mine to a minimum and to define them clearly. Not everyone will agree about their utility, but at least it will be clear what I mean by them. Your instructor may prefer other terms and different ways of explaining a given narrative phenomenon.

Narrative is a kind of *text*, so that is a term we must consider first. Not everything in print is a text. Telephone books and stock market quotations, for example, are not texts but just lists. *Text* comes from a Latin word meaning "to construct" or "to weave." Authors not only weave words into the "cloth" of sentences and paragraphs, but also tailor that cloth into unities of different kinds. For our purposes, three kinds of text, or text-types, are distinguishable — narrative, argument, and description. Though the main subject of this book is narrative, it is useful to learn a bit about argument and description as well. For one thing, knowing about these other text-types can help us better understand narratives. For another, short stories and novels often contain descriptive and argumentative passages that help develop the narrative. In other words, argument and description often serve narrative's ends. The reverse is also possible: A lawyer may *argue* her client's innocence by telling the story of what he really was doing on the night of the murder. Or a travel writer may partially *describe* a certain place by giving its history.

The Text-Types

Let's start with brief definitions of argument and description, the better to see how narrative differs from them. An *argument* presents a case of some kind, urging this or that action or state of mind. A newspaper editorial is a typical argument: It may persuade readers, for example, to vote for a candidate, or to write to their senator in support of a bill. Advertisements are also arguments; even if they seem to be nothing but descriptions of the products, they imply that the reader should rush out and buy that product.

A *description* is a kind of text that renders the properties of things—typically, though not necessarily, objects visible to or imaginable by the senses.

A *narrative*, on the other hand, tells a story. In other words, it presents a unified sequence of events that add up to something, a *plot* with some kind of "point" (I'll define "point" in a moment). The question that narrative asks and answers is not argument's "Why should I do X?" or description's "What is X like?" but rather "What happened?" In doing so, narrative introduces a second dimension of time beyond that employed by the other text-types. Of course, *every* text, regardless of its type, proceeds through a sequence of sentences. Such a sequence must be read in real time, taking up so many minutes or hours of the reader's attention. In other words, the very act of reading has a certain chronology and time span. Narrative, however, adds a second chronology, namely, that of the events that constitute the story told. So we must distinguish a narrative's "outer" time—the time it takes to read the events of the story—from its "inner" time, the time it takes the fictional events inside the world of the story to transpire. These are not commensurate: It may take only a moment of outer reading time to grasp a century of inner story time (as in the sentence "A century passed").

Traditional narratives also connect plot events by *causation*; that is, event Y not only follows event X but is also caused by event X. (In Aesop's fable, the tortoise gets to the finish line not only *before* the hare but *because* the hare naps on the way.) Sometimes it takes a while to grasp a plot's causal structure because the connection between event X and event Y is not clear. Events may succeed each other in seemingly unconnected ways. Their connection may be purposely concealed for reasons of mystery, suspense, or surprise. Detective stories, for example, often confront us with a bewildering variety of apparently unconnected events to heighten the sense of the puzzle facing the detective. Only when the mystery is unraveled does the causal connection among the disparate events become clear. Another reason for an apparently random series of events may be to illustrate a character. Reading Joyce Carol Oates's "Four Summers" (pp. 43–56), we come to understand that the seemingly random events experienced by Sissie reflect a heroine who lives an aimless and confused existence.

To illustrate our discussion, here is a very short story.

❖ ALICE WALKER[1]
The Flowers

It seemed to Myop as she skipped lightly from hen house to pigpen to smokehouse that the days had never been as beautiful as these. The air held a keenness that made her nose twitch. The harvesting of the corn and cotton, peanuts and squash, made each day a golden surprise that caused excited little tremors to run up her jaws.

Myop carried a short, knobby stick. She struck out at random at chickens she liked, and worked out the beat of a song on the fence around the pigpen. She felt light and good in the warm sun. She was ten, and nothing existed for her but her song, the stick clutched in her dark brown hand, and the tat-de-ta-ta-ta of accompaniment.

Turning her back on the rusty boards of her family's sharecropper cabin, Myop walked along the fence till it ran into the stream made by the spring. Around the spring, where the family got drinking water, silver ferns and wildflowers grew. Along the shallow banks pigs rooted. Myop watched the tiny white bubbles disrupt the thin black scale of soil and the water that silently rose and slid away down the stream.

She had explored the woods behind the house many times. Often, in late autumn, her mother took her to gather nuts among the fallen leaves. Today she made her own path, bounding this way and that way, vaguely keeping an eye out for snakes. She found, in addition to various common but pretty ferns and leaves, an armful of strange blue flowers with velvety ridges and a sweetsuds bush full of the brown, fragrant buds.

By twelve o'clock, her arms laden with sprigs of her findings, she was a mile or more from home. She had often been as far before, but the strangeness of the land made it not as pleasant as her usual haunts. It seemed gloomy in the little cove in which she found herself. The air was damp, the silence close and deep.

Myop began to circle back to the house, back to the peacefulness of the morning. It was then she stepped smack into his eyes. Her heel became lodged in the broken ridge between brow and nose, and she reached down quickly, unafraid, to free herself. It was only when she saw his naked grin that she gave a little yelp of surprise.

He had been a tall man. From feet to neck covered a long space. His head lay

[1]Alice Walker (1944–) was born in Eatonton, Georgia, the eighth daughter of a family of sharecroppers. She attended Spelman College in Atlanta and then went to Sarah Lawrence College in New York. She became an instructor at Jackson State University in Mississippi in 1968, during the height of the civil rights movement, in which she was an active participant, registering voters and working in the Head Start program. She has since taught at Tougaloo College, Wellesley College, the University of Massachusetts at Boston, the University of California at Berkeley, and Brandeis University. Hers is a most authoritative voice on the problems faced by black women in our society. Her novels include *The Third Life of Grange Copeland* (1970), *Meridian* (1976), *The Color Purple* (1982, which won the Pulitzer Prize for Literature and was made into a movie), and *The Temple of My Familiar* (1989). Her stories have been collected in *In Love and Trouble: Stories of Black Women* (1973, which includes "The Flowers") and *You Can't Keep a Good Woman Down* (1981). She has also published volumes of poems, essays, and a children's biography of the great black writer Langston Hughes and edited an anthology of the writings of Zora Neale Hurston.

beside him. When she pushed back the leaves and layers of earth and debris Myop saw that he'd had large white teeth, all of them cracked or broken, long fingers, and very big bones. All his clothes had rotted away except some threads of blue denim from his overalls. The buckles of the overalls had turned green.

Myop gazed around the spot with interest. Very near where she'd stepped into the head was a wild pink rose. As she picked it to add to her bundle she noticed a raised mound, a ring, around the rose's root. It was the rotted remains of a noose, a bit of shredding plowline, now blending benignly into the soil. Around an overhanging limb of a great spreading oak clung another piece. Frayed, rotted, bleached, and frazzled — barely there — but spinning restlessly in the breeze. Myop laid down her flowers.

And the summer was over.

(1973)

The story consists of these events: (1) Myop walks about her family's land, playing with her stick — touching chickens, tapping along the fence. (2) She goes into the woods to gather flowers, ending up a mile away in a gloomy little cove. (3) She steps on the skull of a decomposed male corpse. (4) She picks a rose nearby, only to find that it is growing out of the remains of a noose; another piece of the rope hangs from an oak branch above. (5) She puts down her flowers. (6) "And the summer was over."

Notice how description "serves" the cause of narration in "The Flowers." The sentence "Myop walked along the fence" clearly represents an action, hence a plot event; but the sentence "She was ten" is, in itself, purely descriptive. Though the narrative has whetted our desire to learn what happens next, we accept this brief descriptive delay, to understand better who the character is and why she does what she is doing. In nineteenth-century novels, descriptions could delay the action for many pages, and some modern readers become impatient and skip to the next set of quotation marks. By doing so, they may well be missing not only passages of beautiful writing, but also information crucial to an understanding of events and characters, not to mention the themes that emerge from the whole.

Description as such is not limited to expressly descriptive sentences. It may be included in action sentences. At the beginning of "The Flowers," Myop has thoughts and impressions. In other words, just as tapping her stick is a plot event, so are finding the air keen, feeling little tremors running up her jaws, and so on. But these events also entail description: The air is keen, each day is a golden surprise, her stick is short and knobby, the sun is warm, the boards of her family's cabin are rusty, and so on. In its grammatical form, "Along the shallow banks pigs rooted" is an action, but the pigs' rooting is not an essential plot event (as is Myop's discovery of the skeleton). Instead, their actions contribute to a particular scene of farm life, of woods, and of stream. So even though presented as an explicit action, the pigs' rooting is descriptive.

Many short stories and novels begin with explicit descriptions to establish characters and places. Frank O'Connor's "The Drunkard" (pp. 539–

546) begins: "Mr. Dooley was a commercial traveller . . ." "socially he was miles ahead of us," "Mr. Dooley was an intellectual," and so on. These are bits of description so far, not of narration. They tell us only what Mr. Dooley was like, not yet what he has done that is relevant to the plot. Similarly, Carson McCullers's "A Tree A Rock A Cloud" (pp. 27–32) begins not with narration, but with a description of the setting: "It was raining that morning, and still very dark." The weather is described; the first action has not yet occurred. Though short stores concern qualities of characters and settings, their first task, if they are to be narrative at all, is to represent events, actions. When we read "Mr. Dooley was a commercial traveller," we understand that the first event of the story is yet to come.

Getting the Point

A narrative does not merely consist of a sequence of events; these events add up to some *point*. This is an important term that requires some consideration. We all know what we mean when we say "I get the point" or "I don't get the point." We get the point of Alice Walker's "The Flowers" when we understand that the corpse is the remains of a black man who has been lynched by white vigilantes. Further, we understand that the point is not so much the lynching as Myop's reaction to it. After all, the title of the story is "The Flowers," not "The Mystery of the Corpse." We would be missing the point if we didn't understand that Myop's placing her flowers next to the corpse is a symbolic act, much like placing a wreath on a grave at a funeral. And we would also be missing the point if we assumed that the narrator was *only* describing the weather in the last sentence — "And the summer was over." Clearly, that sentence symbolically implies Myop's loss of childish innocence.

Getting or missing the point of a narrative are common experiences for everyone, but the meaning of *point* is easier to illustrate than to define. Perhaps the most we can say is that the point is something like the consequence of the story, the reason that it gets told. If a story doesn't seem to have a point, we are likely to ask "So what?" That question suggests that though we find the events plausibly connected in time-sequence and even causality, they don't add up to anything for us. Point is not the same thing as *theme*, a concept to be discussed at length in chapter 8. For now, the two can be distinguished as follows: Point applies only to the fiction, whereas theme goes beyond the fiction, implying something about the real world. We can talk about a fiction's point only with respect to the imaginary world in which the story occurs, but a discussion of theme takes us beyond the characters and the events out to our own world.

How do we know when we've got the point? It's not easy to say, but we can often distinguish between statements that do and do not express the point. Imagine several possible answers to the question "What's the point of 'The Flowers'?"

1. Myop, a black child in the rural South, lives an unfortunately impoverished life.
2. Myop has more freedom and therefore is more sensitive to nature than are city children.
3. The institution of racial lynching is dreadful.
4. Myop comes of age by finding out how grim life can be for her people.

You will doubtless agree that statements 1 and 2 miss the point. They are true, in some sense, but they don't address the overall intention of the short story. They are not what the story adds up to. They don't account for the whole second part of the story, in which Myop discovers and reacts to the body. The third statement seems closer to the point, but also doesn't quite hit it. Naturally we are shocked and horrified by Myop's discovery, and the meaning of that discovery is essential to her reaction. However, it is her reaction, not the lynching alone, that is the point. The main thrust of the story, we feel, is not a commentary on the practice of lynching: The last two sentences make it more than that. (Final sentences conventionally enjoy a privileged place in fictions.) Rather, the story seems pointed toward the impact on Myop of her discovery. That impact is not spelled out in so many words: The story nowhere baldly states, "Myop realized that it had been a lynching, that no one had mourned the lynched man, that she should do so by placing her flowers next to his body, and that, in doing so, her days of innocent childhood would come to an end." Yet to me that's the point of the story. How do I know? Well, honestly speaking, I can't say that I *do* "know"—with the same certitude that I know that two plus two equals four. Getting the point is never as certain as solving a mathematical problem. I would prefer to say that statement 4 represents my best inference. I prefer that inference to the first three because it includes and explains more than they do and because it makes the story richer and more interesting than they do.

One should be modest about arguing the point of a fiction. For there may well be more than one point, or the point may be complex and manifold. Even if we can think of only one possibility, we should be open to alternative interpretations that are more comprehensive or insightful. (Most teachers can honestly say that, at one time or another, they have changed their minds about a story's point after discussing it with a class.) *Point* is very much determined by context, and, no matter how broadly educated we are, we may fail to reconstruct a comprehensive context. Or the context may be intrinsically unstable, and that instability may be central to the story's intention. Even very good readers are humble about the ever-present possibility of missing the point, whether because they lack an explanatory context or select an erroneous one; or, to put it more positively, they are open to developing new interpretations on the basis of what other readers bring to their attention. In chapter 8 we shall return to the question of point and its relation to broader notions like theme and ideology.

The Meanings of "Fiction"

All the examples we have looked at so far are taken from fictional short stories. We have been using *fiction* in one of its two common senses, namely, as a synonym for "nonfactual." Much of literature is fictional in this sense: Not only are novels and short stories nonfactual but so are plays and poems. However, to say that is *not* to say that fictions are lies. The difference is in the *intention* of the text. A liar *intends* to deceive you by telling you something that he knows to be false and does so to profit in some way from keeping you from the truth. The liar claims to be telling the truth; but a fiction cannot deceive you because it doesn't *claim* to be factual. Because Alice Walker does not claim that a girl named Myop actually existed, she cannot be accused of misrepresenting the facts. (To ensure the fictionality of their works, authors sometimes insert "A Novel" under the title on the title page or even a legalistic disclaimer that any resemblance of their characters to real persons is purely coincidental.) Still, despite their fictionality, great novels and short stories communicate profound truths about life.

We must distinguish the nonfactual sense of fiction from another, narrower sense of the term. In this second sense—a sense that I use extensively in this book—fiction is short for *narrative* fiction. Fiction here is a cover term for all nonfactual narratives, and we can speak of a short story or novel as being *a* fiction. Thus, Alice Walker's "The Flowers" is *a* fiction, as is Mark Twain's *Tom Sawyer*. The library has a section called "Fiction," where you find only novels and short stories.

Fictionality is by no means limited to narrative. Arguments and descriptions may also be fictional. A famous fictional argument is Jonathan Swift's "A Modest Proposal." Swift wrote the essay ironically, assuming the voice of an essayist who seriously proposes to solve the question of Irish overpopulation by butchering Irish babies and selling them as a new and delicate kind of meat.

In "The Flowers" we saw how descriptive elements supported the purposes of the narrative fiction. By contrast, let us turn to Kate Chopin's "Two Portraits" in which narrative subserves the other text-types.

❖ KATE CHOPIN[2]
Two Portraits

I The Wanton

Alberta having looked not very long into life, had not looked very far. She put out her hands to touch things that pleased her and her lips to kiss them. Her eyes were deep brown wells that were drinking, drinking impressions and treasuring them in her soul. They were mysterious eyes and love looked out of them.

Alberta was very fond of her mama who was really not her mama; and the beatings which alternated with the most amiable and generous indulgence, were soon forgotten by the little one, always hoping that there would never be another, as she dried her eyes.

She liked the ladies who petted her and praised her beauty, and the artists who painted it naked, and the student who held her upon his knee and fondled and kissed her while he taught her to read and spell.

There was a cruel beating about that one day, when her mama happened to be in the mood to think her too old for fondling. And the student had called her mama some very vile names in his wrath, and had asked the woman what else she expected.

There was nothing very fixed or stable about her expectations—whatever they were—as she had forgotten them the following day, and Alberta, consoled with a fantastic bracelet for her plump little arm and a shower of bonbons, installed herself again upon the student's knee. She liked nothing better, and in time was willing to take the beating if she might hold his attentions and her place in his affections and upon his knee.

Alberta cried very bitterly when he went away. The people about her seemed to be always coming and going. She had hardly the time to fix her affections upon the men and the women who came into her life before they were gone again.

Her mama died one day—very suddenly; a self-inflicted death, she heard the people say. Alberta grieved sorely, for she forgot the beatings and remembered only the outbursts of a torrid affection. But she really did not belong anywhere then, nor to anybody. And when a lady and gentleman took her to live with them, she went willingly as she would have gone anywhere, with any one. With them she met with more kindness and indulgence than she had ever known before in her life.

---

[2]Kate Chopin (1851–1904) was born Katherine O'Flaherty in St. Louis. Her mother was a French Creole from Louisiana. She was educated as a Catholic. She married Oscar Chopin, a cotton broker from New Orleans. The couple first lived in that city and then moved to rural Louisiana. When her husband died suddenly in 1883, Chopin returned with her six children to St. Louis. She began to publish stories about Creoles in well-known magazines such as the *Atlantic Monthly*. She published the novel *At Fault* in 1890 and her most famous novel, *The Awakening*, in 1899. *The Awakening* was probably the first novel by an American woman to address frankly the question of a woman's right to independence and her own sexuality. Chopin's short stories were collected in *Bayou Folk* (1894) and *A Night in Acadie* (1897), and more recently in a volume called *A Vocation and A Voice: Stories* (1991).

There were no more beatings; Alberta's body was too beautiful to be beaten — it was made for love. She knew that herself; she had heard it since she had heard anything. But now she heard many things and learned many more. She did not lack for instruction in the wiles — the ways of stirring a man's desire and holding it. Yet she did not need instruction — the secret was in her blood and looked out of her passionate, wanton eyes and showed in every motion of her seductive body.

At seventeen she was woman enough, so she had a lover. But as for that, there did not seem to be much difference. Except that she had gold now — plenty of it with which to make herself appear more beautiful, and enough to fling with both hands into the laps of those who came whining and begging to her.

Alberta is a most beautiful woman, and she takes great care of her body, for she knows that it brings her love to squander and gold to squander.

Some one has whispered in her ear:

"Be cautious, Alberta. Save, save your gold. The years are passing. The days are coming when youth slips away, when you will stretch out your hands for money and for love in vain. And what will be left for you but —"

Alberta shrunk in horror before the pictured depths of hideous degradation that would be left for her. But she consoles herself with the thought that such need never be — with death and oblivion always within her reach.

Alberta is capricious. She gives her love only when and where she chooses. One or two men have died because of her withholding it. There is a smooth-faced boy now who teases her with his resistance; for Alberta does not know shame or reserve.

One day he seems to half-relent and another time he plays indifference, and she frets and she fumes and rages.

But he had best have a care; for since Alberta has added much wine to her wantonness she is apt to be vixenish; and she carries a knife.

II The Nun

Alberta having looked not very long into life, had not looked very far. She put out her hands to touch things that pleased her, and her lips to kiss them. Her eyes were deep brown wells that were drinking, drinking impressions and treasuring them in her soul. They were mysterious eyes and love looked out of them.

It was a very holy woman who first took Alberta by the hand. The thought of God alone dwelt in her mind, and his name and none other was on her lips.

When she showed Alberta the creeping insects, the blades of grass, the flowers and trees; the rain-drops falling from the clouds; the sky and the stars and the men and women moving on the earth, she taught her that it was God who had created all; that God was great, was good, was the Supreme Love.

And when Alberta would have put out her hands and her lips to touch the great and all-loving God, it was then the holy woman taught her that it is not with the hands and lips and eyes that we reach God, but with the soul; that the soul must be made perfect and the flesh subdued. And what is the soul but the inward thought? And this the child was taught to keep spotless — pure, and fit as far as a human soul can be, to hold intercourse with the all-wise and all-seeing God.

Her existence became a prayer. Evil things approached her not. The inherited sin of the blood must have been washed away at the baptismal font; for all the things of this world that she encountered — the pleasures, the trials and even temptations, but turned her gaze within, through her soul up to the fountain of all love and every beatitude.

When Alberta had reached the age when with other women the languor of love creeps into the veins and dreams begin, at such a period an overpowering impulse toward the purely spiritual possessed itself of her. She could no longer abide the sights, the sounds, the accidental happenings of life surrounding her, that tended but to disturb her contemplation of the heavenly existence.

It was then she went into the convent — the white convent on the hill that overlooks the river; the big convent whose long, dim corridors echo with the soft tread of a multitude of holy women; whose atmosphere of chastity, poverty and obedience penetrates to the soul through benumbed senses.

But of all the holy women in the white convent, there is none so saintly as Alberta. Any one will tell you that who knows them. Even her pious guide and counsellor does not equal her in sanctity. Because Alberta is endowed with the powerful gift of a great love that lifts her above common mortals, close to the invisible throne. Her ears seem to hear sounds that reach no other ears; and what her eyes see, only God and herself know. When the others are plunged in meditation, Alberta is steeped in an oblivious ecstasy. She kneels before the Blessed Sacrament with stiffened, tireless limbs; with absorbing eyes that drink in the holy mystery till it is a mystery no longer, but a real flood of celestial love deluging her soul. She does not hear the sound of bells nor the soft stir of disbanding numbers. She must be touched upon the shoulder; roused, awakened.

Alberta does not know that she is beautiful. If you were to tell her so she would not blush and utter gentle protest and reproof as might the others. She would only smile, as though beauty were a thing that concerned her not. But she is beautiful, with the glow of a holy passion in her dark eyes. Her face is thin and white, but illumined from within by a light which seems not of this world.

She does not walk upright; she could not, overpowered by the Divine Presence and the realization of her nothingness. Her hands, slender and blue-veined, and her delicate fingers seem to have been fashioned by God to be clasped and uplifted in prayer.

It is said — not broadcast, it is only whispered — that Alberta sees visions. Oh, the beautiful visions! The first of them came to her when she was rapped in suffering, in quivering contemplation of the bleeding and agonizing Christ. Oh, the dear God! Who loved her beyond the power of man to describe, to conceive. The God-Man, the Man-God, suffering, bleeding, dying for her, Alberta, a worm upon the earth; dying that she might be saved from sin and transplanted among the heavenly delights. Oh, if she might die for him in return! But she could only abandon herself to his mercy and his love. "Into thy hands, Oh Lord! Into thy hands!"

She pressed her lips upon the bleeding wounds and the Divine Blood transfigured her. The Virgin Mary enfolded her in her mantle. She could not describe in words the ecstasy; that taste of the Divine love which only the souls of the transplanted could endure in its awful and complete intensity. She, Alberta, had received this sign of

Divine favor; this foretaste of heavenly bliss. For an hour she had swooned in rapture; she had lived in Christ. Oh, the beautiful visions!

The visions come often to Alberta now, refreshing and strengthening her soul; it is being talked about a little in whispers.

And it is said that certain afflicted persons have been helped by her prayers. And others having abounding faith, have been cured of bodily ailments by the touch of her beautiful hands.

(1895)

A portrait is, by definition, a kind of description. "Two Portraits" seems at first to be a narrative. Two different stories are told. The first is about a "wanton." This old-fashioned word (the text was written in 1895) has two possible meanings: (1) "a spoiled and therefore excessively playful child," and (2) a "lascivious and sexually provocative person, especially a woman." Both meanings operate here, as the first Alberta grows from an excessively playful child to a high-priced call girl. The second narrative is about a quite different Alberta, an equally sensitive child who becomes a Catholic nun, indeed, the saintliest woman in her convent, "steeped in oblivious [religious] ecstasy." Two important facts keep us from assuming that these are independent short stories, texts whose intentions are purely narrative. For one thing, the protagonists of both texts have the same name, Alberta. For another, the first paragraphs of each text are absolutely identical in content and phrasing. They describe Alberta's earliest nature and state of mind — her immaturity, her experimental touching and kissing, her beauty and loving manner.

Then the texts diverge: the first Alberta is raised by a "mama who is not her mama" among "ladies who petted her and praised her beauty" and "artists who painted [her beauty] naked." We infer that she was raised in a house of prostitution. (The events occur at a time when artists frequented brothels because only there could they find nude models.) The second Alberta, on the other hand, was raised by a "very holy woman," who set her in the direction of the convent. (Kate Chopin wrote a number of short stories about New Orleans, a city reputed both for its brothels and its French Catholic background.) Why do both texts have an "Alberta" as heroine and identical first paragraphs? It seems reasonable to conclude that the two combine to argue some proposition — for example, that environment is more influential than heredity. The child Alberta is identically characterized in the first paragraph of each text because she is pliable clay, ready to be shaped by early influences. The same sensitive, loving, impressionable young girl can become anything, depending on who influences her and what she sees around her. "Two Portraits" seems to argue that children are completely adaptable and will grow into the sorts of persons who best fit into their surroundings. So two different Albertas are described, but those descriptions, in turn, serve to argue the greater importance of environment over heredity. We can reasonably say that "Two

Portraits" consists of narrative at the service of description which, in turn, is at the service of argument.

Story and Discourse

Let us go back now to the structure of narrative. Scholars have found it useful to distinguish two basic components of narrative. These correspond roughly to *what* a narrative must contain and to *how* the narrative communicates that content. The *what* — or *story* in a special, limited sense — includes the actions, characters, settings, themes. So I shall henceforth avoid using *story* as a simple synonym for *short story*. The word *story* will refer exclusively to the *what* of a narrative, its content.

The second aspect of every narrative, the *how*, is often referred to as the narrative *discourse*. The term *discourse* has many possible meanings, but in this book it will refer exclusively to *the means by which the story is presented*. Included in discourse are the narrator's voice, the character's perspective, the manipulation of time — indeed, anything that is involved in conveying the story to the reader. It is easy to keep these terms clear if you just remember that the discourse delivers the story and that the story is delivered by the discourse. Sometimes this delivery or rendering of the story amounts to a clearly pronounced *telling*. An identifiable narrator seems to be speaking, and she tells us in so many words what happened in the story. At the opposite pole are narratives that are *shown*. The model here is the stage play or movie in which no identifiable narrator can be heard or seen, and all the events seem just to happen on their own, as if before our eyes. A "shown" short story favors *dialogue* — the literal words spoken or written by the characters — because these can be quoted verbatim with little or no intervention by a narrator's voice. Examples in this book are Elizabeth Jolley's "Wednesdays and Fridays" (pp. 98–103), Donald Barthelme's "Me and Miss Mandible" (pp. 348–355), and to a lesser extent Elizabeth Bowen's "Careless Talk" (pp. 370–373) and Ernest Hemingway's "Indian Camp" (pp. 292–295). In the first two, the narrator seems little more than a collector of documents written by the characters; in the latter two, the narrator seems little more than a tape recorder placed in the vicinity of the characters, recording their dialogue.

You may be wondering what practical good this distinction is and how it can help you better understand fictions. For one thing, it gives us names for — and a way to talk about — the two kinds of narrative time that we discussed before. What I earlier called the "internal" time, the time that it takes for the fictional events to occur, I can now call *story-time*. Conversely, the time that it takes for the narrator to tell or show the story and the reader to read it I can call *discourse-time*. A short story may be very short indeed, taking only a few minutes to read, but it may present in summary fashion a whole lifetime of events. Nathaniel Hawthorne's "Wakefield" (pp. 457–462) is an example — only six or so pages of discourse-time tell 20 years of story-time. On the other hand, a discourse of several pages may represent only a few moments of story-time. Ambrose Bierce's "An Occurrence at Owl Creek

Bridge" (pp. 363 – 369) is an example — the few minutes of Peyton Farquhar's hanging require seven pages of discourse-time.

We shall consider the various relations of discourse-time and story-
time in our discussion of *plot* (chapter 2). Thereafter, we shall look at other
aspects of story, such as *character* and *setting* (chapter 3) and *themes* (chapter 8) — the meanings conveyed over and above the plain sense of what is said.
On the *discourse* side, we shall inquire into the process of *narration*, or the
narrator's *voice* (chapter 4), and how the narrative is sometimes communicated through a character's point of view or *filter* (a concept to be defined in
chapter 5). We shall learn how the narrator's *slant* on the events of the story
may differ from a character's filter and how that difference may produce an
effect of *irony* (chapter 6) — as meanings emerge that conflict with what the
narrative overtly expresses. We shall also look at the interesting effect called
unreliable narration (chapter 7), that is, narration that is contrary in fact or
emphasis to what we infer "really happened." Finally, we shall consider how
some fictions seem to assault the basic conventions of narrative (chapter 9).
We shall ask which conventions are being undermined and what the consequences are.

Even though my discussion of narrative technique has the simple
intention of making fiction more comprehensible and therefore more pleasurable, I hope it will prove interesting in its own right. Art, in many ways, is a
kind of play, and looking into artists' inventions and conventions enables us to
understand and even to join in that play. Through studying narrative technique, we can see and appreciate the nuances of the games played by the
masters of fiction.

SUGGESTIONS FOR WRITING

1. Can you turn a narrative fictional text into another form of discourse? Try to
   sum up one of the stories in this section in a sentence, and then develop
   that sentence into a short argument or description.

2. Is it possible to capture a scene or situation that changes over time through
   description alone, or is description only suitable for isolated moments and
   unchanging circumstances? Write a description of something or someone
   that conveys a sense of time passing. Does your description shift over into
   narrative?

3. We don't think of historians and physicists as storytellers, but in a sense they
   are. Find an example of narrative discourse in a text produced by a scientist,
   economist, anthropologist, historian, et cetera. (Look, for instance, at the
   section on cell division in your introductory zoology textbook.) How does
   the narrative differ from a short story? Does it have a time sequence, a plot,
   characters, suspense, a narrator?

4. Have you ever heard (or can you imagine) the same joke told well by one
   person and badly by another? Summarize the joke and try to analyze the
   difference in terms of both *story* and *discourse*.

2 Plot

Narrative turns on the fundamental human need to know what is going to happen next. That need is manipulated by narrative *plot*.

Definition of Plot

The narrative use of *plot* is related to two old meanings of the word: "a measured parcel of ground," and "a secret plan or conspiracy" (originally *complot*). Narrative plot shares both these senses. It is the "measured" plan or pattern of a narrative; unlike a "plot of ground," however, it occurs in time, not in space. It also entails a certain "secret," namely, about what is going to happen next. The sense of secrecy may be quite strong, as in a detective fiction, or relatively weak, as in a short story of humdrum family life. In either case, the motor that drives plot is our curiosity about what will finally happen. Narratives always stimulate our desire to learn the unknown, and we are forever snared by the intriguing situations that authors and filmmakers dream up to provoke our curiosity. Indeed, *intrigue* is the French word for "plot."

All narrative plots start from a certain situation or state of affairs. Jack and Jill need water. Or a father and son decide to hunt for fish along the seashore (Italo Calvino's "Big Fish, Little Fish," pp. 374–379). Or a newspaper boy stops at a café for a cup of coffee (Carson McCullers's "A Tree A Rock A Cloud," pp. 27–32). Immediately, this first event sets up various possible consequences. Jack and Jill might discover gold or see a ghost. What happens instead is that they fall down the hill. In Calvino's short story, the father might have an accident, or the son might get bored and decided to play frisbee. What happens instead is that the boy has a conversation with a plump, tearful lady.

Narrative harnesses curiosity — that powerful human drive — as its motive force, using it in a particular way that can be called *branching*. Think of the plot as a kind of tree on whose trunk grow buds or nodes of plot possibility existing at given story-moments. From each such situation-node any number of event-branches may grow, but these branches are only *possible* events. Only one actually occurs. We are absorbed in an attempt to guess

20

which that will be. The one that occurs gives rise to a new situation, which in turn allows possible further branches.

Each succeeding situation can also be thought of as a question posed by the plot. No sooner is the first question answered but a second one arises. And then a third, fourth, and so on. In "A Tree A Rock A Cloud," the first event, "the boy enters the café for coffee," leads to the initial situation — the boy in the café, along with Leo, soldiers, mill-hands, and an old man in the corner. What happens next? The second event, "the old man calls the boy over." That event leads to a second situation — the conversation between the boy and the old man. And what happens then? The second situation could have led to a third event different from the one that occurs — the body could have ignored the old man. He could have left the café. Or he could have talked to someone else. Instead, the third event is a surprise — the old man tells the boy that he loves him. The others in the café laugh. The boy does not know what to do. And so on. Each event gives rise to a new situation, a new state of affairs, and with it, a new question, until the final situation — the boy, totally confused by the old man's story, makes what he hopes is a neutral and sophisticated comment to Leo.

Closed and Open Plots

The last event of a narrative may answer all our questions, as it does in a traditional short story like Isaac Bashevis Singer's "Short Friday" (pp. 66 – 74). The narrator tells us beyond any doubt that Shmul-Leibele and Shoshe will live in heaven forever. Such short stories have traditional *closure*, that is, they follow a familiar pattern of beginning, middle, and end, which we can often anticipate.[1] A variation on traditional closure is the *surprise ending*, popular at the turn of the century among such short story authors as O. Henry. (An example appears in Edith Wharton's "Roman Fever," pp. 203 – 212).

How do the effects of surprise and suspense arise in a plot? The filmmaker Alfred Hitchcock pointed out that suspense and surprise are mutually exclusive principles. *Suspense* is a particularly intense kind of narrative curiosity. Although the central question of every narrative is What's going to happen next?, suspense stimulates an unusually strong expectation of possible consequences, one of which may be dreadful. The private detective walks up the stairs: He doesn't see the dark shadow following him, but we do. We anticipate something awful; that's suspense. It depends directly on our fearing the worst. *Surprise*, on the other hand, depends on our ignorance. Of all the possible consequences of the situation of the moment, what in fact happens is totally unexpected.

Many short stories, especially modern ones, do not contain suspense, surprise, or even profound changes in an ongoing state of affairs. They prefer to

---

[1]Traditional narrative theory distinguishes five different stages of the plot: *introduction, rising action* (or *complication*), *climax* (or *conflict*), *dénouement*, and *conclusion* (which in classical tragedy was the *catastrophe*, or death of the hero). But it would be artificial to categorize the plots of many short stories in these traditional terms.

offer a slice of life, leaving us in the air, without a definitive conclusion, without a clearly finalizing event such as a wedding or a death. In "A Tree A Rock A Cloud," for example, we are left only with questions. Why doesn't Leo answer the boy's questions? What should we make of the old man's "science of love"? What will happen to the old man? At one level, such indeterminate plots do not satisfy our curiosity. At another, we feel that it's right, somehow, for them to leave us up in the air. We sense that their silence has moved us closer to an important truth, however difficult it might be to state. Such short stories are said to be "like life itself," because life's lessons are often murky or even nonexistent. Can you cure romantic disappointment by learning to love every-thing in the universe? Or is the old man just kidding himself? He says that finding the love of a woman should be the climax of his study of love, but he admits that he has not yet gotten so far. Still, even on this inconclusive final note, "A Tree A Rock A Cloud" somehow jells into a closure, speaking to the human condition in a satisfying way. Indeed, it seems as if any other, more conventional resolution of this plot would have cheapened it. Like many modern short stories, this one raises more questions than it answers but also leaves us with a sense of "the way things are."

James Joyce borrowed a term from Catholic theology to name this sudden discovery of "the way things are." He called it *epiphany*. Originally a term meaning religious "manifestation" or "showing forth," *epiphany* now also has a literary meaning:

> An intuitive grasp of reality achieved in a quick flash of recognition in which something, usually simple and commonplace, is seen in a new light.[2]

In "A Tree A Rock A Cloud," the reader's epiphany (though not the boy's) is a recognition that a person hurt in a relationship may wish to transform that hurt into a generalized love, a love of trees, rocks, clouds — of everything in the universe. At the same time, we recognize that feelings are not so easy to manipulate, to fit into logic or "science," as the old man has attempted to do. He doesn't seem as serene and happy as he claims to be.

Story-Time and Discourse-Time

Because curiosity depends on what we don't know, it is constantly stimulated by the unknown future. So narrative is always heavily involved with time. As I pointed out in chapter 1, all texts — even nonnarrative ones — operate in time. It takes time to read a legal argument or the description in an instruction manual about how to use an electronic calculator. But narrative's involvement with time is greater and more complex than description's or argument's because it has an additional, *inner* time-unfolding.

If a senator is arguing for controls on acid rain, his speech will take time to hear or to read in the *Congressional Record*, but its content is not a

---

[2]C. Hugh Holman and William Harmon, *A Handbook to Literature*, 6th ed. (New York: Macmillan, 1992), p. 174.

sequence of events, not a story. As he provides various reasons for controlling acid rain, his speech follows logic rather than chronology. He speaks about damage to crops, about costs of cleanup, about the rise in respiratory diseases, and the like. These are *reasons*, not events. Argument is the text-type that entails reasoning about something, not telling a story about it.

In description, on the other hand, the basic components are the *qualities* or *aspects* of the thing being described. A description of an apple entails color (green, read, yellow), shape (round), texture (smooth), and so on. Even if the qualities are illustrated by events, it is the qualities that are important, not the events. An article about Hawaii in a travel magazine introduces the reader to life on each of the four principal islands — Oahu, Maui, Hawaii, and Kauai — mentioning various events — a man playing golf on Kauai, a woman climbing a volcano on Maui, or a boy surfing at Waikiki. These events, however, do not constitute a story: They are not connected in a series that adds up to some narrative point. They construct no plot. They simply illustrate some *qualities* of Hawaii, namely, that it is a good place for sports and outdoor activities.

The crucial ingredient of plot is not only a series of *events*, but events so connected that they lead from a beginning to an end, from an initial state of affairs to a concluding one. Sometimes the connection is "tight," as in a detective story. Sometimes it is loose, so loose as to constitute a deliberately chaotic state of affairs. But there must always be some connection.

Narrative Order and Duration

Narrative time is a complicated matter, but it can be broken down into smaller, more digestible components. We have already distinguished between the time taken up by the events, the *story-time*, and the time of the *telling* of those events, or *discourse-time*. This distinction entails a further one, that between narrative *order* and *duration*.

Narrative *order* refers to the parallelism, or lack of parallelism, between the sequence of the events in the discourse and the sequencing of those events by the discourse. Discourse-order parallels story-order when the narrator tells the events in the same order as they occurred — that is, tells the first event first, the second one second, the third one third, and so on. In "A Tree A Rock A Cloud," the first event, the boy entering the café, is told first, the old man addressing him is told second, the old man's explanation of his science of love is told third, and so on. In nonparallel or *inverted narrative order*, the discourse presents the story-events out of sequence: The last event may be told first, and the first event last.

In itself, story-order follows the normal laws of nature (at least in realistic fictions). A woman cannot become a mother before she herself is born, nor can a man die first and then get married. However, discourse-order can *present* these events in a nonchronological order. The narrative may begin with the hero as an old man speaking to his children and then go back to his earlier years. That inversion is usually called a *flashback*. *The God-*

father starts with Don Corleone meeting with various clients on the occasion of his daughter's wedding. Later, the discourse flashes back to his earlier experiences as a boy in Sicily and as a young man on the Lower East Side of Manhattan.

In most of the short stories in this anthology, discourse-order parallels story-order. However, inverted order is a familiar effect. In flashback an earlier story-event is presented out of order, that is, later in the discourse than it "should" occur. One short story in this collection that uses flashbacks is Margaret Atwood's "The Sin Eater" (pp. 34–41). The story concerns the confused feelings of a middle-aged woman, the unnamed narrator, when she learns of the death of her psychotherapist, Joseph. The discourse is divided into 13 brief sections. At a certain moment unstated by the discourse but obviously occurring in the blank space *between* the events narrated in the first and second sections, Joseph dies in a fall from a tree. The discourse-order coincides with the story-order — *except* for the eighth and the eleventh sections. In these, the discourse flashes back to episodes that occurred when Joseph was still alive, counseling the narrator. These are actual events: Joseph actually speaks to the narrator, in the present tense, and she answers him. Even though we have already learned that he has died, it is not Joseph's ghost who speaks in sections 8 and 11. Nor does the narrator dream the events contained in these sections. (In the final section, she *does* dream, but her dream is clearly marked as such, and she awakes to remember that Joseph is really dead.) If this had been a movie, the flashback scenes would be shot in Joseph's office: You would see Joseph alive, even though you would know that he has since died.

Duration is the second important relation between story-time and discourse-time. Duration concerns how long the story and the discourse *last* with respect to each other. Say you've decided to watch a movie on television and you check the television section of the newspaper. You learn that a Cary Grant movie called *Father Goose* is playing at nine and that it lasts 115 minutes; 115 minutes is the discourse-time. The story-events in *Father Goose*, however, are longer than your viewing time; they stretch over days or weeks. Similarly, a short story such as Joyce Carol Oates's "Four Summers" (pp. 43–56) takes less than an hour to read, but it narrates events that lasted 10 years or more in the heroine's life.

The duration of the recounted events, that is, the story-time, the period through which characters live and act, can differ considerably from the duration of the discourse, the time it takes the narrator to tell or show those events. In most narratives, story-time lasts longer than discourse-time, but in some they are equal. In a very few, story-time is actually shorter than discourse-time. Ambrose Bierce's "An Occurrence at Owl Creek Bridge" (pp. 363–369) is an example. Though Peyton Farquhar's "escape" would have lasted hours or even days, we learn at the end of the story that these were all imaginary, occurring in the split second between the moment that the sergeant steps off the plank and the moment the rope jerks taut and breaks Farquhar's neck. But it takes us a half-hour or so to read the story.

To sum up: There are at least four different ways in which story-duration may relate to discourse-duration:

1. *The two durations may be roughly equal*, as in "A Tree A Rock A Cloud." This first possibility corresponds to the *scene* of a stage play or movie. The story happens in "real time," because it takes approximately the same amount of time for the characters to speak their lines of dialogue or think their thoughts as for us to read them.

2. *The discourse-time may be much shorter than the story-time.* This is narrative *summary*. In Anton Chekhov's "The Darling" (pp. 104–112), for example, a discourse-time of a few pages covers a story-time that stretches over many years, from the moment that the young Olenka meets Kukin until the moment when, as an old woman, she hears Sasha crying out in his sleep. Long periods of story-time are summarized in a single sentence or two: "And so the Pustovalovs lived for six years quietly and peaceably in love and complete harmony." Story-time: six years. Discourse-time: the split second it took you to read that sentence.

   Summary may also entail a *repetition* of action. In "Short Friday," Shmul-Leibele *inevitably* "made the garment either too short or too tight." He keeps repeating his mistakes. Or in "The Darling," *whenever* Olenka "took part in the rehearsals, she corrected the actors, she kept an eye on the behavior of the musicians."

   The device of summary is very powerful, because it enables the narrator to present even lengthy events in brief discourse-time. A summary that occurs at the very beginning of a fiction is sometimes given the special name *narrative exposition*. The purpose of exposition is to get the reader into the present moment of the fiction by briefly providing explanatory information about past events.

3. *A period of story-time may be skipped by the discourse entirely.* This is called *ellipsis*. No statement appears in the discourse to account for the skipped, or elided, event, though we know the event must have occurred. There is only a blank space on the page. Movies make heavy use of ellipses, usually through the editing techniques of cut, dissolve, and fade-out.

   In "The Sin Eater," as we have seen, explicit mention of the death of Joseph is elided between the first and second sections of the discourse. "Four Summers" also depends heavily on ellipsis. We are with Sissie at the lake at four different moments in her life: as a small child; as an older child; at fourteen; and as a pregnant wife of nineteen. The discourse marks these sections by roman numerals I through IV. Each section corresponds roughly to a scene, and the empty page space between the last period of one section and the capital letter of the next section contains an ellipsis. Ellipsis is an economical way of deleting irrelevant or self-evident story material, but it may also conceal an important event for some later effect, or make the reader imagine it, thereby giving it an unusual kind of emphasis.

4. The time-relation opposite ellipsis is *pause.* Here *the story-time stops for a moment but the discourse-time continues,* typically to allow the narrator to describe something or to make a comment. For instance, the second sentence in the following passage in "Four Summers" occurs during narrative pause:

> "Why doesn't he hurry up?" Jerry says.
> Jerry is twelve now. He has pimples on his forehead and chin.
> He pushes one of the rowboats with his foot. . . .

In story-time, Jerry's pushing the rowboat follows *immediately* after his saying "Why doesn't he hurry up?" The narrator's intervening description "Jerry is twelve now" takes a time-out in the story. It doesn't "count" in the story's chronology, just as a time-out in football or soccer doesn't count as part of the chronology of the game.

Here is another example, from "The Darling" (pp. 104–112). The narrator tells us what happened after the veterinary surgeon departed, a time during which Olenka was absolutely alone. She got thinner, people stopped smiling at her, she "thought of nothing and wished for nothing." About her state of mind the narrator comments:

> And what was worst of all, she had no opinions of any sort. She saw the objects about her and understood what she saw, but could not form any opinion about them, and did not know what to talk about. And how awful it is not to have any opinions!

The first part of the first sentence and the whole of the last sentence are spoken during narrative pauses, as the narrator takes time out to voice an opinion about Olenka's state of mind.

Narrative time is a fascinating and complex subject, but this is enough to introduce it to you. You will find in this book many interesting treatments of narrative time.

All short stores have plots, though some plots are more eventful than others. We go to some fictions for the sheer excitement and mystery of their events. Others interest us less through the allure of their events than through the kinds of characters they project on the screens of our minds. Fortunately, we don't have to choose; we can enjoy both kinds of narratives. Indeed, many great fictions, such as Joseph Conrad's "The Secret Sharer" (pp. 388–415), manage to give us both thrilling suspense and deep insight into human nature.

❖ CARSON McCULLERS
A Tree · A Rock · A Cloud

Carson McCullers (1917–1967) was born in Columbus, Georgia. She spent her childhood and youth in Columbus, where her mother, convinced of her genius, encouraged her to be a musician. Sent to New York to attend the famed musical academy, the Julliard School, she could not do so because of ill health. Still, she stayed in New York, working during the day and attending writing classes at night at Columbia University. Her life was marked by physical and emotional suffering. She married, divorced, and remarried a depressed man, Reeves McCullers, who ultimately committed suicide. In 1947, at thirty, she suffered the first of a series of strokes that were ultimately to kill her. It blinded her in one eye and paralyzed one arm, reducing her capacity to type to a single page a day. Despite these handicaps, she emerged as one of the most prominent talents of her day. She was especially gifted at conveying the pains and insecurities of children, adolescents, and lost souls. She published the novels *The Heart Is a Lonely Hunter* (1940), *Reflections in a Golden Eye* (1941), *The Member of the Wedding* (1946, which also appeared on the Broadway stage as an acclaimed play), and *The Clock Without Hands* (1961). Her short stories were first collected in *The Ballad of the Sad Café and Collected Short Stories* (1951). The most recent and complete edition of her short fiction is *Collected Stories* (1987). She also wrote a play called *The Square Root of Wonderful* (1958).

It was raining that morning, and still very dark. When the boy reached the streetcar café he had almost finished his route and he went in for a cup of coffee. The place was an all-night café owned by a bitter and stingy man called Leo. After the raw, empty street the café seemed friendly and bright: along the counter there were a couple of soldiers, three spinners from the cotton mill, and in a corner a man who sat hunched over with his nose and half his face down in a beer mug. The boy wore a helmet such as aviators wear. When he went into the café he unbuckled the chin strap and raised the right flap up over his pink little ear; often as he drank his coffee someone would speak to him in a friendly way. But this morning Leo did not look into his face and none of the men were talking. He paid and was leaving the café when a voice called out to him:

"Son! Hey Son!"

He turned back and the man in the corner was crooking his finger and nodding to him. He had brought his face out of the beer mug and he seemed suddenly very happy. The man was long and pale, with a big nose and faded orange hair.

"Hey Son!"

The boy went toward him. He was an undersized boy of about twelve, with one shoulder drawn higher than the other because of the weight of the paper sack. His face was shallow, freckled, and his eyes were round child eyes.

27

"Yeah Mister?"

The man laid one hand on the paper boy's shoulders, then grasped the boy's chin and turned his face slowly from one side to the other. The boy shrank back uneasily.

"Say! What's the big idea?"

The boy's voice was shrill; inside the café it was suddenly very quiet.

The man said slowly: "I love you."

All along the corner the men laughed. The boy, who had scowled and sidled away, did not know what to do. He looked over the counter at Leo, and Leo watched him with a weary, brittle jeer. The boy tried to laugh also. But the man was serious and sad.

"I did not mean to tease you, Son," he said. "Sit down and have a beer with me. There is something I have to explain."

Cautiously, out of the corner of his eye, the paper boy questioned the men along the counter to see what he should do. But they had gone back to their beer or their breakfast and did not notice him. Leo put a cup of coffee on the counter and a little jug of cream.

"He is a minor," Leo said.

The paper boy slid himself up onto the stool. His ear beneath the upturned flap of the helmet was very small and red. The man was nodding at him soberly. "It is important," he said. Then he reached in his hip pocket and brought out something which he held up in the palm of his hand for the boy to see.

"Look very carefully," he said.

The boy stared, but there was nothing to look at very carefully. The man held in his big, grimy palm a photograph. It was the face of a woman, but blurred, so that only the hat and the dress she was wearing stood out clearly.

"See?" the man asked.

The boy nodded and the man placed another picture in his palm. The woman was standing on a beach in a bathing suit. The suit made her stomach very big, and that was the main thing you noticed.

"Got a good look?" He leaned over closer and finally asked: "You ever seen her before?"

The boy sat motionless, staring slantwise at the man. "Not so I know of."

"Very well." The man blew on the photographs and put them back into his pocket. "That was my wife."

"Dead?" the boy asked.

Slowly the man shook his head. He pursed his lips as though about to whistle and answered in a long-drawn way: "Nuuu—" he said. "I will explain."

The beer on the counter before the man was in a large brown mug. He did not pick it up to drink. Instead he bent down and, putting his face over the rim, he rested there for a moment. Then with both hands he tilted the mug and sipped.

"Some night you'll go to sleep with your big nose in a mug and drown," said Leo. "Prominent transient drowns in beer. That would be a cute death."

The paper boy tried to signal to Leo. While the man was not looking he screwed up his face and worked his mouth to question soundlessly: "Drunk?" but Leo only raised his eyebrows and turned away to put some pink strips of bacon on the grill.

The man pushed the mug away from him, straightened himself, and folded his loose crooked hands on the counter. His face was sad as he looked at the paper boy. He did not blink, but from time to time the lids closed down with delicate gravity over his pale green eyes. It was nearing dawn and the boy shifted the weight of the paper sack.

"I am talking about love," the man said. "With me it is a science."

The boy half slid down from the stool. But the man raised his forefinger, and there was something about him that held the boy and would not let him go away.

"Twelve years ago I married the woman in the photograph. She was my wife for one year, nine months, three days, and two nights. I loved her. Yes . . ." He tightened his blurred, rambling voice and said again: "I loved her. I thought also that she loved me. I was a railroad engineer. She had all home comforts and luxuries. It never crept into my brain that she was not satisfied. But do you know what happened?"

"Mgneeow!" said Leo.

The man did not take his eyes from the boy's face. "She left me. I came in one night and the house was empty and she was gone. She left me."

"With a fellow?" the boy asked.

Gently the man placed his palm down on the counter. "Why naturally, Son. A woman does not run off like that alone."

The café was quiet, the soft rain black and endless in the street outside. Leo pressed down the frying bacon with the prongs of his long fork. "So you have been chasing the floozie for eleven years. You frazzled old rascal!"

For the first time the man glanced at Leo. "Please don't be vulgar. Besides, I was not speaking to you." He turned back to the boy and said in a trusting and secretive undertone: "Let's not pay any attention to him. O.K.?"

The paper boy nodded doubtfully.

"It was like this," the man continued. "I am a person who feels many things. All my life one thing after another has impressed me. Moonlight. The leg of a pretty girl. One thing after another. But the point is that when I had enjoyed anything there was a peculiar sensation as though it was laying around loose in me. Nothing seemed to finish itself up or fit in with the other things. Women? I had my portion of them. The same. Afterwards laying around loose in me. I was a man who had never loved."

Very slowly he closed his eyelids, and the gesture was like a curtain drawn at the end of a scene in a play. When he spoke again his voice was excited and the words came fast — the lobes of his large, loose ears seemed to tremble.

"Then I met this woman. I was fifty-one years old and she always said she was thirty. I met her at a filling station and we were married within three days. And do you know what it was like? I just can't tell you. All I had ever felt was gathered together around this woman. Nothing lay around loose in me any more but was finished up by her."

The man stopped suddenly and stroked his long nose. His voice sank down to a steady and reproachful undertone: "I'm not explaining this right. What happened was this. There were these beautiful feelings and loose little pleasures inside me. And this woman was something like an assembly line for my soul. I run these little pieces of myself through her and I come out complete. Now do you follow me?"

"What was her name?" the boy asked.

"Oh," he said. "I called her Dodo. But that is immaterial."

"Did you try to make her come back?"

The man did not seem to hear. "Under the circumstances you can imagine how I felt when she left me."

Leo took the bacon from the grill and folded two strips of it between a bun. He had a gray face, with slitted eyes, and a pinched nose saddled by faint blue shadows. One of the mill workers signaled for more coffee and Leo poured it. He did not give refills on coffee free. The spinner ate breakfast there every morning, but the better Leo knew his customers the stingier he treated them. He nibbled his own bun as though he grudged it to himself.

"And you never got hold of her again?"

The boy did not know what to think of the man, and his child's face was uncertain with mingled curiosity and doubt. He was new on the paper route; it was still strange to him to be out in the town in the black, queer early morning.

"Yes," the man said. "I took a number of steps to get her back. I went around trying to locate her. I went to Tulsa where she had folks. And to Mobile. I went to every town she had ever mentioned to me, and I hunted down every man she had formerly been connected with. Tulsa, Atlanta, Chicago, Cheehaw, Memphis. . . . For the better part of two years I chased around the country trying to lay hold of her."

"But the pair of them had vanished from the face of the earth!" said Leo.

"Don't listen to him," the man said confidentially. "And also just forget those two years. They are not important. What matters is that around the third year a curious thing begun to happen to me."

"What?" the boy asked.

The man leaned down and tilted his mug to take a sip of beer. But as he hovered over the mug his nostrils fluttered slightly; he sniffed the staleness of the beer and did not drink. "Love is a curious thing to begin with. At first I thought only of getting her back. It was a kind of mania. But then as time went on I tried to remember her. But do you know what happened?"

"No," the boy said.

"When I laid myself down on a bed and tried to think about her my mind became a blank. I couldn't see her. I would take out her picture and look. No good. Nothing doing. A blank. Can you imagine it?"

"Say Mac!" Leo called down the counter. "Can you imagine this bozo's mind a blank!"

Slowly, as though fanning away flies, the man waved his hand. His green eyes were concentrated and fixed on the shallow little face of the paper boy.

"But a sudden piece of glass on a sidewalk. Or a nickel tune in a music box. A shadow on a wall at night. And I would remember. It might happen in a street and I would cry or bang my head against a lamppost. You follow me?"

"A piece of glass . . ." the boy said.

"Anything. I would walk around and I had no power of how and when to remember her. You think you can put up a kind of shield. But remembering don't come to a man face forward — it corners around sideways. I was at the mercy of everything I saw and heard. Suddenly instead of me combing the countryside to find her she begun to chase me around in my very soul. *She* chasing *me*, mind you! And in my soul."

The boy asked finally: "What part of the country were you in then?"

"Ooh," the man groaned. "I was a sick mortal. It was like smallpox. I confess, Son, that I boozed. I fornicated. I committed any sin that suddenly appealed to me. I am loath to confess it but I will do so. When I recall that period it is all curdled in my mind, it was so terrible."

The man leaned his head down and tapped his forehead on the counter. For a few seconds he stayed bowed over in this position, the back of his stringy neck covered with orange furze, his hands with their long warped fingers held palm to palm in an attitude of prayer. Then the man straightened himself; he was smiling and suddenly his face was bright and tremulous and old.

"It was in the fifth year that it happened," he said. "And with it I started my science."

Leo's mouth jerked with a pale, quick grin. "Well none of we boys are getting any younger," he said. Then with sudden anger he balled up a dishcloth he was holding and threw it down hard on the floor. "You draggle-tailed old Romeo!"

"What happened?" the boy asked.

The old man's voice was high and clear: "Peace," he answered.

"Huh?"

"It is hard to explain scientifically, Son," he said. "I guess the logical explanation is that she and I had fleed around from each other for so long that finally we just got tangled up together and lay down and quit. Peace. A queer and beautiful blankness. It was spring in Portland and the rain came every afternoon. All evening I just stayed there on my bed in the dark. And that is how the science come to me."

The windows in the streetcar were pale blue with light. The two soldiers paid for their beers and opened the door — one of the soldiers combed his hair and wiped off his muddy puttees before they went outside. The three mill workers bent silently over their breakfasts. Leo's clock was ticking on the wall.

"It is this. And listen carefully. I meditated on love and reasoned it out. I realized what is wrong with us. Men fall in love for the first time. And what do they fall in love with?"

The boy's soft mouth was partly open and he did not answer.

"A woman," the old man said. "Without science, with nothing to go by, they undertake the most dangerous and sacred experience in God's earth. They fall in love with a woman. Is that correct, Son?"

"Yeah," the boy said faintly.

"They start at the wrong end of love. They begin at the climax. Can you wonder it is so miserable? Do you know how men should love?"

The old man reached over and grasped the boy by the collar of his leather jacket. He gave him a gentle little shake and his green eyes gazed down unblinking and grave.

"Son, do you know how love should be begun?"

The boy sat small and listening and still. Slowly he shook his head. The old man leaned closer and whispered:

"A tree. A rock. A cloud."

It was still raining outside in the street: a mild, gray, endless rain. The mill whistle blew for the six o'clock shift and the three spinners paid and went away. There was no one in the café but Leo, the old man, and the little paper boy.

"The weather was like this in Portland," he said. "At the time my science was begun. I meditated and I started very cautious. I would pick up something from the street and take it home with me. I bought a goldfish and I concentrated on the goldfish and I loved it. I graduated from one thing to another. Day by day I was getting this technique. On the road from Portland to San Diego —"

"Aw shut up!" screamed Leo suddenly. "Shut up! Shut up!"

The old man still held the collar of the boy's jacket; he was trembling and his face was earnest and bright and wild. "For six years now I have gone around by myself and built up my science. And now I am a master, Son. I can love anything. No longer do I have to think about it even. I see a street full of people and a beautiful light comes in me. I watch a bird in the sky. Or I meet a traveler on the road. Everything, Son. And anybody. All stranger and all loved! Do you realize what a science like mine can mean?"

The boy held himself stiffly, his hands curled tight around the counter edge. Finally he asked: "Did you ever really find that lady?"

"What? What say, Son?"

"I mean," the boy asked timidly. "Have you fallen in love with a woman again?"

The old man loosened his grasp on the boy's collar. He turned away and for the first time his green eyes had a vague and scattered look. He lifted the mug from the counter, drank down the yellow beer. His head was shaking slowly from side to side. Then finally he answered: "No, Son. You see that is the last step in my science. I go cautious. And I am not quite ready yet."

"Well!" said Leo. "Well well well!"

The old man stood in the open doorway. "Remember," he said. Framed there in the gray damp light of the early morning he looked shrunken and seedy and frail. But his smile was bright. "Remember I love you," he said with a last nod. And the door closed quietly behind him.

The boy did not speak for a long time. He pulled down the bangs on his forehead and slid his grimy little forefinger around the rim of his empty cup. Then without looking at Leo he finally asked:

"Was he drunk?"

"No," said Leo shortly.

The boy raised his clear voice higher. "Then was he a dope fiend?"

"No."

The boy looked up at Leo, and his flat little face was desperate, his voice urgent and shrill. "Was he crazy? Do you think he was a lunatic?" The paper boy's voice dropped suddenly with doubt. "Leo? Or not?"

But Leo would not answer him. Leo had run a night café for fourteen years, and he held himself to be a critic of craziness. There were the town characters and also the transients who roamed in from the night. He knew the manias of all of them. But he did not want to satisfy the questions of the waiting child. He tightened his pale face and was silent.

So the boy pulled down the right flap of his helmet and as he turned to leave he made the only comment that seemed safe to him, the only remark that could not be laughed down and despised:

"He sure has done a lot of traveling."

(1951)

QUESTIONS

1. Much of the mood of this story depends on its clear establishment of a single scene. How does the narrator convey the feeling of an all-night diner and its customers? Why does its discourse-time roughly equal its story-time?

2. The old man uses the word *science* in the sense of "study" or "theory." How would you sum up the old man's "science" of love? Do you think he will *ultimately* take the "last step" in his science and find the woman of his dreams?

3. Why does the narrator present the scene through the eyes of a young boy? Would an adult man see the same things? Would a woman or girl?

4. What is our usual reaction when a man says "I love you" to an adolescent boy? Does the narrator expect us to jump to the wrong conclusions? Does she imply something about what we normally assume to be appropriate love objects?

5. How would you defend this short story against the charge that "nothing happens"? Explain particularly how the short story does lead from an initial situation to a conclusive final one.

❖ MARGARET ATWOOD

The Sin Eater

Margaret Atwood (1939–   ) was born in Ottawa, Canada. She was educated at Victoria College, University of Toronto, Radcliffe, and Harvard. She has taught at the University of British Columbia, Sir George Williams University, York University, the University of Alabama, Tuscaloosa, New York University, and Macquarie University in Australia. Her novels include *The Edible Woman* (1969), *Surfacing* (1972), *Lady Oracle* (1976), *Life before Man* (1979), *Bodily Harm* (1981), *The Handmaid's Tale* (1985), and *Cat's Eye* (1988). As the titles suggest, Atwood is a feminist concerned with the plight of women in a patriarchal, consumer-oriented society. Her most famous novel is probably *The Handmaid's Tale*, which won the Canadian Governor General's award for fiction and which was made into a successful movie. It tells of a future state, Gilead (a successor to the United States), dominated by males, from the perspective of a woman who is an official "mistress" to one of the leaders. Atwood has written many short stories; they appear in the collections *Dancing Girls* (1977), *Murder in the Dark: Short Fictions and Prose Poems* (1983), *Bluebird's Egg* (1983), which contains "The Sin Eater," and *Wilderness Tips* (1991). She has also written several volumes of poetry, and plays for Canadian radio and television (for example, the teleplay *Snowbird*, broadcast in 1981), as well as books of social and literary criticism, for example, *Second Words* (1982).

This is Joseph, in maroon leather bedroom slippers, flattened at the heels, scuffed at the toes, wearing also a seedy cardigan of muddy off-yellow that reeks of bargain basements, sucking at his pipe, his hair greying and stringy, his articulation as beautiful and precise and English as ever:

"In Wales," he says, "mostly in the rural areas, there was a personage known as the Sin Eater. When someone was dying the Sin Eater would be sent for. The people of the house would prepare a meal and place it on the coffin. They would have the coffin all ready, of course: once they'd decided you were going off, you had scarcely any choice in the matter. According to other versions, the meal would be placed on the dead person's body, which must have made for some sloppy eating, one would have thought. In any case the Sin Eater would devour this meal and would also be given a sum of money. It was believed that all the sins the dying person had accumulated during his lifetime would be removed from him and transmitted to the Sin Eater. The Sin Eater thus became absolutely bloated with other people's sins. She'd accumulate such a heavy load of them that nobody wanted to have anything to do with her; a kind of syphilitic of the soul, you might say. They'd even avoid speaking to her, except of course when it was time to summon her to another meal."

"Her?" I say.

34

Joseph smiles, that lopsided grin that shows the teeth in one side of his mouth, the side not engaged with the stem of his pipe. An ironic grin, wolvish, picking up on what? What have I given away this time?

"I think of them as old women," he says, "though there's no reason why they shouldn't have been men, I suppose. They could be anything as long as they were willing to eat the sins. Destitute old creatures who had no other way of keeping body and soul together, wouldn't you think? A sort of geriatric spiritual whoring."

He gazes at me, grinning away, and I remember certain stories I've heard about him, him and women. He's had three wives, to begin with. Nothing with me though, ever, though he does try to help me on with my coat a bit too lingeringly. Why should I worry? It's not as though I'm susceptible. Besides which he's at least sixty, and the cardigan is truly gross, as my sons would say.

"It was bad luck to kill one of them, though," he says, "and there must have been other perks. In point of fact I think Sin Eating has a lot to be said for it."

Joseph's not one of the kind who'll wait in sensitive, indulgent silence when you've frozen on him or run out of things to say. If you won't talk to him, he'll bloody well talk to you, about the most boring things he can think of, usually. I've heard all about his flower beds and his three wives and how to raise calla lilies in your cellar; I've heard all about the cellar, too, I could give guided tours. He says he thinks it's healthy for his patients—he won't call them "clients," no pussyfooting around, with Joseph—to know he's a human being too, and God do we know it. He'll drone on and on until you figure out that you aren't paying him so you can listen to him talk about his house plants, you're paying him so he can listen to you talk about yours.

Sometimes, though, he's really telling you something. I pick up my coffee cup, wondering whether this is one of those occasions.

"Okay," I say, "I'll bite. Why?"

"It's obvious," he says, lighting his pipe again, spewing out fumes. "First, the patients have to wait until they're dying. A true life crisis, no fakery and invention. They aren't permitted to bother you until then, until they can demonstrate that they're serious, you might say. Second, somebody gets a good square meal out of it." He laughs ruefully. We both know that half his patients don't bother to pay him, not even the money the government pays them. Joseph has a habit of taking on people nobody else will touch with a barge pole, not because they're too sick but because they're too poor. Mothers on welfare and so on; bad credit risks, like Joseph himself. He once got fired from a loony bin for trying to institute worker control.

"And think of the time saving," he goes on. "A couple of hours per patient, sum total, as opposed to twice a week for years and years, with the same result in the end."

"That's pretty cynical," I say disapprovingly. I'm supposed to be the cynical one, but maybe he's outflanking me, to force me to give up this corner. Cynicism is a defence, according to Joseph.

"You wouldn't even have to listen to them," he says. "Not a blessed word. The sins are transmitted in the food."

Suddenly he looks sad and tired.

"You're telling me I'm wasting your time?" I say.

"Not mine, my dear," he says. "I've got all the time in the world."

I interpret this as condescension, the one thing above all that I can't stand. I don't throw my coffee cup at him, however. I'm not as angry as I would have been once.

We've spent a lot of time on it, this anger of mine. It was only because I found reality so unsatisfactory; that was my story. So unfinished, so sloppy, so pointless, so endless. I wanted things to make sense.

I thought Joseph would try to convince me that reality was actually fine and dandy and then try to adjust me to it, but he didn't do that. Instead he agreed with me, cheerfully and at once. Life in most ways was a big pile of shit, he said. That was axiomatic. "Think of it as a desert island," he said. "You're stuck on it, now you have to decide how best to cope."

"Until rescued?" I said.

"Forget about the rescue," he said.

"I can't," I said.

This conversation is taking place in Joseph's office, which is just as tatty as he is and smells of unemptied ash-trays, feet, misery and twice-breathed air. But it's also taking place in my bedroom, on the day of the funeral. Joseph's, who didn't have all the time in the world.

"He fell out of a tree," said Karen, notifying me. She'd come to do this in person, rather than using the phone. Joseph didn't trust phones. Most of the message in any act of communication, he said, was non-verbal.

Karen stood in my doorway, oozing tears. She was one of his too, one of us; it was through her I'd got him. By now there's a network of us, it's like recommending a hairdresser, we've passed him from hand to hand like the proverbial eye or tooth. Smart women with detachable husbands or genius afflicted children with nervous tics, smart women with deranged lives, overjoyed to find someone who wouldn't tell us we were too smart for our own good and should all have frontal lobotomies. Smartness was an asset, Joseph maintained. We should only see what happened to the dumb ones.

"Out of a *tree*?" I said, almost screaming.

"Sixty feet, onto his head," said Karen. She began weeping again. I wanted to shake her.

"What the bloody hell was he doing up at the top of a sixty-foot *tree*?" I said.

"Pruning it," said Karen. "It was in his garden. It was cutting off the light to his flower beds."

"The old fart," I said. I was furious with him. It was an act of desertion. What made him think he had the right to go climbing up to the top of a sixty-foot tree, risking all our lives? Did his flower beds mean more to him than we did?

"What are we going to do?" said Karen?"

What am I going to do? is one question. It can always be replaced by *What am I going to wear?* For some people it's the same thing. I go through the cupboard, looking for the blackest things I can find. What I wear will be the non-verbal part of the communication. Joseph will notice. I have a horrible feeling I'll turn up at the funeral home and find they've laid him out in his awful yellow cardigan and those tacky maroon leather bedroom slippers.

I needn't have bothered with the black. It's no longer demanded. The three wives are in pastels, the first in blue, the second in mauve, the third, the current one, in beige. I know a lot about the three wives, from those off-days of mine when I didn't feel like talking.

Karen is here too, in an Indian-print dress, snivelling softly to herself. I envy her. I want to feel grief, but I can't quite believe Joseph is dead. It seems like some joke he's playing, some anecdote that's supposed to make us learn something. Fakery and invention. *All right, Joseph,* I want to call, *we have the answer, you can come out now.* But nothing happens, the closed coffin remains closed, no wisps of smoke issue from it to show there's life.

The closed coffin is the third wife's idea. She thinks it's more dignified, says the grapevine, and it probably is. The coffin is of dark wood, in good taste, no showy trim. No one has made a meal and placed it on this coffin, no one has eaten from it. No destitute old creature, gobbling down the turnips and mash and the heavy secrecies of Joseph's life along with them. I have no idea what Joseph might have had on his conscience. Nevertheless I feel this as an omission: what then have become of Joseph's sins? They hover around us, in the air, over the bowed heads, while a male relative of Joseph's, unknown to me, tells us all what a fine man he was.

After the funeral we go back to Joseph's house, to the third wife's house, for what used to be called the wake. Not any more: now it's coffee and refreshments.

The flower beds are tidy, gladioli at this time of year, already fading and a little ragged. The tree branch, the one that broke, is still on the lawn.

"I kept having the feeling he wasn't really there," says Karen as we go up the walk.

"Really where?" I say.

"There," says Karen. "In the coffin."

"For Christ's sake," I say, "don't start that." I can tolerate that kind of sentimental fiction in myself, just barely, as long as I don't do it out loud. "Dead is dead, that's what he'd say. Deal with here and now, remember?"

Karen, who'd once tried suicide, nodded and started to cry again. Joseph is an expert on people who try suicide. He's never lost one yet.

"How does he do it?" I asked Karen once. Suicide wasn't one of my addictions, so I didn't know.

"He makes it sound so *boring*," she said.

"That can't be all," I said.

"He makes you imagine," she said, "what it's like to be dead."

There are people moving around quietly, in the living room and in the dining room, where the table stands, arranged by the third wife with a silver tea urn and a vase of chrysanthemums, pink and yellow. Noting too funereal, you can hear her thinking. On the white tablecloth there are cups, plates, cookies, coffee, cakes. I don't know why funerals are supposed to make people hungry, but they do. If you can still chew you know you're alive.

Karen is beside me, stuffing down a piece of chocolate cake. On the other side is the first wife.

"I hope you aren't one of the loonies," she says to me abruptly. I've never really met her before, she's just been pointed out to me, by Karen, at the funeral. She's wiping her fingers on a paper napkin. On her powder-blue lapel is a gold brooch in the shape of a bird's nest, complete with the eggs. It reminds me of high school: felt skirts with appliqués of cats and telephones, a world of replicas.

I ponder my reply. Does she mean *client*, or is she asking whether I am by chance genuinely out of my mind?

"No," I say.

"Didn't think so," says the first wife. "You don't look like it. A lot of them were, the place was crawling with them. I was afraid there might be an *incident*. When I lived with Joseph there were always these *incidents*, phone calls at two in the morning, always killing themselves, throwing themselves all over him, you couldn't believe what went on. Some of them were *devoted* to him. If he'd told them to shoot the Pope or something, they'd have done it just like that."

"He was very highly thought of," I say carefully.

"You're telling *me*," says the first wife. "Had the idea he was God himself, some of them. Not that he minded all that much."

The paper napkin isn't adequate, she's licking her fingers. "Too rich," she says. "*Hers*." She jerks her head in the direction of the second wife, who is wispier than the first wife and is walking past us, somewhat aimlessly, in the direction of the living room. "You can have it, I told him finally. I just want some peace and quiet before I have to start pushing up the daisies." Despite the richness, she helps herself to another piece of chocolate cake. "*She* had this nutty idea that we should have some of them stand up and give little testimonies about him, right at the ceremony. Are you totally out of your tree? I told her. It's your funeral, but if I was you I'd try to keep it in mind that some of the people there are going to be a whole lot saner than others. Luckily she listened to me."

"Yes," I say. There's chocolate icing on her cheek: I wonder if I should tell her.

"I did what I could," she says, "which wasn't that much, but still. I was fond of him in a way. You can't just wipe out ten years of your life. I brought the cookies," she adds, rather smugly. "Least I could do."

I look down at the cookies. They're white, cut into the shapes of stars and moons and decorated with coloured sugar and little silver balls. They remind me of Christmas, of festivals and celebrations. They're the kind of cookies you make to please someone; to please a child.

I've been here long enough. I look about for the third wife, the one in charge, to say good-bye. I finally locate her, standing in an open doorway. She's crying, something she didn't do at the funeral. The first wife is beside her, holding her hand.

"I'm keeping it just like this," says the third wife, to no one in particular. Past her shoulder I can see into the room, Joseph's study evidently. It would take a lot of strength to leave that rummage sale untouched, untidied. Not to mention the begonias withering on the sill. But for her it will take no strength at all, because Joseph is in this room, unfinished, a huge boxful of loose ends. He refuses to be packed up and put away.

"Who do you hate the most?" says Joseph. This, in the middle of a lecture he's been giving me about the proper kind of birdbath for one's garden. He knows of course that I don't have a garden.

"I have absolutely no idea," I say.

"Then you should find out," says Joseph. "I myself cherish an abiding hatred for the boy who lived next door to me when I was eight."

"Why is that?" I ask, pleased to be let off the hook.

"He picked my sunflower," he says. "I grew up in a slum, you know. We had an area of sorts at the front, but it was solid cinders. However I did manage to grow this one stunted little sunflower, God knows how. I used to get up early every morning just to look at it. And the little bugger picked it. Pure bloody malice. I've forgiven a lot of later transgressions but if I ran into the little sod tomorrow I'd stick a knife into him."

I'm shocked, as Joseph intends me to be. "He was only a child," I say.

"So was I," he says. "The early ones are the hardest to forgive. Children have no charity; it has to be learned."

Is this Joseph proving yet once more that he's a human being, or am I intended to understand something about myself? Maybe, maybe not. Sometimes Joseph's stories are parables, but sometimes they're just running off at the mouth.

In the front hall the second wife, she of the mauve wisps, ambushes me. "He didn't fall," she whispers.

"Pardon?" I say.

The three wives have a family resemblance — they're all blondish and vague around the edges — but there's something else about this one, a glittering of the eyes. Maybe it's grief; or maybe Joseph didn't always draw a totally firm line between his personal and his professional lives. The second wife has a faint aroma of client.

"He wasn't happy," she says. "I could tell. We were still very close, you know."

What she wants me to infer is that he jumped. "He seemed all right to me," I say.

"He was good at keeping up a front," she says. She takes a breath, she's about to confide in me, but whatever these revelations are I don't want to hear them. I want Joseph to remain as he appeared: solid, capable, wise, and sane. I do not need his darkness.

I go back to the apartment. My sons are away for the weekend. I wonder whether I should bother making dinner just for myself. It's hardly worth it. I wander around the too-small living room, picking things up. No longer my husband's: as befits the half-divorced, he lives elsewhere.

One of my sons has just reached the shower-and-shave phase, the other hasn't, but both of them leave a deposit every time they pass through a room. A sort of bathtub ring of objects — socks, paperback books left face-down and open in the middle, sandwiches with bites taken out of them, and, lately, cigarette butts.

Under a dirty T-shirt I discover the Hare Krishna[1] magazine my younger son

---

[1]One human incarnation of the popular Indian deity, Vishnu.

brought home a week ago. I was worried that it was a spate of adolescent religious mania, but no, he'd given them a quarter because he felt sorry for them. He was a dead-robin-burier as a child. I take the magazine into the kitchen to put it in the trash. On the front there's a picture of Krishna playing the flute, surrounded by adoring maidens. His face is bright blue, which makes me think of corpses: some things are not cross-cultural. If I read on I could find out why meat and sex are bad for you. Not such a poor idea when you think about it: no more terrified cows, no more divorces. A life of abstinence and prayer. I think of myself, standing on a street corner, ringing a bell, swathed in flowing garments. Selfless and removed, free from sin. Sin is this world, says Krishna. This world is all we have, says Joseph. It's all you have to work with. It is not too much for you. You will not be rescued.

I could walk to the corner for a hamburger or I could phone out for pizza. I decide on the pizza.

"Do you like me?" Joseph says from his armchair.

"What do you mean, do I *like* you?" I say. It's early on; I haven't given any thought to whether or not I like Joseph.

"Well, do you?" he says.

"Look," I say. I'm speaking calmly but in fact I'm outraged. This is a demand, and Joseph is not supposed to make demands of me. There are too many demands being made of me already. That's why I'm here, isn't it? Because the demands exceed the supply. "You're like my dentist," I say. "I don't think about whether or not I like my dentist. I don't *have* to like him. I'm paying him to fix my teeth. You and my dentist are the only people in the whole world that I don't *have* to *like*."

"But if you met me under other circumstances," Joseph persists, "would you like me?"

"I have no idea," I say. "I can't imagine any other circumstances."

This is a room at night, a night empty except for me. I'm looking at the ceiling, across which the light from a car passing outside is slowly moving. My apartment is on the first floor: I don't like heights. Before this I always lived in a house.

I've been having a dream about Joseph. Joseph was never much interested in dreams. At the beginning I used to save them up for him and tell them to him, the ones I thought were of interest, but he would always refuse to say what they meant. He'd make me tell him, instead. Being awake, according to Joseph, was more important than being asleep. He wanted me to prefer it.

Nevertheless, there was Joseph in my dream. It's the first time he's made an appearance. I think that it will please him to have made it, finally, after all those other dreams about preparations for dinner parties, always one plate short. But then I remember that he's no longer around to be told. Here it is, finally, the shape of my bereavement: Joseph is no longer around to be told. There is no one left in my life who is there only to be told.

I'm in an airport terminal. The plane's been delayed, all the planes have been delayed, perhaps there's a strike, and people are crammed in and milling around. Some of them are upset, there are children crying, some of the women are crying too, they've lost people, they push through the crowd calling out names, but elsewhere there are clumps of men and women laughing and singing, they've had the foresight to bring cases of beer with them to the airport and they're passing the bottles around. I try to get some information but there's no one at any of the ticket counters. Then I realize I've forgotten my passport. I decide to take a taxi home to get it, and by the time I make it back maybe they'll have everything straightened out.

I push towards the exit doors, but someone is waving to me across the heads of the crowd. It's Joseph. I'm not at all surprised to see him, though I do wonder about the winter overcoat he's wearing, since it's still summer. He also has a yellow muffler wound around his neck, and a hat. I've never seen him in any of these clothes before. Of course, I think, he's cold, but now he's pushed through the people, he's beside me. He's wearing a pair of heavy leather gloves and he takes the right one off to shake my hand. His own hand is bright blue, a flat tempera-paint blue, a picture-book blue. I hesitate, then I shake the hand, but he doesn't let go, he holds my hand, confidingly, like a child, smiling at me as if we haven't met for a long time.

"I'm glad you got the invitation," he says.

Now he's leading me towards a doorway. There are fewer people now. To one side there's a stand selling orange juice. Joseph's three wives are behind the counter, all in identical costumes, white hats and frilly aprons, like waitresses of the forties. We go through the doorway; inside, people are sitting at small round tables, though there's nothing on the tables in front of them, they appear to be waiting.

I sit down at one of the tables and Joseph sits opposite me. He doesn't take off his hat or his coat, but his hands are on the table, no gloves, they're the normal colour again. There's a man standing beside us, trying to attract our attention. He's holding out a small white card covered with symbols, hands and fingers. A deaf-mute, I decide, and sure enough when I look his mouth is sewn shut. Now he's tugging at Joseph's arm, he's holding out something else, it's a large yellow flower. Joseph doesn't see him.

"Look," I say to Joseph, but the man is already gone and one of the waitresses has come instead. I resent the interruption, I have so much to tell Joseph and there's so little time, the plane will go in a minute, in the other room I can already hear the crackle of announcements, but the woman pushes in between us, smiling officiously. It's the first wife; behind her, the other two wives stand in attendance. She sets a large plate in front of us on the table.

"Will that be all?" she says, before she retreats.

The plate is filled with cookies, children's-party cookies, white ones, cut into the shapes of moons and stars, decorated with silver balls and coloured sugar. They look too rich.

"My sins," Joseph says. His voice sounds wistful but when I glance up he's smiling at me. Is he making a joke?

I look down at the plate again. I have a moment of panic: this is not what I ordered, it's too much for me, I might get sick. Maybe I could send it back; but I know this isn't possible.

I remember now that Joseph is dead. The plate floats up towards me, there is no table, around us is dark space. There are thousands of stars, thousands of moons, and as I reach out for one they begin to shine.

(1977)

QUESTIONS

1. What are the narrator's feelings about Joseph? Do they change?

2. List the different time sequences in this story, counting imagined scenes, dreams, and flashbacks. Why is the discourse broken up into these segments?

3. Is psychotherapy a kind of sin eating? Does Joseph's anecdote have more than one application in the story?

4. Why are segments eight and eleven presented by the discourse as flash-backs? Where would they appear if the discourse-order paralleled the story-order? What would the effect be of this "normal" order?

5. How do you think the following readers would react to this story: a priest, a folklorist, a therapist, a therapist's wife or husband, someone contemplating suicide?

❖ Joyce Carol Oates
Four Summers

Joyce Carol Oates (1938–) was born in Lockport, New York, and studied at Syracuse University and the University of Wisconsin. She taught for a number of years in the Detroit area, first at the University of Detroit and then across the river at the University of Windsor in Canada. Some of her stories are set in the area's grim industrial environment. Since 1978 she has taught at Princeton University. She started writing as an undergraduate and won a Mademoiselle College Fiction Award at 21. Oates is amazingly prolific, having written over a dozen novels and over a hundred short stories, not to speak of literary criticism and other nonfiction. Her novels are *With Shuddering Fall* (1964), *A Garden of Earthly Delights* (1967), *Expensive People* (1967), *them* (which won a National Book Award, 1969), *Wonderland* (1971), *Do with Me What You Will* (1973), *The Assassins: A Book of Hours* (1975), *Triumph of the Spider Monkey* (1976), *Childwold* (1976), *Son of the Morning* (1978), *Cybele* (1979), *Unholy Loves* (1979), *Bellefleur* (1980), *Angel of Light* (1981), *A Bloodsmoor Romance* (1982), *Mysteries of Winterthurn* (1984), *Solstice* (1985), *Marya: A Life* (1986), *You Must Remember This* (1987), *American Appetites* (1989), *Because It Is Bitter and Because It Is My Heart* (1990), and *I Lock My Door on Myself* (1990). Her short stories have been collected in *By the North Gate* (1963), *Upon the Sweeping Flood* (1966), *The Wheel of Love* (1970), *Marriages and Infidelities* (1972), *The Goddess and Other Women* (1974), *Where Are You Going, Where Have You Been?* (1974), *The Hungry Ghosts: Seven Allusive Comedies* (1974), *The Poisoned Kiss and Other Stories from the Portuguese* (1975), *The Seduction* (1975), *Crossing the Border* (1976), *Nightside* (1977), *All the Good People I've Left Behind* (1979), *The Lamb of Abyssinia* (1980), *A Sentimental Education* (1981), *Last Days* (1984), *Wild Nights* (1985), *Raven's Wing* (1986), and *The Assignation* (1988). She has also written several volumes of poetry and a collection of plays. Her nonfiction includes *The Edge of Impossibility: Tragic Forms in Literature* (1972), *The Hostile Sun: The Poetry of D. H. Lawrence* (1973), *New Heaven, New Earth: The Visionary Experience in Literature* (1974), *Contraries: Essays* (1981), and *On Boxing* (1987).

It is some kind of special day. "Where's Sissie?" Ma says. Her face gets sharp, she is frightened. When I run around her chair she laughs and hugs me. She is pretty when she laughs. Her hair is long and pretty.

We are sitting at the best table of all, out near the water. The sun is warm and

43

the air smells nice. Daddy is coming back from the building with some glasses of beer, held in his arms. He makes a grunting noise when he sits down.

"Is the lake deep?" I ask them.

They don't hear me, they're talking. A woman and a man are sitting with us. The man marched in the parade we saw just awhile ago; he is a volunteer fireman and is wearing a uniform. Now his shirt is pulled open because it is hot. I can see the dark curly hair way up by his throat; it looks hot and prickly.

A man in a soldier's uniform comes over to us. They are all friends, but I can't remember him. We used to live around here, Ma told me, and then we moved away. The men are laughing. The man in the uniform leans back against the railing, laughing, and I am afraid it will break and he will fall into the water.

"Can we go out in a boat, Dad?" says Jerry.

He and Frank keep running back and forth. I don't want to go with them, I want to stay by Ma. She smells nice. Frank's face is dirty with sweat. "Dad," he says, whining, "can't we go out in a boat? Them kids are going out."

A big lake is behind the building and the open part where we are sitting. Some people are rowing on it. This tavern is noisy and everyone is laughing; it is too noisy for Dad to think about what Frank said.

"Harry," says Ma, "the kids want a boat ride. Why don't you leave off drinking and take them?"

"What?" says Dad.

He looks up from laughing with the men. His face is damp with sweat and he is happy. "Yeah, sure, in a few minutes. Go over there and play and I'll take you out in a few minutes."

The boys run out back by the rowboats, and I run after them. I have a bag of potato chips.

An old man with a white hat pulled down over his forehead is sitting by the boats, smoking. "You kids be careful," he says.

Frank is leaning over and looking at one of the boats. "This here is the best one," he says.

"Why's this one got water in it?" says Jerry.

"You kids watch out. Where's your father?" the man says.

"He's gonna take us for a ride," says Frank.

"Where is he?"

The boys run along, looking at the boats that are tied up. They don't bother with me. The boats are all painted dark green, but the paint is peeling off some of them in little pieces. There is water inside some of them. We watch two people come in, a man and a woman. The woman is giggling. She has on a pink dress and she leans over to trail one finger in the water. "What's all this filthy stuff by the shore?" she says. There is some scum in the water. It is colored a light brown and there are little seeds and twigs and leaves in it.

The man helps the woman out of the boat. They laugh together. Around their rowboat little waves are still moving; they make a churning noise that I like.

"Where's Dad?" Frank says.

"He ain't coming," says Jerry.

They are tossing pebbles out into the water. Frank throws his sideways, twisting his body. He is ten and very big. "I bet he ain't coming," Jerry says, wiping his nose with the back of his hand.

After awhile we go back to the table. Behind the table is the white railing, and then the water, and then the bank curves out so that the weeping willow trees droop over the water. More men in uniforms, from the parade, are walking by.

"Dad," says Frank, "can't we go out? Can't we? There's a real nice boat there—"

"For Christ's sake, get them off me," Dad says. He is angry with Ma. "Why don't you take them out?"

"Honey, I can't row."

"Should we take out a boat, us two?" the other woman says. She has very short, wet-looking hair. It is curled in tiny little curls close to her head and is very bright. "We'll show them, Lenore. Come on, let's give your kids a ride. Show these guys how strong we are."

"That's all you need, to sink a boat," her husband says.

They all laugh.

The table is filled with brown beer bottles and wrappers of things. I can feel how happy they all are together, drawn together by the round table. I lean against Ma's warm leg and she pats me without looking down. She lunges forward and I can tell even before she says something that she is going to be loud.

"You guys're just jealous! Afraid we'll meet some soldiers!" she says.

"Can't we go out, Dad? Please?" Frank says. "We won't fight. . . ."

"Go and play over there. What're those kids doing—over there?" Dad says, frowning. His face is damp and loose, the way it is sometimes when he drinks. "In a little while, okay? Ask your mother."

"She can't do it," Frank says.

"They're just jealous," Ma says to the other woman, giggling. "They're afraid we might meet somebody somewhere."

"Just who's gonna meet this one here?" the other man says, nodding with his head at his wife.

Frank and Jerry walk away. I stay by Ma. My eyes burn and I want to sleep, but they won't be leaving for a long time. It is still daylight. When we go home from places like this it is always dark and getting chilly and the grass by our house is wet.

"Duane Dorsey's in jail," Dad says. "You guys heard about that?"

"Duane? Yeah, really?"

"It was in the newspaper. His mother-in-law or somebody called the police, he was breaking windows in her house."

"That Duane was always a nut!"

"Is he out now, or what?"

"I don't know, I don't see him these days. We had a fight," Dad says.

The woman with the short hair looks at me. "She a real cute little thing," she says, stretching her mouth. "She drink beer, Lenore?"

"I don't know."

"Want some of mine?"

She leans toward me and holds the glass by my mouth. I can smell the beer and the warm stale smell of perfume. There are pink lipstick smudges on the glass.

"Hey, what the hell are you doing?" her husband says.

When he talks rough like that I remember him: we were with him once before.

"Are you swearing at me?" the woman says.

"Leave off the kid, you want to make her a drunk like ourself?"

"It don't hurt, one little sip. . . ."

"It's okay," Ma says. She puts her arm around my shoulders and pulls me closer to the table.

"Let's play cards. Who wants to?" Dad says.

"Sissie wants a little sip, don't you?" the woman says. She is smiling at me and I can see that her teeth are darkish, not nice like Ma's.

"Sure, go ahead," says Ma.

"I said leave off that, Sue, for Christ's sake," the man says. He jerks the table. He is a big man with a thick neck; he is bigger than Dad. His eyebrows are blond, lighter than his hair, and are thick and tufted. Dad is staring at something out on the lake without seeing it. "Harry, look, my goddam wife is trying to make your kid drink beer."

"Who's getting hurt?" Ma says angrily.

Pa looks at me all at once and smiles. "Do you want it, baby?"

I have to say yes. The woman grins and holds the glass down to me, and it clicks against my teeth. They laugh. I stop swallowing right away because it is ugly, and some of the beer drips down on me. "Honey, you're so clumsy," Ma says, wiping me with a napkin.

"She's a real cute girl," the woman says, sitting back in her chair. "I wish I had a nice little girl like that."

"Lay off that," says her husband.

"Hey, did you bring any cards?" Dad says to the soldier.

"They got some inside."

"Look, I'm sick of cards," Ma says.

"Yeah, why don't we all go for a boat ride?" says the woman. "Be real nice, something new. Every time we get together we play cards. How's about a boat ride?"

"It better be a big boat, with you in it," her husband says. He is pleased when everyone laughs, even the woman. The soldier lights a cigarette and laughs. "How come your cousin here's so skinny and you're so fat?"

"She isn't fat," says Ma. "What the hell do you want? Look at yourself."

"Yes, the best days of my life are behind me," the man says. He wipes his face and then presses a beer bottle against it. "Harry, you're lucky you moved out. It's all going downhill, back in the neighborhood."

"You should talk, you let our house look like hell," the woman says. Her face is blotched now, some parts pale and some red. "Harry don't sit out in his back yard all weekend drinking. He gets something done."

"Harry's younger than me."

Ma reaches over and touches Dad's arm. "Harry, why don't you take the kids out? Before it gets dark."

Dad lifts his glass and finishes his beer. "Who else wants more?" he says.

"I'll get them, you went last time," the soldier says.

"Get a chair for yourself," says Dad. "We can play poker."

"I don't want to play poker, I want to play rummy," the woman says.

"At church this morning Father Reilly was real mad," says Ma. "He said some kids or somebody was out in the cemetery and left some beer bottles. Isn't that awful?"

"Duane Dorsey used to do worse than that," the man says, winking.

"Hey, who's that over there?"

"You mean that fat guy?"

"Isn't that the guy at the lumberyard that owes all that money?"

Dad turns around. His chair wobbles and he almost falls; he is angry.

"This goddamn place is too crowded," he says.

"This is a real nice place," the woman says. She is taking something out of her purse. "I always liked it, didn't you, Lenore?"

"Sue and me used to come here a lot," says Ma. "And not just with you two, either."

"Yeah, we're real jealous," the man says.

"You should be," says the woman.

The soldier comes back. Now I can see that he is really a boy. He runs to the table with the beer before he drops anything. He laughs.

"Jimmy, your ma wouldn't like to see you drinking!" the woman says happily.

"Well, she ain't here."

"Are they still living out in the country?" Ma says to the woman.

"Sure. No electricity, no running water, no bathroom — same old thing. What can you do with people like that?"

"She always talks about going back to the Old Country," the soldier says. "Thinks she can save up money and go back."

"Poor old bastards don't know there was a war," Dad says. He looks as if something tasted bad in his mouth. "My old man died thinking he could go back in a year or two. Stupid old bastards!"

"Your father was real nice. . . ." Ma says.

"Yeah, real nice," says Dad. "Better off dead."

Everybody was quiet.

"June Dieter's mother's got the same thing," the woman says in a low voice to Ma. "She had it a year now and don't weigh a hundred pounds — you remember how big she used to be."

"She was big, all right," Ma says.

"Remember how she ran after June and slapped her? We were there — some guys were driving us home."

"Yeah. So she's got it too."

"Hey," says Dad, "why don't you get a chair, Jimmy? Sit down here."

The solder looks around. His face is raw in spots, broken out. But his eyes are nice. He never looks at me.

"Get a chair from that table," Dad says.

"Those people might want it."

"Hell, just take it. Nobody's sitting on it."

"They might—"

Dad reaches around and yanks the chair over. The people look at him, but don't say anything. Dad is breathing hard. "Here, sit here," he says. The soldier sits down.

Frank and Jerry come back. They stand by Dad, watching him, "Can we go out now?" Frank says.

"What?"

"Out for a boat ride."

"What? No, next week. Do it next week. We're going to play cards."

"You said—"

"Shut up, we'll do it next week." Dad looks up and shades his eyes. "The lake don't look right anyway."

"Lots of people are out there—"

"I said shut up."

"Honey," Ma whispers, "let him alone. Go and play by yourselves."

"Can we sit in the car?"

"Okay, but don't honk the horn."

"Ma, can't we go for a ride?"

"Go and play by yourselves, stop bothering us," she says. "Hey, will you take Sissie?"

They look at me. They don't like me, I can see it, but they take me with them. We run through the crowd and somebody spills a drink — he yells at us. "Oops, got to watch it!" Frank giggles.

We run along the walk by the boat. A woman in a yellow dress is carrying a baby. She looks at us like she doesn't like us.

Down at the far end some kids are standing together.

"Hey, lookit that," Frank says.

A blackbird is caught in the scum, by one of the boats. It can't fly up. One of the kids, a long-legged girl in a dirty dress, is poking at it with a stick.

The bird's wings keep fluttering but it can't get out. If it could get free it would fly and be safe, but the scum holds it down.

One of the kids throws a stone at it. "Stupid old goddamn bird," somebody says. Frank throws a stone. They are all throwing stones. The bird doesn't know enough to turn away. Its feathers are all wet and dirty. One of the stones hits the bird's head.

"Take that!" Frank says, throwing a rock. The water splashes up and some of the girls scream.

I watch them throwing stones. I am standing at the side. If the bird dies, then everything can die. I think. Inside the tavern there is music from the jukebox.

II

We are at the boathouse tavern again. It is a mild day, a Sunday afternoon. Dad is talking with some men; Jerry and I are waiting by the boats. Mommy is at home with the new baby. Frank has gone off with some friends of his, to a stock-car race. There are some people here, sitting out at the tables, but they don't notice us.

"Why doesn't he hurry up?" Jerry says.

Jerry is twelve now. He has pimples on his forehead and chin.

He pushes one of the rowboats with his foot. He is wearing sneakers that are dirty. I wish I could get in that boat and sit down, but I am afraid. A boy not much older than Jerry is squatting on the boardwalk, smoking. You can tell he is in charge of the boats.

"Daddy, come on. Come on," Jerry says, whining. Daddy can't hear him.

I have mosquito bites on my arms and legs. There are mosquitoes and flies around here; the flies crawl around the sticky mess left on tables. A car over in the parking lot has its radio on loud. You can hear the music all this way. "He's coming," I tell Jerry so he won't be mad. Jerry is like Dad, the way his eyes look.

"Oh, that fat guy keeps talking to him," Jerry says.

The fat man is one of the bartenders; he has on a dirty white apron. All these men are familiar. We have been seeing them for years. He punches Dad's arm, up by the shoulder, and Dad pushes him. They are laughing, though. Nobody is mad.

"I'd sooner let a nigger—" the bartender says. We can't hear anything more, but the men laugh again.

"All he does is drink," Jerry says. "I hate him."

At school, up on the sixth-grade floor, Jerry got in trouble last month. The principal slapped him. I am afraid to look at Jerry when he's mad.

"I hate him, I wish he'd die," Jerry says.

Dad is trying to come to us, but every time he takes a step backward and gets ready to turn, one of the men says something. There are three men beside him. Their stomachs are big, but Dad's isn't. He is wearing dark pants and a white shirt; his tie is in the car. He wears a tie to church, then takes it off. He has his shirt sleeves rolled up and you can see how strong his arms must be.

Two women cross over from the parking lot. They are wearing high-heeled shoes and hats and bright dresses — orange and yellow — and when they walk past the men look at them. They go into the tavern. The men laugh about something. The way they laugh makes my eyes focus on something away from them — a bird flying in the sky — and it is hard for me to look anywhere else. I feel as if I'm falling asleep.

"Here he comes!" Jerry says.

Dad walks over to us, with his big steps. He is smiling and carrying a bottle of beer. "Hey, kid," he says to the boy squatting on the walk, "how's about a boat?"

"This one is the best," Jerry says.

"The best, huh? Great." Dad grins at us. "Okay, Sissie, let's get you in. Be careful now." He picks me up even though I am too heavy for it, and sets me in the boat. It hurts a little where he held me, under the arms, but I don't care.

Jerry climbs in. Dad steps and something happens — he almost slips, but he catches himself. With the wet oar he pushes us off from the boardwalk.

Dad can row fast. The sunlight is gleaming on the water. I sit very still, facing him, afraid to move. The boat goes fast, and Dad is leaning back and forth and pulling on the oars, breathing hard, doing everything fast like he always does. He is always in a hurry to get things done. He has set the bottle of beer down by his leg, pressed against the side of the boat so it won't fall.

"There's the guys we saw go out before," Jerry says. Coming around the island is a boat with three boys in it, older than Jerry. "They went to the island. Can we go there too?"

"Sure," says Dad. His eyes squint in the sun. He is suntanned, and there are freckles on his forehead. I am sitting close to him, facing him, and it surprises me what he looks like — he is a stranger, with his eyes narrowed. The water beneath the boat makes me feel funny. It keeps us up now, but if I fell over the side I would sink and drown.

"Nice out here, huh?" Dad says. He is breathing hard.

"We should go over that way to get on the island," Jerry says.

"This goddamn oar has splinters in it," Dad says. He hooks the oar up and lets us glide. He reaches down to get the bottle of beer. Though the lake and some trees and the buildings back on shore are in front of me, what makes me look at it is my father's throat, the way it bobs when he swallows. He wipes his forehead. "Want to row, Sissie?" he says.

"Can I?"

"Let me do it," says Jerry.

"Naw, I was just kidding," Dad says.

"I can do it. It ain't hard."

"Stay where you are," Dad says.

He starts rowing again, faster. Why does he go so fast? His face is getting red, the way it does at home when he has trouble with Frank. He clears his throat and spits over the side; I don't like to see that but I can't help but watch. The other boat glides past us, heading for shore. The boys don't look over at us.

Jerry and I look to see if anyone else is on the island, but no one is. The island is very small. You can see around it.

"Are you going to land on it, Dad?" Jerry says.

"Sure okay." Dad's face is flushed and looks angry.

The boat scrapes bottom and bumps. "Jump out and pull it in," Dad says. Jerry jumps out. His shoes and socks are wet now, but Dad doesn't notice. The boat bumps; it hurts me. I am afraid. But then we're up on the land and Dad is out and lifting me. "Nice ride, sugar?" he says.

Jerry and I run around the island. It is different from what we thought, but we don't know why. There are some trees on it, some wild grass, and then bare caked mud that goes down to the water. The water looks dark and deep on the other side, but when we get there it's shallow. Lily pads grow there; everything is thick and tangled. Jerry wades in the water and gets his pants legs wet. "There might be money in the water," he says.

Some napkins and beer cans are nearby. There is part of a hotdog bun, with flies buzzing around it.

When we go back by Dad, we see him squatting over the water doing something. His back jerks. Then I see that he is being sick. He is throwing up in the water and making a noise like coughing.

Jerry turns around right away and runs back. I follow him, afraid. On the other side we can look back at the boathouse and wish we were there.

III

Marian and Betty went to the show, but I couldn't. She made me come along here with them. "And cut out that snippy face," Ma said, to let me know she's watching. I have to help her take care of Linda — poor fat Linda, with her runny nose! So here we are inside the tavern. There's too much smoke, I hate smoke. Dad is smoking a cigar. I won't drink any more root beer, it's flat, and I'm sick of potato chips. Inside me there is something that wants to run away, that hates them. How loud they are, my parents! My mother spilled something on the front of her dress, but does she notice? And my aunt Lucy and uncle Joe, they're here. Try to avoid them. Lucy has false teeth that make everyone stare at her. I know that everyone is staring at us. I could hide my head in my arms and turn away, I'm so tired and my legs hurt from sunburn and I can't stand them any more.

"So did you ever hear from them? That letter you wrote?" Ma says to Lucy.

"I'm still waiting. Somebody said you got to have connections to get on the show. But I don't believe it. That Howie Masterson that's the emcee, he's a real nice guy. I can tell."

"It's all crap," Dad says. "You women believe anything."

"I don't believe it," I say.

"Phony as hell," says my uncle.

"You do too believe it, Sissie," says my mother. "Sissie thinks he's cute. I know she does.

"I hate that guy!" I tell her, but she and my aunt are laughing. "I said I hate him! He's greasy."

"All that stuff is phony as hell," says my Uncle Joe. He is tired all the time, and right now he sits with his head bowed. I hate his bald head with the little fringe of gray hair on it. At least my father is still handsome. His jaws sag and there are lines in his neck — edged with dirt, I can see, embarrassed — and his stomach is bulging a little against the table, but still he is a handsome man. In a place like this women look at him. What's he see in *her*? they think. My mother had her hair cut too short last time; she looks queer. There is a photograph taken of her when she was young, standing by someone's motorcycle, with her hair long. In the photograph she was pretty, almost beautiful, but I don't believe it. Not really. I can't believe it, and I hate her. Her forehead gathers itself up a little in wrinkles whenever she glances down at Linda, as if she can't remember who Linda is.

"Well, nobody wanted you, kid," she once said to Linda. Linda was a baby then, one year old. Ma was furious, standing in the kitchen where she was washing the floor, screaming: "Nobody wanted you, it was a goddamn accident! An accident!" That surprised me so I didn't know what to think, and I didn't know if I hated Ma or not; but I kept it all a secret . . . only my girl friends know, and I won't tell the priest either. Nobody can make me tell. I narrow my eyes and watch my mother leaning forward to say something — it's like she's going to toss something out on the table — and think that maybe she isn't my mother after all, and she isn't that pretty girl in the photograph, but someone else.

"A woman was on the show last night that lost two kids in a fire. Her house burned down," my aunt says loudly. "And she answered the questions right off and got a lot of money and the audience went wild. You could see she was a real lady. I love that guy, Howie Masterson. He's real sweet."

"He's a bastard," Dad says.

"Harry, what the hell? You never even see him," Ma says.

"I sure as hell never did. Got better things to do at night." Dad turns to my uncle and his voice changes. "I'm on the night shift, now."

"Yeah, I hate that, I—"

"I can sleep during the day. What's the difference?"

"I hate those night shifts."

"What's there to do during the day?" Dad says flatly. His eyes scan us at the table as if he doesn't see anything, then they seem to fall off me and go behind me, looking at nothing.

"Not much," says my uncle, and I can see his white scalp beneath his hair. Both men are silent.

Dad pours beer into his glass and spills some of it. I wish I could look away. I love him, I think, but I hate to be here. Where would I rather be? With Marian and Betty at the movies, or in my room, lying on the bed and staring at the photographs of movie stars on my walls — those beautiful people that never say anything — while out in the kitchen my mother is waiting for my father to come home, so they can continue their quarrel. It never stops, that quarrel. Sometimes they laugh together, kid around, they kiss. Then the quarrel starts up again in a few minutes.

"Ma, can I go outside and wait in the car?" I say. "Linda's asleep."

"What's so hot about the car?" she says, looking at me.

"I'm tired. My sunburn hurts."

Linda is sleeping in Ma's lap, with her mouth open and drooling on the front of her dress. "Okay, go on," Ma says. "But we're not going to hurry just for you." When she has drunk too much there is a struggle in her between being angry and being affectionate; she fights both of them, as if standing with her legs apart and her hands on her hips, bracing a strong wind.

When I cross through the crowded tavern I'm conscious of people looking at me. My hair lost its curl because it was so humid today, my legs are too thin, my figure is flat and not nice like Marian's — I want to hide somewhere, hide my face from them. I hate this noisy place and these people. Even the music is ugly because it belongs to them. Then, when I'm outside, the music gets faint right away and it doesn't sound so bad. It's cooler out here. No one is around. Out back, the old rowboats are tied up. Nobody's on the lake. There's no moon, the sky is overcast, it was raining earlier.

When I turn around, a man is standing by the door watching me.

"What're you doing?" he says.

"Nothing."

He has dark hair and a tanned face, I think, but everything is confused because the light from the door is pinkish — there's a neon sign there. My heart starts to pound. The man leans forward to stare at me. "Oh, I thought you were somebody else," he says.

I want to show him I'm not afraid. "Yeah, really? Who did you think I was?" When we ride on the school bus we smile out the windows at strange men, just for fun. We do that all the time. I'm not afraid of any of them.

"You're not her," he says.

Some people come out the door and he has to step out of their way. I say to him, "Maybe you seen me around here before. We come here pretty often."

"Who do you come with?" He is smiling as if he thinks I'm funny. "Anybody I know?"

"That's my business."

It's a game. I'm not afraid. When I think of my mother and father inside, something makes me want to step closer to this man — why should I be afraid? I could be wild like some of the other girls. Nothing surprises me.

We keep on talking. At first I can tell he wants me to come inside the tavern with him, but then he forgets about it; he keeps talking. I don't know what we say, but we talk in drawling voices, smiling at each other but in a secret, knowing way, as if each one of us knew more than the other. My cheeks start to burn. I could be wild like Betty is sometimes — like some of the other girls. Why not? Once before I talked with a man like this, on the bus. We were both sitting in the back. I wasn't afraid. This man and I keep talking and we talk about nothing, he wants to know how old I am, but it makes my heart pound so hard that I want to touch my chest to calm it. We are walking along the old boardwalk and I say: "Somebody took me out rowing once here."

"Is that so?" he says. "You want me to take you out?"

He has a hard, handsome face. I like that face. Why is he alone? When he smiles I know he's laughing at me, and this makes me stand taller, walk with my shoulders raised.

"Hey, are you with somebody inside there?" he says.

"I left them."

"Have a fight?"

"A fight, yes."

He looks at me quickly. "How old are you anyway?"

"That's none of your business."

"Girls your age are all alike."

"We're not all alike?" I arch my back and look at him in a way I must have learned somewhere — where? — with my lips not smiling but ready to smile, and my eyes narrowed. One leg is turned as if I'm ready to jump from him. He sees all this. He smiles.

"Say, you're real cute."

We're walking over by the parking lot now. He touches my arm. Right away my heart trips, but I say nothing, I keep walking. High above us the tree branches are moving in the wind. It's cold for June. It's late — after eleven. The man is wearing a jacket, but I have on a sleeveless dress and there are goose-pimples on my arms.

"Cold, huh?" he says.

He takes hold of my shoulders and leans toward me. This is to show me, he's no kid, he's grown-up, this is how they do things; when he kisses me his grip on my shoulders gets tighter. "I better go back," I say to him. My voice is queer.

"What?" he says.

I am wearing a face like one of the faces pinned up in my room, and what if I lose it? This is not my face. I try to turn away from him.

He kisses me again. His breath smells like beer, maybe, it's like my father's breath, and my mind is empty; I can't think what to do. Why am I here? My legs feel numb, my fingers are cold. The man rubs my arms and says, "You should have a sweater or something. . . ."

He is waiting for me to say something, to keep on the way I was before. But I have forgotten how to do it. Before, I was Marian or one of the older girls; now I am just myself. I am fourteen. I think of Linda sleeping in my mother's lap, and something frightens me.

"Hey, what's wrong?" the man says.

He sees I'm afraid but pretends he doesn't. He comes to me again and embraces me, his mouth presses against my neck and shoulder, I feel as if I'm suffocating. "My car's over here," he says, trying to catch his breath. I can't move. Something dazzling and icy rises up in me, an awful fear, but I can't move and can't say anything. He is touching me with his hands. His mouth is soft but wants too much from me. I think, What is he doing? Do they all do this? Do I have to have it done to me too?

"You cut that out," I tell him.

He steps away. His chest is heaving and his eyes look like a dog's eyes, surprised and betrayed. The last thing I see of him is those eyes, before I turn and run back to the tavern.

IV

Jesse says, "Let's stop at this place. I been here a few times before."

It's the Lakeside Bar. That big old building with the grubby siding, and a big pink neon sign in front, and the cinder driveway that's so bumpy. Yes, everything the same. But different too — smaller, dirtier. There is a custard stand nearby with a glaring orange roof, and people are crowded around it. That's new. I haven't been here for years.

"I feel like a beer," he says.

He smiles at me and caresses my arm. He treats me as if I were something that might break; in my cheap linen maternity dress I feel ugly and heavy. My flesh is so soft and thick that nothing could hurt it.

"Sure, honey, Pa used to stop in here too.'

We cross through the parking lot to the tavern. Wild grass grows along the sidewalk and in the cracks of the sidewalk. Why is this place so ugly to me? I feel as if a hand were pressing against my chest, shutting off my breath. Is there some secret here? Why am I afraid?

I catch sight of myself in a dusty window as we pass. My hair is long, down to my shoulders. I am pretty, but my secret is that I am pretty like everyone is. My husband loves me for this but doesn't know it. I have a pink mouth and plucked darkened eyebrows and soft bangs over my forehead; I know everything, I have no need to learn from anyone else now. I am one of those girls younger girls study closely, to learn from. On buses, in five-and-tens, thirteen-year-old girls must look at me solemnly, learning, memorizing.

"Pretty Sissie!" my mother likes to say when we visit, though I told her how I hate that name. She is proud of me for being pretty, but thinks I'm too thin. "You'll fill out nice, after the baby," she says. Herself, she is fat and veins have begun to darken on her legs; she scuffs around the house in bedroom slippers. Who is my mother? When I think of her I can't think of anything — do I love her or hate her, or is there nothing there?

Jesse forgets and walks ahead of me, I have to walk fast to catch up. I'm wearing pastel-blue high heels—that must be because I am proud of my legs. I have little else. Then he remembers and turns to put out his hand for me, smiling to show he is sorry. Jesse is the kind of young man thirteen-year-old girls stare at secretly; he is not a man, not old enough, but not a boy either. He is a year older than I am, twenty. When I met him he was wearing a navy uniform and he was with a girl friend of mine.

Just a few people sitting outside at the tables. They're afraid of rain—the sky doesn't look good. And how bumpy the ground is here, bare spots and little holes and patches of crab grass, and everywhere napkins and junk. Too many flies outside. Has this place changed hands? The screens at the window don't fit right; you can see why flies get inside. Jesse opens the door for me and I go in. All bars smell alike. There is a damp, dark odor of beer and something indefinable—spilled soft drinks, pretzels getting stale? This bar is just like any other. Before we were married we went to places like this, Jesse and me and other couples. We had to spend a certain amount of time doing things like that—and going to movies, playing miniature golf, bowling, dancing, swimming—then we got married, now we're going to have a baby. I think of the baby all the time, because my life will be changed then; everything will be different. Four months from now. I should be frightened, but a calm laziness has come over me. It was so easy for my mother. . . . But it will be different with me because my life will be changed by it, and nothing ever changed my mother. You couldn't change her! Why should I think? Why should I be afraid? My body is filled with love for this baby, and I will never be the same again.

We sit down at a table near the bar. Jesse is in a good mood. My father would have liked him, I think; when he laughs Jesse reminds me of him. Why is a certain kind of simple, healthy, honest man always destined to lose everything? Their souls are as clean and smooth as the muscular line of their arms. At night I hold Jesse, thinking of my father and what happened to him—all that drinking, then the accident at the factory—and I pray that Jesse will be different. I hope that his quick, open, loud way of talking is just a disguise, that really he is someone else—slower and calculating. That kind of man grows old without jerks and spasms. Why did I marry Jesse?

Someone at the bar turns around, and it's a man I think I know—I have known. Yes. That man outside, the man I met outside, I stare at him, my heart pounding, and he doesn't see me. He is dark, his hair is neatly combed but is thinner than before; he is wearing a cheap gray suit. But is it the same man? He is standing with a friend and looking around, as if he doesn't like what he sees. He is tired too. He has grown years older.

Our eyes meet. He glances away. He doesn't remember—that frightened girl he held in his arms.

I am tempted to put my hand on Jesse's arm and tell him about that man, but how can I? Jesse is talking about trading in our car for a new one. . . . I can't move, my mind seems to be coming to a stop. Is that the man I kissed, or someone else? A feeling of angry loss comes over me. Why should I lose everything? Everything? Is it the same man, and would he remember? My heart bothers me, it's stupid to be like this: here I sit, powdered and sweet, a girl safely married, pregnant and secured to the earth, with my husband beside me. He still loves me. Our love keeps on. Like my parents' love, it will subside someday, but nothing surprises me because I have learned everything.

The man turns away, talking to his friend. They are weary, tired of some-thing. He isn't married yet, I think, and that pleases me. Good. But why are these men always tired? Is it the jobs they hold, the kind of men who stop in at this tavern? Why do they flash their teeth when they smile, but stop smiling so quickly? Why do their children cringe from them sometimes—an innocent upraised arm a frightening thing? Why do they grow old so quickly, sitting at kitchen tables with bottles of beer? They are everywhere, in every house. All of the houses in this neighborhood and all neighborhoods around here. Jesse is young, but the outline of what he will be is already in his face; do you think I can't see it? Their lives are like hands dealt out to them in their innumerable card games. You pick up the sticky cards, and there it is: there it is. Can't change anything, all you can do is switch some cards around, stick one in here, one over here . . . pretend there is some sense, a secret scheme.

The man at the bar tosses some coins down and turns to go. I want to cry out to him, "Wait, wait?" But I cannot. I sit helplessly and watch him leave. Is it the same man? If he leaves I will be caught here, what can I do? I can almost hear my mother's shrill laughter coming in from outside, and some drawling remark of my father's—lifting for a moment above the music. Those little explosions of laughter, the slap of someone's hand on the damp table in anger, the clink of bottles accidentally touching—and there, there, my drunken aunt's voice, what is she saying? I am terrified at being left with them. I watch the man at the door and think that I could have loved him. I know it.

He has left, he and his friend. He is nothing to me, but suddenly I feel tears in my eyes. What's wrong with me? I hate everything that springs upon me and seems to draw itself down and oppress me in a way I could never explain to anyone. . . . I am crying because I am pregnant, but not with that man's child. It could have been his child, I could have gone with him to his car; but I did nothing, I ran away, I was afraid, and now I'm sitting here with Jesse, who is picking the label off his beer bottle with his thick squarish fingernails. I did nothing. I was afraid. Now he has left me here and what can I do?

I let my hand fall onto my stomach to remind myself that I am in love: with this baby, with Jesse, with everything. I am in love with our house and our life and the future and even this moment—right now—that I am struggling to live through.

(1967)

QUESTIONS

1. How does the author indicate the passage of time between sections of the story? How much story-time elapses between the sections? Is this an effec-tive means of telling this particular short story, as opposed, say, to summar-izing events in Sissie's life? Why?

2. Does the style change from section to section to indicate the age of the narrator? How?

3. Why do these four slices of time constitute a whole short story? What holds them together? What about all the times we don't hear about?

4. What life options are open to Sissie? How does she learn what is expected of her?

5. Does everything in the story and every word in the discourse belong to the young girl who is supposed to be telling it? Are there any indications of another consciousness, of someone more like the author (older, better educated, urban, with different values and expectations), peeking over her shoulder and guiding her pen? If so, what are they? If not, why not?

SUGGESTIONS FOR WRITING

1. What happens after the narrative secrets are given away? When you reread a story, you already know what is going to take place. Analyze the difference in your reactions between your first reading of a story and subsequent readings. Were you still interested? Did you deliberately "forget" the ending in order to enjoy the plot? Is there something else that replaces simple curiosity that keeps you going?

2. Most stories invite us to speculate beyond the ending. Pick one of the stories in this section and sketch some events that might follow the last words in this story. What is the evidence to support your speculation?

3. Test your sense of fictional closure. Using one of the short stories in this section, see if it could be ended satisfactorily by giving it another point. Would the story have equal impact?

4. Compare story-time and discourse-time by constructing two time lines for any short story in this book. On one, show the events in the order they occurred; on the other, show the order in which we come to know them. Try to make your discourse time line show the relative duration of reading time, so that a fully developed *scene* is shown as longer than a *summary*, even though the scene may represent only a few moments, whereas the summary covers several years. How different are the two time lines? What does that tell you about the author's methods of storytelling?

3 Character and Setting

An event in a narrative doesn't happen by itself. Somebody or something makes it happen. In other words, plot actions require *agents*. These agents are usually human, but need not be: most of the agents in Aesop's *Fables* are animals. So is Lassie, the collie who stars in several novels and films. The principal agent of Herman Melville's *Moby-Dick* is a whale, and of Peter Benchley's *Jaws*, a shark. Remember, too, Bugs Bunny, White Fang, and Rudolph the Red-Nosed Reindeer. Narrative agents don't even have to be made flesh and blood: a tin man and a scarecrow are agents in *The Wizard of Oz*, robots play leading roles in *Star Wars*, and a computer named Hal is the villain of *2001*. A forest fire and a tropical storm are important agents in two modern novels. Literature and films are filled with supernatural creatures who are important agents. There is also a category of narrative, called *allegory*, populated by abstract qualities, for instance, Mr. Worldly Wiseman and Mrs. Timorous in John Bunyan's *Pilgrim's Progress*.

Character: A Definition

A narrative agent may be merely instrumental to the plot, for example, a "spear-carrier" or an unnamed messenger in a play. Such agents are totally colorless, without personality. The actions they perform completely explain their narrative purpose. We go to fictions to learn about more important agents, those we call *characters*. Our interest in characters stretches beyond their actions. For they possess *traits*, distinguishing qualities that give them some kind of identity and personality. Though always connected to the plot, a character has something of an independent existence. We may remember a character like Sissie or Shmul-Leibele or Huck Finn long after we have forgotten plot details.

Traits—whether "brave" or "cowardly," "honest" or "crooked," "debonair" or "bumptious"—are lasting qualities, not merely transitory moods or emotions. Some characters, like the *resourceful* Robinson Crusoe or the *ingenious* Sherlock Holmes or the *inept* but *saintly* Shmul-Leibele or the

58

loving but *meddlesome* Olenka, manifest strongly marked traits that are easy to cite and describe. Some display their chief trait in their very names: Charles Dickens named characters "Mr. Gradgrind" and "Mr. M'Choakumchild" (men committed to an absurdly strict and repressive educational system), "Bounderby" (who is very much a bounder), "Skimpole," "Jellyby," "Turveydrop," "Krook," "Cuttle," "Nipper," "Chuzzlewit," "Pecksniff," and many more.

Other characters, especially in modern fiction, are harder to describe, their traits more difficult to name. Characters like Joseph in Margaret Atwood's "The Sin Eater" or Wakefield, in Hawthorne's story of that name (pp. 457–462), or the old man in Carson McCullers's "A Tree A Rock A Cloud" are so complex, even enigmatic, that it is difficult to sum them up in a word or two. Other characters are difficult to categorize precisely because they are humdrum, ordinary, nondescript—those in "Careless Talk," for example, or in "Big Fish, Little Fish." Such short stories are marked more by the interest of the situation than by that of the characters' personalities. Characters themselves may be unclear about their personalities—indeed, the point of many modern short stories is a character's search for identity (Sissie in "Four Summers" is a good example).

In our attempt to understand a character, we look for direct clues, like explicit pronouncements of the narrator, but we also rely heavily on the character's actions. What a character does or says or thinks implies what she is like. Take Sissie in "Four Summers": It is not easy to say what makes her tick or to find exact adjectives to describe her, and we can only infer an impression. We see already in the first reported event that she is neglected by her parents. This neglect seems to have made her insecure, driving her into an early, unconsidered marriage and pregnancy. At nineteen she is already world-weary and unhappy about the future. She knows she is pretty, or at least she "knows everything" about how to look pretty, but that knowledge doesn't seem to make her very happy. The trait "insecure" seems appropriate to explain her various thoughts and actions, especially her overly hasty marriage, dissatisfaction with her husband, and fantasies of an affair with a man she met in the parking lot when she was fourteen.

Though we can distinguish them in theory, plot and character are in practice never separated. The actions of a character serve to characterize her. Conversely, her traits, whether stated explicitly by the narrator or only implied, set up plot expectations that she will in fact *do* something that illustrates the kind of person she is. If she is described as vengeful, we expect her to perform some act of revenge. Conversely, if she contemplates or performs an act of revenge, we can comfortably assign the trait "vengeful." In either direction, whether from action to trait or trait to action, we can say that one narrative component *motivates* the other. Many fictions establish motivation clearly, and deciphering motive is part of the pleasure that reading fiction gives us. Even when we cannot explain why, we feel that events happen for some reason, that if a character performs a given action, that action must be characteristic of her.

The chief character of a narrative is often called the *hero* or *heroine*.

Because *hero* implies virtue, and many chief characters are far from virtuous, a better term is *protagonist*. *Agon*, a Greek word, means "contest." The ancient Greeks thought of plot as a conflict or contest between the "first" or chief player (*proto* means "first") and his or her contender, the *antagonist* (*anti* means "against"). These terms should not be taken literally, not, at least, with respect to the modern short story. The protagonist may not be a hero in the moral sense, and the antagonist may not be a villain. Further, though some fictions entail a clear-cut conflict (like that between Fortunato and Montresor in Edgar Allan Poe's "The Cask of Amontillado," pp. 558–562), many do not.

Another important aspect of characters is their relative *complexity*. Complex characters like Sissie are often called *round characters*. *Flat characters*, on the other hand, possess a single marked trait that can be captured in a word or phrase — the miser, the prostitute with the heart of gold, the mad doctor, the cop that can't be bribed. Many of the Dickens characters cited above manifest only the single trait bound up in their names. Round characters are not so easy to sum up. Their traits are many, divergent, or even conflicting. Consider the complexity of Polzunkov in Dostoevsky's story (pp. 430–440); the narrator can barely find words to portray the contradictions of this "comic martyr." Or the characters may be nondescript, yet compellingly alive. Round characters, like people in real life, can be very complicated and not easy to explain. Learning about them, however, is a fascinating and absorbing experience, no less absorbing, once one gets into it, than discovering the solution to a murder mystery.

We can also distinguish between *major* characters and *minor*, according to their importance to the plot. These are independent properties: A character may be round and major, or flat and major, round and minor or flat and minor. The first and last combinations are the most frequent. A final distinction can be made between *dynamic* and *static* characters. Dynamic characters change over the course of the plot and usually as a consequence of what happens. Static characters remain the same.

How can we describe the characters we've met so far? Shmul-Leibele seems relatively round and major. The narrator explicitly calls him "slow," "small," and "clumsy," and we easily gather that he is also inept in his trade; but clearly he is devout and loving. His wife, Shoshe, is also round and major: She is devoted, efficient, helpful, tall, competent at her work. Both are static rather than dynamic characters, because their personalities do not change over the course of the short story. The character of Sissie, on the other hand, is not only round and major, but also dynamic: We see her evolve from a child without distinct traits to a young woman of some complexity.

Why do sophisticated readers and filmgoers prefer round and dynamic characters such as Sissie or the old man in "A Tree A Rock A Cloud" or Joseph and the unnamed narrator of Margaret Atwood's "The Sin Eater" to flat or static characters? Because they find in more complex characters something of the complexity of real life. It is easy to become engrossed with Sissie's confusion and dead-end despair, or with the pathetic attempts of the old man in "A Tree A Rock A Cloud" to come to terms with love. Conversely, I don't feel any such involvement with the handsome but inane characters who appears in television soap operas. Even if their *situations* are intriguing, they are not interesting as *people*; they seem all surface. How different is my pleasure in struggling to understand some complex character in a great short story or novel. Even if I don't totally fathom Joseph or the narrator of "The Sin Eater," or the schoolmaster or the Arab prisoner in Albert Camus's "The Guest" (pp. 193–202), or many of the characters who inhabit the great novels of Fyodor Dostoevsky or Marcel Proust or James Joyce, they remain more vivid in my memory than most people I have met in real life. Indeed, it seems precisely the uncertainty and enigma of their characters that makes me want to read about them more than once.

Characterization

Characters are given traits by a process called *characterization*. They may be characterized in a variety of ways. The most obvious is the narrator's *direct naming* of a trait, as we saw in the list of adjectives which the narrator applies to Shmul-Leibele. Another characterizing device is the trait-naming of one character *by another character*. However, can we trust the reliability and the motives of this second character? Sometimes we can and sometimes we can't. He may be objective, or he may be telling us more about his own prejudices than about the character that he describes. In "A Tree A Rock A Cloud" Leo's sneering remarks about the old man don't seem to characterize the old man fairly, but they speak worlds about Leo's own cynicism and bitterness.

Both of these characterizing devices are *direct*, that is, they work through actual words, typically adjectives, which the narrator assigns as trait-names. But traits are also *implied*. For example, we can infer from the actions, speeches, and thoughts of characters what they are like. If a character assaults several people, we may safely conclude that he is "violent." If he is afraid to speak his mind, we may well conclude that he is "timid." When I read in the very title that the first Alberta is a "wanton," I anticipate acts of wantonness; when I read that she is a nun, I anticipate acts of spiritual devotion.

These three kinds of characterization are all used in "Short Friday." At the beginning, the narrator tells us in so many words what kind of man Shmul-Leibele is—"small," "clumsy," and so on. We also learn about Shmul-Leibele from the traits applied to him by his wife, Shoshe, who finds him "quiet," "pious," and "retiring." Because Shoshe herself is characterized by her employers as "honest" and "diligent," we accept the validity of *her* characterization of her husband. Finally, the actions, dialogue, and thoughts of Shmul-Leibele and Shoshe contribute to our perception of their characters, whether by confirming the explicitly named traits or by adding ramifications and further details. That Shoshe makes such elaborate plans for the Sabbath, skimping the whole week in order to be lavish on the day of rest, confirms and illustrates her piety. Shmul-Leibele's devotion to his wife and his capacity for gratitude, as well as his own piety, are illustrated by his speech "Ah, Shoshe love, it's food fit for a king! Nothing less than a taste of Paradise!" And perhaps the best illustration of their devotion to God and to each other is their ultimate fate: to die a painless death in each other's arms and to be received into heaven by an angel of God.

In "Four Summers," on the other hand, Sissie is characterized indirectly—mostly by the way she tells her own story. The general atmosphere in which she grows up—her father's unpredictability and the general neglect that she and her brothers suffer—rob her of real values and a sense of security. Her thoughts in the fourth section provide confirming details. From the way she thinks about how she has made herself "pretty like everyone is" we infer that she has become cynical. She thinks of beauty as a game that young women learn from older women and then play on men. Her dead-end attitude appears in the remark "I know everything now." We are not taken in by such bravado, which obviously masks a deep uncertainty and even fear about her future. She doesn't know why she has married Jesse. That Jesse is like her father, "destined to lose everything," is hardly a good omen for her future. Her insecurity and dissatisfaction are also reflected in her romantic fantasy about a man who tried to pick her up when she was fourteen.

So Sissie is characterized *implicitly*. We infer her traits from her thoughts—thoughts that occurred to her back when she was younger and thoughts that she has now, in the final section, as she contemplates her present situation. Why is she characterized implicitly and not explicitly? Because insecurity and a lack of a clear sense of identity cloud one's objectivity. It makes sense for the narrator of "Short Friday" to characterize Shmul-Leibele and Shoshe definitively, but not for Sissie to be definitive about her own character.

Setting

The task of a fiction is to create a world that is believable. By "believable," I don't mean "realistic." The fictive world need not duplicate the real world. Fantasy and the supernatural have always been popular subjects for serious fiction, but even a supernatural fictional world needs to have its own consistency and autonomy. If they are to be magical at all, characters and events, such as those in the world of Oz, must be uniformly magical. Even fantasies have their rules of *verisimilitude*, a concept vitally important to fiction. Verisimilitude is not literal truth but the *appearance or semblance of truth*. It is "truth-seeming." In *Alice's Adventures in Wonderland*, the March Hare and the Cheshire Cat may be rather bizarre figments of Alice's (and Lewis Carroll's) imagination—but they are consistent figments. The Cheshire Cat never stops being odd; for example, he never suddenly becomes like our own tabbies, sniffing around pet food cans or scratching at the patio door to get out.

We have seen how the fictional world is inhabited by significant agents of action, or characters. That world, of course, also contains places and objects appropriate to the plot. To use words from the stage, we may call these *settings* and *props*. *Setting* is the larger backdrop against which the events transpire. *Props* are the objects handled or otherwise encountered by the characters. The choice of setting and props is crucial. Try to imagine Sam Spade occupying any world other than the one typified by his seedy office and old car. Except in a parody, a Sam Spade in orbit around the moon or in the jungles of New Guinea seems inconceivable. The same is true of props: We can imagine Sam with a phone or a gun in his hand, but not a lace doily or a fencing rapier. Conversely, telephones or other modern gadgets would be out of place in Isaac Bashevis Singer's "Short Friday."

Setting is a very elastic property of story. Some fictions take great pains to establish place; others sketch it in the briefest of terms. Some make no reference to place at all. Some lie between these two extremes. Isaac Babel's "How It Was Done in Odessa" (pp. 75–81), for example, uses relatively few but highly telling details. The settings are only named: two cemeteries, the meeting place of Benya and his men, Tartakovsky's office, Seredinskaya Square. A few props, however, are vivid and precisely evoked by adjectives: Benya wears "a chocolate jacket, cream pants, and raspberry boots." He drives a red automobile with a music box for a horn which plays a march from the opera *Pagliacci*. These sharp details vividly evoke the sense of Benya Krik's flashy appearance as new czar of the Jewish underworld of Odessa.

Setting entails the historical era during which the events transpire. Obviously we have different expectations about what would be a likely occurrence in the nineteenth-century Russia of Anton Chekhov's "The Darling" (pp. 104–112) and the twentieth-century New York City of James Baldwin's "The Rockpile" (pp. 153–159).

Setting also refers to climates of emotion, opinion, and attitude that hover about the fiction. The word *atmosphere* is sometimes used to refer to such climates, to the tone or mood of a narrative. Some of the short stories of Edgar Allan Poe, like "The Tell-Tale Heart" (pp. 226–229), evoke a weird, macabre atmosphere, whereas many stories by Mark Twain (pp. 380–384) and Stephen Crane (pp. 416–424) exude the dusty, rough-and-ready atmosphere of the American frontier. Other writers are not concerned about evoking a distinctive atmosphere; they prefer neutral settings.

We tend to take props and settings for granted. Sometimes we're even impatient with them because they seem to "slow down" the action. Raised as most of us are on movies and television, we expect to grasp the setting in a single glance. So, when we read, we may purposely skip descriptive passages. Clearly that way of reading robs us of potential pleasures. Without their descriptive passages many fictions would be shortchanged. Some, like Virginia Woolf's "Kew Gardens" (pp. 83–87), would be totally ruined. Imagine Albert Camus's "The Guest" (pp. 193–201) without its high snowy plateau, where the schoolmaster lives in such solitude. Or William Faulkner's "Delta Autumn" (pp. 281–290) without the landing on the river where the hunters pitch their camp. Or Gabriel Garcia Márquez's "Monologue of Isabel Watching It Rain in Macondo" (pp. 452–456) without a passage like this:

> After mass, before we women had time to find the catches on our parasols, a thick, dark wind blew, which with one broad, round swirl swept away the dust and hard tinder of May.

Ignoring a fiction's description of setting and atmosphere is like tuning out the mood music of a movie or television drama. That music may not seem strictly "necessary" to the unfolding of the plot, but think how weakened the film would be if it were eliminated from the sound track.

In fact, some fictions so highlight setting that it seems more important than the plot and characters. Virginia Woolf's "Kew Gardens" is an interesting example. The short story begins with a description of a flower-bed. There follow four short tales, consisting entirely of the conversations of passersby — a married couple, Eleanor and Simon, reminiscing about the past; an eccentric old man led by his attendant William through the gardens; two elderly working-class ladies; and a pair of young lovers. No, make that five tales: We must not forget the adventures of the snail, for the snail is very much a character in "Kew Gardens." Not only is its tale given equal place in the series between the first and third tales, but, as if to assure us of the snail's importance, the narrator describes the surroundings from its tiny perspective. What to us would be mere bits of soil are to the snail "brown cliffs," drops of water are "deep green lakes," and blades of grass are "flat, blade-like trees."

Yet, a traditional reader might complain, none of these conversations nor the snail's adventure really "go anywhere." There seems no particular reason for the order in which they are presented. Nor are any of the characters more important than any others: no protagonist emerges. These are random events, simply the kinds of happenings that one would expect in a public park on a sunny day. And that's the whole point! The conversations are incidental, but the setting is central. When we finish the story we feel less that the flower-bed provides the setting for a plot than that the conversations of the passersby and the desperate voyage of the snail are disturbances of the beautiful and tranquil setting of the flower-bed. The setting emerges as paramount. The flower garden, the park, the people, the sounds of London, the flicker of light and color — all form an impression of a fine day in that city. The text is a study in the beauty of the sheer existence of people, animals, and things, but a study from an odd perspective — that of the flower-bed. Unlike most short stories, where the narrator moves along with the characters, the narrator here stays with this single patch of garden. To make a cinematic comparison, it's as if the camera refused to "track" or "dolly" along with the human beings, thus making the flower-bed the enduring element, and beyond it, the impression of the blotches of color and the muffled sounds of the city. In a way, these become the characters — if we can speak of mere figures on a landscape as characters.

Some novels and short stories seem to demand a knowledge of places that we don't possess. It can be frustrating to feel that you must have seen the streets of Madrid or the steppes of Russia to understand the significance of plot events. Some great classics of fiction, fortunately, come in editions with explanatory notes. Though we may not have the time to consult an encyclopedia or an atlas, we may learn much about a place from reading a novel. Indeed, one of the most pleasant ways to learn about geography is to read fiction. Even if the information is impressionistic from a strictly geographic point of view, it's better to have a fictional sense of Paris or St. Petersburg than none at all. What we learn from novels and short stories is not as visually explicit as what movies and television spend millions to show us, but think of all the movies that are bad despite their scrupulously accurate attention to the setting. The rich descriptions of gifted verbal artists, on the other hand, provide a source of perennial nourishment for the visual imagination.

❖ ISAAC BASHEVIS SINGER
Short Friday*

Isaac Bashevis Singer (1904–1991) was born in Radzymin, Poland, the son of an orthodox rabbi but also a writer, as was his brother, Israel Joshua Singer. He began writing stories and poems at fourteen. He attended the Tachkemoni Rabbinical Seminary in Warsaw, as his father wished, but soon left for a full-time career as author, translator, and editor. He immigrated to Brooklyn in 1935 where he worked for the Yiddish-language newspaper *Jewish Daily Forward*. Despite advice to give up on Yiddish because it was dying, he continued to write in his native language. As his fiction got translated into English the greatness of his genius as an interpreter of Jewish life in Europe and America came to be recognized. Perhaps his greatest gift is to present deep and serious human problems in fiction that seems deceptively simple and straightforward. His novels include *Satan in Goray* (1935), *The Family Moskat* (1950), *The Magician of Lublin* (1960), *The Slave* (1962), *The Manor* (1967), *The Estate* (1969), *Enemies: A Love Story* (1972, since made into a film), *Shosha* (1978), and *The Penitent* (1983). His short stories have been collected in *Gimpel the Fool* (1957, the title story of which was translated by Saul Bellow), *The Spinoza of Market Street* (1961), *Short Friday* (1964), *Selected Short Stories* (1966), *The Seance* (1968), *A Friend of Kafka* (1970), *A Crown of Feathers* (1973, which won the National Book Award), *Passions* (1975), *Old Love* (1979), *The Collected Stories of I. B. Singer* (1982, which won the Pulitzer Prize for literature), and *The Image* (1985). Singer has also written many children's stories, as well as plays and books of autobiography. He was awarded the Nobel Prize for literature in 1978.

In the village of Lapschitz[1] lived a tailor named Shmul-Leibele with his wife, Shoshe. Shmul-Leibele was half tailor, half furrier, and a complete pauper. He had never mastered his trade. When filling an order for a jacket or a gaberdine, he inevitably made the garment either too short or too tight. The belt in the back would hang either too high or too low, the lapels never matched, the vent was off center. It was said that he had once sewn a pair of trousers with the fly off to one side. Shmul-Leibele could not count the wealthy citizens among his customers. Common people brought him their shabby garments to have patched and turned, and the peasants gave him their old

---

*Translated by Joseph Singer and Roger Klein.
[1]A small town in Poland.

pelts to reverse. As is usual with bunglers, he was also slow. He would dawdle over a garment for weeks at a time. Yet despite his shortcomings, it must be said that Shmul-Leibele was an honorable man. He used only strong thread and none of his seams ever gave. If one ordered a lining from Shmul-Leibele, even one of common sackcloth or cotton, he bought only the very best material, and thus lost most of his profit. Unlike other tailors who hoarded every last bit of remaining cloth, he returned all scraps to his customers.

Had it not been for his competent wife, Shmul-Leibele would certainly have starved to death. Shoshe helped him in whatever way she could. On Thursdays she hired herself out to wealthy families to knead dough, and on summer days went off to the forest to gather berries and mushrooms, as well as pinecones and twigs for the stove. In winter she plucked down for brides' featherbeds. She was also a better tailor than her husband, and when he began to sigh, or dally and mumble to himself, an indication that he could no longer muddle through, she would take the chalk from his hand and show him how to continue. Shoshe had no children, but it was common knowledge that it wasn't she who was barren, but rather her husband who was sterile, since all of her sisters had borne children, while his only brother was likewise childless. The townswomen repeatedly urged Shoshe to divorce him, but she turned a deaf ear, for the couple loved one another with a great love.

Shmul-Leibele was small and clumsy. His hands and feet were too large for his body, and his forehead bulged on either side as is common in simpletons. His cheeks, red as apples, were bare of whiskers, and but a few hairs sprouted from his chin. He had scarcely any neck at all; his head sat upon his shoulders like a snowman's. When he walked, he scraped his shoes along the ground so that every step could be heard far away. He hummed continuously and there was always an amiable smile on his face. Both winter and summer he wore the same caftan[2] and sheepskin cap with earlaps. Whenever there was any need for a messenger, it was always Shmul-Leibele who was pressed into service, and however far away he was sent, he always went willingly. The wags[3] saddled him with a variety of nicknames and made him the butt of all sorts of pranks, but he never took offense. When others scolded his tormentors, he would merely observe: "What do I care? Let them have their fun. They're only children, after all. . . ."

Sometimes he would present one or another of the mischief makers with a piece of candy or a nut. This he did without any ulterior motive, but simply out of good-heartedness.

Shoshe towered over him by a head. In her younger days she had been considered a beauty, and in the households where she worked as a servant they spoke highly of her honesty and diligence. Many young men had vied for her hand, but she had selected Shmul-Leibele because he was quiet and because he never joined the other town boys who gathered on the Lublin road at noon Saturdays to flirt with the girls. His piety and retiring nature pleased her. Even as a girl Shoshe had taken pleasure in studying the Pentateuch,[4] in nursing the infirm at the almshouse, in

---

[2]A long coatlike garment tied at the waist with a sash.
[3]People given to droll or mischievous humor.
[4]The first five books of the Old Testament.

listening to the tales of the old women who sat before their houses darning stockings. She would fast on the last day of each month, the Minor Day of Atonement, and often attended the services at the women's synagogue. The other servant girls mocked her and thought her old-fashioned. Immediately following her wedding she shaved her head and fastened a kerchief firmly over her ears, never permitting a stray strand of hair from her matron's wig to show as did some of the other young women. The bath attendant praised her because she never frolicked at the ritual bath, but performed her ablutions[5] according to the laws. She purchased only indisputably kosher meat, though it was a half-cent more per pound, and when she was in doubt about the dietary laws she sought out the rabbi's advice. More than once she had not hesitated to throw out all the food and even to smash the earthen crockery. In short, she was a capable, God-fearing woman, and more than one man envied Shmul-Leibele his jewel of a wife.

Above all of life's blessings the couple revered the Sabbath. Every Friday noon Shmul-Leibele would lay aside his tools and cease all work. He was always among the first at the ritual bath, and he immersed himself in the water four times for the four letters of the Holy Name. He also helped the beadle[6] set the candles in the chandeliers and the candelabra. Shoshe scrimped throughout the week, but on the Sabbath she was lavish. Into the heated oven went cakes, cookies and the Sabbath loaf. In winter she prepared puddings made of chicken's neck stuffed with dough and rendered fat. In summer she made puddings with rice or noodles, greased with chicken fat and sprinkled with sugar or cinnamon. The main dish consisted of potatoes and buck-wheat, or pearl barley with beans, in the midst of which she never failed to set a marrowbone. To insure that the dish would be well cooked, she sealed the oven with loose dough. Shmul-Leibele treasured every mouthful, and at every Sabbath meal he would remark: "Ah, Shoshe love, it's food fit for a king! Nothing less than a taste of Paradise!" to which Shoshe replied, "Eat hearty. May it bring you good health."

Although Shmul-Leibele was a poor scholar, unable to memorize a chapter of the Mishnah,[7] he was well versed in all the laws. He and his wife frequently studied *The Good Heart* in Yiddish. On half-holidays, holidays, and on each free day, he studied the Bible in Yiddish. He never missed a sermon, and though a pauper, he bought from peddlers all sorts of books of moral instructions and religious tales, which he then read together with his wife. He never wearied of reciting sacred phrases. As soon as he arose in the morning he washed his hands and began to mouth the preamble to the prayers. Then he would walk over to the study house and worship as one of the quorum. Every day he recited a few chapters of the Psalms, as well as those prayers which the less serious tended to skip over. From his father he had inherited a thick prayer book with wooden covers, which contained the rites and laws pertaining to each day of the year. Shmul-Leibele and his wife heeded each and every one of these. Often he would observe to his wife: "I shall surely end up in Gehenna,[8] since there'll be no one on earth to say Kaddish[9] over me." "Bite your tongue, Shmul-Leibele," she would

---

[5]A cleansing with water as a religious ritual.
[6]A parish officer who keeps order during services, waits on the clergyman, etc.
[7]The section of the Talmud consisting of the collection of oral laws edited by Rabbi Judah ha-Nasi (AD c. 135–c. 210).
[8]The valley of Hinnom, near Jerusalem, where conciliatory sacrifices were made to Moloch.
[9]A prayer for the dead.

counter, "For one, everything is possible under God. Secondly, you'll live until the Messiah comes. Thirdly, it's just possible that I will die before you and you will marry a young woman who'll bear you a dozen children." When Shoshe said this, Shmul-Leibele would shout: "God forbid! You must remain in good health. I'd rather rot in Gehenna!"

Although Shmul-Leibele and Shoshe relished every Sabbath, their greatest satisfaction came from the Sabbaths in wintertime. Since the day before the Sabbath evening was a short one, and since Shoshe was busy until late Thursday at her work, the couple usually stayed up all of Thursday night. Shoshe kneaded dough in the trough, covering it with cloth and a pillow so that it might ferment. She heated the oven with kindling-wood and dry twigs. The shutters in the room were kept closed, the door shut. The bed and bench-bed remained unmade, for at daybreak the couple would take a nap. As long as it was dark Shoshe prepared the Sabbath meal by the light of a candle. She plucked a chicken or a goose (if she had managed to come by one cheaply), soaked it, salted it and scraped the fat from it. She roasted a liver for Shmul-Leibele over the glowing coals and baked a small Sabbath loaf for him. Occasionally she would inscribe her name upon the loaf with letters of dough, and then Shmul-Leibele would tease her: "Shoshe, I am eating you up. Shoshe, I have already swallowed you." Shmul-Leibele loved warmth, and he would climb up on the oven and from there look down as his spouse cooked, baked, washed, rinsed, pounded and carved. The Sabbath loaf would turn out round and brown. Shoshe braided the loaf so swiftly that it seemed to dance before Shmul-Leibele's eyes. She bustled about efficiently with spatulas, pokers, ladles and goosewing dusters, and at times even snatched up a live coal with her bare fingers. The pots perked and bubbled. Occasionally a drop of soup would spill and the hot tin would hiss and squeal. And all the while the cricket continued its chirping. Although Shmul-Leibele had finished his supper by this time, his appetite would be whetted afresh, and Shoshe would throw him a knish, a chicken gizzard, a cookie, a plum from the plum stew or a chunk of the pot-roast. At the same time she would chide him, saying that he was a glutton. When he attempted to defend himself she would cry: "Oh, the sin is upon me, I have allowed you to starve . . ."

At dawn they would both lie down in utter exhaustion. But because of their efforts Shoshe would not have to run herself ragged the following day, and she could make the benediction over the candles a quarter of an hour before sunset.

The Friday on which this story took place was the shortest Friday of the year. Outside, the snow had been falling all night and had blanketed the house up to the windows and barricaded the door. As usual, the couple had stayed up until morning, then had lain down to sleep. They had arisen later than usual, for they hadn't heard the rooster's crow, and since the windows were covered with snow and frost, the day seemed as dark as night. After whispering, "I thank Thee," Shmul-Leibele went outside with a broom and shovel to clear a path, after which he took a bucket and fetched water from the well. Then, as he had no pressing work, he decided to lay off for the whole day. He went to the study house for the morning prayers, and after breakfast wended his way to the bathhouse. Because of the cold outside, the patrons kept up an eternal plaint: "A bucket! A bucket!" and the bath attendant poured more and more water over the glowing stones so that the steam grew constantly denser. Shmul-Leibele located a scraggly willow-broom, mounted to the highest bench and whipped himself until his skin glowed red. From the bathhouse, he hurried over to the study house where the beadle had already swept and sprinkled the floor with sand. Shmul-Leibele set the candles and helped spread the tablecloths over the tables. Then he went home again and changed into his Sabbath clothes. His boots, resoled but a few days before, no longer let the wet through. Shoshe had done her washing for the week, and had given him a fresh shirt, underdrawers, a fringed garment, even a clean pair of stockings. She had already performed the benediction over the candles, and the spirit of the Sabbath emanated from every corner of the room. She was wearing her silk kerchief with the silver spangles, a yellow and gray dress, and shoes with gleaming, pointed tips. On her throat hung the chain that Shmul-Leibele's mother, peace be with her, had given her to celebrate the signing of the wedding contract. The marriage band sparkled on her index finger. The candlelight reflected in the window panes, and Shmul-Leibele fancied that there was a duplicate of this room outside and that another Shoshe was out there lighting the Sabbath candles. He yearned to tell his wife how full of grace she was, but there was no time for it, since it is specifically stated in the prayer book that it is fitting and proper to be amongst the first ten worshipers at the synagogue; as it so happened, going off to prayers he was the tenth man to arrive. After the congregation had intoned the Song of Songs, the cantor sang, "Give thanks," and "O come, let us exult." Shmul-Leibele prayed with fervor. The words were sweet upon his tongue, they seemed to fall from his lips with a life of their own, and he felt that they soared to the eastern wall, rose above the embroidered curtain of the Holy Ark, the gilded lions, and the tablets, and floated up to the ceiling with its painting of the twelve constellations. From there, the prayers surely ascended to the Throne of Glory.

The cantor chanted, "Come, my beloved," and Shmul-Leibele trumpeted along in accompaniment. Then came the prayers, and the men recited, "It is our duty to praise . . ." to which Shmul-Leibele added a "Lord of the Universe." Afterwards, he wished everyone a good Sabbath: the rabbi, the ritual slaughterer, the head of the community, the assistant rabbi, everyone present. The *cheder*[10] lads shouted, "Good Sabbath, Shmul-Leibele," while they mocked him with gestures and grimaces, but Shmul-Leibele answered them all with a smile, even occasionally pinched a boy's cheek affectionately. Then he was off for home. The snow was piled high so that one could barely make out the contours of the roofs, as if the entire settlement had been immersed in white. The sky, which had hung low and overcast all day, now grew clear. From among white clouds a full moon peered down, casting a day-like brilliance over the snow. In the west, the edge of a cloud still held the glint of sunset. The stars on this Friday seemed larger and sharper, and through some miracle Lapschitz seemed to have blended with the sky. Shmul-Leibele's hut, which was situated not far from the synagogue, now hung suspended in space, as it is written: "He suspendeth the earth on nothingness." Shmul-Leibele walked slowly since, according to law, one must not hurry when coming from a holy place. Yet he longed to be home. "Who knows?" he thought. "Perhaps Shoshe has become ill? Maybe she's gone to fetch water and, God forbid, has fallen into the well? Heaven save us, what a lot of troubles can befall a man."

On the threshold he stamped his feet to shake off the snow, then opened the

---

[10]A Jewish school for teaching children Hebrew, Bible, and prayers.

door and saw Shoshe. The room made him think of Paradise. The oven had been freshly whitewashed, the candles in the brass candelabras cast a Sabbath glow. The aromas coming from the sealed oven blended with the scents of the Sabbath supper. Shoshe sat on the bench-bed apparently awaiting him, her cheeks shining with the freshness of a young girl's. Shmul-Leibele wished her a happy Sabbath and she in turn wished him a good year. He began to hum, "Peace upon ye ministering angels . . ." and after he had said his farewells to the invisible angels that accompany each Jew leaving the synagogue, he recited: "The worthy woman." How well he understood the meaning of these words, for he had read them often in Yiddish, and each time reflected anew on how aptly they seemed to fit Shoshe.

Shoshe was aware that these holy sentences were being said in her honor, and thought to herself, "Here am I, a simple woman, an orphan, and yet God has chosen to bless me with a devoted husband who praises me in the holy tongue."

Both of them had eaten sparingly during the day so that they would have an appetite for the Sabbath meal. Shmul-Leibele said the benediction over the raisin wine and gave Shoshe the cup so that she might drink. Afterwards, he rinsed his fingers from a tin dipper, then she washed hers, and they both dried their hands with a single towel, each at either end. Shmul-Leibele lifted the Sabbath loaf and cut it with the bread knife, a slice for himself and one for his wife.

He immediately informed her that the loaf was just right, and she countered: "Go on, you say that every Sabbath."

"But it happens to be the truth," he replied.

Although it was hard to obtain fish during the cold weather, Shoshe had purchased three-fourths of a pound of pike from the fishmonger. She had chopped it with onions, added an egg, salt and pepper, and cooked it with carrots and parsley. It took Shmul-Leibele's breath away, and after it he had to drink a tumbler of whiskey. When he began the table chants, Shoshe accompanied him quietly. Then came the chicken soup with noodles and tiny circlets of fat which glowed on the surface like golden ducats.[11] Between the soup and the main course, Shmul-Leibele again sang Sabbath hymns. Since goose was cheap at this time of year, Shoshe gave Shmul-Leibele an extra leg for good measure. After the dessert, Shmul-Leibele washed for the last time and made a benediction. When he came to the words: "Let us not be in need either of the gifts of flesh and blood nor of their loans," he rolled his eyes upward and brandished his fists. He never stopped praying that he be allowed to continue to earn his own livelihood and not, God forbid, become an object of charity.

After grace, he said yet another chapter of the Mishnah, and all sorts of other prayers which were found in his large prayer book. Then he sat down to read the weekly portion of the Pentateuch twice in Hebrew and once in Aramaic.[12] He enunciated every word and took care to make no mistake in the difficult Aramaic paragraphs of the Onkelos. When he reached the last section, he began to yawn and tears gathered in his eyes. Utter exhaustion overcame him. He could barely keep his eyes open and between one passage and the next he dozed off for a second or two. When Shoshe

---

[11]Various gold coins formerly issued in various parts of Europe.

[12]A Semitic language that was the everyday speech of Syria, Mesopotamia, and Palestine from c. 300 BC to AD 650.

noticed this, she made up the bench-bed for him and prepared her own featherbed with clean sheets. Shmul-Leibele barely managed to say the retiring prayers and began to undress. When he was already lying on his bench-bed he said: "A good Sabbath, my pious wife. I am very tired . . ." and turning to the wall, he promptly began to snore.

Shoshe sat a while longer gazing at the Sabbath candles which had already begun to smoke and flicker. Before getting into bed, she placed a pitcher of water and a basin at Shmul-Leibele's bedstead so that he would not rise the following morning without water to wash with. Then she, too, lay down and fell asleep.

They had slept an hour or two or possibly three — what does it matter, actually? — when suddenly Shoshe heard Shmul-Leibele's voice. He waked her and whispered her name. She opened one eye and asked, "What is it?"

"Are you clean?" he mumbled.

She thought for a moment and replied, "Yes."

He rose and came to her. Presently he was in bed with her. A desire for her flesh had roused him. His heart pounded rapidly, the blood coursed in his veins. He felt a pressure in his loins. His urge was to mate with her immediately, but he remembered the law which admonished a man not to copulate with a woman until he had first spoken affectionately to her, and he now began to speak of his love for her and how this mating could possibly result in a male-child.

"And a girl you wouldn't accept?" Shoshe chided him, and he replied, "Whatever God deigns to bestow would be welcome."

"I fear this privilege isn't mine anymore," she said with a sigh.

"Why not?" he demanded. "Our mother Sarah was far older than you."

"How can one compare oneself to Sarah? Far better you divorce me and marry another."

He interrupted her, stopping her mouth with his hand. "Were I sure that I could sire the twelve tribes of Israel with another, I still would not leave you. I cannot even imagine myself with another woman. You are the jewel of my crown."

"And what if I were to die?" she asked.

"God forbid! I would simply perish from sorrow. They would bury us both on the same day."

"Don't speak blasphemy. May you outlive my bones. You are a man. You would find somebody else. But what would I do without you?"

He wanted to answer her, but she sealed his lips with a kiss. He went to her then. He loved her body. Each time she gave herself to him, the wonder of it astonished him anew. How was it possible, he would think, that he, Shmul-Leibele, should have such a treasure all to himself? He knew the law, one dared not surrender to lust for pleasure. But somewhere in a sacred book he had read that it was permissible to kiss and embrace a wife to whom one had been wed according to the laws of Moses and Israel, and he now caressed her face, her throat and her breasts. She warned him that this was frivolity. He replied, "So I'll lie on the torture rack. The great saints also loved their wives." Nevertheless, he promised himself to attend the ritual bath the following morning, to intone psalms and to pledge a sum to charity. Since she loved him also and enjoyed his caresses, she let him do his will.

After he had satiated his desire, he wanted to return to his own bed, but a heavy sleepiness came over him. He felt a pain in his temples. Shoshe's head ached as well. She suddenly said, "I'm afraid something is burning in the oven. Maybe I should open the flue?"

"Go on, you're imagining it," he replied. "It'll become too cold in here."

And so complete was his weariness that he fell asleep, as did she.

That night Shmul-Leibele suffered an eerie dream. He imagined that he had passed away. The Burial-Society brethren came by, picked him up, lit candles by his head, opened the windows, intoned the prayer to justify God's ordainment. Afterwards, they washed him on the ablution board, carried him on a stretcher to the cemetery. There they buried him as the gravedigger said Kaddish over his body.

"That's odd," he thought, "I hear nothing of Shoshe lamenting or begging forgiveness. Is it possible that she would so quickly grow unfaithful? Or has she, God forbid, been overcome by grief?"

He wanted to call her name, but he was unable to. He tried to tear free of the grave, but his limbs were powerless. All of a sudden he awoke.

"What a horrible nightmare!" he thought. "I hope I come out of it all right."

At that moment Shoshe also awoke. When he related his dream to her, she did not speak for a while. Then she said, "Woe is me. I had the very same dream."

"Really? You too?" asked Shmul-Leibele, now frightened. "This I don't like."

He tried to sit up, but he could not. It was as if he had been shorn of all his strength. He looked towards the window to see if it were day already, but there was no window visible, nor any windowpane. Darkness loomed everywhere. He cocked his ears. Usually he would be able to hear the chirping of a cricket, the scurrying of a mouse, but this time only a dead silence prevailed. He wanted to reach out to Shoshe, but his hand seemed lifeless.

"Shoshe," he said quietly, "I've grown paralyzed."

"Woe is me, so have I," she said. "I cannot move a limb."

They lay there for a long while, silently, feeling their numbness. Then Shoshe spoke: "I fear that we are already in our graves for good."

"I'm afraid you're right," Shmul-Leibele replied in a voice that was not of the living.

"Pity me, when did it happen? How?" Shoshe asked. "After all, we went to sleep hale and hearty."

"We must have been asphyxiated by the fumes from the stove," Shmul-Leibele said.

"But I said I wanted to open the flue."

"Well, it's too late for that now."

"God have mercy upon us, what do we do now? We were still young people . . ."

"It's no use. Apparently it was fated."

"Why? We arranged a proper Sabbath. I prepared such a tasty meal. An entire chicken neck and tripe."

"We have no further need of food."

Shoshe did not immediately reply. She was trying to sense her own entrails. No, she felt no appetite. Not even for a chicken neck and tripe. She wanted to weep, but she could not.

"Shmul-Leibele, they've buried us already. It's all over."

"Yes, Shoshe, praised be the true Judge! We are in God's hands."

"Will you be able to recite the passage attributed to your name before the Angel Dumah?"

"Yes."

"It's good that we are lying side by side," she muttered.

"Yes, Shoshe," he said, recalling a verse: *Lovely and pleasant in their lives, and in their death they were not divided.*

"And what will become of our hut? You did not even leave a will."

"It will undoubtedly go to your sister."

Shoshe wished to ask something else, but she was ashamed. She was curious about the Sabbath meal. Had it been removed from the oven? Who had eaten it? But she felt that such a query would not be fitting of a corpse. She was no longer Shoshe the dough-kneader, but a pure, shrouded corpse with shards covering her eyes, a cowl[13] over her head, and myrtle twigs between her fingers. The Angel Dumah would appear at any moment with his fiery staff, and she would have to be ready to give an account of herself.

Yes, the brief years of turmoil and temptation had come to an end. Shmul-Leibele and Shoshe had reached the true world. Man and wife grew silent. In the stillness they heard the flapping of wings, a quiet singing. An angel of God had come to guide Shmul-Leibele the tailor and his wife, Shoshe, into Paradise.

(1964)

QUESTIONS

1. The setting of this story is distant from most American readers in place, time, and culture. What sorts of details about setting does the narrator provide? Are they the sorts of details that a stranger would notice?

2. What would the characters Shmul-Leibele and Shoshe be like in a different setting, for instance, an urban ghetto? Could their story be the same?

3. At the beginning of the story, from whose perspective do we perceive things? How about at the end of the story? Why the change?

4. Why does the action and setting turn so much on food and food preparation? What is the connection between food and the other concerns of the story, such as religion, incompetence, marriage, and death?

5. How do the traits of the characters, both stated and implied, motivate the plot, especially the ending?

---

[13]A hooded garment.

❖ ISAAC BABEL
How It Was Done in Odessa*,1

Isaac Babel (1894–1939 or 1940) was born in Odessa, Russia. A victim of Stalin's purges, little is known of Babel's life except what can be reconstructed from his short stories (which seem autobiographical). During World War I he served in the czar's army in Rumania. He joined the Bolshevik army during the Revolution, becoming an officer in the cossacks. He fought in the ill-fated Russian-Polish war of 1920. It was, of course, strange to be a Jew in the traditionally anti-Semitic cossack regiment at a time when the cossacks themselves had turned from the czarist to the Communist side. That experience inspired a collection of stories entitled *Red Cavalry* (1929). Babel's ironic stance in these stories enabled him to reflect the paradoxes of his situation. Two other collections contain his short stories about the rich life of the Jewish community in Odessa: *Odessa Tales* (1924) and *Jewish Tales* (1927). A volume of his *Collected Stories* was published in 1955, and another collection, under the title *You Must Know Everything,* in 1969.

It was I that began.

"Reb Arye-Leib," I said to the old man, "let us talk of Benya Krik. Let us talk of his thunderclap beginning and his terrible end. Three black shadows block up the paths of my imagination. Here is the one-eyed Ephraim Rook. The russet steel of his actions, can it really not bear comparison with the strength of the King? Here is Nick Pakovsky. The simple-minded fury of that man held all that was necessary for him to wield power. And did not Haim Drong know how to distinguish the brilliance of the rising star? Why then did Benya Krik alone climb to the top of the rope ladder, while all the rest hung swaying on the lower rungs?"

Reb Arye-Leib was silent, sitting on the cemetery wall. Before us stretched the green stillness of the graves. A man who thirsts for an answer must stock himself with patience. A man possessing knowledge is suited by dignity. For this reason Reb Arye-Leib was silent, sitting on the cemetery wall. Finally he said:

"Why he? Why not they, you wish to know? Then see here, forget for a while that you have spectacles on your nose and autumn in your heart. Cease playing the rowdy at your desk and stammering while others are about. Imagine for a moment that you play the rowdy in public places and stammer on paper. You are a tiger, you are a

---

*Translated by Walter Morison.
1A city on the Black Sea in Ukrania.

lion, you are a cat. You can spend the night with a Russian woman, and satisfy her. You are twenty-five. If rings were fastened to heaven and earth, you would grasp them and draw heaven and earth together. And your father is Mendel Krik the drayman.[2] What does such a father think about? He thinks about drinking a good glass of vodka, of smashing somebody in the face, of his horses — and nothing more. You want to live, and he makes you die twenty times a day. What would you have done in Benya Krik's place? You would have done nothing. But *he* did something. That's why he's the King, while you thumb your nose in the privy.[3]

He — Benya Krik — went to see Ephraim Rook, who, already in those days looking at the world out of only one eye, was already then what he is now. He said to Ephraim:

"Take me on. I want to moor to your bollard.[4] The bollard I moor to will be the winning one."

Rook asked him:

"Who are you, where do you come from, and what do you use for breath?"

"Give me a try, Ephraim," replied Benya, "and let us stop smearing gruel over a clean table."

"Let us stop smearing gruel," assented Rook. "I'll give you a try."

And the gangsters went into conference to consider the matter of Benya Krik. I wasn't at that conference, but they say that a conference was held. Chairman at that time was Lyovka Bullock.

"What goes on under his hat, under little Benya's hat?" asked the late Bullock.

And the one-eyed Rook gave his opinion:

"Benya says little, but what he says is tasty. He says little, and one would like him to say more."

"If so," exclaimed the late Bullock, "then let's try him on Tartakovsky."

"Let's try him on Tartakovsky," resolved the conference, and all in whom conscience still had lodgings blushed when they heard this decision. Why did they blush? You will learn this if you come where I shall lead you.

We used to call Tartakovsky "Jew-and-a-Half" or "Nine Holdups." "Jew-and-a-Half" he was called because no single Jew could have had so much dash and so much cash as Tartakovsky. He was taller than the tallest cop in Odessa, and weighed more than the fattest of Jewesses. And "Nine Holdups" he was called because the firm of Lyovka Bullock and Co. had made on his office not eight nor yet ten raids, but nine precisely. To the lot of Benya Krik, who was not yet the King, fell the honor of carrying out the tenth raid on Jew-and-a-Half. When Ephraim informed him accordingly, he said "O.K." and went out, banging the door. Why bang the door? You will learn this if you come where I shall lead you.

Tartakovsky has the soul of a murderer, but he is one of us. He originated with us. He is our blood. He is our flesh, as though one momma had born us. Half Odessa serves in his shops. And it was through his own Moldavanka lads that he

---

[2]A man who drives a low, strong cart carrying heavy loads.
[3]Outhouse.
[4]A post mounted on a wharf, to which mooring lines from vessels are attached.

suffered. Twice they held him for ransom, and once during a pogrom[5] they buried him with a choir. The Sloboda thugs were then beating up the Jews on Bolshaya Arnautskaya. Tartakovsky escaped from them, and on Sofiyskaya met a funeral procession with a choir. He asked:

"Who's that they're burying with a choir?"

The passers-by replied that it was Tartakovsky they were burying. The procession got to the Sloboda Cemetery. Then our chaps produced a machine gun from the coffin and started plastering the Sloboda thugs. But Jew-and-a-Half had not forseen this. Jew-and-a-Half was scared to death. And what boss would not have been scared in his place?

The tenth raid on a man who has already once been buried was a coarse action. Benya, who was not then the King, understood this better than anyone. But he said "O.K." to Rook, and that day wrote Tartakovsky a letter similar to all letters of this sort:

"Highly respected Ruvim son of Joseph! Be kind enough to place, on Saturday, under the rain barrel, etc. If you refuse, as last time you refused, know that a great disappointment awaits you in your private life. Respects from the Bentzion Krik you know of."

Tartakovsky did not play the sluggard, and replied without delay:

"Benya! If you were a half-wit I should write to you as to a half-wit. But I do not know you as such, and God forfend[6] I ever shall! You, it is evident, want to play the child. Do you really mean you don't know that this year there is such a crop in the Argentine that there's enough to drown in, and we sitting with all our wheat and no customers? And I will tell you, hand on heart, that in my old age I am finding it tedious to swallow so bitter a piece of bread and to experience these unpleasantnesses, having worked all my life as hard as the least of draymen. And what have I from all this endless convict-labor? Ulcers, sores, troubles, and insomnia. Give up this nonsense, Benya. Your friend (much more than you suppose) Ruvim Tartakovsky."

Jew-and-a-Half had done what he could. He had written a letter. But the letter wasn't delivered to the right address. Receiving no reply, Benya waxed wroth.[7] Next day he turned up with four pals at Tartakovsky's office. Four youths in masks and with revolvers bowled into the office.

"Hands up!" they cried, and started waving their pistols about.

"A little more *Sang-frwa*,[8] Solomon," observed Benya to one who was shouting louder than the rest. "Don't make a habit of being nervous on the job." And turning to the clerk, who was white as death and yellow as clay, he asked him:

"Is Jew-and-a-Half on the premises?"

"No, sir," replied the clerk, one Muginstein by name. His first name was Joseph, and he was the bachelor son of Aunt Pesya the poultry-dealer on Seredinskaya Square.

---

[5] An organized massacre.
[6] Defend or protect.
[7] Wrathful.
[8] Phonetic approximation of the French *sangfroid*, which means coolness of mind.

"Well then, who's in charge in the old man's absence?" they started third-degreeing the wretched Muginstein.

"I am," said the clerk, green as green grass.

"Then with God's help open up the safe!" Benya ordered, and the curtain rose on a three-act opera.

The nervous Solomon was packing cash, securities, watches, and monograms in a suitcase; the late Joseph stood before him with his hands in the air, and at that moment Benya was telling anecdotes about Jews.

"Since he's forever playing the Rothschild," Benya was saying of Tartakovsky, "let him burn on a slow fire. Explain this to me, Muginstein, as to a friend: if he receives, as he has, a businesslike letter from me, why shouldn't he take a five-copeck[9] streetcar-ride and come over and see me at my place and drink a glass of vodka with my family and take potluck? What prevented him from opening his heart to me? 'Benya,' he might have said, 'so on and so forth, here's my balance-sheet, gimme a coupla days to draw breath and see how things stand.' What should I have replied? Pig does not see eye to eye with pig, but man with man does. Muginstein, do you catch my drift?"

"I d-do," stuttered Muginstein, but he lied, for he hadn't the remotest idea why Jew-and-a-Half the wealthy and respected should want to take a streetcar-ride to eat a snack with the family of Mendel Krik the drayman.

And meantime misfortune lurked beneath the window like a pauper at daybreak. Misfortune broke noisily into the office. And though on this occasion it bore the shape of the Jew Savka Butsis, this misfortune was as drunk as a water-carrier.

"Ho-hoo-ho," cried the Jew Savka, "forgive me, Benya, I'm late." And he started stamping his feet and waving his arms about. Then he fired, and the bullet landed in Muginstein's belly.

Are words necessary? A man was, and is no more. A harmless bachelor was living his life like a bird on a bough, and had to meet a nonsensical end. There came a Jew looking like a sailor and took a potshot not at some clay pipe or dolly but at a live man. Are words necessary?

"Let's scram," cried Benya, and ran out last. But as he departed he managed to say to Butsis:

"I swear by my mother's grave, Savka, that you will lie next to him . . ."

Now tell me, young master, you who snip coupons on other people's shares, how would you have acted in Benya's place? You don't know how you would have acted. But he knew. That's why he's the King, while you and I are sitting on the wall of the Second Jewish Cemetery and keeping the sun off with our palms.

Aunt Pesya's unfortunate son did not die straightaway. An hour after they had got him to the hospital, Benya appeared there. He asked for the doctor in charge and the nurse to be sent out to him, and said to them, not taking his hands out of his cream pants:

"It is in my interest," he said, "that the patient Joseph Muginstein should recover. Let me introduce myself, just in case: Bentzion Krik. Camphor,[10] air-cushions,

---

[9]A coin of the Soviet Union, the 100th part of a ruble.
[10]A substance used as a counterirritant.

a private ward—supply them with liberal hands. Otherwise every Tom, Dick, and Harry of a doctor, even if he's a doctor of philosophy, will get no more than six feet of earth."

But Muginstein died that night. And only then did Jew-and-a-Half raise a stink through all Odessa.

"Where do the police begin," he wailed, "and where does Benya end?"

"The police end where Benya begins," replied sensible folk, but Tartakovsky refused to take the hint, and he lived to see the day when a red automobile with a music box for horn played its first march from the opera *Pagliacci* on Seredinskaya Square. In broad daylight the car flew up to the little house in which Aunt Pesya dwelt.

The automobile cast thunderbolts with its wheels, spat fumes, shone brassily, stank of gasoline, and performed arias on its horn. From the car someone sprang out and passed into the kitchen, where little Aunt Pesya was throwing hysterics on the earthen floor. Jew-and-a-Half was sitting in a chair waving his hands about.

"You hooligan!" he cried, perceiving the visitor, "you bandit, may the earth cast you forth! A fine trick you've thought up, killing live people."

"Monsieur Tartakovsky," Benya Krik replied quietly, "it's forty-eight hours now that I've been weeping for the dear departed as for my own brother. But I know that you don't give a damn for my youthful tears. Shame, Monsieur Tartakovsky. In what sort of safe have you locked up your sense of shame? You had the gall to send the mother of our deceased Joseph a hundred paltry roubles. My brains shivered along with my hair when I heard this."

Here Benya paused. He was wearing a chocolate jacket, cream pants, and raspberry boots.

"Ten thousand down," he roared, "ten thousand down and a pension till she dies, and may she live to a hundred and twenty. Otherwise we will depart from this residence, Monsieur Tartakovsky, and we will sit in my limousine."

Then they used bad language at one another hammer and tongs, Jew-and-a-Half and Benya. I wasn't present at this quarrel, but those who were remember it. They compromised on five thousand in cash and fifty roubles a month.

"Aunt Pesya," Benya said to the disheveled old woman who was rolling on the floor, "if you need my life you may have it, but all make mistakes, God included. A terrible mistake has been made, Aunt Pesya. But wasn't it a mistake on the part of God to settle Jews in Russia, for them to be tormented worse than in Hell? How would it hurt if the Jews lived in Switzerland, where they would be surrounded by first-class lakes, mountain air, and nothing but Frenchies? All make mistakes, God not excepted. Listen to me with all your ears, Aunt Pesya. You'll have five thousand down and fifty roubles a month till you croak. Live to a hundred and twenty if you like. Joseph shall have a Number One funeral: six horses like six lions, two carriages with flowers, the choir from the Brody Synagogue. Minkovsky in person will sing at your deceased son's funeral."

And the funeral was performed next morning. Ask the cemetery beggars about that funeral. Ask the shamessim[11] from the synagogue of the dealers in kosher poultry about it, or the old women from the Second Almshouse. Odessa had never

---

[11]Custodians of a synagogue (Hebrew).

before seen such a funeral, the world will never see such a funeral. On that day the cops wore cotton gloves. In the synagogues, decked with greenstuff and wide open, the electric lights were burning. Black plumes swayed on the white horses harnessed to the hearse. A choir of sixty headed the cortege: a choir of boys, but they sang with the voice of women. The Elders of the synagogue of the dealers in kosher poultry helped Aunt Pesya along. Behind the elders walked members of the Association of Jewish Shop Assistants, and behind the Jewish Shop Assistants walked the lawyers, doctors of medicine, and certified midwives. On one side of Aunt Pesya were the women who trade in poultry on the Old Market, and on the other side, draped in orange shawls, were the honorary dairymaids from Bugayevka. They stamped their feet like gendarmes[12] parading on a holiday. From their wide hips wafted the odors of the sea and of milk. And behind them all plodded Ruvim Tartakovsky's employees. There were a hundred of them, or two hundred, or two thousand. They wore black frock coats with silk lapels and new shoes that squeaked like sacked sucking-pigs.

And now I will speak as the Lord God spoke on Mount Sinai from the Burning Bush. Put my words in your ears. All I saw, I saw with my own eyes, sitting here on the wall of the Second Cemetery next to Little Lisping Mose and Samson from the undertaker's. I, Arye-Leib, saw this—I, a proud Jew dwelling by the dead.

The hearse drove up to the cemetery synagogue. The coffin was placed on the steps. Aunt Pesya was trembling like a little bird. The cantor crawled out of the carriage and began the service. Sixty singers seconded him. And at this moment a red automobile flew around the turning. It played "Laugh, clown" and drew up. People were as silent as the dead. Silent were the trees, the choir, the beggars. Four men climbed out of the red car and at a slow pace bore to the hearse a wreath of roses such as was never seen before. And when the service ended the four men inserted their steel shoulders beneath the coffin and with burning eyes and swelling breasts walked side by side with the members of the Association of Jewish Shop Assistants.

In front walked Benya Krik, whom no one as yet called the King. He was the first to approach the grave. He climbed the mound of earth and spread out his arms.

"What have you in mind, young man?" cried Kofman of the Burial Brotherhood, running over to him.

"I have it in mind to make a funeral oration," replied Benya Krik.

And a funeral oration he made. All who wished listened to it. I listened to it; I, Arye-Leib, and Little Lisping Mose, who was sitting on the wall beside me.

"Ladies and gentlemen, and dames," said Benya Krik. "Ladies and gentlemen, and dames," said he, and the sun rose above his head like an armed sentry. "You have come to pay your last respects to a worthy laborer who perished for the sake of a copper penny. In my name, and in the name of all those not here present, I thank you. Ladies and gentlemen! What did our dear Joseph get out of life? Nothing worth mentioning. How did he spend his time? Counting other people's cash. What did he perish for? He perished for the whole of the working class. There are people already condemned to death, and there are people who have not yet begun to live. And lo and behold a bullet flying into a condemned breast pierces our Joseph, who in his whole life had seen nothing worth mentioning, and comes out on the other side. There are people

---

[12]Policemen or soldiers (French).

who know how to drink vodka, and there are people who don't know how to drink vodka but drink it all the same. And the first lot, you see, get satisfaction from joy and from sorrow, and the second lot suffer for all those who drink vodka without knowing how to. And so, ladies and gentlemen, and dames, after we have said a prayer for our poor Joseph I will ask you to accompany to his last resting-place one unknown to you but already deceased, one Savely Butsis."

And having finished his oration Benya Krik descended from the mound. No sound came from the people, the trees, or the cemetery beggars. Two gravediggers bore an unpainted coffin to the next grave. The cantor, stammering, finished his prayers. Benya threw in the first spadeful of soil and crossed over to Savka's grave. After him like sheep went all the lawyers, all the ladies with brooches. He made the cantor sing the full funeral service over Savka, and the sixty choirboys seconded the cantor. Savka had never dreamed of having such a funeral — take it from Arye-Leib, an old man who has seen many things.

They say that on that day Jew-and-a-Half decided to shut up shop. I wasn't present. But that neither the cantor, nor the choir, nor the Funeral Brotherhood charged anything for the funeral, this I saw with the eyes of Arye-Leib. Arye-Leib, that's what they call me. And more than that I couldn't see, for the people, creeping quietly at first from Savka's grave, then started running as from a house on fire. They flew off in carriages, in carts, and on foot. And only the four who had driven up in the red automobile also drove off in it. The music box played its march, the car shuddered and was gone.

"A King," said Little Lisping Mose, looking after the car — Little Mose who does me out of the best seats on the wall.

Now you know all. You know who first uttered the word 'King.' It was Little Mose. You know why he didn't give that name to One-Eyed Rook, or to Crazy Nick. You know all. But what's the use, if you still have spectacles on your nose and autumn in your heart?"

(1923)

QUESTIONS

1. Benya Krik met with Tartakovsky and Aunt Pesya before the funeral. As a consequence of his conversation with Benya Krik, what did Tartakovsky do? Why is there no explicit mention of his activities in preparation for the funeral?

2. What seem to be the predominant traits of Benya Krik? Does a comparison between him and what you know of, say, Al Capone or other American gangsters help you understand what a Jewish gangster in Odessa might have been like? How?

3. Who is telling the main part of the story? Who is listening? What is their reaction to Benya Krik and his exploits? Why does the author choose to use a framing story to help achieve verisimilitude in plot and characterization?

4. How would you place Benya Krik on the scale of complexity (round/flat), importance (major/minor), and change (dynamic/static)? How does the

particular configuration of these three dimensions correspond to the point of the story?

5. How would you describe the story's atmosphere? What is the narrator's prevailing tone or attitude toward characters, setting, and incidents? Does the (implied) author *share* the narrator's attitude? What details indicate that tone?

❖ VIRGINIA WOOLF

Kew Gardens

Virginia Woolf (1882–1941) was born in London, the daughter of the distinguished author Sir Leslie Stephen. When her father died in 1904, she moved to the section of London called Bloomsbury where she helped found the famous Bloomsbury Group of writers, artists, and intellectuals. In 1912, she married Leonard Woolf, journalist, political thinker, and educator, a man who was to support both her writing and her troubled personality for the rest of her life. Together they established the Hogarth Press, which published some of the most important English literature of the twentieth century. After some conventional novels— *The Voyage Out* (1915) and *Night and Day* (1919) —Woolf turned to experimentation, especially in fiction that took deep plunges into characters' minds. Her first novel in this vein was *Jacob's Room* (1922); it was followed by the highly acclaimed *Mrs. Dalloway* (1925) and *To the Lighthouse* (1927). *Orlando: A Biography* (1928) is a fantasy whose protagonist not only lives many centuries but changes sexes in the course of his/her life. *The Waves* (1931) was even more experimental than Woolf's previous novels, but her last two novels, *The Years* (1937) and *Between the Acts* (1941) returned to more traditional storytelling form. In her short stories she experimented with the innovative techniques that were to crown her novelistic achievement. The stories were collected in *Kew Gardens* (1919), *The Mark on the Wall* (1919), and *Monday or Tuesday* (1921); a complete collection of her short fiction was published under the title *The Complete Shorter Fiction of Virginia Woolf* in 1985. Woolf was also an important essayist and literary critic who articulated her literary practice in books such as *Mr. Bennett and Mrs. Brown* (1924), *The Common Reader* (in two series 1925, 1932), and *Three Guineas* (1938). She also was an ardent voice for the cause of feminism, especially in such books as *A Room of One's Own* (1929).

From the oval-shaped flower-bed there rose perhaps a hundred stalks spreading into heart-shaped or tongue-shaped leaves half-way up and unfurling at the tip red or blue or yellow petals marked with spots of colour raised upon the surface; and from the red, blue or yellow gloom of the throat emerged a straight bar, rough with gold dust and slightly clubbed at the end. The petals were voluminous enough to be stirred by the summer breeze, and when they moved the red, blue and yellow lights passed one over the other, staining an inch of the brown earth beneath with a spot of the most intricate colour. The light fell either upon the smooth, grey back of a pebble, or, the shell of a snail with its brown, circular veins, or falling into a raindrop, it expanded with such intensity of red, blue and yellow the thin walls of water that one expected them to burst and disappear. Instead, the drop was left in a second silver grey once more, and the light now settled upon the flesh of a leaf, revealing the branching thread of fibre beneath the surface, and again it moved on and spread its illumination in the vast green spaces beneath the dome of the heart-shaped and tongue-shaped leaves. Then the breeze stirred rather more briskly overhead and the colour was flashed into the air above, into the eyes of the men and women who walk in Kew Gardens in July.

The figures of these men and women straggled past the flower-bed with a curiously irregular movement not unlike that of the white and blue butterflies who crossed the turf in zig-zag flights from bed to bed. The man was about six inches in front of the woman, strolling carelessly, while she bore on with greater purpose, only turning her head now and then to see that the children were not too far behind. The man kept this distance in front of the woman purposely, though perhaps unconsciously, for he wished to go on with his thoughts.

"Fifteen years ago I came here with Lily," he thought. "We sat somewhere over there by a lake and I begged her to marry me all through the hot afternoon. How the dragonfly kept circling round us: how clearly I see the dragonfly and her shoe with the square silver buckle at the toe. All the time I spoke I saw her shoe and when it moved impatiently I knew without looking up what she was going to say: the whole of her seemed to be in her shoe. And my love, my desire, were in the dragonfly; for some reason I thought that if it settled there, on that leaf, the broad one with the red flower in the middle of it, if the dragonfly settled on the leaf she would say 'Yes' at once. But the dragonfly went round and round: it never settled anywhere — of course not, happily not, or I shouldn't be walking here with Eleanor and the children. Tell me, Eleanor. D'you ever think of the past?"

"Why do you ask, Simon?"

"Because I've been thinking of the past. I've been thinking of Lily, the woman I might have married. . . . Well, why are you silent? Do you mind my thinking of the past?"

"Why should I mind, Simon? Doesn't one always think of the past, in a garden with men and women lying under the trees? Aren't they one's past, all that remains of it, those men and women, those ghosts lying under the trees, . . . one's happiness, one's reality?"

"For me, a square silver shoe buckle and a dragonfly — "

"For me, a kiss. Imagine six little girls sitting before their easels twenty years ago, down by the side of a lake, painting the water-lilies, the first red water-lilies I'd ever seen. And suddenly a kiss, there on the back of my neck. And my hand shook all the afternoon so that I couldn't paint. I took out my watch and marked the hour when I would allow myself to think of the kiss for five minutes only — it was so precious — the kiss of an old grey-haired woman with a wart on her nose, the mother of all my kisses all my life. Come, Caroline, come, Hubert."

They walked on past the flower-bed, now walking four abreast, and soon diminished in size among the trees and looked half transparent as the sunlight and shade swam over their backs in large trembling irregular patches.

In the oval flower-bed the snail, whose shell had been stained red, blue and yellow for the space of two minutes or so, now appeared to be moving very slightly in its shell, and next began to labour over the crumbs of loose earth which broke away and rolled down as it passed over them. It appeared to have a definite goal in front of it, differing in this respect from the singular high stepping angular green insect who attempted to cross in front of it, and waited for a second with its antennae trembling as if in deliberation, and then stepped off as rapidly and strangely in the opposite direction. Brown cliffs with deep green lakes in the hollows, flat, blade-like trees that waved from root to tip, round boulders of grey stone, vast crumpled surfaces of a thin crackling texture — all these objects lay across the snail's progress between one stalk and another to his goal. Before he had decided whether to circumvent the arched tent of a dead leaf or to breast it there came past the bed the feet of other human beings.

This time they were both men. They younger of the two wore an expression of perhaps unnatural calm; he raised his eyes and fixed them very steadily in front of him while his companion spoke, and directly his companion had done speaking he looked on the ground again and sometimes opened his lips only after a long pause and sometimes did not open them at all. The elder man had a curiously uneven and shaky method of walking, jerking his hand forward and throwing up his head abruptly, rather in the manner of an impatient carriage horse tired of waiting outside a house; but in the man these gestures were irresolute and pointless. He talked almost incessantly; he smiled to himself and again began to talk, as if the smile had been an answer. He was talking about spirits — the spirits of the dead, who according to him, were even now telling him all sorts of odd things about their experiences in Heaven.

"Heaven was known to the ancients as Thessaly,[1] William, and now, with this war, the spirit matter is rolling between the hills like thunder." He paused, seemed to listen, smiled, jerked his head and continued:

"You have a small electric battery and a piece of rubber to insulate the wire — isolate? — insulate? — well, we'll skip the details, no good going into details that wouldn't be understood — and in short the little machine stands in any convenient position by the head of the bed, we will say, on a neat mahogany stand. All arrangements being properly fixed by workmen under my direction, the widow applies her ear and summons the spirit by sign as agreed. Women! Widows! Women in black — "

Here he seemed to have caught sight of a woman's dress in the distance, which in the shade looked a purple black. He took off his hat, placed his hand upon his heart, and hurried towards her muttering and gesticulating feverishly. But William caught him by the sleeve and touched a flower with the tip of his walking-stick in order to divert the old man's attention. After looking at it for a moment in some confusion the old man bent his ear to it and seemed to answer a voice speaking from it, for he began talking about the forests of Uruguay which he had visited hundreds of years ago in company with the most beautiful young woman in Europe. He could be heard murmuring about forests of Uruguay blanketed with the wax petals of tropical roses, nightingales, sea beaches, mermaids, and women drowned at sea, as he suffered himself to be moved on by William, upon whose face the look of stoical patience grew slowly deeper and deeper.

Following his steps so closely as to be slightly puzzled by his gestures came two elderly women of the lower middle class, one stout and ponderous, the other rosy cheeked and nimble. Like most people of their station they were frankly fascinated by

---

[1] A former division of ancient Greece.

any signs of eccentricity betokening a disordered brain, especially in the well-to-do; but they were too far off to be certain whether the gestures were merely eccentric or genuinely mad. After they had scrutinized the old man's back in silence for a moment and given each other a queer, sly look, they went on energetically piecing together their very complicated dialogue:

"Nell, Bert, Lot, Cess, Phil, Pa, he says, I says, she says, I says, I says—"

"My Bert, Sis, Bill, Grandad, the old man, sugar,

Sugar, flour, kippers, greens,

Sugar, sugar, sugar."

The ponderous woman looked through the pattern of falling words at the flowers standing cool, firm, and upright in the earth, with a curious expression. She saw them as a sleeper waking from a heavy sleep sees a brass candlestick reflecting the light in an unfamiliar way, and closes his eyes and opens them, and seeing the brass candlestick again, finally starts broad awake and stares at the candlestick with all his powers. So the heavy woman came to a standstill opposite the oval-shaped flower-bed, and ceased even to pretend to listen to what the other woman was saying. She stood there letting the words fall over her, swaying the top part of her body slowly backwards and forwards, looking at the flowers. Then she suggested that they should find a seat and have their tea.

The snail had now considered every possible method of reaching his goal without going round the dead leaf or climbing over it. Let alone the effort needed for climbing a leaf, he was doubtful whether the thin texture which vibrated with such an alarming crackle when touched even by the tips of his horns would bear his weight; and this determined him finally to creep beneath it, for there was a point where the leaf curved high enough from the ground to admit him. He had just inserted his head in the opening and was taking stock of the high brown roof and was getting used to the cool brown light when two other people came past outside on the turf. This time they were both young, a young man and a young woman. They were both in the prime of youth, or even in that season which precedes the prime of youth, the season before the smooth pink folds of the flower have burst their gummy case, when the wings of the butterfly, though fully grown, are motionless in the sun.

"Lucky it isn't Friday," he observed.

"Why? D'you believe in luck?"

"They make you pay sixpence on Fridays."

"What's sixpence anyway? Isn't it worth sixpence?"

"What's 'it'—what do you mean by 'it'?"

"O, anything—I mean—you know what I mean."

Long pauses came between each of these remarks; they were uttered in toneless and monotonous voices. The couple stood still on the edge of the flower-bed, and together pressed the end of her parasol deep down into the soft earth. The action and the fact that his hand rested on the top of hers expressed their feelings in a strange way, as these short insignificant words also expressed something, words with short wings for their heavy body of meaning, inadequate to carry them far and thus alighting awkwardly upon the very common objects that surrounded them, and were to their inexperienced touch so massive; but who knows (so they thought as they pressed the parasol into the earth) what precipices aren't concealed in them, or what slopes of ice don't shine in the sun on the other side? Who knows? Who has ever seen this before? Even when she wondered what sort of tea they gave you at Kew, he felt that something loomed up behind her words, and stood vast and solid behind them; and the mist very slowly rose and uncovered — O, Heavens, what were those shapes? — little white tables, and waitresses who looked first at her and then at him; and there was a bill that he would pay with a real two shilling piece, and it was real, all real, he assured himself, fingering the coin in his pocket, real to everyone except to him and to her; even to him it began to seem real; and then — but it was too exciting to stand and think any longer, and he pulled the parasol out of the earth with a jerk and was impatient to find the place where one had tea with other people, like other people.

"Come along, Trissie; it's time we had our tea."

"Wherever *does* one have one's tea?" she asked with the oddest thrill of excitement in her voice, looking vaguely round and letting herself be drawn on down the grass path, trailing her parasol; turning her head this way and that way forgetting her tea, wishing to go down there and then down there, remembering orchids and cranes among wild flowers, a Chinese pagoda[2] and a crimson crested bird; but he bore her on.

Thus one couple after another with much the same irregular and aimless movement passed the flower-bed and were enveloped in layer after layer of green blue vapour, in which at first their bodies had substance and a dash of colour, but later both substance and colour dissolved in the green-blue atmosphere. How hot it was! So hot that even the thrush chose to hop, like a mechanical bird, in the shadow of the flowers, with long pauses between one movement and the next; instead of rambling vaguely the white butterflies danced one above another, making with their white shifting flakes the outline of a shattered marble column above the tallest flowers; the glass roofs of the palm house shone as if a whole market full of shiny green umbrellas had opened in the sun; and in the drone of the aeroplane the voice of the summer sky murmured its fierce soul. Yellow and black, pink and snow white, shapes of all these colours, men, women, and children were spotted for a second upon the horizon, and then, seeing the breadth of yellow that lay upon the grass, they wavered and sought shade beneath the trees, dissolving like drops of water in the yellow and green atmosphere, staining it faintly with red and blue. It seemed as if all gross and heavy bodies had sunk down in the heat motionless and lay huddled upon the ground, but their voices went wavering from them as if they were flames lolling from the thick waxen bodies of candles. Voices. Yes, voices. Wordless voices, breaking the silence suddenly with such depth of contentment, such passion of desire, or, in the voices of children, such freshness of surprise; breaking the silence? But there was no silence; all the time the motor omnibuses were turning their wheels and changing their gear; like a vast nest of Chinese boxes all of wrought steel turning ceaselessly one within another the city murmured; on the top of which the voices cried aloud and the petals of myriads of flowers flashed their colours into the air.

(1919)

---

[2]A temple or sacred building, usually a pyramidlike tower.

QUESTIONS

1. Imagine that you are filming the story. Where would you place the camera for the opening scene? Why?

2. The names of colors recur many times in the story. Does a single color stand for a single idea or object, or do the colors and meanings shift? Why?

3. Does the narrator distinguish between human characters and the objects and animals in the garden? Is the division a clear-cut one? Why or why not?

4. Is the narrator quoting the elderly women directly when they say, "Sugar, flour, kippers, greens" and so on? What point is being made about their conversation? Why do their remarks fall into lines like a poem?

5. It seems to be up to the reader to make connections among the story's images and ideas. How do you think the snail is related to the pair of lovers? The spiritualist to the forests of Uruguay? The cup of tea to the vision of the city of London?

SUGGESTIONS FOR WRITING

1. Even though it seems natural to separate setting from character, sometimes the two can merge. Try two experiments with the stories in this section. First, pick a character whose main function seems to be establishing the setting. In other words, argue that the character is no different from any other prop. Second, pick a setting that seems to develop characterlike traits (for example, "sympathetic," "capricious," or "hostile"). Show how those traits are conveyed to the reader.

2. Compare three or four characters from different short stories in this and preceding chapters. Name some of their traits, and classify them as flat or round, static or dynamic, major or minor. Try to explain why — in terms of the point of the whole story — they are constructed that way.

3. Interesting things happen when you take characters out of their normal settings. Pick a character from a story in this section and represent him or her in the plot and setting of another story. What changes would you have to make to fit the character into the new context?

4. Describe how a given character in any short story in this book is characterized. Quote illustrative examples. In a paragraph or two, try to characterize a given trait using another method. Explain the appropriateness of the original method to the story's overall point.

5. How much difference does your own experience make in imagining a fictional setting? If a story is set in your home town, the writer can simply name a street corner and let you imagine the whole scene. But what if you have never been in Odessa or London? Pick a short story with an unfamiliar setting and describe what sorts of clues help you to construct the scene in your imagination.

6. Settings are both physical and cultural. Characters' actions are only meaningful in the context of their cultural settings. A burp might be polite or
   rude, according to the cultural code that operates in a particular setting.
   Asking a question might be a friendly or a hostile act. Pick a story whose
   cultural presuppositions seem different from the ones you are familiar with.
   Explain how the story reveals its cultural code.

4 Narration: Narrator and Narratee

We ordinarily assume that authors speak directly to us. We say "Julius Caesar informs us in *The Gallic Wars* that . . ." or "Winston Churchill tells us in *The Gathering Storm* that . . ." So it seems natural to extend that way of speaking to fictions: "In 'Delta Autumn,' Faulkner says that . . ." or "In 'Short Friday,' Isaac Bashevis Singer tells us that . . ." For a variety of reasons, however, the assumption that the real author tells us the fiction is misleading. We need to distinguish between the actual, biographical author and the fictional *narrator*. Even a moment's reflection suggests that the two are quite separate individuals. For example, "Je Ne Parle Pas Français" (pp. 494–512) was written by a woman, Katherine Mansfield, but the "I" narrator is a male character named Raoul Duquette. The author was a real historical personage, but the narrator is part of the fiction. Even if the narrator's voice is unidentified or muted, or the story is completely shown rather than told, it is better to speak of the "narrator" than of the "author" as the immediate communicator of the fiction. Unlike authors of nonfictional texts, who communicate in their own persons, authors of fictions invent spokespersons — narrators — to present the story.

Telling: Internal and External Narrators

Such terms as *author, narrator, speaks,* and the like need careful examination. In chapter 1, I pointed out that the narrator's "voice" may either "tell" the story or "show" it. Clearly these terms are metaphorical. There is nothing wrong with metaphorical terms unless they obscure the subject that they are intended to illuminate. They should not block our understanding of what is going on when we read a fictional narrative. Though short stories and novels come to us in print, we often employ the metaphor of oral discourse, saying that a narrator "tells" or "speaks" — rather than "writes" — the story. We may say that the narrator "tells" the narrative even in a short story whose form is a written diary, like Donald Barthelme's "Me and Miss Mandible" (pp. 348–355), or a series of letters, like Elizabeth Jolley's "Wednesdays and Fridays" (pp. 98–103).

The notion that the narrator "speaks" probably carries over from an earlier time when fictions were indeed spoken aloud rather than written. In the Middle Ages, professional oral storytellers, whom the Anglo-Saxons called *scops*, told tales to assembled audiences. The practice is recorded in the very word *tale*, which comes from Old English *talu*, the noun form of the verb "to tell." "That which is told" came to mean a kind of narrative. The tradition still flourishes in various places, for example, among the Bedouin nomads of the Sahara Desert. Even cultures without writing systems enjoy the pleasures of storytelling.

Though terms like *tell* and *show* are metaphorical, we can distinguish between them with reasonable precision. A narrator who "tells" the story is one whose presence is more or less evident. For instance, if she refers to herself as "I," offers opinions, makes comments about a character's behavior or about the nature of the world, and so on, we feel that the narrator is some specific person addressing us. That person may be someone in the story, even the protagonist. Consider the second sentence of Ralph Ellison's "The Battle Royal" (pp. 441–451): "All my life I had been looking for something, and everywhere I turned someone tried to tell me what it was." We infer not only that this "I" *is* the teller of the story "now" (that is, during the present moment of the discourse), but also that he *was* a character "back then" during the story-time. He is both the person who lived the events and the teller of those events.

Such first-person narrators may be called *character-narrators*. Character-narrators typically tell the story retrospectively, after the fact (though concurrent or even prophetic narratives are also possible). Like "The Battle Royal," Tillie Olsen's "I Stand Here Ironing" (pp. 122–127) is retrospectively narrated by a character-narrator. In this kind of fiction, the narrator and the character are biologically the same person, but for purposes of narratological discussion, we can distinguish between the older *narrator-I* and the younger *character-I*. The *narrator-I* speaks during the discourse-time, "now," as she irons, whereas the *character-I* experienced the story-events "back then" when she was trying to raise Emily.

Some character-narrators, however, are not protagonists but lesser characters. We can call these *witness-narrators*. The narrator of Margaret Atwood's "The Sin Eater" (pp. 34–41), for example, is a witness to the recent life and times of Joseph, her psychotherapist, whose death disturbs her profoundly, and whom she tries to understand through memories and dreams. The enigma of Joseph's personality is central to the story. (In that sense, "The Sin Eater" resembles F. Scott Fitzgerald's *The Great Gatsby*, whose first-person narrator is a writer and neighbor trying to figure out, after Gatsby's death, what made him tick.)

Whether protagonists or witnesses, character-narrators may be called *internal* because they formerly lived "inside" the story.

In other cases, the person narrating the story is not a character at all. An example is the narrator of Nathaniel Hawthorne's "Wakefield" (pp. 457–462). This narrator recalls some story he read in a magazine or newspaper about a man "who absented himself for a long time, from his wife." Clearly, though he refers to himself as "I," the narrator of "Wakefield" is not a party to the events, that is, he did not live inside the story-world inhabited by the absent husband. So the use of "I" for a narrator is not a simple and sure sign that he is a character-narrator. Unlike Sissie or the narrators of "The Battle Royal" or "The Sin Eater" or *The Great Gatsby*, the narrator of "Wakefield" exists only in the discourse, not in the story. Isaac Bashevis Singer's "Short Friday" has the same kind of narrator. We can call such a narrator *external*. The external narrator may refer to herself as "the author," or "your author," or not refer to herself at all. We can call her or him an *authorial narrator* providing we remember that "authorial" refers not to the real author, Nathaniel Hawthorne or Isaac Bashevis Singer, but to a conventional figure, the teller of the tale, who is no less fictional than Wakefield or Shmul-Leibele.

Showing: Impersonal Narration

Still another possibility is that the narrator may not be a person at all, either a character or the "author." Some short stories and novels seem to unfold, like plays or movies, as if *no one* were telling them. Mrs. Morgan cannot be called the narrator of Elizabeth Jolley's "Wednesdays and Fridays" because her letters don't *tell* the story but *are* the story, the story of a mother's attempt to communicate with her live-in son by writing him letters. Elizabeth Bowen's "Careless Talk" (pp. 370–373) is also mostly shown. It consists mainly of quoted dialogue among the characters, giving little sense of a human teller, even a shadowy one. Except for a sentence or two, it could be the tape recording of the conversation between the protagonist and her friends.

Such a short story is said to be *shown* rather than *told*. Obviously, to "show" a short story is also a metaphor because "to show" means literally to give a visual presentation. But in literature the author presents words, not people and objects, or even pictures of them. Readers read those words, and from them reconstruct the events, characters, and settings. The easy applicability of "show" suggests the close relation of a short story's "showing" to the more literal showing of a stage play or movie. In plays or movies, "showing" is not metaphoric, because the characters—or at least human surrogates or photographs—*do* appear before our eyes. Still, in movies and television, the word *show* operates somewhat metaphorically, because it applies not only to visible but also to audible events such as characters' speeches. To "show" a sound is a rather odd way of speaking, but it is not too difficult to understand the metaphor.

What's really at issue, however, is not the metaphoric distinction between "telling" and "showing" but that between *personal* and *impersonal narration*. Personal narration implies that the narrator is a person, a "speaker" or "teller." Impersonal narration implies that there is no such person. Still, we need a verb to explain how impersonal narration comes about—and the one that has arisen in narrative theory is "to show." Other metaphors have been used, some of them quite colorful, like "camera-eye" or "fly-on-the-wall" narration, but however we name it, the crucial distinction is between narrations articulated by some recognizable person inhabiting a time and place in the discourse, and those that do not imply such a person. The latter fictions give the illusion of just "happening by themselves."

Some narratives occupy a middle ground. On the one hand, their narrators do not identify themselves or refer to themselves as "I." On the other hand, they do seem to exist as human beings, not merely as tape recorders or camera eyes. The narrator of "The Darling," (pp. 104–112) though unnamed and without explicit character traits, comments occasionally on the behavior of the protagonist Olenka. Describing her life after the departure of the veterinary surgeon, the narrator says: "And what was worst, she had no opinions of any sort." "What was worst" is clearly a value judgment, and it can only be the narrator's own value judgment. Even though the narrator does not name himself[1] or refer to himself as "I," the act of making such a judgment clearly implies that he *is* a person. Whoever he may be, the narrator of "The Darling" is someone who thinks it important for people to have their own opinions. Still, he remains external to the story. He inhabits only the realm of the discourse, unlike the internal narrators of Ralph Ellison's "The Battle Royal" (pp. 441–451) or Amy Tan's "Jin-Mei Woo: Two Kinds" (pp. 570–577). Personal narrators live both "now," in the discourse, but also "back then," in the story.

Some people call external narrators "third-person" narrators, but that is not a very good term. Third-person (as opposed to first-person) narration would imply that the narrator refers to himself or herself as "he" or "she." But it is not "he" or "she" that makes a narrator external. On the contrary, many external narrators don't refer to themselves at all. And if they do, as does the narrator of "Wakefield," they refer to themselves as "I." Critics who speak of the third-person narrator probably mean the *character*, not the narrator, especially the "point-of-view" or "filter" character whose thoughts dominate the story. We shall learn about that kind of character in the next chapter. We must always be very clear about the difference between characters and narrators — between those who tell or show the story and those who live it. The character lives in the story-world; the narrator speaks from a place in the discourse-world.

Omniscience and Limitation

Another important distinction concerns the amount and quality of information that narrators convey. Obviously, our reading of a fiction is very much controlled by what the narrator shows or tells, or to anticipate the discussion of chapter 6, what the narrator is *authorized* to show or tell. For the narrator is no less a fictional being than the characters. It is the (implied) author who chooses what — and how much — the narrator may explicitly tell and/or show. Camera-eye narrators are authorized to furnish only what a

---

[1]Actually, we have no way of knowing whether the narrator is male or female. It is simply conventional to refer to the unidentified "authorial" narrator by the same gender terms that would refer to the real author.

camera or tape recorder or Xerox machine can record. Elizabeth Bowen's "Careless Talk" (pp. 370–373) mainly quotes characters' speeches and describes physical actions (like "She signalled a waiter"). It is not a pure camera-eye short story, however, because the narrator tells us a bit (though only a bit) about what the protagonist Joanna *thinks* (". . . Joanna might easily have felt out of it," "[Eric] reminded her of one of the pictures" in a party game, and so on). The narrator's power to express what a character is thinking is called *mental access* or *inner view*.

Obviously, mental access cannot be recorded by a camera or tape-recorder. It implies a human narrator who can plumb a character's consciousness. But how deeply and widely can he do so?

In one kind of novel or short story, the narrator accesses only a single character's thinking. This access is called *limited filter*. When an entire short story or novel limits its access to one character's consciousness, we say that the story is told through the "point of view" or "filter" of that character's mind. The next chapter will discuss this important effect in great detail and examine how it works in a story like James Joyce's "A Little Cloud."

On the other hand, the narrator may present much broader information. She may tell us about what *any* character is thinking, and she may switch freely among various characters' minds without explanation or apology. She may also summarize long periods of time and describe vast spatial panoramas as if from the high perspective of a bird or airplane. She may have the authority to judge the characters, interpret their actions, or relate the fictional events to happenings in the real world. She may be granted the power to explain, in so many words, the meaning of events and the motives and personalities of characters in the larger scheme of things. Such powers constitute a narrator's *omniscience*, a Latin word for "all-knowing." If we think of the narrator's powers as a spectrum of possibilities, camera-eye reporting would mark the negative pole of the narrator's involvement, and omniscience would mark the positive. Omniscience is more characteristic of older fiction than of modern, though recent novels show a revival of interest in its possibilities.

A very clear example of narratorial omniscience occurs in Sarah Orne Jewett's "A White Heron" (pp. 114–120). The narrator describes the setting —the woods filled with shadows—as from a distance. She also has total access to every character's mind, telling us not only what Sylvia, Mrs. Tilley, and the hunter are thinking, but even what the *cow's* "greatest pleasure" is (hiding among the bushes and standing still so its bell won't ring). We are taken from one mind to another with the greatest of ease — for example, in the second paragraph, from Sylvia's to Mistress Moolly's (the cow's), to Mrs. Tilley's, in order to understand how the girl and cow could be out in the woods so long without causing concern to the grandmother. When the young hunter appears, he is represented as "the stranger" at first, because we are still in Sylvia's mind. Soon we move over into his mind; now he is simply "the young man," and we notice that the language becomes more elegant to suit his obvious good breeding and education. The narrator also knows, and tells us, that the great pine-tree that Sylvia climbs is "the last of its generation" and that no one knows why it still stands. The narrator is authorized to report not only the contents of the minds of the main characters but of everyone who lives in the neighborhood. She also has the power to comment on Sylvia's unwillingness to reveal the heron's whereabouts. It is a case, she says, of "Dear loyalty." At the same time, she notes that Sylvia must feel a conflicting loyalty to the young man. Finally, she speculates on the comparative value of human companionship (the hunter) and the companionship of Nature (the birds, the woodlands), implying that in growing up, a young person's interests inevitably shift to other human beings.

When we speak of the narrator's "knowledge," we are again not speaking literally. The amount of "knowledge" at the narrator's command is controlled by the (implied) author,[2] not by the narrator himself. Just as the (implied) author creates characters who know or do not know something in the plot, so the (implied) author creates a narrator capable of communicating just *this* amount of story information — no more and no less. The (implied) author controls the narrator's knowledge for a variety of reasons — reasons of suspense, surprise, artistry, and so on. Obviously, the (implied) author of a traditional detective novel cannot allow the narrator to tell the solution to the murder before the detective begins his investigation. Even if the detective is an internal, first-person narrator, who *must* know the solution because he himself has already solved the murder, he cannot be allowed to reveal the murderer's name prematurely.

The Narratee

We've been talking so far about the "voice" that presents the story, but we haven't said much about the "ear" that hears it. Whose ear is it? Actually, "reader" is not the best term, because the audience might not be a reader at all, but a listener, hearing the story around the campfire or over the radio, or a viewer watching the story on television. On the other hand, she may actually be named in the narrative itself. Just as we need to separate the real author from the "teller" of the story, we need to separate the real audience from the "listening ear" built into the discourse, and sometimes directly named and characterized by the narrator. A good term for this listener is *narratee*. Not only is the term less metaphorical than "ear," but it also ensures that we see the correspondence of the "ear" to the "voice" — thus, of the narrat-ee to the narrat-or. The narrator presents ("shows," "tells") and the narratee receives ("hears," "sees") the story.

A story that signals a narratee's presence very clearly is Tillie Olsen's "I Stand Here Ironing" (pp. 122 – 127). That presence is marked in the very first sentences:

---

[2] I shall explain in chapter 7 why it is useful to distinguish between the (real) author and the (implied) author — at which point I shall unwrap the parentheses. The implied author is not a historical human being, but rather the agent through whom we re-create the fiction — both story and discourse. It is the agent who, we infer, *intended* such-and-such an effect.

>   I stand here ironing, and what you asked me moves tormented back and
> forth with the iron.
>   "I wish you would manage the time to come in and talk with me about your
> daughter. I'm sure you can help me understand her. She's a youngster who
> needs help and whom I'm deeply interested in helping."

Clearly the woman ironing is not addressing a real you or me, or any other real
reader of this text, but rather the person who has asked her the tormenting
question about her daughter quoted in the second paragraph. From that question we infer that the narratee is someone dedicated to helping young people,
perhaps a teacher or social worker. We cannot know for sure, but given the
context, let us assume the latter. The narratee is not a character in the story that
the mother tells, but rather a figure in the discourse who hears the story. It is a
story of how she, the woman at the ironing board, has tried to be a good
mother, to raise her eldest daughter, Emily, properly, despite the hardships of
crushing poverty and abandonment by her first husband. The mother's story is
tinged with guilt. She realizes that even though life has gotten easier for her
and she has more time for Emily, it is too late to help her daughter. She admits
that Emily "was a child of anxious, not proud, love." Her other children
learned how to smile and be happy, but not Emily. There were too many
others, and Emily had to help out too soon, to the detriment of her own
development.

Still, the mother is not overwhelmed by that guilt. Though her "wisdom came too late," it did come. The mother appreciates Emily's talent to
amuse people, but experience persuades her that "nothing will come of it."
For to become a comedienne one needs training, and training requires
"money, or knowing how," and Emily has neither. Still, the mother is a
survivor (as one guesses Emily will be): "Why did you want me to come in at
all?" she asks the narratee. "Why were you concerned? She will find her way."
She will do so even though "she is a child of her age, of depression, of war, of
fear."

The form of this short story could be a monologue, spoken aloud, in
soliloquy, or silently thought by the mother as she stands alone in her kitchen
ironing. She seems to be mulling over what the narratee has said: this is her
response. She may or may not ultimately deliver it to the narratee, but clearly at
this moment, the moment of telling, of discourse, the story is at least mentally
addressed to the social worker.

In a sense, every "told" narrative implies a narratee, for the act of
telling does not happen in a void. It presupposes someone, some audience,
interested enough to hear. More often than not, narrative fictions do not name
or even allude to narratees. When the narratee becomes a full-blown person in
the discourse, we need to ask why the (implied) author invented her. Perhaps,
in "I Stand Here Ironing," it was to enhance our understanding of the range
and poignancy of the mother's feelings. The social worker has offered to help
the daughter become a success in life. This offer elicits the complex feelings
that are the subject of the short story: the mother's guilt, her sense of lost
opportunity to show love, her wish to avoid raising Emily's hopes about

becoming a comedienne only to see her defeated once again. The (implied) author obviously believes that these feelings are best dramatized by having them spoken to a provocative outsider who wants to help the daughter "make something of her life." Though the mother obviously wishes the best for Emily, the family has had its fill of institutional do-gooders, those who raise money for foster homes in the country for indigent children. The homes may be materially pleasant, but they end up alienating the children from their families. The mother has reason to be suspicious of fantasies of glorious success for Emily, and she doesn't want her daughter to continue being disappointed by life.

It is not clear that the narratee of "I Stand Here Ironing" speaks — his/her words may simply be repeated in the mother's consciousness. When narratees do speak, however, an interesting thing happens. Because dialogue tends to dramatize a text, thus turning it into a story, the dialogue between narrator and narratee becomes a little narrative in its own right. The narrative of the telling of the story becomes a kind of *frame-narrative* for the main story. The main story then becomes a *framed*-narrative. The frame-narrative technique is used by three short stories in this book: Fyodor Dostoevsky's "Polzunkov" (pp. 430–440), Mark Twain's "The Celebrated Jumping Frog of Calaveras County" (pp. 380–384), and Isaac Babel's "How It Was Done in Odessa" (pp. 75–81). In each case the first-person narrator repeats a story that he has heard as a narratee of the framed-narrative. In "Polzunkov," the unnamed I-narrator of the frame-narrative story tells "us" the saga of the buffoon's humiliation as he heard it from Polzunkov's own lips. In the framed-narrative, he had been Polzunkov's narratee. Similarly, in the framed-narrative of "The Celebrated Jumping Frog of Calaveras County," Simon Wheeler tells the "I"-narratee the absurd adventures of Smiley and the frog; the "I" in turn becomes the narrator of the frame-narrative who tells it to "us" narratees. In "How It Was Done in Odessa," Reb Arye-Leib tells the "I"-narratee the story of Benya Krik, but the narratee does not become an overt narrator. We simply join him as narratees, *overhearing* the Reb's narration, so to speak.

The narratee may be explicitly named, as in these three short stories, or her presence only acknowledged, as in "I Stand Here Ironing." A narratee may not be suggested at all, but still we may invent one by speaking of "ourselves" as the addressees of the story. Because narratives are communications of some sort, a narratee is always at least *potentially* present. That someone tells or shows a story logically entails a someone who hears or sees it.

❖ ELIZABETH JOLLEY
Wednesdays and Fridays

Elizabeth Jolley (1923–   ) was born in Birmingham, England. She was trained as a nurse, a profession that she practiced during World War II. She migrated to Western Australia in 1959, where she first worked as a housecleaner and salesperson. She did not publish her first fiction until she was 52, in 1975. Since then, she has been very prolific, publishing the following novels: *The Travelling Entertainer* (1979), *Palomino* (1980), *The Newspaper of Claremont Street* (1981), *Mr. Scobie's Riddle* (1983), *Miss Peabody's Inheritance* (1983), *Milk and Honey* (1984), *Foxybaby* (1985), *The Well* (1986), *The Sugar Mother* (1988), *My Father's Moon* (1989), and *Cabin Fever* (1990). "Wednesdays and Fridays" appeared in her short story collection *Woman in the Lampshade* (1983). Later short story collections include *Stories* (1984) and *Five Acre Virgin* (1989). Jolley is presently Writer-in-Residence at Curtin University of Technology in Perth, Australia.

Wednesday 4 June
Dear Mr Morgan,
          You will be surprised to have a letter from me since we are living in the same house but I should like to remind you that you have not paid me board for last week.
Yours sincerely,
Mabel Doris Morgan
(landlady)

Wednesday 11 June
Dear Mr Morgan,
          This is to remind you that you are now owing two weeks' board and I should like to take the opportunity to ask you to remove the outboard motor from your room. There is an oil stain on the rug already and I'm afraid for my curtains and bedspread.
Yours sincerely,
Mabel Doris Morgan
(landlady)

Friday 13 June
Dear Mr Morgan,
          I know there isn't anything in the 'Rules of the House' to say outboard motors cannot be kept in bedrooms. I didn't think any one would want to. Since you mention the rules I would like to draw your attention first to rule number nine which refers to empty beer cans, female visitors and cigarette ends, and to point out that rule eleven

98

states quite clearly the hour for breakfast. It is simply not possible, I am sorry, to serve breakfasts after twelve noon.

Yours sincerely,
Mabel D. Morgan
(landlady)

Wednesday 18 June
Dear Mr Morgan,
        I am writing to remind you that you now owe three weeks' board and the price of one single bed sheet which is ruined. Please note that bed linen is not to be used for other purposes. Thank you for moving the outboard motor.

Yours sincerely,
Mabel Doris Morgan
(landlady)

Friday 20 June
Dear Mr Morgan,
        No. Black oil and grease will not wash out of a sheet furthermore it's torn badly in places. I can't think how it's possible to damage a sheet as much as this one has been damaged.
        I am afraid I shall have to ask you to move the outboard motor again as it is impossible for anyone to sit in the lounge room to watch TV the way you have the propellor balanced between the two easy chairs.

Yours sincerely,
Mabel D. Morgan
(landlady)

Wednesday 25 June
Dear Mr Morgan,
        Thank you for the two dollars. I should like to remind you that you now owe four weeks' board less two dollars.

Yours sincerely,
Mabel D. Morgan
(landlady)

Friday 27 June
Dear Mr Morgan,
        Leaving a note on the mantelpiece does not excuse anyone for taking two dollars which does not belong to them even if you are only borrowing it back as you say till next week. Board is at four weeks now. I'm sorry to have to tell you that the hall is too narrow for the storage of an outboard motor. And, would you please replace your bedspread and put up your curtains again as I am afraid they will spoil and they

do not in any way help to prevent people from falling over the outboard as they go in and out of this house.

Yours sincerely,
Mabel D. Morgan
(landlady)

Wednesday 2 July
Dear Mr Morgan,

Board is up to five weeks. With respect, Mr Morgan, I'd like to suggest you try to get a job. I'd like to suggest the way to do this is to get up early and get the paper and read the *Situations Vacant, Men and Boys*, and go after something. I'd like to say this has to be done early and quick. Mr Morgan, five weeks' board is five weeks' board. And Mr Morgan what's been going on in the bathroom. I think I am entitled to an explanation.

Yours sincerely
Mabel Doris Morgan
(landlady)

Friday 4 July
Dear Mr Morgan,

Thank you for your very kind thought. The chocolates really look very nice though, as you know, I don't eat sweet things as I have to watch my weight but as I said it's the thought that counts. Do you think it's possible you might be smoking a bit too much. Perhaps you could cut it down to say sixty a day for a start.

Yours sincerely
Mabel Doris Morgan
(landlady)

Wednesday 9 July
Dear Mr Morgan

I'm still waiting for an explanation about the bathroom. I must remind you that you now owe me six weeks' board and the cost of one single bed sheet ruined plus the cost of one bottle carpet cleaning detergent plus the price of the four pounds of gift-wrapped confectionery charged to my account at the Highway General Store. Early payment would be appreciated.

Yours sincerely,
Mabel Doris Morgan
(landlady)

Friday 11 July
Mr Morgan

Get a Job. And clean your room. I never saw such a mess of chocolate papers under anyone's bed, ever. In my whole life I never saw such a mess. Never. I must point out too that I do not intend to spend hours in the kitchen over the hot roast and two veg. for someone who is too full up with rubbish to eat what's good for them. I'd like to remind you how to get a job. You get up early to get a job. I see in the paper concrete hands are wanted, this should suit you, so GET UP EARLY as it's a question of being first on site.

Yours sincerely,
Mabel Doris Morgan
(landlady)

And Mr Morgan, Bathroom? Explanation? And Mr Morgan. Smoking!

Wednesday 16 July
Dear Mr Morgan,

I appreciate you have troubles. We all have our troubles and I do see you have yours and it was kind of you to think of sending me flowers when you have so much on your mind. Thank you for the thought.

Miss, I forget, if you said, what you said her name was, had no business to miss her last bus. In future no guests are to stay in this house without me. See that this does not happen again. You seem to have forgotten the outboard motor. There simply is not room for it in the hall and it's all wet. Please see that it is removed immediately. And please Mr Morgan, Board seven weeks.

Yours sincerely,
Mabel D. Morgan
(landlady)

Friday 18 July
Dear Mr Morgan,

First I must ask for an immediate explanation about the bathroom please. And secondly, I must ask you to ask Miss whatever her name is to leave. I suggest you ask her what her name is if you didn't get it the first time.

I hope you won't feel offended about this but there really is not room for you to sleep in the hall, you know it has always been too narrow. There simply is not room there for you and the outboard motor. One of you will have to go. And see that young Miss, leaves at once. And, Donald, always make sure you know what a girl's name is beforehand. You not knowing her name makes me feel I haven't brought you up right.

Yours sincerely,
Mabel Doris Morgan
(landlady)

Wednesday 23 July
Dear Mr Morgan,

I have to remind you Board eight weeks and Board one week for Extra Person. Perhaps you could persuade Pearl to go back to her lovely boarding school? Could you? I'm sure she's a nice girl but I really can't do with the two of you lazing round the house all day using up all my electricity and hot water. And I don't need to tell you that there really isn't enough space in the hall for your bed, her bicycle and her extra cases and the outboard motor.

Donald it's silly blocking up the hall with your bed. The neighbours will talk in any case. They'll think immorality is going on and what about young Mary? What ideas is she going to get? Donald I'm warning you I'm putting my foot down furthermore the outboard motor is not to be used in the bath. Where can it get you? AND what about a Job?

> Yours sincerely,
> Mabel Doris Morgan
> (landlady)

Friday 25 July
   Donald, No more roses please. I haven't got vases. Besides how am I going to pay for them? You know me, I'd just as soon see a flower growing in someone's garden. Thank you all the same for your lovely thought.

> Your loving landlady,
> Mabel Doris Morgan

Wednesday 30 July
   Mr Morgan, This is to remind you Board nine weeks and Board two weeks for one Extra Person. I must say young Pearl has a healthy appetite. I wish you would eat properly.
   As I was saying. Board as above, also cost of one single bed sheet, one bottle carpet cleaning detergent plus the price of the four-pound box of assorted confectionery and four dozen red roses, two deliveries, long stalks extra, and to dry cleaning and dyeing one chenille bedspread (purple) and two pairs curtains (electric green). With dry cleaning the price it is it would have been better to consult me first and about the extraordinary choice of colours, especially as I don't think the oil and grease stains will be hidden at all.
   Donald, I do seriously think a Job is a good thing. Get a Job. Do try to get a Job.

> Yours sincerely,
> Mabel Doris Morgan
> (landlady)

Friday 1 August
Donald, No more presents please. You know I never use lipsticks and certainly never a phosphorescent one. You must be off your brain. Though I suppose there is always a first time.

> Your loving landlady,
> Mabel Doris Morgan

Wednesday 6 August
Dear Donald,
   I'm pushing this note under your door since you won't come out. I'm leaving a tray on the table outside. Do try and eat something. I'm sorry I said what I said. I am sorry too about the outboard motor. I suppose it wasn't fixed on to the boat properly. You say it's about thirty-five feet down? I didn't know the river was so deep there. Of course I'll lend you twenty dollars to hire a boat and a grappling iron. We'll simply add it onto the Board which is at ten weeks now and three weeks for one Extra Person, plus the cost of one single bed sheet, one bottle carpet cleaning detergent, one four-pound

box assorted confectionery gift wrapped, and four dozen red roses, two deliveries (long stalks extra) and to the dry cleaning of one chenille bedspread and two pairs of curtains and the dyeing of the above, purple and electric green, respectively, plus the cost of one Midnight Ecstasy lipstick (phosphorescent frosted ice). I do hope we can find the outboard motor. I'm really looking forward to going on the river in a row boat, it's years since I was in a boat. We'll take Pearl and Mary with us and our lunch.

Your loving mother,
Mabel Doris Morgan
(landlady)
(1983)

QUESTIONS

1. What difficulties are there in writing a story entirely through letters? What advantages?
2. Is there any reason for the various ways Mabel Doris Morgan opens and closes her letters?
3. No narrator speaks in this short story. If that is so, how can you explain how the short story becomes available to you? Can a narrator simply be a collector of "already written" documents?
4. Does the letter writer think the story is funny? Does the letter receiver? Does the (implied) author? Do you? Why the disparity?
5. A short story this brief must be very selective. Name some of the details that are cited and then name some that are only implied but that are crucial to the point. Can you say anything about the results?

❖ ANTON CHEKHOV
The Darling*

Anton Chekhov (1860–1904) was born in Taganrog, Russia, into a poor family. He earned a degree as a physician at Moscow University, but he did not practice extensively. Still, he felt that his medical training helped him become a writer by providing him with insights into human psychology. He published his first collection of short stories, *Tales of Melpomone* (1884) while still in college. Thereafter he wrote literally hundreds of stories, which can be found in English translation in his *Collected Works* (five volumes, 1987). For all intents and purposes, Chekhov along with Guy de Maupassant, invented the modern short story, or a least the short story of ironic and subtle cast. Chekhov had trouble with his lungs most of his life and died at 44 at his home in Yalta. He was not even able to go to Moscow to see his wife, an actress, perform in his many successful plays, among which are *The Sea Gull* (1896), *Uncle Vanya* (1899), *The Three Sisters* (1901), and *The Cherry Orchard* (1904).

Olenka, the daughter of the retired collegiate assessor, Plemyanniakov, was sitting in her back porch, lost in thought. It was hot, the flies were persistent and teasing, and it was pleasant to reflect that it would soon be evening. Dark rain clouds were gathering from the east, and bringing from time to time a breath of moisture in the air.

Kukin, who was the manager of an open-air theatre called the Tivoli, and who lived in the lodge, was standing in the middle of the garden looking at the sky.

"Again!" he observed despairingly. "It's going to rain again! Rain every day, as though to spite me. I might as well hang myself! It's ruin! Fearful losses every day."

He flung up his hands, and went on, addressing Olenka:

"There! that's the life we lead, Olga Semyonovna. It's enough to make one cry. One works and does one's utmost, one wears oneself out, getting no sleep at night, and racks one's brain what to do for the best. And then what happens? To begin with, one's public is ignorant, boorish. I give them the very best operetta, a dainty masque, first rate music-hall artists. But do you suppose that's what they want! They don't understand anything of that sort. They want a clown; what they ask for is vulgarity. And then look at the weather! Almost every evening it rains. It started on the tenth of May, and it's kept it up all May and June. It's simply awful! The public doesn't come, but I've to pay the rent just the same, and pay the artists."

The next evening the clouds would gather again, and Kukin would say with an hysterical laugh:

"Well, rain away, then! Flood the garden, drown me! Damn my luck in this

---

*Translated by Constance Garnett.

world and the next! Let the artists have me up! Send me to prison! — to Siberia! — the scaffold! Ha, ha, ha!"

And next day the same thing.

Olenka listened to Kukin with silent gravity, and sometimes tears came into her eyes. In the end his misfortunes touched her; she grew to love him. He was a small thin man, with a yellow face, and curls combed forward on his forehead. He spoke in a thin tenor; as he talked his mouth worked on one side, and there was always an expression of despair on his face; yet he aroused a deep and genuine affection in her. She was always fond of some one, and could not exist without loving. In earlier days she had loved her papa, who now sat in a darkened room, breathing with difficulty; she had loved her aunt who used to come every other year from Bryansk[1]; and before that, when she was at school, she had loved her French master. She was a gentle, soft-hearted, compassionate girl, with mild, tender eyes and very good health. At the sight of her full rosy cheeks, her soft white neck with a little dark mole on it, and the kind, naïve smile, which came into her face when she listened to anything pleasant, men thought, "Yes, not half bad," and smiled too, while lady visitors could not refrain from seizing her hand in the middle of a conversation, exclaiming in a gush of delight, "You darling!"

The house in which she had lived from her birth upwards, and which was left her in her father's will, was at the extreme end of the town, not far from the Tivoli. In the evenings and at night she could hear the band playing, and the crackling and banging of fireworks, and it seemed to her that it was Kukin struggling with his destiny, storming the entrenchments of his chief foe, the indifferent public; there was a sweet thrill at her heart, she had no desire to sleep, and when he returned home at day-break, she tapped softly at her bedroom window, and showing him only her face and one shoulder through the curtain, she gave him a friendly smile. . . .

He proposed to her, and they were married. And when he had a closer view of her neck and her plump, fine shoulders, he threw up his hands, and said:

"You darling!"

He was happy, but as it rained on the day and night of his wedding, his face still retained an expression of despair.

They got on very well together. She used to sit in his office, to look after things in the Tivoli, to put down the accounts and pay the wages. And her rosy cheeks, her sweet, naïve, radiant smile, were to be seen now at the office window, now in the refreshment bar or behind the scenes of the theatre. And already she used to say to her acquaintances that the theatre was the chief and most important thing in life, and that it was only through the drama that one could derive true enjoyment and become cultivated and humane.

"But do you suppose the public understands that?" she used to say. "What they want is a clown. Yesterday we gave 'Faust Inside Out,' and almost all the boxes were empty; but if Vanitchka and I had been producing some vulgar thing, I assure you the theatre would have been packed. Tomorrow Vanitchka and I are doing 'Orpheus in Hell.'[2] Do come."

---

[1] A small city southwest of Moscow.
[2] Popular theatrical pieces of the nineteenth century.

And what Kukin said about the theatre and the actors she repeated. Like him she despised the public for their ignorance and their indifference to art; she took part in the rehearsals, she corrected the actors, she kept an eye on the behavior of the musicians, and when there was an unfavorable notice in the local paper, she shed tears, and then went to the editor's office to set things right.

The actors were fond of her and used to call her "Vanitchka and I," and "the darling"; she was sorry for them and used to lend them small sums of money, and if they deceived her, she used to shed a few tears in private, but did not complain to her husband.

They got on well in the winter too. They took the theatre in the town for the whole winter, and let it for short terms to a Little Russian company, or to a conjurer, or to a local dramatic society. Olenka grew stouter, and was always beaming with satisfaction, while Kukin grew thinner and yellower, and continually complained of their terrible losses, although he had not done badly all the winter. He used to cough at night, and she used to give him hot raspberry tea or limeflower water, to rub him with eau-de-Cologne and to wrap him in her warm shawls.

"You're such a sweet pet!" she used to say with perfect sincerity, stroking his hair. "You're such a pretty dear!'

Towards Lent he went to Moscow to collect a new troupe, and without him she could not sleep, but sat all night at her window, looking at the stars, and she compared herself with the hens, who are awake all night and uneasy when the cock is not in the hen-house. Kukin was detained in Moscow, and wrote that he would be back at Easter, adding some instructions about the Tivoli. But on the Sunday before Easter, late in the evening, came a sudden ominous knock at the gate; some one was hammering on the gate as though on a barrel — boom, boom, boom! The drowsy cook went flopping with her bare feet through the puddles, as she ran to open the gate.

"Please open," said some one outside in a thick bass. "There is a telegram for you."

Olenka had received telegrams from her husband before, but this time for some reason she felt numb with terror. With shaking hands she opened the telegram and read as follows:

"Ivan Petrovitch died suddenly today. Awaiting immate instructions fufuneral Tuesday."

That was how it was written in the telegram — "fufuneral," and the utterly incomprehensible word "immate." It was signed by the stage manager of the operatic company.

"My darling!" sobbed Olenka. "Vanitchka, my precious, my darling! Why did I ever meet you! Why did I know you and love you! Your poor heart-broken Olenka is all alone without you!"

Kukin's funeral took place on Tuesday in Moscow, Olenka returned home on Wednesday, and as soon as she got indoors she threw herself on her bed and sobbed so loudly that it could be heard next door, and in the street.

"Poor darling!" the neighbors said, as they crossed themselves. "Olga Semyonovna, poor darling! How she does take on!"

Three months later Olenka was coming home from mass, melancholy and in deep mourning. It happened that one of her neighbors, Vassily Andreitch Pustovalov, returning home from church, walked back beside her. He was the manager at Baba-kayev's, the timber merchant's. He wore a straw hat, a white waistcoat, and a gold watchchain, and looked more like a country gentleman than a man in trade.

"Everything happens as it is ordained, Olga Semyonovna," he said gravely, with a sympathetic note in his voice; "and if any of our dear ones die, it must be because it is the will of God, so we ought to have fortitude and bear it submissively."

After seeing Olenka to her gate, he said goodbye and went on. All day afterwards she heard his sedately dignified voice, and whenever she shut her eyes she saw his dark beard. She liked him very much. And apparently she had made an impression on him too, for not long afterwards an elderly lady, with whom she was only slightly acquainted, came to drink coffee with her, and as soon as she was seated at table began to talk about Pustovalov, saying that he was an excellent man whom one could thoroughly depend upon, and that any girl would be glad to marry him. Three days later Pustovalov came himself. He did not stay long, only about ten minutes, and he did not say much, but when he left, Olenka loved him — loved him so much that she lay awake all night in a perfect fever, and in the morning she sent for the elderly lady. The match was quickly arranged, and then came the wedding.

Pustovalov and Olenka got on very well together when they were married.

Usually he sat in the office till dinnertime, then he went out on business, while Olenka took his place, and sat in the office till evening, making up accounts and booking orders.

"Timber gets dearer every year; the price rises twenty per cent," she would say to her customers and friends. "Only fancy we used to sell local timber, and now Vassitchka always has to go for wood to the Mogilev district.[3] And the freight!" she would add, covering her cheeks with her hands in horror. "The freight!"

It seemed to her that she had been in the timber trade for ages and ages, and that the most important and necessary thing in life was timber; and there was something intimate and touching to her in the very sound of words such as "baulk," "post," "beam," "pole," "scantling," "batten," "lath," "plank," etc.

At night when she was asleep she dreamed of perfect mountains of planks and boards, and long strings of wagons, carting timber somewhere far away. She dreamed that a whole regiment of six-inch beams forty feet high, standing on end, was marching upon the timber-yard; that logs, beams, and boards knocked together with the resounding crash of dry wood, kept falling and getting up again, piling themselves on each other. Olenka cried out in her sleep, and Pustovalov said to her tenderly: "Olenka, what's the matter, darling? Cross yourself!"

Her husband's ideas were hers. If he thought the room was too hot, or that business was slack, she thought the same. Her husband did not care for entertainments, and on holidays he stayed at home. She did likewise.

"You are always at home or in the office," her friends said to her. "You should go to the theatre, darling, or to the circus."

"Vassitchka and I have no time to go to theatres," she would answer sedately. "We have no time for nonsense. What's the use of these theatres?"

On Saturdays Pustovalov and she used to go to the evening service; on

---

[3] A city on the Dnieper River, west of Moscow.

holidays to early mass, and they walked side by side with softened faces as they came home from church. There was a pleasant fragrance about them both, and her silk dress rustled agreeably. At home they drank tea, with fancy bread and jams of various kinds, and afterwards they ate pie. Every day at twelve o'clock there was a savoury smell of beet-root soup and of mutton or duck in their yard, and on fast-days of fish, and no one could pass the gate without feeling hungry. In the office the samovar[4] was always boiling, and customers were regaled with tea and cracknels.[5] Once a week the couple went to the baths and returned side by side, both red in the face.

"Yes, we have nothing to complain of, thank God." Olenka used to say to her acquaintances. "I wish every one were as well off as Vassitchka and I."

When Pustovalov went away to buy wood in the Mogilev district, she missed him dreadfully, lay awake and cried. A young veterinary surgeon in the army, called Smirnin, to whom they had let their lodge, used sometimes to come in in the evening. He used to talk to her and play cards with her, and this entertained her in her husband's absence. She was particularly interested in what he told her of his home life. He was married and had a little boy, but was separated from his wife because she had been unfaithful to him, and now he hated her and used to send her forty roubles a month for the maintenance of their son. And hearing of all this, Olenka sighed and shook her head. She was sorry for him.

"Well, God keep you," she used to say to him at parting, as she lighted him down the stairs with a candle. "Thank you for coming to cheer me up, and may the Mother of God give you health."

And she always expressed herself with the same sedateness and dignity, the same reasonableness, in imitation of her husband. As the veterinary surgeon was disappearing behind the door below, she would say:

"You know, Vladimir Platonitch, you'd better make it up with your wife. You should forgive her for the sake of your son. You may be sure the little fellow understands."

And when Pustovalov came back, she told him in a low voice about the veterinary surgeon and his unhappy home life, and both sighed and shook their heads and talked about the boy, who, no doubt, missed his father, and by some strange connection of ideas, they went up to the holy ikons,[6] bowed to the ground before them and prayed that God would give them children.

And so the Pustovalovs lived for six years quietly and peaceably in love and complete harmony.

But behold! one winter day after drinking hot tea in the office, Vassily Andreitch went out into the yard without his cap on to see about sending off some timber, caught cold and was taken ill. He had the best doctors, but he grew worse and died after four months' illness. And Olenka was a widow once more.

"I've nobody, now you've left me, my darling," she sobbed, after her husband's funeral. "How can I live without you, in wretchedness and misery! Pity me, good people, all alone in the world!"

---

[4] A metal urn for heating water.
[5] Hard, brittle cakes.
[6] Religious images.

She went about dressed in black with long "weepers,"[7] and gave up wearing hat and gloves for good. She hardly ever went out, except to church, or to her husband's grave, and led the life of a nun. It was not till six months later that she took off the weepers and opened the shutters of the windows. She was sometimes seen in the mornings, going with her cook to market for provisions, but what went on in her house and how she lived now could only be surmised. People guessed, from seeing her drinking tea in her garden with the veterinary surgeon, who read the newspaper aloud to her, and from the fact that, meeting a lady she knew at the post-office, she said to her: "There is no proper veterinary inspection in our town, and that's the cause of all sorts of epidemics. One is always hearing of people's getting infection from the milk supply, or catching diseases from horses and cows. The health of domestic animals ought to be as well cared for as the health of human beings."

She repeated the veterinary surgeon's words, and was of the same opinion as he about everything. It was evident that she could not live a year without some attachment, and had found new happiness in the lodge. In any one else this would have been censured, but no one could think ill of Olenka; everything she did was so natural. Neither she nor the veterinary surgeon said anything to other people of the change in their relations, and tried, indeed, to conceal it, but without success, for Olenka could not keep a secret. When he had visitors, men serving in his regiment, and she poured out tea or served the supper, she would begin talking of the cattle plague, of the foot and mouth disease, and of the municipal slaughterhouses. He was dreadfully embarrassed, and when the guests had gone, he would seize her by the hand and hiss angrily:

"I've asked you before not to talk about what you don't understand. When we veterinary surgeons are talking among ourselves, please don't put your word in. It's really annoying."

And she would look at him with astonishment and dismay, and ask him in alarm: "But, Voloditchka, what *am* I to talk about?"

And with tears in her eyes she would embrace him, begging him not to be angry, and they were both happy.

But this happiness did not last long. The veterinary surgeon departed, departed for ever with his regiment, when it was transferred to a distant place — to Siberia, it may be. And Olenka was left alone.

Now she was absolutely alone. Her father had long been dead, and his armchair lay in the attic, covered with dust and lame of one leg. She got thinner and plainer, and when people met her in the street they did not look at her as they used to, and did not smile to her; evidently her best years were over and left behind, and now a new sort of life had begun for her, which did not bear thinking about. In the evening Olenka sat in the porch, and heard the band playing and the fireworks popping in the Tivoli, but now the sound stirred no response. She looked into her yard without interest, thought of nothing, wished for nothing, and afterwards, when night came on she went to bed and dreamed of her empty yard. She ate and drank as it were unwillingly.

And what was worst of all, she had no opinions of any sort. She saw the

---

[7] Hanging garments worn in mourning, as a widow's black veil.

objects about her and understood what she saw, but could not form any opinion about them, and did not know what to talk about. And how awful it is not to have any opinions! One sees a bottle, for instance, or the rain, or a peasant driving in his cart, but what the bottle is for, or the rain, or the peasant, and what is the meaning of it, one can't say, and could not even for a thousand roubles. When she had Kukin, or Pustovalov, or the veterinary surgeon, Olenka could explain everything, and give her opinion about anything you like, but now there was the same emptiness in her brain and in her heart as there was in her yard outside. And it was as harsh and as bitter as wormwood in the mouth.

Little by little the town grew in all directions. The road became a street, and where the Tivoli and the timber-yard had been, there were new turnings and houses. How rapidly time passes! Olenka's house grew dingy, the roof got rusty, the shed sank on one side, and the whole yard was overgrown with docks and stinging-nettles.[8] Olenka herself had grown plain and elderly; in summer she sat in the porch, and her soul, as before, was empty and dreary and full of bitterness. In winter she sat at her window and looked at the snow. When she caught the scent of spring, or heard the chime of the church bells, a sudden rush of memories from the past came over her, there was a tender ache in her heart, and her eyes brimmed over with tears; but this was only for a minute, and then came emptiness again and the sense of the futility of life. The black kitten, Briska, rubbed against her and purred softly, but Olenka was not touched by these feline caresses. That was not what she needed. She wanted a love that would absorb her whole being, her whole soul and reason — that would give her ideas and an object in life, and would warm her old blood. And she would shake the kitten off her skirt and say with vexation:

"Get along; I don't want you!"

And so it was, day after day and year after year, and no joy, and no opinions. Whatever Mavra, the cook, said she accepted.

One hot July day, towards evening, just as the cattle were being driven away, and the whole yard was full of dust, some one suddenly knocked at the gate. Olenka went to open it herself and was dumbfounded when she looked out: she saw Smirnin, the veterinary surgeon, grey-headed, and dressed as a civilian. She suddenly remembered everything. She could not help crying and letting her head fall on his breast without uttering a word, and in the violence of her feeling she did not notice how they both walked into the house and sat down to tea.

"My dear Vladimir Platonitch! What fate has brought you?" she muttered, trembling with joy.

"I want to settle here for good, Olga Semyonovna," he told her. "I have resigned my post, and have come to settle down and try my luck on my own account. Besides, it's time for my boy to go to school. He's a big boy. I am reconciled with my wife, you know."

"Where is she?" asked Olenka.

"She's at the hotel with the boy, and I'm looking for lodgings."

"Good gracious, my dear soul! Lodgings? Why not have my house? Why

[8]Prickly plants.

shouldn't that suit you? Why, my goodness, I wouldn't take any rent!" cried Olenka in a flutter, beginning to cry again. "You live here, and the lodge will do nicely for me. Oh dear! how glad I am!"

Next day the roof was painted and the walls were whitewashed, and Olenka with her arms akimbo, walked about the yard giving directions. Her face was beaming with her old smile, and she was brisk and alert as though she had waked from a long sleep. The veterinary's wife arrived — a thin, plain lady, with short hair and a peevish expression. With her was her little Sasha, a boy of ten, small for his age, blue-eyed, chubby, with dimples in his cheeks. And scarcely had the boy walked into the yard when he ran after the cat, and at once there was the sound of his gay, joyous laugh.

"Is that your puss, auntie?" he asked Olenka. "When she has little ones, do give us a kitten. Mamma is awfully afraid of mice."

Olenka talked to him, and gave him tea. Her heart warmed and there was a sweet ache in her bosom, as though the boy had been her own child. And when he sat at the table in the evening, going over his lessons, she looked at him with deep tenderness and pity as she murmured to herself:

"You pretty pet! . . . my precious! . . . Such a fair little thing, and so clever."

" 'An island is a piece of land which is entirely surrounded by water,' " he read aloud.

"An island is a piece of land," she repeated, and this was the first opinion to which she gave utterance with positive conviction after so many years of silence and dearth of ideas.

Now she had opinions of her own, and at supper she talked to Sasha's parents, saying how difficult the lessons were at the high schools, but that yet the high school was better than a commercial one, since with a high-school education all careers were open to one, such as being a doctor or an engineer.

Sasha began going to the high school. His mother departed to Harkov to her sister's and did not return; his father used to go off every day to inspect cattle, and would often be away from home for three days together, and it seemed to Olenka as though Sasha was entirely abandoned, that he was not wanted at home, that he was being starved, and she carried him off to her lodge and gave him a little room there.

And for six months Sasha had lived in the lodge with her. Every morning Olenka came into his bedroom and found him fast asleep, sleeping noiselessly with his hand under his cheek. She was sorry to wake him.

"Sashenka," she would say mournfully, "get up, darling. It's time for school."

He would get up, dress and say his prayers, and then sit down to breakfast, drink three glasses of tea, and eat two large cracknels and a half a buttered roll. All this time he was hardly awake and a little ill-humoured in consequence.

"You don't quite know your fable, Sashenka," Olenka would say, looking at him as though he were about to set off on a long journey. "What a lot of trouble I have with you! You must work and do your best, darling, and obey your teachers."

"Oh, do leave me alone!" Sasha would say.

Then he would go down the street to school, a little figure, wearing a big cap and carrying a satchel on his shoulder. Olenka would follow him noiselessly.

"Sashenka!" she would call after him, and she would pop into his hand a date or a caramel. When he reached the street where the school was, he would feel ashamed of being followed by a tall, stout woman; he would turn round and say:

"You'd better go home, auntie. I can go the rest of the way alone."

She would stand still and look after him fixedly till he had disappeared at the school-gate.

Ah, how she loved him! Of her former attachments not one had been so deep; never had her soul surrendered to any feeling so spontaneously, so disinterestedly, and so joyously as now that her maternal instincts were aroused. For this little boy with the dimple in his cheek and the big school cap, she would have given her whole life, she would have given it with joy and tears of tenderness. Why? Who can tell why?

When she had seen the last of Sasha, she returned home, contented and serene, brimming over with love; her face, which had grown younger during the last six months, smiled and beamed; people meeting her looked at her with pleasure.

"Good morning, Olga Semyonovna, darling. How are you, darling?"

"The lessons at the high school are very difficult now," she would relate at the market. "It's too much; in the first class yesterday they gave him a fable to learn by heart, and a Latin translation and a problem. You know it's too much for a little chap."

And she would begin talking about the teachers, the lessons, and the school books, saying just what Sasha said.

At three o'clock they had dinner together: in the evening they learned their lessons together and cried. When she put him to bed, she would stay a long time making the Cross over him and murmuring a prayer; then she would go to bed and dream of that far-away misty future when Sasha would finish his studies and become a doctor or an engineer, would have a big house of his own with horses and a carriage, would get married and have children. . . . She would fall asleep still thinking of the same thing, and tears would run down her cheeks from her closed eyes, while the black cat lay purring beside her: "Mrr, mrr, mrr."

Suddenly there would come a loud knock at the gate.

Olenka would wake up breathless with alarm, her heart throbbing. Half a minute later would come another knock.

"It must be a telegram from Harkov," she would think, beginning to tremble from head to foot. "Sasha's mother is sending for him from Harkov. . . . Oh, mercy on us!"

She was in despair. Her head, her hands, and her feet would turn chill, and she would feel that she was the most unhappy woman in the world. But another minute would pass, voices would be heard: it would turn out to be the veterinary surgeon coming home from the club.

"Well, thank God!" she would think.

And gradually the load in her heart would pass off, and she would feel at ease. She would go back to bed thinking of Sasha, who lay sound asleep in the next room, sometimes crying out in his sleep:

"I'll give it you! Get away! Shut up!"

(1899)

QUESTIONS

1. Are we intended to think that Sasha is asleep when he addresses Olenka at the end? Why does the narrator use Sasha's words to close the story?

2. Try ending this story at different moments, such as after Olenka's marriage to Pustovalov or just before the return of the veterinary surgeon. Would the story feel finished? Would it have the same point?

3. Is the narrator external or internal? Characterial or authorial? How can you tell? Is any particular narrator implied?

4. Does the narrator seem to be viewing Olenka's story from a masculine or feminine perspective? What evidence can you find in choice of details, wording, or judgments?

5. Argue one of the following, or a claim of your own, using details of the story for support:
   a. Olenka is an emotional vampire.
   b. Olenka is a perfect wife and mother deprived of the opportunity to use her gifts.
   c. Olenka is the product of a social system that leaves women with no lives of their own.

❖ SARAH ORNE JEWETT
A White Heron

Sarah Orne Jewett (1849–1909) was born and raised in Berwick, Maine, and spent her adult life in that small town, except for visits to Boston and Europe. She attended Berwick Academy, but acquired most of her education through the books in her family's library. Much of what she learned about life was the result of accompanying her father, a physician, on his rounds. She published her first story at nineteen in the prestigious *Atlantic Monthly*, whose famous editor, William Dean Howells, gave her encouragement. Her first stories were collected in *Deephaven* (1877). She published the novels *A Country Doctor* (1884), based on her father's life, and *A Marsh Island* in 1886. Her latest stories appeared in the collections *A White Heron* (1886), *Tales of New England* (1890), *Strangers and Wayfarers* (1890), and *The Country of Pointed Firs* (1896).

The woods were already filled with shadows one June evening, just before eight o'clock, though a bright sunset still glimmered faintly among the trunks of the trees. A little girl was driving home her cow, a plodding, dilatory, provoking creature in her behavior, but a valued companion for all that. They were going away from the western light, and striking deep into the dark woods, but their feet were familiar with the path, and it was no matter whether their eyes could see it or not.

There was hardly a night the summer through when the old cow could be found waiting at the pasture bars; on the contrary, it was her greatest pleasure to hide herself away among the high huckleberry bushes, and though she wore a loud bell she had made the discovery that if one stood perfectly still it would not ring. So Sylvia had to hunt for her until she found her, and call Co'! Co'! with never an answering Moo, until her childish patience was quite spent. If the creature had not given good milk and plenty of it, the case would have seemed very different to her owners. Besides, Sylvia had all the time there was, and very little use to make of it. Sometimes in pleasant weather it was a consolation to look upon the cow's pranks as an intelligent attempt to play hide and seek, and as the child had no playmates she lent herself to this amusement with a good deal of zest. Though this chase had been so long that the wary animal herself had given an unusual signal of her whereabouts, Sylvia had only laughed when she came upon Mistress Moolly at the swamp-side, and urged her affectionately homeward with a twig of birch leaves. The old cow was not inclined to wander farther, she even turned in the right direction for once as they left the pasture, and stepped along the road at a good pace. She was quite ready to be milked now, and seldom stopped to browse. Sylvia wondered what her grandmother would say because they were so late. It was a great while since she had left home at half past five o'clock, but everybody knew the difficulty of making this errand a short one. Mrs. Tilley had chased the horned torment too many summer evenings herself to blame any one else for lingering, and was only thankful as she waited that she had Sylvia, nowadays, to give such valuable assistance. The good woman suspected that Sylvia loitered occasionally on her own account; there never was such a child for straying about out-of-doors since the world was made! Everybody said that it was a good change for a little maid who had tried to grow for eight years in a crowded manufacturing town, but, as for Sylvia herself, it seemed as if she never had been alive at all before she came to live at the farm. She thought often with wistful compassion of a wretched dry geranium that belonged to a town neighbor.

"'Afraid of folks,'" old Mrs. Tilley said to herself, with a smile, after she had made the unlikely choice of Sylvia from her daughter's houseful of children, and was returning to the farm. " 'Afraid of folks,' they said! I guess she won't be troubled no great with 'em up to the old place!" When they reached the door of the lonely house and stopped to unlock it, and the cat came to purr loudly, and rub against them, a deserted pussy, indeed, but fat with young robins, Sylvia whispered that this was a beautiful place to live in, and she never should wish to go home.

The companions followed the shady wood-road, the cow taking slow steps, and the child very fast ones. The cow stopped long at the brook to drink, as if the pasture were not half a swamp, and Sylvia stood still and waited, letting her bare feet cool themselves in the shoal water, while the great twilight moths struck softly against her. She waded on through the brook as the cow moved away, and listened to the thrushes with a heart that beat fast with pleasure. There was a stirring in the great boughs overhead. They were full of little birds and beasts that seemed to be wide-awake, and going about their world, or else saying good-night to each other in sleepy twitters. Sylvia herself felt sleepy as she walked along. However, it was not much farther to the house, and the air was soft and sweet. She was not often in the woods so late as this, and it made her feel as if she were a part of the gray shadows and the moving leaves. She was just thinking how long it seemed since she first came to the farm a year ago, and wondering if everything went on in the noisy town just the same as when she was there; the thought of the great red-faced boy who used to chase and frighten her made her hurry along the path to escape from the shadow of the trees.

Suddenly this little woods-girl is horror-stricken to hear a clear whistle not very far away. Not a bird's whistle, which would have a sort of friendliness, but a boy's whistle, determined, and somewhat aggressive. Sylvia left the cow to whatever sad fate might await her, and stepped discreetly aside into the bushes, but she was just too late. The enemy had discovered her, and called out in a very cheerful and persuasive tone, "Halloa, little girl, how far is it to the road?" and trembling Sylvia answered almost inaudibly, "A good ways."

She did not dare to look boldly at the tall young man, who carried a gun over his shoulder, but she came out of her bush and again followed the cow, while he walked alongside.

"I have been hunting for some birds," the stranger said kindly, "and I have lost my way, and need a friend very much. Don't be afraid," he added gallantly. "Speak up and tell me what your name is, and whether you think I can spend the night at your house, and go out gunning early in the morning."

Sylvia was more alarmed than before. Would not her grandmother consider her much to blame? But who could have foreseen such an accident as this? It did not appear to be her fault, and she hung her head as if the stem of it were broken, but managed to answer, "Sylvy," with much effort when her companion again asked her name.

Mrs. Tilley was standing in the doorway when the trio came into view. The cow gave a loud moo by way of explanation.

"Yes, you'd better speak up for yourself, you old trial! Where'd she tucked herself away this time, Sylvy?" Sylvia kept an awed silence; she knew by instinct that her grandmother did not comprehend the gravity of the situation. She must be mistaking the stranger for one of the farmer-lads of the region.

The young man stood his gun beside the door, and dropped a heavy game-bag beside it; then he bade Mrs. Tilley good-evening, and repeated his wayfarer's story, and asked if he could have a night's lodging.

"Put me anywhere you like," he said. "I must be off early in the morning, before day; but I am very hungry, indeed. You can give me some milk at any rate, that's plain."

"Dear sakes, yes," responded the hostess, whose long slumbering hospitality seemed to be easily awakened. "You might fare better if you went out on the main road a mile or so, but you're welcome to what we've got. I'll milk right off, and you make yourself at home. You can sleep on husks or feathers," she proffered graciously. "I raised them all myself. There's good pasturing for geese just below here towards the ma'sh. Now step round and set a plate for the gentleman, Sylvy!" And Sylvia promptly stepped. She was glad to have something to do, and she was hungry herself.

It was a surprise to find so clean and comfortable a dwelling in this New England wilderness. The young man had known the horrors of its most primitive housekeeping, and the dreary squalor of that level of society which does not rebel at the companionship of hens. This was the best thrift of an old-fashioned farmstead, though on such a small scale that it seemed like a hermitage. He listened eagerly to the old woman's quaint talk, he watched Sylvia's pale face and shining gray eyes with ever growing enthusiasm, and insisted that this was the best supper he had eaten for a month; then, afterward, the new-made friends sat down in the doorway together while the moon came up.

Soon it would be berry-time, and Sylvia was a great help at picking. The cow was a good milker, though a plaguy thing to keep track of, the hostess gossiped frankly, adding presently that she had buried four children, so that Sylvia's mother, and a son (who might be dead) in California were all the children she had left. "Dan, my boy, was a great hand to go gunning," she explained sadly. "I never wanted for pa'tridges or gray squer'ls while he was to home. He's been a great wand'rer, I expect, and he's no hand to write letters. There, I don't blame him, I'd ha' seen the world myself if it had been so I could.

"Sylvia takes after him," the grandmother continued affectionately, after a minute's pause. "There ain't a foot o'ground she don't know her way over, and the wild creatur's counts her one o'themselves. Squer'ls she'll tame to come an' feed right out o' her hands, and all sorts o'birds. Last winter she got the jay-birds to bangeing here, and I believe she'd 'a' scanted herself of her own meals to have plenty to throw out amongst 'em, if I hadn't kep' watch. Anything but crows, I tell her, I'm willin' to help support — though Dan he went an' tamed one o' them that did seem to have reason same as folks. It was round here a good spell after he went away. Dan an' his father they didn't hitch — but he never held up his head ag'in after Dan had dared him an' gone off."

The guest did not notice this hint of family sorrows in his eager interest in something else.

"So Sylvy knows all about birds, does she?" he exclaimed, as he looked round at the little girl who sat, very demure but increasingly sleepy, in the moonlight. "I am making a collection of birds myself. I have been at it ever since I was a boy." (Mrs. Tilley smiled.) "There are two or three very rare ones I have been hunting for these five years. I mean to get them on my own ground if they can be found."

"Do you cage 'em up?" asked Mrs. Tilley doubtfully, in response to this enthusiastic announcement.

"Oh, no, they're stuffed and preserved, dozens and dozens of them," said the ornithologist, "and I have shot or snared every one myself. I caught a glimpse of a white heron three miles from here on Saturday, and I have followed it in this direction. They have never been found in this district at all. The little white heron, it is," and he turned again to look at Sylvia with the hope of discovering that the rare bird was one of her acquaintances.

But Sylvia was watching a hop-toad in the narrow footpath.

"You would know the heron if you saw it," the stranger continued eagerly. "A queer tall white bird with soft feathers and long thin legs. And it would have a nest perhaps in the top of a high tree, made of sticks, something like a hawk's nest."

Sylvia's heart gave a wild beat; she knew that strange white bird, and had once stolen softly near where it stood in some bright green swamp grass, away over at the other side of the woods. There was an open place where the sunshine always seemed strangely yellow and hot, where tall, nodding rushes grew, and her grandmother had warned her that she might sink in the soft black mud underneath and never be heard of more. Not far beyond were the salt marshes and beyond those was the sea, the sea which Sylvia wondered and dreamed about, but never had looked upon, though its great voice could often be heard above the noise of the woods on stormy nights.

"I can't think of anything I should like so much as to find that heron's nest," the handsome stranger was saying. "I would give ten dollars to anybody who could show it to me," he added desperately, "and I mean to spend my whole vacation hunting for it if need be. Perhaps it was only migrating, or had been chased out of its own region by some bird of prey."

Mrs. Tilley gave amazed attention to all this, but Sylvia still watched the toad, not divining, as she might have done at some calmer time, that the creature wished to get to its hole under the doorstep, and was much hindered by the unusual spectators at that hour of the evening. No amount of thought, that night, could decide how many wished-for-treasures the ten dollars, so lightly spoken of, would buy.

The next day the young sportsman hovered about the woods, and Sylvia kept him company, having lost her first fear of the friendly lad, who proved to be most kind and sympathetic. He told her many things about the birds and what they knew and where they lived and what they did with themselves. And he gave her a jack-knife, which she thought as great a treasure as if she were a desert-islander. All day long he did not once make her troubled or afraid except when he brought down some unsuspecting singing creature from its bough. Sylvia would have liked him vastly better without his gun; she could not understand why he killed the very birds he seemed to like so much. But as the day waned, Sylvia still watched the young man with loving admiration. She had never seen anybody so charming and delightful; the woman's heart, asleep in the child, was vaguely thrilled by a dream of love. Some premonition of that great power stirred and swayed these young foresters who traversed the solemn woodlands with soft-footed silent care. They stopped to listen to a bird's song; they pressed forward again eagerly, parting the branches — speaking to each other rarely and in whispers; the young man going first and Sylvia following, fascinated, a few steps behind, with her gray eyes dark with excitement.

She grieved because the longed-for white heron was elusive, but she did not lead the guest, she only followed, and there was no such thing as speaking first. The sound of her own unquestioned voice would have terrified her — it was hard enough to answer yes or no when there was need of that. At last evening began to fall, and they drove the cow home together, and Sylvia smiled with pleasure when they came to the place where she heard the whistle and was afraid only the night before.

Half a mile from home, at the farther edge of the woods, where the land was highest, a great pine-tree stood, the last of its generation. Whether it was left for a boundary mark, or for what reason, no one could say; the woodchoppers who had felled its mates were dead and gone long ago, and a whole forest of sturdy trees, pines and oaks and maples, had grown again. But the stately head of this old pine towered above them all and made a landmark for sea and shore miles and miles away. Sylvia knew it well. She had always believed that whoever climbed to the top of it could see the ocean; and the little girl had often laid her hand on the great rough trunk and looked up wistfully at those dark boughs that the wind always stirred, no matter how hot and still the air might be below. Now she thought of the tree with a new excitement, for why, if one climbed it at break of day, could not one see all the world, and easily discover whence the white heron flew, and mark the place, and find the hidden nest?

What a spirit of adventure, what wild ambition! What fancied triumph and delight and glory for the later morning when she could make known the secret! It was almost too real and too great for the childish heart to bear.

All night the door of the little house stood open, and the whippoorwills came and sang upon the very step. The young sportsman and his old hostess were sound asleep, but Sylvia's great design kept her broad awake and watching. She forgot to think of sleep. The short summer night seemed as long as the winter darkness, and at last when the whippoorwills ceased, and she was afraid the morning would after all come too soon, she stole out of the house and followed the pasture path through the woods, hastening toward the open ground beyond, listening with a sense of comfort and companionship to the drowsy twitter of a half-awakened bird, whose perch she had jarred in passing. Alas, if the great wave of human interest which flooded for the first time this dull little life should sweep away the satisfactions of an existence heart to heart with nature and the dumb life of the forest!

There was the huge tree asleep yet in the paling moonlight, and small and hopeful Sylvia began with utmost bravery to mount to the top of it, with tingling, eager blood coursing the channels of her whole frame, with her bare feet and fingers, that pinched and held like bird's claws to the monstrous ladder reaching up, up, almost to the sky itself. First she must mount the white oak tree that grew alongside, where she was almost lost among the dark branches and the green leaves heavy and wet with dew; a bird fluttered off its nest, and a red squirrel ran to and fro and scolded pettishly at the harmless housebreaker. Sylvia felt her way easily. She had often climbed there, and knew that higher still one of the oak's upper branches chafed against the pine trunk, just where its lower boughs were set close together. There, when she made the dangerous pass from one tree to the other, the great enterprise would really begin.

She crept out along the swaying oak limb at last, and took the daring step across into the old pine-tree. The way was harder than she thought; she must reach far and hold fast, the sharp dry twigs caught and held her and scratched her like angry talons, the pitch made her thin little fingers clumsy and stiff as she went round and round the tree's great stem, higher and higher upward. The sparrows and robins in the woods below were beginning to wake and twitter to the dawn, yet it seemed much lighter there aloft in the pine-tree, and the child knew that she must hurry if her project were to be of any use.

The tree seemed to lengthen itself out as she went up, and to reach farther and farther upward. It was like a great main-mast to the voyaging earth; it must truly have been amazed that morning through all its ponderous frame as it felt this determined spark of human spirit creeping and climbing from higher branch to branch. Who knows how steadily the least twigs held themselves to advantage this light, weak creature on her way! The old pine must have loved his new dependent. More than all the hawks, and bats, and moths, and even the sweet-voiced thrushes, was the brave, beating heart of the solitary gray-eyed child. And the tree stood still and held away the winds that June morning while the dawn grew bright in the east.

Sylvia's face was like a pale star, if one had seen it from the ground, when the last thorny bough was past, and she stood trembling and tired but wholly triumphant, high in the tree-top. Yes, there was the sea with the dawning sun making a golden dazzle over it, and toward that glorious east flew two hawks with slow-moving pinions. How low they looked in the air from that height when before one had only seen them far up, and dark against the blue sky. Their gray feathers were as soft as moths; they seemed only a little way from the tree, and Sylvia felt as if she too could go flying away among the clouds. Westward, the woodlands and farms reached miles and miles into the distance; here and there were church steeples, and white villages; truly it was a vast and awesome world.

The birds sang louder and louder. At last the sun came up bewilderingly bright. Sylvia could see the white sails of ships out at sea, and the clouds that were purple and rose-colored and yellow at first began to fade away. Where was the white heron's nest in the sea of green branches, and was this wonderful sight and pageant of the world the only reward for having climbed to such a giddy height? Now look down again, Sylvia, where the green marsh is set among the shining birches and dark hemlocks; there where you saw the white heron once you will see him again; look, look! a white spot of him like a single floating feather comes up from the dead hemlock and grows larger, and rises, and comes close at last, and goes by the landmark pine with a steady sweep of wing and outstretched slender neck and crested head. And wait! wait! do not move a foot or a finger, little girl, do not send an arrow of light and consciousness from your two eager eyes, for the heron has perched on a pine bough not far beyond yours, and cries back to his mate on the nest, and plumes his feathers for the new day!

The child gives a long sigh a minute later when a company of shouting cat-birds comes also to the tree, and vexed by their fluttering and lawlessness the solemn heron goes away. She knows his secret now, the wild, light, slender bird that floats and wavers, and goes back like an arrow presently to his home in the green world beneath. Then Sylvia, well satisfied, makes her perilous way down again, not daring to look far below the branch she stands on, ready to cry sometimes because her fingers ache and her lamed feet slip. Wondering over and over again what the stranger would say to her, and what he would think when she told him how to find his way straight to the heron's nest.

"Sylvy, Sylvy!" called the busy old grandmother again and again, but nobody answered, and the small husk bed was empty, and Sylvia had disappeared.

The guest waked from a dream, and remembering his day's pleasure hurried to dress himself that it might sooner begin. He was sure from the way the shy little girl looked once or twice yesterday that she had at least seen the white heron, and now she must really be persuaded to tell. Here she comes now, paler than ever, and her worn old frock is torn and tattered, and smeared with pine pitch. The grandmother and the sportsman stand in the door together and question her, and the splendid moment has come to speak of the dead hemlock-tree by the green marsh.

But Sylvia does not speak after all, though the old grandmother fretfully rebukes her, and the young man's kind appealing eyes are looking straight in her own. He can make them rich with money; he was promised it, and they are poor now. He is so well worth making happy, and he waits to hear the story she can tell.

No, she must keep silence! What is it that suddenly forbids her and makes her dumb? Has she been nine years growing, and now, when the great world for the first time puts out a hand to her, must she thrust it aside for a bird's sake? The murmur of the pine's green branches is in her ears, she remembers how the white heron came flying through the golden air and how they watched the sea and the morning together, and Sylvia cannot speak, she cannot tell the heron's secret and give its life away.

Dear loyalty, that suffered a sharp pang as the guest went away disappointed later in the day, that could have served and followed him and loved him as a dog loves! Many a night Sylvia heard the echo of his whistle haunting the pasture path as she came home with the loitering cow. She forgot even her sorrow at the sharp report of his gun and the piteous sight of thrushes and sparrows dropping silent to the ground, their songs hushed and their pretty feathers stained and wet with blood. Were the birds better friends than their hunter might have been — who can tell? Whatever treasures were lost to her, woodlands and summer-time, remember! Bring your gifts and graces and tell your secrets to this lonely country child!

(1886)

QUESTIONS

1. How much time do the events of the story cover? What do we learn of events before the story proper? After? How?

2. What does the name "Sylvia" mean? Are there other clues that Sylvia's strongest attachment is to the natural world? Does she resemble the white heron?

3. Why does the narrator move from conventional past-tense storytelling into present (paragraph 5) and even future tense (part II, paragraph 8)? How would you describe a narrator who speaks this way?

4. The narrator hints that Sylvia must make a choice that will affect her entire life. What are the alternatives open to her? Would a male character be required to make such choices?

5. Who or what is the "dear loyalty" mentioned by the narrator in the final paragraph? The last sentence, again, is addressed to someone through the imperative form of the verb "remember!" That person is further told to "Bring his or her gifts" to the child. Are these two people the same? If not, which is *in* the *story* (a character or trait) and which in the *discourse* (a narrator)?

❖ TILLIE OLSEN
I Stand Here Ironing

Tillie Olsen (1913–) was born in Omaha, Nebraska. Her immigrant family was poor, and she could not finish high school. She was a political radical and labor organizer, who was once jailed for her activism. Abandoned by her first husband, she married another labor activist, Jack Olsen. Financial needs, political struggles, and responsibilities as a mother kept her from devoting full time to her fiction until she was 43, when she was awarded a Stanford fellowship in creative writing. She has taught at Amherst, University of Massachusetts, Stanford, MIT, and the University of California at Berkeley where she was Regent Professor. She published the uncompleted novel *Yonnondio* in 1974 and the short story collection *Tell Me a Riddle* in 1961. She has also "selected and shaped" a book called *Mother to Daughter, Daughter to Mother, Mothers on Mothering* (1984) and written a book on the difficulties that women writers face called *Silences* (1978). Olsen is very much the spokesperson for underclass women, especially those who never got the chance to communicate their feelings, who feel (in her phrase) "the unnatural thwarting of what struggles to come into being but cannot."

I stand here ironing, and what you asked me moves tormented back and forth with the iron.

"I wish you would manage the time to come in and talk with me about your daughter. I'm sure you can help me understand her. She's a youngster who needs help and whom I'm deeply interested in helping."

"Who needs help." Even if I came, what good would it do? You think because I am her mother I have a key, or that in some way you could use me as a key? She has lived for nineteen years. There is all that life that has happened outside of me, beyond me.

And when is there time to remember, to sift, to weigh, to estimate, to total? I will start and there will be an interruption and I will have to gather it all together again. Or I will become engulfed with all I did or did not do, with what should have been and what cannot be helped.

She was a beautiful baby. The first and only one of our five that was beautiful at birth. You do not guess how new and uneasy her tenancy in her now-loveliness. You did not know her all those years she was thought homely, or see her poring over her baby pictures, making me tell her over and over how beautiful she had been — and would be, I would tell her — and was now, to the seeing eye. But the seeing eyes were few or nonexistent. Including mine.

I nursed her. They feel that's important nowadays. I nursed all the children, but with her, with all the fierce rigidity of first motherhood, I did like the books then said. Though her cries battered me to trembling and my breasts ached with swollenness, I waited till the clock decreed.

Why do I put that first? I do not even know if it matters, or if it explains anything.

She was a beautiful baby. She blew shining bubbles of sound. She loved motion, loved light, loved color and music and textures. She would lie on the floor in her blue overalls patting the surface so hard in ecstasy her hands and feet would blur. She was a miracle to me, but when she was eight months old I had to leave her daytimes with the woman downstairs to whom she was no miracle at all, for I worked or looked for work and for Emily's father, who "could no longer endure" (he wrote in his good-bye note) "sharing want with us."

I was nineteen. It was the pre-relief, pre-WPA[1] world of the depression. I would start running as soon as I got off the streetcar, running up the stairs, the place smelling sour, and awake or asleep to startle awake, when she saw me she would break into a clogged weeping that could not be comforted, a weeping I can hear yet.

After a while I found a job hashing at night so I could be with her days, and it was better. But it came to where I had to bring her to his family and leave her.

It took a long time to raise the money for her fare back. Then she got chicken pox and I had to wait longer. When she finally came, I hardly knew her, walking quick and nervous like her father, looking like her father, thin, and dressed in a shoddy red that yellowed her skin and glared at the pockmarks. All the baby loveliness gone.

She was two. Old enough for nursery school they said, and I did not know then what I know now — the fatigue of the long day, and the lacerations of group life in nurseries that are only parking places for children.

Except that it would have made no difference if I had known. It was the only place there was. It was the only way we could be together, the only way I could hold a job.

And even without knowing, I knew. I knew the teacher that was evil because all these years it has curdled into my memory, the little boy hunched in the corner, her rasp, "why aren't you outside, because Alvin hits you? that's no reason, go out, scaredy." I knew Emily hated it even if she did not clutch and implore "don't go Mommy" like the other children, mornings.

She always had a reason why we should stay home. Momma, you look sick, Momma. I feel sick. Momma, the teachers aren't there today, they're sick. Momma, we can't go, there was a fire there last night. Momma, it's a holiday today, no school, they told me.

But never a direct protest, never rebellion. I think of our others in their three-, four-year-oldness — the explosions, the tempers, the denunciations, the demands — and I feel suddenly ill. I put the iron down. What in me demanded that goodness in her? And what was the cost, the cost to her of such goodness?

The old man living in the back once said in his gentle way: "You should smile at Emily more when you look at her." What *was* in my face when I looked at her? I loved her. There were all the acts of love.

---

[1] Work Projects Administration: the former federal agency (1935–43) charged with instituting and administering public works to relieve national unemployment.

It was only with the others I remembered what he said, and it was the face of joy, and not of care or tightness or worry I turned to them — too late for Emily. She does not smile easily, let alone almost always as her brothers and sisters do. Her face is closed and sombre, but when she wants, how fluid. You must have seen it in her pantomimes, you spoke of her rare gift for comedy on the stage that rouses a laughter out of the audience so dear they applaud and applaud and do not want to let her go.

Where does it come from, that comedy? There was none of it in her when she came back to me that second time, after I had had to send her away again. She had a new daddy now to learn to love, and I think perhaps it was a better time.

Except when we left her alone nights, telling ourselves she was old enough.

"Can't you go some other time, Mommy, like tomorrow?" she would ask. "Will it be just a little while you'll be gone? Do you promise?"

The time we came back, the front door open, the clock on the floor in the hall. She rigid awake. "It wasn't just a little while. I didn't cry. Three times I called you, just three times, and then I ran downstairs to open the door so you could come faster. The clock talked loud. I threw it away, it scared me what it talked."

She said the clock talked loud again that night I went to the hospital to have Susan. She was delirious with the fever that comes before red measles, but she was fully conscious all the week I was gone and the week after we were home when she could not come near the new baby or me.

She did not get well. She stayed skeleton thin, not wanting to eat, and night after night she had nightmares. She would call for me, and I would rouse from exhaustion to sleepily call back: "You're all right, darling, go to sleep, it's just a dream," and if she still called, in a sterner voice, "now go to sleep, Emily, there's nothing to hurt you." Twice, only twice, when I had to get up for Susan anyhow, I went in to sit with her.

Now when it is too late (as if she would let me hold and comfort her like I do the others) I get up and go to her at once at her moan or restless stirring. "Are you awake, Emily? Can I get you something?" And the answer is always the same: "No, I'm all right, go back to sleep, Mother."

They persuaded me at the clinic to send her away to a convalescent home in the country where "she can have the kind of food and care you can't manage for her, and you'll be free to concentrate on the new baby." They still send children to that place. I see pictures on the society page of sleek young women planning affairs to raise money for it, or dancing at the affairs, or decorating Easter eggs or filling Christmas stockings for the children.

They never have a picture of the children so I do not know if the girls still wear those gigantic red bows and the ravaged looks on the every other Sunday when parents can come to visit "unless otherwise notified" — as we were notified the first six weeks.

Oh it is a handsome place, green lawns and tall trees and fluted flower beds. High up on the balconies of each cottage the children stand, the girls in their red bows and white dresses, the boys in white suits and giant red ties. The parents stand below shrieking up to be heard and the children shriek down to be heard, and between them the invisible wall "Not To Be Contaminated by Parental Germs or Physical Affection."

There was a tiny girl who always stood hand in hand with Emily. Her parents never came. One visit she was gone. "They moved her to Rose Cottage" Emily shouted in explanation. "They don't like you to love anybody here."

She wrote once a week, the labored writing of a seven-year-old. "I am fine. How is the baby. If I write my leter nicly I will have a star. Love." There never was a star. We wrote every other day, letters she could never hold or keep but only hear read — once. "We simply do not have room for children to keep any personal possessions," they patiently explained when we pieced one Sunday's shrieking together to plead how much it would mean to Emily, who loved so to keep things, to be allowed to keep her letters and cards.

Each visit she looked frailer. "She isn't eating," they told us.

(They had runny eggs for breakfast or mush with lumps, Emily said later, I'd hold it in my mouth and not swallow. Nothing ever tasted good, just when they had chicken.)

It took us eight months to get her released home, and only the fact that she gained back so little of her seven lost pounds convinced the social worker.

I used to try to hold and love her after she came back, but her body would stay stiff, and after a while she'd push away. She ate little. Food sickened her, and I think much of life too. Oh she had physical lightness and brightness, twinkling by on skates, bouncing like a ball up and down up and down over the jump rope, skimming over the hill; but these were momentary.

She fretted about her appearance, thin and dark and foreign-looking at a time when every little girl was supposed to look or thought she should look a chubby blonde replica of Shirley Temple. The doorbell sometimes rang for her, but no one seemed to come and play in the house or be a best friend. Maybe because we moved so much.

There was a boy she loved painfully through two school semesters. Months later she told me how she had taken pennies from my purse to buy him candy. "Licorice was his favorite and I brought him some every day, but he still liked Jennifer better'n me. Why, Mommy?" The kind of question for which there is no answer.

School was a worry to her. She was not glib or quick in a world where glibness and quickness were easily confused with ability to learn. To her overworked and exasperated teachers she was an overconscientious "slow learner" who kept trying to catch up and was absent entirely too often.

I let her be absent, though sometimes the illness was imaginary. How different from my now-strictness about attendance with the others. I wasn't working. We had a new baby, I was home anyhow. Sometimes, after Susan grew old enough, I would keep her home from school, too, to have them all together.

Mostly Emily had asthma, and her breathing, harsh and labored, would fill the house with a curiously tranquil sound. I would bring the two old dresser mirrors and her boxes of collections to her bed. She would select beads and single earrings, bottle tops and shells, dried flowers and pebbles, old postcards and scraps, all sorts of oddments; then she and Susan would play Kingdom, setting up landscapes and furniture, peopling them with action.

Those were the only times of peaceful companionship between her and Susan. I have edged away from it, that poisonous feeling between them, that terrible balancing of hurts and needs I had to do between the two, and did so badly, those earlier years.

Oh there are conflicts between the others too, each one human, needing, demanding, hurting, taking—but only between Emily and Susan, no, Emily toward Susan that corroding resentment. It seems so obvious on the surface, yet it is not obvious. Susan, the second child, Susan, golden- and curly-haired and chubby, quick and articulate and assured, everything in appearance and manner Emily was not; Susan, not able to resist Emily's precious things, losing or sometimes clumsily breaking them; Susan telling jokes and riddles to company for applause while Emily sat silent (to say to me later: that was *my* riddle, Mother, I told it to Susan); Susan, who for all the five years' difference in age was just a year behind Emily in developing physically.

I am glad for that slow physical development that widened the difference between her and her contemporaries, though she suffered over it. She was too vulnerable for that terrible world of youthful competition, of preening and parading, of constant measuring of yourself against every other, of envy, "If I had that copper hair," "If I had that skin. . . ." She tormented herself enough about not looking like the others, there was enough of the unsureness, the having to be conscious of words before you speak, the constant caring—what are they thinking of me? without having it all magnified by the merciless physical drives.

Ronnie is calling. He is wet and I change him. It is rare there is such a cry now. That time of motherhood is almost behind me when the ear is not one's own but must always be racked and listening for the child cry, the child call. We sit for a while and I hold him, looking out over the city spread in charcoal with its soft aisles of light. *"Shoogily,"* he breathes and curls closer. I carry him back to bed, asleep. *Shoogily.* A funny word, a family word, inherited from Emily, invented by her to say: *comfort.*

In this and other ways she leaves her seal, I say aloud. And startle at my saying it. What do I mean? What did I start to gather together, to try and make coherent? I was at the terrible, growing years. War years. I do not remember them well. I was working, there were four smaller ones now, there was not time for her. She had to help be a mother, and housekeeper, and shopper. She had to set her seal. Mornings of crisis and near hysteria trying to get lunches packed, hair combed, coats and shoes found, everyone to school or Child Care on time, the baby ready for transportation. And always the paper scribbled on by a smaller one, the book looked at by Susan then mislaid, the homework not done. Running out to that huge school where she was one, she was lost, she was a drop; suffering over the unpreparedness, stammering and unsure in her classes.

There was so little time left at night after the kids were bedded down. She would struggle over books, always eating (it was in those years she developed her enormous appetite that is legendary in our family) and I would be ironing, or preparing food for the next day, or writing V-mail to Bill, or tending the baby. Sometimes, to make me laugh, or out of her despair, she would imitate happenings or types at school.

I think I said once: "Why don't you do something like this in the school amateur show?" One morning she phoned me at work, hardly understandable through the weeping: "Mother, I did it. I won, I won; they gave me first prize; they clapped and clapped and wouldn't let me go."

Now suddenly she was Somebody, and as imprisoned in her difference as she had been in anonymity.

She began to be asked to perform at other high schools, even in colleges, then at city and statewide affairs. The first one we went to, I only recognized her that first moment when thin, shy, she almost drowned herself into the curtains. Then: Was this Emily? The control, the command, the convulsing and deadly clowning, the spell, then the roaring, stamping audience, unwilling to let this rare and precious laughter out of their lives.

Afterwards: You ought to do something about her with a gift like that — but without money or knowing how, what does one do? We have left it all to her, and the gift has as often eddied inside, clogged and clotted, as been used and growing.

She is coming. She runs up the stairs two at a time with her light graceful step, and I know she is happy tonight. Whatever it was that occasioned your call did not happen today.

"Aren't you ever going to finish the ironing, Mother? Whistler painted his mother in a rocker. I'd have to paint mine standing over an ironing board." This is one of her communicative nights and she tells me everything and nothing as she fixes herself a plate of food out of the icebox.

She is so lovely. Why did you want me to come in at all? Why were you concerned? She will find her way.

She starts up the stairs to bed. "Don't get me up with the rest in the morning." "But I thought you were having midterms." "Oh, those," she comes back in, kisses me, and says quite lightly, "in a couple of years when we'll all be atom-dead they won't matter a bit."

She has said it before. She *believes* it. But because I have been dredging the past, and all that compounds a human being is so heavy and meaningful in me, I cannot endure it tonight.

I will never total it all. I will never come in to say: She was a child seldom smiled at. Her father left me before she was a year old. I had to work her first six years when there was work, or I sent her home and to his relatives. There were years she had care she hated. She was dark and thin and foreign-looking in a world where the prestige went to blondeness and curly hair and dimples, she was slow where glibness was prized. She was a child of anxious, not proud, love. We were poor and could not afford for her the soil of easy growth. I was a young mother, I was a distracted mother. There were the other children pushing up, demanding. Her younger sister seemed all that she was not. There were years she did not want me to touch her. She kept too much in herself, her life was such she had to keep too much in herself. My wisdom came too late. She has much to her and probably nothing will come of it. She is a child of her age, of depression, of war, of fear.

Let her be. So all that is in her will not bloom — but in how many does it? There is still enough left to live by. Only help her to know — help make it so there is cause for her to know — that she is more than this dress on the ironing board, helpless before the iron.

(1953–1954)

QUESTIONS

1. Can you pinpoint the era during which the events of this short story occurred? Try matching Emily's life (and the narrator's) against historical events in America. Why is it necessary to know something about the era to understand the short story?

2. How does the narrator judge herself? Do you always agree with her judgments?

3. Why should Emily's gift be one of making people laugh? What could the story be implying about the sources of humor?

4. Are you satisfied that the narratee implied by this short story is a social worker? Who else might it be? Does the narrator speak to the narratee directly? If not, how are we to understand her response to the narratee's request?

5. Weigh the language the narrator uses to portray highly charged events and scenes. Are the words generally abstract or concrete, overstated or understated, plain or elegant? What is the effect?

SUGGESTIONS FOR WRITING

1. Change the narrator of a story that you like, rewriting a page or two in the new style. For example, change an externally narrated short story to an internally narrated story whose narrator is a witness. Explain how the point of the story alters.

2. Pick a short story with no obvious clues as to the narrator's identity. Are there more subtle indications? Look, for instance, at the different ways the narrator describes male and female characters. Does that difference make you think of the narrator as masculine or feminine? Is the narrator happy about the events he or she is narrating? Does the narrator notice the same kinds of details you would notice? How well educated is the narrator?

3. Pick a short story whose narratee is identified or implied and substitute another one. If the narratee seems to be female, what would happen if the story were told to a man? What if the narratee were a child, a Tibetan monk, an informer for the secret police, someone with no sense of humor, or an ex-lover of the main character? Change some sentences to accommodate the difference in narratee.

4. Find a short story in which no frame or storytelling situation is described and invent one for it. Who is telling or writing or thinking the story? Who is hearing or reading or overhearing? In what circumstances? In other words, write your own frame story.

5. There are as many kinds of telling as there are reasons to tell a story. In a conversation you might tell an anecdote to make someone laugh, to illustrate a point, to threaten your listeners, or to issue an invitation. In other

words, storytelling might be considered an act of amusing, explaining, bullying, or inviting. Pick a story with a strongly identifiable narratee, such as "I Stand Here Ironing," and see if you can identify the act (or acts) the narrator is performing by telling the story.

6. Like most critical terms, *frame* is a metaphor. It says that the storytelling situation surrounds the story the way a frame surrounds a painting. But a frame does not merely surround a painting; it affects the way we see the painting. An elaborate frame with gold paint and carved cherubs tells us to look for certain qualities in the painting. A sleek steel frame emphasizes quite different effects. Pick a story with a frame and explain how the frame affects your reading of the inner narrative.

5 Point of View: Character's Filter and Narrator's Slant

Sometimes the narrator recounts events without reference to the mind or interests of any character. In Jack London's science-fiction fantasy, "The Unparalleled Invasion" (pp. 248–256), a short story that predicts the destruction of China by biological warfare, the characters are nations: China, France, Russia, the United States.[1] In such a story, which pretends to the objectivity of actual history, the inner lives of individuals have little place.

Character's Filter

More usually, short stories communicate the thoughts and feelings of characters, sometimes with uncanny precision. Authors evoke a vivid sense of the life of the mind by creating an illusion called *filter*. Filter turns the character's consciousness into a kind of "screen" through which we learn of the events of the story and their impact on her. Like any screen, it lets only some things through. What the character doesn't perceive or doesn't understand doesn't get stated. Still, we are free to speculate. We learn much about the character's personality by observing how and which experiences seep through her mind.

Obviously, thoughts are events. No less than weddings or battles, they qualify as building blocks of plot. In some fictions a character's thinking constitutes the principal action. The character comes to understand his situation or to remain unconscious of it, to make decisions or to accept his fate. And that's the whole point of the short story.

Conveying thoughts is not an easy task. Do you ever introspect about your own thinking process? When I do, I usually find myself chasing a will-o'-the-wisp. For example, I can't be sure that I even think in words. I may catch a word or two but usually I'm conscious only of a vague flow of thoughts and feelings. Perception is an example: I may be conscious of seeing a humming-

---

[1]The racist ideology implicit in this short story will be discussed in chapter 7.

bird, but I don't *say* to myself "Look! there's a hummingbird" or "Gee, I'm seeing a hummingbird."

However, an author's only materials are words, and only through words can she register characters' inner experiences. The question is Whose words should she use? There are two main options. A narrator may quote the very words that a character "says" to himself in the privacy of his mind. Or she may supply her own words to articulate the character's thought or feeling. The choice is deliberate, calculated to achieve specific artistic effects. The answer to "Whose language conveys the character's thoughts?" heavily influences the larger movements and intentions of a fiction.

When an entire fiction (or large portion thereof) quotes only the literal words passing through a character's mind, the effect is called *interior monologue*. We can see interior monologue beginning in the middle two sentences of the first paragraph of Katherine Anne Porter's "The Jilting of Granny Weatherall" (pp. 563 – 569), a short story about an old woman's dying moments:

> She flicked her wrist neatly out of Doctor Harry's pudgy careful fingers and pulled the sheet up to her chin. The brat ought to be in knee breeches. Doctoring around the country with spectacles on his nose! "Get along now, take your schoolbooks and go. There's nothing wrong with me."

Obviously, it is Granny Weatherall, not the narrator, who feels that the "brat," Doctor Harry (whom she confuses with the child he once was), ought to be in knee breeches. The final sentence, in quotation marks, is what she says to him in consequence of her thoughts. Interior monologue is the technique used by some of the most important novels of our century, such as James Joyce's *Ulysses* and William Faulkner's *The Sound and the Fury*.

Most short stories, however, use a mixed technique to represent characters' filter. Let us consider the masterful treatment of the protagonist's thinking in James Joyce's "A Little Cloud" (pp. 142 – 151). "A Little Cloud" is one of those stories in which, some readers might say, "nothing happens." A man has a drink with an old friend. When he gets home, he is scolded by his wife for forgetting to buy tea. As he tries to read a poem, his baby starts crying. He shouts at the baby and is again reprimanded by his wife, whereupon tears of remorse fill his eyes. Period. Nothing has really changed. These few events, however, seem to convey a whole life of thwarted ambition, frustration, and failure. The protagonist is a victim of the "moral paralysis" suffered, according to Joyce, by the whole of Dublin. Such a story turns necessarily on the thoughts and feelings of the victim. It is in the representation of these thoughts and feelings that much of the art of "A Little Cloud" lies.

The first paragraph of the short story plunges us immediately into the consciousness of the protagonist, Little Chandler. His name is not given, because in the privacy of his own mind, he would not refer to himself as "Chandler." Further, the sentences seem to contain his very words. For example: "It was something to have a friend like that." This must be a shortened version of "Little Chandler said to himself 'It's something to have a friend like that.'" It cannot be the narrator's independent observation. Obviously, it is Little Chandler, not the narrator, who feels honored to have a friend like Gallaher.

Having placed us clearly in the character's mind, the narrator can now step back and describe Chandler objectively, stressing his "littleness," his fragility, his fastidiousness. By using these words, the narrator asserts these traits authoritatively, the better to motivate later events. Continuing in his own voice, the narrator lays out the material facts of Chandler's daily life, his drab job, and the squalid neighborhood surrounding his workplace (the Dublin law courts called "King's Inns"). The narrator continues to describe these in his own words, for some of the sights, like the "horde of grimy children," seem purposely ignored by Chandler. Intermittently, however, the narrator reports Chandler's feelings about *selected* portions of his environment, for example, his "poetic" perceptions of the "glow of late autumn sunset" and the "kindly" golden dust. Chandler avoids the unpleasant sights. Above all, his thoughts are vague:

> He . . . thought of life; and (as always happened when he thought of life) he became sad. A gentle melancholy took possession of him.

Chandler's thoughts are still couched in the narrator's words, for somebody who thinks of life and becomes sad does not *say* to himself "I'm thinking of life and becoming sad." As the short story develops, it becomes clear that Chandler is only a would-be poet who will never succeed, will perhaps never publish a single poem. The seeds of his failure are already sown. The very vagueness of the expression "thinking of life" suggests how far he is from poetic creativity. True poets, we suspect, don't think vaguely about life and become sad. Rather, they busily seek out precise phrases to capture their experiences. The vagueness of Chandler's reactions suggest that his future as a poet is dim.

As he approaches Corless's restaurant for his meeting with Gallaher, however, Chandler's thoughts become more lively, though not poetic:

> He turned to the right towards Capel Street. Ignatius Gallaher on the London Press! Who would have thought it possible eight years before? Still, now that he reviewed the past, Little Chandler could remember many signs of future greatness in his friend.

The second and third sentences obviously quote the very words passing through Chandler's mind. It is the narrator who says that Chandler turned toward Capel Street, but surely only Chandler would say to himself "Ignatius Gallaher on the London Press!" That is, only the character would *exclaim* incredulously. Impersonal narrators have no reason to exclaim. Similarly, only the character would ask himself a rhetorical question, like "Who would have thought it possible eight years before?" or would curse mildly as he reminisces, a few sentences later, about Gallaher's lightheartedness in tight situations: "That was Ignatius Gallaher all out; and, damn it, you couldn't but admire him for it." Chandler's excitement is best expressed by his own inner monologue, but it is not a poetic excitement, nor is the language suggestive of poetic powers.

The Filter-Character Is Not the Narrator

Whether by quotation or report, so much of "A Little Cloud" takes place inside Little Chandler's mind that it is tempting to say that it is actually he who *tells* the story. However, to put things that way blurs an important distinction. Unlike a true internal narrator (say, the first-person narrators of Ralph Ellison's "The Battle Royal," pp. 441–451, or of Katherine Mansfield's "Je Ne Parle Pas Français," pp. 494–512), Chandler is not consciously telling anybody (even himself) a *story*. He is simply living his life, fantasizing about being a poet, feeling upset about Gallaher and then about his wife and baby. To see how different the short story would be if Chandler *were* narrating, all we need do is change self-references from the third-person pronoun to the first. Here is a transformed version of the second paragraph:

> My thoughts ever since lunch-time were of my meeting with Gallaher, of Gallaher's invitation and of the great city London where Gallaher lived. I am called Little Chandler because, though I am but slightly under the average stature, I give one the idea of being a little man. My hands are white . . .

How profoundly the short story has changed! Instead of a character-Chandler who is simply living his life and thinking his thoughts, here is a narrator-Chandler who is telling a story about himself. In the process he *explains* himself to someone, to some narratee. Note particularly how problematic the second sentence becomes. It would be quite another kind of "Little Cloud" if the protagonist *acquiesced* to his own "littleness." The capacity to explain himself would imply a Chandler who saw himself more objectively than the short story intends. With deeper understanding of himself, Chandler might also recognize his self-delusions about becoming a poet. He might recognize the secret jealousy behind his admiration of Gallaher. He might recognize how henpecked he is. It just wouldn't be the same short story, nor, obviously, would it be as good as it is. However much it plunges us into the depths of Chandler's soul, "A Little Cloud" requires that we keep a certain detachment from him. We are not hearing Little Chandler's story from his own lips but rather *overhearing* his inner voice pouring over his situation. An independent if shadowy narrator communicates it to us. The narrator's objectivity helps us recognize that Chandler's frustrations, no less than his fantasies, are self-induced. It is precisely the narrator's distance that ironizes Chandler (see chapter 6 on irony). A Chandler-as-narrator could not remain the small man who tries to escape from his petty life with vague dreams of creativity and exciting travel. So Chandler must be filter-character, not internal narrator.

Is there a surefire way of distinguishing narrator from filter-character? Nothing in this world is surefire, but there is a useful question we can ask: "Who speaks? as opposed to Who sees?" Answer: It is the narrator who *speaks* the story—it is the filter-character who *sees*, that is, *experiences* the events.

What about internal narration, where the speaker and the see-er are the same person? Even in such stories, as I shall explain below, there is usually a time lag that enables us to separate the I-narrator ("now") from the I-character ("back then"). In that case, we can ask "Who speaks?" Answer: The I-narrator ("now"). "Who *saw*?" Answer: The I-character ("back then").

Narrator's Slant

What I call *filter* is sometimes called "point of view." But "point of view" is a confusing term, because it is also used to refer to the *narrator's slant* or attitude toward the events and characters. Let us distinguish between these two kinds of "point of view." Recall how Olenka, the protagonist of Anton Chekhov's "The Darling" (pp. 104–112), approaches life solely through her "love" for and identification with a male. Remember, too, how the narrator implicitly—and in a few sentences explicitly—deplores the selfishness and parasitism of Olenka's love. Clearly, Olenka and the narrator have entirely different attitudes, different "points of view," about love. "Filter" and "slant" help us distinguish these attitudes by explaining that it is only in Olenka's *filter* that love is a natural outpouring of a warm heart and a deep involvement in her partner's every interest. In the narrator's *slant*, Olenka's kind of love is selfish and smothering—an emotional sponging off the loved one, so to speak.

Filter promotes our *identification* with this or that character in a fiction. By "identification" I mean the reader's close mental association with that character (or group of characters) as opposed to others. We usually make this association unconsciously, in the most "natural" way, but a good writer works hard to prompt us to do so. Sometimes, as in Alice Walker's "The Flowers" (pp. 9–10), there is only one character *to* identify with. Sometimes, however, there are several, and the author uses various means to help identify with one rather than another.

One means is simply immersing us constantly in that character's thoughts. Because sharing thoughts and feelings is the most intimate relation we can have with another person, keeping us in a character's mind gets us to identify with him. Such short stories as "A Little Cloud," "The Darling," Ama Ata Aidoo's "Certain Winds from the South" (pp. 296–302), Ambrose Bierce's "An Occurrence at Owl Creek Bridge" (pp. 363–369), Albert Camus's "The Guest" (pp. 193–201), and many others in this book identify us with the protagonist through sustained access to his or her thoughts.

Remember how limited narration was defined—as a restriction on the kind of information the narrator could report. Most of the short stories in this book restrict us to the consciousness of a single character. Others, however, like Sarah Orne Jewett's "A White Heron" (pp. 114–120) or D. H. Lawrence's "Two Blue Birds" (pp. 483–493), skip from one filter to another as suits their purposes. Sometimes the filter conveys the thinking of a whole community, as in Stephen Crane's "Moonlight on the Snow" (pp. 416–424), where we read the collective mind of the village of War Post. When many minds are entered, the filter is called *omniscient*, a word that means "knowing all." The omniscient narrator can arbitrarily shift from the mind of a given character or group of characters to the minds of others.

Filter is more than simply entering a character's consciousness, however. Other signs may also help us understand the story events and characters from the perspective of a given character. Sometimes the very content of the story requires us to identify with her. In Elizabeth Bowen's "Careless Talk" (pp. 370–373) we identify with Joanna (rather than, say, with Mary Dash), not only because of our entry into Joanna's consciousness (which is very brief) but because of her situation. She is the stranger in the group, the one who has just come from the country, bringing her three precious eggs into a heavily rationed wartime London. The war has changed London for her: She has become an ignorant country bumpkin, so to speak. Because, as readers, we are as ignorant as Joanna of this beleaguered city, we tend to feel a natural alliance with her. We join her in trying to understand how, despite the desperateness of the situation, upper-crust Londoners such as Mary, Eric, and Ponsonby carry on their old snobbish ways.

Though technically omniscient, James Baldwin's "The Rockpile" (pp. 153–159) also uses content and context to make us identify with John, even though we enter the mind of his brother, Roy, first and spend much time in the thoughts of his mother, Elizabeth. For instance, we "stay" with John on the fire escape watching Roy's exploits from a distance, instead of joining Roy down on the rockpile. Clearly the story intends to make us feel as keenly as does John the injustice of his father's treatment. After all, it is his brother who has disobeyed, yet John is the one who gets blamed for Roy's injury. The short story plays on our natural inclination to side with the underdog. Even though we are not told John's final thoughts, clearly we are being *invited* to imagine his overwhelming sense of oppression as he picks up his father's lunchbox, "bending his dark head near the toe of his father's heavy shoe."

A cleverly built-up sense of filter can help us imagine a character's thoughts even when they go unnarrated. Recall how, in the final moments of "The Flowers" (pp. 9–10), the reader is expressly excluded from Myop's mind as she places the flowers next to the body. Through our previous access to her consciousness we came to appreciate her sensitivity to nature, her sense of adventure, and her sturdy fearlessness at the sight of the body. Those traits prepare us for her respect for the victim of the lynching and for her sense that the grisly discovery ends the summer of her childhood. Precisely our ability to *imagine* her unstated final thoughts makes their impact on us very strong.

The Grammar of Filter

What are the author's techniques for representing a character's thought process? I have already explained the basic distinction between couching the character's thought in the narrator's words — which we can call the *report* method — and couching them in the character's words — the *quotation* method. As we have seen, the *report* method is useful for representing sensations and perceptions, which by their nature do not occur to us in actual words. In "A Little Cloud," for example, "his sight was confused by the shining of many red and green wineglasses" or "Little Chandler felt his cheeks suffused with shame." The report method also provides a handy means for *summarizing* thoughts or feelings: "He remembered the books of poetry upon his shelves at home. . . . many an evening . . . he had been tempted to take one down from the bookshelf and read out something to his wife. But shyness had always held him back."

Quotation techniques are more complex. There are several ways to represent a character's thoughts in his or her own words. The most obvious is the direct quotation. For example, in Isaac Bashevis Singer's "Short Friday," as Shoshe listens to her husband's recitation of the Hebrew prayer "The worthy woman":

> . . . she thought to herself, "Here am I, a simple woman, an orphan, and yet God has chosen to bless me with a devoted husband who praises me in the holy tongue."

This is a *direct* quotation: We recognize it as such not only because of the quotation marks, but because the character refers to herself as "I" and uses the present tense of the verbs ("am" and "praises").

Another way of quoting a thought is *indirect*. In indirect quotation, the character refers to himself or herself in the *third* person ("he/his/him" or "she/her") and the verb occurs in the past tense. In indirect quotation, Shoshe's thought would have read as follows:

> . . . she thought to herself that here she was, a simple woman, an orphan, and yet God had shown to bless her with a devoted husband who praised her in the holy tongue.

All first-person pronouns become third person, and all present-tense verbs become past tense. (Those verbs that are *already* past tense become past perfects: thus "*has* chosen" becomes "*had* chosen.")

We have identified two different means for expressing a character's mental experience. In the first, the narrator uses his own words. In the second, the narrator quotes the character's words. Our account of the means for expressing consciousness, however, is still not complete. There is an additional distinction between two kinds of indirect quotation that turns on the notion of *tag*.[2] A *tag* is a phrase such as "he said" or "she thought" that immediately marks what adjoins it as a quotation. Consider this quotation from "A Little Cloud":

> Melancholy was the dominant note of his temperament, he thought, but it was a melancholy tempered by recurrences of faith and resignation and simple joy.

"He thought" tells us that this is a tagged indirect quotation of Little Chandler's thought. In contrast, the last sentence of the short story's first paragraph reads:

---

[2]Or *inquit*, if you want to impress your friends with a fancy Latin term.

> It was something to have a friend like that.

No tag marks this quotation of Chandler's own mental words. So how do we know that they *are* his and not the narrator's? By the context. For there is nowhere in "A Little Cloud" — or in the whole of *Dubliners* — the kind of narrator who would intervene to make such a judgment.

So we must distinguish between indirect quotations that are *tagged* and those that are *untagged*. Untagged quotations are also called *free quotations*. The thought is "free" in the sense that there is no tag of thinking, no "he thought" or "he remembered."[3]

Notice how the representation of Little Chandler's filter shifts from tagged indirect to free indirect representation — from

> Melancholy was the dominant note, he thought . . .

to

> If he could give expression to it in a book of poems perhaps men would listen.

Clearly the latter sentence represents Chandler speculating to himself about how he could capture an audience's interest, not the narrator assuring us about that possibility. The sentence does not mean "Dear reader, I, your trustworthy narrator, assure you that if our friend Chandler could express himself, the audience would read him." As if to help us keep our bearings, the sentence that follows, "He would never be popular: he saw that," reinserts a tag. Clearly the point of the story is that Chandler will have *no* success at all.

Having established that these are Chandler's own thoughts, the narrator can cast the remainder of the paragraph in free indirect style:

> He could not sway the crowd but he might appeal to a little circle of kindred minds. The English critics, perhaps, would recognise him as one of the Celtic school by reason of the melancholy tone of his poems; besides that, he would put in allusions. He began to invent sentences and phrases from the notice which his book would get. *Mr. Chandler has the gift of easy and graceful verse. . . . A wistful sadness pervades these poems. . . . The Celtic note*. It was a pity his name was not more Irish-looking. Perhaps it would be better to insert his mother's name before the surname: Thomas Malone Chandler, or better still: T. Malone Chandler. He would speak to Gallaher about it.

These quotations are in free indirect form to preserve the exact flavor of Chandler's self-deluding fantasies. Here he is, quoting favorable reviews by nonexistent "English critics" and thinking about a pen name — before he has even written the poems! Even the very last sentence, "He would speak to Gallaher about it," is a free version of "[He told himself that] he would speak

---

[3]Direct quotations may also be free. For example, the quotation from Shoshe's filter cited above could have occurred without "She thought to herself" — indeed, it could have occurred without quotation marks. Shoshe's self-reference by "I" and her use of the present tense would alone ensure our understanding that it was her very thought in her very words. But free direct forms do not give rise to the kind of interpretational problems that free indirect forms do, so it is not necessary to discuss them in any detail.

to Gallaher about it.'' The irony here is delicious, because we suspect that the hard-drinking and cynical womanizer Gallaher would laugh if asked how to publish wistful romantic poetry.

Free indirect thought differs from tagged indirect thought in an interesting way. The tag identifies the thought as exclusively the character's, but the absence of a tag can lead to a certain uncertainty or ambiguity. The free indirect form *may* be the character's words to himself, but it may alternatively be the narrator's language addressed to the narratee. Or it may be indeterminately *both!* For not all short stories ironize the filter of a character. Often, the narrator is perfectly sympathetic with the filter character's views. In that case there is no way of — nor any point in — distinguishing whether a certain sentence represents the character's filter or the narrator's slant. Elizabeth Bowen's ''Careless Talk'' (pp. 370–373) is a good example of this kind of short story.

In any event, it is always context that helps us understand whether a given passage represents filter or slant or both. Indeed, context may be the *only* clue, for example, when the diction of the character and narrator is similar. Because Little Chandler is well-educated, we cannot distinguish his mental words from those of the well-spoken narrator on the basis of dialect or accent alone. (The external narrator is generally assumed, by convention, to be well-spoken.)

In fictions where the character's diction is other than well-spoken, of course, no such ambiguity arises. In ''The Rockpile,'' for example, we can be pretty sure whose language we are reading at any given moment. The *speech* of the mother, Elizabeth, is characterized by such sentences as ''You ain't going to take no strap to this boy, not today you ain't.'' Her *thoughts* are communicated by such sentences as

> . . . she found in [Gabriel's] face not fury alone, which would not have surprised her; but hatred so deep as to become insupportable in its lack of personality. His eyes were struck alive, unmoving, blind with malevolence . . .

The diction is quite different. It is unlikely that the words *insupportable* and *malevolence* are in Elizabeth's vocabulary, even though the sentiments signaled by those words are. So the sentence must represent a *report* of her thoughts by the well-spoken narrator, who is *interpreting* how Elizabeth feels, even though Elizabeth does not have these precise words to express her feelings.

This is not a textbook of English grammar or rhetoric, and it is less important that you know terms like *''free indirect thought''* than that you recognize the different possible meanings that such a construction may give rise to. Why? To guard against mistaken interpretations. If you interpret a passage as the explicit pronouncement of the narrator, but it is really the character's attitude, expressed in the privacy of her own filter, you obviously risk a serious misunderstanding of the fiction.

Consider, for example, Nadine Gordimer's ''Town and Country

Lovers" (pp. 160 – 172), a short story that turns on the nuances of racism in South Africa. Here is the context: Dr. von Leinsdorf, a German geologist on an expedition to South Africa, is approached by an unnamed "colored"[4] girl who works at a supermarket where he has tried unsuccessfully to purchase some razor blades. She tells him the blades are now in, that she has saved some for him, and offers to fetch them. He acquiesces "in the kindly tone of assumption used for an obliging underling." This is an explicit clue to Dr. von Leinsdorf's social attitudes. That von Leinsdorf thinks of people of color in terms of "underlings" already tells us much about him. But the (implied) author has been careful not to suggest that the narrator endorses von Leinsdorf's attitudes.

The narrator then switches to the girl's thinking as she delivers the blades, up the elevator segregated for whites, through the glassed-in corridors of the luxurious Atlantis apartment house, to Dr. von Leinsdorf's door. Then the narrator returns to Dr. von Leinsdorf's mind, as he wonders whether to tip her. It is in that context that we read the following free indirect thought:

> It was difficult to know how to treat these people, in this country . . .

If we assume that the *narrator* says this — that is, presents it as a general truth that she too believes — we seriously misinterpret the short story. We might make that mistake if we were not alert to the potential ambiguity of free indirect thought, and the constant question that the form poses, namely, "Whose language *is* this?" If we look carefully at the context, we must realize that the remark represents Dr. von Leinsdorf's, not the narrator's, opinion.[5] We must recognize that the narrator preserves a clear distance between her own slant and the protagonist's filter and by no means shares Dr. von Leinsdorf's racial and class prejudices.

Filter in Internal Narration

So far we have been considering how filter works in externally narrated stories, where the filter-character is referred to in the third person and is clearly separated from the narrator. What happens if the narrator and the filter-character are the same person? Internal narration, where the I-narrator is the I-protagonist grown older, introduces an interestingly different question. In some short stories, such as "The Tell-Tale Heart" (pp. 226 – 229), the narrative discourse occurs so soon after the story-events that narrator and character are substantially the same person. In others, a period of time has passed, so "older" and "younger" do have some meaning. About such short stories we can ask whether they are conveyed through the filter of the younger character "back then," in the throes of the experiences themselves, or retrospectively through her slant as an older, wiser narrator.

---

[4]"Colored" in South Africa refers not to blacks but to other nonwhite races, in particular, the many Asian Indians who have settled there.
[5]If this were the narrator's opinion, the racist sentence would have to be cast in the present, not the past tense: "It *is* difficult to know how to treat these people."

The first possibility is illustrated by V. S. Naipaul's "The Thing Without a Name" (pp. 174–178). It uses the filter of the narrator's younger self, his self-as-character. All the words attributed to the character's thinking (with the possible exception of "loquacious") are simple enough for the vocabulary of a relatively young boy, for example:

> I thought Popo was a much nicer man than Bogart.

or

> The only thing I didn't like was the way she sat and watched me while I ate. It was as though I was eating for her. She asked me to call her Auntie.

or

> But I didn't mind. I was glad. It was good to see Popo.

The story is told very much in the language of the *character*-I, not the narrator-I. That seems appropriate to a fiction about the experiences of a simple man whom the narrator met as a boy and whose story even a boy could understand and would not have to decipher later in life.

Mary McCarthy's "C.Y.E." (pp. 179–184) uses the other possibility. It is presented through the slant of a narrator who looks back at her past and judges it from her present strength and maturity. Indeed, the short story turns on the narrator-I's rejection of her former, insecure, mousey, character-I self. Confronted with the letters "CYE" on a sign in Manhattan, the narrator-I remembers how, years ago in parochial school (back when she was character-I), she felt cowed by two girl classmates who gave her that nickname. The girls managed to keep the meaning of the nickname a secret from her, and she never knew what it meant. As character-I "back then," she always assumed that C.Y.E. referred to something unpleasant. Now, as a confident and successful adult, she *elects* to put a good interpretation on the letters. She *wills* them to mean "Clever Young Egg." Regardless of what her classmates might have meant by them, the adult narrator asserts the strength and self-confidence that she has acquired. In so doing, the narrator-I rejects the "pale, plain" character-I in such vivid terms that it is as if the two were totally different individuals. The narrator-I leaves her younger self in an unending time warp, forever timorous, forever unable to puzzle out the letters.

In a short story like "C.Y.E.," where the adult narrator rejects the young character that she once was, it makes artistic sense to express the whole story, including the character-I's thoughts, in the narrator's language. Couching those thoughts in the elegant diction of the person she has become — a sophisticated professional writer — confirms her success. Note the elaborate diction through which the narrator-I recalls how the character-I lay awake trying to figure out what "C.Y.E." stood for:

> My fault was nothing ordinary that you could do something about, like washing your ears. Plainly, it was something immanent and irremediable, a spiritual taint. And though I could not have told precisely what my wrongness consisted in, I felt its existence almost tangible during those nights . . .

Even a gifted eleven-year-old, as the character-I doubtless was, would probably not use words like "immanent and irremediable, a spiritual taint." As an adult, however, she now has the vocabulary to characterize her earlier vague feelings with great precision.

Though characters' thoughts have always been important in fiction, short stories of the twentieth century are particularly concerned with them. Indeed, many stories consist of little else than the stream of a character's thought. This preoccupation reflects the belief that the deepest truths about human beings are to be discovered not in what they do in the physical world but in what (and how) they think. Their thoughts reflect their innermost beings, their real selves. The concept of filter helps us understand the various ways in which the character's mind is the focus of the story (whether or not he or she is also the narrator). A cleverly used filter is a neat and efficient way to plunge the reader deeply into the innermost recesses of a character's personality.

❖ JAMES JOYCE
A Little Cloud[1]

James Joyce (1882–1941) was born in Dublin, Ireland, and educated at two Jesuit schools and then at University College, Dublin. Though the son of an impoverished family, he was determined to become a man of letters. He rejected both his religion and his country, taking up life on the continent, first in Trieste, Italy, then in Paris and Zurich. Until the thirties, he had to eke out a meager living as a teacher of English as a foreign language. Though he wrote two volumes of poems, *Pomes Penyeach* (1927) and *Chamber Music* (1907) and the play *Exiles* (1918), his true gift was fiction. After an enormous struggle with censorious publishers and even typesetters, he managed to see into print the collection of short stories *Dubliners* (1914), some of whose stories had been written ten years before ("A Little Cloud" is part of that collection). *Dubliners* as a whole documents in telling detail Joyce's image of the "spiritual paralysis" suffered by the citizens of his home city. His first novel, *A Portrait of the Artist as a Young Man* (1916), was an autobiographical account of a writer's struggle to free himself of family, religious, and political restraints so that he might make himself into a true artist. Despite self-imposed exile, Joyce could not tear himself away from the Dublin scene, and its streets, buildings, and parks form the setting of his two great novels, *Ulysses* (completed in 1922, first published in 1934) and *Finnegans Wake* (1939). Because of their technical experimentation, these are difficult and challenging novels, requiring the use of special glossaries, but no one should miss the opportunity to read them. Many critics consider Joyce to be the greatest novelist of the twentieth century.

Eight years before he had seen his friend off at the North Wall[2] and wished him godspeed, Gallaher has got on. You could tell that at once by his travelled air, his well-cut tweed suit and fearless accent. Few fellows had talents like his and fewer still could remain unspoiled by such success. Gallaher's heart was in the right place and he had deserved to win. It was something to have a friend like that.

Little Chandler's thoughts ever since lunch-time had been of his meeting with Gallaher, of Gallaher's invitation and of the great city London where Gallaher lived. He was called Little Chandler because, though he was but slightly under the average stature, he gave one the idea of being a little man. His hands were white and small, his frame was fragile, his voice was quiet and his manners were refined. He took the greatest care of his fair silken hair and moustache and used perfume discreetly on his handkerchief. The half-moons of his nails were perfect and when he smiled you caught a glimpse of a row of childish white teeth.

---

[1]From a verse in the Old Testament (Kings 18:44).
[2]The dock area along the bank of the River Liffey in Dublin.

As he sat at his desk in the King's Inns[3] he thought what changes those eight years had brought. The friend whom he had known under a shabby and necessitous guise had become a brilliant figure on the London Press. He turned often from his tiresome writing to gaze out of the office window. The glow of a late autumn sunset covered the grass plots and walks. It cast a shower of kindly golden dust on the untidy nurses and decrepit old men who drowsed on the benches; it flickered upon all the moving figures—on the children who ran screaming along the gravel paths and on everyone who passed through the gardens. He watched the scene and thought of life; and (as always happened when he thought of life) be became sad. A gentle melancholy took possession of him. He felt how useless it was to struggle against fortune, this being the burden of wisdom which the ages had bequeathed to him.

He remembered the books of poetry upon his shelves at home. He had bought them in his bachelor days and many an evening, as he sat in the little room off the hall, he had been tempted to take one down from the bookshelf and read out something to his wife. But shyness had always held him back; and so the books had remained on their shelves. At times he repeated lines to himself and this consoled him.

When his hour had struck he stood up and took leave of his desk and of his fellow-clerks punctiliously. He emerged from under the feudal arch of the King's Inns, a neat modest figure, and walked swiftly down Henrietta Street. The golden sunset was waning and the air had grown sharp. A horde of grimy children populated the street. They stood or ran in the roadway or crawled up the steps before the gaping doors or squatted like mice upon the thresholds. Little Chandler gave them no thought. He picked his way deftly through all that minute vermin-like life and under the shadow of the gaunt spectral mansions in which the old nobility of Dublin had roistered. No memory of the past touched him, for his mind was full of a present joy.

He had never been in Corless's but he knew the value of the name. He knew that people went there after the theatre to eat oysters and drink liqueurs; and he had heard that the waiters there spoke French and German. Walking swiftly by at night he had seen cabs drawn up before the door and richly dressed ladies, escorted by cavaliers, alight and enter quickly. They wore noisy dresses and many wraps. Their faces were powdered and they caught up their dresses, when they touched the earth, like alarmed Atalantas.[4] He had always passed without turning his head to look. It was his habit to walk swiftly in the street even by day and whenever he found himself in the city late at night he hurried on his way apprehensively and excitedly. Sometimes, however, he courted the causes of his fear. He chose the darkest and narrowest streets and, as he walked boldly forward, the silence that was spread about his footsteps troubled him, the wandering silent figures troubled him; and at times a sound of low fugitive laughter made him tremble like a leaf.

He turned to the right towards Capel Street. Ignatius Gallaher on the London Press! Who would have thought it possible eight years before? Still, now that he reviewed the past, Little Chandler could remember many signs of future greatness in his friend. People used to say that Ignatius Gallaher was wild. Of course, he did mix with a rakish set of fellows at that time, drank freely and borrowed money on all sides.

---

[3]A residence for lawyers, like London's Inns of Court.
[4]A huntress of Greek mythology who kept her suitors at bay by outrunning them.

In the end he had got mixed up in some shady affair, some money transaction: at least, that was one version of his flight. But nobody denied him talent. There was always a certain . . . something in Ignatius Gallaher that impressed you in spite of yourself. Even when he was out at elbows and at his wits' end for money he kept up a bold face. Little Chandler remembered (and the remembrance brought a slight flush of pride to his cheek) one of Ignatius Gallaher's sayings when he was in a tight corner:

—Half time, now, boys, he used to say light-heartedly. Where's my considering cap?

That was Ignatius Gallaher all out; and, damn it, you couldn't but admire him for it.

Little Chandler quickened his pace. For the first time in his life he felt superior to the people he passed. For the first time his soul revolted against the dull inelegance of Capel Street. There was no doubt about it: if you wanted to succeed you had to go away. You could do nothing in Dublin. As he crossed Grattan Bridge he looked down the river towards the lower quays and pitied the poor stunted houses. They seemed to him a band of tramps, huddled together along the river-banks, their old coats covered with dust and soot, stupefied by the panorama of sunset and waiting for the first chill of night to bid them arise, shake themselves and begone. He wondered whether he could write a poem to express his idea. Perhaps Gallaher might be able to get it into some London paper for him. Could he write something original? He was not sure what idea he wished to express but the thought that a poetic moment had touched him took life within him like an infant hope. He stepped onward bravely.

Every step brought him nearer to London, farther from his own sober inartistic life. A light began to tremble on the horizon of his mind. He was not so old — thirty-two. His temperament might be said to be just at the point of maturity. There were so many different moods and impressions that he wished to express in verse. He felt them within him. He tried to weigh his soul to see if it was a poet's soul. Melancholy was the dominant note of his temperament, he thought, but it was a melancholy tempered by recurrences of faith and resignation and simple joy. If he could give expression to it in a book of poems perhaps men would listen. He could never be popular: he saw that. He could not sway the crowd but he might appeal to a little circle of kindred minds. The English critics, perhaps, would recognise him as one of the Celtic school[5] by reason of the melancholy tone of his poems; besides that, he would put in allusions. He began to invent sentences and phrases from the notices which his book would get. *Mr Chandler has the gift of easy and graceful verse. . . . A wistful sadness pervades these poems. . . . The Celtic note.* It was a pity his name was not more Irish-looking. Perhaps it would be better to insert his mother's name before the surname: Thomas Malone Chandler, or better still: T. Malone Chandler. He would speak to Gallaher about it.

He pursued his revery so ardently that he passed his street and had to turn back. As he came near Corless's his former agitation began to overmaster him and he halted before the door in indecision. Finally he opened the door and entered.

The light and noise of the bar held him at the doorway for a few moments. He

---

[5]Irish poets of the 1890s such as W. B. Yeats and George "A. E." Russell, whose poems were based on Irish legend. They were softly romantic and melancholy.

looked about him, but his sight was confused by the shining of many red and green wineglasses. The bar seemed to him to be full of people and he felt that the people were observing him curiously. He glanced quickly to right and left (frowning slightly to make his errand appear serious), but when his sight cleared a little he saw that nobody had turned to look at him: and there, sure enough, was Ignatius Gallaher leaning with his back against the counter and his feet planted far apart.

—Hallo, Tommy, old hero, here you are! What is it to be? What will you have? I'm taking whisky: better stuff than we get across the water. Soda? Lithia?[6] No mineral? I'm the same. Spoils the flavour. . . . Here, *garçon*,[7] bring us two halves of malt whisky, like a good fellow. . . . Well, and how have you been pulling along since I saw you last? Dear God, how old we're getting! Do you see any signs of aging in me — eh, what? A little grey and thin on the top — what?

Ignatius Gallaher took off his hat and displayed a large closely cropped head. His face was heavy, pale and clean-shaven. His eyes, which were of bluish slate-colour, relieved his unhealthy pallor and shone out plainly above the vivid orange tie[8] he wore. Between these rival features the lips appeared very long and shapeless and colourless. He bent his head and felt with two sympathetic fingers the thin hair at the crown. Little Chandler shook his head as a denial. Ignatius Gallaher put on his hat again.

—It pulls you down, he said, Press life. Always hurry and scurry, looking for copy and sometimes not finding it: and then, always to have something new in your stuff. Damn proofs and printers, I say, for a few days. I'm deuced glad, I can tell you, to get back to the old country. Does a fellow good, a bit of a holiday. I feel a ton better since I landed again in dear dirty Dublin. . . . Here you are, Tommy. Water? Say when.

Little Chandler allowed his whisky to be very much diluted.

—You don't know what's good for you, my boy, said Ignatius Gallaher. I drink mine neat.

—I drink very little as a rule, said Little Chandler modestly. An odd half-one or so when I meet any of the old crowd: that's all.

—Ah, well, said Ignatius Gallaher, cheerfully, here's to us and to old times and old acquaintance.

They clinked glasses and drank the toast.

—I met some of the old gang to-day, said Ignatius Gallaher. O'Hara seems to be in a bad way. What's he doing?

—Nothing, said Little Chandler. He's gone to the dogs.

—But Hogan has a good sit,[9] hasn't he?

—Yes; he's in the Land Commission.[10]

—I met him one night in London and he seemed to be very flush. . . . Poor O'Hara! Boose, I suppose?

---

[6]A kind of mineral water.

[7]Waiter (French).

[8]Worn by Orangemen (named after William of Orange), Anglo-Irish Protestants. The color suggests that Gallaher prefers England to his home country.

[9]A good position or situation.

[10]The government office created to help transfer lands held by the Irish landed aristocracy to their tenant farmers.

—Others things, too, said Little Chandler shortly.

Ignatius Gallaher laughed.

—Tommy, he said, I see you haven't changed an atom. You're the very same serious person that used to lecture me on Sunday mornings when I had a sore head and a fur on my tongue. You'd want to knock about a bit in the world. Have you never been anywhere, even for a trip?

—I've been to the Isle of Man,[11] said Little Chandler.

Ignatius Gallaher laughed.

—The Isle of Man! he said. Go to London or Paris: Paris, for choice. That'd do you good.

—Have you seen Paris?

—I should think I have! I've knocked about there a little.

—And is it really so beautiful as they say? asked Little Chandler.

He sipped a little of his drink while Ignatius Gallaher finished his boldly.

—Beautiful? said Ignatius Gallaher, pausing on the word and on the flavour of his drink. It's not so beautiful, you know. Of course, it is beautiful. . . . But it's the life of Paris; that's the thing. Ah, there's no city like Paris for gaiety, movement, excitement. . . .

Little Chandler finished his whisky and, after some trouble, succeeded in catching the barman's eye. He ordered the same again.

—I've been to the Moulin Rouge,[12] Ignatius Gallaher continued when the barman had removed their glasses, and I've been to all the Bohemian cafés. Hot stuff! Not for a pious chap like you, Tommy.

Little Chandler said nothing until the barman returned with the two glasses: then he touched his friend's glass lightly and reciprocated the former toast. He was beginning to feel somewhat disillusioned. Gallaher's accent and way of expressing himself did not please him. There was something vulgar in his friend which he had not observed before. But perhaps it was only the result of living in London amid the bustle and competition of the Press. The old personal charm was still there under this new gaudy manner. And, after all, Gallaher had lived, he had seen the world. Little Chandler looked at his friend enviously.

—Everything in Paris is gay, said Ignatius Gallaher. They believe in enjoying life—and don't you think they're right? If you want to enjoy yourself properly you must go to Paris. And, mind you, they've a great feeling for the Irish there. When they heard I was from Ireland they were ready to eat me, man.

Little Chandler took four or five sips from his glass.

—Tell me, he said, is it true that Paris is so . . . immoral as they say?

Ignatius Gallaher made a catholic gesture with his right arm.

—Every place is immoral, he said. Of course you do find spicy bits in Paris. Go to one of the students' balls, for instance. That's lively, if you like, when the *cocottes*[13] begin to let themselves loose. You know what they are, I suppose?

—I've heard of them, said Little Chandler.

---

[11]An island off the English coast.

[12]A dance hall in Paris, well-known through the posters of Henri de Toulouse-Lautrec (1864–1901).

[13]Prostitutes (French).

Ignatius Gallaher drank off his whisky and shook his head.

—Ah, he said, you may say what you like. There's no woman like the Parisienne—for style, for go.

—Then it is an immoral city, said Little Chandler, with timid insistence—I mean, compared with London or Dublin?

—London! said Ignatius Gallaher. It's six of one and half-a-dozen of the other. You ask Hogan, my boy. I showed him a bit about London when he was over there. He'd open your eye. . . . I say, Tommy, don't make punch of that whisky: liquor up.

—No, really. . . .

—O, come on, another one won't do you any harm. What is it? The same again, I suppose?

—Well . . . all right.

—*François*, the same again. . . . Will you smoke, Tommy?

Ignatius Gallaher produced his cigar-case. The two friends lit their cigars and puffed at them in silence until their drinks were served.

—I'll tell you my opinion, said Ignatius Gallaher, emerging after some time from the clouds of smoke in which he had taken refuge, it's a rum world. Talk of immorality! I've heard of cases—what am I saying?—I've known them: cases of . . . immorality. . . .

Ignatius Gallaher puffed thoughtfully at his cigar and then, in a calm historian's tone, he proceeded to sketch for his friend some pictures of the corruption which was rife abroad. He summarised the vices of many capitals and seemed inclined to award the palm to Berlin. Some things he could not vouch for (his friends had told him), but of others he had had personal experience. He spared neither rank nor caste. He revealed many of the secrets of religious houses on the Continent and described some of the practices which were fashionable in high society and ended by telling, with details, a story about an English duchess—a story which he knew to be true. Little Chandler was astonished.

—Ah, well, said Ignatius Gallaher, here we are in old jog-along Dublin where nothing is known of such things.

—How dull you must find it, said Little Chandler, after all the other places you've seen!

—Well, said Ignatius Gallaher, it's a relaxation to come over here, you know. And, after all, it's the old country, as they say, isn't it? You can't help having a certain feeling for it. That's human nature. . . . But tell me something about yourself. Hogan told me you had . . . tasted the joys of connubial bliss. Two years ago, wasn't it?

Little Chandler blushed and smiled.

—Yes, he said. I was married last May twelve months.

—I hope it's not too late in the day to offer my best wishes, said Ignatius Gallaher. I didn't know your address or I'd have done so at the time.

He extended his hand, which Little Chandler took.

—Well, Tommy, he said, I wish you and yours every joy in life, old chap, and tons of money, and may you never die till I shoot you. And that's the wish of a sincere friend, an old friend. You know that?

—I know that, said Little Chandler.

—Any youngsters? said Ignatius Gallaher.

Little Chandler blushed again.

—We have one child, he said.

—Son or daughter?

—A little boy.

Ignatius Gallaher slapped his friend sonorously on the back.

—Bravo, he said, I wouldn't doubt you, Tommy.

Little Chandler smiled, looked confusedly at his glass and bit his lower lip with three childishly white front teeth.

—I hope you'll spend an evening with us, he said, before you go back. My wife will be delighted to meet you. We can have a little music and—

—Thanks awfully, old chap, said Ignatius Gallaher, I'm sorry we didn't meet earlier. But I must leave to-morrow night.

—To-night, perhaps . . . ?

—I'm awfully sorry, old man. You see I'm over here with another fellow, clever young chap he is too, and we arranged to go to a little card-party. Only for that . . .

—O, in that case. . . .

—But who knows? said Ignatius Gallaher considerately. Next year I may take a skip over here now that I've broken the ice. It's only a pleasure deferred.

—Very well, said Little Chandler, the next time you come we must have an evening together. That's agreed now, isn't it?

—Yes, that's agreed, said Ignatius Gallaher. Next year if I come, *parole d'honneur*.[14]

—And to clinch the bargain, said Little Chandler, we'll just have one more now.

Ignatius Gallaher took out a large gold watch and looked at it.

—Is it to be the last? he said. Because you know, I have an a.p.[15]

—O, yes, positively, said Little Chandler.

—Very well, then, said Ignatius Gallaher, let us have another one as a *deoc an doruis*[16]—that's good vernacular for a small whisky, I believe.

Little Chandler ordered the drinks. The blush which had risen to his face a few moments before was establishing itself. A trifle made him blush at any time: and now he felt warm and excited. Three small whiskies had gone to his head and Gallaher's strong cigar had confused his mind, for he was a delicate and abstinent person. The adventure of meeting Gallaher after eight years, of finding himself with Gallaher in Corless's surrounded by lights and noise, of listening to Gallaher's stories and of sharing for a brief space Gallaher's vagrant and triumphant life, upset the equipoise of his sensitive nature. He felt acutely the contrast between his own life and his friend's, and it seemed to him unjust. Gallaher was his inferior in birth and education. He was sure that he could do something better than his friend had ever done, or could ever do, something higher than mere tawdry journalism if he only got the chance. What was it that stood in his way? His unfortunate timidity! He wished to

---

[14]Word of honor (French).

[15]Appointment.

[16]A farewell drink (Gaelic).

vindicate himself in some way, to assert his manhood. He saw behind Gallaher's refusal of his invitation. Gallaher was only patronising him by his friendliness just as he was patronising Ireland by his visit.

The barman brought their drinks. Little Chandler pushed one glass towards his friend and took up the other boldly.

— Who knows? he said, as they lifted their glasses. When you come next year I may have the pleasure of wishing long life and happiness to Mr and Mrs Ignatius Gallaher.

Ignatius Gallaher in the act of drinking closed one eye expressively over the rim of his glass. When he had drunk he smacked his lips decisively, set down his glass and said:

— No blooming fear of that, my boy. I'm going to have my fling first and see a bit of life and the world before I put my head in the sack — if I ever do.

— Some day you will, said Little Chandler calmly.

Ignatius Gallaher turned his orange tie and slate-blue eyes full upon his friend.

— You think so? he said.

— You'll put your head in the sack, repeated Little Chandler stoutly, like everyone else if you can find the girl.

He had slightly emphasised his tone and he was aware that he had betrayed himself; but, though the colour had heightened in his cheek, he did not flinch from his friend's gaze. Ignatius Gallaher watched him for a few moments and then said:

— If ever it occurs, you may bet your bottom dollar there'll be no mooning and spooning about it. I mean to marry money. She'll have a good fat account at the bank or she won't do for me.

Little Chandler shook his head.

— Why, man alive, said Ignatius Gallaher, vehemently, do you know what it is? I've only to say the word and to-morrow I can have the woman and the cash. You don't believe it? Well, I know it. There are hundreds — what am I saying? — thousands of rich Germans and Jews, rotten with money, that'd only be too glad. . . . You wait a while, my boy. See if I don't play my cards properly. When I go about a thing I mean business, I tell you. You just wait.

He tossed his glass to his mouth, finished his drink and laughed loudly. Then he looked thoughtfully before him and said in a calmer tone:

— But I'm in no hurry. They can wait. I don't fancy tying myself up to one woman, you know.

He imitated with his mouth the act of tasting and made a wry face.

— Must get a bit stale, I should think, he said.

Little Chandler sat in the room off the hall, holding a child in his arms. To save money they kept no servant but Annie's young sister Monica came for an hour or so in the morning and an hour or so in the evening to help. But Monica had gone home long ago. It was a quarter to nine. Little Chandler had come home late for tea and, moreover, he had forgotten to bring Annie home the parcel of coffee from Bewley's. Of course she was in a bad humour and gave him short answers. She said she would do without any tea but when it came near the time at which the shop at the corner closed she decided to go out herself for a quarter of a pound of tea and two pounds of sugar. She put the sleeping child deftly in his arms and said:

—Here. Don't waken him.

A little lamp with a white china shade stood upon the table and its light fell over a photograph which was enclosed in a frame of crumpled horn. It was Annie's photograph. Little Chandler looked at it, pausing at the thin tight lips. She wore the pale blue summer blouse which he had brought her home as a present one Saturday. It had cost him ten and elevenpence; but what an agony of nervousness it had cost him! How he had suffered that day, waiting at the shop door until the shop was empty, standing at the counter and trying to appear at his ease while the girl piled ladies' blouses before him, paying at the desk and forgetting to take up the odd penny of his change, being called back by the cashier, and, finally, striving to hide his blushes as he left the shop by examining the parcel to see if it was securely tied. When he brought the blouse home Annie kissed him and said it was very pretty and stylish; but when she heard the price she threw the blouse on the table and said it was a regular swindle to charge ten and elevenpence for that. At first she wanted to take it back but when she tried it on she was delighted with it, especially with the make of the sleeves, and kissed him and said he was very good to think of her.

Hm! . . .

He looked coldly into the eyes of the photograph and they answered coldly. Certainly they were pretty and the face itself was pretty. But he found something mean in it. Why was it so unconscious and lady-like? The composure of the eyes irritated him. They repelled him and defied him: there was no passion in them, no rapture. He thought of what Gallaher had said about rich Jewesses. Those dark Oriental eyes, he thought, how full they are of passion, of voluptuous longing! . . . Why had he married the eyes in the photograph?

He caught himself up at the question and glanced nervously round the room. He found something mean in the pretty furniture which he had bought for his house on the hire system.[17] Annie had chosen it herself and it reminded him of her. It too was prim and pretty. A dull resentment against his life awoke within him. Could he not escape from his little house? Was it too late for him to try to live bravely like Gallaher? Could he go to London? There was the furniture still to be paid for. If he could only write a book and get it published, that might open the way for him.

A volume of Byron's poems[18] lay before him on the table. He opened it cautiously with his left hand lest he should waken the child and began to read the first poem in the book:

> Hushed are the winds and still the evening gloom,
> Not e'en a Zephyr wanders through the grove,
> Whilst I return to view my Margaret's tomb
> And scatter flowers on the dust I love.

He paused. He felt the rhythm of the verse about him in the room. How melancholy it was! Could he, too, write like that, express the melancholy of his soul in verse? There

---

[17]On the installment plan.

[18]Lord Byron (1788–1824). The lines following are from a poem that opens his first collection, *Hours of Idleness* (1807).

were so many things he wanted to describe: his sensation of a few hours before on Grattan Bridge, for example. If he could get back again into that mood. . . .

The child awoke and began to cry. He turned from the page and tried to hush it: but it would not be hushed. He began to rock it to and fro in his arms but its wailing cry grew keener. He rocked it faster while his eyes began to read the second stanza:

> Within this narrow cell reclines her clay,
> That clay where once . . .

It was useless. He couldn't read. He couldn't do anything. The wailing of the child pierced the drum of his ear. It was useless, useless! He was a prisoner for life. His arms trembled with anger and suddenly bending to the child's face he shouted:

—Stop!

The child stopped for an instant, had a spasm of fright and began to scream. He jumped up from his chair and walked hastily up and down the room with the child in his arms. It began to sob piteously, losing its breath for four or five seconds, and then bursting out anew. The thin walls of the room echoed the sound. He tried to soothe it but it sobbed more convulsively. He looked at the contracted and quivering face of the child and began to be alarmed. He counted seven sobs without a break between them and caught the child to his breast in fright. If it died! . . .

The door was burst open and a young woman ran in, panting.

—What is it? What is it? she cried.

The child, hearing its mother's voice, broke out into a paroxysm of sobbing.

—It's nothing, Annie . . . it's nothing. . . . He began to cry . . .

She flung her parcels on the floor and snatched the child from him.

—What have you done to him? she cried, glaring into his face.

Little Chandler sustained for one moment the gaze of her eyes and his heart closed together as he met the hatred in them. He began to stammer:

—It's nothing. . . . He . . . he began to cry. . . . I couldn't . . . I didn't do anything. . . . What?

Giving no heed to him she began to walk up and down the room, clasping the child tightly in her arms and murmuring:

—My little man! My little mannie! Was 'ou frightened, love? . . . There now, love! There now! . . . Lambabaun![19] Mamma's little lamb of the world! . . . There now!

Little Chandler felt his cheeks suffused with shame and he stood back out of the lamplight. He listened while the paroxysm of the child's sobbing grew less and less; and tears of remorse started to his eyes.

(1914)

QUESTIONS

1. Many readers would say that "A Little Cloud" is the kind of short story in which "nothing happens." How would you defend the story against that charge?

---

[19]Lamb-child (Irish).

2. What traits characterize Ignatius Gallaher? How much can we rely on Little Chandler's attitudes about him? Is Gallaher characterized by any other means than Chandler's reactions?

3. The settings of this short story are profoundly important to its effect. How would you describe them? By what means does the narrator distinguish between the various locales? Is descriptive *pause* the device of choice for depicting these locales? Why or why not?

4. The narrator of "A Little Cloud" is very much effaced, but still we seem able to infer some of his beliefs and attitudes from the way he tells the story. Sketch out some and explain how you infer them.

5. Read another short story in James Joyce's collection *Dubliners*, say "Eveline" or "The Gallants." Even though the protagonists are very different from Little Chandler, can you find some resemblance between the stories with respect to the theme of "moral paralysis" which, Joyce says, dominates *Dubliners*?

❖ JAMES BALDWIN
The Rockpile

James Baldwin (1924–1987) was born in Harlem, the son of a minister. From 1948 to 1957, he lived in France, where he found less racial
prejudice and hence a freer atmosphere in which to write. His first
novel, *Go Tell It on the Mountain* (1953) concerns the religion that so
dominated his childhood. *Giovanni's Room* (1956) and *Another Country* (1962) turn on racial and sexual questions. Later novels are *Tell Me
How Long the Train's Been Gone* (1968), *If Beale Street Could Talk*
(1974), and *Just Above My Head* (1979). "The Rockpile" appeared in
his short story collection *Going to Meet the Man* (1965). Baldwin
wrote two plays: *Blues for Mister Charley* (1964) and *The Amen
Corner* (1968). Baldwin was also a prolific writer of essays, in which
he passionately discussed the black cause. His most famous collections of essays are *Notes of a Native Son* (1955), *Nobody Knows My
Name* (1961), and *The Fire Next Time* (1963). Many of these and later
essays are collected in *The Price of the Ticket: Collected Nonfiction
1948–1985* (1985).

Across the street from their house, in an empty lot between two houses, stood the
rockpile. It was a strange place to find a mass of natural rock jutting out of the ground;
and someone, probably Aunt Florence, had once told them that the rock was there and
could not be taken away because without it the subway cars underground would fly
apart, killing all the people. This, touching on some natural mystery concerning the
surface and the center of the earth, was far too intriguing an explanation to be
challenged, and it invested the rockpile, moreover, with such mysterious importance
that Roy felt it to be his right, not to say his duty, to play there.

Other boys were to be seen there each afternoon after school and all day
Saturday and Sunday. They fought on the rockpile. Sure footed, dangerous, and
reckless, they rushed each other and grappled on the heights, sometimes disappearing
down the other side in a confusion of dust and screams and upended flying feet. "It's a
wonder they don't kill themselves," their mother said, watching sometimes from the
fire escape. "You children stay away from there, you hear me?" Though she said
"children," she was looking at Roy, where he sat beside John on the fire escape. "The
good Lord knows," she continued, "I don't want you to come home bleeding like a hog
every day the Lord sends." Roy shifted impatiently, and continued to stare at the
street, as though in this gazing he might somehow acquire wings. John said nothing.
He had not really been spoken to: he was afraid of the rockpile and of the boys who
played there.

Each Saturday morning John and Roy sat on the fire escape and watched the
forbidden street below. Sometimes their mother sat in the room behind them, sewing,
or dressing their younger sister, or nursing the baby, Paul. The sun fell across them and

153

across the fire escape with a high, benevolent indifference; below them, men and women, and boys and girls, sinners all, loitered; sometimes one of the church-members passed and saw them and waved. Then, for the moment that they waved decorously back, they were intimidated. They watched the saint, man or woman, until he or she had disappeared from sight. The passage of one of the redeemed made them consider, however vacantly, the wickedness of the street, their own latent wickedness in sitting where they sat; and made them think of their father, who came home early on Saturdays and who would soon be turning this corner and entering the dark hall below them.

But until he came to end their freedom, they sat, watching and longing above the street. At the end of the street nearest their house was the bridge which spanned the Harlem River and led to a city called the Bronx; which was where Aunt Florence lived. Nevertheless, when they saw her coming, she did not come from the bridge, but from the opposite end of the street. This, weakly, to their minds, she explained by saying that she had taken the subway, not wishing to walk, and that, besides, she did not live in *that* section of the Bronx. Knowing that the Bronx was across the river, they did not believe this story ever, but, adopting toward her their father's attitude, assumed that she had just left some sinful place which she dared not name, as, for example, a movie palace.

In the summertime boys swam in the river diving off the wooden dock, or wading in from the garbage-heavy bank. Once a boy, whose name was Richard, drowned in the river. His mother had not known where he was; she had even come to their house, to ask if he was there. Then, in the evening, at six o'clock, they had heard from the street a woman screaming and wailing; and they ran to the windows and looked out. Down the street came the woman, Richard's mother, screaming, her face raised to the sky and tears running down her face. A woman walked beside her, trying to make her quiet and trying to hold her up. Behind them walked a man, Richard's father, with Richard's body in his arms. There were two white policemen walking in the gutter, who did not seem to know what should be done. Richard's father and Richard were wet, and Richard's body lay across his father's arms like a cotton baby. The woman's screaming filled all the street; cars slowed down and the people in the cars stared; people opened their windows and looked out and came rushing out of doors to stand in the gutter, watching. Then the small procession disappeared within the house which stood beside the rockpile. Then, *"Lord, Lord, Lord!"* cried Elizabeth, their mother, and slammed the window down.

One Saturday, an hour before his father would be coming home, Roy was wounded on the rockpile and brought screaming upstairs. He and John had been sitting on the fire escape and their mother had gone into the kitchen to sip tea with Sister McCandless. By and by Roy became bored and sat beside John in restless silence; and John began drawing into his schoolbook a newspaper advertisement which featured a new electric locomotive. Some friends of Roy passed beneath the fire escape and called him. Roy began to fidget, yelling down to them through the bars. Then a silence fell. John looked up. Roy stood looking at him.

"I'm going downstairs," he said.

"You'd better stay where you is, boy. You know Mama don't want you going downstairs."

"I be right *back*. She won't even know I'm gone, less you run and tell her."

"I ain't *got* to tell her. What's going to stop her from coming in here and looking out the window?"

"She's talking," Roy said. He started into the house.

"But Daddy's going to be home soon!"

"I be back before *that*. What you all the time got to be so *scared* for?" He was already in the house and he now turned, leaning on the windowsill, to swear impatiently, "I be back in *five* minutes."

John watched him sourly as he carefully unlocked the door and disappeared. In a moment he saw him on the sidewalk with his friends. He did not dare to go and tell his mother that Roy had left the fire escape because he had practically promised not to. He started to shout, *Remember, you said five minutes!* but one of Roy's friends was looking up at the fire escape. John looked down at his schoolbook: he became engrossed again in the problem of the locomotive.

When he looked up again he did not know how much time had passed, but now there was a gang fight on the rockpile. Dozens of boys fought each other in the harsh sun: clambering up the rocks and battling hand to hand, scuffed shoes sliding on the slippery rock; filling the bright air with curses and jubilant cries. They filled the air, too, with flying weapons: stones, sticks, tin cans, garbage, whatever could be picked up and thrown. John watched in a kind of absent amazement—until he remembered that Roy was still downstairs, and that he was one of the boys on the rockpile. Then he was afraid; he could not see his brother among the figures in the sun; and he stood up, leaning over the fire-escape railing. Then Roy appeared from the other side of the rocks; John saw that his shirt was torn; he was laughing. He moved until he stood at the very top of the rockpile. Then, something, an empty tin can, flew out of the air and hit him on the forehead, just above the eye. Immediately, one side of Roy's face ran with blood, he fell and rolled on his face down the rocks. Then for a moment there was no movement at all, no sound, the sun, arrested, lay on the street and the sidewalk and the arrested boys. Then someone screamed or shouted; boys began to run away, down the street, toward the bridge. The figure on the ground, having caught its breath and felt its own blood, began to shout. John cried, "Mama! Mama!" and ran inside.

"Don't fret, don't fret," panted Sister McCandless as they rushed down the dark, narrow, swaying stairs, "don't fret. Ain't a boy been born don't get his knocks every now and again. *Lord!*" they hurried into the sun. A man had picked Roy up and now walked slowly toward them. One or two boys sat silent on their stoops; at either end of the street there was a group of boys watching. "He ain't hurt bad," the man said. "Wouldn't be making this kind of noise if he was hurt real bad."

Elizabeth, trembling, reached out to take Roy, but Sister McCandless, bigger, calmer, took him from the man and threw him over her shoulder as she once might have handled a sack of cotton. "God bless you," she said to the man, "God bless you son." Roy was still screaming. Elizabeth stood behind Sister McCandless to stare at his bloody face.

"It's just a flesh wound," the man kept saying "just broke the skin, that's all." They were moving across the sidewalk, toward the house. John, not now afraid of the staring boys, looked toward the corner to see if his father was yet in sight.

Upstairs, they hushed Roy's crying. They bathed the blood away, to find, just above the left eyebrow, the jagged, superficial scar. "Lord, have mercy," murmured Elizabeth, "another inch and it would've been his eye." And she looked with apprehension toward the clock. "Ain't it the truth," said Sister McCandless, busy with bandages and iodine.

"When did he go downstairs?" his mother asked at last.

Sister McCandless now sat fanning herself in the easy chair at the head of the sofa where Roy lay, bound and silent. She paused for a moment to look sharply at John. John stood near the window, holding the newspaper advertisement and the drawing he had done.

"We was sitting on the fire escape," he said. "Some boys he knew called him."

"When?"

"He said he'd be back in five minutes."

"Why didn't you tell me he was downstairs?"

He looked at his hands, clasping his notebook, and did not answer.

"Boy," said Sister McCandless, "you hear your mother a-talking to you?"

He looked at his mother. He repeated:

"He said he'd be back in five minutes."

"He said he'd be back in five minutes," said Sister McCandless with scorn, "don't look to me like that's no right answer. You's the man of the house, you supposed to look after your baby brothers and sisters—you ain't supposed to let them run off and get half-killed. But I expect," she added, rising from the chair, dropping the cardboard fan, "your Daddy'll make you tell the truth. Your Ma's way too soft with you."

He did not look at her, but at the fan where it lay in the dark red, depressed seat where she had been. The fan advertised a pomade for the hair and showed a brown woman and her baby, both with glistening hair, smiling happily at each other.

"Honey," said Sister McCandless, "I got to be moving along. Maybe I drop in later tonight. I don't reckon you going to be at Tarry Service tonight?"

Tarry Service was the prayer meeting held every Saturday night at church to strengthen believers and prepare the church for the coming of the Holy Ghost on Sunday.

"I don't reckon," said Elizabeth. She stood up; she and Sister McCandless kissed each other on the cheek. "But you be sure to remember me in your prayers."

"I surely will do that." She paused, with her hand on the door knob, and looked down at Roy and laughed. "Poor little man," she said, "reckon he'll be content to sit on the fire escape *now*."

Elizabeth laughed with her. "It sure ought to be a lesson to him. You don't reckon," she asked nervously, still smiling, "he going to keep that scar, do you?"

"Lord, no," said Sister McCandless, "ain't nothing but a scratch. I declare, Sister Grimes, you worse than a child. Another couple of weeks and you won't be able to *see* no scar. No, you go on about your housework honey, and thank the Lord it weren't no worse." She opened the door; they heard the sound of feet on the stairs. "I expect that's the Reverend," said Sister McCandless, placidly. "I *bet* he's going to raise cain."

"Maybe it's Florence," Elizabeth said. "Sometimes she get here about this time." They stood in the doorway, staring, while the steps reached the landing below and began again climbing to their floor. "No," said Elizabeth then, "that ain't her walk. That's Gabriel."

"Well, I'll just go on," said Sister McCandless, "and kind of prepare his mind." She pressed Elizabeth's hand as she spoke and started into the hall, leaving the door behind her slightly ajar. Elizabeth turned slowly back into the room. Roy did not open his eyes, or move; but she knew that he was not sleeping; he wished to delay until the last possible moment any contact with his father. John put his newspaper and his notebook on the table and stood, leaning on the table, staring at her.

"It wasn't my fault," he said, "I couldn't stop him from going downstairs."

"No," she said, "you ain't got nothing to worry about. You just tell your Daddy the truth."

He looked directly at her, and she turned to the window, staring into the street. What was Sister McCandless saying? Then from her bedroom she heard Delilah's thin wail and she turned, frowning, looking toward the bedroom and toward the still open door. She knew that John was watching her. Delilah continued to wail, she thought, angrily, *Now that girl's getting too big for that*, but she feared that Delilah would awaken Paul and she hurried into the bedroom. She tried to soothe Delilah back to sleep. Then she heard the front door open and close — too loud, Delilah raised her voice, with an exasperated sigh Elizabeth picked the child up. Her child and Gabriel's, her children and Gabriel's: Roy, Delilah, Paul. Only John was nameless and a stranger, living, unalterable testimony to his mother's days in sin.

"What happened?" Gabriel demanded. He stood, enormous, in the center of the room, his black lunchbox dangling from his hand, staring at the sofa where Roy lay. John stood just before him, it seemed to her astonished vision just below him, beneath his fist, his heavy shoe. The child stared at the man in fascination and terror — when a girl down home she had seen rabbits stand so paralyzed before the barking dog. She hurried past Gabriel to the sofa, feeling the weight of Delilah in her arms like the weight of a shield, and stood over Roy, saying:

"Now, ain't a thing to get upset about, Gabriel. This boy sneaked downstairs while I had my back turned and got hisself hurt a little. He's alright now."

Roy, as though in confirmation, now opened his eyes and looked gravely at his father. Gabriel dropped his lunchbox with a clatter and knelt by the sofa.

"How you feel, son? Tell your Daddy what happened?"

Roy opened his mouth to speak and then, relapsing into panic, began to cry. His father held him by the shoulder.

"You don't want to cry. You's Daddy's little man. Tell your Daddy what happened."

"He went downstairs," said Elizabeth, "where he didn't have no business to be, and got to fighting with them bad boys playing on that rockpile. That's what happened and it's a mercy it weren't nothing worse."

He looked up at her. "Can't you let this boy answer me for hisself?"

Ignoring this, she went on, more gently: "He got cut on the forehead, but it ain't nothing to worry about."

"You call a doctor? How you know it ain't nothing to worry about?"

"Is you got money to be throwing away on doctors? No, I ain't called no doctor. Ain't nothing wrong with my eyes that I can't tell whether he's hurt bad or not. He got a fright more'n anything else, and you ought to pray God it teaches him a lesson."

"You got a lot to say *now*," he said, "but I'll have *me* something to say in a minute. I'll be wanting to know when all this happened, what you was doing with your eyes *then*." He turned back to Roy, who had lain quietly, sobbing eyes wide open and body held rigid: and who now, at his father's touch, remembered the height, the sharp, sliding rock beneath his feet, the sun, the explosion of the sun, his plunge into darkness and his salty blood; and recoiled, beginning to scream, as his father touched his forehead. "Hold still, hold still," crooned his father, shaking, "hold still. Don't cry. Daddy ain't going to hurt you, he just wants to see this bandage, see what they've done to his little man." But Roy continued to scream and would not be still and Gabriel dared not lift the bandage for fear of hurting him more. And he looked at Elizabeth in fury: "Can't you put that child down and help me with this boy? John, take your baby sister from your mother—don't look like neither of you got good sense."

John took Delilah and sat down with her in the easy chair. His mother bent over Roy, and held him still, while his father, carefully—but still Roy screamed—lifted the bandage and stared at the wound. Roy's sobs began to lessen. Gabriel readjusted the bandage. "You see," said Elizabeth, finally, "he ain't nowhere near dead."

"It sure ain't your fault that he ain't dead." He and Elizabeth considered each other for a moment in silence. "He came mightly close to losing an eye. Course, his eyes ain't as big as your'n, so I reckon you don' think it matters so much." At this her face hardened; he smiled. "Lord, have mercy," he said, "you think you ever going to learn to do right? Where was you when all this happened? Who let him go downstairs?"

"Ain't nobody let him go downstairs, he just went. He got a head just like his father, it got to be broken before it'll bow. I was in the kitchen."

"Where was Johnnie?"

"He was in here?"

"Where?"

"He was on the fire escape."

"Didn't he know Roy was downstairs?"

"I reckon."

"What you mean, you reckon? He ain't got your big eyes for nothing, does he?" He looked over at John. "Boy, you see your brother go downstairs?"

"Gabriel, ain't no sense in trying to blame Johnnie. You know right well if you have trouble making Roy behave, he ain't going to listen to his brother. He don't hardly listen to me."

"How come you didn't tell your mother Roy was downstairs?"

John said nothing, staring at the blanket which covered Delilah.

"Boy, you hear me? You want me to take a strap to you?"

"No, you ain't," she said. "You ain't going to take no strap to this boy, not today you ain't. Ain't a soul to blame for Roy's lying up there now but you—you because you done spoiled him so that he thinks he can do just anything and get away with it. I'm here to tell you that ain't no way to raise no child. You don't pray to the Lord to help you do better than you been doing, you going to live to shed bitter tears that the Lord didn't take his soul today." And she was trembling. She moved, unseeing, toward John and took Delilah from his arms. She looked back at Gabriel, who had risen, who stood near the sofa, staring at her. And she found in his face not fury alone, which would not have surprised her; but hatred so deep as to become insupportable in its lack of personality. His eyes were struck alive, unmoving, blind with malevolence — she felt, like the pull of the earth at her feet, his longing to witness her perdition. Again, as though it might be propitiation, she moved the child in her arms. And at this his eyes changed, he looked at Elizabeth, the mother of his children, the helpmeet given by the Lord. Then her eyes clouded; she moved to leave the room; her foot struck the lunchbox lying on the floor.

"John," she said, "pick up your father's lunchbox like a good boy."

She heard, behind her, his scrambling movement as he left the chair, the scrape and jangle of the lunchbox as he picked it up, bending his dark head near the toe of his father's heavy shoe.

(1965)

QUESTIONS

1. How would you describe the neighborhood described in this story? How would its inhabitants describe it? In terms of some combination of religion, racial makeup, friendships, families, entertainments, poverty, security, or violence?

2. Where does Gabriel's sudden look of hatred come from? Toward whom or what is it directed? Why is its object not stated?

3. Whose perspective dominates the early part of the story? At what point does the filter shift? Why?

4. Is the rockpile of the title important in the story's plot? In its theme? Does it have symbolic associations? What are they?

5. Think through the story several times, each time identifying with a different character: John, Elizabeth, Roy, Gabriel, Sister McCandless, Aunt Florence. Does the narrator make some of these characters easier to identify with than others? Does the story's meaning change depending on whose viewpoint is adopted? How about judging it from a perspective outside the story, such as that of a middle-class white reader or a successful Harlem-born writer living in France?

❖ NADINE GORDIMER
Town and Country Lovers

Nadine Gordimer (1923–) was born near Johannesburg, South Africa, and attended the University of Witwatersrand in that city. She has published many works of fiction about life in South Africa, mostly examining the impact on people of all colors by the doctrine of racial segregation or *apartheid* which has plagued her nation for so many years. She won the Nobel Prize for literature in 1991. Her novels are *The Lying Days* (1953), *A World of Strangers* (1958), *Occasion for Loving* (1963), *The Late Bourgeois World* (1966), *A Guest of Honour* (1970), *The Conservationist* (1974), *Burger's Daughter* (1979), *July's People* (1981), *A Sport of Nature* (1987), and *My Son's Story* (1990). Her short stories appear in the collections *Face to Face* (1949), *The Soft Voice of the Serpent* (1952), *Six Feet of the Country* (1956), *Friday's Footprint* (1960), *Not for Publication* (1965), *Livingstone's Companions* (1971), *Selected Stories* (1975), *A Soldier's Embrace* (1980, which includes "Town and Country Lovers"), *Something Out There* (1984), *Crimes of Conscience* (1991), and *Jump and Other Stories* (1991). She has also published essays, especially on political subjects, and an autobiography.

One

Dr Franz-Josef von Leinsdorf is a geologist absorbed in his work; wrapped up in it, as the saying goes — year after year the experience of this work enfolds him, swaddling him away from landscapes, the cities and the people, wherever he lives: Peru, New Zealand, the United States. He's always been like that, his mother could confirm from their native Austria. There, even as a handsome small boy he presented only his profile to her: turned away to his bits of rock and stone. His few relaxations have not changed much since then. An occasional skiing trip, listening to music, reading poetry — Rainer Maria Rilke once stayed in his grandmother's hunting lodge in the forests of Styria and the boy was introduced to Rilke's poems while very young.

Layer upon layer, country after country, wherever his work takes him — and now he has been almost seven years in Africa. First the Côte d'Ivoire,[1] and for the past five years, South Africa. The shortage of skilled manpower brought about his recruitment here. He has no interest in the politics of the countries he works in. His private preoccupation-within-the-preoccupation of his work has been research into underground water-courses, but the mining company that employs him in a senior though not executive capacity is interested only in mineral discovery. So he is much out in the field — which is the veld,[2] here — seeking new gold, copper, platinum and uranium deposits. When he is at home — on this particular job, in this particular country, this

---

[1]Ivory Coast, a republic in West Africa.
[2]The open country, thinly forested, characteristic of parts of South Africa.

160

city — he lives in a two-roomed flat in a suburban block with a landscaped garden, and does his shopping at a supermarket conveniently across the street. He is not married —yet. That is how his colleagues, and the typists and secretaries at the mining company's head office, would define his situation. Both men and women would describe him as a good-looking man, in a foreign way, with the lower half of the face dark and middle-aged (his mouth is thin and curving, and no matter how close-shaven his beard shows like fine shot embedded in the skin round mouth and chin) and the upper half contradictorily young, with deep-set eyes (some would say grey, some black), thick eyelashes and brows. A tangled gaze: through which concentration and gleaming thoughtfulness perhaps appear as fire and languor. It is this that the women in the office mean when they remark he's not unattractive. Although the gaze seems to promise, he has never invited any one of them to go out with him. There is the general assumption he probably has a girl who's been picked for him, he's bespoken by one of his own kind, back home in Europe where he comes from. Many of these well-educated Europeans have no intention of becoming permanent immigrants; neither the remnant of white colonial life nor idealistic involvement with Black Africa appeals to them.

One advantage, at least, of living in underdeveloped or half-developed countries is that flats are serviced. All Dr von Leinsdorf has to do for himself is buy his own supplies and cook an evening meal if he doesn't want to go to a restaurant. It is simply a matter of dropping in to the supermarket on his way from his car to his flat after work in the afternoon. He wheels a trolley up and down the shelves, and his simple needs are presented to him in the form of tins, packages, plastic-wrapped meat, cheeses, fruit and vegetables, tubes, bottles . . . At the cashiers' counters where customers must converge and queue there are racks of small items uncategorized, for last-minute purchase. Here, as the coloured girl cashier punches the adding machine, he picked up cigarettes and perhaps a packet of salted nuts or a bar of nougat. Or razor-blades, when he remembers he's running short. One evening in winter he saw that the cardboard display was empty of the brand of blades he preferred, and he drew the cashier's attention to this. These young coloured girls are usually pretty unhelpful, taking money and punching their machines in a manner that asserts with the time-serving obstinacy of the half-literate the limit of any responsibility towards customers, but this one ran an alert glance over the selection of razor-blades, apologized that she was not allowed to leave her post, and said she would see that the stock was replenished 'next time.' A day or two later she recognized him, gravely, as he took his turn before her counter — 'I ahssed them, but it's out of stock. You can't get it. I did ahss about it.' He said this didn't matter. 'When it comes in, I can keep a few packets for you.' He thanked her.

He was away with the prospectors the whole of the next week. He arrived back in town just before nightfall on Friday, and was on his way from car to flat with his arms full of briefcase, suitcase and canvas bags when someone stopped him by standing timidly in his path. He was about to dodge round unseeingly on the crowded pavement but she spoke. 'We got the blades in now. I didn't see you in the shop this week, but I kept some for you when you come. So . . .'

He recognized her. He had never seen her standing before, and she was wearing a coat. She was rather small and finely-made, for one of them. The coat was skimpy but no big backside jutted. The cold brought an apricot-graining of warm colour to her cheekbones, beneath which a very small face was quite delicately hollowed, and the skin was smooth, the subdued satiny colour of certain yellow wood. That crêpey hair, but worn drawn back flat and in a little knot pushed into one of the cheap wool chignons that (he recognized also) hung in the miscellany of small goods along with the razor-blades, at the supermarket. He said thanks, he was in a hurry, he'd only just got back from a trip — shifting the burdens he carried, to demonstrate. 'Oh shame.' She acknowledged his load. 'But if you want I can run in and get it for you quickly. If you want.'

He saw at once it was perfectly clear that all the girl meant was that she would go back to the supermarket, buy the blades and bring the packet to him there where he stood, on the pavement. And it seemed that it was this certainty that made him say, in the kindly tone of assumption used for an obliging underling, 'I live just across there — *Atlantis* — that flat building. Could you drop them by, for me — number seven-hundred-and-eighteen, seventh floor — '

She had not before been inside one of these big flat buildings near where she worked. She lived a bus- and train-ride away to the West of the city, but this side of the black townships, in a township for people her tint. There was a pool with ferns, not plastic, and even a little waterfall pumped electrically over rocks, in the entrance of the building *Atlantis*; she didn't wait for the lift marked GOODS but took the one meant for whites and a white woman with one of those sausage-dogs on a lead got in with her but did not pay her any attention. The corridors leading to the flats were nicely glassed-in, not draughty.

He wondered if he should give her a twenty-cent piece for her trouble — ten cents would be right for a black; but she said, 'Oh no — please, here — ' standing outside his open door and awkwardly pushing back at his hand the change from the money he'd given her for the razor-blades. She was smiling, for the first time, in the dignity of refusing a tip. It was difficult to know how to treat these people, in this country; to know what they expected. In spite of her embarrassing refusal of the coin, she stood there, completely unassuming, fists thrust down the pockets of her cheap coat against the cold she'd come in from, rather pretty thin legs neatly aligned, knee to knee, ankle to ankle.

'Would you like a cup of coffee or something?'

He couldn't very well take her into his study-cum-living-room and offer her a drink. She followed him to his kitchen, but at the sight of her pulling out the single chair to drink her cup of coffee at the kitchen table, he said, 'No — bring it in here — ' and led the way into the big room where, among his books and his papers, his files of scientific correspondence (and the cigar boxes of stamps from the envelopes) his racks of records, his specimens of minerals and rocks, he lived alone.

It was no trouble for her; she saved him the trips to the supermarket and brought him his groceries two or three times a week. All he had to do was to leave a list and the key under the doormat, and she would come up in her lunch-hour to collect them, returning to put his supplies in the flat after work. Sometimes he was home and sometimes not. He bought a box of chocolates and left it, with a note, for her to find; and that was acceptable, apparently, as a gratuity.

Her eyes went over everything in the flat although her body tried to conceal its sense of being out of place by remaining as still as possible, holding its contours in the chair offered her as a stranger's coat is set aside and remains exactly as left until the owner takes it up to go. 'You collect?'

'Well, these are specimens — connected with my work.'

'My brother used to collect. Miniatures. With brandy and whisky and that, in them. From all over. Different countries.'

The second time she watched him grinding coffee for the cup he had offered her she said, 'You always do that? Always when you make coffee?'

'But of course. Is it no good, for you? Do I make it too strong?'

'Oh it's just I'm not used to it. We buy it ready — you know, it's in a bottle, you just add a bit to the milk or water.'

He laughed, instructive: 'That's not coffee, that's a synthetic flavouring. In my country we drink only real coffee, fresh, from the beans — you smell how good it is as it's being ground?'

She was stopped by the caretaker and asked what she wanted in the building? Heavy with the *bona fides*[3] of groceries clutched to her body, she said she was working at number 718, on the seventh floor. The caretaker did not tell her not to use the whites' lift; after all, she was not black; her family was very light-skinned.

There was the item 'grey button for trousers' on one of his shopping lists. She said as she unpacked the supermarket carrier, 'Give me the pants, so long, then,' and sat on his sofa that was always gritty with fragments of pipe tobacco, sewing in and out through the four holes of the button with firm, fluent movements of the right hand, gestures supplying the articulacy missing from her talk. She had a little yokel's, peasant's (he thought of it) gap between her two front teeth when she smiled that he didn't much like, but, face ellipsed to three-quarter angle, eyes cast down in concentration with soft lips almost closed, this didn't matter. He said, watching her sew, 'You're a good girl'; and touched her.

She remade the bed every late afternoon when they left it and she dressed again before she went home. After a week there was a day when late afternoon became evening, and they were still in the bed.

'Can't you stay the night?'

'My mother,' she said.

'Phone her. Make an excuse.' He was a foreigner. He had been in the country five years, but he didn't understand that people don't usually have telephones in their houses, where she lived. She got up to dress. He didn't want that tender body to go out in the night cold and kept hindering her with the interruption of his hands; saying nothing. Before she put on her coat, when the body had already disappeared, he spoke. 'But you must make some arrangement.'

'Oh my mother!' Her face opened to fear and vacancy he could not read.

He was not entirely convinced the woman would think of her daughter as some pure and unsullied virgin . . . 'Why?'

---

[3]Objects showing good faith.

The girl said, 'S'e'll be scared. S'e'll be scared we get caught.'

'Don't tell her anything. Say I'm employing you.' In this country he was working in now there were generally rooms on the roofs of flat buildings for tenants' servants.

She said: 'That's what I told the caretaker.'

She ground fresh coffee beans every time he wanted a cup while he was working at night. She never attempted to cook anything until she had watched in silence while he did it the way he liked, and she learned to reproduce exactly the simple dishes he preferred. She handled his pieces of rock and stone, at first admiring the colours — 'It'd make a beautiful ring or a necklace, ay.' Then he showed her the striations, the formation of each piece, and explained what each was, and how, in the long life of the earth, it had been formed. He named the mineral it yielded, and what that was used for. He worked at his papers, writing, writing, every night, so it did not matter that they could not go out together to public places. On Sundays she got into his car in the basement garage and they drove to the country and picnicked away up in the Magaliesberg, where there was no one. He read or poked about among the rocks; they climbed together, to the mountain pools. He taught her to swim. She had never seen the sea. She squealed and shrieked in the water, showing the gap between her teeth, as — it crossed his mind — she must do when among her own people. Occasionally he had to go out to dinner at the houses of colleagues from the mining company; she sewed and listened to the radio in the flat and he found her in the bed, warm and already asleep, by the time he came in. He made his way into her body without speaking; she made him welcome without a word. Once he put on evening dress for a dinner at his country's consulate; watching him brush one or two fallen hairs from the shoulders of the dark jacket that sat so well on him, she saw a huge room, all chandeliers and people dancing some dance from a costume film — stately, hand-to-hand. She supposed he was going to fetch, in her place in the car, a partner for the evening. They never kissed when either left the flat; he said, suddenly, kindly, pausing as he picked up cigarettes and keys, 'Don't be lonely.' And added, 'Wouldn't you like to visit your family sometimes, when I have to go out?'

He had told her he was going home to his mother in the forests and mountains of his country near the Italian border (he showed her on the map) after Christmas. She had not told him how her mother, not knowing there was any other variety, assumed he was a medical doctor, so she had talked to her about the doctor's children and the doctor's wife who was a very kind lady, glad to have someone who could help out in the surgery as well as the flat.

She remarked wonderingly on his ability to work until midnight or later, after a day at work. She was so tired when she came home from her cash register at the supermarket that once dinner was eaten she could scarcely keep awake. He explained in a way she could understand that while the work she did was repetitive, undemanding of any real response from her intelligence, requiring little mental or physical effort and therefore unrewarding, his work was his greatest interest, it taxed his mental capacities to their limit, exercised all his concentration, and rewarded him constantly as much with the excitement of a problem presented as with the satisfaction of a problem solved. He said later, putting away his papers, speaking out of a silence: 'Have you done other kinds of work?' She said, 'I was in a clothing factory before. Sportbeau shirts; you know? But the pay's better in the shop.'

Of course. Being a conscientious newspaper-reader in every country he lived in, he was aware that it was only recently that the retail consumer trade in this one had been allowed to employ coloureds as shop assistants; even punching a cash register represented advancement. With the continuing shortage of semiskilled whites a girl like this might be able to edge a little farther into the white-collar category. He began to teach her to type. He was aware that her English was poor, even though, as a foreigner, in his ears her pronunciation did not offend, nor categorize her as it would in those of someone of his education whose mother tongue was English. He corrected her grammatical mistakes but missed the less obvious ones because of his own some-times exotic English usage — she continued to use the singular pronoun 'it' when what was required was the plural 'they'. Because he was a foreigner (although so clever, as she saw) she was less inhibited than she might have been by the words she knew she misspelled in her typing. While she sat at the typewriter she thought how one day she would type notes for him, as well as making coffee the way he liked it, and taking him inside her body without saying anything, and sitting (even if only through the empty streets of quiet Sundays) besides him in his car, like a wife.

On a summer night near Christmas — he had already bought and hidden a slightly showy but nevertheless good watch he thought she would like — there was a knocking at the door that brought her out of the bathroom and him to his feet, at his work-table. No one ever came to the flat at night; he had no friends intimate enough to drop in without warning. The summons was an imperious banging that did not pause and clearly would not stop until the door was opened.

She stood in the open bathroom doorway gazing at him across the passage into the living-room; her bare feet and shoulders were free of a big bath-towel. She said nothing, did not even whisper. The flat seemed to shake with the strong unhurried blows.

He made as if to go to the door, at last, but now she ran and clutched him by both arms. She shook her head wildly; her lips drew back but her teeth were clenched, she didn't speak. She pulled him into the bedroom, snatched some clothes from the clean laundry laid out on the bed and got into the wall-cupboard, thrusting the key at his hand. Although his arms and calves felt weakly cold he was horrified, distastefully embarrassed at the sight of her pressed back crouching there under his suits and coat; it was horrible and ridiculous. *Come out!* he whispered. *No! Come out!* She hissed: *Where? Where can I go?*

Never mind! Get out of there!

He put out his hand to grasp her. At bay, she said with all the force of her terrible whisper, baring the gap in her teeth: *I'll throw myself out the window.*

She forced the key into his hand like the handle of a knife. He closed the door on her face and drove the key home in the lock, then dropped it among his coins in his trouser pocket.

He unslotted the chain that was looped across the flat door. He turned the serrated knob of the Yale lock. The three policemen, two in plain clothes, stood there without impatience although they had been banging on the door for several minutes.

The big dark one with an elaborate moustache held out in a hand wearing a plaited gilt ring some sort of identity card.

Dr von Leinsdorf said quietly, the blood coming strangely back to legs and arms, 'What is it?'

The sergeant told him they knew there was a coloured girl in the flat. They had had information; 'I been watching this flat three months, I know.'

'I am alone here.' Dr von Leinsdorf did not raise his voice.

'I know, I know who is here. Come — ' And the sergeant and his two assistants went into the living-room, the kitchen, the bathroom (the sergeant picked up a bottle of after-shave cologne, seemed to study the French label) and the bedroom. The assistants removed the clean laundry that was laid upon the bed and then turned back the bedding, carrying the sheets over to be examined by the sergeant under the lamp. They talked to one another in Afrikaans, which the Doctor did not understand. The sergeant himself looked under the bed, and lifted the long curtains at the window. The wall cupboard was of the kind that has no knobs; he saw that it was locked and began to ask in Afrikaans, then politely changed to English, 'Give us the key.'

Dr von Leinsdorf said, 'I'm sorry, I left it at my office — I always lock and take my keys with me in the mornings.'

'It's no good, man, you better give me the key.'

He smiled a little, reasonably. 'It's on my office desk.'

The assistants produced a screwdriver and he watched while they inserted it where the cupboard doors met, gave it quick, firm but not forceful leverage. He heard the lock give.

She had been naked, it was true, when they knocked. But now she was wearing a long-sleeved T-shirt with an appliquéd butterfly motif on one breast, and a pair of jeans. Her feet were still bare; she had managed, by feel, in the dark, to get into some of the clothing she had snatched from the bed, but she had no shoes. She had perhaps been weeping behind the cupboard door (her cheeks looked stained) but now her face was sullen and she was breathing heavily, her diaphragm contracting and expanding exaggeratedly and her breasts pushing against the cloth. It made her appear angry; it might simply have been that she was half-suffocated in the cupboard and needed oxygen. She did not look at Dr von Leinsdorf. She would not reply to the sergeant's questions.

They were taken to the police station where they were at once separated and in turn led for examination by the district surgeon. The man's underwear was taken away and examined, as the sheets had been, for signs of his seed. When the girl was undressed, it was discovered that beneath her jeans she was wearing a pair of men's briefs with his name on the neatly-sewn laundry tag; in her haste, she had taken the wrong garment to her hiding-place.

Now she cried, standing there before the district surgeon in a man's underwear.

He courteously pretended not to notice. He handed briefs, jeans and T-shirt round the door, and motioned her to lie on a white-sheeted high table where he placed her legs apart, resting in stirrups, and put into her where the other had made his way so warmly a cold hard instrument that expanded wider and wider. Her thighs and knees trembled uncontrollably while the doctor looked into her and touched her deep inside with more hard instruments, carrying wafers of gauze.

When she came out of the examining room back to the charge office, Dr von Leinsdorf was not there; they must have taken him somewhere else. She spent what was left of the night in a cell, as he must be doing; but early in the morning she was released and taken home to her mother's house in the coloured township by a white man who explained he was the clerk of the lawyer who had been engaged for her by Dr von Leinsdorf. Dr von Leinsdorf, the clerk said, had also been bailed out that morning. He did not say when, or if she would see him again.

A statement made by the girl to the police was handed in to Court when she and the man appeared to meet charges of contravening the Immorality Act in a Johannesburg flat on the night of—December, 19—. *I lived with the white man in his flat. He had intercourse with me sometimes. He gave me tablets to take to prevent me becoming pregnant.*

Interviewed by the Sunday papers, the girl said, 'I'm sorry for the sadness brought to my mother.' She said she was one of nine children of a female laundry worker. She had left school in Standard Three because there was no money at home for gym clothes or a school blazer. She had worked as a machinist in a factory and a cashier in a supermarket. Dr von Leinsdorf taught her to type his notes.

Dr Franz-Josef von Leinsdorf, described as the grandson of a baroness, a cultured man engaged in international mineralogical research, said he accepted social distinctions between people but didn't think they should be legally imposed. 'Even in my own country it's difficult for a person from a higher class to marry one from a lower class.'

The two accused gave no evidence. They did not greet or speak to each other in Court. The Defense argued that the sergeant's evidence that they had been living together as man and wife was hearsay. (The woman with the dachshund, the care-taker?) The magistrate acquitted them because the State failed to prove carnal inter-course had taken place on the night of—December, 19—.

The girl's mother was quoted, with photograph, in the Sunday papers: 'I won't let my daughter work as a servant for a white man again.'

Two

The farm children play together when they are small; but once the white children go away to school they soon don't play together any more, even in the holidays. Although most of the black children get some sort of schooling, they drop every year farther behind the grades passed by the white children; the childish vocabulary, the child's exploration of the adventurous possibilities of dam, koppies,[4] mealie lands[5] and veld—there comes a time when the white children have surpassed these with the vocabulary of boarding-school and the possibilities of inter-school

---

[4]Small hills.
[5]Cornfields.

sports matches and the kind of adventures seen at the cinema. This usefully coincides with the age of twelve or thirteen; so that by the time early adolescence is reached, the black children are making, along with the bodily changes common to all, an easy transition to adult forms of address, beginning to call their old playmates *missus* and *baasie* — little master.

The trouble was Paulus Eysendyck did not seem to realize that Thebedi was now simply one of the crowd of farm children down at the kraal,[6] recognizable in his sisters' old clothes. The first Christmas holidays after he had gone to boarding-school he brought home for Thebedi a painted box he had made in his wood-work class. He had to give it to her secretly because he had nothing for the other children at the kraal. And she gave him, before he went back to school, a bracelet she had made of thin brass wire and the grey-and-white beans of the castor-oil crop his father cultivated. (When they used to play together, she was the one who had taught Paulus how to make clay oxen for their toy spans.)[7] There was a craze, even in the *platteland*[8] towns like the one where he was at school, for boys to wear elephant-hair and other bracelets beside their watch-straps; his was admired, friends asked him to get similar ones for them. He said the natives made them on his father's farm and he would try.

When he was fifteen, six feet tall, and tramping round at school dances with the girls from the 'sister' school in the same town; when he had learnt how to tease and flirt and fondle quite intimately these girls who were the daughters of prosperous farmers like his father; when he had even met one who, at a wedding he had attended with his parents on a nearby farm, had let him do with her in a locked storeroom what people did when they made love — when he was as far from his childhood as all this, he still brought home from a shop in town a red plastic belt and gilt hoop ear-rings for the black girl, Thebedi. She told her father the missus had given these to her as a reward for some work she had done — it was true she sometimes was called to help out in the farmhouse. She told the girls in the kraal that she had a sweetheart nobody knew about, far away, away on another farm, and they giggled, and teased, and admired her. There was a boy in the kraal called Njabulo who said he wished he could have bought her a belt and ear-rings.

When the farmer's son was home for the holidays she wandered far from the kraal and her companions. He went for walks alone. They had not arranged this; it was an urge each followed independently. He knew it was she, from a long way off. She knew that his dog would not bark at her. Down at the dried-up river-bed where five or six years ago the children had caught a leguaan one great day — a creature that combined ideally the size and ferocious aspect of the crocodile with the harmlessness of the lizard — they squatted side by side on the earth bank. He told her traveller's tales: about school, about the punishments at school, particularly, exaggerating both their nature and his indifference to them. He told her about the town of Middleburg, which she had never seen. She had nothing to tell but she prompted with many questions, like any good listener. While he talked he twisted and tugged at the roots of white stinkwood and Cape willow trees that looped out of the eroded earth around them. It

---

[6]A village of South African natives, usually surrounded by a stockage or the like.
[7]Harnesses for pairs of animals.
[8]Countryside.

had always been a good spot for children's games, down there hidden by the mesh of old, ant-eaten trees held in place by vigorous ones, wild asparagus bushing up between the trunks, and here and there prickly-pear cactus sunken-skinned and bristly, like an old man's face, keeping alive sapless until the next rainy season. She punctured the dry hide of a prickly-pear again and again with a sharp stick while she listened. She laughed a lot at what he told her, sometimes dropping her face on her knees, sharing amusement with the cool shady earth beneath her bare feet. She put on her pair of shoes — white sandals, thickly Blanco-ed against the farm dust — when he was on the farm, but these were taken off and laid aside, at the river-bed.

One summer afternoon when there was water flowing there and it was very hot she waded in as they used to do when they were children, her dress bunched modestly and tucked into the legs of her pants. The schoolgirls he went swimming with at dams or pools on neighbouring farms wore bikinis but the sight of their dazzling bellies and thighs in the sunlight had never made him feel what he felt now, when the girl came up the bank and sat beside him, the drops of water beading off her dark legs the only points of light in the earth-smelling, deep shade. They were not afraid of one another, they had known one another always; he did with her what he had done that time in the storeroom at the wedding, and this time it was so lovely, so lovely, he was surprised . . . and she was surprised by it, too — he could see in her dark face that was part of the shade, with her big dark eyes, shiny as soft water, watching him attentively: as she had when they used to huddle over their teams of mud oxen, as she had when he told her about detention weekends at school.

They went to the river-bed often through those summer holidays. They met just before the light went, as it does quite quickly, and each returned home with the dark — she to her mother's hut, he to the farmhouse — in time for the evening meal. He did not tell her about school or town any more. She did not ask questions any longer. He told her, each time, when they would meet again. Once or twice it was very early in the morning; the lowing of the cows being driven to graze came to them where they lay, dividing them with unspoken recognition of the sound read in their two pairs of eyes, opening so close to each other.

He was a popular boy at school. He was in the second, then the first soccer team. The head girl of the 'sister' school was said to have a crush on him; he didn't particularly like her, but there was a pretty blonde who put up her long hair into a kind of doughnut with a black ribbon round it, whom he took to see films when the schoolboys and girls had a free Saturday afternoon. He had been driving tractors and other farm vehicles since he was ten years old, and as soon as he was eighteen he got a driver's licence and in the holidays, this last year of his school life, he took neighbours' daughters to dances and to the drive-in cinema that had just opened twenty kilometres from the farm. His sisters were married, by then; his parents often left him in charge of the farm over the weekend while they visited the young wives and grandchildren.

When Thebedi saw the farmer and his wife drive away on a Saturday afternoon, the boot of their Mercedes filled with fresh-killed poultry and vegetables from the garden that it was part of her father's work to tend, she knew that she must come not to the river-bed but up to the house. The house was an old one, thick-walled, dark against the heat. The kitchen was its lively thoroughfare, with servants, food supplies, begging cats and dogs, pots boiling over, washing being damped for ironing, and the big deep-freeze the missus had ordered from town, bearing a crocheted mat and a vase of plastic irises. But the dining-room with the bulging-legged heavy table was shut up in its rich, old smell of soup and tomato sauce. The sitting-room curtains were drawn and the T.V. set silent. The door of the parents' bedroom was locked and the empty rooms where the girls had slept had sheets of plastic spread over the beds. It was in one of these that she and the farmer's son stayed together whole nights — almost: she had to get away before the house servants, who knew her, came in at dawn. There was a risk someone would discover her or traces of her presence if he took her to his own bedroom, although she had looked into it many times when she was helping out in the house and knew well, there, the row of silver cups he had won at school.

When she was eighteen and the farmer's son nineteen and working with his father on the farm before entering a veterinary college, the young man Njabulo asked her father for her. Njabulo's parents met with hers and the money he was to pay in place of the cows it is customary to give a prospective bride's parents was settled upon. He had no cows to offer; he was a labourer on the Eysendyck farm, like her father. A bright youngster; old Eysendyck had taught him brick-laying and was using him for odd jobs in construction, around the place. She did not tell the farmer's son that her parents had arranged for her to marry. She did not tell him, either, before he left for his first term at the veterinary college, that she thought she was going to have a baby. Two months after her marriage to Njabulo, she gave birth to a daughter. There was no disgrace in that; among her people it is customary for a young man to make sure, before marriage, that the chosen girl is not barren, and Njabulo had made love to her then. But the infant was very light and did not quickly grow darker as most African babies do. Already at birth there was on its head a quantity of straight, fine floss, like that which carries the seeds of certain weeds in the veld. The unfocused eyes it opened were gray flecked with yellow. Njabulo was the matt, opaque coffee-grounds colour that has always been called black; the colour of Thebedi's legs on which beaded water looked oyster-shell blue, the same colour as Thebedi's face, where the black eyes, with their interested gaze and clear whites, were so dominant.

Njabulo made no complaint. Out of his farm labourer's earnings he bought from the Indian store a cellophane-windowed pack containing a pink plastic bath, six napkins, a card of safety pins, a knitted jacket, cap and bootees, a dress, and a tin of Johnson's Baby Powder, for Thebedi's baby.

When it was two weeks old Paulus Eysendyck arrived home from the veterinary college for the holidays. He drank a glass of fresh, still-warm milk in the childhood familiarity of his mother's kitchen and heard her discussing with the old house-servant where they could get a reliable substitute to help out now that the girl Thebedi had had a baby. For the first time since he was a small boy he came right into the kraal. It was eleven o'clock in the morning. The men were at work in the lands. He looked about him, urgently; the women turned away, each not wanting to be the one approached to point out where Thebedi lived. Thebedi appeared, coming slowly from the hut Njabulo had built in white man's style, with a tin chimney, and a proper window with glass panes set in straight as walls made of unfired bricks would allow. She greeted him with hands brought together and a token movement representing the respectful bob with which she was accustomed to acknowledge she was in the presence of his father or mother. He lowered his head under the doorway of her home and went in. He said, 'I want to see. Show me.'

She had taken the bundle off her back before she came out into the light to face him. She moved between the iron bedstead made up with Njabulo's checked blankets and the small wooden table where the pink plastic bath stood among food and kitchen pots, and picked up the bundle from the snugly-blanketed grocer's box where it lay. The infant was asleep; she revealed the closed, pale, plump tiny face, with a bubble of spit at the corner of the mouth, the spidery pink hands stirring. She took off the woollen cap and the straight fine hair flew up after it in static electricity, showing gilded strands here and there. He said nothing. She was watching him as she had done when they were little, and the gang of children had trodden down a crop in their games or transgressed in some other way for which he, as the farmer's son, the white one among them, must intercede with the farmer. She disturbed the sleeping face by scratching or tickling gently at a cheek with one finger, and slowly the eyes opened, saw nothing, were still asleep, and then, awake, no longer narrowed, looked out at them, grey with yellowish flecks, his own hazel eyes.

He struggled for a moment with a grimace of tears, anger and self-pity. She could not put out her hand to him. He said, 'You haven't been near the house with it?'

She shook her head.

'Never?'

Again she shook her head.

'Don't take it out. Stay inside. Can't you take it away somewhere. You must give it to someone—'

She moved to the door with him.

He said, 'I'll see what I will do. I don't know.' And then he said: 'I feel like killing myself.'

Her eyes began to glow, to thicken with tears. For a moment there was the feeling between them that used to come when they were alone down at the river-bed.

He walked out.

Two days later, when his mother and father had left the farm for the day, he appeared again. The women were away on the lands, weeding, as they were employed to do as casual labour in summer; only the very old remained, propped up on the ground outside the huts in the flies and the sun. Thebedi did not ask him in. The child had not been well; it had diarrhoea. He asked where its food was. She said, 'The milk comes from me.' He went into Njabulo's house, where the child lay; she did not follow but stayed outside the door and watched without seeing an old crone who had lost her mind, talking to herself, talking to the fowls who ignored her.

She thought she heard small grunts from the hut, the kind of infant grunt that indicates a full stomach, a deep sleep. After a time, long or short she did not know, he came out and walked away with plodding stride (his father's gait) out of sight, towards his father's house.

The baby was not fed during the night and although she kept telling Njabulo it was sleeping, he saw for himself in the morning that it was dead. He comforted her with words and caresses. She did not cry but simply sat, staring at the door. Her hands were cold as dead chickens' feet to his touch.

Njabulo buried the little baby where farm workers were buried, in the place in the veld the farmer had given them. Some of the mounds had been left to weather away unmarked, others were covered with stones and a few had fallen wooden crosses. He was going to make a cross but before it was finished the police came and dug up the grave and took away the dead baby: someone — one of the other labourers? their women? — had reported that the baby was almost white, that, strong and healthy, it had died suddenly after a visit by the farmer's son. Pathological tests on the infant corpse showed intestinal damage not always consistent with death by natural causes.

Thebedi went for the first time to the country town where Paulus had been to school, to give evidence at the preparatory examination into the charge of murder brought against him. She cried hysterically in the witness box, saying yes, yes (the gilt hoop ear-rings swung in her ears), she saw the accused pouring liquid into the baby's mouth. She said he had threatened to shoot her if she told anyone.

More than a year went by before, in that same town, the case was brought to trial. She came to Court with a new-born baby on her back. She wore gilt hoop ear-rings; she was calm; she said she had not seen what the white man did in the house.

Paulus Eysendyck said he had visited the hut but had not poisoned the child.

The Defence did not contest that there had been a love relationship between the accused and the girl, or that intercourse had taken place, but submitted there was no proof that the child was the accused's.

The judge told the accused there was strong suspicion against him but not enough proof that he had committed the crime. The Court could not accept the girl's evidence because it was clear she had committed perjury either at his trial or at the preparatory examination. There was the suggestion in the mind of the Court that she might be an accomplice in the crime; but, again, insufficient proof.

The judge commended the honourable behaviour of the husband (sitting in court in a brown-and-yellow-quartered golf cap bought for Sundays) who had not rejected his wife and had 'even provided clothes for the unfortunate infant out of his slender means.'

The verdict on the accused was 'not guilty.'

The young white man refused to accept the congratulations of press and public and left the Court with his mother's raincoat shielding his face from photographers. His father said to the press, 'I will try and carry on as best I can to hold up my head in the district.'

Interviewed by the Sunday papers, who spelled her name in a variety of ways, the black girl, speaking in her own language, was quoted beneath her photograph: 'It was a thing of our childhood, we don't see each other any more.'

(1980)

QUESTIONS

1. Untagged sentences may often be interpreted in more than one way. When the short story says, on page 162, "It was no trouble for her . . ." how would you interpret that statement if it is the narrator's judgment? Dr. von Leinsdorf's? The unnamed woman's?

2. What does the short story imply will happen to the first two lovers? To the second two lovers?

3. Whose filter seems to be represented at the end of the first part of the short story? The second part? Why?

4. What sorts of relationships are being described in this story? How are the relationships affected by each protagonist's cultural background? Their different economic status? The apartheid system? Why are the two stories combined?

5. How does the (implied) author want you to judge the events and characters? Would a purely aesthetic response be appropriate or must it include some social judgment?

❖ V. S. NAIPAUL
The Thing Without a Name

V. S. Naipaul (1932–) was born Vidiadhar Surajprasad Naipaul in Trinidad. He attended Queen's Royal College in Trinidad and then University College, Oxford. He did free-lance broadcasting for a number of years on the BBC. His novels include *The Mystic Masseur* (1957), *Mr. Stone and the Knights Companion* (1963), *The Mimic Men* (1967), *A House for Mr. Biswas* (1969), *Guerrillas* (1977), *A Bend in the River* (1980), *The Suffrage of Elvira* (1981), and *The Enigma of Arrival* (1987). *Miguel Street* (1971), from which "The Thing Without a Name" is taken, is variously described as a novella and a unified short story collection. Naipaul is very much engaged in political discussion, especially on topics concerning the Third World. His nonfiction includes *In a Free State* (1978) and *Among the Believers* (1981).

The only thing that Popo, who called himself a carpenter, ever built was the little galvanised-iron workshop under the mango tree at the back of his yard. And even that he didn't quite finish. He couldn't be bothered to nail on the sheets of galvanised-iron for the roof, and kept them weighted down with huge stones. Whenever there was a high wind the roof made a frightening banging noise and seemed ready to fly away.

And yet Popo was never idle. He was always busy hammering and sawing and planning. I liked watching him work. I liked the smell of the woods — cyp and cedar and crapaud. I liked the colour of the shavings, and I liked the way the sawdust powdered Popo's kinky hair.

'What you making, Mr Popo?' I asked.

Popo would always say, 'Ha, boy! That's the question. I making the thing without a name.'

I liked Popo for that. I thought he was a poetic man.

One day I said to Popo, 'Give me something to make.'

'What you want to make?' he said.

It was hard to think of something I really wanted.

'You see,' Popo said. 'You thinking about the thing without a name.'

Eventually I decided on an egg-stand.

'Who you making it for?' Popo asked.

'Ma.'

He laughed. 'Think she going to use it?'

My mother was pleased with the egg-stand, and used it for about a week. Then she seemed to forget all about it; and began putting the eggs in bowls or plates, just as she did before.

And Popo laughed when I told him. He said, 'Boy, the only thing to make is the thing without a name.'

174

After I painted the tailoring sign for Bogart, Popo made me do one for him as well.

He took the little red stump of a pencil he had stuck over his ear and puzzled over the words. At first he wanted to announce himself as an architect; but I managed to dissuade him. He wasn't sure about the spelling. The finished sign said:

BUILDER AND CONTRACTOR
Carpenter
And Cabinet-Maker

And I signed my name, as sign-writer, in the bottom right-hand corner.

Popo liked standing up in front of the sign. But he had a little panic when people who didn't know about him came to inquire.

'The carpenter fellow?' Popo would say. 'He don't live here again.'

I thought Popo was a much nicer man than Bogart. Bogart said little to me; but Popo was always ready to talk. He talked about serious things, like life and death and work, and I felt he really liked talking to me.

Yet Popo was not a popular man in the street. They didn't think he was mad or stupid. Hat used to say, 'Popo too conceited, you hear.'

It was an unreasonable thing to say. Popo had the habit of taking a glass of rum to the pavement every morning. He never sipped the rum. But whenever he saw someone he knew he dipped his middle finger in the rum, licked it, and then waved to the man.

'We could buy rum too,' Hat used to say. 'But we don't show off like Popo.'

I myself never thought about it in that way, and one day I asked Popo about it.

Popo said, 'Boy, in the morning, when the sun shining and it still cool, and you just get up, it make you feel good to know that you could go out and stand up in the sun and have some rum.'

Popo never made any money. His wife used to go out and work, and this was easy, because they had no children. Popo said, 'Women and them like work. Man not make for work.'

Hat said, 'Popo is a man-woman. Not a proper man.'

Popo's wife had a job as a cook in a big house near my school. She used to wait for me in the afternoons and take me into the big kitchen and give me a lot of nice things to eat. The only thing I didn't like was the way she sat and watched me while I ate. It was as though I was eating for her. She asked me to call her Auntie.

She introduced me to the gardener of the big house. He was a good-looking brown man, and he loved his flowers. I liked the gardens he looked after. The flower-beds were always black and wet; and the grass green and damp and always cut. Sometimes he let me water the flower-beds. And he used to gather the cut grass into little bags which he gave me to take home to my mother. Grass was good for the hens.

One day I missed Popo's wife. She wasn't waiting for me.

Next morning I didn't see Popo dipping his finger in the glass of rum on the pavement.

And that evening I didn't see Popo's wife.

I found Popo sad in his workshop. He was sitting on a plank and twisting a bit of shaving around his fingers.

Popo said, 'Your auntie gone, boy.'

'Where, Mr Popo?'

'Ha, boy! That's the question,' and he pulled himself up there.

Popo found himself then a popular man. The news got around very quickly. And when Eddoes said one day, 'I wonder what happen to Popo. Like he got no more rum,' Hat jumped up and almost cuffed him. And then all the men began to gather in Popo's workshop, and they would talk about cricket and football and pictures — everything except women — just to try to cheer Popo up.

Popo's workshop no longer sounded with hammering and sawing. The sawdust no longer smelled fresh, and became black, almost like dirt. Popo began drinking a lot, and I didn't like him when he was drunk. He smelled of rum, and he used to cry and then grow angry and want to beat up everybody. That made him an accepted member of the gang.

Hat said, 'We was wrong about Popo. He is a man, like any of we.'

Popo liked the new companionship. He was at heart a loquacious man, and always wanted to be friendly with the men of the street and he was always surprised that he was not liked. So it looked as though he had got what he wanted. But Popo was not really happy. The friendship had come a little too late, and he found he didn't like it as much as he'd expected. Hat tried to get Popo interested in other women, but Popo wasn't interested.

Popo didn't think I was too young to be told anything.

'Boy, when you grow old as me,' he said once, 'you find that you don't care for the things you thought you woulda like if you coulda afford them.'

That was his way of talking, in riddles.

Then one day Popo left us.

Hat said, 'He don't have to tell me where he gone. He gone looking for he wife.'

Edward said, 'Think she going come back with he?'

Hat said, 'Let we wait and see.'

We didn't have to wait long. It came out in the papers. Hat said it was just what he expected. Popo had beaten up a man in Arima, the man had taken his wife away. It was the gardener who used to give me bags of grass.

Nothing much happened to Popo. He had to pay a fine, but they let him off otherwise. The magistrate said that Popo had better not molest his wife again.

They made a calypso about Popo that was the rage that year. It was the road-march for the Carnival, and the Andrews Sisters sang it for an American recording company:

> A certain carpenter feller went to Arima
> Looking for a mopsy called Emelda.

It was a great thing for the street.

At school, I used to say, 'The carpenter feller was a good, good friend of mine.'

And, at cricket matches, and at the races, Hat used to say, 'Know him? God, I used to drink with that man night and day. Boy, he could carry his liquor.'

Popo wasn't the same man when he came back to us. He growled at me when I tried to talk to him, and he drove out Hat and the others when they brought a bottle of rum to the workshop.

Hat said, 'Woman send that man mad, you hear.'

But the old noises began to be heard once more from Popo's workshop. He was working hard, and I wondered whether he was still making the thing without a name. But I was too afraid to ask.

He ran an electric light to the workshop and began working in the night-time. Vans stopped outside his house and were always depositing and taking away things. Then Popo began painting his house. He used a bright green, and he painted the roof a bright red. Hat said, 'The man really mad.'

And added, 'Like he getting married again.'

Hat wasn't too far wrong. One day, about two weeks later, Popo returned, and he brought a woman with him. It was his wife. My auntie.

'You see the sort of thing woman is,' Hat commented. 'You see the sort of thing they like. Not the man. But the new house paint up, and all the new furniture inside it. I bet you if the man in Arima had a new house and new furnitures, she wouldnta come back with Popo.'

But I didn't mind. I was glad. It was good to see Popo standing outside with his glass of rum in the mornings and dipping his finger into the rum and waving at his friends; and it was good to ask him again, 'What you making, Mr Popo?' and to get the old answer, 'Ha, boy! That's the question. I making the thing without a name.'

Popo returned very quickly to his old way of living, and he was still devoting his time to making the thing without a name. He had stopped working, and his wife got her job with the same people near my school.

People in the street were almost angry with Popo when his wife came back. They felt that all their sympathy had been mocked and wasted. And again Hat was saying, 'That blasted Popo too conceited, you here.'

But this time Popo didn't mind.

He used to tell me, 'Boy, go home and pray tonight that you get happy like me.'

What happened afterwards happened so suddenly that we didn't even know it had happened. Even Hat didn't know about it until he read it in the papers. Hat always read the papers. He read them from about ten in the morning until about six in the evening.

Hat shouted out, 'But what is this I seeing?' and he showed us the headlines: CALYPSO CARPENTER JAILED.

It was a fantastic story. Popo had been stealing things left and right. All the new furnitures, as Hat called them, hadn't been made by Popo. He had stolen things and simply remodelled them. He had stolen too much as a matter of fact, and had had to sell the things he didn't want. That was how he had been caught. And we understand now why the vans were always outside Popo's house. Even the paint and the brushes with which he had redecorated the house had been stolen.

Hat spoke for all of us when he said, 'That man too foolish. Why he had to sell what he thief? Just tell me that. Why?'

We agreed it was a stupid thing to do. But we felt deep inside ourselves that Popo was really a man, perhaps a bigger man than any of us.

And as for my auntie . . .

Hat said, 'How much jail he get? A year? With three months off for good behaviour, that's nine months in all. And I give she three months good behaviour too. And after that, it ain't going have no more Emelda in Miguel Street, you hear.'

But Emelda never left Miguel Street. She not only kept her job as cook, but she started taking in washing and ironing as well. No one in the street felt sorry that Popo had gone to jail because of the shame; after all that was a thing that could happen to any of us. They felt sorry only that Emelda was going to be left alone for so long.

He came back as a hero. He was one of the boys. He was a better man than either Hat or Bogart.

But for me, he had changed. And the change made me sad.

For Popo began working.

He began making morris chairs and tables and wardrobes for people.

And when I asked him, 'Mr Popo, when you going start making the thing without a name again?' he growled at me.

'You too troublesome,' he said. 'Go away quick, before I lay my hand on you.

(1959)

QUESTIONS

1. The narrator of this story does not begin by describing the Caribbean setting or spend much time explaining the characters' actions and relationships. Does the physical and cultural setting come through? How?

2. The characters speak a language that is a little different from standard North American or British English. How does it differ? Why doesn't the narrator tell the story in the same dialect that the characters speak?

3. How do the neighbors respond to the changes in Popo's situation and behavior? Did you react the same way? Does the narrator?

4. Is there a difference between the ''I'' who is a character in the story and the ''I'' who is telling it? Which one is the screen (filter or slant) through which the story reaches us? Why?

5. This short story presents a complex cultural situation. The real author's ancestors were from India; he grew up in Trinidad; he lives in England and writes for a primarily British audience; you who are reading the story are most likely American. How do these various cultural facets contribute to the short story's impact?

❖ MARY McCARTHY

C.Y.E.

Mary McCarthy (1912–1989) was born in Seattle, Washington, and became an orphan at six. She was first put in the care of relatives who mistreated her (see her autobiographical *Memories of a Catholic Girlhood*, 1957) but then raised by sympathetic grandparents. She was educated at Vassar College (see *How I Grew*, 1987). Graduating in 1933, she went to New York where she wrote essays and reviews, especially on the theater, for liberal publications. She was also an editor of the *Partisan Review*. For a time she was married to the noted critic and author Edmund Wilson, who was the first to encourage her to write fiction. She also taught courses at Bard College and Sarah Lawrence College. McCarthy's novels include *The Company She Keeps* (1942), *The Oasis* (1949), *The Groves of Academe* (1952), *A Charmed Life* (1955), *The Group*, her best-selling novel (1963), *Birds of America* (1971), and *Cannibals and Missionaries* (1979). She published the short story collection *Cast a Cold Eye* in 1950, which includes "C.Y.E." This volume was reprinted in expanded form under the title *The Hounds of Summer* in 1981. McCarthy wrote much nonfiction, in particular autobiography, reportage, travel sketches, and art and literary criticism. Especially spirited were her writings against the Vietnam War and the Watergate scandal.

Near the corner of Fourteenth Street and Fourth Avenue, there is a store called Cye Bernard. I passed it the other day on my way to the Union Square[1] subway station. To my intense surprise, a heavy blush spread over my face and neck, and my insides contorted in that terrible grimace of shame that is generally associated with hangovers. I averted my eyes from the sign and hurried into the subway, my head bent so that no observer should discover my secret identity, which until that moment I had forgotten myself. Now I pass this sign every day, and it is always a question whether I shall look at it or not. Usually I do, but hastily, surreptitiously, with an ineffective air of casualness, lest anybody suspect that I am crucified there on that building, hanging exposed in black script lettering to advertise bargains in men's haberdashery.

The strangest part about it is that this unknown clothier on Fourteenth Street should not only incorporate in his name the mysterious, queerly spelled nickname I was given as a child in the convent, but that he should add to this the name of my patron saint, St. Bernard of Clairvaux,[2] whom I chose for my special protector at a time when I was suffering from the nickname. It is nearly enough to convince me that life is a system of recurrent pairs, the poison and the antidote being externally packaged

---

[1]A square in New York City.

[2]French monk, preacher, and mystical writer (1090–1153).

together by some considerate heavenly druggist. St. Bernard, however, was, from my point of view, never so useful as the dog that bears his name, except in so far as he represented the contemplative, bookish element in the heavenly hierarchy, as opposed, say, to St. Martin of Tours, St. Francis Xavier or St. Aloysius of Gonzaga,[3] who was of an ineffable purity and died young. The life of action was repellent to St. Bernard, though he engaged in it from time to time; on the other hand, he was not a true *exalté*[4] — he was, in short, a secondary man, and it was felt, in the convent, I think, that he was a rather odd choice for an eleven-year-old girl, the nuns themselves expressing some faint bewilderment and concern, as older people do when a child is presented with a great array of toys and selects from among them a homely and useful object.

It was marvelous, I said to myself that day on the subway, that I could have forgotten so easily. In the official version of my life the nickname does not appear. People have asked me, now and then, whether I have ever had a nickname and I have always replied, No, it is funny but I do not seem to be the type that gets one. I have even wondered about it a little myself, asking, Why is it that I have always been Mary, world without end, Amen, feeling a faint pinch of regret and privation, as though a cake had been cut and no favor, not even the old maid's thimble or the miser's penny, been found in my piece. How political indeed is the personality, I thought. What coalitions and cabals the party in power will not make to maintain its uncertain authority! Nothing is sacred. The past is manipulated to serve the interests of the present. For any bureaucracy, amnesia is convenient. The name of Trotsky[5] drops out of the chapter on the revolution in the Soviet textbooks — what shamelessness, we say, while in the meantime our discarded selves languish in the Lubianka[6] of the unconscious. But a moment comes at last, after the régime has fallen, after all interested parties are dead, when the archives are opened and the old ghosts walk, and history must be rewritten in the light of fresh discoveries.

It was happening to me then, as I sat frozen in my seat, staring at the picture of Miss Subways, February 1943, who loves New York and spends her spare time writing to her two officer-brothers in the Army and Navy. The heavy doors of the mind swung on their hinges. I was back in the convent, a pale new girl sitting in the front of the study hall next to a pretty, popular eighth-grader, whom I bored and who resented having me for a deskmate. I see myself perfectly: I am ambitious, I wish to make friends with the most exciting and powerful girls; at the same time, I am naive, without stratagems, for I think that I have only to be myself. The first rebuffs startle me. I look around and see that there is a social pyramid here and that I and my classmates are on the bottom. I study the disposition of stresses and strains and discover that two girls, Elinor Henehan and Mary Heinrichs, are important, and that their approval is essential to my happiness.

There were a great many exquisite and fashionable-looking girls in the

---

[3]Saints who lived more active lives than St. Bernard.
[4]An exalted person (French).
[5]Leon Trotsky, one of the original leaders of the Russian Revolution who fell out of favor, was exiled and ultimately assassinated by Stalin's agents.
[6]Russian prison camp.

convent, girls with Irish or German names, who used make-up in secret, had suitors, and always seemed to be on the verge of a romantic elopement. There were also some very pretty Protestant girls, whose personal charms were enhanced for us by the exoticism of their religion — the nuns telling us that we should always be especially considerate of them because they were Protestants, and, so to speak, our guests, with the result that we treated them reverently, like French dolls. These two groups made up the élite of the convent; the nuns adored them for their beauty, just as we younger girls did; and they enjoyed far more réclame[7] than the few serious students who were thought to have the vocation.

Elinor Henehan and Mary Heinrichs fell into neither category. They were funny, lazy, dangling girls, fourteen or fifteen years old, with baritone voices, very black hair, and an insouciant attitude toward convent life. It was said that they came from east of the mountains. Elinor Henehan was tall and bony, with horn-rimmed glasses; Mary Heinrichs was shorter and plump. Their blue serge uniforms were always a mess, the collars and cuffs haphazardly sewn on and worn a day or so after they ought to have been sent to the laundry. They broke rules constantly, talking in study hall, giggling in chapel.

Yet out of these unpromising personal materials, they had created a unique position for themselves. They were the school clowns. And like all clowns they had made a shrewd bargain with life, exchanging dignity for power, and buying with servility to their betters immunity from the reprisals of their equals or inferiors. For the upper school they travestied themselves, exaggerating their own odd physical characteristics, their laziness, their eccentric manner of talking. With the lower school, it was another story: we were the performers, the school the audience, they the privileged commentators from the royal box. Now it was our foibles, our vanities, our mannerisms that were on display, and the spectacle was apparently so hilarious that it was a continual challenge to the two girls' self-control. They lived in a recurrent spasm of mirth. On the playground, at the dinner-table, laughter would dangerously overtake them; one would whisper to the other and then a wordless rocking would begin, till finally faint anguished screams were heard, and the nun in charge clapped her clapper for silence.

What was unnerving about this laughter — unnerving especially for the younger girls — was its general, almost abstract character. More often than not, we had no idea what it was that Elinor and Mary were laughing at. A public performance of any sort — a recital, a school play — instantly reduced them to jelly. Yet what was there about somebody's humble and pedestrian performance of *The Merry Peasant* that was so uniquely comic? Nobody could tell, least of all the performer. To be the butt of this kind of joke was a singularly painful experience, for you were never in a position to turn the tables, to join in the laughter at your own expense, because you could not possibly pretend to know what the joke was. Actually, as I see now, it was the intimacy of the two girls that set their standard: from the vantage point of their private world, anything outside seemed strange and ludicrous. It was our very existence they laughed at, as the peasant laughs at the stranger from another province. The occasions of mirth — a request for the salt, a trip to the dictionary in the study hall — were mere

---

[7]Fame (French).

pretexts; our personalities *in themselves* were incredible to them. At the time, however, it was very confusing. Their laughter was a kind of crazy compass that was steering the school. Nobody knew, ever, where the whirling needle would stop, and many of us lived in a state of constant apprehension, lest it should point to *our* desk, lest we become, if only briefly, the personification of all that was absurd, the First Cause of this cosmic mirth.

Like all such inseparable friends, they delighted in nicknames, bestowing them in godlike fashion, as though by renaming their creatures they could perform a new act of creation, a secular baptism. And as at the baptismal font we had passed from being our parents' children to being God's children, so now we passed from God's estate to a societal trolls' world presided over by these two unpredictable deities. They did not give nicknames to everybody. You had to have some special quality to be singled out by Elinor and Mary, but what that quality was only Elinor and Mary could tell. I saw very soon (the beginnings of wisdom) that I had two chances of finding an honorable place in the convent system: one was to escape being nicknamed altogether, the other was to earn for myself an appellation that, while humorous, was still benevolent; rough, perhaps, but tender. On the whole, I would have preferred the first alternative, as being less chancy. Months passed, and no notice was taken of me; my anxiety diminished; it seemed as though I might get my wish.

They broke the news to me one night after study hall. We were filing out of the large room when Elinor stepped out of the line to speak to me. "We have got one for you," she said. "Yes?" I said calmly, for really (I now saw) I had known it all along, known that there was something about me that would inevitably appeal to these two strange girls. I stiffened up in readiness, feeling myself to be a sort of archery target: there was no doubt that they could hit me (I was an easy mark), but, pray God, it be one of the larger concentric circles, not, oh Blessed Virgin, the red, tender bull's-eye at the heart. I could not have imagined what was in store for me. "Cye," said Elinor and began to laugh, looking at me oddly because I did not laugh too. "Si?" I asked, puzzled. I was a new girl, it was true, but I did not come from the country. "C-Y-E," said Elinor, spelling. "But what does it mean?" I asked the two of them, for Mary had now caught up with her. They shook their dark heads and laughed. "Oh no," they said. "We can't tell you. But it's very, very good. Isn't it?" they asked each other. "It's one of our best."

I saw at once that it was useless to question them. They would never tell me, of course, and I would only make myself ridiculous, even more Cye-like, if I persisted. It occurred to me that if I showed no anxiety, they would soon forget about it, but my shrewdness was no match for theirs. The next day it was all over the school. It was called to me on the baseball field, when the young nun was at bat; it was whispered from head to head down the long refectory table at dinner. It rang through the corridors in the dormitory. "What does it mean?" I would hear a girl ask. Elinor or Mary would whisper in her ear, and the girl would cast me a quick glance, and then laugh. Plainly, they had hit me off to a T, and as I saw this my curiosity overcame my fear and my resentment. I no longer cared how derogatory the name might be; I would stand anything, I said to myself, if only I could know it. If only I had some special friend who could find out and then tell me. But I was new and a little queer, anyway, it seemed; I had no special friends, and now it was part of the joke that the whole school should know, and know that I wanted to know and not tell me. My isolation, which had been obscure, was now conspicuous, and, as it were, axiomatic. Nobody could ever become my friend, because to do so would involve telling me and Elinor and Mary would never forgive that.

It was up to me to guess it, and I would lie in bed at night, guessing wildly, as though against time, like the miller's upstart daughter in Rumpelstiltskin. Outlandish phrases would present themselves: "Catch your elbow," "Cheat your end." Or, on the other hand, sensible ones that were humiliating: "Clean your ears." One night I got up and poured water into the china basin and washed my ears in the dark, but when I looked at the washcloth in the light the next morning, it was perfectly clean. And in any case, it seemed to me that the name must have some more profound meaning. My fault was nothing ordinary that you could do something about, like washing your ears. Plainly, it was something immanent and irremediable, a spiritual taint. And though I could not have told precisely what my wrongness consisted in, I felt its existence almost tangible during those nights, and knew that it had always been with me, even in the other school, where I had been popular, good at games, good at dramatics; I had always had it, a kind of miserable effluvium[8] of the spirit that the ordinary sieves of report cards and weekly confessions had been powerless to catch.

Now I saw that I could never, as I had hoped, belong to the convent's inner circles, not to the tier of beauty, nor to the tier of manners and good deportment, which was signalized by wide moiré[9] ribbons, awarded once a week, blue, green, or pink, depending on one's age, that were worn in a sort of bandolier style, crosswise from shoulder to hip. I could take my seat in the dowdy tier of scholarship, but my social acquaintance would be limited to a few frowzy little girls of my own age who were so insignificant, so contemptible, that they did not even know what my nickname stood for. Even they, I thought, were better off than I, for they knew their place, they accepted the fact that they were unimportant little girls. No older girl would bother to jeer at them, but in me there was something overweening, over-eager, over-intense, that had brought upon me the hateful name. Now my only desire was to be alone, and in the convent this was difficult, for the nuns believed that solitude was appropriate for anchorites,[10] but for growing girls, unhealthy. I went to the library a great deal and read all of Cooper, and *Stoddard's Lectures*.[11] I became passionately religious, made a retreat with a fiery missionary Jesuit, spent hours on my knees in adoration of the Blessed Sacrament, but even in the chapel, the name pursued me: glancing up at the cross, I would see the initials, I.N.R.I.[12]; the name that had been given Christ in mockery now mocked me, for I was not a prig and I knew that my sufferings were ignoble and had nothing whatever in common with God's. And, always, there was no avoiding the communal life, the older girls passing as I crept along the corridor with a little knot of my classmates. "Hello, Cye."

Looking back, I see that if I had ever burst into tears publicly, begged for quarter, compunction would have been felt. Some goddess of the college department

---

[8] A disagreeable vapor.
[9] Wavy like silk.
[10] Religious recluse.
[11] A series of books on travel, c. 1898–1909.
[12] Iesus Nazarenus Rex Iudaeorum, which means "Jesus of Nazareth, King of the Jews."

would have comforted me, spoken gently to Elinor and Mary, and the nickname would have been dropped. Perhaps it might even have been explained to me. But I did not cry, even alone in my room. I chose what was actually the more shameful part. I accepted the nickname, made a sort of joke of it, used it brazenly myself on the telephone, during vacations, calling up to ask a group of classmates to the movies: "This is Cye speaking." But all the time I was making plans, writing letters home, arranging my escape. I resolved that once I was out of the convent, I would never, never, never again let anybody see what I was like. That, I felt, had been my mistake.

The day I left the Mother Superior cried. "I think you will grow up to be a novelist," she said, "and that can be a fine thing, but I want you to remember all your life the training you have had here in the convent."

I was moved and thrilled by the moment, the prediction, the parting adjuration. "Yes," I said, weeping, but I intended to forget the convent within twenty-four hours. And in this I was quite successful.

The nickname followed me for a time, to the public high school I entered. One of the girls said to me, "I hear you are called Cye." "Yes," I replied easily. "How do you spell it?" she asked. "S-I," I said. "Oh," she said. "That's funny." "Yes," I said. "I don't know why they called me that." This version of the nickname lasted perhaps three weeks. At the end of that time, I dropped the group of girls who used it, and I never heard it again.

Now, however, the question has been reopened. What do the letters stand for? A happy solution occurred to me yesterday, on Fifteenth Street and Fourth Avenue. "Clever Young Egg," I said to myself out loud. The words had arranged themselves without my volition, and instantly I felt that sharp, cool sense of relief and triumph that one has on awakening from a nightmare. Could that have been it? Is it possible that that was all? Is it possible that Elinor and Mary really divined nothing, that they were paying me a sort of backhanded compliment, nothing certainly that anybody could object to? I began to laugh at myself, affectionately, as one does after a long worry, saying, "You fool, look how silly you've been." "Now I can go back," I thought happily, without reflection, just as though I were an absconding bank teller who had been living for years with his spiritual bags packed, waiting for the charges against him to be dropped that he might return to his native town. A vision of the study hall rose before me, with my favorite nun on the platform and the beautiful girls in their places. My heart rushed forward to embrace it.

But, alas, it is too late. Elinor Henehan is dead, my favorite nun has removed to another convent, the beautiful girls are married — I have seen them from time to time and no longer aspire to their friendship. And as for the pale, plain girl in the front of the study hall, her, too, I can no longer reach. I see her creeping down the corridor with a little knot of her classmates. "Hello, Cye," I say with a touch of disdain for her rawness, her guileless ambition. I should like to make her a pie-bed, or drop a snake down her back, but unfortunately the convent discipline forbids such open brutality. I hate her, for she is my natural victim, and it is I who have given her the name, the shameful, inscrutable name that she will never, sleepless in her bed at night, be able to puzzle out.

(1950)

QUESTIONS

1. What is the bureaucracy mentioned in paragraph 3? What is the narrator saying about psychology?
2. What evidence can you find in the story's language or imagery that the narrator has been influenced by her Catholic education?
3. Is the kind of power exercised by Elinor Henehan and Mary Heinrichs unique to boarding schools? How much of this story could be transferred to another setting, such as a sorority house, a department store, or a government office?
4. How does the narrator's view of her former self change throughout the story? Why?
5. Is a story about a childhood nickname as interesting or important as a story about war or love? What else besides subject matter might make a story worth reading?

SUGGESTIONS FOR WRITING

1. Write a narrative of one of your own actions that you remember clearly. Write it first as an internal narrator, with your earlier self as the filter character. Now try rewriting the paragraph from the outside, either filtered through someone else's perceptions or as a camera might have recorded the events. How do your two paragraphs differ? Does it seem like the same event?
2. Find a passage in any short story in this book in which a narrator tells us what a character is thinking. Does the narrator quote the character's thoughts directly, slip into free or tagged indirect quotation, or report the thoughts through paraphrase? Try transforming a passage using any one of these techniques into one of the others, and explain the consequences of the changes. Do the changes make you feel closer to the character or more distant?
3. Do you ever find yourself identifying with a character whom you wouldn't like if you met in person? How do writers create such characters? Imagine a really despicable person and write a scene through that person's filter. Is it easy to "listen" to the character's thoughts?
4. Find a short story in this book that uses more than one character as filter. Look at the way each character's viewpoint is translated into words and sentences. Does the narrator's style change to adapt to each filter? Does the narrator's slant change?

6 Narrative Irony

We all know how to tell stories that make fun of a character or of the narrator we are pretending to be, without explicitly saying that's what we're doing. Even children can be quite clever in imitating some idiosyncrasy of a character's speech — a lisp or stutter or characteristic turn of phrase. Such mockery is a form of *irony*, a figure of speech whose relevance to narrative structure is profound. *Irony* is a disparity between what occurs and what one would expect to occur. The target of the irony can be anything or anyone — even the speaker himself. "Self-irony" is commonplace, even among public figures. Remember President Bush's remark to reporters as he ended a press conference — "Read my hips." That was a self-ironic pun on a campaign slogan that he had earlier used in promising to raise no new taxes: "Read my lips." Irony operates as much in ordinary conversation as in literature. Nor is it restricted to jokes. Though it is commonly used for comic effect, irony can just as easily contribute to a sense of the tragic.

In this book we are especially concerned with how irony is used to shape our attitudes toward such structures as plots, characters, and narrators. Even when limited to narrative, irony is a complex term, referring to many kinds of effects. I shall limit my own discussion, however, to two — *situational irony* and *verbal irony*.

Definitions of Situational and Verbal Irony

Situational irony is irony of the "funny coincidence" variety. This is what people often mean when they use the term in everyday conversation. For example, an article in the newspaper reports: "It's ironic that the day after the brush fire, the county had its biggest rainstorm of the year." Here an event occurs that would have solved a problem, but a day too late. Another example: You bump into a friend and ask what she has been doing, and she says she spent the last month in New York: "How ironic!" you respond. "I was there too, and we could have gotten together." Again, a mere accident of fate prevented an event, namely, your meeting your friend in a distant city.

186

In *verbal irony*, on the other hand, the disparity concerns not events and accidents of fate, but language used by human beings. An ironic speaker conveys a meaning that is different from, even opposite to, the literal meaning of his words. If your friend drives up to your house in a new Porsche and you say "That's quite a heap you've got there," you have ironically expressed your admiration for the car in the pseudo-disparaging word "heap." Contrarily, if he has just purchased a wreck that requires a lot of renovation, you might ironically compliment him on his "magnificent new chariot." To repeat, verbal irony is *a consciously intended statement* by the ironist, not an accident of destiny. It relies completely on the audience's ability to grasp an unexpected meaning by rejecting the usual interpretation of a word or phrase.

Situational and Verbal Irony in Narrative Fiction

Let's start with situational irony, because it is simpler and easier to recognize. Situational irony concerns events, not statements, so its narrative use involves plot. For example, it is the basis of the "surprise ending" kind of short story made famous around the turn of the century by such authors as O. Henry.

Situational irony drives the plot of Albert Camus's "The Guest" (pp. 193–202). In this short story, the actual fate of the characters differs considerably from that merited by their traits. It is ironic, to begin with, that the Arab prisoner should be unable to accept what presumably he most desires, freedom, even though the French schoolmaster, Daru, offers it to him. All the Arab has to do is *choose* to be free, and then act accordingly. However, choice and action, the essence of freedom, are apparently not possible for him, whether because of fear, the mores of his culture, or other factors that we do not know. It is also ironic that Daru, though he gives the Arab freedom, is singled out as the Arab's enemy. The scrawled message on the blackboard shows that the Arabs fail to understand that Daru is trying to help, that he is not a racist, unlike the rest of the colonialist Frenchmen who rule their country. Some critics might object to calling these ironies, or at least "situational" ironies, because they seem so deeply rooted in the psychology of colonialism. However, the point of the story still turns on the fact that the Arabs act contrarily to what most readers would expect, and the fate of the schoolmaster seems unfair, given what we know of his character.

An even clearer example of situational irony occurs in Edith Wharton's "Roman Fever" (pp. 203–212). Because that irony turns on a surprise ending, however, I shall not reveal it. But I invite you to read the story right now: I'm sure you'll be able to point to the irony of fate that befalls the protagonist, Mrs. Slade.

Verbal irony, on the other hand, occurs when we recognize that someone says one thing but means something else. To understand this effect we must distinguish the two parties to an irony. The one who speaks the irony we may call the *ironist*; the object of the irony we may call the *target*. If Mary says that her 300-pound friend John dances like a gazelle, Mary is the ironist and John is the target. (Saying that he dances like a bear entails another figure of speech, namely, *simile*, because there is some justice in the comparison.) Verbal ironies are by definition intentional. The ironist intends that somebody (though not necessarily the target) grasp the disparity between the words she utters and the underlying reality that she wishes to convey.

In a fictional narrative, either a character or the narrator may be an ironist. The general context of plot helps us to recognize the ironization of one character by another. In Carson McCullers's "A Tree A Rock A Cloud," for example, the cynical owner of the diner, Leo, explicitly ironizes the old man, making fun of his drinking habits and predicting that someday he will fall asleep with his nose in a beer mug and drown. Leo quotes an imaginary newspaper headline reporting the event: "Prominent transient drowns in beer." "Prominent" is a word applicable to respectable citizens, not drifters. It is not a word usually coupled with "transient." Leo obviously means that the old man is less than "prominent" in the usual social sense.

The irony in this case is spoken by an unlikable character, so its justice is not established, as it would tend to be if pronounced by a narrator. For, unless we have evidence to the contrary, we assume that a narrator gives us the "true" story—that is, what really happened within the fictional world of the story. (Even the narrator may be ironized: I'll discuss the "unreliable narrator" later in this chapter.) The credence we grant to a character-ironist depends very much on how willing or unwilling we are to identify with him. For many readers, the old man is more likable than Leo, so we tend to discount the irony. The degree to which we are willing to accept the irony depends on how the ironist and the target are otherwise characterized. The narrator may or may not help out. Even if the ironist is believable, the narrator may remain neutral, only reporting the ironic remark. Or he may endorse it.

Fallible Filters

Often the narrator is the ironist, and a character the target. A good term to describe such a character is *fallible*, that is, "liable to err." *Fallible* is a better word for this effect than *unreliable*, a term more appropriately applied to a *narrator* who is the target. Why are filters only fallible, not unreliable? Because the term *unreliable* presupposes an *expectation* of reliability. That expectation is reasonable for narrators, because narrational reliability is the norm. A powerful reading convention makes us assume that a narrator contracts with us to give an accurate account of what happened. But the character has signed no such contract. Indeed, by the logic of narrative, she is not even aware that her mind is being entered. It would be unfair to accuse her of a breach of reliability when she has never promised such reliability and may even be constitutionally incapable of it. Little Chandler, in "A Little Cloud," is a clear example of a fallible filter.

Irony generated by the narrator may be *explicit* or *implicit*. Explicit irony can be traced to an actual passage in the text. Guy de Maupassant's "Love Awakening" (pp. 513–517) *explicitly* evokes the characters' fallibility in its very title.[1] Love is supposed to arise naturally between people, as naturally as awakening from a sleep, but the "love" of Henry for his cousin Jeanne, a woman just abandoned by her newly wed husband, can hardly be described as natural. On the contrary, Henry's intention is clearly to take sexual advantage of Jeanne's misfortune, the loss of both husband and dowry. What "awakens" in Henry is not love but lechery. So the title "Love's Awakening" is ironic, meaning something quite "other than" (opposite to) its usual meaning. Similarly, the word *great* in Ruth Prawer Jhabvala's "In a Great Man's House" (pp. 463–475) is also ironically used, for Khan Sahib's "greatness" is very much in question.

More often fallible filtration is *not* confirmed by a narrator's word or phrase. We have to sense that the character's behavior as a whole shows itself to be flawed. Irony occurs, for example, when the filter-character is too ignorant or naive to understand the full import of his actions. Fictions illustrating the naiveté of children provide clear examples. In Italo Calvino's "Big Fish, Little Fish" (pp. 374–379) we understand and chuckle at Zeffirino's fallible interpretation of the plump lady's behavior. As much as he longs to return to his undersea world, he stays onshore, fascinated by the spectacle of her tears. It is not that he feels an adult's sympathy; it is just that the sight of this woman is more spellbinding than anything he sees under the water. He is totally innocent of the source of her tears, even though she tells him that she is not a "signora" (a "Mrs.") but a "signorina" (a "Miss"). He can't understand why the undersea world doesn't please her as much as it does him. He feels uneasy, not so much out of sympathy for her suffering as out of filial responsibility. He feels duty-bound to help an adult in trouble, even if he doesn't understand the source of the trouble. When he asks why she's crying and is told that it's because she's unlucky in love, the only thing he can think of doing is to offer her his diving mask.

A child's filter may be tragically ironized. In Flannery O'Connor's "The River" (pp. 213–225), the four-year-old protagonist goes with an elderly baby-sitter to a religious revival meeting at the river, where an itinerant preacher named Bevel Summers baptizes born-again Christians. Harry is totally neglected by his parents, who party every night. He feels so alienated from his family that on hearing the preacher's name, he rechristens himself "Bevel." The preacher says: " 'If I Baptize you . . . you'll be able to go to the Kingdom of Christ. You'll be washed in the river of suffering, son, and you'll go by the deep river of life.' " Harry/Bevel unfortunately takes the preacher's words literally, for he thinks "I won't go back to the apartment then, I'll go under the river." And, indeed, the next morning he goes "under" the river. That's certainly not what Preacher Summers meant by "going by the deep river of life." Bevel is not consciously committing suicide; he is simply searching for a

---

[1]At least it does in the English translation. The exact meaning of the French title, "Le Dot," is "The Dowry."

better place to live, which he thinks exists under the water. The verbal irony lies in his overly literal interpretation of phrases like "river of suffering," "going by the deep river of life," "go under," and so on.[2]

The ironization of a character's filter is by no means limited to children. We have already examined the misguided self-communing of characters like Chekhov's Olenka and Joyce's Little Chandler. Though "A Little Cloud" contains no direct comment by the narrator, we cannot doubt that Little Chandler is the target of irony. He is self-deluded: For all his ambitions, he shall never become a poet of any value. Nor can we sympathize very much with his soft fantasies of a glamorous life in another country. Though we have only Chandler's thoughts to go on, we are made to feel that it is his own timidity and weakness that have turned family responsibilities into a trap blocking his creative urges. (Joyce himself, whom some call the greatest novelist of the twentieth century, was a committed husband and father, yet he did not let his family duties stand in the way of his writing.)

Unreliable Narration

Sometimes it is not a character's filter but the very narration of a fiction that is ironized. That is, the narrator himself is the target. His version of what happened is somehow suspect. The true story seems to be other — more (or perhaps less) complex, subtle, grim — than the way the narrator represents it. His version of events calls itself into question: I say "calls *itself* into question" because unreliable narration can only be *inferred* by the reader. However, if the narrator is the target of the narrative irony, how do we infer that? Who is the ironist? It can only be the (implied) author.[3] The (implied) author has created a story, but the story as the narrator tells it somehow doesn't hold water. So the reader begins to wonder if this inconsistency isn't due to the narrator. If the story is fishy, she reasons, perhaps it is the *teller* of the story who makes it so.

Consider, for example, Edgar Allan Poe's "The Tell-Tale Heart" (pp. 226–229). Because there is obviously something terribly wrong with the "I"-narrator-protagonist, we suspect that there might be something wrong with the story he tells. It would be surprising if his account of the events were more reliable than his deeds. He keeps reassuring us that he is calm and sane, but he doesn't sound like it. His defense of his murder is strange indeed. Protesting that he loved the old man, who had never done anything to harm

---

[2]Some readers would find a deeper irony still in this story. Flannery O'Connor was a devout Catholic, and those who know her work might argue that the story's meaning is that "we must lose our lives to gain our Life." That irony operates at a deeper level in the sense that it *depends* on our acceptance of the lesser irony I have suggested above, namely, that the preacher meant "the river of life" in a spiritual, not a literal, sense.

[3]I continue to wrap "implied" in parentheses until, in chapter 7, I provide a formal definition and explanation.

him, and that he had no designs on the old man's fortune, he says that he killed him only because one of the old man's eyes had a film over it (probably the consequence of some disease, such as a cataract). He repeatedly denies that he is crazy, but surely it is an act of insanity to focus on one physical trait and to kill someone for having it. The narrator confuses madness with caution, with foresight, with acuteness of perception, and so on. When the police come, he is confident of his ability to fool them, but then he begins to hear the heart beating again. Once more his mania isolates one feature from the rest: the body is dead, but the heart beats on. It is the noise of the beating heart — which only he in his madness hears — that drives him to confess his crime.

You might ask: Does mental aberration *ipso facto* qualify a narrator as unreliable? Not necessarily. The narrator of Vladimir Nabokov's novel *Lolita*, for example, is a child molester, but we cannot help believing that he tells the painful truth as he sees it. In "The Tell-Tale Heart," however, the narrator surely distorts the events. He claims that the heart is beating but the officers do not hear it: they chat pleasantly and smile. We can only conclude that in reality the heart is not beating. It is not only that the character-I has committed a murder, but also that the narrator-I distorts the events of the story in the telling. An event, the beating of the heart, is recounted as happening, but that event never happened. So "I" is not only a murder but also an unreliable narrator.

The mad narrator of "The Tell-Tale Heart" is an extreme case. Often there are other, less heinous explanations for narrative unreliability. Some narrators are unreliable because they are liars or prejudiced. Others, such as Huckleberry Finn or Holden Caulfield (character-narrator of J. D. Salinger's *Catcher in the Rye*) are unreliable out of immaturity and naiveté. (Though often such texts offer a kind of counter-irony: The apparently misguided views of the narrator prove to be "truer" in some sense than those of more sophisticated people.)

Obtuseness is sometimes the source of unreliability, as in Ring Lardner's "Haircut" (pp. 231 – 238). Whitey, the narrator, defends the behavior of his dead friend, Jim Kendall, but few readers would agree that Jim's behavior was defensible. Jim not only crudely teases his friends in the barbershop (mocking Whitey's red nose and Milt Shepard's prominent Adam's apple), but also performs random acts of cruelty. These acts include sending anonymous postcards to shopkeepers whose names he sees as his train passes through their town, postcards aimed at stirring up jealousy and dissension. He is cruel even to his own children, standing them up at the circus after promising to meet them at the entrance with the tickets. He plays a mean practical joke on Julie Gregg after forcing his attentions on her. Yet, despite all these offensive tricks, Whitey still expresses fondness for Kendall, calls him "comical," a source of "fun," though "kind of rough . . . a good fella at heart." Obviously, anyone who believes that such a person is still "a good fella at heart" suffers from a serious defect of judgment. He is either vicious himself or morally stupid. We decide it must be the latter, again not because anybody actually *says* that Whitey is obtuse, but because his own words — that is, his very narration and interpretation of the events — reveal it. This trait is confirmed by his interpretation of the final events. He shows himself to be totally gullible in swallowing Doc Foote's judgment about Paul's shooting of Kendall, and he does so even after he himself has shown how much Kendall's taunting might have given Paul a reason for murder. Whitey clearly has trouble putting two and two together.

❖ ALBERT CAMUS
The Guest*

Albert Camus (1913–1960) was born in Algeria at a time when it was still a colony of France. He studied philosophy in college and then worked for a while on a newspaper. He was very active in the French resistance movement during World War II. His partisan attitude informed the novel *The Plague* (1947), in which the Nazis were alluded to under the symbol of an epidemic. Prior to that he had written *The Stranger* (or *Outsider*, 1942), which embodies his existentialist ideas, ideas that allied him with Jean-Paul Sartre. His last novel was *The Fall* (1956). His collected short stories, including "The Guest," were published under the title *Exile and the Kingdom* (1957). His *Collected Fiction* appeared in 1960. He also published plays, including *Caligula* (1944) and *Stage of Siege* (1948), as well as much nonfiction, notably the philosophical treatises *The Myth of Sisyphus* (1943) and *The Rebel* (1951). Camus was killed in a car accident at the age of 47.

The schoolmaster was watching the two men climb towards him. One was on horseback, the other on foot. They had not yet tackled the abrupt rise leading to the schoolhouse built on the hillside. They were toiling onwards, making slow progress in the snow, among the stones, on the vast expanse of the high, deserted plateau. From time to time the horse stumbled. Without hearing anything yet, he could see the breath issuing from the horse's nostrils. One of the men, at least, knew the region. They were following the trail although it had disappeared days ago under a layer of dirty white snow. The schoolmaster calculated that it would take them half an hour to get on to the hill. It was cold; he went back into the school to get a sweater.

He crossed the empty, frigid classroom. On the blackboard the four rivers of France, drawn with four different coloured chalks, had been flowing towards their estuaries for the past three days. Snow had suddenly fallen in mid October after eight months of drought without the transition of rain, and the twenty pupils, more or less, who lived in the villages scattered over the plateau had stopped coming. With fair weather they would return. Daru now heated only the single room that was his lodging, adjoining the classroom and giving also on to the plateau to the east. Like the class windows, his window looked to the south too. On that side the school was a few kilometres from the point where the plateau began to slope towards the south. In clear weather could be seen the purple mass of the mountain range where the gap opened on to the desert.

Somewhat warmed, Daru returned to the window from which he had first seen the two men. They were no longer visible. Hence they must have tackled the rise. The sky was not so dark, for the snow had stopped falling during the night. The

---

*Translated by Justin O'Brien.

morning had opened with a dirty light which had scarcely become brighter as the ceiling of clouds lifted. At two in the afternoon it seemed as if the day were merely beginning. But still this was better than those three days when the thick snow was falling amidst unbroken darkness with little gusts of wind that rattled the double door of the classroom. Then Daru had spent long hours in his room, leaving it only to go to the shed and feed the chickens or get some coal. Fortunately the delivery truck from Tadjid, the nearest village to the north, had brought his supplies two days before the blizzard. It would return in forty-eight hours.

Besides, he had enough to resist a siege, for the little room was cluttered with bags of wheat that the administration left as a stock to distribute to those of his pupils whose families had suffered from the drought. Actually they had all been victims because they were all poor. Every day Daru would distribute a ration to the children. They had missed it, he knew, during these bad days. Possibly one of the fathers or big brothers would come this afternoon and he could supply them with grain. It was just a matter of carrying them over to the next harvest. Now shiploads of wheat were arriving from France and the worst was over. But it would be hard to forget that poverty, that army of ragged ghosts wandering in the sunlight, the plateaux burned to a cinder month after month, the earth shrivelled up little by little, literally scorched, every stone bursting into dust under one's foot. The sheep had died then by thousands and even a few men, here and there, sometimes without anyone's knowing.

In contrast with such poverty, he who lived almost like a monk in his remote schoolhouse, none the less satisfied with the little he had and with the rough life, had felt like a lord with his whitewashed walls, his narrow couch, his upainted shelves, his well, and his weekly provision of water and food. And suddenly this snow, without warning, without the foretaste of rain. This is the way the region was, cruel to live in, even without men—who didn't help matters either. But Daru had been born here. Everywhere else, he felt exiled.

He stepped out on to the terrace in front of the schoolhouse. The two men were now half-way up the slope. He recognized the horseman as Balducci, the old gendarme[1] he had known for a long time. Balducci was holding on the end of a rope an Arab who was walking behind him with hands bound and head lowered. The gendarme waved a greeting to which Daru did not reply, lost as he was in contemplation of the Arab dressed in a faded blue jellaba,[2] his feet in sandals but covered with socks of heavy raw wool, his head surmounted by a narrow, short chèche.[3] They were approaching. Balducci was holding back his horse in order not to hurt the Arab, and the group was advancing slowly.

Within earshot, Balducci shouted: 'One hour to do the three kilometres from El Ameur!' Daru did not answer. Short and square in his thick sweater, he watched them climb. Not once had the Arab raised his head. 'Hello,' said Daru when they got up on to the terrace. 'Come in and warm up.' Balducci painfully got down from his horse without letting go the rope. From under his bristling moustache he smiled at the schoolmaster. His little dark eyes, deep-set under a tanned forehead, and his mouth

---

[1]Policeman (French).
[2]Woolen cloak (Arabic).
[3]Turban used as a military cap.

surrounded with wrinkles made him look attentive and studious. Daru took the bridle, led the horse to the shed, and came back to the two men, who were now waiting for him in the school. He led them into his room. 'I am going to heat up the classroom,' he said. 'We'll be more comfortable there.' When he entered the room again, Balducci was on the couch. He had undone the rope tying him to the Arab, who had squatted near the stove. His hands still bound, the *chèche* pushed back on his head, he was looking towards the window. At first Daru noticed only his huge lips, fat, smooth, almost negroid; yet his nose was straight, his eyes were dark and full of fever. The *chèche* revealed an obstinate forehead and, under the weathered skin now rather discoloured by the cold, the whole face had a restless and rebellious look that stuck Daru when the Arab, turning his face towards him, looked him straight in the eyes. 'Go into the other room,' said the schoolmaster, 'and I'll make you some mint tea.' 'Thanks,' Balducci said. 'What a nuisance! How I long for retirement.' And addressing his prisoner in Arabic: 'Come on, you.' The Arab got up and, slowly, holding his bound wrists in front of him, went into the classroom.

With the tea, Daru brought a chair. But Balducci was already enthroned on the nearest pupil's desk and the Arab had squatted against the teacher's platform facing the stove, which stood between the desk and the window. When he held out the glass of tea to the prisoner, Daru hesitated at the sight of his bound hands. 'He might perhaps be untied.' 'Certainly,' said Balducci. 'That was for the journey.' He started to get to his feet. But Daru, setting the glass on the floor, had knelt beside the Arab. Without saying anything, the Arab watched him with his feverish eyes. Once his hands were free, he rubbed his swollen wrists against each other, took the glass of tea, and sucked up the burning liquid in swift little sips.

'Good,' said Daru. 'And where are you headed for?'

Balducci withdrew his moustache from the tea. 'Here, my boy.'

'Odd pupils! And you're spending the night?'

'No. I'm going back to El Ameur. And you will deliver this fellow to Tinguit. He is expected at police headquarters.'

Balducci was looking at Daru with a friendly little smile.

'What's this story?' asked the schoolmaster. 'Are you pulling my leg?'

'No, my boy. Those are the orders.'

'The orders? I'm not . . .' Daru hesitated not wanting to hurt the old Corsican. 'I mean, that's not my job.'

'What! What's the meaning of that? In wartime people do all kinds of jobs.'

'Then I'll wait for the declaration of war!'

Balducci nodded.

'O.K. But the orders exist and they concern you too. Things are brewing, it appears. There is talk of a forthcoming revolt. We are mobilized, in a way.'

Daru still had his obstinate look.

'Listen, my boy,' Balducci said. 'I like you and you must understand. There's only a dozen of us at El Ameur[4] to patrol throughout the whole territory of a small department and I must get back in a hurry. I was told to hand this man over to you and return without delay. He couldn't be kept there. His village was beginning to stir; they

---

[4]A village in Algeria.

wanted to take him back. You must take him to Tinguit[5] tomorrow before the day is over. Twenty kilometres shouldn't worry a husky fellow like you. After that, all will be over. You'll come back to your pupils and your comfortable life.'

Behind the wall the horse could be heard snorting and pawing the earth. Daru was looking out of the window. Decidedly, the weather was clearing and the light was increasing over the snowy plateau. When all the snow was melted, the sun would take over again and once more would burn the fields of stone. For days, still, the unchanging sky would shed its dry light on the solitary expanse where nothing had any connexion with man.

'After all,' he said, turning around towards Balducci, 'what did he do?' And, before the gendarme had opened his mouth, he asked: 'Does he speak French?'

'No, not a word. We had been looking for him for a month, but they were hiding him. He killed his cousin.'

'Is he against us?'

'I don't think so. But you can never be sure.'

'Why did he kill?'

'A family squabble, I think. One owed the other grain, it seems. It's not at all clear. In short, he killed his cousin with a billhook.[6] You know, like a sheep, *kreezk!*'

Balducci made the gesture of drawing a blade across his throat and the Arab, his attention attracted, watched him with a sort of anxiety. Daru felt a sudden wrath against the man, against all men with their rotten spite, their tireless hates, their blood lust.

But the kettle was singing on the stove. He served Balducci more tea, hesitated, then served the Arab again, who, a second time, drank avidly. His raised arms made the jellaba fall open and the schoolmaster saw his thin, muscular chest.

'Thanks, my boy,' Balducci said. 'And now, I'm off.'

He got up and went towards the Arab, taking a small rope from his pocket.

'What are you doing?' Daru asked dryly.

Balducci, disconcerted, showed him the rope.

'Don't bother.'

The old gendarme hesitated. 'It's up to you. Of course, you are armed?'

'I have my shot gun.'

'Where?'

'In the trunk.'

'You ought to have it near your bed.'

'Why? I have nothing to fear.'

'You're mad. If there's an uprising, no one is safe, we're all in the same boat.'

'I'll defend myself. I'll have time to see them coming.'

Balducci began to laugh, then suddenly the moustache covered the white teeth.

'You'll have time? O.K. That's just what I was saying. You have always been a little cracked. That's why I like you, my son was like that.'

At the same time he took out his revolver and put it on the desk.

---

[5] A village in Algeria.
[6] A sharp, hooked instrument used for pruning and cutting.

'Keep it; I don't need two weapons from here to El Ameur.'

The revolver shone against the black paint of the table. When the gendarme turned towards him, the schoolmaster caught the smell of leather and horseflesh.

'Listen, Balducci,' Daru said suddenly, 'every bit of this disgusts me, and most of all your fellow here. But I won't hand him over. Fight, yes, if I have to. But not that.'

The old gendarme stood in front of him and looked at him severely.

'You're being a fool,' he said slowly. 'I don't like it either. You don't get used to putting a rope on a man even after years of it, and you're even ashamed—yes, ashamed. But you can't let them have their way.'

'I won't hand him over,' Daru said again.

'It's an order, my boy, and I repeat it.'

'That's right. Repeat to them what I've said to you: I won't hand him over.'

Balducci made a visible effort to reflect. He looked at the Arab and at Daru. At last he decided.

'No, I won't tell them anything. If you want to drop us, go ahead; I'll not denounce you. I have an order to deliver the prisoner and I'm doing so. And now you'll just sign this paper for me.'

'There's no need. I'll not deny that you left him with me.'

'Don't be mean with me. I know you'll tell the truth. You're from hereabouts and you are a man. But you must sign, that's the rule.'

Daru opened his drawer, took out a little square bottle of purple ink, the red wooden penholder with the 'sergeant-major' pen he used for making models of penmanship, and signed. The gendarme carefully folded the paper and put it into his wallet. Then he moved towards the door.

'I'll see you off,' Daru said.

'No,' said Balducci. 'There's no use being polite. You insulted me.'

He looked at the Arab, motionless in the same spot, sniffed peevishly, and turned away towards the door. 'Good-bye, son,' he said. The door shut behind him. Balducci appeared suddenly outside the window and then disappeared. His footsteps were muffled by the snow. The horse stirred on the other side of the wall and several chickens fluttered in fright. A moment later Balducci reappeared outside the window leading the horse by the bridle. He walked towards the little rise without turning round and disappeared from sight with the horse following him. A big stone could be heard bouncing down. Daru walked back towards the prisoner, who, without stirring, never took his eyes off him. 'Wait,' the schoolmaster said in Arabic and went towards the bedroom. As he was going through the door, he had a second thought, went to the desk, took the revolver, and stuck it in his pocket. Then, without looking back, he went into his room.

For some time he lay on his couch watching the sky gradually close over, listening to the silence. It was this silence that had seemed painful to him during the first days here, after the war. He had requested a post in the little town at the base of the foothills separating the upper plateaux from the desert. There, rocky walls, green and black to the north, pink and lavender to the south, marked the frontier of eternal summer. He had been named to a post farther north, on the plateau itself. In the beginning, the solitude and the silence had been hard for him on these wastelands peopled only by stones. Occasionally, furrows suggested cultivation, but they had been dug to uncover a certain kind of stone good for building. The only ploughing here was to harvest rocks. Elsewhere a thin layer of soil accumulated in the hollows would be scraped out to enrich paltry village gardens. This is the way it was: bare rock covered three-quarters of the region. Towns sprang up, flourished, then disappeared; men came by, loved one another or fought bitterly, then died. No one in this desert, neither he nor his guest, mattered. And yet, outside this desert neither of them, Daru knew, could have really lived.

When he got up, no noise came from the classroom. He was amazed at the unmixed joy he derived from the mere thought that the Arab might have fled and that he would be alone with no decision to make. But the prisoner was there. He had merely stretched out between the stove and the desk. With eyes open, he was staring at the ceiling. In that position, his thick lips were particularly noticeable, giving him a pouting look. 'Come,' said Daru. The Arab got up and followed him. In the bedroom, the schoolmaster pointed to a chair near the table under the window. The Arab sat down without taking his eyes off Daru.

'Are you hungry?'

'Yes,' the prisoner said.

Daru set the table for two. He took flour and oil, shaped a cake in a frying-pan, and lighted the little stove that functioned on bottled gas. While the cake was cooking, he went out to the shed to get cheese, eggs, dates, and condensed milk. When the cake was done he set it on the window sill to cool, heated some condensed milk diluted with water, and beat up the eggs into an omelet. In one of his motions he knocked against the revolver stuck in his right pocket. He set the bowl down, went into the classroom, and put the revolver in his desk drawer. When he came back to the room, night was falling. He put on the light and served the Arab. 'Eat,' he said. The Arab took a piece of the cake, lifted it eagerly to his mouth, and stopped short.

'And you?' he asked.

'After you. I'll eat too.'

The thick lips opened slightly. The Arab hesitated, then bit into the cake determinedly.

The meal over, the Arab looked at the schoolmaster. 'Are you the judge?'

'No, I'm simply keeping you until tomorrow.'

'Why do you eat with me?'

'I'm hungry.'

The Arab fell silent. Daru got up and went out. He brought back a folding bed from the shed, set it up between the table and the stove, at right-angles to his own bed. From a large suitcase which, upright in a corner, served as a shelf for papers, he took two blankets and arranged them on the camp bed. Then he stopped, felt useless, and sat down on his bed. There was nothing more to do or to get ready. He had to look at this man. He looked at him, therefore, trying to imagine his face bursting with rage. He couldn't do so. He could see nothing but the dark yet shining eyes and the animal mouth.

'Why did you kill him?' he asked in a voice whose hostile tone surprised him. The Arab looked away.

'He ran away. I ran after him.'

He raised his eyes to Daru again and they were full of a sort of woeful interrogation. 'Now what will they do to me?'

'Are you afraid?'

He stiffened, turning his eyes away.

'Are you sorry?'

The Arab stared at him open-mouthed. Obviously he did not understand. Daru's annoyance was growing. At the same time he felt awkward and self-conscious with his big body wedged between the two beds.

'Lie down there,' he said impatiently. 'That's your bed.'

The Arab didn't move. He called to Daru:

'Tell me!'

The schoolmaster looked at him.

'Is the gendarme coming back tomorrow?'

'I don't know.'

'Are you coming with us?'

'I don't know. Why?'

The prisoner got up and stretched out on top of the blankets, his feet towards the window. The light from the electric bulb shone straight into his eyes and he closed them at once.

'Why?' Daru repeated, standing beside the bed.

The Arab opened his eyes under the blinding light and looked at him, trying not to blink.

'Come with us,' he said.

In the middle of the night, Daru was still not asleep. He had gone to bed after undressing completely; he generally slept naked. But, when he suddenly realized that he had nothing on, he hesitated. He felt vulnerable and the temptation came to him to put on his clothes again. Then he shrugged his shoulders; after all, he wasn't a child and, if need be, he could break his adversary in two. From his bed he could observe him, lying on his back, still motionless with his eyes closed under the harsh light. When Daru turned out the light, the darkness seemed to coagulate all of a sudden. Little by little, the night came back to life in the window where the starless sky was stirring gently. The schoolmaster soon made out the body lying at his feet. The Arab still did not move, but his eyes seemed open. A faint wind was prowling around the schoolhouse. Perhaps it would drive away the clouds and the sun would reappear.

During the night the wind increased. The hens fluttered a little and then were silent. The Arab turned over on his side with his back to Daru, who thought he heard him moan. Then he listened for his guest's breathing, become heavier and more regular. He listened to that breath so close to him and mused without being able to go to sleep. In this room where he had been sleeping alone for a year, this presence bothered him. But it bothered him also by imposing on him a sort of brotherhood he knew well but refused to accept in the present circumstances. Men who share the same rooms, soldiers or prisoners, develop a strange alliance as if, having cast off their armour with their clothing, they fraternized every evening, over and above their differences, in the ancient community of dream and fatigue. But Daru shook himself; he didn't like such musings, and it was essential to sleep.

A little later, however, when the Arab stirred slightly, the schoolmaster was still not asleep. When the prisoner made a second move, he stiffened, on the alert. The Arab was lifting himself slowly on his arms with almost the motion of a sleepwalker. Seated upright in bed, he waited motionless without turning his head towards Daru, as if he were listening attentively. Daru did not stir; it had just occurred to him that the revolver was still in the drawer of his desk. It was better to act at once. Yet he continued to observe the prisoner, who, with the same slithery motion, put his feet on the ground, waited again, then began to stand up slowly. Daru was about to call out to him when the Arab began to walk, in a quite natural but extraordinarily silent way. He was heading towards the door at the end of the room that opened into the shed. He lifted the latch with precaution and went out, pushing the door behind him but without shutting it. Daru had not stirred. 'He is running away,' he merely thought. 'Good riddance!' Yet he listened attentively. The hens were not fluttering; the guest must be on the plateau. A faint sound of water reached him, and he didn't know what it was until the Arab again stood framed in the doorway, closed the door carefully, and came back to bed without a sound. Then Daru turned his back on him and fell asleep. Still later he seemed, from the depths of his sleep, to hear furtive steps around the schoolhouse. 'I'm dreaming! I'm dreaming!' he repeated to himself. And he went on sleeping.

When he awoke, the sky was clear; the loose window let in a cold, pure air. The Arab was asleep, hunched up under the blankets now, his mouth open, utterly relaxed. But when Daru shook him, he started dreadfully, staring at Daru with wild eyes as if he had never seen him and such a frightened expression that the schoolmaster stepped back. 'Don't be afraid. It's me. You must eat.' The Arab nodded his head and said yes. Calm had returned to his face, but his expression was vacant and listless.

The coffee was ready. They drank it seated together on the folding bed as they munched their pieces of the cake. Then Daru led the Arab under the shed and showed him the tap where he washed. He went back into the room, folded the blankets and the bed, made his own bed and put the room in order. Then he went through the classroom and out on to the terrace. The sun was already rising in the blue sky; a soft, bright light was bathing the deserted plateau. On the ridge the snow was melting in spots. The stones were about to reappear. Crouched on the edge of the plateau, the schoolmaster looked at the deserted expanse. He thought of Balducci. He had hurt him, for he had sent him off in a way as if he didn't want to be associated with him. He could still hear the gendarme's farewell and, without knowing why, he felt strangely empty and vulnerable. At that moment, from the other side of the schoolhouse, the prisoner coughed. Daru listened to him almost despite himself and then, furious, threw a pebble that whistled through the air before sinking into the snow. That man's stupid crime revolted him, but to hand him over was contrary to honour. Merely thinking of it made him smart with humiliation. And he cursed at one and the same time his own people who had sent him this Arab and the Arab too who had dared to kill and not managed to get away. Daru got up, walked in a circle on the terrace, waited motionless, and then went back into the schoolhouse.

The Arab, leaning over the cement floor of the shed, was washing his teeth with two fingers. Daru looked at him and said: 'Come.' He went back into the room ahead of the prisoner. He slipped a hunting-jacket on over his sweater and put on walking-shoes. Standing, he waited until the Arab had put on his *chèche* and sandals. They went into the classroom and the schoolmaster pointed to the exit, saying: 'Go ahead.' The fellow didn't budge. 'I'm coming,' said Daru. The Arab went out. Daru went back into the room and made a package of pieces of rusk, dates, and sugar. In the classroom, before going out, he hesitated a second in front of his desk, then crossed the threshold and locked the door. 'That's the way,' he said. He started towards the east, followed by the prisoner. But, a short distance from the schoolhouse, he thought he heard a slight sound behind them. He retraced his steps and examined the surroundings of the house; there was no one there. The Arab watched him without seeming to understand. 'Come on,' said Daru.

They walked for an hour and rested beside a sharp peak of limestone. The snow was melting faster and faster and the sun was drinking up the puddles at once, rapidly cleaning the plateau, which gradually dried and vibrated like the air itself. When they resumed walking, the ground rang under their feet. From time to time a bird rent the space in front of them with a joyful cry. Daru breathed in deeply the fresh morning light. He felt a sort of rapture before the vast familiar expanse, now almost entirely yellow under its dome of blue sky. They walked an hour more, descending towards the south. They reached a level height made up of crumbly rocks. From there on, the plateau sloped down, eastward, towards a low plain where there were a few spindly trees and, to the south, towards outcroppings of rock that gave the landscape a chaotic look.

Daru surveyed the two directions. There was nothing but the sky on the horizon. Not a man could be seen. He turned towards the Arab, who was looking at him blankly. Daru held out the packages to him. 'Take it,' he said. 'There are dates, bread, and sugar. You can hold out for two days. Here are a thousand francs too.' The Arab took the package and the money but kept his full hands at chest level as if he didn't know what to do with what was being given him. 'Now look,' the schoolmaster said as he pointed in the direction of the east, 'there's the way to Tinguit. You have a two-hour walk. At Tinguit you'll find the administration and the police. They are expecting you.' The Arab looked towards the east, still holding the package and the money against his chest. Daru took his elbow and turned him rather roughly towards the south. At the foot of the height on which they stood could be seen a faint path. 'That's the trail across the plateau. In a day's walk from here you'll find pasture lands and the first nomads. They'll take you in and shelter you according to their law.' The Arab had now turned towards Daru and a sort of panic was visible in his expression. 'Listen,' he said. Daru shook his head: 'No, be quiet. Now I'm leaving you.' He turned his back on him, took two long steps in the direction of the school, looked hesitantly at the motionless Arab, and started off again. For a few minutes he heard nothing but his own step resounding on the cold ground and did not turn his head. A moment later, however, he turned around. The Arab was still there on the edge of the hill, his arms hanging now, and he was looking at the schoolmaster. Daru felt something rise in his throat. But he swore with impatience, waved vaguely, and started off again. He had already gone some distance when he again stopped and looked. There was no longer anyone on the hill.

Daru hesitated. The sun was now rather high in the sky and was beginning to beat down on his head. The schoolmaster retraced his steps, at first somewhat uncertainly, then with decision. When he reached the little hill, he was bathed in sweat. He climbed it as fast as he could and stopped, out of breath, at the top. The rock-fields to the south stood out sharply against the blue sky, but on the plain to the east a steamy heat was already rising. And in that slight haze, Daru, with heavy heart, made out the Arab walking slowly on the road to prison.

A littler later, standing before the window of the classroom, the schoolmaster was watching the clear light bathing the whole surface of the plateau, but he hardly saw it. Behind him on the blackboard, among the winding French rivers, sprawled the clumsily chalked-up words he had just read: 'You handed over our brother. You will pay for this.' Daru looked at the sky, the plateau, and, beyond, the invisible lands stretching all the way to the sea. In this vast landscape he had loved so much, he was alone.

(1957)

QUESTIONS

1. How do you prefer to remember this short story? Does it make you want to continue speculating about Daru's fate, or are you content to leave him forever standing in your memory, alone, "look[ing] at the sky, the plateau, and, beyond, the invisible lands stretching all the way to the sea"? Why?

2. How does the narrator create the effect of the vast emptiness of the North African plateau that so dominates "The Guest"? How does that emptiness contribute to its psychological and emotional atmosphere?

3. Look up the word *existentialism* in a large dictionary, such as Webster's *Unabridged*. Along with Jean-Paul Sartre, Camus was known as one of the founders of the existentialist philosophical movement. How does even a brief dictionary definition help you formulate the themes of the short story?

4. There are three characters in this short story — Daru, Balducci, and the Arab. Why are the first two assigned names but the third only referred to generically as "the Arab"? Does the refusal to assign the character a name contribute to the psychological atmosphere and theme of the short story? Does it suggest that the (implied) author has a negative attitude toward ethnic minorities or does it imply something else? If so, what?

5. Why would omniscient narration undermine the intention of this short story?

❖ EDITH WHARTON
Roman Fever

Edith Wharton (1862–1937) was born Edith Newbold Jones in New York City and was educated by private tutors. She married the banker Edward Wharton in 1885 and divorced him in 1913, after which she moved to France. She did volunteer work during World War I for which she was awarded the French Cross of the Legion of Honor. She was a great friend of Henry James, and in some ways his disciple. She wrote fiction prolifically. Her novels include *The House of Mirth* (1905), *Ethan Frome* (1911), *The Custom of the Country* (1913), *Summer* (1917), *The Marne* (1918), and her masterpiece, *The Age of Innocence* (1920, which won the Pulitzer Prize for literature). *Old New York* (1924) was a collection of four novellas. Her short stories appeared in *Crucial Instances* (1901), *The Hermit and the Wild Woman* (1908), *Tales of Men and Ghosts* (1910), and *The World Over* (1936, which included "Roman Fever"). Wharton also wrote an important work of literary theory, *The Writing of Fiction* (1925).

I

From the table at which they had been lunching two American ladies of ripe but well-cared-for middle age moved across the lofty terrace of the Roman restaurant and, leaning on its parapet, looked first at each other, and then down on the outspread glories of the Palatine[1] and the Forum,[2] with the same expression of vague but benevolent approval.

As they leaned there a girlish voice echoed up gaily from the stairs leading to the court below. "Well, come along, then," it cried, not to them but to an invisible companion, "and let's leave the young things to their knitting"; and a voice as fresh laughed back: "Oh, look here, Babs, not actually *knitting*—"Well, I mean figuratively," rejoined the first. "After all, we haven't left our poor parents much else to do. . . ." and at that point the turn of the stairs engulfed the dialogue.

The two ladies looked at each other again, this time with a tinge of smiling embarrassment, and the smaller and paler one shook her head and colored slightly.

"Barbara!" she murmured, sending an unheard rebuke after the mocking voice in the stairway.

The other lady, who was fuller, and higher in color, with a small determined nose supported by vigorous black eyebrows, gave a good-humored laugh. "That's what our daughters think of us!"

Her companion replied by a deprecating gesture. "Not of us individually. We must remember that. It's just the collective modern idea of Mothers. And you see—" Half-guiltily she drew from her handsomely mounted black handbag a twist of

---

[1]One of the seven hills on which ancient Rome was built.
[2]The public square of ancient Rome.

crimson silk run through by two fine knitting needles. "One never knows," she murmured. "The new system has certainly given us a good deal of time to kill; and sometimes I get tired just looking — even at this." Her gesture was now addressed to the stupendous scene at their feet.

The dark lady laughed again, and they both relapsed upon the view, contemplating it in silence, with a sort of diffused serenity which might have been borrowed from the spring effulgence of the Roman skies. The luncheon hour was long past, and the two had their end of the vast terrace to themselves. At its opposite extremity a few groups, detained by a lingering look at the outspread city, were gathering up guidebooks and fumbling for tips. The last of them scattered, and the two ladies were alone on the air-washed height.

"Well, I don't see why we shouldn't just stay here," said Mrs. Slade, the lady of the high color and energetic brows. Two derelict basket chairs stood near, and she pushed them into the angle of the parapet, and settled herself in one, her gaze upon the Palatine. "After all, it's still the most beautiful view in the world."

"It always will be, to me," assented her friend Mrs. Ansley, with so slight a stress on the "me" that Mrs. Slade, though she noticed it, wondered if it were not merely accidental, like the random underlinings of old-fashioned letter writers.

"Grace Ansley was always old-fashioned," she thought; and added aloud, with a retrospective smile: "It's a view we've both been familiar with for a good many years. When we first met here we were younger than our girls are now. You remember?"

"Oh, yes, I remember," murmured Mrs. Ansley, with the same undefinable stress. "There's that headwaiter wondering," she interpolated. She was evidently far less sure than her companion of herself and of her rights in the world.

"I'll cure him of wondering," said Mrs. Slade, stretching her hand toward a bag as discreetly opulent-looking as Mrs. Ansley's. Signing to the headwaiter, she explained that she and her friend were old lovers of Rome, and would like to spend the end of the afternoon looking down on the view — that is, if it did not disturb the service? The headwaiter, bowing over her gratuity, assured her that the ladies were most welcome, and would be still more so if they would condescend to remain for dinner. A full-moon night, they would remember. . . .

Mrs. Slade's black brows drew together, as though references to the moon were out of place and even unwelcome. But she smiled away her frown as the headwaiter retreated. "Well, why not? We might do worse. There's no knowing, I suppose, when the girls will be back. Do you even know back from *where*? I don't!"

Mrs. Ansley again colored slightly. "I think those young Italian aviators we met at the Embassy invited them to fly to Tarquinia for tea. I suppose they'll want to wait and fly black by moonlight."

"Moonlight — moonlight! What a part it still plays. Do you suppose they're as sentimental as we were?"

"I've come to the conclusion that I don't in the least know what they are," said Mrs. Ansley. "And perhaps we didn't know much more about each other."

"No; perhaps we didn't."

Her friend gave her a shy glance. "I never should have supposed you were sentimental, Alida."

"Well, perhaps I wasn't." Mrs. Slade drew her lids together in retrospect; and for a few moments the two ladies, who had been intimate since childhood, reflected how little they knew each other. Each one, of course, had a label ready to attach to the other's name; Mrs. Delphin Slade, for instance, would have told herself, or anyone who asked her, that Mrs. Horace Ansley, twenty-five years ago, had been exquisitely lovely — no, you wouldn't believe it, would you? . . . though, of course, still charming, distinguished. . . . Well, as a girl she had been exquisite; far more beautiful than her daughter Barbara, though certainly Babs, according to the new standards at any rate, was more effective — had more *edge*, as they say. Funny where she got it, with those two nullities as parents. Yes; Horace Ansley was — well, just the duplicate of his wife. Museum specimens of old New York. Good-looking, irreproachable, exemplary. Mrs. Slade and Mrs. Ansley had lived opposite each other — actually as well as figuratively — for years. When the drawing-room curtains in No. 20 East 73rd Street were renewed, No. 23, across the way, was always aware of it. And of all the movings, buyings, travels, anniversaries, illnesses — the tame chronicle of an estimable pair. Little of it escaped Mrs. Slade. But she had grown bored with it by the time her husband made his big *coup* in Wall Street, and when they bought in upper Park Avenue had already begun to think: "I'd rather live opposite a speakeasy for a change; at least one might see it raided." The idea of seeing Grace raided was so amusing that (before the move) she launched it at a woman's lunch. It made a hit, and went the rounds — she sometimes wondered if it had crossed the street, and reached Mrs. Ansley. She hoped not, but didn't much mind. Those were the days when respectability was at a discount, and it did the irreproachable no harm to laugh at them a little.

A few years later, and not many months apart, both ladies lost their husbands. There was an appropriate exchange of wreaths and condolences, and a brief renewal of intimacy in the half-shadow of their mourning; and now, after another interval, they had run across each other in Rome, at the same hotel, each of them the modest appendage of a salient daughter. The similarity of their lot had again drawn them together, lending itself to mild jokes, and the mutual confession that, if in old days it must have been tiring to "keep up" with daughters, it was now, at times, a little dull not to.

No doubt, Mrs. Slade reflected, she felt her unemployment more than poor Grace ever would. It was a big drop from being the wife of Delphin Slade to being his widow. She had always regarded herself (with a certain conjugal pride) as his equal in social gifts, as contributing her full share to the making of the exceptional couple they were: but the difference after his death was irremediable. As the wife of the famous corporation lawyer, always with an international case or two on hand, every day brought its exciting and unexpected obligation: the impromptu entertaining of eminent colleagues from abroad, the hurried dashes on legal business to London, Paris or Rome, where the entertaining was so handsomely reciprocated; the amusements of hearing in her wake: "What, that handsome woman with the good clothes and the eyes is Mrs. Slade — *the* Slade's wife? Really? Generally the wives of celebrities are such frumps."

Yes; being *the* Slade's widow was a dullish business after that. In living up to such a husband all her faculties had been engaged; now she had only her daughter to live up to, for the son who seemed to have inherited his father's gifts had died suddenly in boyhood. She had fought through that agony because her husband was there, to be helped and to help; now, after the father's death, the thought of the boy had become unbearable. There was nothing left but to mother her daughter; and dear Jenny was such a perfect daughter that she needed no excessive mothering. "Now with Babs Ansley I don't know that I *should* be so quiet," Mrs. Slade sometimes half-enviously reflected; but Jenny, who was younger than her brilliant friend, was that rare accident, an extremely pretty girl who somehow made youth and prettiness seem as safe as their absence. It was all perplexing — and to Mrs. Slade a little boring. She wished that Jenny would fall in love — with the wrong man, even; that she might have to be watched, out-maneuvered, rescued. And instead, it was Jenny who watched her mother, kept her out of drafts, made sure that she had taken her tonic. . . .

Mrs. Ansley was much less articulate than her friend, and her mental portrait of Mrs. Slade was slighter, and drawn with fainter touches. "Alida Slade's awfully brilliant; but not as brilliant as she thinks," would have summed it up; though she would have added, for the enlightenment of strangers, that Mrs. Slade had been an extremely dashing girl; much more so than her daughter, who was pretty, of course, and clever in a way, but had none of her mother's — well, "vividness," someone had once called it. Mrs. Ansley would take up current words like this, and cite them in quotation marks, as unheard-of audacities. No; Jenny was not like her mother. Sometimes Mrs. Ansley thought Alida Slade was disappointed; on the whole she had had a sad life. Full of failures and mistakes; Mrs. Ansley had always been rather sorry for her. . . .

So these two ladies visualized each other, each through the wrong end of her little telescope.

II

For a long time they continued to sit side by side without speaking. It seemed as though, to both, there was a relief in laying down their somewhat futile activities in the presence of the vast Memento Mori which faced them. Mrs. Slade sat quite still, her eyes fixed on the golden slope of the Palace of Caesars, and after a while Mrs. Ansley ceased to fidget with her bag, and she too sank into meditation. Like many intimate friends, the two ladies had never before had occasion to be silent together, and Mrs. Ansley was slightly embarrassed by what seemed, after so many years, a new stage in their intimacy, and one with which she did not yet know how to deal.

Suddenly the air was full of that deep clangor of bells which periodically covers Rome with a roof of silver. Mrs. Slade glanced at her wristwatch. "Five o'clock already," she said, as though surprised.

Mrs. Ansley suggested interrogatively: "There's bridge at the Embassy at five." For a long time Mrs. Slade did not answer. She appeared to be lost in contemplation, and Mrs. Ansley thought the remark had escaped her. But after a while she said, as if speaking out of a dream: "Bridge, did you say? Not unless you want to. . . . But I don't think I will, you know."

"Oh, no," Mrs. Ansley hastened to assure her. "I don't care to at all. It's so lovely here; and so full of old memories, as you say." She settled herself in her chair, and almost furtively drew forth her knitting. Mrs. Slade took sideway note of this activity, but her own beautifully cared-for hands remained motionless on her knee.

"I was just thinking," she said slowly, "what different things Rome stands for to each generation of travelers. To our grandmothers, Roman fever; to our mothers, sentimental dangers—how we used to be guarded!—to our daughters, no more dangers than the middle of Main Street. They don't know it—but how much they're missing!"

The long golden light was beginning to pale, and Mrs. Ansley lifted her knitting a little closer to her eyes. "Yes; how we were guarded!"

"I always used to think," Mrs. Slade continued, "that our mothers had a much more difficult job than our grandmothers. When Roman fever stalked the streets it must have been comparatively easy to gather in the girls at the danger hour; but when you and I were young, with such beauty calling us, and the spice of disobedience thrown in, and no worse risk than catching cold during the cool hour after sunset, the mothers used to be put to it to keep us in—didn't they?"

She turned again toward Mrs. Ansley, but the latter had reached a delicate point in her knitting. "One, two, three—slip two; yes, they must have been," she assented, without looking up.

Mrs. Slade's eyes rested on her with a deepened attention. "She can knit—in the face of *this*! How like her. . . ."

Mrs. Slade leaned back, brooding, her eyes ranging from the ruins which faced her to the long green hollow of the Forum, the fading glow of the church fronts beyond it, and the outlying immensity of the Colosseum.[3] Suddenly she thought: "It's all very well to say that our girls have done away with sentiment and moonlight. But if Babs Ansley isn't out to catch that young aviator—the one who's a Marchese—then I don't know anything. And Jenny has no chance beside her. I know that too. I wonder if that's why Grace Ansley likes the two girls to go everywhere together? My poor Jenny as a foil—!" Mrs. Slade gave a hardly audible laugh, and at the sound Mrs. Ansley dropped her knitting.

"Yes—?"

"I—oh, nothing. I was only thinking how your Babs carries everything before her. That Campolieri boy is one of the best matches in Rome. Don't look so innocent, my dear—you know he is. And I was wondering, ever so respectfully, you understand . . . wondering how two such exemplary characters as you and Horace had managed to produce anything quite so dynamic." Mrs. Slade laughed again, with a touch of asperity.

Mrs. Ansley's hands lay inert across her needles. She looked straight out at the great accumulated wreckage of passion and splendor at her feet. But her small profile was almost expressionless. At length she said: "I think you overrate Babs, my dear."

Mrs. Slade's tone grew easier. "No; I don't. I appreciate her. And perhaps envy you. Oh, my girl's perfect; if I were a chronic invalid I'd—well, I think I'd rather be in Jenny's hands. There must be times . . . but there! I always wanted a brilliant daughter . . . and never quite understood why I got an angel instead."

Mrs. Ansley echoed her laugh in a faint murmur. "Babs is an angel too."

"Of course—of course! But she's got rainbow wings. Well, they're wandering

---

[3]An ancient amphitheater in Rome.

by the sea with their young men; and here we sit . . . and it all brings back the past a little too acutely."

Mrs. Ansley had resumed her knitting. One might almost have imagined (if one had known her less well, Mrs. Slade reflected) that, for her also, too many memories rose from the lengthening shadows of those august ruins. But no; she was simply absorbed in her work. What was there for her to worry about? She knew that Babs would almost certainly come back engaged to the extremely eligible Campolieri. "And she'll sell the New York house, and settle down near them in Rome, and never be in their way . . . she's much too tactful. But she'll have an excellent cook, and just the right people in for bridge and cocktails . . . and a perfectly peaceful old age among her grandchildren."

Mrs. Slade broke off this prophetic flight with a recoil of self-disgust. There was no one of whom she had less right to think unkindly than of Grace Ansley. Would she never cure herself of envying her? Perhaps she had begun too long ago.

She stood up and leaned against the parapet, filling her troubled eyes with the tranquilizing magic of the hour. But instead of tranquilizing her the sight seemed to increase her exasperation. Her gaze turned toward the Colosseum. Already its golden flank was drowned in purple shadow, and above it the sky curved crystal clear, without light or color. It was the moment when afternoon and evening hang balanced in midheaven.

Mrs. Slade turned back and laid her hand on her friend's arm. The gesture was so abrupt that Mrs. Ansley looked up, startled.

"The sun's set. You're not afraid, my dear?"

"Afraid — ?"

"Of Roman fever or pneumonia? I remember how ill you were that winter. As a girl you had a very delicate throat, hadn't you?"

"Oh, we're all right up here. Down below, in the Forum, it does get deathly cold, all of a sudden . . . but not here."

"Ah, of course you know because you had to be so careful." Mrs. Slade turned back to the parapet. She thought: "I must make one more effort not to hate her." Aloud she said: "Whenever I look at the Forum from up here, I remember that story about a great-aunt of yours, wasn't she? A dreadfully wicked great-aunt?"

"Oh, yes; great-aunt Harriet. The one who was supposed to have sent her young sister out to the Forum after sunset to gather a night-blooming flower for her album. All our great-aunts and grandmothers used to have albums of dried flowers."

Mrs. Slade nodded. "But she really sent her because they were in love with the same man —"

"Well, that was the family tradition. They said Aunt Harriet confessed it years afterward. At any rate, the poor little sister caught the fever and died. Mother used to frighten us with the story when we were children."

"And you frightened *me* with it, that winter when you and I were here as girls. The winter I was engaged to Delphin."

Mrs. Ansley gave a faint laugh. "Oh, did I? Really frightened you? I don't believe you're easily frightened."

"Not often; but I was then. I was easily frightened because I was too happy. I wonder if you know what that means?"

"I — yes . . ." Mrs. Ansley faltered.

"Well, I suppose that was why the story of your wicked aunt made such an impression on me. And I thought: "There's no more Roman fever, but the Forum is deathly cold after sunset — especially after a hot day. And the Colosseum's even colder and damper."

"The Colosseum — ?"

"Yes. It wasn't easy to get in, after the gates were locked for the night. Far from easy. Still, in those days it could be managed; it *was* managed, often. Lovers met there who couldn't meet elsewhere. You knew that?"

"I — I dare say. I don't remember."

"You don't remember? You don't remember going to visit some ruins or other one evening, just after dark, and catching a bad chill? You were supposed to have gone to see the moon rise. People always said that expedition was what caused your illness."

There was a moment's silence; then Mrs. Ansley rejoined: "Did they? It was all so long ago."

"Yes. And you got well again — so it didn't matter. But I suppose it struck your friends — the reason given for your illness, I mean — because everybody knew you were so prudent on account of your throat, and your mother took such care of you. . . . You *had* been out late sight-seeing, hadn't you, that night?"

"Perhaps I had. The most prudent girls aren't always prudent. What made you think of it now?"

Mrs. Slade seemed to have no answer ready. But after a moment she broke out: "Because I simply can't bear it any longer — !"

Mrs. Ansley lifted her head quickly. Her eyes were wide and very pale. "Can't bear what!"

"Why — your not knowing that I've always known why you went."

"Why I went — ?"

"Yes. You think I'm bluffing, don't you? Well, you went to meet the man I was engaged to — and I can repeat every word of the letter that took you there."

While Mrs. Slade spoke Mrs. Ansley had risen unsteadily to her feet. Her bag, her knitting and gloves, slid in a panic-stricken heap to the ground. She looked at Mrs. Slade as though she were looking at a ghost.

"No, no — don't," she faltered out.

"Why not? Listen, if you don't believe me. 'My one darling, things can't go on like this. I must see you alone. Come to the Colosseum immediately after dark tomorrow. There will be somebody to let you in. No one whom you need fear will suspect' — but perhaps you've forgotten what the letter said?"

Mrs. Ansley met the challenge with an unexpected composure. Steadying herself against the chair she looked at her friend, and replied: "No; I know it by heart too."

"And the signature? 'Only *your* D.S.' Was that it? I'm right, am I? That was the letter that took you out that evening after dark?"

Mrs. Ansley was still looking at her. It seemed to Mrs. Slade that a slow struggle was going on behind the voluntarily controlled mask of her small quiet face. "I shouldn't have thought she had herself so well in hand," Mrs. Slade reflected, almost resentfully. But at this moment Mrs. Ansley spoke. "I don't know how you knew. I burnt that letter at once."

"Yes; you would, naturally — you're so prudent!" The sneer was open now.

"And if you burnt the letter you're wondering how on earth I know what was in it. That's it, isn't it?"

Mrs. Slade waited, but Mrs. Ansley did not speak.

"Well, my dear, I know what was in the letter because I wrote it!"

"You wrote it?"

"Yes."

The two women stood for a minute staring at each other in the last golden light. Then Mrs. Ansley dropped back into her chair. "Oh," she murmured, and covered her face with her hands.

Mrs. Slade waited nervously for another word or movement. None came, and at length she broke out: "I horrify you."

Mrs. Ansley's hands dropped to her knee. The face they uncovered was streaked with tears. "I wasn't thinking of you. I was thinking — it was the only letter I ever had from him!"

"And I wrote it. Yes; I wrote it! But I was the girl he was engaged to. Did you happen to remember that?"

Mrs. Ansley's head drooped again. "I'm not trying to excuse myself . . . I remembered. . . ."

"And still you went?"

"Still I went."

Mrs. Slade stood looking down on the small bowed figure at her side. The flame of her wrath had already sunk, and she wondered why she had ever thought there would be any satisfaction in inflicting so purposeless a wound on her friend. But she had to justify herself.

"You do understand? I'd found out — and I hated you, hated you. I knew you were in love with Delphin — and I was afraid; afraid of you, of your quiet ways, your sweetness . . . your . . . well, I wanted you out of the way, that's all. Just for a few weeks; just till I was sure of him. So in a blind fury I wrote that letter. . . . I don't know why I'm telling you now."

"I suppose," said Mrs. Ansley slowly, "it's because you've always gone on hating me."

"Perhaps. Or because I wanted to get the whole thing off my mind." She paused. "I'm glad you destroyed the letter. Of course I never thought you'd die."

Mrs. Ansley relapsed into silence, and Mrs. Slade, leaning above her, was conscious of a strange sense of isolation, of being cut off from the warm current of human communication. "You think me a monster!"

"I don't know. . . . It was the only letter I had, and you say he didn't write it?"

"Ah, how you care for him still!"

"I cared for that memory," said Mrs. Ansley.

Mrs. Slade continued to look down on her. She seemed physically reduced by the blow — as if, when she got up, the wind might scatter her like a puff of dust. Mrs. Slade's jealousy suddenly leapt up again at the sight. All these years the woman had been living on that letter. How she must have loved him, to treasure the mere memory of its ashes! The letter of the man her friend was engaged to. Wasn't it she who was the monster?

"You tried your best to get him away from me, didn't you? But you failed; and I kept him. That's all."

"Yes. That's all."

"I wish now I hadn't told you. I'd no idea you'd feel about it as you do; I thought you'd be amused. It all happened so long ago, as you say; and you must do me the justice to remember that I had no reason to think you'd ever taken it seriously. How could I, when you were married to Horace Ansley two months afterward? As soon as you could get out of bed your mother rushed you off to Florence and married you. People were rather surprised — they wondered at its being done so quickly; but I thought I knew. I had an idea you did it out of *pique* — to be able to say you'd got ahead of Delphin and me. Girls have such silly reasons for doing the most serious things. And your marrying so soon convinced me that you'd never really cared."

"Yes. I suppose it would," Mrs. Ansley assented.

The clear heaven overhead was emptied of all its gold. Dusk spread over it, abuptly darkening the Seven Hills. Here and there lights began to twinkle through the foliage at their feet. Steps were coming and going on the deserted terrace — waiters looking out of the doorway at the head of the stairs, then reappearing with trays and napkins and flasks of wine. Tables were moved, chairs straightened. A feeble string of electric lights flickered out. Some vases of faded flowers were carried away, and brought back replenished. A stout lady in a dust coat suddenly appeared, asking in broken Italian if anyone had seen the elastic band which held together her tattered Baedeker.[4] She poked with her stick under the table at which she had lunched, the waiters assisting.

The corner where Mrs. Slade and Mrs. Ansley sat was still shadowy and deserted. For a long time neither of them spoke. At length Mrs. Slade began again: "I suppose I did it as a sort of joke — "

"A joke?"

"Well, girls are ferocious sometimes, you know. Girls in love especially. And I remember laughing to myself all that evening at the idea that you were waiting around there in the dark, dodging out of sight, listening for every sound, trying to get in — Of course I was upset when I heard you were so ill afterward."

Mrs. Ansley had not moved for a long time. But now she turned slowly toward her companion. "But I didn't wait. He'd arranged everything. He was there. We were let in at once," she said.

Mrs. Slade sprang up from her leaning position. "Delphin there? They let you in? — Ah, now you're lying!" she burst out with violence.

Mrs. Ansley's voice grew clearer, and full of surprise. "But of course he was there. Naturally he came — "

"Came? How did he know he'd find you there? You must be raving!"

Mrs. Ansley hesitated, as though reflecting. "But I answered the letter. I told him I'd be there. So he came."

Mrs. Slade flung her hands up to her face. "Oh, God — you answered! I never thought of your answering. . . ."

---

[4]A series of guidebooks for travelers.

"It's odd you never thought of it, if you wrote the letter."

"Yes. I was blind with rage."

Mrs. Ansley rose, and drew her fur scarf about her. "It is cold here. We'd better go. . . . I'm sorry for you," she said, as she clasped the fur about her throat.

The unexpected words sent a pang through Mrs. Slade. "Yes; we'd better go." She gathered up her bag and cloak. "I don't know why you should be sorry for me," she muttered.

Mrs. Ansley stood looking away from her toward the dusky secret mass of the Colosseum. "Well — because I didn't have to wait that night."

Mrs. Slade gave an unquiet laugh. "Yes; I was beaten there. But I oughtn't to begrudge it to you, I suppose. At the end of all these years. After all, I had everything; I had him for twenty-five years. And you had nothing but that one letter that he didn't write."

Mrs. Ansley was again silent. At length she turned toward the door of the terrace. She took a step, and turned back, facing her companion.

"I had Barbara," she said, and began to move ahead of Mrs. Slade toward the stairway.

(1936)

QUESTIONS

1. What is a *memento mori*? Why does the narrator use the term to describe the scene below the terrace?

2. What details take on new significance after you know the ending? What is it like to reread the story once the surprise is gone?

3. Mrs. Slade thinks of her widowhood as "unemployment." What sort of "employment" did she have as a socialite wife? In what ways could that be considered "employment"?

4. The narrator moves between the two women as filter-characters. How are the shifts in filter indicated? How are they justified? Do the narrator's sympathies shift or are they lodged in one filter?

5. How do the Americans in this story view Europe? Is there any irony in the use of the setting?

❖ FLANNERY O'CONNOR

The River

Flannery O'Connor (1925–1964) was born in Savannah, Georgia, where she lived until 1938. She studied at the Georgia State College for Women and then on a fellowship in the Writer's Workshop of the University of Iowa, from which she received a Master of Fine Arts degree in 1947. She moved to New York where she started publishing in important literary journals. In 1950 she discovered that she had inherited a blood disease from which her father died. She returned to her mother's farm near Macon, Georgia, where she spent the last 14 years of her life. Though in constant pain, she managed to write continually and even to give lectures. She published two novels, *Wise Blood* (1952) and *The Violent Bear It Away* (1960). The first was made into a film by John Huston. Her short stories were published in *A Good Man Is Hard to Find* (1955) and *Everything That Rises Must Converge* (1965). Her *Complete Stories* appeared in 1971 and won her, posthumously, the National Book Award. Her collected letters were published in 1979 in a volume entitled *The Habit of Being.* Being a Roman Catholic in heavily Baptist country gave O'Connor a peculiar vantage on life in the South. Her fiction often concerns the violent and the grotesque, but manages to evoke in the reader a strange sense of empathy and even sympathy for the plights of her bizarre characters.

The child stood glum and limp in the middle of the dark living room while his father pulled him into a plaid coat. His right arm was hung in the sleeve but the father buttoned the coat anyway and pushed him forward toward a pale spotted hand that stuck through the half-open door.

"He ain't fixed right," a loud voice said from the hall.

"Well then for Christ's sake fix him," the father muttered. "It's six o'clock in the morning." He was in his bathrobe and barefooted. When he got the child to the door and tried to shut it, he found her looming in it, a speckled skeleton in a long pea-green coat and felt helmet.

"And his and my carfare," she said. "It'll be twict we have to ride the car."

He went in the bedroom again to get the money and when he came back, she and the boy were both standing in the middle of the room. She was taking stock. "I couldn't smell those dead cigarette butts long if I was ever to come sit with you," she said, shaking him down in his coat.

"Here's the change," the father said. He went to the door and opened it wide and waited.

After she had counted the money she slipped it somewhere inside her coat and walked over to a watercolor hanging near the phonograph. "I know what time it is," she said, peering closely at the black lines crossing into broken planes of violent color.

"I ought to. My shift goes on at 10 P.M. and don't get off till 5 and it takes me one hour to ride the Vine Street car."

"Oh, I see," he said; "well, we'll expect him back tonight, about eight or nine?"

"Maybe later," she said. "We're going to the river to a healing. This particular preacher don't get around this way often. I wouldn't have paid for that," she said, nodding at the painting, "I would have drew it myself."

"All right, Mrs. Connin, we'll see you then," he said, drumming on the door. A toneless voice called from the bedroom, "Bring me an icepack."

"Too bad his mamma's sick," Mrs. Connin said. "What's her trouble?"

"We don't know," he muttered.

"We'll ask the preacher to pray for her. He's healed a lot of folks. The Reverend Bevel Summers. Maybe she ought to see him sometime."

"Maybe so," he said. "We'll see you tonight," and he disappeared into the bedroom and left them go.

The little boy stared at her silently, his nose and eyes running. He was four or five. He had a long face and bulging chin and half-shut eyes set far apart. He seemed mute and patient, like an old sheep waiting to be let out.

"You'll like this preacher," she said. "The Reverend Bevel Summers. You ought to hear him sing."

The bedroom door opened suddenly and the father stuck his head out and said, "Good-by, old man. Have a good time."

"Good-by," the little boy said and jumped as if he had been shot.

Mrs. Connin gave the watercolor another look. Then they went out into the hall and rang for the elevator. "I wouldn't have drew it," she said.

Outside the gray morning was blocked off on either side by the unlit empty buildings. "It's going to fair up later," she said, "but this is the last time we'll be able to have any preaching at the river this year. Wipe your nose, Sugar Boy."

He began rubbing his sleeve across it but she stopped him. "That ain't nice," she said. "Where's your handkerchief?"

He put his hands in his pockets and pretended to look for it while she waited. "Some people don't care how they send one off," she murmured to her reflection in the coffee shop window. "You pervide." She took a red and blue flowered handkerchief out of her pocket and stooped down and began to work on his nose. "Now blow," she said and he blew. "You can borry it. Put it in your pocket."

He folded it up and put it in his pocket carefully and they walked on to the corner and leaned against the side of a closed drugstore to wait for the car. Mrs. Connin turned up her coat collar so that it met her hat in the back. Her eyelids began to droop and she looked as if she might go to sleep against the wall. The little boy put a slight pressure on her hand.

"What's your name?" she asked in a drowsy voice. "I don't know but only your last name. I should have found out your first name."

His name was Harry Ashfield and he had never thought at any time before of changing it. "Bevel," he said.

Mrs. Connin raised herself from the wall. "Why ain't that a coincident!" she said. "I told you that's the name of this preacher!"

"Bevel," he repeated.

She stood looking down at him as if he had become a marvel to her. "I'll have to see you meet him today," she said. "He's no ordinary preacher. He's a healer. He couldn't do nothing for Mr. Connin though. Mr. Connin didn't have the faith but he said he would try anything once. He had this griping in his gut."

The trolley appeared as a yellow spot at the end of the deserted street.

"He's gone to the government hospital now," she said, "and they taken one-third of his stomach. I tell him he better thank Jesus for what he's got left but he says he ain't thanking nobody. Well I declare," she murmured, "Bevel!"

They walked out to the tracks to wait. "Will he heal me?" Bevel asked.

"What you got?"

'I'm hungry," he decided finally.

"Didn't you have your breakfast?"

"I didn't have time to be hungry yet then," he said.

"Well when we get home we'll both have us something," she said. "I'm ready myself."

They got on the car and sat down a few seats behind the driver and Mrs. Connin took Bevel on her knees. "Now you be a good boy," she said, "and let me get some sleep. Just don't get off my lap." She lay her head back and as he watched, gradually her eyes closed and her mouth fell open to show a few long scattered teeth, some gold and some darker than her face; she began to whistle and blow like a musical skeleton. There was no one in the car but themselves and the driver and when he saw she was asleep, he took out the flowered handkerchief and unfolded it and examined it carefully. Then he folded it up again and unzipped a place in the innerlining of his coat and hid it in there and shortly he went to sleep himself.

Her house was a half-mile from the end of the car line, set back a little from the road. It was tan paper brick with a porch across the front of it and a tin top. On the porch there were three little boys of different sizes with identical speckled faces and one tall girl who had her hair up in so many aluminum curlers that it glared like the roof. The three boys followed them inside and closed in on Bevel. They looked at him silently, not smiling.

"That's Bevel," Mrs. Connin said, taking off her coat. "It's a coincident he's named the same as the preacher. These boys are J. C., Spivey, and Sinclair, and that's Sarah Mildred on the porch. Take off that coat and hang it on the bed post, Bevel."

The three boys watched him while he unbuttoned the coat and took it off. Then they watched him hang it on the bed post and then they stood, watching the coat. They turned abruptly and went out the door and had a conference on the porch.

Bevel stood looking around him at the room. It was part kitchen and part bedroom. The entire house was two rooms and two porches. Close to his foot the tail of a light-colored dog moved up and down between two floor boards as he scratched his back on the underside of the house. Bevel jumped on it but the hound was experienced and had already withdrawn when his feet hit the spot.

The walls were filled with pictures and calendars. There were two round photographs of an old man and woman with collapsed mouths and another picture of a man whose eyebrows dashed out of two bushes of hair and clashed in a heap on the bridge of his nose; the rest of his face stuck out like a bare cliff to fall from. "That's Mr.

Connin," Mrs. Connin said, standing back from the stove for a second to admire the face with him, "but it don't favor him any more." Bevel turned from Mr. Connin to a colored picture over the bed of a man wearing a white sheet. He had long hair and a gold circle around his head and he was sawing on a board while some children stood watching him. He was going to ask who that was when the three boys came in again and motioned for him to follow them. He thought of crawling under the bed and hanging onto one of the legs but the three boys only stood there, speckled and silent, waiting, and after a second he followed them at a little distance out on the porch and around the corner of the house. They started off through a field of rough yellow weeds to the hog pen, a five-foot boarded square full of shoats, which they intended to ease him over into. When they reached it, they turned and waited silently, leaning against the side.

He was coming very slowly, deliberately bumping his feet together as if he had trouble walking. Once he had been beaten up in the park by some strange boys when his sitter forgot him, but he hadn't known anything was going to happen that time until it was over. He began to smell a strong odor of garbage and to hear the noises of a wild animal. He stopped a few feet from the pen and waited, pale but dogged.

The three boys didn't move. Something seemed to have happened to them. They stared over his head as if they saw something coming behind him but he was afraid to turn his own head and look. Their speckles were pale and their eyes were still and gray as glass. Only their ears twitched slightly. Nothing happened. Finally, the one in the middle said, "She'd kill us," and turned, dejected and hacked, and climbed up on the pen and hung over, staring in.

Bevel sat down on the ground, dazed with relief, and grinned up at them.

The one sitting on the pen glanced at him severely. "Hey you," he said after a second, "if you can't climb up and see these pigs you can lift that bottom board off and look in thataway." He appeared to offer this as a kindness.

Bevel had never seen a real pig but he had seen a pig in a book and knew they were small fat pink animals with curly tails and round grinning faces and bow ties. He leaned forward and pulled eagerly at the board.

"Pull harder," the littlest boy said. "It's nice and rotten. Just lift out thet nail."

He eased a long reddish nail out of the soft wood.

"Now you can lift up the board and put your face to the . . ." a quiet voice began.

He had already done it and another face, gray, wet and sour, was pushing into his, knocking him down and back as it scraped out under the plank. Something snorted over him and charged back again, rolling him over and pushing him up from behind and then sending him forward, screaming through the yellow field, while it bounded behind.

The three Connins watched from where they were. The one sitting on the pen held the loose board back with his dangling foot. Their stern faces didn't brighten any but they seemed to become less taut, as if some great need had been partly satisfied. "Maw ain't going to like him lettin out thet hawg," the smallest one said.

Mrs. Connin was on the back porch and caught Bevel up as he reached the steps. The hog ran under the house and subsided, panting, but the child screamed for five minutes. When she had finally calmed him down, she gave him his breakfast and let him sit on her lap while he ate it. The shoat climbed the two steps onto the back porch and stood outside the screen door, looking in with his head lowered sullenly. He was long-legged and hump-backed and part of one of his ears had been bitten off.

"Git away!" Mrs. Connin shouted. "That one yonder favors Mr. Paradise that has the gas station," she said. "You'll see him today at the healing. He's got the cancer over his ear. He always comes to show he ain't been healed."

The shoat stood squinting a few seconds longer and then moved off slowly. "I don't want to see him," Bevel said.

They walked to the river, Mrs. Connin in front with him and the three boys strung out behind and Sarah Mildred, the tall girl, at the end to holler if one of them ran out on the road. They looked like the skeleton of an old boat with two pointed ends, sailing slowly on the edge of the highway. The white Sunday sun followed at a little distance, climbing fast through a scum of gray cloud as if it meant to overtake them. Bevel walked on the outside edge, holding Mrs. Connin's hand and looking down into the orange and purple gulley that dropped off from the concrete.

It occurred to him that he was lucky this time that they had found Mrs. Connin who would take you away for the day instead of an ordinary sitter who only sat where you lived or went to the park. You found out more when you left where you lived. He had found out already this morning that he had been made by a carpenter named Jesus Christ. Before he had thought it had been a doctor named Sladewall, a fat man with a yellow mustache who gave him shots and thought his name was Herbert, but this must have been a joke. They joked a lot where he lived. If he had thought about it before, he would have thought Jesus Christ was a word like "oh" or "damm" or "God," or maybe somebody who had cheated them out of something sometime. When he had asked Mrs. Connin who the man in the sheet in the picture over her bed was, she had looked at him a while with her mouth open. Then she had said, "That's Jesus," and she had kept on looking at him.

In a few minutes she had got up and got a book out of the other room. "See here," she said, turning over the cover, "this belonged to my great grandmamma. I wouldn't part with it for nothing on earth." She ran her finger under some brown writing on a spotted page. "Emma Stevens Oakley, 1832," she said. "Ain't that something to have? And every word of it the gospel truth." She turned the next page and read him the name: "The Life of Jesus Christ for Readers Under Twelve." Then she read him the book.

It was a small book, pale brown on the outside with gold edges and a smell like old putty. It was full of pictures, one of the carpenter driving a crowd of pigs out of a man. They were real pigs, gray and sour-looking, and Mrs. Connin said Jesus had driven them all out of this one man. When she finished reading, she let him sit on the floor and look at the pictures again.

Just before they left for the healing, he had managed to get the book inside his innerlining without her seeing him. Now it made his coat hang down a little farther on one side than the other. His mind was dreamy and serene as they walked along and when they turned off the highway onto a long red clay road winding between banks of honeysuckle, he began to make wild leaps and pull forward on her hand as if he wanted to dash off and snatch the sun which was rolling away ahead of them now.

They walked on the dirt road for a while and then they crossed a field stippled with purple weeds and entered the shadows of a wood where the ground was covered with thick pine needles. He had never been in woods before and he walked carefully, looking from side to side as if he were entering a strange country. They moved along a bridle path that twisted downhill through crackling red leaves, and once, catching at a branch to keep himself from slipping, he looked into two frozen green-gold eyes enclosed in the darkness of a tree hole. At the bottom of the hill, the woods opened suddenly onto a pasture dotted here and there with black and white cows and sloping down, tier after tier, to a broad orange stream where the reflection of the sun was set like a diamond.

There were people standing on the near bank in a group, singing. Long tables were set up behind them and a few cars and trucks were parked in a road that came up by the river. They crossed the pasture, hurrying, because Mrs. Connin, using her hand for a shed over her eyes, saw the preacher already standing out in the water. She dropped her basket on one of the tables and pushed the three boys in front of her into the knot of people so that they wouldn't linger by the food. She kept Bevel by the hand and eased her way up to the front.

The preacher was standing about ten feet out in the stream where the water came up to his knees. He was a tall youth in khaki trousers that he had rolled up higher than the water. He had on a blue shirt and a red scarf around his neck but no hat and his light-colored hair was cut in sideburns that curved into the hollows of his cheeks. His face was all bone and red light reflected from the river. He looked as if he might have been nineteen years old. He was singing in a high twangy voice, above the singing on the bank, and he kept his hands behind him and his head tilted back.

He ended the hymn on a high note and stood silent, looking down at the water and shifting his feet in it. Then he looked up at the people on the bank. They stood close together, waiting; their faces were solemn but expectant and every eye was on him. He shifted his feet again.

"Maybe I know why you come," he said in the twangy voice, "maybe I don't.

"If you ain't come for Jesus, you ain't come for me. If you just come to see can you leave your pain in the river, you ain't come for Jesus. You can't leave your pain in the river," he said. "I never told nobody that." He stopped and looked down at his knees.

"I seen you cure a woman oncet!" a sudden high voice shouted from the hump of people. "Seen that woman git up and walk out straight where she had limped in!"

The preacher lifted one foot and then the other. He seemed almost but not quite to smile. "You might as well go home if that's what you come for," he said.

Then he lifted his head and arms and shouted, "Listen to what I got to say, you people! There ain't but one river and that's the River of Life, made out of Jesus' Blood. That's the river you have to lay your pain in, in the River of Faith, in the River of Life, in the River of Love, in the rich red river of Jesus' Blood, you people!"

His voice grew soft and musical. "All the rivers come from that one River and go back to it like it was the ocean sea and if you believe, you can lay your pain in that River and get rid of it because that's the River that was made to carry sin. It's a River full of pain itself, pain itself, moving toward the Kingdom of Christ, to be washed away, slow, you people, slow as this here old red water river round my feet."

"Listen," he sang, "I read in Mark about an unclean man, I read in Luke about a blind man, I read in John about a dead man! Oh you people hear! The same blood that makes this River red, made that leper clean, made that blind man stare, made that dead man leap! You people with trouble," he cried, "lay it in that River of Blood, lay it in that River of Pain, and watch it move away toward the Kingdom of Christ."

While he preached, Bevel's eyes followed drowsily the slow circles of two silent birds revolving high in the air. Across the river there was a low red and gold grove of sassafras with hills of dark blue trees behind it and an occasional pine jutting over the skyline. Behind, in the distance, the city rose like a cluster of warts on the side of the mountain. The birds revolved downward and dropped lightly in the top of the highest pine and sat hunch-shouldered as if they were supporting the sky.

"If it's this River of Life you want to lay your pain in, then come up," the preacher said, "and lay your sorrow here. But don't be thinking this is the last of it because this old red river don't end here. This old red suffering stream goes on, you people, slow to the Kingdom of Christ. This old red river is good to Baptize in, good to lay your faith in, good to lay your pain in, but it ain't this muddy water here that saves you. I been all up and down this river this week," he said. "Tuesday I was in Fortune Lake, next day in Ideal, Friday me and my wife drove to Lulawillow to see a sick man there. Them people didn't see no healing," he said and his face burned redder for a second. "I never said they would."

While he was talking a fluttering figure had begun to move forward with a kind of butterfly movement — an old woman with flapping arms whose head wobbled as if it might fall off any second. She managed to lower herself at the edge of the bank and let her arms churn in the water. Then she bent farther and pushed her face down in it and raised herself up finally, streaming wet; and still flapping, she turned a time or two in a blind circle until someone reached out and pulled her back into the group.

"She's been that way for thirteen years," a rough voice shouted. "Pass the hat and give this kid his money. That's what he's here for." The shout, directed out to the boy in the river, came from a huge old man who sat like a humped stone on the bumper of a long ancient gray automobile. He had on a gray hat that was turned down over one ear and up over the other to expose a purple bulge on his left temple. He sat bent forward with his hands hanging between his knees and his small eyes half closed.

Bevel stared at him once and then moved into the folds of Mrs. Connin's coat and hid himself.

The boy in the river glanced at the old man quickly and raised his fist. "Believe Jesus or the devil!" he cried. "Testify to one or the other!"

"I know from my own self-experience," a woman's mysterious voice called from the knot of people, "I know from it that this preacher can heal. My eyes have been opened! I testify to Jesus!"

The preacher lifted his arms quickly and began to repeat all that he had said before about the River and the Kingdom of Christ and the old man sat on the bumper, fixing him with a narrow squint. From time to time Bevel stared at him again from around Mrs. Connin.

A man in overalls and a brown coat leaned forward and dipped his hand in the water quickly and shook it and leaned back, and a woman held a baby over the edge of the bank and splashed its feet with water. One man moved a little distance away and sat down on the bank and took off his shoes and waded out into the stream; he stood there for a few minutes with his face tilted as far back as it would go, then he waded back and put on his shoes. All this time, the preacher sang and did not appear to watch what went on.

As soon as he stopped singing, Mrs. Connin lifted Bevel up and said, "Listen here, preacher, I got a boy from town today that I'm keeping. His mamma's sick and he wants you to pray for her. And this is a coincident — his name is Bevel! Bevel," she said, turning to look at the people behind her, "same as his. Ain't that a coincident, though?"

There were some murmurs and Bevel turned and grinned over her shoulder at the faces looking at him. "Bevel," he said in a loud jaunty voice.

"Listen," Mrs. Connin said, "have you ever been Baptized, Bevel?"

He only grinned.

"I suspect he ain't ever been Baptized," Mrs. Connin said, raising her eyebrows at the preacher.

"Swang him over here," the preacher said and took a stride forward and caught him.

He held him in the crook of his arm and looked at the grinning face. Bevel rolled his eyes in a comical way and thrust his face forward, close to the preacher's. "My name is Bevvvuuuuul," he said in a loud deep voice and let the tip of his tongue slide across his mouth.

The preacher didn't smile. His bony face was rigid and his narrow gray eyes reflected the almost colorless sky. There was a loud laugh from the old man sitting on the car bumper and Bevel grasped the back of the preacher's collar and held it tightly. The grin had already disappeared from his face. He had the sudden feeling that this was not a joke. Where he lived everything was a joke. From the preacher's face, he knew immediately that nothing the preacher said or did was a joke. "My mother named me that," he said quickly.

"Have you ever been Baptized?" the preacher asked.

"What's that?" he murmured.

"If I Baptize you," the preacher said, "you'll be able to go to the Kingdom of Christ. You'll be washed in the river of suffering, son, and you'll go by the deep river of life. Do you want that?"

"Yes," the child said, and thought, I won't go back to the apartment then, I'll go under the river.

"You won't be the same again," the preacher said. "You'll count." Then he turned his face to the people and began to preach and Bevel looked over his shoulder at the pieces of the white sun scattered in the river. Suddenly the preacher said, "All right, I'm going to Baptize you now," and without more warning, he tightened his hold an swung him upside down and plunged his head into the water. He held him under while he said the words of Baptism and then he jerked him up again and looked sternly at the gasping child. Bevel's eyes were dark and dilated. "You count now," the preacher said. "You didn't even count before."

The little boy was too shocked to cry. He spit out the muddy water and rubbed his wet sleeve into his eyes and over his face.

"Don't forget his mamma," Mrs. Connin called. "He wants you to pray for his mamma. She's sick."

"Lord," the preacher said, "we pray for somebody in affliction who isn't here to testify. Is your mother sick in the hospital?" he asked. "Is she in pain?"

The child stared at him. "She hasn't got up yet," he said in a high dazed voice. "She has a hangover." The air was so quiet he could hear the broken pieces of the sun knocking in the water.

The preacher looked angry and startled. The red drained out of his face and the sky appeared to darken in his eyes. There was a loud guffaw from the bank and Mr. Paradise shouted, "Haw! Cure the afflicted woman with the hangover!" and began to beat his knee with his fist.

"He's had a long day," Mrs. Connin said, standing with him in the door of the apartment and looking sharply into the room where the party was going on. "I reckon it's past his regular bedtime." One of Bevel's eyes was closed and the other half closed; his nose was running and he kept his mouth open and breathed through it. The damp plaid coat dragged down on one side.

That would be her, Mrs. Connin decided, in the black britches—long black satin britches and barefoot sandals and red toenails. She was lying on half the sofa, with her knees crossed in the air and her head propped on the arm. She didn't get up.

"Hello Harry," she said. "Did you have a big day?" She had a long pale face, smooth and blank, and straight sweet-potato-colored hair, pulled back.

The father went off to get the money. There were two other couples. One of the men, blond with little violet-blue eyes, leaned out of his chair and said, "Well Harry, old man, have a big day?"

"His name ain't Harry. It's Bevel," Mrs. Connin said.

"His name is Harry," *she* said from the sofa. "Whoever heard of anybody named Bevel?"

The little boy had seemed to be going to sleep on his feet, his head drooping farther and farther forward; he pulled it back suddenly and opened one eye; the other was stuck.

"He told me this morning his name was Bevel," Mrs. Connin said in a shocked voice. "The same as our preacher. We been all day at a preaching and healing at the river. He said his name was Bevel, the same as the preacher's. That's what he told me."

"Bevel!" his mother said. "My God! what a name."

"This preacher is name Bevel and there's no better preacher around," Mrs. Connin said. "And furthermore," she added in a defiant tone, "he Baptized this child this morning!"

His mother sat straight up. "Well the nerve!" she muttered.

"Furthermore," Mrs. Connin said, "he's a healer and he prayed for you to be healed."

"Healed!" she almost shouted. "Healed of what for Christ's sake?"

"Of your affliction," Mrs. Connin said icily.

The father had returned with the money and was standing near Mrs. Connin waiting to give it to her. His eyes were lined with red threads. "Go on, go on," he said, "I want to hear more about her affliction. The exact nature of it has escaped . . ." He waved the bill and his voice trailed off. "Healing by prayer is mighty inexpensive," he murmured.

Mrs. Connin stood a second, staring into the room, with a skeleton's appearance of seeing everything. Then, without taking the money, she turned and shut the door behind her. The father swung around, smiling vaguely, and shrugged. The rest of them were looking at Harry. The little boy began to shamble toward the bedroom.

"Come here, Harry," his mother said. He automatically shifted his direction toward her without opening his eye any farther. "Tell me what happened today," she said when he reached her. She began to pull off his coat.

"I don't know," he muttered.

"Yes you do know," she said, feeling the coat heavier on one side. She unzipped the innerlining and caught the book and a dirty handkerchief as they fell out. "Where did you get these?"

"I don't know," he said and grabbed for them. "They're mine. She gave them to me."

She threw the handkerchief down and held the book too high for him to reach and began to read it, her face after a second assuming an exaggerated comical expression. The others moved around and looked at it over her shoulder. "My God," somebody said."

One of the men peered at it sharply from behind a thick pair of glasses. "That's valuable," he said. "That's a collector's item," and he took it away from the rest of them and retired to another chair.

"Don't let George go off with that," his girl said.

"I tell you it's valuable," George said. "1832."

Bevel shifted his direction again toward the room where he slept. He shut the door behind him and moved slowly in the darkness to the bed and sat down and took off his shoes and got under the cover. After a minute a shaft of light let in the tall silhouette of his mother. She tiptoed lightly across the room and sat down on the edge of his bed. "What did that dolt of a preacher say about me?" she whispered. "What lies have you been telling today, honey?"

He shut his eye and heard her voice from a long way away, as if he were under the river and she on top of it. She shook his shoulder. "Harry," she said, leaning down and putting her mouth to his ear, "tell me what he said." She pulled him into a sitting position and he felt as if he had been drawn up from under the river. "Tell me," she whispered and her bitter breath covered his face.

He saw the pale oval close to him in the dark. "He said I'm not the same now," he muttered. "I count."

After a second, she lowered him by his shirt front onto the pillow. She hung over him an instant and brushed her lips against his forehead. Then she got up and moved away, swaying her hips lightly through the shaft of light.

He didn't wake up early but the apartment was still dark and close when he did. For a while he lay there, picking his nose and eyes. Then he sat up in bed and looked out the window. The sun came in palely, stained gray by the glass. Across the street at the Empire Hotel, a colored cleaning woman was looking down from an upper window, resting her face on her folded arms. He got up and put on his shoes and went to the bathroom and then into the front room. He ate two crackers spread with anchovy paste, that he found on the coffee table, and drank some ginger ales left in a bottle and looked around for his book but it was not there.

The apartment was silent except for the faint humming of the refrigerator. He went into the kitchen and found some raisin bread heels and spread a half jar of peanut butter between them and climbed up on the tall kitchen stool and sat chewing the sandwich slowly, wiping his nose every now and then on this shoulder. When he finished he found some chocolate milk and drank that. He would rather have had the ginger ale he saw but they left the bottle openers where he couldn't reach them. He studied what was left in the refrigerator for a while — some shriveled vegetables that she had forgot were there and a lot of brown oranges that she bought and didn't squeeze; there were three or four kinds of cheese and something fishy in a paper bag; the rest was a pork bone. He left the refrigerator door open and wandered back into the dark living room and sat down on the sofa.

He decided they would be out cold until one o'clock and that they would all have to go to a restaurant for lunch. He wasn't high enough for the table yet and the waiter would bring a highchair and he was too big for a highchair. He sat in the middle of the sofa, kicking it with his heels. Then he got up and wandered around the room, looking into the ashtrays at the butts as if this might be a habit. In his own room he had picture books and blocks but they were for the most part torn up; he found the way to get new ones was to tear up the ones he had. There was very little to do at any time but eat; however, he was not a fat boy.

He decided he would empty a few of the ashtrays on the floor. If he only emptied a few, she would think they had fallen. He emptied two, rubbing the ashes carefully into the rug with his finger. Then he lay on the floor for a while, studying his feet which he held up in the air. His shoes were still damp and he began to think about the river.

Very slowly, his expression changed as if he were gradually seeing appear what he didn't know he'd been looking for. Then all of a sudden he knew what he wanted to do.

He got up and tiptoed into their bedroom and stood in the dim light there, looking for her pocketbook. His glance passed her long pale arm hanging off the edge of the bed down to the floor, and across the white mound his father made, and past the crowded bureau, until it rested on the pocketbook hung on the back of a chair. He took a car-token out of it and half a package of Life Savers. Then he left the apartment and caught the car at the corner. He hadn't taken a suitcase because there was nothing from there he wanted to keep.

He got off the car at the end of the line and started down the road he and Mrs.

Connin had taken the day before. He knew there wouldn't be anybody at her house because the three boys and the girl went to school and Mrs. Connin had told him she went out to clean. He passed her yard and walked on the way they had gone to the river. The paper brick houses were far apart and after a while the dirt place to walk on ended and he had to walk on the edge of the highway. The sun was pale yellow and high and hot.

He passed a shack with an orange gas pump in front of it but he didn't see the old man looking out at nothing in particular from the doorway. Mr. Paradise was having an orange drink. He finished it slowly, squinting over the bottle at the small plaid-coated figure disappearing down the road. Then he set the empty bottle on a bench and, still squinting, wiped his sleeve over his mouth. He went in the shack and picked out a peppermint stick, a foot long and two inches thick, from the candy shelf, and stuck it in his hip pocket. Then he got in his car and drove slowly down the highway after the boy.

By the time Bevel came to the field speckled with purple weeds, he was dusty and sweating and he crossed it at a trot to get into the woods as fast as he could. Once inside, he wandered from tree to tree, trying to find the path they had taken yesterday. Finally he found a line worn in the pine needles and followed it until he saw the steep trail twisting down through the trees.

Mr. Paradise had left his automobile back some way on the road and had walked to the place where he was accustomed to sit almost every day, holding an unbaited fishline in the water while he stared at the river passing in front of him. Anyone looking at him from a distance would have seen an old boulder half hidden in the bushes.

Bevel didn't see him at all. He only saw the river, shimmering reddish yellow, and bounded into it with his shoes and his coat on and took a gulp. He swallowed some and spit the rest out and then he stood there in water up to his chest and looked around him. The sky was clear pale blue, all in one piece — except for the hole the sun made — and fringed around the bottom with treetops. His coat floated to the surface and surrounded him like a strange gay lily pad and he stood grinning in the sun. He intended not to fool with preachers any more but to Baptize himself and to keep on going this time until he found the Kingdom of Christ in the river. He didn't mean to waste any more time. He put his head under the water at once and pushed forward.

In a second he began to gasp and sputter and his head reappeared on the surface; he started under again and the same thing happened. The river wouldn't have him. He tried again and came up, choking. This was the way it had been when the preacher held him under — he had had to fight with something that pushed him back in the face. He stopped and thought suddenly: it's another joke, it's just another joke! He thought how far he had come for nothing and he began to hit and splash and kick the filthy river. His feet were already treading on nothing. He gave one low cry of pain and indignation. Then he heard a shout and turned his head and saw something like a giant pig bounding after him, shaking a red and white club and shouting. He plunged under once and this time, the waiting current caught him like a long gentle hand and pulled him swiftly forward and down. For an instant he was overcome with surprise; then since he was moving quickly and knew that he was getting somewhere, all his fury and his fear left him.

Mr. Paradise's head appeared from time to time on the surface of the water. Finally, far downstream, the old man rose like some ancient water monster and stood empty-handed, staring with his dull eyes as far down the river line as he could see.

(1953)

QUESTIONS

1. Does Harry know why he calls himself Bevel? Why does the narrator begin to call him Bevel?

2. At the beginning of the short story, did you understand why the boy was being taken care of by a series of baby-sitters? Is the narrator deliberately misleading you, withholding information to create suspense, adopting the limited perspective of a filter-character, or doing something else?

3. How do you react when a detail or image keeps reappearing in a story? Think about the number of times you encounter water, or, for that matter, pigs, in this story. Do these images take on extra meaning by reappearing in different contexts? Can you pin down a specific meaning for either one?

4. Is this a sad story? A funny one? An ironic one? What do you look for in deciding on a short story's tone?

5. Much of the imagery and content of this story turns on a specific kind of Christianity. Compare O'Connor's use of Christian symbols and beliefs with that of another writer, such as Mary McCarthy in "C.Y.E." (pp. 179–184) or James Baldwin in "The Rockpile" (pp. 153–159).

❖ EDGAR ALLAN POE
The Tell-Tale Heart

Edgar Allan Poe (1809–1849) was born in Boston. After his father, an actor, deserted the family, and his mother, an actress, died in 1811, Poe was adopted by John Allan, of Richmond, Virginia. Allan supported Poe's education, in England and at the University of Virginia. He served in the army from 1827 to 1829, but ruined his chances at West Point by excessive drinking and gambling. Allan then disowned him as a profligate. Poe moved in with an aunt in Baltimore and set up as a writer. His short stories—a genre he did much to invent—began to appear in newspapers and literary magazines. In 1835 he became editor of *The Southern Literary Messenger* and later of his own magazine, *The Stylus*. In 1836 he married his thirteen-year-old cousin, Virginia. He moved to New York City but suffered terrible personal problems—the death of his wife and his own ongoing addiction to alcohol and drugs. Still, he published much work in the last years of his short life: the novel *The Narrative of Arthur Gordon Pym* (1838) and two collections of short stories and poems, *Tales of the Grotesque and Arabesque* (1840) and *The Raven and Other Poems* (1845). In 1849, he was found unconscious in a Baltimore gutter and died a few days later. Like Dostoevsky, Poe had great insight into the neurotic mind. Despite the amorality of his life and the preoccupation of his fiction with evil, his reputation has grown over the century and a half since his death. He has been of particular interest to the French, through the translations of Charles Baudelaire. Poe not only invented the detective story but also was a formidable literary critic and theorist.

True!—nervous—very, very dreadfully nervous I had been and am; but why *will* you say that I am mad? The disease had sharpened my senses—not destroyed—not dulled them. Above all was the sense of hearing acute. I heard all things in the heaven and in the earth. I heard many things in hell. How, then, am I mad? Hearken! and observe how healthy—how calmly I can tell you the whole story.

It is impossible to say how first the idea entered my brain; but once conceived, it haunted me day and night. Object there was none. Passion there was none. I loved the old man. He had never wronged me. He had never given me insult. For his gold I had no desire. I think it was his eye! yes, it was this! One of his eyes resembled that of a vulture—a pale blue eye, with a film over it. Whenever it fell upon me, my blood ran cold; and so by degrees—very gradually—I made up my mind to take the life of the old man, and thus rid myself of the eye for ever.

Now this is the point. You fancy me mad. Madmen know nothing. But you should have seen *me*. You should have seen how wisely I proceeded—with what caution—with what foresight—with what dissimulation I went to work! I was never

kinder to the old man than during the whole week before I killed him. And every
night, about midnight, I turned the latch of his door and opened it—oh, so gently!
And then, when I had made an opening sufficient for my head, I put in a dark lantern,
all closed, closed, so that no light shone out, and then I thrust in my head. Oh, you
would have laughed to see how cunningly I thrust it in! I moved it slowly—very, very
slowly, so that I might not disturb the old man's sleep. It took me an hour to place my
whole head within the opening so far that I could see him as he lay upon his bed.
Ha!—would a madman have been so wise as this? And then, when my head was well
in the room, I undid the lantern cautiously—oh, so cautiously—cautiously (for the
hinges creaked)—I undid it just so much that a single thin ray fell upon the vulture
eye. And this I did for seven long nights—every night just at midnight—but I found
the eye always closed; and so it was impossible to do the work; for it was not the old
man who vexed me, but his Evil Eye. And every morning, when the day broke, I went
boldly into the chamber, and spoke courageously to him, calling him by name in a
hearty tone, and inquiring how he had passed the night. So you see he would have been
a very profound old man, indeed, to suspect that every night, just at twelve, I looked in
upon him while he slept.

Upon the eighth night I was more than usually cautious in opening the door.
A watch's minute hand moves more quickly than did mine. Never before that night
had I *felt* the extent of my own powers—of my sagacity. I could scarcely contain my
feelings of triumph. To think that there I was, opening the door, little by little, and he
not even to dream of my secret deeds or thoughts. I fairly chuckled at the idea; and
perhaps he heard me; for he moved on the bed suddenly, as if startled. Now you may
think that I drew back—but no. His room was as black as pitch with the thick
darkness (for the shutters were close fastened, through fear of robbers), and so I knew
that he could not see the opening of the door, and I kept pushing it on steadily,
steadily.

I had my head in, and was about to open the lantern, when my thumb slipped
upon the tin fastening, and the old man sprang up in the bed, crying out—"Who's
there?"

I kept quite still and said nothing. For a whole hour I did not move a muscle,
and in the meantime I did not hear him lie down. He was still sitting up in the bed
listening;—just as I have done, night after night, hearkening to the death watches[1] in
the wall.

Presently I heard a slight groan, and I knew it was the groan of mortal terror.
It was not a groan of pain or of grief—oh, no!—it was the low stifled sound that arises
from the bottom of the soul when overcharged with awe. I knew the sound well. Many
a night, just at midnight, when all the world slept, it has welled up from my own
bosom, deepening, with its dreadful echo, the terrors that distracted me. I say I knew it
well. I knew what the old man felt, and pitied him, although I chuckled at heart. I
knew that he had been lying awake ever since the first slight noise, when he had
turned in the bed. His fears had been ever since growing upon him. He had been trying
to fancy them causeless, but could not. He had been saying to himself—"It is nothing

[1]Beetles that make a ticking sound as they bore through wood. This sound was believed to be an omen of
death.

but the wind in the chimney — it is only a mouse crossing the floor," or "it is merely a cricket which has made a single chirp." Yes, he had been trying to comfort himself with these suppositions; but he had found all in vain. *All in vain*; because Death, in approaching him, had stalked with his black shadow before him, and enveloped the victim. And it was the mournful influence of the unperceived shadow that caused him to feel — although he neither saw nor heard — to *feel* the presence of my head within the room.

When I had waited a long time, very patiently, without hearing him lie down, I resolved to open a little — a very, very little crevice in the lantern. So I opened it — you cannot imagine how stealthily, stealthily — until, at length, a single dim ray, like the thread of the spider, shot from out the crevice and full upon the vulture eye.

It was open — wide, wide open — and I grew furious as I gazed upon it. I saw it with perfect distinctness — all a dull blue, with a hideous veil over it that chilled the very marrow in my bones; but I could see nothing else of the old man's face or person: for I had directed the ray as if by instinct, precisely upon the damned spot.

And now have I not told you that what you mistake for madness is but over-acuteness of the senses? — now, I say, there came to my ears a low, dull, quick sound, such as a watch makes when enveloped in cotton. I knew *that* sound well too. It was the beating of the old man's heart. It increased my fury, as the beating of a drum stimulates the soldier into courage.

But even yet I refrained and kept still. I scarcely breathed. I held the lantern motionless. I tried how steadily I could maintain the ray upon the eye. Meantime the hellish tattoo of the heart increased. It grew quicker and quicker, and louder and louder every instant. The old man's terror *must* have been extreme! It grew louder, I say, louder every moment! — do you mark me well? I have told you that I am nervous: so I am. And now at the dead hour of the night, amid the dreadful silence of that old house, so strange a noise as this excited me to uncontrollable terror. Yet, for some minutes longer I refrained and stood still. But the beating grew louder, louder! I thought the heart must burst. And now a new anxiety seized me — the sound would be heard by a neighbor! The old man's hour had come! With a loud yell, I threw open the lantern and leaped into the room. He shrieked once — once only. In an instant I dragged him to the floor, and pulled the heavy bed over him. I then smiled gaily, to find the deed so far done. But, for many minutes, the heart beat on with a muffled sound. This, however, did not vex me; it would not be heard through the wall. At length it ceased. The old man was dead. I removed the bed and examined the corpse. Yes, he was stone, stone dead. I placed my hand upon the heart and held it there many minutes. There was no pulsation. He was stone dead. His eye would trouble me no more.

If still you think me mad, you will think so no longer when I describe the wise precautions I took for the concealment of the body. The night waned, and I worked hastily, but in silence. First of all I dismembered the corpse. I cut off the head and the arms and the legs.

I then took up three planks from the flooring of the chamber, and deposited all between the scantlings.[2] I then replaced the boards so cleverly, so cunningly, that no

---

[2] Narrow timbers.

human eye — not even *his* — could have detected anything wrong. There was nothing to wash out — no stain of any kind — no bloodspot whatever. I had been too wary for that. A tub had caught all — ha! ha!

When I had made an end of these labors, it was four o'clock — still dark as midnight. As the bell sounded the hour, there came a knocking at the street door. I went down to open it with a light heart, — for what had I *now* to fear? There entered three men, who introduced themselves, with perfect suavity, as officers of the police. A shriek had been heard by a neighbor during the night; suspicion of foul play had been aroused; information had been lodged at the police office, and they (the officers) had been deputed to search the premises.

I smiled, — for *what* had I to fear? I bade the gentlemen welcome. The shriek, I said, was my own in a dream. The old man, I mentioned, was absent in the country. I took my visitors all over the house. I bade them search — search *well*. I led them, at length, to *his* chamber. I showed them his treasures, secure, undisturbed. In the enthusiasm of my confidence, I brought chairs into the room, and desired them *here* to rest from their fatigues, while I myself, in the wild audacity of my perfect triumph, placed my own seat upon the very spot beneath which reposed the corpse of the victim.

The officers were satisfied. My *manner* had convinced them. I was singularly at ease. They sat, and while I answered cheerily, they chatted familiar things. But, ere long, I felt myself getting pale and wished them gone. My head ached, and I fancied a ringing in my ears: but still they sat and still chatted. The ringing became more distinct: — it continued and became more distinct: I talked more freely to get rid of the feeling: but it continued and gained definitiveness — until, at length, I found that the noise was *not* within my ears.

No doubt I now grew *very* pale: — but I talked more fluently, and with a heightened voice. Yet the sound increased — and what could I do? It was *a low, dull, quick sound — much such a sound as a watch makes when enveloped in cotton.* I gasped for breath — and yet the officers heard it not. I talked more quickly — more vehemently; but the noise steadily increased. I arose and argued about trifles, in a high key and with violent gesticulations, but the noise steadily increased. Why *would* they not be gone? I paced the floor to and fro with heavy strides, as if excited to fury by the observation of the men — but the noise steadily increased. Oh God! what *could* I do? I foamed — I raved — I swore! I swung the chair upon which I had been sitting, and grated it upon the boards, but the noise arose over all and continually increased. It grew louder — louder — *louder!* And still the men chatted pleasantly, and smiled. Was it possible they heard not? Almighty God! — no, no! They heard! — they suspected! — they *knew!* — they were making a mockery of my horror! — this I thought, and this I think. But any thing was better than this agony! Any thing was more tolerable than this derision! I could bear those hypocritical smiles no longer! I felt that I must scream or die! — and now — again! — hark! louder! louder! louder! *louder!* —

"Villains!" I shrieked, "dissemble no more! I admit the deed! — tear up the planks! — here, here! — it is the beating of his hideous heart!"

(1850)

QUESTIONS

1. What does the immediate use of the word "true!" suggest about this short story? Does the narrator make any overtly untrue statements?

2. Poe is often credited with inventing the detective story. Besides the fact that this story is about a murder, is there anything about the way it is constructed or told that is reminiscent of detective fiction?

3. Is the "old man" the narrator's Old Man, in the slang sense — his father? Can this question be answered from evidence within the story? Does it make a difference to the story's theme or its psychological content?

4. What is the story's psychological content? Is it about abnormal or normal psyches, or both?

5. In a famous essay, Poe claims that every element of a good story must contribute to a single effect. Does this short story achieve a single effect? Does every word contribute to it? Is Poe's a good test for judging short stories?

❖ RING LARDNER
Haircut

Ring Lardner (1885–1933) was born and raised in Niles, Michigan. His career was centered on journalism, especially baseball reporting. He also wrote a humorous newspaper column for many years. Many of his short stories have as heroes baseball players, golfers, bridge-players, and boxers. Like Samuel Clemens (Mark Twain), Lardner became cynical over the years and his fictional world came to be populated by "mental sadists, flour-flushers, intolerable gossipers, meal ticket females, interfering morons, brainless flirts, liars, brutes, spiteful snobs, vulgar climbers, dishonest jockeys" (the list was compiled by the critic Clifton Fadiman). Despite their bitter tone, many of his stories remain funny. His short story collections include *You Know Me, Al* (1916), *Own Your Own Home* (1919), *How to Write Short Stories* (1924), *Round Up* (1929), and *Ring Lardner's Best Short Stories* (1938).

I got another barber that comes over from Carterville and helps me out Saturdays, but the rest of the time I can get along all right alone. You can see for yourself that this ain't no New York City and besides that, the most of the boys works all day and don't have no leisure to drop in here and get themselves prettied up.

You're a newcomer, ain't you? I thought I hadn't seen you round before. I hope you like it good enough to stay. As I say, we ain't no New York City or Chicago, but we have pretty good times. Not as good, though, since Jim Kendall got killed. When he was alive, him and Hod Meyers used to keep this town in an uproar. I bet they was more laughin' done here than any town its size in America.

Jim was comical, and Hod was pretty near a match for him. Since Jim's gone, Hod tries to hold his end up just the same as ever, but it's tough goin' when you ain't got nobody to kind of work with.

They used to be plenty fun in here Saturdays. This place is jam-packed Saturdays, from four o'clock on. Jim and Hod would show up right after their supper, round six o'clock. Jim would set himself down in that big chair, nearest the blue spittoon. Whoever had been settin' in that chair, why they'd get up when Jim come in and give it to him.

You'd of thought it was a reserved seat like they have sometimes in a theayter. Hod would generally always stand or walk up and down, or some Saturdays, of course, he'd be settin' in this chair part of the time, gettin' a haircut.

Well, Jim would set there a w'ile without openin' his mouth only to spit, and then finally he'd say to me, "Whitey," — my right name, that is, my right first name, is Dick, but everybody round here calls me Whitey — Jim would say, "Whitey, your nose looks like a rosebud tonight. You must of been drinkin' some of your aw de cologne."

So I'd say, "No, Jim, but you look like you'd been drinkin' somethin' of that kind or somethin' worse."

Jim would have to laugh at that, but then he'd speak up and say, "No, I ain't had nothin' to drink, but that ain't sayin' I wouldn't like somethin'. I wouldn't even mind if it was wood alcohol."

Then Hod Meyers would say, "Neither would your wife." That would set everybody to laughin' because Jim and his wife wasn't on very good terms. She'd of divorced him only they wasn't no chance to get alimony and she didn't have no way to take care of herself and the kids. She couldn't never understand Jim. He *was* kind of rough, but a good fella at heart.

Him and Hod had all kinds of sport with Milt Sheppard. I don't suppose you've seen Milt. Well, he's got an Adam's apple that looks more like a mushmelon. So I'd be shavin' Milt and when I'd start to shave down here on his neck, Hod would holler, "Hey, Whitey, wait a minute! Before you cut into it, let's make up a pool and see who can guess closest to the number of seeds."

And Jim would say, "If Milt hadn't of been so hoggish, he'd of ordered a half a cantaloupe instead of a whole one and it might not of stuck in his throat."

All the boys would roar at this and Milt himself would force a smile, though the joke was on him. Jim certainly was a card!

There's his shavin' mug, settin' on the shelf, right next to Charley Vail's. "Charles M. Vail." That's the druggist. He comes in regular for his shave, three times a week. And Jim's is the cup next to Charley's. "James H. Kendall." Jim won't need no shavin' mug no more, but I'll leave it there just the same for old time's sake. Jim certainly was a character!

Years ago, Jim used to travel for a canned goods concern over in Carterville. They sold canned goods. Jim had the whole northern half of the State and was on the road five days out of every week. He'd drop in here Saturdays and tell his experiences for that week. It was rich.

I guess he paid more attention to playin' jokes than makin' sales. Finally the concern let him out and he come right home here and told everybody he'd been fired instead of sayin' he'd resigned like most fellas would of.

It was a Saturday and the shop was full and Jim got up out of that chair and says, "Gentlemen, I got an important announcement to make. I been fired from my job."

Well, they asked him if he was in earnest and he said he was and nobody could think of nothin' to say till Jim finally broke the ice himself. He says, "I been sellin' canned goods and now I'm canned goods myself."

You see, the concern he'd been workin' for was a factory that made canned goods. Over in Carterville. And now Jim said he was canned himself. He was certainly a card!

Jim had a great trick that he used to play w'ile he was travelin'. For instance, he'd be ridin' on a train and they'd come to some little town like — well, like — we'll say, like Benton. Jim would look out the train window and read the signs on the stores.

For instance, they'd be a sign, "Henry Smith, Dry Goods." Well, Jim would write down the name and the name of the town and when he got to wherever he was goin' he'd mail back a postal card to Henry Smith at Benton and not sign no name to it, but he'd write on the card, well, somethin' like "Ask your wife about that book agent that spent the afternoon last week," or "Ask your Missus who kept her from gettin' lonesome the last time you was in Carterville." And he'd sign the card, "A Friend."

Of course, he never knew what really come of none of these jokes, but he could picture what *probably* happened and that was enough.

Jim didn't work very steady after he lost his position with the Carterville people. What he did earn, doin' odd jobs round town, why he spent pretty near all of it on gin and his family might of starved if the stores hadn't of carried them along. Jim's wife tried her hand at dressmakin', but they ain't nobody goin' to get rich makin' dresses in this town.

As I say, she'd of divorced Jim, only she seen that she couldn't support herself and the kids and she was always hopin' that some day Jim cut out his habits and give her more than two or three dollars a week.

They was a time when she would go to whoever he was workin' for and ask them to give her his wages, but after she done this once or twice, he beat her to it by borrowin' most of his pay in advance. He told it all round town, how he had outfoxed his Missus. He certainly was a caution!

But he wasn't satisfied with just outwittin' her. He was sore the way she had acted, tryin' to grab off his pay. And he made up his mind he'd get even. Well, he waited till Evan's Circus was advertised to come to town. Then he told his wife and two kiddies that he was goin' to take them to the circus. The day of the circus, he told them he would get the tickets and meet them outside the entrance to the tent.

Well, he didn't have no intentions of bein' there or buyin' tickets or nothin'. He got full of gin and laid round Wright's poolroom all day. His wife and the kids waited and waited and of course he didn't show up. His wife didn't have a dime with her, or nowhere else, I guess. So she finally had to tell the kids it was all off and they cried like they wasn't never goin' to stop.

Well, it seems, w'ile they was cryin', Doc Stair came along and he asked what was the matter, but Mrs. Kendall was stubborn and wouldn't tell him, but the kids told him and he insisted on takin' them and their mother in the show. Jim found this out afterwards and it was one reason why he had it in for Doc Stair.

Doc Stair come here about a year and a half ago. He's a mighty handsome young fella and his clothes always look like he has them made to order. He goes to Detroit two or three times a year and w'ile he's there he must have a tailor take his measure and then make him a suit to order. They cost pretty near twice as much, but they fit a whole lot better than if you just bought them in a store.

For a w'ile everybody was wonderin' why a young doctor like Doc Stair should come to a town like this where we already got old Doc Gamble and Doc Foote that's both been here for years and all the practice in town was always divided between the two of them.

Then they was a story got around that Doc Stair's gal had throwed him over, a gal up in the Northern Peninsula somewheres, and the reason he come here was to hide himself away and forget it. He said himself that he thought they wasn't nothin' like general practice in a place like ours to fit a man to be a good all round doctor. And that's why he'd came.

Anyways, it wasn't long before he was makin' enough to live on, though they tell me that he never dunned nobody for what they owed him, and the folks here certainly has got the owin' habit, even in my business. If I had all that was comin' to me for just shaves alone, I could go to Carterville and put up at the Mercer for a week and see a different picture every night. For instance, they's old George Purdy — but I guess I shouldn't ought to be gossipin'.

Well, last year, our coroner died, died of the flu. Ken Beatty, that was his name. He was the coroner. So they had to choose another man to be coroner in his place and they picked Doc Stair. He laughed at first and said he didn't want it, but they made him take it. It ain't no job that anybody would fight for and what a man makes out of it in a year would just about buy seeds for their garden. Doc's the kind, though, that can't say no to nothin' if you keep at him long enough.

But I was goin' to tell you about a poor boy we got here in town — Paul Dickson. He fell out of a tree when he was about ten years old. Lit on his head and it done somethin' to him and he ain't never been right. No harm in him, but just silly. Jim Kendall used to call him cuckoo; that's a name Jim had for anybody that was off their head, only he called people's head their bean. That was another of his gags, callin' head bean and callin' crazy people cuckoo. Only poor Paul ain't crazy, but just silly.

You can imagine that Jim used to have all kinds of fun with Paul. He's send him to the White Front Garage for a left-handed monkey wrench. Of course they ain't no such thing as a left-handed monkey wrench.

And once we had a kind of a fair here and they was a baseball game between the fats and the leans and before the game started Jim called Paul over and sent him way down to Schrader's hardware store to get a key for the pitcher's box.

They wasn't nothin' in the way of gags that Jim couldn't think up, when he put his mind to it.

Poor Paul was always kind of suspicious of people, maybe on account of how Jim had kept foolin' him. Paul wouldn't have much to do with anybody only his own mother and Doc Stair and a girl here in town named Julie Gregg. That is, she ain't a girl no more, but pretty near thirty or over.

When Doc first come to town, Paul seemed to feel like here was a real friend and he hung round Doc's office most of the w'ile; the only time he wasn't there was when he'd go home to eat or sleep or when he seen Julie Gregg doin' her shoppin'.

When he looked out Doc's window and seen her, he'd run downstairs and join her and tag along with her to the different stores. The poor boy was crazy about Julie and she always treated him mighty nice and made him feel like he was welcome, though of course it wasn't nothin' but pity on her side.

Doc done all he could to improve Paul's mind and he told me once that he really thought the boy was gettin' better, that they was times when he was as bright and sensible as anybody else.

But I was goin' to tell you about Julie Gregg. Old Man Gregg was in the lumber business, but got to drinkin' and lost the most of his money and when he died, he didn't leave nothin' but the house and just enough insurance for the girl to skimp along on.

Her mother was a kind of a half invalid and didn't hardly ever leave the house. Julie wanted to sell the place and move somewheres else after the old man died, but the mother said she was born here and would die here. It was tough on Julie, as the young people round this town — well, she's too good for them.

She's been away to school and Chicago and New York and different places and they ain't no subject she can't talk on, where you take the rest of the young folks here and you mention anything to them outside of Gloria Swanson or Tommy Meighan and they think you're delirious. Did you see Gloria in *Wages of Virtue?* You missed somethin'!

Well, Doc Stair hadn't been here more than a week when he come in one day to get shaved and I recognized who he was as he had been pointed out to me, so I told him about my old lady. She's been ailin' for a couple years and either Doc Gambler or Doc Foote, neither one, seemed to be helpin' her. So he said he would come out and see her, but if she was able to get out herself, it would be better to bring her to his office where he could make a completer examination.

So I took her to his office and w'ile I was waitin' for her in the reception room, in come Julie Gregg. When somebody comes in Doc Stair's office, they's a bell that rings in his inside office so as he can tell they's somebody to see him.

So he left my old lady inside and come out to the front office and that's the first time him and Julie met and I guess it was what they call love at first sight. But it wasn't fifty-fifty. This young fella was the slickest lookin' fella she'd ever seen in this town and she went wild over him. To him she was just a young lady that wanted to see the doctor.

She'd came on about the same business I had. Her mother had been doctorin' for years with Doc Gamble and Doc Foote and without no results. So she'd heard they was a new doc in town and decided to give him a try. He promised to call and see her mother that same day.

I said a minute ago that it was love at first sight on her part. I'm not only judgin' by how she acted afterwards but how she looked at him that first day in his office. I ain't no mind reader, but it was wrote all over her face that she was gone.

Now Jim Kendall, besides bein' a jokesmith and a pretty good drinker, well, Jim was quite a lady-killer. I guess he run pretty wild durin' the time he was on the road for them Carterville people, and besides that, he'd had a couple little affairs of the heart right here in town. As I say, his wife would of divorced him, only she couldn't.

But Jim was like the majority of men, and women, too, I guess. He wanted what he couldn't get. He wanted Julie Gregg and worked his head off tryin' to land her. Only he'd of said bean instead of head.

Well, Jim's habits and his jokes didn't appeal to Julie and of course he was a married man, so he didn't have no more chance than, well, than a rabbit. That's an expression of Jim's himself. When somebody didn't have no chance to get elected or somethin', Jim would always say they didn't have no more chance than a rabbit.

He didn't make no bones about how he felt. Right in here, more than once, in front of the whole crowd, he said he was stuck on Julie and anybody that could get her for him was welcome to his house and his wife and kids included. But she wouldn't have nothin' to do with him; wouldn't even speak to him on the street. He finally seen he wasn't gettin' nowheres with his usual line so he decided to try the rough stuff. He went right up to her house one evenin' and when she opened the door he forced his way in and grabbed her. But she broke loose and before he could stop her, she run in the next room and locked the door and phoned to Joe Barnes. Joe's the marshal. Jim could hear who she was phonin' to and he beat it before Joe got there.

Joe was an old friend of Julie's pa. Joe went to Jim the next day and told him what would happen if he ever done it again.

I don't know how the news of this little affair leaked out. Chances is that Joe Barnes told his wife and she told somebody else's wife and they told their husband. Anyways, it did leak out and Hod Meyers had the nerve to kid Jim about it, right here in this shop. Jim didn't deny nothin' and kind of laughed it off and said for us all to wait; that lots of people had tried to make a monkey out of him, but he always got even.

Meanw'ile everybody in town was wise to Julie's bein' wild mad over the Doc. I don't suppose she had any idear how her face changed when him and her was together; of course she couldn't of, or she'd of kept away from him. And she didn't know that we was all noticin' how many times she made excuses to go up to his office or pass it on the other side of the street and look up in his window to see if he was there. I felt sorry for her and so did most other people.

Hod Meyers kept rubbin' it into Jim about how the Doc had cut him out. Jim didn't pay no attention to the kiddin' and you could see he was plannin' one of his jokes.

One trick Jim had was the knack of changin' his voice. He could make you think he was a girl talkin' and he could mimic any man's voice. To show you how good he was along this line, I'll tell you the joke he played on me once.

You know, in most towns of any size, when a man is dead and needs a shave, why the barber that shaves him soaks him five dollars for the job; that is, he don't soak *him*, but whoever ordered the shave. I just charge three dollars because personally I don't mind much shavin' a dead person. They lay a whole lot stiller than live customers. The only thing is that you don't feel like talkin' to them and you get kind of lonesome.

Well, about the coldest day we ever had here, two years ago last winter, the phone rung at the house w'ile I was home to dinner and I answered the phone and it was a woman's voice and she said she was Mrs. John Scott and her husband was dead and would I come out and shave him.

Old John had always been a good customer of mine. But they live seven miles out in the country, on the Streeter road. Still I didn't see how I could say no.

So I said I would be there, but would have to come in a jitney and it might cost three or four dollars besides the price of the shave. So she, or the voice, it said that was all right, so I got Frank Abbott to drive me out to the place and when I got there, who should open the door but old John himself! He wasn't no more dead than, well, than a rabbit.

It didn't take no private detective to figure out who had played me this little joke. Nobody could of thought it up but Jim Kendall. He certainly was a card!

I tell you this incident just to show you how he could disguise his voice and make you believe it was somebody else talkin'. I'd of swore it was Mrs. Scott had called me. Anyways, some woman.

Well, Jim waited till he had Doc Stair's voice down pat; then he went after revenge.

He called Julie up on a night when he knew Doc was over in Carterville. She never questioned but what it was Doc's voice. Jim said he must see her that night; he couldn't wait no longer to tell her somethin'. She was all excited and told him to come to the house. But he said he was expectin' an important long distance call and wouldn't she please forget her manners for once and come to his office. He said they couldn't nothin' hurt her and nobody would see her and he just *must* talk to her a little w'ile. Well, poor Julie fell for it.

Doc always keeps a night light in his office, so it looked to Julie like they was somebody there.

Meanw'ile Jim Kendall had went to Wright's poolroom, where they was a whole gang amusin' themselves. The most of them had drank plenty of gin, and they was a rough bunch even when sober. They was always strong for Jim's jokes and when he told them to come with him to see some fun they give up their card games and pool games and followed along.

Doc's office is on the second floor. Right outside his door they's a flight of stairs leadin' to the floor above. Jim and his gang hid in the dark behind these stairs.

Well, Julie come up to Doc's door and rung the bell and they was nothin' doin'. She rung it again and she rung it seven or eight times. Then she tried the door and found it locked. Then Jim made some kind of a noise and she heard it and waited a minute, and then she says, "Is that you, Ralph?" Ralph is Doc's first name.

They was no answer and it must of came to her all of a sudden that she'd been bunked. She pretty near fell downstairs and the whole gang after her. They chased her all the way home, hollerin', "Is that you, Ralph?" and "Oh, Ralphie, dear, is that you?" Jim says he couldn't holler it himself, as he was laughin' too hard.

Poor Julie! She didn't show up here on Main Street for a long, long time afterward.

And of course Jim and his gang told everybody in town, everybody but Doc Stair. They was scared to tell him, and he might of never knowed only for Paul Dickson. The poor cuckoo, as Jim called him, he was here in the shop one night when Jim was still gloatin' yet over what he'd done to Julie. And Paul took in as much of it as he could understand and he run to Doc with the story.

It's a cinch Doc went up in the air and swore he'd make Jim suffer. But it was a kind of a delicate thing, because if it got out that he had beat Jim up, Julie was bound to hear of it and then she'd know that Doc knew and of course knowin' that he knew would make it worse for her than ever. He was goin' to do somethin', but it took a lot of figurin'.

Well, it was a couple days later when Jim was here in the shop again, and so was the cuckoo. Jim was goin' duck-shootin' the next day and had came in lookin' for Hod Meyers to go with him. I happened to know that Hod had went over to Carterville and wouldn't be home till the end of the week. So Jim said he hated to go alone and he guessed he would call it off. Then poor Paul spoke up and said if Jim would take him he would go along. Jim thought a w'ile and then he said, well, he guessed a half-wit was better than nothin'.

I suppose he was plottin' to get Paul out in the boat and play some joke on him, like pushin' him in the water. Anyways, he said Paul could go. He asked him had he ever shot a duck and Paul said no, he'd never even had a gun in his hands. So Jim said he could set in the boat and watch him and if he behaved himself, he might lend him his gun for a couple of shots. They made a date to meet in the mornin' and that's the last I seen of Jim alive.

Next mornin', I hadn't been open more than ten minutes when Doc Stair come in. He looked kind of nervous. He asked me had I seen Paul Dickson. I said no, but I knew where he was, out duck-shootin' with Jim Kendall. So Doc says that's what he had heard, and he couldn't understand it because Paul had told him he wouldn't never have no more to do with Jim as long as he lived.

He said Paul had told him about the joke Jim had played on Julie. He said Paul had asked him what he thought of the joke and the Doc had told him that anybody that would do a thing like that ought not to be let live.

I said it had been a kind of a raw thing, but Jim just couldn't resist no kind of a joke, no matter how raw. I said I thought he was all right at heart, but just bubblin' over with mischief. Doc turned and walked out.

At noon he got a phone call from old John Scott. The lake where Jim and Paul had went shootin' is on John's place. Paul had came runnin' up to the house a few minutes before and said they'd been an accident. Jim had shot a few ducks and then give the gun to Paul and told him to try his luck. Paul hadn't never handled a gun and he was nervous. He was shakin' so hard that he couldn't control the gun. He let fire and Jim sunk back in the boat, dead.

Doc Stair, bein' the coroner, jumped in Frank Abbott's flivver and rushed out to Scott's farm. Paul and old John was down on the shore of the lake. Paul had rowed the boat to shore, but they'd left the body in it, waitin' for Doc to come.

Doc examined the body and said they might as well fetch it back to town. They was no use leavin' it there or callin' a jury, as it was a plain case of accidental shootin'.

Personally I wouldn't never leave a person shoot a gun in the same boat I was in unless I was sure they knew somethin' about guns. Jim was a sucker to leave a new beginner have his gun, let alone a half-wit. It probably served Jim right, what he got. But still we miss him round here. He certainly was a card!

Comb it wet or dry?

(1925)

QUESTIONS

1. What do you learn about the narrator Whitey from his language? What does it indicate about his social class, his regional background, his education, his interests, his personality?

2. If the narrator is unreliable, how can we trust anything he says? Can a narrator be *totally* unreliable? If not, which aspects of his account must be reasonably reliable?

3. What does the (implied) author want us to think about the events, the characters, the community in this short story?

4. Imagine that you are reading the short story for the first time, and that you are under the impression that Jim Kendall is going to be an admirable character. Does your impression change all at once or gradually? Which details bring about your changed attitude?

5. Ring Lardner is generally known as a humorous writer. Is there humor in this story? If so, what kind of humor is it?

SUGGESTIONS FOR WRITING

1. Many people use the words *irony* and *sarcasm* interchangeably. *Sarcasm*, which comes from a Greek word meaning "to tear flesh," specifically refers to the use of language to humiliate or wound someone. Is all irony sarcastic? Find three or four examples of irony in the short stories in this book. In each case, explain the target of the irony and decide whether the irony is abusive enough to be called sarcastic.

2. Find an example of situational irony in any story in this book. Explain what you would have to change to make the situation nonironic: all or some of the events? the dialogue? a character's traits? a character's knowledge?

3. Irony is the source of many disagreements among readers who may find virtually opposite meanings in a story according to whether they think the behavior of a particular character or a narrator's statement is meant ironically or not. How would you convince someone who believes a story is ironic when you think otherwise, or vice versa? Illustrate with respect to any story in this book.

4. Titles are often clues to ironic meanings. Look through the titles of stories in this book and find some that are at least partly ironic. Is it the narrator or the (implied) author who has picked that title? Is the narrator aware of its ironic dimension? (Who is the "tell-tale heart" telling on?) What different title might the narrator give the story and why?

7 Authors and Readers: Real and Implied

It is now time to unwrap the parentheses that have enclosed the word *implied* and to distinguish between the *real author* and the *implied author*, and also between the implied author and the narrator. I shall also explain why, in actual reading, we are more concerned with the implied than the real author. Once those distinctions are established, we can look at parallel differences on the reader's side.

The Real Author

The *real author* is (or was) the flesh-and-blood person who sat down and wrote the fiction, whose biography we can discuss quite separately from her work. For example, a little rummaging in the library will tell us that Virginia Woolf, the author of "Kew Gardens" and many other fictions, was born in 1882; that she was the daughter of Sir Leslie Stephen and married Leonard Woolf, another author, in 1912; and that she wrote a certain number of novels and short stories, kept an elaborate journal, and died by drowning in 1941. Biography is an important and fascinating branch of literary studies, and facts from the real author's life may help us understand her fictions.

In another respect, we often need to know surprisingly little about the real author to make reasonable sense of a narrative fiction, to understand its plot and characters, its intentions, and the themes it wishes to communicate. We may never have heard of the real Ring Lardner, let alone his feelings about small-town America, yet it is not difficult to gather that "Haircut" implicitly condemns rather than endorses the attitudes of Jim Kendall and even those of its own narrator, Whitey. How are we able to draw such an inference?

The Implied Author

We can draw inferences about authors' attitudes by the way in which the fiction *itself* communicates something about how we should read it. It is the fiction that does that, even though we assign the communication to an

240

"author." We speak so readily of the author — even if we know absolutely nothing about him — because in the ordinary business of life we have learned to infer people's intentions from their acts. Because the text is the product of an act, it seems natural to speak as much about the actor as about the act. But if we know nothing about the real Ring Lardner, it cannot really be *he* that we refer to when we say "Ring Lardner does not endorse Whitey's attitudes." Rather, the name "Ring Lardner" here must refer to some hypothetical person, or agency, whose intentions we infer from the text.

A biographer regularly uses an author's fiction as evidence for writing about her life, but the ordinary reader, interested primarily in the fiction, has a quite different goal, namely, to develop assumptions that lead to a satisfying interpretation. In other words, we look for clues within the fiction itself for what we are to make of it. Intention and agency are abstract notions, so we tend to say that we are looking for what "the author" had in mind. Unless we do some extra reading, however, there is no (real) author who will tell us. We normally read fictions and watch movies without bothering to make outside inquiries about the real author's or director's intentions. Still, the fiction itself *implies* certain attitudes — this set of beliefs, as opposed to that. It is we who impute those beliefs to the "author," even if we have never heard of her. In other words, we *imply* an author who is responsible for choosing this plot and these characters and for devising the discourse in this way to achieve a certain kind of illusion and theme.

The "author" implied by "Town and Country Lovers," (pp. 160– 172) for example, obviously holds racial views quite different from those of the "author" of "Delta Autumn" (pp. 281–290). The "author" implied by "Indian Camp" (pp. 292–295) holds gender views quite different from those of the "author" implied by "Certain Winds from the South" (pp. 296–302). We sense all those differences even if we know little or nothing about the real people named Nadine Gordimer, William Faulkner, Ernest Hemingway, and Ama Ata Aidoo. It is only out of habit that we say that the attitudes conveyed by a fiction are generated by some person whom we call the "author," or "Faulkner," "Hemingway," "Gordimer," or "Aidoo." It would be more accurate (and more honest, if we know little or nothing about Faulkner, Hemingway, Gordimer, or Aidoo) to say that these attitudes are generated by the fiction itself. "The fiction itself," of course, means the fiction as we interpret it. The implied author's intentions derive from the reader's construction of the text's meaning. Or, better, *reconstruction*, because the real author was the original constructor. As we observed in previous chapters, readers look for and reconstruct an intention, a point to each narrative fiction they read, but our reconstruction doesn't just materialize out of thin air. Rather, it entails our recognition that a certain kind of agent must have created it, one who allows it to be re-created on each reading. It is that agent that we call the *implied author*.

It is to the implied author, this imaginary person whom we reconstruct as we read, that we attribute the set of choices that makes the story what it is. Those choices include not only the events and the characters, but also the narrator who tells or shows them and all the narrative techniques by which she does so.

The Implied Author Is Not the Narrator

The implied author is not the same person as the narrator, for the narrator is part of what the implied author constructs (and we reconstruct). The narrator is only the *transmitter* of the story, whereas the implied author is responsible for its whole design — *including the decision to use that particular narrator and not some other*. In chapter 5, for example, we saw that the implied author of "A Little Cloud" chose an anonymous external narrator instead of Little Chandler to narrate the events, the better to ensure our detached and ironic interpretation of Chandler's thoughts.

But, you might ask, doesn't the narrator always reflect the values of the implied author? Not necessarily. Usually she does, but in unreliable narration, she does not. It is the implied author who shows the narrator to be unreliable. In other words, unreliable narration arises precisely because an implied author has created a narrator who voices facts and values that do not correspond to the larger intentions of the fiction, as we make them out in reading. One of those intentions may be precisely to cast doubt on the narrator's integrity, sanity, maturity, astuteness, sobriety, intelligence, or whatever. Even when we have no reason to suspect the narrator's reliability, even when she seems to convey the implied author's attitudes faithfully (as the total effect of the fiction confirms), we must understand that it is the narrator, not the implied author, who "speaks" the story. By definition, the implied author does not "speak," does not deliver direct messages to the reader. The implied author only *implies* messages, and we understand those messages only by *inferring* them from the total fiction — not only from what the narrator says, but from what happens, what the characters are like, what they say about each other, what the setting and atmosphere suggest, and so on.

The concept of implied author assumes that each work of narrative fiction lives its own life. That life is relived each time a reader reads it. For it is the real readers, the real you and I, who breathe life into the marks on the page as we read and attempt to make sense of them. Of course, it is a historical fact that a real author *originally* created the fiction. But we do not obtain the fiction directly from the real author — the real Virginia Woolf or the real Ernest Hemingway — but rather from the books that she or he left behind. These books record and preserve their real authors' original intentions. We re-create an intention when we read the story. It is that intention, ever implicit in the fiction and ever ready to explain itself, that is conveyed by the implied author.

Problems Solved by the Notion of Implied Author

What practical good is all this theory about the implied author? It solves a lot of problems for us. For example, it explains our sense that a narrative composed by a group of *different* real authors still seems the product of a single intention. Many a Hollywood movie has been created by a collaboration of several real authors. There is always a screenwriter (sometimes several). There is the director and the producer (sometimes several). There are film editors and sound editors. The actors contribute to authorship by the way they interpret the characters. And many other people contribute to the final narrative product. Even "sneak preview" audiences may get involved in modifying the film, through suggestions they jot down on ballots distributed after the projection. Most films reflect a compromise among these various people. Yet, we think of the movie as having a single implied author (though we are more likely to speak of "the director").

The notion of implied author also explains how narratives whose authors are unknown or anonymous still seem "authored" in an ordinary sense of the word. And it accounts for the odd fact that readers may decide that a certain fiction has a meaning quite different from what the real author *said* that he intended. And it explains how two fictions by the same real author may seem to be by two totally different implied authors.

The Real Jack London and Two Different Implied "Jack Londons"

This last possibility may be illustrated by a pair of stories by Jack London, "The Apostate" (pp. 258–270) and "The Unparalleled Invasion" (pp. 248–257). "The Apostate" is a short story by an implied author deeply concerned about the evils of child labor. Such an implied author could only be called a political liberal. The story-events are constructed to reveal a life of unmitigated misery. Every day, day after day, young Johnny reluctantly awakes to wash up at a greasy, foul-smelling sink; to eat a miserable breakfast of muddy coffee, bread, and a bit of cold pork; to take a long walk to work under horrendous conditions at a lint-filled, pneumonia- and tuberculosis-breeding factory; to return home exhausted with no hope of rest and relaxation. In the factory, Johnny is himself a machine, losing all interest in developing his mind or character, and at home he is irritable and out of sorts. He is old far beyond his sixteen years. Feeling totally worn out, Johnny just gives up, refuses to work anymore. He leaves his home to lead the life of a tramp. There is no reason to believe that Johnny is going to his salvation. How could he?

> He was a travesty of the human. It was a twisted and stunted and nameless piece of life that shambled like a sickly ape, arms loose-hanging, stoop-shouldered, narrow-chested, grotesque and terrible.

Johnny's life is over, ruined. He has nothing to show for all his labor but a fatigue so complete that he never wants to work again, no matter what happens to him or his family. The short story's theme is the devastating effect of child labor. The effect is not only devastating but also counterproductive, even from the capitalist point of view, because he is the factory's most efficient worker. A system that ruins its own best workers can hardly be called successful.

It is clearly the intention of the story, and hence of the implied author, to condemn the institution of child labor. That intention prescribes the choice of a character who begins factory work at seven and is burned out at sixteen. It prescribes much of the story's detail—the close description of the kinds of jobs Johnny has performed, of his maimed physical and mental condition, of the premature loss of the hopes and dreams that every child is entitled to, of the early and unexplained disappearance of his father, of the pitiful situation of his mother, of his bad relations with his siblings, and so on. It also prescribes the choice of narrator, one who is mostly "objective," that is, content to present without much comment the facts of the case, because the facts alone are sufficient to convey its horror. The narrator is simply a mouthpiece of the liberal implied author, for nothing in the story suggests a conflict between the narrator's and the implied author's attitudes. Once we have understood the story, we come to realize that its title, "The Apostate," can only be ironic. *Apostasy* means "the abandonment of religious faith, vows, and principles," but capitalism is no religion, at least not to the narrator, the implied author, and finally, to Johnny. His "apostasy" is Johnny's feeble attempt to escape the slavery that society has subjected him to.

Biographical information adds to our reading of the story by confirming a relationship between the views of the real Jack London and those implicit in the story. We learn that London read Marx, once got arrested for speaking at a Socialist meeting, and wrote Socialist tracts such as *The War of the Classes* (1905) and *The Human Drift* (1917). We can even find parallels between Johnny's experiences and London's own. He once suffered from scurvy, and he did not know his real father. He is reported to have felt that he had no boyhood. Now this information is interesting and supportive, but it is not essential to our interpretation of the short story. "The Apostate" would communicate its liberal orientation even if we had found it in a book lying in the street with the author's name missing.

The attitudes implicit in London's "The Unparalleled Invasion" cook quite another kettle of fish. The short story purports to be an actual historical account of events pertaining to China from 1904 to 1987 reprinted from an imaginary book called *Certain Essays in History*, by one Walt Mervin. Because it originally appeared in a magazine in July 1910, we understand immediately that the short story was published as a piece of futuristic science fiction. It claims to report only the facts of history as interpreted by Walt Mervin, but there seems no reason to disbelieve that the implied author endorses his narrator's views.

These views are highly reactionary, virtually fascistic. They smack strongly of racism, even genocidal racism, both in the overall text and in individual phrases and expressions. The implied author organizes a tale in which an appalling biological weapon kills most of the Chinese population. The remaining few are "mopped up" by more conventional forces. What is particularly unpleasant is that no explanation is offered for the necessity of total genocide. It simply "goes without saying" that the entire vast nation, to the last man, woman, and child, has to be wiped out. Walt Mervin does not explain why the Chinese never thought of surrendering, or why, even after being clearly defeated, the allies decided that every last Chinese had to be hunted down and killed. When an implied author feels that there is no *need* for his narrator to explain the motive for an action, it must be because that motive is so firmly established in his attitudes, so "self-evident," as to be "beyond question." An attitude that assumes that *every last Chinese* must be eliminated is clearly racist by any definition of the word. It differs in no respect from Hitler's conclusion that the "final solution" to the "problem" of the Jews was to eliminate them, every *last* Jew.

Whatever the *real* Jack London may have felt or said about the Chinese, however much he may have denied that he was a racist espousing genocide, normal reading conventions open the *implied* author to such charges. For the work exists, and the implied author invents it as we read. It is he who dreams up the events, who decides to make it a "historical fact" that only the elimination of the Chinese will solve the "inevitable" problem of world domination that they pose. It is the implied author who constructs a world in which humankind can only be "saved" by the total annihilation of a whole nation. It is only *after* and as a consequence of eliminating the Chinese that the remaining nations "solemnly pledged themselves never to use against one another the laboratory methods of warfare they had employed in the invasion of China."

In short, because the implied author does not give us any reason to assume that he is undercutting his narrator and the history that the narrator tells, a history in which the Chinese "peril" is eliminated by biological warfare, we must conclude that the implied author condones such warfare as a historically necessary act. Nothing in the short story suggests that the narrator's account should be ironically dismissed as the words of a madman (like Poe's story) or of a bigot or fool (like Lardner's story).

What is true of the general design of the short story seems confirmed by its details. Consider some of the prejudices expressed and implied by the narrator. The account is very much white-supremacist: "the comity of nations" is a white comity consisting of the United States and Europe. There is no mention of other countries in the world, no value attributed to skin colors other than white. Even when a "yellow" country, such as Japan, does something good, for instance, opening itself to the West, it is treated as a kind of "freak" or "biological sport," an accident of nature. Underneath the text lie certain assumptions about the world that most decent people today would find highly questionable if not downright obnoxious. One is that the only kind of progress is "Western" progress. Another is that sheer numbers and "breeding" power (in the wretched metaphor "the fecundity of [China's] loins") would inevitably lead the most populous nation to *increase* her population in order to dominate the world. (Actually, recognizing that the population has grown beyond Mervin's dreaded one billion, the Chinese have imposed severe birth-control measures on themselves.) A third is that such biological warfare represents one more of the marvels of science, that Jacobus Laningdale is as important as Edison and Pasteur.

For this story, too, there are biographical details about Jack London that are interesting. For example, London's mother taught him that fair-haired Anglo-Saxons were a kind of master race, a belief that would jibe nicely with his reading in Nietzsche about the superman. But we do not *require* such information to make out the beliefs of the implied author of "The Unparalleled Invasion." They are implicitly there in the text.

Though these two fictions are by the same *real* author, we infer from them totally different *implied* authors, one liberal and one quite the opposite. Simply referring to Jack London as the author of these short stories explains little or nothing about their vastly different ideologies. The stories still need to be interpreted on the basis of their own inner workings, that is, the intentions of their different implied authors.

The Real Reader and the Implied Reader

The implied author presupposes not only a certain set of beliefs, but also a certain kind of reader sympathetic to her purposes. We may call this reader the *implied reader*. Obviously, the implied reader of Ring Lardner's "Haircut" cannot himself be a vicious practical joker because such a person would miss the implied author's irony. Nor can the implied reader of "Short Friday" be anti-Semitic, or so antireligious as to ridicule the possibility of entrance into heaven as a reward for a devout life. The implied reader of "The Darling" must agree that women *should* have their own opinions. The implied reader of "Town and Country Lovers" cannot be a racist. The implied reader of "The Unparalleled Invasion" must be a racist or at least tolerate genocide for political reasons. The implied reader of "Delta Autumn" (pp. 281–290) cannot be *so* furious about the protagonist's racism as to find McCaslin beneath contempt, not even worth thinking about. The implied reader of Isak Dinesen's "The Ring" (pp. 425–429) must believe in symbolism and accept, imaginatively at least, the supernatural. The implied reader of "The River" must believe that overly literal interpretations of metaphors can be tragically fatal.

The implied reader then may be defined as a member of an "optimal audience," one who understands the fiction in the spirit in which it is intended, one who is able to perceive its irony, one whose own values do not so dominate his thinking as to cause him to reject out of hand the beliefs that the fiction asks him implicitly to entertain. For being able to *entertain* beliefs — though not accepting them as our own — is a minimal requirement for reading a fiction. Some fictions, however, require more than that: They want us to change our beliefs and to agree with theirs. Insofar as they do that, they provide a kind of argument for those beliefs. These fictions are propagandistic in character.

In coming to a narrative fiction, then, we real readers take on the task of first discovering and then imaginatively accommodating ourselves to the beliefs required for the fiction to work. We have seen that there are various kinds and degrees of accommodation. Despite differences in age, sex, education, cultural background, and the like, a group of real readers can read a story and come to similar, if not identical, feelings about it. Insofar as they do so, they approximate the reader implied by the text.[1] It is the mark of an experienced reader that she can assume the mind-sets of a wide variety of implied readers. Does that mean that reading fiction makes you a more knowledgeable or tolerant person? Perhaps, for beyond learning concepts or facts from fictions, as one does from scientific textbooks, one stretches one's mind by imaginatively *trying out* various approaches to life implicit in them.

One might argue that the reading of a fiction succeeds when a real reader becomes an *appropriate* implied reader, that is, temporarily adopts the attitudes that the fiction calls for. That does not mean taking the fiction as gospel. The real reader need not even like the ideas that it espouses, but he must be able to concede that *someone*—and someone worth reading about —might feel and act that way. If the real reader cannot do so, he can make no contract with the fiction. He will reject it out of hand. Morally and humanly, rejecting a fiction may be a necessary act.[2] But it is an act that goes beyond the bounds of narrative theory to explain.

The Implied Reader Is Not the Narratee

Finally, we must distinguish between the implied reader and the narratee. The implied reader is the counterpart, on the receiving end, of the implied author. On the other hand, as we saw in chapter 4, the narrator's counterpart is the narratee. The narratee is the audience directly addressed by the narrator. Sometimes this audience is named and identified. For example, Whitey, the narrator of Ring Lardner's "Haircut" addresses an unnamed narratee who is a customer:

> You can see for yourself that this ain't no New York City and besides that, the most of the boys works all day and don't have no leisure to drop in here and get themselves prettied up.
> You're a newcomer, ain't you? I thought I hadn't seen you round before. I hope you like it good enough to stay.

Because the narratee never speaks, we have no way of knowing how he feels about Whitey's story (for instance, we don't know whether *he* is unreliable too), but clearly the narratee is not to be identified with the implied reader. The implied reader is not having a haircut. Rather, he/she is the one who observes this barbershop monologue from a distance, and comes to conclude, as the implied author intends, that Whitey's narration misses the real point of the story.

---

[1] I don't mean to suggest that there is some single "correct" reader (and therefore reading) of the text. The notion of implied readership works best when we think of a *range* of readers who can negotiate the fiction with some degree of success. I know that "success" is a loaded word, but its definition is beyond the scope of this book.

[2] Recently, a novel appeared that was so gratuitously and grotesquely violent that many bookstores refused to sell it. I have not read the novel, but if it is anything like what its critics describe, I might very well join the large numbers of real readers who have refused to become its implied reader.

❖ JACK LONDON
The Unparalleled Invasion

Jack London (1876–1916) was born in poverty in San Francisco and raised in Oakland, California. He had little formal education and was on his own from a very early age. At seventeen he became a sailor and then worked haphazardly at low-paying jobs. He returned to high school at nineteen and then spent a semester at the University of California at Berkeley. London was lured to Alaska in the Klondike gold rush. He found no gold, but did begin to write stories, which were published in the collection *The Son of the Wolf* (1900). The collection was very popular, and London's writing career began. He wrote quickly and profitably but also spent his money lavishly. His fiction is characterized by the sheer love of adventure and (usually) by sympathy for the downtrodden classes and for animals. His novels include *The Call of the Wild* (1903), *The Sea-Wolf* (1904), *White Fang* (1906), *The Iron Heel* (1908), and *Martin Eden* (1909). In addition to *The Son of the Wolf*, his short story collections include *Children of the Frost* (1902), *When God Laughs* (1911), and *South Sea Tales* (1911).

It was in the year 1976 that the trouble between the world and China reached its culmination. It was because of this that the celebration of the Second Centennial of American Liberty was deferred. Many other plans of the nations of the earth were twisted and tangled and postponed for the same reason. The world awoke rather abruptly to its danger; but for over seventy years, unperceived, affairs had been shaping toward this very end.

The year 1904 logically marks the beginning of the development that, seventy years later, was to bring consternation to the whole world. The Japanese-Russian War took place in 1904, and the historians of the time gravely noted it down that that event marked the entrance of Japan into the comity of nations. What it really did mark was the awakening of China. This awakening, long expected, had finally been given up. The Western nations had tried to arouse China, and they had failed. Out of their native optimism and race-egotism they had therefore concluded that the task was impossible, that China would never awaken.

What they had failed to take into account was this: *that between them and China was no common psychological speech*. Their thought-processes were radically dissimilar. There was no intimate vocabulary. The Western mind penetrated the Chinese mind but a short distance when it found itself in a fathomless maze. The Chinese mind penetrated the Western mind an equally short distance when it fetched up against a blank, incomprehensible wall. It was all a matter of language. There was no way to communicate Western ideas to the Chinese mind. China remained asleep. The material achievement and progress of the West was a closed book to her; nor could the West open the book. Back and deep down on the tie-ribs of consciousness, in the mind, say, of the English-speaking race, was a capacity to thrill to short, Saxon words; back and deep-down on the tie-ribs of consciousness of the Chinese mind was a capacity to thrill to its own hieroglyphics; but the Chinese mind could not thrill to short, Saxon words; nor could the English-speaking mind thrill to hieroglyphics. The fabrics of their minds were woven from totally different stuffs. They were mental aliens. And so it was that Western material achievement and progress made no dent on the rounded sleep of China.

Came Japan and her victory over Russia in 1904. Now the Japanese race was the freak and paradox among Eastern peoples. In some strange way Japan was receptive to all the West had to offer. Japan swiftly assimilated the Western ideas, and digested them, and so capably applied them that she suddenly burst forth, full-panoplied, a world-power. There is no explaining this peculiar openness of Japan to the alien culture of the West. As well might be explained any biological sport in the animal kingdom.

Having decisively thrashed the great Russian Empire, Japan promptly set about dreaming a colossal dream of empire for herself. Korea she had made into a granary and a colony; treaty privileges and vulpine diplomacy gave her the monopoly of Manchuria. But Japan was not satisfied. She turned her eyes upon China. There lay a vast territory, and in that territory were the hugest deposits in the world of iron and coal — the backbone of industrial civilization. Given natural resources, the other great factor in industry is labor. In that territory was a population of 400,000,000 souls — one quarter of the then total population of the earth. Furthermore, the Chinese were excellent workers, while their fatalistic philosophy (or religion) and their stolid nervous organization constituted them splendid soldiers — if they were properly managed. Needless to say, Japan was prepared to furnish that management.

But best of all, from the standpoint of Japan, the Chinese was a kindred race. The baffling enigma of the Chinese character to the West was no baffling enigma to the Japanese. The Japanese understood as we could never school ourselves or hope to understand. Their mental processes were the same. The Japanese thought with the same thought-symbols as did the Chinese, and they thought in the same peculiar grooves. Into the Chinese mind the Japanese went on where we were balked by the obstacle of incomprehension. They took the turning which we could not perceive, twisted around the obstacle, and were out of sight in the ramifications of the Chinese mind where we could not follow. They were brothers. Long ago one had borrowed the other's written language, and, untold generations before that, they had diverged from the common Mongol stock. There had been changes, differentiations brought about by diverse conditions and infusions of other blood; but down at the bottom of their beings, twisted into the fibers of them, was a heritage in common, a sameness in kind that time had not obliterated.

And so Japan took upon herself the management of China. In the years immediately following the war with Russia, her agents swarmed over the Chinese Empire. A thousand miles beyond the last mission station toiled her engineers and spies, clad as coolies, under the guise of itinerant merchants or proselyting Buddhist priests, noting down the horsepower of every waterfall, the likely sites for factories, the heights of mountains and passes, the strategic advantages and weaknesses, the wealth of the farming valleys, the number of bullocks in a district or the number of laborers that could be collected by forced levies. Never was there such a census, and it could have been taken by no other people than the dogged, patient, patriotic Japanese.

But in short time secrecy was thrown to the winds. Japan's officers reorganized the Chinese army; her drill sergeants made the mediæval warriors over into twentieth century soldiers, accustomed to all the modern machinery of war and with a higher average of marksmanship than the soldiers of any Western nation. The engineers of Japan deepened and widened the intricate system of canals, built factories and foundries, netted the empire with telegraphs and telephones, and inaugurated the era of railroad-building. It was these same protagonists of machine-civilization that discovered the great oil deposits of Chunsan, the iron mountains of Whang-Sing, the copper ranges of Chinchi, and they sank the gas wells of Wow-Wee, that most marvelous reservoir of natural gas in all the world.

In China's councils of empire were the Japanese emissaries. In the ears of the statesmen whispered the Japanese statesmen. The political reconstruction of the Empire was due to them. They evicted the scholar class, which was violently reactionary, and put into office progressive officials. And in every town and city of the Empire newspapers were started. Of course, Japanese editors ran the policy of these papers, which policy they got direct from Tokio. It was these papers that educated and made progressive the great mass of the population.

China was at last awake. Where the West had failed, Japan succeeded. She had transmuted Western culture and achievement into terms that were intelligible to the Chinese understanding. Japan herself, when she so suddenly awakened, had astounded the world. But at the time she was only forty millions strong. China's awakening, what of her four hundred millions and the scientific advance of the world, was frightfully astounding. She was the colossus of the nations, and swiftly her voice was heard in no uncertain tones in the affairs and councils of the nations. Japan egged her on, and the proud Western peoples listened with respectful ears.

China's swift and remarkable rise was due, perhaps more than to anything else, to the superlative quality of her labor. The Chinese was the perfect type of industry. He had always been that. For sheer ability to work, no worker in the world could compare with him. Work was the breath of his nostrils. It was to him what wandering and fighting in far lands and spiritual adventure had been to other peoples. Liberty, to him, epitomized itself in access to the means of toil. To till the soil and labor interminably was all he asked of life and the powers that be. And the awakening of China had given its vast population not merely free and unlimited access to the means of toil, but access to the highest and most scientific machine-means of toil.

China rejuvenescent! It was but a step to China rampant. She discovered a new pride in herself and a will of her own. She began to chafe under the guidance of Japan, but she did not chafe long. On Japan's advice, in the beginning, she had expelled from the Empire all Western missionaries, engineers, drill sergeants, merchants, and teachers. She now began to expel the similar representatives of Japan. The latter's advisory statesmen were showered with honors and decorations, and sent home. The West had awakened Japan, and, as Japan had then requited the West, Japan was now requited by China. Japan was thanked for her kindly aid and flung out bag and baggage by her gigantic protégé. The Western nations chuckled. Japan's rainbow dream had gone glimmering. She grew angry. China laughed at her. The blood and the swords of the Samurai would out, and Japan rashly went to war. This occurred in 1922, and in seven bloody months Manchuria, Korea, and Formosa were taken away from her and she was hurled back, bankrupt, to stifle in her tiny, crowded islands. Exit Japan from the world drama. Thereafter she devoted herself to art, and her task became to please the world greatly with her creations of wonder and beauty.

Contrary to expectation, China did not prove warlike. She had no Napoleonic dream, and was content to devote herself to the arts of peace. After a time of disquiet, the idea was accepted that China was to be feared, not in war, but in commerce. It will be seen that the real danger was not apprehended. China went on consummating her machine-civilization. Instead of a large standing army, she developed an immensely larger and splendidly efficient militia. Her navy was so small that it was the laughing stock of the world; nor did she attempt to strengthen her navy. The treaty ports of the world were never entered by her visiting battleships.

The real danger lay in the fecundity of her loins, and it was in 1970 that the first cry of alarm was raised. For some time all territories adjacent to China had been grumbling at Chinese immigration; but now it suddenly came home to the world that China's population was 500,000,000. She had increased by a hundred millions since her awakening. Burchaldter called to attention the fact that there were more Chinese in existence than white-skinned people. He performed a simple sum in arithmetic. He added together the populations of the United States, Canada, New Zealand, Australia, South Africa, England, France, Germany, Italy, Austria, European Russia, and all Scandinavia. The result was 495,000,000. And the population of China over-topped this tremendous total by 5,000,000. Burchaldter's figures went around the world, and the world shivered.

For many centuries China's population had been constant. Her territory had been saturated with population; that is to say, her territory, with the primitive method of production, had supported the maximum limit of population. But when she awoke and inaugurated the machine-civilization, her productive power had been enormously increased. Thus, on the same territory, she was able to support a far larger population. At once the birth rate began to rise and the death rate to fall. Before, when population pressed against the means of subsistence, the excess population had been swept away by famine. But now, thanks to the machine-civilization, China's means of subsistence had been enormously extended, and there were no famines; her population followed on the heels of the increase in the means of subsistence.

During this time of transition and development of power, China had entertained no dreams of conquest. The Chinese was not an imperial race. It was industrious, thrifty, and peace-loving. War was looked upon as an unpleasant but necessary task that at times must be performed. And so, while the Western races had squabbled and fought, and world-adventured against one another, China had calmly gone on working at her machines and growing. Now she was spilling over the boundaries of her Empire — that was all, just spilling over into the adjacent territories with all the certainty and terrifying slow momentum of a glacier.

Following upon the alarm raised by Burchaldter's figures, in 1970, France made a long-threatened stand. French Indo-China had been over-run, filled up, by Chinese immigrants. France called a halt. The Chinese wave flowed on. France assembled a force of a hundred thousand on the boundary between her unfortunate colony and China, and China sent down an army of militia-soldiers a million strong. Behind came the wives and sons and daughters and relatives, with their personal household luggage, in a second army. The French force was brushed aside like a fly. The Chinese militia-soldiers, along with their families, over five millions all told, coolly took possession of French Indo-China and settled down to stay for a few thousand years.

Outraged France was in arms. She hurled fleet after fleet against the coast of China, and nearly bankrupted herself by the effort. China had no navy. She withdrew like a turtle into her shell. For a year the French fleets blockaded the coast and bombarded exposed towns and villages. China did not mind. She did not depend upon the rest of the world for anything. She calmly kept out of range of the French guns and went on working. France wept and wailed, wrung her impotent hands and appealed to the dumbfounded nations. Then she landed a punitive expedition to march to Peking. It was two hundred and fifty thousand strong, and it was the flower of France. It landed without opposition and marched into the interior. And that was the last ever seen of it. The line of communication was snapped on the second day. Not a survivor came back to tell what had happened. It had been swallowed up in China's cavernous maw, that was all.

In the five years that followed, China's expansion, in all land directions, went on apace. Siam was made part of the Empire, and, in spite of all that England could do, Burma and the Malay Peninsula were over-run; while all along the long south boundary of Siberia, Russia was pressed severely by China's advancing hordes. The process was simple. First came the Chinese immigration (or, rather, it was already there, having come there slowly and insidiously during the previous years). Next came the clash at arms and the brushing away of all opposition by a monster army of militia-soldiers, followed by their families and household baggage. And finally came their settling down as colonists in the conquered territory. Never was there so strange and effective a method of world conquest.

Napal and Bhutan were over-run, and the whole northern boundary of India pressed against by this fearful tide of life. To the west, Bokhara, and, even to the south and west, Afghanistan, were swallowed up. Persia, Turkestan, and all Central Asia felt the pressure of the flood. It was at this time that Burchaldter revised his figures. He had been mistaken. China's population must be seven hundred millions, eight hundred millions, nobody knew how many millions, but at any rate it would soon be a billion. There were two Chinese for every white-skinned human in the world, Burchaldter announced, and the world trembled. China's increase must have begun immediately, in 1904. It was remembered that since that date there had not been a single famine. At 5,000,000 a year increase, her total increase in the intervening seventy years must be 350,000,000. But who was to know? It might be more. Who was to know anything of this strange new menace of the twentieth century — China, old China, rejuvenescent, fruitful, and militant!

The Convention of 1975 was called at Philadelphia. All the Western nations, and some few of the Eastern, were represented. Nothing was accomplished. There was talk of all countries putting bounties on children to increase the birth rate, but it was laughed to scorn by the arithmeticians, who pointed out that China was too far in the lead in that direction. No feasible way of coping with China was suggested. China was appealed to and threatened by the United Powers, and that was all the Convention of Philadelphia came to; and the Convention and the Powers were laughed at by China. Li Tang Fwung, the power behind the Dragon Throne, deigned to reply.

"What does China care for the comity of nations?" said Li Tang Fwung. "We are the most ancient, honorable, and royal of races. We have our own destiny to accomplish. It is unpleasant that our destiny does not jibe with the destiny of the rest of the world, but what would you? You have talked windily about the royal races and the heritage of the earth, and we can only reply that that remains to be seen. You cannot invade us. Never mind about your navies. Don't shout. We know our navy is small. You see, we use it for police purposes. We do not care for the sea. Our strength is in our population, which will soon be a billion. Thanks to you, we are equipped with all modern war-machinery. Send your navies. We will not notice them. Send your punitive expeditions, but first remember France. To land half a million soldiers on our shores would strain the resources of any of you. And our thousand millions would swallow them down in a mouthful. Send a million; send five million, and we will swallow them down just as readily. Pouf! A mere nothing, a meager morsel. Destroy, as you have threatened, you United States, the ten million coolies we have forced upon your shores — why, the amount scarcely equals half of our excess birth rate for a year."

So spoke Li Tang Fwung. The world was nonplussed, helpless, terrified. Truly had he spoken. There was no combating China's amazing birth rate. If her population was a billion, and was increasing twenty millions a year, in twenty-five years it would be a billion and a half — equal to the total population of the world in 1904. And nothing could be done. There was no way to dam up the over-spilling monstrous flood of life. War was futile. China laughed at a blockade of her coasts. She welcomed invasion. In her capacious maw was room for all the hosts of earth that could be hurled at her. And in the meantime her flood of yellow life poured out and on over Asia. China laughed and read in their magazines the learned lucubrations of the distracted Western scholars.

But there was one scholar China failed to reckon on — Jacobus Laningdale. Not that he was a scholar, except in the widest sense. Primarily, Jacobus Laningdale was a scientist, and, up to that time, a very obscure scientist, a professor employed in the laboratories of the Health Office of New York City. Jacobus Laningdale's head was very like any other head, but in that head was evolved an idea. Also, in that head was the wisdom to keep that idea secret. He did not write an article for the magazines. Instead, he asked for a vacation. On September 19, 1975, he arrived in Washington. It was evening, but he proceeded straight to the White House, for he had already arranged an audience with the President. He was closeted with President Moyer for three hours. What passed between them was not learned by the rest of the world until long after; in fact, at that time the world was not interested in Jacobus Laningdale. Next day the President called in his Cabinet. Jacobus Laningdale was present. The proceedings were kept secret. But that very afternoon Rufus Cowdery, Secretary of State, left Washington and early the following morning sailed for England. The secret that he carried began to spread, but it spread only among the heads of governments. Possibly half a dozen men in a nation were intrusted with the idea that had formed in Jacobus Laningdale's head. Following the spread of the secret, sprang up great activity in all the dock-yards, arsenals, and navy-yards. The people of France and Austria became suspicious, but so sincere were their governments' calls for confidence that they acquiesced in the unknown project that was afoot.

This was the time of the Great Truce. All countries pledged themselves solemnly not to go to war with any other country. The first definite action was the gradual mobilization of the armies of Russia, Germany, Austria, Italy, Greece, and Turkey. Then began the eastward movement. All railroads into Asia were glutted with troop trains. China was the objective, that was all that was known. A little later began the great sea movement. Expeditions of war ships were launched from all countries. Fleet followed fleet, and all proceeded to the coast of China. The nations cleaned out their navy-yards. They sent their revenue cutters and dispatch boats and lighthouse tenders, and they sent their last antiquated cruisers and battleships. Not content with this, they impressed the merchant marine. The statistics show that 58,640 merchant steamers, equipped with searchlights and rapid-fire guns, were dispatched by the various nations to China.

And China smiled and waited. On her land side, along her boundaries, were millions of the warriors of Europe. She mobilized five times as many millions of her militia and waited the invasion. On her sea coasts she did the same. But China was puzzled. After all this enormous preparation, there was no invasion. She could not understand. Along the great Siberian frontier all was quiet. Along her coasts the towns and villages were not even shelled. Never, in the history of the world, had there been so mighty a gathering of war fleets. The fleets of all the world were there, and day and night millions of tons of battleships plowed the brine of her coasts, and nothing happened. Nothing was attempted. Did they think to make her emerge from her shell? China smiled. Did they think to tire her out, or starve her out? China smiled again.

But on May 1, 1976, had the reader been in the imperial city of Peking, with its then population of eleven millions, he would have witnessed a curious sight. He would have seen the streets filled with the chattering yellow populace, every queued head tilted back, every slant eye turned skyward. And high up in the blue he would have beheld a tiny dot of black, which, because of its orderly evolutions, he would have identified as an airship. From this airship, as it curved its flight back and forth over the city, fell missiles — strange, harmless missiles, tubes of fragile glass that shattered into thousands of fragments on the streets and house-tops. But there was nothing deadly about these tubes of glass. Nothing happened. There were no explosions. It is true, several Chinese were killed by the tubes dropping on their heads from so enormous a height; but what were three Chinese against an excess birth rate of twenty millions? One tube struck perpendicularly in a fish pond in a garden and was not broken. It was dragged ashore by the master of the house. He did not dare to open it, but, accompanied by his friends, and surrounded by an ever-increasing crowd, he carried the mysterious tube to the magistrate of the district. The latter was a brave man. With all eyes upon him, he shattered the tube with a blow from his brass-bowled pipe. Nothing happened. Of those who were very near, one or two thought they saw some mosquitos fly out. That was all. The crowd set up a great laugh and dispersed.

As Peking was bombarded by glass tubes, so was all China. The tiny airships, dispatched from the warships, contained but two men each, and over all cities, towns, and villages they wheeled and curved, one man directing the ship, the other man throwing over the glass tubes.

Had the reader again been in Peking, six weeks later, he would have looked in vain for the eleven million inhabitants. Some few of them he would have found, a few hundred thousand, perhaps, their carcasses festering in the houses and in the deserted streets, and piled high on the abandoned death wagons. But for the rest he would have had to seek along the highways and byways of the Empire. And not all would he have found fleeing from plague-stricken Peking, for behind them, by hundreds of thousands of unburied corpses by the wayside, he could have marked their flight. And as it was with Peking, so was it with all the cities, towns, and villages of the Empire. The plague smote them all. Nor was it one plague, nor two plagues; it was a score of plagues. Every virulent form of infectious death stalked through the land. Too late the Chinese government apprehended the meaning of the colossal preparations, the marshaling of the world hosts, the flights of the tiny airships, and the rain of the tubes of glass. The proclamations of the government were vain. They could not stop the eleven million plague-stricken wretches, fleeing from the one city of Peking to spread disease through all the land. The physicians and health officers died at their posts; and death, the all-conqueror, rode over the decrees of the Emperor and Li Tang Fwung. It rode over them as well, for Li Tang Fwung died in the second week, and the Emperor, hidden away in the Summer Palace, died in the fourth week.

Had there been one plague, China might have coped with it. But from a score of plagues no creature was immune. The man who escaped smallpox went down before scarlet fever. The man who was immune to yellow fever was carried away by cholera; and if he were immune to that, too, the Black Death, which was the bubonic plague, swept him away. For it was these bacteria, and germs, and microbes, and bacilli, cultured in the laboratories of the West, that had come down upon China in the rain of glass.

All organization vanished. The government crumbled away. Decrees and proclamations were useless when the men who made them and signed them one moment were dead the next. Nor could the maddened millions, spurred on to flight by death, pause to heed anything. They fled from the cities to infect the country, and wherever they fled they carried the plagues with them. The hot summer was on — Jacobus Laningdale had selected the time shrewdly — and the plague festered everywhere. Much is conjectured of what occurred, and much has been learned from the stories of the few survivors. The wretched creatures stormed across the Empire in many-millioned flight. The vast armies China had collected on her frontiers melted away. The farms were ravaged for food, and no more crops were planted, while the crops already in were left unattended and never came to harvest. The most remarkable thing, perhaps, was the flights. Many millions engaged in them, charging to the bounds of the Empire to be met and turned back by the gigantic armies of the West. The slaughter of the mad hosts on the boundaries was stupendous. Time and again the guarding line was drawn back twenty or thirty miles to escape the contagion of the multitudinous dead.

Once the plague broke through and seized upon the German and Austrian soldiers who were guarding the borders of Turkestan. Preparations had been made for such a happening, and though sixty thousand soldiers of Europe were carried off, the international corps of physicians isolated the contagion and dammed it back. It was during this struggle that it was suggested that a new plague-germ had originated, that in some way or other a sort of hybridization between plague-germs had taken place, producing a new and frightfully virulent germ. First suspected by Vomberg, who became infected with it and died, it was later isolated and studied by Stevens, Hazenfelt, Norman, and Landers.

Such was the unparalleled invasion of China. For that billion of people there was no hope. Pent in their vast and festering charnel house, all organization and cohesion lost, they could do naught but die. They could not escape. As they were flung back from their land frontiers, so were they flung back from the sea. Seventy-five thousand vessels patroled the coasts. By day their smoking funnels dimmed the sea-rim, and by night their flashing searchlights plowed the dark and harrowed it for the tiniest escaping junk. The attempts of the immense fleets of junks were pitiful. Not one ever got by the guarding sea-hounds. Modern war-machinery held back the disorganized mass of China, while the plagues did the work.

But old War was made a thing of laughter. Naught remained to him but patrol duty. China had laughed at war, and war she was getting, but it was ultra-modern war, twentieth century war, the war of the scientist and the laboratory, the war of Jacobus Laningdale. Hundred-ton guns were toys compared with the micro-organic projectiles hurled from the laboratories, the messengers of death, the destroying angels that stalked through the empire of a billion souls.

During all the summer and fall of 1976 China was an inferno. There was no eluding the microscopic projectiles that sought out the remotest hiding places. The hundreds of millions of dead remained unburied and the germs multiplied themselves, and, toward the last, millions died daily of starvation. Besides, starvation weakened the victims and destroyed their natural defences against the plagues. Cannibalism, murder, and madness reigned. And so perished China.

Not until the following February, in the coldest weather, were the first expeditions made. These expeditions were small, composed of scientists and bodies of troops; but they entered China from every side. In spite of the most elaborate precautions against infection, numbers of soldiers and a few of the physicians were stricken. But the exploration went bravely on. They found China devastated, a howling wilderness through which wandered bands of wild dogs and desperate bandits who had survived. All survivors were put to death wherever found. And then began the great task, the sanitation of China. Five years and hundreds of millions of treasure were consumed, and then the world moved in — not in zones, as was the idea of Baron Albrecht, but heterogeneously, according to the democratic American program. It was a vast and happy intermingling of nationalities that settled down in China in 1982 and the years that followed — a tremendous and successful experiment in cross-fertilization. We know to-day the splendid mechanical, intellectual, and art output that followed.

It was in 1987, the Great Truce having been dissolved, that the ancient quarrel between France and Germany over Alsace and Lorraine recrudesced. The war-cloud grew dark and threatening in April, and on April 17 the Convention of Copenhagen was called. The representatives of the nations of the world being present, all nations solemnly pledged themselves never to use against one another the laboratory methods of warfare they had employed in the invasion of China.

—*Excerpt from Walt Mervin's "Certain Essays in History."*

(1910)

QUESTIONS

1. Who is supposed to be telling the story? Under what circumstances? What nonfictional form is London imitating and why?

2. How does London's view of the world of 1976, as seen from 1914, compare with our own view looking backward to the seventies? Were any of London's prophecies correct? Do his predictions about society differ from his predictions about science?

3. Do you think national characters are as clear-cut and monolithic as the narrative suggests? Can you combine J. S. Bach and Adolf Hitler to produce a picture of the "German mind"? People in England and in North America speak the same "Saxon" language — does that mean we have the same worldview?

4. What sense do you get from this story of its implied author's beliefs, values, and sympathies? How does this portrait compare with the one you derive from London's story "The Apostate" (pp. 258–270) or from some of his more famous stories such as "To Build a Fire" and *The Call of the Wild?*

5. What moral principles are used to justify the extermination of an entire nation? For example, does the phrase "the sanitation of China" refer to germs and dirt? Had such genocides occurred at the time London was writing?

The Apostate

Now I wake me up to work;
I pray the Lord I may not shirk.
If I should die before the night,
I pray the Lord my work's all right.
                                    Amen.

If you don't git up, Johnny, I won't give you a bite to eat!"

The threat had no effect on the boy. He clung stubbornly to sleep, fighting for its oblivion as the dreamer fights for his dream. The boy's hands loosely clenched themselves, and he made feeble, spasmodic blows at the air. These blows were intended for his mother, but she betrayed practised familiarity in avoiding them as she shook him roughly by the shoulder.

"Lemme 'lone!"

It was a cry that began, muffled, in the deeps of sleep, that swiftly rushed upward, like a wail, into passionate belligerence, and that died away and sank down into an inarticulate whine. It was a bestial cry, as of a soul in torment, filled with infinite protest and pain.

But she did not mind. She was a sad-eyed, tired-faced woman, and she had grown used to this task, which she repeated every day of her life. She got a grip on the bed-clothes and tried to strip them down; but the boy, ceasing his punching, clung to them desperately. In a huddle, at the foot of the bed, he still remained covered. Then she tried dragging the bedding to the floor. The boy opposed her. She braced herself. Hers was the superior weight, and the boy and bedding gave, the former instinctively following the latter in order to shelter against the chill of the room that bit into his body.

As he toppled on the edge of the bed it seemed that he must fall head-first to the floor. But consciousness fluttered up in him. He righted himself and for a moment perilously balanced. Then he struck the floor on his feet. On the instant his mother seized him by the shoulders and shook him. Again his fists struck out, this time with more force and directness. At the same time his eyes opened. She released him. He was awake.

"All right," he mumbled.

She caught up the lamp and hurried out, leaving him in darkness.

"You'll be docked," she warned back to him.

He did not mind the darkness. When he had got into his clothes, he went out into the kitchen. His tread was very heavy for so thin and light a boy. His legs dragged with their own weight, which seemed unreasonable because they were such skinny legs. He drew a broken-bottomed chair to the table.

"Johnny!" his mother called sharply.

He arose as sharply from the chair, and, without a word, went to the sink. It was a greasy, filthy sink. A smell came up from the outlet. He took no notice of it. That a sink should smell was to him part of the natural order, just as it was a part of the natural order that the soap should be grimy with dish-water and hard to lather. Nor did he try very hard to make it lather. Several splashes of the cold water from the running faucet completed the function. He did not wash his teeth. For that matter he had never seen a tooth-brush, nor did he know that there existed beings in the world who were guilty of so great a foolishness as tooth washing.

"You might wash yourself wunst a day without bein' told," his mother complained.

She was holding a broken lid on the pot as she poured two cups of coffee. He made no remark, for this was a standing quarrel between them, and the one thing upon which his mother was hard as adamant. "Wunst" a day it was compulsory that he should wash his face. He dried himself on a greasy towel, damp and dirty and ragged, that left his face covered with shreds of lint.

"I wish we didn't live so far away," she said, as he sat down. "I try to do the best I can. You know that. But a dollar on the rent is such a savin', an' we've more room here. You know that."

He scarcely followed her. He had heard it all before, many times. The range of her thought was limited, and she was ever harking back to the hardship worked upon them by living so far from the mills.

"A dollar means more grub," he remarked sententiously. "I'd sooner do the walkin' an' git the grub."

He ate hurriedly, half chewing the bread and washing the unmasticated chunks down with coffee. The hot and muddy liquid went by the name of coffee. Johnny thought it was coffee — and excellent coffee. That was one of the few of life's illusions that remained to him. He had never drunk real coffee in his life.

In addition to the bread, there was a small piece of cold pork. His mother refilled his cup with coffee. As he was finishing the bread, he began to watch if more was forthcoming. She intercepted his questioning glance.

"Now, don't be hoggish, Johnny," was her comment. "You've had your share. Your brothers an' sisters are smaller'n you."

He did not answer the rebuke. He was not much of a talker. Also, he ceased his hungry glancing for more. He was uncomplaining, with a patience that was as terrible as the school in which it had been learned. He finished his coffee, wiped his mouth on the back of his hand, and started to rise.

"Wait a second," she said hastily. "I guess the loaf kin stand you another slice — a thin un."

There was legerdemain in her actions. With all the seeming of cutting a slice from the loaf for him, she put loaf and slice back in the bread box and conveyed to him one of her own two slices. She believed she had deceived him, but he had noted her sleight-of-hand. Nevertheless, he took the bread shamelessly. He had a philosophy that his mother, what of her chronic sickliness, was not much of an eater anyway.

She saw that he was chewing the bread dry, and reached over and emptied her coffee cup into his.

"Don't set good somehow on my stomach this morning," she explained.

A distant whistle, prolonged and shrieking, brought both of them to their feet.

She glanced at the tin alarm-clock on the shelf. The hands stood at half-past five. The rest of the factory world was just arousing from sleep. She drew a shawl about her shoulders, and on her head put a dingy hat, shapeless and ancient.

"We've got to run," she said, turning the wick of the lamp and blowing down the chimney.

They groped their way out and down the stairs. It was clear and cold, and Johnny shivered at the first contact with the outside air. The stars had not yet begun to pale in the sky, and the city lay in blackness. Both Johnny and his mother shuffled their feet as they walked. There was no ambition in the leg muscles to swing the feet clear of the ground.

After fifteen silent minutes, his mother turned off to the right.

"Don't be late," was her final warning from out of the dark that was swallowing her up.

He made no response, steadily keeping on his way. In the factory quarter, doors were opening everywhere, and he was soon one of a multitude that pressed onward through the dark. As he entered the factory gate the whistle blew again. He glanced at the east. Across a ragged sky-line of housetops a pale light was beginning to creep. This much he saw of the day as he turned his back upon it and joined his work gang.

He took his place in one of many long rows of machines. Before him, above a bin filled with small bobbins, were large bobbins revolving rapidly. Upon these he wound the jute-twine of the small bobbins. The work was simple. All that was required was celerity. The small bobbins were emptied so rapidly, and there were so many large bobbins that did the emptying, that there were no idle moments.

He worked mechanically. When a small bobbin ran out, he used his left hand for a brake, stopping the large bobbin and at the same time, with thumb and forefinger, catching the flying end of twine. Also, at the same time, with his right hand, he caught up the loose twine-end of a small bobbin. These various acts with both hands were performed simultaneously and swiftly. Then there would come a flash of his hands as he looped the weaver's knot and released the bobbin. There was nothing difficult about weaver's knots. He once boasted he could tie them in his sleep. And for that matter, he sometimes did, toiling centuries long in a single night at tying an endless succession of weaver's knots.

Some of the boys shirked, wasting time and machinery by not replacing the small bobbins when they ran out. And there was an overseer to prevent this. He caught Johnny's neighbor at the trick, and boxed his ears.

"Look at Johnny there — why ain't you like him?" the overseer wrathfully demanded.

Johnny's bobbins were running full blast, but he did not thrill at the indirect praise. There had been a time . . . but that was long ago, very long ago. His apathetic face was expressionless as he listened to himself being held up as a shining example. He was the perfect worker. He knew that. He had been told so, often. It was a commonplace, and besides it didn't seem to mean anything to him any more. From the perfect worker he had evolved into the perfect machine. When his work went wrong, it was with him as with the machine, due to faulty material. It would have been as possible for a perfect nail-die to cut imperfect nails as for him to make a mistake.

THE APOSTATE   261

And small wonder. There had never been a time when he had not been in intimate relationship with machines. Machinery had almost been bred into him, and at any rate he had been brought up on it. Twelve years before, there had been a small flutter of excitement in the loom room of this very mill. Johnny's mother had fainted. They stretched her out on the floor in the midst of the shrieking machines. A couple of elderly women were called from their looms. The foreman assisted. And in a few minutes there was one more soul in the loom room than had entered by the doors. It was Johnny, born with the pounding, crashing roar of the looms in his ears, drawing with his first breath the warm, moist air that was thick with flying lint. He had coughed that first day in order to rid his lungs of the lint; and for the same reason he had coughed ever since.

The boy alongside of Johnny whimpered and sniffed. The boy's face was convulsed with hatred for the overseer who kept a threatening eye on him from a distance; but every bobbin was running full. The boy yelled terrible oaths into the whirling bobbins before him; but the sound did not carry half a dozen feet, the roaring of the room holding it in and containing it like a wall.

Of all this Johnny took no notice. He had a way of accepting things. Besides, things grow monotonous by repetition, and this particular happening he had witnessed many times. It seemed to him as useless to oppose the overseer as to defy the will of a machine. Machines were made to go in certain ways and to perform certain tasks. It was the same with the overseer.

But at eleven o'clock there was excitement in the room. In an apparently occult way the excitement instantly permeated everywhere. The one-legged boy who worked on the other side of Johnny bobbed swiftly across the floor to a bin truck that stood empty. Into this he dived out of sight, crutch and all. The superintendent of the mill was coming along, accompanied by a young man. He was well dressed and wore a starched shirt—a gentleman, in Johnny's classification of men, and also, "the Inspector."

He looked sharply at the boys as he passed along. Sometimes he stopped and asked questions. When he did so, he was compelled to shout at the top of his lungs, at which moments his face was ludicrously contorted with the strain of making himself heard. His quick eye noted the empty machine alongside of Johnny's, but he said nothing. Johnny also caught his eye, and he stopped abruptly. He caught Johnny by the arm to draw him back a step from the machine; but with an exclamation of surprise he released the arm.

"Pretty skinny," the superintendent laughed anxiously.

"Pipe stems," was the answer. "Look at those legs. The boy's got the rickets —incipient, but he's got them. If epilepsy doesn't get him in the end, it will be because tuberculosis gets him first."

Johnny listened, but did not understand. Furthermore he was not interested in future ills. There was an immediate and more serious ill that threatened him in the form of the inspector.

"Now, my boy, I want you to tell me the truth," the inspector said, or shouted, bending close to the boy's ear to make him hear. "How old are you?"

"Fourteen," Johnny lied, and he lied with the full force of his lungs. So loudly did he lie that it started him off in a dry, hacking cough that lifted the lint which had been settling in his lungs all morning.

"Looks sixteen at least," said the superintendent.

"Or sixty," snapped the inspector.

"He's always looked that way."

"How long?" asked the inspector, quickly.

"For years. Never gets a bit older."

"Or younger, I dare say. I suppose he's worked here all those years?"

"Off and on — but that was before the new law was passed," the superintendent hastened to add.

"Machine idle?" the inspector asked, pointing at the unoccupied machine beside Johnny's, in which the part-filled bobbins were flying like mad.

"Looks that way." The superintendent motioned the overseer to him and shouted in his ear and pointed at the machine. "Machine's idle," he reported back to the inspector.

They passed on, and Johnny returned to his work, relieved in that the ill had been averted. But the one-legged boy was not so fortunate. The sharp-eyed inspector haled him out at arm's length from the bin truck. His lips were quivering, and his face had all the expression of one upon whom was fallen profound and irremediable disaster. The overseer looked astounded, as though for the first time he had laid eyes on the boy, while the superintendent's face expressed shock and displeasure.

"I know him," the inspector said. "He's twelve years old. I've had him discharged from three factories inside the year. This makes the fourth."

He turned to the one-legged boy. "You promised me, word and honor, that you'd go to school."

The one-legged boy burst into tears. "Please, Mr. Inspector, two babies died on us, and we're awful poor."

"What makes you cough that way?" the inspector demanded, as though charging him with crime.

And as in denial of guilt, the one-legged boy replied: "It ain't nothin'. I jes' caught a cold last week, Mr. Inspector, that's all."

In the end the one-legged boy went out of the room with the inspector, the latter accompanied by the anxious and protesting superintendent. After that monotony settled down again. The long morning and the longer afternoon wore away and the whistle blew for quitting time. Darkness had already fallen when Johnny passed out through the factory gate. In the interval the sun had made a golden ladder of the sky, flooded the world with its gracious warmth, and dropped down and disappeared in the west behind a ragged sky-line of housetops.

Supper was the family meal of the day — the one meal at which Johnny encountered his younger brothers and sisters. It partook of the nature of an encounter, to him, for he was very old, while they were distressingly young. He had no patience with their excessive and amazing juvenility. He did not understand it. His own childhood was too far behind him. He was like an old and irritable man, annoyed by the turbulence of their young spirits that was to him arrant silliness. He glowered silently over his food, finding compensation in the thought that they would soon have to go to work. That would take the edge off of them and make them sedate and dignified — like him. Thus it was, after the fashion of the human, that Johnny made of himself a yardstick with which to measure the universe.

During the meal, his mother explained in various ways and with infinite repetition that she was trying to do the best she could; so that it was with relief, the scant meal ended, that Johnny shoved back his chair and arose. He debated for a moment between bed and the front door, and finally went out the latter. He did not go far. He sat down on the stoop, his knees drawn up and his narrow shoulders drooping forward, his elbows on his knees and the palms of his hands supporting his chin.

As he sat there, he did no thinking. He was just resting. So far as his mind was concerned, it was asleep. His brothers and sisters came out, and with other children played noisily about him. An electric globe on the corner lighted their frolics. He was peevish and irritable, that they knew; but the spirit of adventure lured them into teasing him. They joined hands before him, and, keeping time with their bodies, chanted in his face weird and uncomplimentary doggerel. At first he snarled curses at them — curses he had learned from the lips of various foremen. Finding this futile, and remembering his dignity, he relapsed into dogged silence.

His brother Will, next to him in age, having just passed his tenth birthday, was the ring-leader. Johnny did not possess particularly kindly feelings toward him. His life had early been embittered by continual giving over and giving way to Will. He had a definite feeling that Will was greatly in his debt and was ungrateful about it. In his own playtime, far back in the dim past, he had been robbed of a large part of that playtime by being compelled to take care of Will. Will was a baby then, and then, as now, their mother had spent her days in the mills. To Johnny had fallen the part of little father and little mother as well.

Will seemed to show the benefit of the giving over and the giving way. He was well-built, fairly rugged, as tall as his elder brother and even heavier. It was as though the lifeblood of the one had been diverted into the other's veins. And in spirits it was the same. Johnny was jaded, worn out, without resilience, while his younger brother seemed bursting and spilling over with exuberance.

The mocking chant rose louder and louder. Will leaned closer as he danced, thrusting out his tongue. Johnny's left arm shot out and caught the other around the neck. At the same time he rapped his bony fist to the other's nose. It was a pathetically bony fist, but that it was sharp to hurt was evidenced by the squeal of pain it produced. The other children were uttering frightened cries, while Johnny's sister, Jennie, had dashed into the house.

He thrust Will from him, kicked him savagely on the shins, then reached for him and slammed him face downward in the dirt. Nor did he release him till the face had been rubbed into the dirt several times. Then the mother arrived, an anaemic whirlwind of solicitude and maternal wrath.

"Why can't he leave me alone?" was Johnny's reply to her upbraiding. "Can't he see I'm tired?"

"I'm as big as you," Will raged in her arms, his face a mess of tears, dirt, and blood. "I'm as big as you now, an' I'm goin' to git bigger. Then I'll lick you — see if I don't."

"You ought to be to work, seein' how big you are," Johnny snarled. "That's what's the matter with you. You ought to be to work. An' it's up to your ma to put you to work."

"But he's too young," she protested. "He's only a little boy."

"I was younger'n him when I started to work."

Johnny's mouth was open, further to express the sense of unfairness that he felt, but the mouth closed with a snap. He turned gloomily on his heel and stalked into the house and to bed. The door of his room was open to let in warmth from the kitchen. As he undressed in the semi-darkness he could hear his mother talking with a neighbor woman who had dropped in. His mother was crying, and her speech was punctuated with spiritless sniffles.

"I can't make out what's gittin' into Johnny," he could hear her say. "He didn't used to be this way. He was a patient little angel."

"An' he *is* a good boy," she hastened to defend. "He's worked faithful, an' he did go to work too young. But it wasn't my fault. I do the best I can, I'm sure."

Prolonged sniffling from the kitchen, and Johnny murmured to himself as his eyelids closed down, "You betcher life I've worked faithful."

The next morning he was torn bodily by his mother from the grip of sleep. Then came the meagre breakfast, the tramp through the dark, and the pale glimpse of day across the housetops as he turned his back on it and went in through the factory gate. It was another day, of all the days, and all the days were alike.

And yet there had been variety in his life — at the times he changed from one job to another, or was taken sick. When he was six, he was little mother and father to Will and the other children still younger. At seven he went into the mills — winding bobbins. When he was eight, he got work in another mill. His new job was marvellously easy. All he had to do was to sit down with a little stick in his hand and guide a stream of cloth that flowed past him. This stream of cloth came out of the maw of a machine, passed over a hot roller, and went on its way elsewhere. But he sat always in the one place, beyond the reach of daylight, a gas-jet flaring over him, himself part of the mechanism.

He was very happy at that job, in spite of the moist heat, for he was still young and in possession of dreams and illusions. And wonderful dreams he dreamed as he watched the streaming cloth streaming endlessly by. But there was no exercise about the work, no call upon his mind, and he dreamed less and less, while his mind grew torpid and drowsy. Nevertheless, he earned two dollars a week, and two dollars represented the difference between acute starvation and chronic underfeeding.

But when he was nine, he lost his job. Measles was the cause of it. After he recovered, he got work in a glass factory. The pay was better, and the work demanded skill. It was piece-work, and the more skilful he was, the bigger wages he earned. Here was incentive. And under this incentive he developed into a remarkable worker.

It was simple work, the tying of glass stoppers into small bottles. At his waist he carried a bundle of twine. He held the bottles between his knees so that he might work with both hands. Thus, in a sitting position and bending over his own knees, his narrow shoulders grew humped and his chest was contracted for ten hours each day. This was not good for the lungs, but he tied three hundred dozen bottles a day.

The superintendent was very proud of him, and brought visitors to look at him. In ten hours three hundred dozen bottles passed through his hands. This meant that he had attained machine-like perfection. All waste movements were eliminated. Every motion of his thin arms, every movement of a muscle in the thin fingers, was swift and accurate. He worked at high tension, and the result was that he grew nervous. At night his muscles twitched in his sleep, and in the daytime he could not relax and rest. He remained keyed up and his muscles continued to twitch. Also he grew sallow and his lint-cough grew worse. Then pneumonia laid hold of the feeble lungs within the contracted chest, and he lost his job in the glass-works.

Now he had returned to the jute mills where he had first begun with winding bobbins. But promotion was waiting for him. He was a good worker. He would next go on the starcher, and later he would go into the loom room. There was nothing after that except increased efficiency.

The machinery ran faster than when he had first gone to work, and his mind ran slower. He no longer dreamed at all, though his earlier years had been full of dreaming. Once he had been in love. It was when he first began guiding the cloth over the hot roller, and it was with the daughter of the superintendent. She was much older than he, a young woman, and he had seen her at a distance only a paltry half-dozen times. But that made no difference. On the surface of the cloth stream that poured past him, he pictured radiant futures wherein he performed prodigies of toil, invented miraculous machines, won to the mastership of the mills, and in the end took her in his arms and kissed her soberly on the brow.

But that was all in the long ago, before he had grown too old and tired to love. Also, she had married and gone away, and his mind had gone to sleep. Yet it had been a wonderful experience, and he used often to look back upon it as other men and women look back upon the time they believed in fairies. He had never believed in fairies nor Santa Claus; but he had believed implicitly in the smiling future his imagination had wrought into the steaming cloth stream.

He had become a man very early in life. At seven, when he drew his first wages, began his adolescence. A certain feeling of independence crept up in him, and the relationship between him and his mother changed. Somehow, as an earner and breadwinner, doing his own work in the world, he was more like an equal with her. Manhood, full-blown manhood, had come when he was eleven, at which time he had gone to work on the night shift for six months. No child works on the night shift and remains a child.

There had been several great events in his life. One of these had been when his mother bought some California prunes. Two others had been the two times when she cooked custard. Those had been events. He remembered them kindly. And at that time his mother had told him of a blissful dish she would sometime make — "floating island," she had called it, "better than custard." For years he had looked forward to the day when he would sit down to the table with floating island before him, until at last he had relegated the idea of it to the limbo of unattainable ideals.

Once he found a silver quarter lying on the sidewalk. That, also, was a great event in his life, withal a tragic one. He knew his duty on the instant the silver flashed on his eyes, before even he had picked it up. At home, as usual, there was not enough to eat, and home he should have taken it as he did his wages every Saturday night. Right conduct in this case was obvious; but he never had any spending of his money, and he was suffering from candy hunger. He was ravenous for the sweets that only on red-letter days he had ever tasted in his life.

He did not attempt to deceive himself. He knew it was sin, and deliberately he sinned when he went on a fifteen-cent candy debauch. Ten cents he saved for a future orgy; but not being accustomed to the carrying of money, he lost the ten cents. This occurred at the time when he was suffering all the torments of conscience, and it was to him an act of divine retribution. He had a frightened sense of the closeness of an awful and wrathful God. God had seen, and God had been swift to punish, denying him even the full wages of sin.

In memory he always looked back upon that event as the one great criminal deed of his life, and at the recollection his conscience always awoke and gave him another twinge. It was the one skeleton in his closet. Also, being so made and circumstanced, he looked back upon the deed with regret. He was dissatisfied with the manner in which he had spent the quarter. He could have invested it better, and, out of his later knowledge of the quickness of God, he would have beaten God out by spending the whole quarter at one fell swoop. In retrospect he spent the quarter a thousand times, and each time to better advantage.

There was one other memory of the past, dim and faded, but stamped into his soul everlasting by the savage feet of his father. It was more like a nightmare than a remembered vision of a concrete thing — more like the race-memory of man that makes him fall in his sleep and that goes back to his arboreal ancestry.

This particular memory never came to Johnny in broad daylight when he was wide awake. It came at night, in bed, at the moment that his consciousness was sinking down and losing itself in sleep. It always aroused him to frightened wakefulness, and for the moment, in the first sickening start, it seemed to him that he lay crosswise on the foot of the bed. On the bed were the vague forms of his father and mother. He never saw what his father looked like. He had but one impression of his father, and that was that he had savage and pitiless feet.

His earlier memories lingered with him, but he had no late memories. All days were alike. Yesterday or last year were the same as a thousand years — or a minute. Nothing ever happened. There were no events to mark the march of time. Time did not march. It stood always still. It was only the whirling machines that moved, and they moved nowhere — in spite of the fact that they moved faster.

*   *   *

When he was fourteen, he went to work on the starcher. It was a colossal event. Something had at last happened that could be remembered beyond a night's sleep or a week's payday. It marked an era. It was a machine Olympiad, a thing to date from. "When I went to work on the starcher," or, "after," or "before I went to work on the starcher," were sentences often on his lips.

He celebrated his sixteenth birthday by going into the loom room and taking a loom. Here was an incentive again, for it was piece-work. And he excelled, because the clay of him had been moulded by the mills into the perfect machine. At the end of three months he was running two looms, and, later, three and four.

At the end of his second year at the looms he was turning out more yards than any other weaver, and more than twice as much as some of the less skilful ones. And at home things began to prosper as he approached the full stature of his earning power. Not, however, that his increased earnings were in excess of need. The children were growing up. They ate more. And they were going to school, and school-books cost money. And somehow, the faster he worked, the faster climbed the prices of things. Even the rent went up, though the house had fallen from bad to worse disrepair.

He had grown taller; but with his increased height he seemed leaner than ever. Also, he was more nervous. With the nervousness increased his peevishness and irritability. The children had learned by many bitter lessons to fight shy of him. His mother respected him for his earning power, but somehow her respect was tinctured with fear.

There was no joyousness in life for him. The procession of the days he never saw. The nights he slept away in twitching unconsciousness. The rest of the time he worked, and his consciousness was machine consciousness. Outside this his mind was a blank. He had no ideals, and but one illusion; namely, that he drank excellent coffee. He was a work-beast. He had no mental life whatever; yet deep down in the crypts of his mind, unknown to him, were being weighed and sifted every hour of his toil, every movement of his hands, every twitch of his muscles, and preparations were making for a future course of action that would amaze him and all his little world.

It was in the late spring that he came home from work one night aware of unusual tiredness. There was a keen expectancy in the air as he sat down to the table, but he did not notice. He went through the meal in moody silence, mechanically eating what was before him. The children um'd and ah'd and made smacking noises with their mouths. But he was deaf to them.

"D'ye know what you're eatin'?" his mother demanded at last, desperately.

He looked vacantly at the dish before him, and vacantly at her.

"Floatin' island," she announced triumphantly.

"Oh," he said.

"Floating island!" the children chorused loudly.

"Oh," he said. And after two or three mouthfuls, he added, "I guess I ain't hungry to-night."

He dropped the spoon, shoved back his chair, and arose wearily from the table.

"An' I guess I'll go to bed."

His feet dragged more heavily than usual as he crossed the kitchen floor. Undressing was a Titan's task, a monstrous futility, and he wept weakly as he crawled into bed, one shoe still on. He was aware of a rising, swelling something inside his head that made his brain thick and fuzzy. His lean fingers felt as big as his wrist, while in the ends of them was a remoteness of sensation vague and fuzzy like his brain. The small of his back ached intolerably. All his bones ached. He ached everywhere. And in his head began the shrieking, pounding, crashing, roaring of a million looms. All space was filled with flying shuttles. They darted in and out, intricately, amongst the stars. He worked a thousand looms himself, and ever they speeded up, faster and faster, and his brain unwound, faster and faster, and became the thread that fed the thousand flying shuttles.

He did not go to work next morning. He was too busy weaving colossally on the thousand looms that ran inside his head. His mother went to work, but first she sent for the doctor. It was a severe attack of la grippe, he said. Jennie served as nurse and carried out his instructions.

It was a very severe attack, and it was a week before Johnny dressed and tottered feebly across the floor. Another week, the doctor said, and he would be fit to return to work. The foreman of the loom room visited him on Sunday afternoon, the first day of his convalescence. The best weaver in the room, the foreman told his mother. His job would be held for him. He could come back to work a week from Monday.

"Why don't you thank 'im, Johnny?" his mother asked anxiously.

"He's ben that sick he ain't himself yet," she explained apologetically to the visitor.

Johnny sat hunched up and gazing steadfastly at the floor. He sat in the same position long after the foreman had gone. It was warm outdoors, and he sat on the stoop in the afternoon. Sometimes his lips moved. He seemed lost in endless calculations.

Next morning, after the day grew warm, he took his seat on the stoop. He had pencil and paper this time with which to continue his calculations, and he calculated painfully and amazingly.

"What comes after millions?" he asked at noon, when Will came home from school. "An' how d'ye work 'em?"

That afternoon finished his task. Each day, but without paper and pencil, he returned to the stoop. He was greatly absorbed in the one tree that grew across the street. He studied it for hours at a time, and was unusually interested when the wind swayed its branches and fluttered its leaves. Throughout the week he seemed lost in a great communion with himself. On Sunday, sitting on the stoop, he laughed aloud, several times, to the perturbation of his mother, who had not heard him laugh in years.

Next morning, in the early darkness, she came to his bed to rouse him. He had had his fill of sleep all week, and awoke easily. He made no struggle, nor did he attempt to hold on to the bedding when she stripped it from him. He lay quietly, and spoke quietly.

"It ain't no use, ma."

"You'll be late," she said, under the impression that he was still stupid with sleep.

"I'm awake, ma, an' I tell you it ain't no use. You might as well lemme alone. I ain't goin' to git up."

"But you'll lose your job!" she cried.

"I ain't goin' to git up," he repeated in a strange, passionless voice.

She did not go to work herself that morning. This was sickness beyond any sickness she had ever known. Fever and delirium she could understand; but this was insanity. She pulled the bedding up over him and sent Jennie for the doctor.

When that person arrived, Johnny was sleeping gently, and gently he awoke and allowed his pulse to be taken.

"Nothing the matter with him," the doctor reported. "Badly debilitated, that's all. Not much meat on his bones."

"He's always been that way," his mother volunteered.

"Now go 'way, ma, an' let me finish my snooze."

Johnny spoke sweetly and placidly, and sweetly and placidly he rolled over on his side and went to sleep.

At ten o'clock he awoke and dressed himself. He walked out into the kitchen, where he found his mother with a frightened expression on her face.

"I'm goin' away, ma," he announced, "an' I jes' want to say good-by."

She threw her apron over her head and sat down suddenly and wept. He waited patiently.

"I might a-known it," she was sobbing.

"Where?" she finally asked, removing the apron from her head and gazing up at him with a stricken face in which there was little curiosity.

"I don't know — anywhere."

As he spoke, the tree across the street appeared with dazzling brightness on his inner vision. It seemed to lurk just under his eyelids, and he could see it whenever he wished.

"An' your job?" she quavered.

"I ain't never goin' to work again."

"My God, Johnny!" she wailed, "don't say that!"

What he had said was blasphemy to her. As a mother who hears her child deny God, was Johnny's mother shocked by his words.

"What's got into you, anyway?" she demanded, with a lame attempt at imperativeness.

"Figures," he answered. "Jes' figures. I've ben doin' a lot of figurin' this week, an' it's most surprisin'."

"I don't see what that's got to do with it," she sniffled.

Johnny smiled patiently, and his mother was aware of a distinct shock at the persistent absence of his peevishness and irritability.

"I'll show you," he said. "I'm plum' tired out. What makes me tired? Moves. I've ben movin' ever since I was born. I'm tired of movin', an' I ain't goin' to move any more. Remember when I worked in the glass-house? I used to do three hundred dozen a day. Now I reckon I made about ten different moves to each bottle. That's thirty-six thousan' moves a day. Ten days, three hundred an' sixty thousan' moves a day. One month, one million an' eighty thousan' moves. Chuck out the eighty thousan'—" he spoke with the complacent beneficence of a philanthropist — "chuck out the eighty thousan', that leaves a million moves a month — twelve million moves a year.

"At the looms I'm movin' twic'st as much. That makes twenty-five million moves a year, an' it seems to me I've ben a movin' that way 'most a million years.

"Now this week I ain't moved at all. I ain't made one move in hours an' hours. I tell you it was swell, jes' settin' there, hours an' hours, an' doin' nothin'. I ain't never ben happy before. I never had any time. I've ben movin' all the time. That ain't no way to be happy. An' I ain't goin' to do it any more. I'm jes' goin' to set, an' set, an' rest, an' rest, and then rest some more."

"But what's goin' to come of Will an' the children?" she asked despairingly.

"That's it, 'Will an' the children,'" he repeated.

But there was no bitterness in his voice. He had long known his mother's ambition for the younger boy, but the thought of it no longer rankled. Nothing mattered any more. Not even that.

"I know, ma, what you've ben plannin' for Will — keepin' him in school to make a bookkeeper out of him. But it ain't no use, I've quit. He's got to go to work."

"An' after I have brung you up the way I have," she wept, starting to cover her head with the apron and changing her mind.

"You never brung me up," he answered with sad kindliness. "I brung myself up, ma, an' I brung up Will. He's bigger'n me, an' heavier, an' taller. When I was a kid, I reckon I didn't git enough to eat. When he come along an' was a kid, I was workin' an' earnin' grub for him too. But that's done with. Will can go to work, same as me, or he can go to hell, I don't care which. I'm tired. I'm goin' now. Ain't you goin' to say good-by?"

She made no reply. The apron had gone over her head again, and she was crying. He paused a moment in the doorway.

"I'm sure I done the best I knew how," she was sobbing.

He passed out of the house and down the street. A wan delight came into his face at the sight of the lone tree. "Jes' ain't goin' to do nothin'," he said to himself, half aloud, in a crooning tone. He glanced wistfully up at the sky, but the bright sun dazzled and blinded him.

It was a long walk he took, and he did not walk fast. It took him past the jute-mill. The muffled roar of the loom room came to his ears, and he smiled. It was a gentle, placid smile. He hated no one, not even the pounding, shrieking machines. There was no bitterness in him, nothing but an inordinate hunger for rest.

The houses and factories thinned out and the open spaces increased as he approached the country. At last the city was behind him, and he was walking down a leafy lane beside the railroad track. He did not walk like a man. He did not look like a man. He was a travesty of the human. It was a twisted and stunted and nameless piece of life that shambled like a sickly ape, arms loose-hanging, stoop-shouldered, narrow-chested, grotesque and terrible.

He passed by a small railroad station and lay down in the grass under a tree. All afternoon he lay there. Sometimes he dozed, with muscles that twitched in his sleep. When awake, he lay without movement, watching the birds or looking up at the sky through the branches of the tree above him. Once or twice he laughed aloud, but without relevance to anything he had seen or felt.

After twilight had gone, in the first darkness of the night, a freight train rumbled into the station. When the engine was switching cars on to the side-track, Johnny crept along the side of the train. He pulled open the side-door of an empty box-car and awkwardly and laboriously climbed in. He closed the door. The engine whistled. Johnny was lying down, and in the darkness he smiled.

(1906)

QUESTIONS

1. "Apostate" is a word usually used in a religious context. How does it apply to the situation in this story? What sort of analogy is London making between religion and something else?

2. Study the language used in the opening scene. How much violence is implied in the words? How violent are the events actually being narrated?

How, then, do you explain the difference between *what* is being said and the *way* it is being said?

3. How does the narrator encourage you to feel toward Johnny? Do your feelings change throughout the story? Do you ever have conflicting reactions? What does Johnny's smile at the end suggest?

4. How would you describe the political content of the story? Imagine that you could enact any law you wished in response to it. What would you legislate?

5. Compare this story with one in which the characters face difficult moral choices, such as "A White Heron" (pp. 114–120) or "Town and Country Lovers" (pp. 160–172). What kind of choices are available to Johnny or his family? Would any individual choice make a difference in the world London is depicting? What does that indicate about London's ideology and about how ideology affects literary form?

SUGGESTIONS FOR WRITING

1. One way we distinguish between the implied and real authors of a text is to use different verb tenses in talking about them. We say, "Virginia Woolf *wrote To the Lighthouse* in 1927," but we say, "In 'Kew Gardens,' the implied author *constructs* a narrator who *describes* the various characters that pass by a particular flower bed." Why do we use past tense for the former and present tense for the latter?

2. The concept of implied author is useful in answering a common student question: "Do authors really think about all that stuff when they write?" Let us assume that the person who actually wrote a story had no idea that she was creating a symbol for women's struggles to express themselves, and yet a majority of readers find such a symbol in the story. Does the *implied* author of the story intend us to find the symbol? How could a meaning get into the story other than by the real author's intention?

3. Sometimes a reader feels that he comes to "know" a real author as well as he knows his friends. He will seek out everything the author wrote and read it for the author's company as much as for the characters and situations. Would you recommend that this reader read the author's diaries? Her letters? A biography written by someone else? Why or why not?

4. When the implied authors of two different texts by the same writer (such as the two "Jack Londons") seem to have quite different traits or hold opposite views, how do you reconcile them? Do you decide that the man who wrote "The Apostate" had changed by the time he wrote "The Unparalleled Invasion"? That he was serious when he wrote the one but not when he wrote the other? That he was simply following the logic of the story rather than expressing a personal opinion? That he somehow defined his human responsibilities in such a way that he saw no conflict between compassion

for the working class and intolerance of ethnic groups? Can these questions be answered by studying biographical documents about Jack London?

5. Find something you wrote a long time ago or invent something you might have written. Imagine that you are a stranger reading it. What sort of author would you as a stranger infer to be the implied author? How does that implied author differ from the self you remember being when you wrote the text?

8 Theme and Ideology

A friend says "I see you're reading Faulkner's 'Delta Autumn' (pp. 281–290). I hear it's a good story. What's it about?" You proceed to tell her that it's about an old man named McCaslin who, on an annual hunting trip in the Mississippi marshlands, learns of a love affair between a younger companion, Don Boyd, and a black woman. McCaslin, you go on, warns the woman to get out of the affair and ends up meditating about the destruction of the wilderness that he loves so much. What you have given your friend is a summary of the story's *subject matter*. You have simply retold the story in fewer words, that is, *paraphrased* it.

Her curiosity aroused, your friend reads the short story for herself. The next time she sees you, she says "I liked the story, but I'm not sure what it means. What do you think?" This is clearly different from her first question. A paraphrase of "Delta Autumn" concerns what McCaslin did and thought, but to answer the question "What does the story *mean?*" one must leave the specific fictional world and consider more generally the ideas or notions that the fiction propounds — sometimes explicitly but more often implicitly. These ideas or notions, which relate as much to the real as to the fictional world, are often called *themes*.

The Definition of "Theme"

A theme refers outward from the fictional world to the world of real-life experience. There are several themes that we might infer from "Delta Autumn." (I put them in quotation marks merely to identify them, not to suggest that these are the only sentences in which to formulate them, or that all readers would agree that these are good formulations.) One is "old prejudices die hard, even among those who might suspect that they are wrong" (McCaslin admits in his own mind that racial intermarriage is possible, but wants to delay it long beyond his death, indeed, "a thousand or two thousand years"). Another is "the line between good intentions and bigotry is sometimes difficult to draw" (McCaslin is surely a racist, and speaks cruelly to the woman, but

273

inwardly he feels a concern, even a certain sympathy about her love: "But God," he thinks, "pity these"). A third is suggested by McCaslin's love of the wetlands and his fear of what commercial developers might do to them: "A person can be bigoted about human relations but still have admirable attitudes about preserving the natural environment." The themes of racial and sexual bigotry and that of love of the land may combine, as in the statement: "Elderly people tend to be very conservative, both in a bad and a good sense: they reject inevitable social change but they also want to conserve things that more progressive, younger people may destroy without realizing their irreplaceability."

Themes do not repeat the story in other words, as do paraphrases, but rather reach outward from the specifics of the story to life in general, life as we in the nonfictional world experience it. Though often only by implication, themes "speak" to real psychological, social, and moral questions. That's one of the precious qualities of fictions: they intersect with our lives. We are intimately touched by them. Consider the words *intersect* and *touch*. Even if we have never been to the Deep South and were born long after the era evoked by "Delta Autumn," we may well know something about prejudice and bigotry and ecology. Perhaps we have seen naked prejudice firsthand, or the ruin of a beautiful natural terrain. We may have met people who were bigoted, but who struck us as pleasant, even admirable in other ways. We may have an elderly relative or family friend whose attitudes toward foreigners or immigrants or people of other races are deplorable, but who is otherwise the kindest of persons. In a superhonest moment, we ourselves may remember feeling a bit of prejudice or ruining a bit of nature. It is through these experiences that "Delta Autumn" "speaks" to us, tells us more than the mere subject of the story— "There was once an old man named McCaslin who . . ."

Most fictions, especially modern fictions, are relatively open-ended, that is, suggest several themes. Readers may well differ about a fiction's meaning, because themes intersect our backgrounds in different and complex ways. Obviously, a conservation-minded reader will read the short story differently than will a reader who favors urbanization of the landscape. A white person will read it differently from a person of color. Indeed, a racist land developer might not even sense a racist theme in "Delta Autumn," but might object to what he considers its thematic bias against land development.

Thesis

Sometimes fictions present only a single, unambiguous theme. Such a theme is called a *moral* or *thesis* and is expressed or implied by fictional genres such as the allegory, the parable, and the fable. An *allegory* is a kind of narrative whose characters stand for abstract qualities, typically vices and virtues. A *parable* presents, for the purposes of generalization, a typical moral situation (an example is the biblical parable of the prodigal son). A *fable* offers a moral lesson in terms of supernatural characters, typically animals who can speak and think.

For example, the fable "The Tortoise and the Hare" ends with the explicitly stated thesis "Slow and steady wins the race." Other fables, such as the following, do not explicitly express a moral but clearly imply one (and only one):

> A dispute arose between the North Wind and the Sun, each claiming that he was stronger than the other. At last they agreed to try their powers upon a traveller, to see which could soonest strip him of his cloak. The North Wind had the first try; and, gathering up all his force for the attack, he came whirling furiously down upon the man, and caught up his cloak as though he would wrest it from him by one single effort: but the harder he blew, the more closely the man wrapped it round himself. Then came the turn of the Sun. At first he beamed gently upon the traveller, who soon unclasped his cloak and walked on with it hanging loosely about his shoulders: then he shone forth in his full strength, and the man, before he had gone many steps, was glad to throw his cloak right off and complete his journey more lightly clad.[1]

The thesis is fairly obvious, isn't it? How would you formulate it?

The difference between theme and thesis is more a question of degree than of kind. Some short stories have relatively specific themes. One could state them in a sentence or two and expect to get fairly common agreement. Examples are Isaac Bashevis Singer's "Short Friday" (pp. 66–74) and Leo Tolstoy's "Three Deaths" (pp. 578–588). Though the themes of these stories do not reduce to a simple moral or thesis, they suggest definitely fewer possibilities than "Delta Autumn." However we phrase it, the theme of "Short Friday" turns on the painlessness of the death of the pious and their assured place in heaven. The theme of "Three Deaths" is that no matter who or what you are, death will reduce you finally to a heap of dust. The themes of other short stories, such as "Delta Autumn" and many others in this collection, are more numerous and more difficult to pin down.

How to Formulate a Theme

Formulating a theme is not an exact science. Don't expect to find some magic sequence of words that everyone will agree to. However, constructing a thematic sentence is a useful starting point for talking about a short story, for answering the vital question "What does this fiction mean to me?"

How do you decide on a short story's theme? What evidence helps you formulate your understanding of its intentions? An obvious place to begin is the title. From the outset, the title "Delta Autumn" focuses our attention on the wetlands that McCaslin loves and whose loss he fears. We sense that the Delta setting is not just utilitarian but plays an important symbolic role in the theme. "Autumn" suggests both the season of the traditional hunt and McCaslin's time of life, a time given to nostalgia and brooding about the pleasures of the past and the follies of the present and the future.

---

[1]From Jean La Fontaine, *Fables of La Fontaine*, translated Elizur Wright (New York: Derby & Jackson, 1860).

Another potential source of thematic intention is the direct commentary of the narrator. Consider, for example, "The Darling" (pp. 104–112), one of whose themes we might state as follows: "People should not define themselves solely in terms of their lovers' personalities." Though this theme is primarily evoked by what happens in the story, phrases scattered here and there clearly point to the narrator's attitude. Remember the narrator's remark: "And what was worst of all, she had no opinions of any sort"? Olenka's only opinions are those that echo opinions held by her man of the moment. When she is without a man, she has no opinions. The narrator notes that this is "worst of all." The absence of opinion is one mark of a person's total incapacity for independence.

Sometimes the theme inheres in a symbol that is obviously important to the story. A *symbol* is "something that is itself and also stands for something else . . ."[2] For example, a flag, which is only a piece of colored cloth, stands for a whole nation. In Isak Dinesen's "The Ring" (pp. 425–429), the young bride's wedding ring is such a symbol. She offers it to the strange being who accosts her in the woods. He refuses it, though he touches her and takes her handkerchief. The ring falls, and the bride makes no effort to retrieve it. When her husband finds her she thinks "all is over." We sense that what is over is not her frightening adventure but her marriage — or at least her romance with her husband. The loss of the ring has wedded her not to family bliss but "to poverty, persecution, total loneliness. To the sorrows and the sinfulness of this earth." The ring, then, symbolizes a traditional romantic ideal, that is, a value that the bride's extraordinary experience leads her to reject.

Ideology

Themes always arise in a larger structure of ideas. Every text has a *context*. A context is literally what surrounds the text — in other words, the set of assumptions and beliefs that must operate for the text to be comprehensible. I have discussed beliefs before in this book, for example, in the chapter on irony. Now I would like to refer to them by means of a new term. The totality of beliefs that constitute an all-encompassing system dominant in a culture is called an *ideology. The American College Dictionary* defines ideology as follows:

> The body of doctrine, myth, and symbols of a social movement, institution, class or large group.

Ideology so dominates our thinking that we usually don't even think of it as such, simply referring instead to the "way things are." Obviously even the briefest study of another culture will demonstrate the relativity of ideologies. Roland Barthes, a French critic, wrote a wonderful essay examining "the way wine is" to the average French person. It is an amazing composite: the best thirst-quencher; a "dense and vital fluid" like blood, which it helps fortify; a

---

[2]C. Hugh Holman and William Harmon, *A Handbook to Literature*, 6th ed. (New York: Macmillan, 1992), p. 466.

"converting substance" that reverses states, making a weak person strong; and so on. Compare that with the negative attitude of what wine "is" to an American community where alcoholic beverages are prohibited. Or compare our own attitudes about the appropriate street dress of women to those held by many Saudi Arabians.

Authors spend a lot of energy fine-tuning the ideological presuppositions of their fictions. As science-fiction movies never tire of showing us, aliens from outer space must learn the ideology of modern American life before coming down to mingle with us. In the same way, we can only understand the events and motives of characters in a story by Mark Twain by knowing something about the ideology of the American frontier of the nineteenth century. Often you may learn all you need to know about a fiction's ideology simply in the course of reading it. That's why reading fiction offers educational benefits beyond the pleasure that it gives us. By the same token, the more you already know about an ideology, the richer the experience of reading a fiction imbued with it.

Ideological assumptions may actually be spelled out in a fiction; more often they are presupposed. Either way, themes rest on the ideology evoked by the fiction. The ideology of "Short Friday," for example, necessarily includes a belief in God, heaven, and immortality. It insists that devoutness is unrelated to worldly competence and that competent women might be attracted to incompetent but devout men. The ideology of "The Sin Eater" includes a belief in the value of psychotherapy. The ideology implicit in "Town and Country Lovers" is profoundly critical of *apartheid*.

Because the ideology of a fiction is its set of ideas about the world, the implied author must be assumed to hold these attitudes. (The narrator may or may not hold them, depending on whether he or she is reliable.)

We assimilate a text's ideology, often without thinking consciously about it. We do so because we can barely understand or say anything without evoking an ideology. Even a single sentence frames the terms of a discourse. Take the old legal chestnut: "Have you stopped beating your wife?" Whether you answer yes or no, you are tacitly acceding to an ideology in which wife-beating is both possible and reprehensible. A more positive example: "When did you finally realize the need for sexual equality?" The ideology implicit here takes as a given the equal rights of both genders.

By the very act of narrating, a narrator, like any speaker, presupposes not only a certain state of affairs but also a certain set of ideas or notions that explain why things are the way they are. The world of a fiction is made up not only of its time and setting but also of the behavior and ideas that are acceptable in such a world.

The Invisibility of Ideology

A text's ideology is not always easy to determine. Oddly enough, it can be especially hard to piece out when it is close to our own. Because ideology is "that which goes without saying," we may have trouble seeing the woods for the trees. We tend to take our own ideology as the "natural" one, the one that accounts for things as they *really* are. We confuse opinion with reality. For Americans, for example, the rights guaranteed by the Constitution go without saying. Everyone is entitled to freedom of speech, assembly, press, and the like. Similarly, it goes without saying that it's good to be rich and famous, that a college education is worth having, that moms and dads should be easygoing and have a sense of humor. These ideas are so widespread and so ingrained in current American thinking—in our ideology—that we assume that everyone everywhere has always shared them. Obviously that assumption makes it hard to grasp stories that rest on different ideologies, especially ideologies that conflict with our own.

One of the great virtues of literature (and of all art) is that it tempts us to see life through the eyes of other ideologies, thereby making us aware of the presuppositions of our own. That may lead us to reaffirm what our culture has taught us as "only natural," but it may also lead us to some meditation on our attitudes, helping us grow in spirit and humanity.

Obviously, at some level we need to understand the ideology of a fiction to make much sense of it. That does not mean, of course, that we have to be practicing believers of the ideology. Christians or Muslems or Buddhists can accept the ideology of "Short Friday" without converting to Judaism. We do not even have to believe in God to accept the story as a moving expression of faith. We may have faith in other kinds of ideas and beliefs and be able to transfer the energy behind our faith to imaginative sympathy with an ideology that we do not literally accept. Even if we do not believe in God and heaven, we may find it pleasant and comforting, and perhaps in some sense true, that being a good person and faithfully practicing a certain tradition enables one to accept death with equanimity.

On the other hand, our religious (or antireligious) feelings may be so strong as to prevent us from accepting the presuppositions of a story like "Short Friday," even imaginatively. Still, that need not lead us to total rejection of the story. We may treat it as a pleasing *myth*, that is, a fanciful story that cannot be believed literally, but that somehow speaks meaningfully to a real-life concern. For instance, we may accept the ideology of *Star Wars* because we think it important to believe in some "force" of personal strength and integrity that can be "with" us, as long as we commit ourselves to it.

Some, however, may find the ideology evoked by fictions like "Short Friday" or "Delta Autumn" or *Star Wars* so offensive that they cannot accept it, even imaginatively. They simply reject the fictions out of hand. This is not an unusual experience, and it is not necessarily blameworthy. Fictional ideologies are not like traffic laws: they do not *have* to be obeyed. Who has not said to herself "That movie was totally worthless; I got nothing out of it; it was a complete waste of time"? Every reader or viewer has the sacred right to throw the book into the trash or walk out of the theater.

However, a compromise is possible: we may accept an ideology intellectually even as we reject it emotionally. For most of us, especially those who have been victimized by bigotry, it may be very difficult to muster the objectivity to appreciate a short story like "Delta Autumn," but we should try. Many critics would argue that there is no necessary connection between the beauty of a fiction and the ideology that it rests upon. Let's face it (they would say), great works of art have been created by bigots. Being an artist does not make a person a saint, or even somebody you'd be willing to drink a cup of coffee with. Artistic talent has nothing to do with virtue. Or to put it in other terms, *artistic* integrity is not the same thing as *personal* integrity. I doubt, for example, that I would relish having Dostoevsky, a very troubled man, as a friend, but the world would be much poorer for me if I could not read his novels. Great novels and short stories often deal with very troubling issues and portray ugly events and characters, sometimes from a point of view that we find offensive. Yet, if we are serious about learning to appreciate literature and the other arts, we cannot afford to confuse objectionable subject matter with the beauty of the artist's representation. Though we may be upset by what a fiction seems to mean, we should stay open to the possible beauty of how it leads us to that meaning. I object to much of the ideology implicit in "Delta Autumn," but I so admire the skill with which the short story is constructed and the larger human truths that it touches on that I am willing to "go along" with its premises — that is, to entertain them imaginatively, even as I protest against them intellectually.

Dealing with the Ideologies of Fictions

Let's come down out of the clouds of theory and do an interesting exercise. Let's compare two short stories ostensibly on the same subject that reveal markedly different ideologies. They are Ernest Hemingway's "Indian Camp" and "Certain Winds from the South," by the African author Ama Ata Aidoo, both of which concern birth. In Hemingway's story (pp. 292–295), the young protagonist Nick goes to an Indian camp with his doctor father, who has been called to deliver a baby. To calm Nick's dismay, the doctor tells his son that the pregnant squaw's screams "are not important. I don't hear them because they are not important." In saying that, he expresses the attitude of many white male American physicians of the early part of this century. He understands birth only in his own personal context. Though he knows intellectually that giving birth is a very painful experience, to him the pain is not medically significant, and therefore he excludes it from his emotional life. There may be good reasons for his doing so. Medical people need to steel themselves against human misery if they are to maintain their professional cool. But Nick is not a doctor; he keenly senses the woman's excruciating pain and feels appalled by the whole business. He looks away. He doesn't want to see what his father is doing as he performs a Caesarean birth, cuts the umbilical cord, cleans the baby, gets rid of the afterbirth, stitches the squaw up, and so on. His father, however, feels professional pride in delivering the baby under such primitive conditions. Of course, he sobers up when he realizes that the father of the child has committed suicide, presumably because *he* could not stand to hear his wife's screams. Still, the doctor succeeds in comforting Nick, who sits back in the boat feeling so reassured by his father's strength, intelligence, and skill that he is convinced of his own immortality.

"Indian Camp" presupposes an ideology of white male strength and bonding, and of the power of an "enlightened" scientific attitude about nature. Though the story is about giving birth, a difficult and momentous experience that only women undergo, the focus is on the responses of white American upper-class males. The birth of the baby and the Indian husband's suicide are only the occasion or backdrop for a young man's coming of age through bonding with his father's professional competence. The story seems to imply the superiority of the white race's ability to deal with nature. The father understands the need for scrupulous cleanliness, whereas the Indians are dirty, and their houses smell. The Indians have no power of their own: in every respect, they are dependent on the whites. The young brave who guides the doctor, Nick, and Uncle George to the village laughs when Uncle George gets bitten by the pregnant woman. We don't know whether he is laughing at the bite (as a rare and excusable occasion when an Indian can "get back" at a white man without suffering the consequences) or at Uncle George's cursing the squaw, but whatever it is about, the laughter wells up from powerlessness, not strength.

Ama Ata Aidoo's "Certain Winds from the South" (pp. 296–302), on the other hand, implies a totally different ideology. Here power, solidarity, and bonding are in the hands of women, not men. M'ma Asana, mother of Hawa and grandmother of the infant boy Fuseni, holds together whatever is left of the family, as her son-in-law, Issa, like her own husband before him, goes off to the south (that is, the white man's country, South Africa). M'ma Asana's husband left her to fight in an overseas war against the Germans, a war that was meaningless from M'ma Asana's point of view. Her husband never returned. Though Issa is only going south to work, not to fight, M'ma Asana is pessimistic about the prospects of his return, and she resolves to continue caring for her daughter and grandson on her own.

The ideology of this short story contrasts sharply with that of "Indian Camp." The short story does not presuppose that power is in the hands of males. On the contrary, the men do nothing but go off, abandoning the village for idle hopes of glory or money. The only stability rests with the women, who recognize the need to stay at home and fight to survive, to bring in the cola crop. The power of these women inheres not only in their greater stability but also in their greater wisdom and knowledge. It is the grandmother, not some white doctor, who attends to the birth of the child. The birth is successful, and M'ma Asana knows how to take care of the baby's healing navel. None of the countless babies whose birth she has assisted has ever had an infected navel. Similarly, though they are very poor, the inhabitants of this village are independent. They do not rely on a superior class of educated whites. It seems unlikely that M'ma Asana and her family will die of famine, no matter how cruelly nature treats them. Fuseni, we feel, will grow up strong and healthy. The ideology also suggests that he too may go off because of some temptation from the outside world. And the power in the village will pass from M'ma Asana to Hawa, because, it seems, men cannot resist their impulse to leave.

❖ WILLIAM FAULKNER
Delta Autumn

William Faulkner (1897–1962) was born in Albany, Mississippi, and educated at the University of Mississippi at Oxford. He was a fighter pilot during World War I and worked for a time on a New Orleans newspaper. He achieved his first great critical success with the novel *The Sound and the Fury* (1929). Later novels include *As I Lay Dying* (1930), *Light in August* (1932), *Absolom, Absolom* (1936), and a trilogy following the fortunes of a conniving family called the Snopes. He wrote almost 100 short stories, many of which appear in *Collected Short Stories* (1950). His fiction turns mostly on events in a mythical Mississippi county which he named Yoknapatawpha, whose entire history unfolds in the course of his novels and stories. Despite his concern with the traditional values, his fiction is often highly experimental. He was especially interested in representing the minds of characters, for example, through the technique of interior monologue. Despite his critical success, Faulkner had financial difficulties and was forced to work in Hollywood, writing or doctoring screenplays. It was an experience he largely disliked, preferring to spend his time in Mississippi. Many critics feel that Faulkner is the best American novelist of the twentieth century. He was awarded the Nobel Prize for literature in 1949.

Soon now they would enter the Delta. The sensation was familiar to him, renewed like this each last week in November for more than fifty years — the last hill at the foot of which the rich unbroken alluvial[1] flatness began as the sea began at the base of its cliffs, dissolving away beneath the unhurried November rain as the sea itself would dissolve away. At first they had come in wagons — the guns, the bedding, the dogs, the food, the whiskey, the anticipation of hunting — the young men who could drive all night and all the following day in the cold rain and pitch camp in the rain and sleep in the wet blankets and rise at daylight the next morning to hunt. There had been bear then, and a man shot a doe or a fawn as quickly as he did a buck, and in the afternoons they shot wild turkey with pistols to test their stalking skill and marksmanship, feeding all but the breast to the dogs. But that time was gone now and now they went in cars, driving faster and faster each year because the roads were better and they had farther to drive, the territory in which game still existed drawing yearly inward as his life was drawing in, until now he was the last of those who had once made the journey in wagons without feeling it and now those who accompanied him were the sons and even the grandsons of the men who had ridden for twenty-four hours in rain and sleet behind the steaming mules, calling him Uncle Ike now, and he no longer told anyone

---

[1]Characterized by the deposit of sand and mud formed by flowing water.

how near seventy he actually was because he knew as well as they did that he no longer had any business making such expeditions, even by car. In fact, each time now, on that first night in camp, lying aching and sleepless in the harsh blankets, his blood only faintly warmed by the single thin whiskey-and-water which he allowed himself, he would tell himself that this would be his last. But he would stand that trip (he still shot almost as well as he had ever shot, he still killed almost as much of the game he saw as he had ever killed; he no longer knew how many deer had fallen before his gun) and the fierce long heat of the next summer would somehow renew him. Then November would come again and again in the car with two of the sons of his old companions, whom he had taught not only how to distinguish between the prints left by a buck and a doe but between the sound they made in moving, he would look ahead past the jerking arc of the windshield wiper and see the land flatten suddenly, dissolving away beneath the rain as the sea itself would dissolve, and he would say, "Well boys, there it is again."

This time though he didn't have time to speak. The driver of the car stopped it, slamming it to a skidding halt on the greasy pavement without warning, so that old McCaslin, first looking ahead at the empty road, glanced sharply past the man in the middle until he could see the face of the driver, the youngest face of them all, darkly aquiline, handsome and ruthless and saturnine[2] and staring sombrely ahead through the steaming windshield across which the twin arms of the wiper flicked and flicked. "I didn't intend to come in here this time," he said. His name was Boyd. He was just past forty. He owned the car as well as two of the three Walker hounds in the rumble behind them, just as he owned, or at least did the driving of, anything—animal, machine or human—which he happened to be using.

"You said that back in Jefferson last week," McCaslin said. "Then you changed your mind. Have you changed it again?"

"Oh, Don's coming," the third man said. His name was Legate. He seemed to be speaking to no one. "If it was just a buck he was coming all this distance for now. But he's got a doe in here. On two legs—when she's standing up. Pretty light-colored too. The one he was after them nights last fall when he said he was coon-hunting. The one I figured maybe he was still chasing when he was gone all that month last January." He chortled, still in that voice addressed to no one, not quite completely jeering.

"What?" McCaslin said. "What's that?"

"Now, Uncle Ike," Legate said, "that's something a man your age ain't supposed to had no interest in in twenty years." But McCaslin had not even glanced at Legate. He was still watching Boyd's face, the eyes behind the spectacles, the blurred eyes of an old man but quite sharp too; eyes which could still see a gun barrel and what ran beyond it as well as any of them could. He was remembering himself now: how last year, during the final stage by motor boat to where they would camp, one of the boxes of food had been lost overboard and how on the second day Boyd had gone back to the nearest town for supplies and had been gone overnight and when he did return, something had happened to him: he would go into the woods each dawn with his gun when the others went, but McCaslin, watching him, knew that he was not hunting.

---

[2] Having a gloomy temperament.

"All right," he said. "Take Will and me on to shelter where we can wait for the truck, and you can go back."

"I'm going in," Boyd said harshly. "I'm going to get mine too. Because this will be the last of it."

"The last of deer hunting, or of doe hunting?" Legate said. This time McCaslin paid no attention to him even in speech. He still watched Boyd's savage and immobile face.

"Why?" he said.

"After Hitler gets through with it? Or Yokohama or Pelley or Smith or Jones or whatever he will call himself in this country."

"We'll stop him in this country," Legate said. "Even if he calls himself George Washington."

"How?" Boyd said. "By singing God Bless America in bars at midnight and wearing dime-store flags in our lapels?"

"So that's what's worrying you," McCaslin said. "I ain't noticed this country being short of defenders yet when it needed them. You did some of it yourself twenty years ago and did it well, if those medals you brought back home mean anything. This country is a little mite stronger and bigger than any one man or even group of men outside or inside of it either. I reckon it can cope with one Austrian paper hanger, no matter what he calls himself. My pappy and some other better men than any of them you named tried once to tear it in two with a war, and they failed."

"And what have you got left?" Boyd said. "Half the people without jobs and half the factories closed by strikes. Too much cotton and corn and hogs, and not enough for all the people to wear and eat. Too much not-butter and not even the guns. . . ."

"We got a deer camp—if we ever get to it," Legate said. "Not to mention does."

"It's a good time to mention does," McCaslin said. "Does and fawns both. The only fighting anywhere that ever had anything of God's blessing on it has been when men fought to protect does and fawns. If it's going to come to fighting, that's a good thing to mention and remember."

"Haven't you discovered in sixty years that women and children are one thing there's never any scarcity of?" Boyd said.

"Maybe that's why all I am worrying about right now is that ten miles of river we still got to run before we can make camp," McCaslin said. "Let's get on."

They went on. Soon they were going fast again—that speed at which Boyd drove, about which he had consulted neither of them just as he had given neither of them any warning when he had slammed the car to a stop. McCaslin relaxed again, watching, as he did each recurrent November while more than fifty of them passed, the land which he had seen change. At first there had been only the old towns along the river and the old towns along the edge of the hills, from each of which the planters with their gangs of slaves and then of hired labor had wrested from the impenetrable jungle of waterstanding cane and cypress, gum and holly and oak and ash, cotton patches which as the years passed became fields and then plantations, the paths made by deer and bear becoming roads and then highways, with towns in turn springing up along them and along the rivers Tallahatchie and Sunflower which joined and became the Yazoo, the River of the Dead of the Choctaws — the thick, slow, black, unsunned streams almost without current, which once each year actually ceased to flow and then moved backward, spreading, drowning the rich land and then subsiding again, leaving it still richer. Most of that was gone now. Now a man drove two hundred miles from Jefferson before he found wilderness to hunt in; now the land lay open from the cradling hills on the east to the rampart of levee on the west, standing horseman-tall with cotton for the world's looms — the rich black land, imponderable and vast, fecund up to the very cabin doorsteps of the Negroes who worked it and the domiciles of the white men who owned it, which exhausted the hunting life of a dog in one year, the working life of a mule in five and of a man in twenty — the land in which neon flashed past them from the little countless towns and constant this-year's cars sped over the broad plumb-ruled highways, yet in which the only permanent mark of man's occupation seemed to be the tremendous gins, constructed in sections of sheet iron and in a week's time though they were, since no man, millionaire though he be, would build more than a roof and walls to live in, with camping equipment to live with, because he knew that once each ten years or so his house would be flooded to the second story and all within it ruined; — the land across which there came now no scream of panther but instead the long hooting of locomotives: trains of incredible length and drawn by a single engine since there was no gradient anywhere and no elevation save those raised by forgotten aboriginal hands as refuges from the yearly water and used by their Indian successors to sepulchure their fathers' bones, and all that remained of that old time were the Indian names on the little towns and usually pertaining to water — Aluschaskuna, Tillatoba, Homachitto, Yazoo.

By early afternoon they were on water. At the last little Indian-named town at the end of the pavement they waited until the other car and the two trucks — the one containing the bedding and tents, the other carrying the horses — overtook them. Then they left the concrete and, after a mile or so, the gravel too, and in caravan they ground on through the ceaselessly dissolving afternoon with chained wheels in the lurching and splashing ruts, until presently it seemed to him that the retrograde of his recollection had gained an inverse velocity from their own slow progress and that the land had retreated not in minutes from the last spread of gravel, but in years, decades, back toward what it had been when he first knew it — the road they now followed once more the ancient pathway of bear and deer, the diminishing fields they now passed once more scooped punily and terrifically by axe and saw and mule drawn plow from the brooding and immemorial tangle instead of ruthless mile-wide parallelograms wrought by ditching and dyking machinery.

They left the cars and trucks at the landing, the horses to go overland down the river to a point opposite the camp and swim the river, themselves and the bedding and food and tents and dogs in the motor launch. Then, his old hammer double gun which was better than half as old as he between his knees, he watched even these last puny marks of man — cabin, clearing, the small and irregular fields which a year ago were jungle and in which the skeleton stalks of this year's cotton stood almost as tall and rank as the old cane had stood, as if man had had to marry his planting to the wilderness in order to conquer it — fall away and vanish until the twin banks marched with wilderness as he remembered it; the tangle of brier and cane impenetrable even to sight twenty feet away, the tall tremendous soaring of oak and gum and ash and hickory which had rung to no axe save the hunter's, had echoed to no machinery save the beat of old-time steamboats traversing it or the snarling of launches like their own of people going into it to dwell for a week or two weeks because it was still wilderness. There was still some of it left, although now it was two hundred miles from Jefferson when once it had been thirty. He had watched it, not being conquered, destroyed, so much as retreating since its purpose was now done and its time an outmoded time, retreating southward through this shaped section of earth between hills and river until what was left of it seemed now to be gathered and for the time arrested in one tremendous density of brooding and inscrutable impenetrability at the ultimate funnelling tip.

They reached the site of their last year's camp with still two hours left of light. "You go on over under that driest tree and set down," Legate told him. "Me and these other young boys will do this." He did neither. In his slicker he directed the unloading of the boat — the tents, the stove, the bedding, the food for themselves and the dogs until there should be meat in camp. He sent two of the Negroes to cut firewood; he had the cook-tent raised and the stove set up and a fire going and a meal cooking while the big tent was still being staked down. Then in the beginning of dusk he crossed in the boat to where the horses waited, backing and snorting at the water. He took the lead-ropes and with no more weight than that and his voice he drew them down into the water and held them beside the boat with only their heads above the surface as though they actually were suspended from his frail and strengthless old man's hands while the boat recrossed and each horse in turn lay prone in the shallows, panting and trembling, its eyes rolling in the dusk until the same weightless hand and the unraised voice gathered surging upward, splashing and thrashing up the bank.

Then the meal was ready. The last of light was gone now save the thin stain of it snared somewhere between the river's surface and the rain. He had the glass of thin whiskey-and-water and they ate standing in the mud beneath the stretched tarpaulin. The oldest Negro, Isham, had already made his bed — the strong, battered iron cot, the stained mattress which was not quite soft enough, the worn, washed blankets which as the years passed were less and less warm enough. Wearing only his bagging woolen underclothes, his spectacles folded away in the worn case beneath the pillow where he could reach them readily and his lean body fitted into the old worn groove of mattress and blankets, he lay on his back, his hands crossed on his breast and his eyes closed while the others went to bed and the last of the talking died into snoring. Then he opened his eyes and lay looking up at the motionless belly of canvas upon which the constant rain murmured, upon which the glow of the sheet-iron heater died slowly away and would fade still further until the youngest Negro, lying on planks before it for that purpose, would sit up and stoke it again and lie back down.

They had had a house once. That was twenty and thirty and forty years ago, when the big bottom was only thirty miles from Jefferson and old Major de Spain, who had been his father's cavalry commander in '61 and –2 and –3 and –4 and who had taken him into the woods his first time, had owned eight or ten sections of it. Old Sam Fathers was alive then, half Chickasaw Indian, grandson of a chief, and half Negro, who had taught him how and when to shoot; such a November dawn as tomorrow would be and the old man had led him straight to the great cypress and he had known the buck would pass exactly there because there was something running in Sam

Fathers' veins which ran in the veins of the buck and they stood there against the tremendous trunk, the old man and the boy of twelve, and there was nothing but the dawn and then suddenly the buck was there, smoke-colored out of nothing, magnificent with speed, and Sam Fathers said, "Now. Shoot quick and shoot slow," and the gun leveled without hurry and crashed and he walked to the buck lying still intact and still in the shape of that magnificent speed and he bled it with his own knife and Sam Fathers dipped his hands in the hot blood and marked his face forever while he stood trying not to tremble, humbly and with pride too though the boy of twelve had been unable to phrase it then, "I slew you; my bearing must not shame your quitting life. My conduct forever onward must become your death." They had the house then. That roof, the two weeks of each fall which they spent under it, had become his home; although since that time they had lived during the two fall weeks in tents and not always in the same place two years in succession, and now his companions were the sons and even the grandsons of those with whom he had lived in the house and the house itself no longer existed, the conviction, the sense of home, had been merely transferred into the canvas. He owned a house in Jefferson, where he had had a wife and children once though no more, and it was kept for him by his dead wife's niece and her family and he was comfortable in it, his wants and needs looked after by blood at least related to the blood which he had elected out of all the earth to cherish. But he spent the time between those walls waiting for November, because even this tent with its muddy floor and the bed which was not soft enough nor warm enough was his home and these men, some of whom he only saw during these two weeks, were more his kin. Because this was his land. . . .

The shadow of the youngest Negro loomed, blotting the heater's dying glow from the ceiling, the wood billets thumping into it until the glow, the flame, leaped high and bright across the canvas. But the Negro's shadow still remained, until after a moment McCaslin, rising onto one elbow, saw that it was not the Negro, it was Boyd; when he spoke the other turned his head and he saw in the red firelight the sullen and ruthless profile. "Nothing," Boyd said. "Go on back to sleep."

"Since Will Legate mentioned it," McCaslin said, "I remember you had some trouble sleeping in here last fall too. Only you called it coon-hunting then. Or was it Will Legate that called it that?" Boyd didn't answer. He turned and went back to his bed. McCaslin, propped on his elbow, watched until the other's shadow sank down the wall and vanished. "That's right," he said. "Try to get some sleep. We must have meat in camp tomorrow. You can do all the setting up you want to after that." Then he too lay back down, his hands crossed again on his breast, watching the glow of the heater. It was steady again now, the fresh wood accepted, being assimilated, soon it would begin to fade again, taking with it the last echo of that sudden upflare of a young man's passion and unrest. Let him lie awake for a little while, he thought. He would lie still some day for a long time without even dissatisfaction to disturb him. And lying awake here, in these surroundings, would soothe him if anything could, if anything could soothe a man just forty years old. The tent, the rain-murmured canvas globe, was filled with it once more now. He lay on his back, his eyes closed, his breathing quiet and peaceful as a child's, listening to it — that silence which was never silence but was myriad. He could almost see it, tremendous, primeval, looming, musing downward upon this puny evanescent clutter of human sojourn which after a single brief week would vanish and in another week would be completely healed, traceless in the unmarked solitude. Because it was his land, although he had never owned a foot of it. He had never wanted to, even after he saw its ultimate doom, began to watch it retreating year by year before the onslaught of axe and saw and log-lines and then dynamite and tractor plows, because it belonged to no man. It belonged to all; they had only to use it well, humbly and with pride. Then suddenly he knew why he had never wanted to own any of it, arrest at least that much of what people called progress. It was because there was just exactly enough of it. He seemed to see the two of them— himself and the wilderness—as coevals,[3] his own span as a hunter, a woodsman not contemporary with his first breath but transmitted to him, assumed by him gladly, humbly, with joy and pride, from that old Major de Spain and Sam Fathers who had taught him to hunt, the two spans running out together, not into oblivion, nothing- ness, but into a scope free of both time and space where once more the untreed land warped and wrung to mathematical squares of rank cotton for the frantic old-world peoples to turn into shells to shoot at one another, would find ample room for both—the shades of the tall unaxed trees and the sightless brakes where the wild strong immortal animals ran forever before the tireless belling immortal hounds, falling and rising phoenix-like[4] before the soundless guns.

Then he had slept. The lantern was lighted, the tent was full of the movement of men getting up and dressing and outside in the darkness the oldest Negro, Isham, was beating with a spoon on the bottom of a tin pan and crying, "Raise up and get yo fo clock coffy. Raise up and get yo fo clock coffy."

He heard Legate too. "Get on out of here now and let Uncle Ike sleep. If you wake him up, he'll want to go on stand. And he aint got any business in the woods this morning." So he didn't move. He heard them leave the tent; he listened to the breakfast sounds from the table beneath the tarpaulin. Then he heard them depart— the horses, the dogs, the last voice dying away; after a while he might possibly even hear the first faint clear cry of the first hound ring through the wet woods from where the buck had bedded, then he would go back to sleep again. Then the tent flap swung in and fell, something jarred against the end of the cot and a hand grasped his knee through the blanket and shook him before he could open his eyes. It was Boyd, carrying a shotgun instead of his rifle. He spoke in a harsh, rapid voice. "Sorry I had to wake you. There will be a. . . ."

"I was awake," McCaslin said. "Are you going to shoot that today?"

"You just told me last night you want meat," Boyd said. "There will be a. . . ."

"Since when did you start having trouble getting meat with your rifle?"

"All right," the other said, with that harsh, restrained, furious impatience. Then McCaslin saw in his other hand a thick oblong, an envelope. "There will be a woman here some time this morning, looking for me. Give her this and tell her I said no."

"What?" McCaslin said. "A what?" He half rose onto his elbow as the other

---

[3]Equals.
[4]Like the mythical bird of great beauty fabled to live 500 or so years, to burn itself to death, and to rise from its ashes in the freshness of youth, and live through another life cycle.

jerked the envelope onto the blanket in front of him, already turning toward the entrance, the envelope striking solid and heavy and soundless and already sliding from the bed until McCaslin caught it, feeling through the paper the thick sheaf of bank-notes. "Wait," he said. "Wait." The other stopped, looking back. They stared at one another — the old face, wan, sleep-raddled above the tumbled bed, the dark handsome younger one at once furious and cold. "Will Legate was right," McCaslin said. "This is what you called coon-hunting. And now this." He didn't lift the envelope nor indicate it in any way. "What did you promise her that you haven't the courage to face her and retract?"

"Nothing," Boyd said. "This is all of it. Tell her I said no." He was gone; the tent flap lifted on a waft of faint light and the constant murmur of the rain and fell again while McCaslin still lay half-raised on his elbow, the envelope clutched in his shaking hand. It seemed to him later that he began to hear the approaching boat almost immediately, before Boyd could have got out of sight even. It seemed to him that there had been no interval whatever: the mounting snarl of the engine, increasing, nearer and nearer and then cut short off, ceasing into the lap and plop of water under the bows as the boat slid in to the bank, the youngest Negro, the youth, raising the tent flap beyond which for an instant he saw the boat — a small skiff with a Negro man sitting in the stern beside the upslanted motor — then the woman entering, in a man's hat and a man's slicker and rubber boots, carrying the blanket-and-tarpaulin-wrapped bundle and bringing something else, something intangible, an effluvium[5] which he knew he would recognize in a moment because he knew now that Isham had already told him, warned him, by sending the young Negro to the tent instead of coming himself — a face young and with dark eyes, queerly colorless but not ill and not that of a country woman despite the garments she wore, looking down at him where he sat upright on the cot now, clutching the envelope, the soiled underclothes bagging about him and the twisted blankets huddled about his hips.

"Is that his?" he said. "Don't lie to me!"

"Yes," she said. "He's gone."

"He's gone," he said. "You won't jump him here. He left you this. He said to tell you no." He extended the envelope. It was sealed and it bore no superscription. Nevertheless he watched her take it in one hand and manage to rip it open and tilt the neat sheaf of bound notes onto the blanket without even glancing at them and then look into the empty envelope before she crumpled and dropped it.

"Just money," she said.

"What did you expect?" he said. "You have known him long enough or at least often enough to have got that child, and you don't know him that well?"

"Not very often," she said. "Not very long. Just that week here last fall, and in January he sent for me and we went West, to New Mexico, and lived for six weeks where I could cook for him and look after his clothes. . . ."

"But no marriage," he said. "He didn't promise you that. Don't lie to me. He didn't have to."

"He didn't have to," she said. "I knew what I was doing. I knew that to begin

---

[5]Noxious vapor.

with, before we agreed. Then we agreed again before he left New Mexico that that would be all of it. I believed him. I must have believed him. I don't see how I could have helped but believe him. I wrote him last month to make sure and the letter came back unopened and I was sure. So I didn't even know I was coming back here until last week. I was waiting there by the road yesterday when the car passed and he saw me and I was sure."

"Then what do you want?" he said. "What do you want?"

"Yes," she said. He glared at her, his white hair awry from the pillow, his eyes, lacking the spectacles to focus them, blurred, irisless and apparently pupilless.

"He met you on a street one afternoon just because a box of groceries happened to fall out of a boat. And a month later you went off and lived with him until you got a child from it. Then he took his hat and said good-bye and walked out. Haven't you got any folks at all?"

"Yes. My aunt, in Vicksburg. I came to live with her two years ago when my father died; we lived in Indianapolis until then. But my aunt had a family and she took in washing herself, so I got a job teaching school in Aluschaskuna. . . ."

"Took in what?" he said. "Took in washing?" He sprang, flinging himself backward onto one arm, awry-haired, glaring. Now he understood what it was she had brought in with her, what old Isham had already told him—the lips and skin pallid and colorless yet not ill, the tragic and foreknowing eyes. *Maybe in a thousand or two thousand years it will have blended in America and we will have forgotten it,* he thought. *But God pity these.* He cried, not loud, in a voice of amazement, pity and outrage, "You're a nigger!"

"Yes," she said.

"Then what did you expect here?"

"Nothing."

"Then why did you come here? You said you were waiting in Aluschaskuna yesterday and he saw you."

"I'm going back North," she said. "My cousin brought me up from Vicksburg the day before yesterday in his boat. He's going to take me on to Leland to get the train."

"Then go," he said. Then he cried again in that thin, not loud voice, "Get out of here; I can do nothing for you! Can't nobody do nothing for you!" She moved, turning toward the entrance. "Wait," he said. She paused, turning. He picked up the sheaf of bank notes and laid it on the blanket at the foot of the cot and drew his hand back beneath the blanket. "Here."

"I don't need it," she said. "He gave me money last winter. Provided. That was all arranged when we agreed that would have to be all."

"Take it," he said. His voice began to rise again, but he stopped it. "Take it out of my tent." She came back and took the money. "That's right," he said. "Go back North. Marry, a man in your own race. That's the only salvation for you. Marry a black man. You are young, handsome, almost white; you could find a black man who would see in you whatever it was you saw in him, who would ask nothing from you and expect less and get even still less if it's revenge you want. And then in a year's time you will have forgotten all this; you will forget it even happened, that he ever existed. . . ." He ceased; for an instant he almost sprang again for it seemed to him that, without moving at all, she had blazed silently at him. But she had not. She had not even moved, looking quietly down at him from beneath the sodden hat.

"Old man," she said, "have you lived so long that you have forgotten all you ever knew or felt or even heard about love?" Then she was gone too; the waft of light and the hushed constant rain flowed into the tent, then the flap fell again. Lying back again, trembling, panting, the blanket huddled to his chin and his hands crossed on his breast, he heard the pop and snarl, the mounting then the descending whine of the motor until it died away and once again the tent held only silence and the sound of the rain. And the cold too: he lay shaking faintly and steadily in it, rigid save for the shaking. 'This Delta,' he thought. 'This Delta.' *This land, which man has deswamped and denuded and deriverred in two generations so that white men can own plantations and commute every night to Memphis and black men can own plantations and even towns and keep their town houses in Chicago, where white men rent farms and live like niggers and niggers crop on shares and live like animals, where cotton is planted and grows man-tall in the very cracks in the sidewalks, where usury and mortgage and bankruptcy and measureless wealth, Chinese and African and Aryan and Jew, all breed and spawn together until no man has time to say which is which, or cares. . . .* 'No wonder the ruined woods I used to know don't cry for retribution,' he thought. 'The people who have destroyed it will accomplish its revenge.'

The tent flap swung rapidly in and fell. He did not move save to turn his head and open his eyes. Legate was stooping over Boyd's bed, rummaging hurriedly in it. "What is it?" McCaslin said.

"Looking for Don's skinning knife," Legate said. "We got a deer on the ground. I come in to get the horses." He rose, the knife in his hand and went toward the door.

"Who killed it?" McCaslin said. "It was Don," he said.

"Yes," Legate said, lifting the tent flap.

"Wait," McCaslin said. "What was it?" Legate paused for an instant in the entrance. He did not look back.

"Just a deer, Uncle Ike," he said impatiently. "Nothing extra." He was gone; the flap fell behind him, wafting out of the tent again the faint light, the constant and grieving rain. McCaslin lay back on the cot.

"It was a doe," he said to the empty tent.

(1942)

QUESTIONS

1. Would you describe the plot of "Delta Autumn" as "open" or "closed"? Speculate on the kinds of events that might occur in a sequel to the short story.

2. Clearly the setting is vital to the short story. How does the narrator present it to maximize the story's thematic impact?

3. "Delta Autumn" manages somehow to invoke a unified theme or set of themes out of two very different plot elements — McCaslin's dismay over

his friend's interracial affair and his preoccupation over the disappearance of his beloved wetlands. How does the narrator achieve this synthesis? How does the title "Delta Autumn" contribute to the synthesis?

4. How would you characterize the relation of the narrator's slant to the character's filter? What seems to be the ideology of the implied author? How does it compare with the actual pronouncements on racial matters made by the real William Faulkner, for example, in his famous speech upon accepting the Nobel Prize?

5. How might someone read this short story "against the grain" of its ideology and still find it rewarding?

❖ ERNEST HEMINGWAY

Indian Camp

Ernest Hemingway (1899–1961) was born in Oak Park, Illinois. He did not attend college but started his professional life as a reporter for the Kansas City *Star.* He volunteered as an ambulance driver in France and then as a soldier in Italy in World War I. After the war he lived in Paris, becoming a central figure in the colony of American artists, sometimes called the "Lost Generation." His first novel, *The Sun Also Rises* (1926), reflected his expatriate experience, and his second, *A Farewell to Arms* (1929), was based on his wartime experience in Italy. He also wrote two important collections of short stories, *In Our Time* (1924), about the coming to maturity of Nick Adams, and *Men and Women* (1927). Hemingway's later fiction reflects his widespread and restless travels: *To Have and Have Not* (1937), set in the Caribbean; *For Whom the Bell Tolls* (1940), about the Spanish Civil War; *The Old Man and the Sea* (1952), which won the Pulitzer Prize for best novel. Two novels have appeared posthumously: *Islands in the Stream* (1970) and *The Garden of Eden* (1986). He also wrote nonfictional books on big-game hunting, fishing, and travel. Hemingway won the Nobel Prize for literature in 1954.

At the lake shore there was another rowboat drawn up. The two Indians stood waiting.

Nick and his father got in the stern of the boat and the Indians shoved it off and one of them got in to row. Uncle George sat in the stern of the camp rowboat. The young Indian shoved the camp boat off and got in to row Uncle George.

The two boats started off in the dark. Nick heard the oar-locks of the other boat quite a way ahead of them in the mist. The Indians rowed with quick choppy strokes. Nick lay back with his father's arm around him. It was cold on the water. The Indian who was rowing them was working very hard, but the other boat moved further ahead in the mist all the time.

"Where are we going, Dad?" Nick asked.

"Over to the Indian camp. There is an Indian lady very sick."

"Oh," said Nick.

Across the bay they found the other boat beached. Uncle George was smoking a cigar in the dark. The young Indian pulled the boat way up the beach. Uncle George gave both the Indians cigars.

They walked up from the beach through a meadow that was soaking wet with dew, following the young Indian who carried a lantern. Then they went into the woods and followed a trail that led to the logging road that ran back into the hills. It was much lighter on the logging road as the timber was cut away on both sides. The young Indian stopped and blew out his lantern and they all walked on along the road.

292

They came around a bend and a dog came out barking. Ahead were the lights of the shanties where the Indian bark-peelers lived. More dogs rushed out at them. The two Indians sent them back to the shanties. In the shanty nearest the road there was a light in the window. An old woman stood in the doorway holding a lamp.

Inside on a wooden bunk lay a young Indian woman. She had been trying to have her baby for two days. All the old women in the camp had been helping her. The men had moved off up the road to sit in the dark and smoke out of range of the noise she made. She screamed just as Nick and the two Indians followed his father and Uncle George into the shanty. She lay in the lower bunk, very big under a quilt. Her head was turned to one side. In the upper bunk was her husband. He had cut his foot very badly with an ax three days before. He was smoking a pipe. The room smelled very bad.

Nick's father ordered some water to be put on the stove, and while it was heating he spoke to Nick.

"This lady is going to have a baby, Nick," he said.

"I know," said Nick.

"You don't know," said his father. "Listen to me. What she is going through is called being in labor. The baby wants to be born and she wants it to be born. All her muscles are trying to get the baby born. That is what is happening when she screams."

"I see," Nick said.

Just then the woman cried out.

"Oh, Daddy, can't you give her something to make her stop screaming?" asked Nick.

"No. I haven't any anaesthetic," his father said. "But her screams are not important. I don't hear them because they are not important."

The husband in the upper bunk rolled over against the wall.

The woman in the kitchen motioned to the doctor that the water was hot. Nick's father went into the kitchen and poured about half of the water out of the big kettle into a basin. Into the water left in the kettle he put several things he unwrapped from a handkerchief.

"Those must boil," he said, and began to scrub his hands in the basin of hot water with a cake of soap he had brought from the camp. Nick watched his father's hands scrubbing each other with the soap. While his father washed his hands very carefully and thoroughly, he talked.

"You see, Nick, babies are supposed to be born head first but sometimes they're not. When they're not they make a lot of trouble for everybody. Maybe I'll have to operate on this lady. We'll know in a little while."

When he was satisfied with his hands he went in and went to work.

"Pull back that quilt, will you, George?" he said. "I'd rather not touch it."

Later when he started to operate Uncle George and three Indian men held the woman still. She bit Uncle George on the arm and Uncle George said, "Damn squaw bitch!" and the young Indian who had rowed Uncle George over laughed at him. Nick held the basin for his father. It all took a long time.

His father picked the baby up and slapped it to make it breathe and handed it to the old woman.

"See, it's a boy, Nick," he said. "How do you like being an interne?"

Nick said, "All right." He was looking away so as not to see what his father was doing.

"There. That gets it," said his father and put something into the basin.

Nick didn't look at it.

"Now," his father said, "there's some stitches to put in. You can watch this or not, Nick, just as you like. I'm going to sew up the incision I made."

Nick did not watch. His curiosity has been gone for a long time.

His father finished and stood up. Uncle George and the three Indian men stood up. Nick put the basin out in the kitchen.

Uncle George looked at his arm. The young Indian smiled reminiscently.

"I'll put some peroxide on that, George," the doctor said.

He bent over the Indian woman. She was quiet now and her eyes were closed. She looked very pale. She did not know what had become of the baby or anything.

"I'll be back in the morning," the doctor said, standing up. "The nurse should be here from St. Ignace by noon and she'll bring everything we need."

He was feeling exalted and talkative as football players are in the dressing room after a game.

"That's one for the medical journal, George," he said. "Doing a Caesarian with a jack-knife and sewing it up with nine-foot, tapered gut leaders."

Uncle George was standing against the wall, looking at his arm.

"Oh, you're a great man, all right," he said.

"Ought to have a look at the proud father. They're usually the worst sufferers in these little affairs," the doctor said. "I must say he took it all pretty quietly."

He pulled back the blanket from the Indian's head. His hand came away wet. He mounted on the edge of the lower bunk with the lamp in one hand and looked in. The Indian lay with his face toward the wall. His throat had been cut from ear to ear. The blood had flowed down into a pool where his body sagged the bunk. His head rested on his left arm. The open razor lay, edge up, in the blankets.

"Take Nick out of the shanty, George," the doctor said.

There was no need of that. Nick, standing in the door of the kitchen, had a good view of the upper bunk when his father, the lamp in one hand, tipped the Indian's head back.

It was just beginning to be daylight when they walked along the logging road back toward the lake.

"I'm terribly sorry I brought you along, Nickie," said his father, all his post-operative exhilaration gone. "It was an awful mess to put you through."

"Do ladies always have such a hard time having babies?" Nick asked.

"No, that was very, very exceptional."

"Why did he kill himself, Daddy?"

"I don't know, Nick. He couldn't stand things, I guess."

"Do many men kill themselves, Daddy?"

"Not very many, Nick."

"Do many women?"

"Hardly ever."

"Don't they ever?"

"Oh, yes. They do sometimes."

"Daddy?"

"Yes."

"Where did Uncle George go?"

"He'll turn up all right."

"Is dying hard, Daddy?"

"No, I think it's pretty easy, Nick. It all depends."

They were seated in the boat, Nick in the stern, his father rowing. The sun was coming up over the hills. A bass jumped, making a circle in the water. Nick trailed his hand in the water. It felt warm in the sharp chill of the morning.

In the early morning on the lake sitting in the stern of the boat with his father rowing, he felt quite sure that he would never die.

(1925)

QUESTIONS

1. Which event seems to invoke the main point of this short story: the birth, the successful operation, the suicide, the taking of a step toward maturity, or something else? How does the narrator direct our attention toward or away from these different events? Do we gain equal access to the minds of the characters involved in each action? Why or why not?

2. The sentences in this story are short and simple, and the descriptions are sparse. Does this style represent the way Nick would tell the story? What other functions could it have?

3. Who is the implied reader of this story, the one who will understand all its references, accept its judgments, and find its conflicts significant? What happens when the actual reader differs from the ideal by being, for instance, a woman or a person of color?

4. Does your reading of the story change if you know that Hemingway's father was a doctor? That both Hemingway and his father committed suicide? That this story is part of a collection of stories centered around World War I? What sort of "outside" information is relevant to a fictional text?

5. The story presupposes American ideology of the 1920s. Have there been changes in our ideology that make it difficult for you to read it with sympathy for the boy? What are they?

❖ AMA ATA AIDOO
Certain Winds from the South

Ama Ata (Christina) Aidoo (1942–) was born in Abeadzi Kyiakor,
Ghana. She was educated at the University of Ghana, where she is
currently an instructor. She also spent time at Stanford University. She
has written a novel—*Our Sister Killjoy; or Reflections from a Black-
Eyed Squint* (1966)—and a collection of short stories, *No Sweetness
Here* (1970), which includes "Certain Winds from the South." She also
published a collection of short stories for children, *The Eagle and the
Chickens*, two plays—*Dilemma of a Ghost* (1964) and *Anowa* (1970)
—and a collection of poems called *Someone Talking to Sometime*
(1985).

M'ma Asana eyed the wretched pile of cola-nuts,[1] spat, and picked up the reed-bowl.
Then she put down the bowl, picked up one of the nuts, bit at it, threw it back, spat
again, and stood up. First, a sharp little ache, just a sharp little one, shot up from
somewhere under her left ear. Then her eyes became misty.

'I must check on those logs,' she thought, thinking this misting of her eyes
was due to the chill in the air. She stooped over the nuts.

'You never know what evil eyes are prowling this dust over these grasslands, I
must pick them up quickly.'

On the way back to the kraal[2] her eyes fell on the especially patchy circles that
marked where the old pits had been. At this time, in the old days, they would have
been nearly bursting and as one scratched out the remains of the out-going season, one
felt a near-sexual thrill of pleasure looking at these pits, just as one imagines a man
might feel who looks upon his wife in the ninth month of pregnancy.

Pregnancy and birth and death and pain; and death again . . . when there
are no more pregnancies, there are no more births, and therefore, no more deaths. But
there is only one death and only one pain.

Show me a fresh corpse, my sister, so I can weep you old tears.

The pit of her belly went cold, then her womb moved and she had to lean by
the doorway. In twenty years Fuseni's has been the only pregnancy and the only birth.
Twenty years, and the first child and a male! In the old days, there would have been
bucks and you got scolded for serving a woman in maternity a duicker.[3] But these days
those mean poachers on the government reserves sneak away their miserable duickers,
such wretched hinds! Yes they sneak away even the duickers to the houses of those
sweet-toothed southerners.

In the old days, how time goes, and how quickly age comes. But then does one

---

[1] A brownish seed, about the size of a chestnut, found in western tropical Africa, the West Indies, and Brazil.
[2] A village of South African natives, usually surrounded by a stockade or the like.
[3] A small African antelope.

expect to grow younger when one starts getting grandchildren? Allah be praised for a grandson.

The fire was still strong when she returned to the room. M'ma Asana put the nuts down. She craned her neck into the corner. At least those logs should take them to the following week. For the rest of the evening, she sat about preparing for the morrow's marketing.

The evening prayers were done. The money was in the bag. The grassland was still, Hawa was sleeping and so was Fuseni. M'ma came out to the main gate, first to check up if all was well outside and then to draw the door across. It was not the figure, but rather the soft rustle of light footsteps trying to move still more lightly over the grass, that caught her attention.

'If only it could be my husband.'

But of course it was not her husband!

'Who comes?'

'It is me, M'ma.'

'You, Issa, my son?'

'Yes, M'ma.'

'They are asleep.'

'I thought so. That is why I am coming now.'

There was a long pause in the conversation as they both hesitated about whether the son-in-law should go in to see Hawa and the baby or not. Nothing was said about this struggle but then one does not say everything.

M'ma Asana did not see but felt him win the battle. She crossed the threshold outside and drew the door behind her. Issa led the way. They did not walk far, however. They just turned into a corner between two of the projecting pillars in the wall of the kraal. It was as it should have been for it was he who needed the comforting coolness of it for his backbone.

'M'ma, is Fuseni well?'

'Yes.'

'M'ma, is Hawa well?'

'Yes.'

'M'ma please tell me, is Fuseni very well?'

'A-ah, my son. For what are you troubling yourself so much? Fuseni is a new baby who was born not more than ten days ago. How can I tell you he is very well? When a grown-up goes to live in other people's village . . .'

'M'ma?'

'What is it?'

'No. Please, it is nothing.'

'My son, I cannot understand you this evening . . . yes, if you, a grown-up person, go to live in another village, will you say after the first few days that you are perfectly well?'

'No.'

'Shall you not get yourself used to their food? Shall you not find first where you can get water for yourself and your sheep?'

'Yes, M'ma.'

'Then how is it you ask me if Fuseni is very well? The navel is healing very fast . . . and how would it not? Not a single navel of all that I have cut here got infected. Shall I now cut my grandson's and then sit and see it rot? But it is his male that I can't say. Mallam did it neat and proper and it must be all right. Your family is not noted for males that rot, is it now?'

'No, M'ma.'

'Then let your heart lie quiet in your breast. Fuseni is well but we cannot say how well yet.'

'I have heard you, M'ma. M'ma?'

'Yes, my son.'

'M'ma, I am going south.'

'Where did you say?'

'South.'

'How far?'

'As far as the sea. M'ma, I thought you would understand.'

'Have I spoken yet?'

'No, you have not.'

'Then why did you say that?'

'That was not well said.'

'And what are you going to do there?'

'Find some work.'

'What work?'

'I do not know.'

'Yes, you know, you are going to cut grass.'

'Perhaps.'

'But my son, why must you travel that far just to cut grass? Is there not enough of it all round here? Around this kraal, your father's and all the others in the village? Why do you not cut these?'

'M'ma, you know it is not the same. If I did that here people would think I was mad. But over there, I have heard that not only do they like it but the government pays you to do it.'

'Even so, our men do not go south to cut grass. This is for those further north. They of the wilderness, it is they who go south to cut grass. This is not for our men.'

'Please M'ma, already time is going. Hawa is a new mother and Fuseni my first child.'

'And yet you are leaving them to go south and cut grass.'

'But M'ma, what will be the use of my staying here and watching them starve? You yourself know that all the cola went bad, and even if they had not, with trade as it is, how much money do you think I would have got from them? And that is why I am going. Trade is broken and since we do not know when things will be good again, I think it will be better for me to go away.'

'Does Hawa know?'

'No, she does not.'

'Are you coming to wake her up at this late hour to tell her?'

'No.'

'You are wise.'

'M'ma, I have left everything in the hands of Amadu. He will come and see Hawa tomorrow.'

'Good.'

'When shall we expect you back?'

'Issa.'

'M'ma.'

'When shall we expect you back?'

'M'ma, I do not know. Perhaps next Ramadan.'[4]

'Good.'

'So I go now.'

'Allah go with you.'

'And may His prophet look after you all.'

M'ma went straight back to bed, but not to sleep. And how could she sleep? At dawn, her eyes were still wide open.

'Is his family noted for males that rot? No, certainly not. It is us who are noted for our unlucky females. There must be something wrong with them . . . Or how is it we cannot hold our men? Allah, how is it?

'Twenty years ago. Twenty years, perhaps more than twenty years . . . perhaps more than twenty years and Allah, please, give me strength to tell Hawa.

'Or shall I go to the market now and then tell her when I come back? No. Hawa, Hawa, now look at how you are stretched down there like a log! Does a mother sleep like this? Hawa, H-a-a-w-a! Oh, I shall not leave you alone . . . and how can you hear your baby when it cries in the night since you die when you sleep?

'Listen to her asking me questions! Yes, it is broad daylight. I thought you really were dead. If it is cold, draw your blanket round you and listen to me for I have something to tell you.

'Hawa, Issa has gone south.

'And why do you stare at me with such shining eyes. I am telling you that Issa is gone south.

'And what question do you think you are asking me? How could he take you along when you have a baby whose navel wound has not even healed yet?

'He went away last night.

'Don't ask me why I did not come and wake you up. What should I have woken you up for? Listen, Issa said he could not stay here and just watch you and Fuseni starve.

'He is going south to find work, and . . . Hawa, where do you think you are getting up to go? Issa is not at the door waiting for you. The whole neighbourhood is not up yet, so do not let me shout . . . and why are you behaving like a baby? Now you are a mother and you must decide to grow up . . . where are you getting up to go? Listen to me telling you this. Issa is gone. He went last night because he wants to catch the government bus that leaves Tamale very early in the morning. So . . .

'Hawa, ah-ah, are you crying? Why are you crying? That your husband has left you to go and work? Go on weeping, for he will bring the money to look after me and not you . . .

'I do not understand, you say? Maybe I do not . . . See, now you have woken up Fuseni. Sit down and feed him and listen to me.

---

[4]The ninth month of the Islamic calendar.

'Listen to me and I will tell you of another man who left his newborn child and went away.

'Did he come back? No, he did not come back. But do not ask me any more questions for I will tell you all.

'He used to go and come, then one day he went away and never came back. Not that he had to go like the rest of them . . .

'Oh, they were soldiers. I am talking of a soldier. He need not have gone to be a soldier. After all, his father was one of the richest men of this land. He was not the eldest son, that is true, but still there were so many things he could have done to look after himself and his wife when he came to marry. But he would not listen to anybody. How could he sit by and have other boys out-do him in smartness?

'Their clothes that shone and shone with pressing . . . I say, you could have looked into any of them and put khole[5] under your eyes. And their shoes, how they roared! You know soldiers for yourself. Oh, the stir on the land when they came in from the south! Mothers spoke hard and long to daughters about the excellencies of proper marriages, while fathers hurried through with betrothals. Most of them were afraid of getting a case like that of Memunat on their hands. Her father had taken the cattle and everything and then Memunat goes and plays with a soldier. Oh, the scandal she caused herself then!

'Who was this Memunat? No, she is not your friend's mother. No, this Memunat in the end ran away south herself. We hear she became a bad woman in the city and made a lot of money.

'No, we do not hear of her now. She is not dead either, for we hear such women usually go to their homes to die, and she has not come back here yet.

'But us, we are different. I had not been betrothed.

'Do you ask me why I say "we"? Because this man was your father. Ah-ah, you open your mouth and eyes wide? Yes, my child, it is of your father I am speaking.

'No, I was not lying when I told you that he died. But keep quiet and listen. He was going south to get himself a house for married soldiers.

'No, it was not that time he did not come back. He came here, but not to fetch me.

'He asked us if we had heard of the war.

'Had we not heard of the war? Was it not difficult to get things like tinned fish, kerosene and cloth?

'Yes, we said, but we thought it was only because the traders were not bringing them in.

'Well yes, he said, but the traders do not get them even in the south.

'And why, we asked.

'Oh you people, have you not heard of the German people? He had no patience with us. He told us that in the south they were singing dirty songs with their name.

'But when are we going, I asked him?

'What he told me was that that was why he had come. He could not take me

---

[5](Usually spelled *kohl*) a fine cosmetic powder used to darken the eyelids and eyebrows.

along with him. You see, he said we were under the Anglis-people's rule and they were fighting with the German-people.

'Ask me, my child, for that was exactly what I asked him. What has all that got to do with you and me? Why can I not come south with you?'

'Because I have to travel to the lands beyond the sea and fight.

'In other people's war? My child, it is as if you were there, that is what I asked him.

'But it is not as simple as that, he said.

'We could not understand him. You shall not go, said his father. You shall not go, for it is not us fighting with the Grunshies or the Gonjas.

'I know about the Anglis-people but not about any German-people, but anyway they are in their country.

'Of course his father was playing, and so was I.

'A soldier must obey at all times, he said.

'I wanted to give him so many things to take with him but he said he could only take cola.

'Then the news came. It did not enter my head, for it was all empty. Everything went into my womb. You were just three days old.

'The news was like fire which settled in the pit of my belly. And from time to time, some will shoot up, searing my womb, singeing my intestines and burning up and up and up until I screamed with madness when it got into my head.

'I had told myself when you were born that it did not matter you were a girl. All gifts from Allah are good and anyway he was coming back and we were going to have many more children, lots of sons.

'But Hawa, you had a lot of strength, for how you managed to live I do not know. Three days you were and suddenly like a rivulet that is hit by an early harmattan,[6] my breasts went dry. Hawa, you have a lot of strength.

'Later, they told me that if I could go south and prove to the government's people that I was his wife I would get a lot of money.

'But I did not go. It was him I wanted not his body turned into gold.

'I never saw the south.

'Do you say "oh"? My child I am always telling you that the world was created a long while ago and it is old-age one has seen but not youth. So do not say "oh".

'Those people, the government's people, who come and go, tell us trade is bad now, and once again there is no tinned fish and no cloth. But this time they say this is because our children are going to get them in abundance one day.

'Issa has gone south now because he cannot afford even goat flesh for his wife in maternity. This has to be, so that Fuseni can stay with his wife and eat cow-meat with her? Hmm. And he will come back alive . . . perhaps not next Ramadan but the next. Now my daughter, you know of another man who went to fight. And he went to fight in other people's war and he never came back.

'I am going to the market now. Get up early to wash Fuseni. I hope to get something for those miserable colas. There is enough rice for two, is there not?

---

[6]A dry dust-laden wind blowing out of the southern African interior.

'Good. Today even if it takes all the money, I hope to get us some smoked fish, the biggest I can find, to make us a real good sauce.'

(1970)

QUESTIONS

1. What happened to M'ma Asana's husband? Is the pattern repeating itself exactly with her daughter and son-in-law?
2. This story is full of cultural references unfamiliar to most North Americans: cola nuts, duickers, kraal, Ramadan. Are you given enough clues in the text to interpret these references? Are they a hindrance to your enjoyment of the story or part of its value? Aside from reading the footnotes, how might you find out what these words mean?
3. The final section of the story is a dialogue between Asana and her daughter. Why have the daughter's responses not been included?
4. What are the "winds from the south"? How are events in other parts of Africa and the world affecting the lives of the characters? Do they have to be aware of the outside world to be influenced by it?
5. How do you weigh the value of a story like this one? How much emphasis would you place on its distinctive cultural perspective and how much on its literary skill? Are the two separable?

SUGGESTIONS FOR WRITING

1. Have you ever been asked to find *the* theme of a fiction? Did that assignment make you uncomfortable? Aside from fables and allegories (and perhaps not even all of them), does any fiction have just a single theme? Offer an opinion about why.
2. Pick two short stories in the Further Reading section. Try expressing their major themes as nouns or noun phrases, such as "justice" or "the difficulty of communicating with persons from another culture." Then try expressing them as full sentences, such as "The price for independence may be loneliness," or "Heredity may account for differences in temperament, but environment determines how they will be expressed." The difference is that the full sentence makes an assertion about something, whereas the noun merely points to it. Are there "asserting" stories and "pointing" stories?
3. If the implied reader of a fiction is someone who agrees with its themes and with the ideology from which they grow, then what kind of reader can you be if you reject either ideology or theme? A suggestion made by a critic named Judith Fetterly is that texts allow readers to find themes different from those the implied author intends. Such a "resisting reader" can deliberately identify with a character different from the one that the implied

author favors, or can provide a moral context that the implied author did not anticipate. Try to be a resisting reader of one of the stories in this book. Write a brief account of your "against-the-grain" interpretation. Did you first have to figure out how the implied reader was supposed to experience the short story, and then go your own way?

4. Read a short story several times as if you were different readers, with different backgrounds, ages, social positions, and beliefs. Or, discuss the story with other readers with different backgrounds. Do you all agree on certain themes? Or do you posit different themes? Of several themes suggested by a story, is there unanimity about which are most important?

5. Find a short story in which one of the themes is something you have experienced firsthand. For instance, choose a war story if you are a veteran, a story about ethnic conflict if you have experienced such conflict, a story about parental responsibilities if you are a parent. Then find a story with a theme that you don't have direct knowledge of. How does your reading of the two stories differ?

9 Narrative Limits: Experimental and Postmodern Fiction

From Edgar Allan Poe to Roald Dahl, authors have used the short story as a vehicle for the strange, the eerie, the bizarre. But what is "narrative strangeness"? We can usefully distinguish two kinds — strangeness of content and strangeness of form. Strangeness of content is the more familiar. Most of television's tales from outer space or "beyond the crypt" present odd events and characters, but few of them are *formally* odd. Their forms are generally conventional: narrators tend to be reliable, plots have strongly marked beginnings and endings, characters (however weird) stay consistently themselves, usually behaving in ways recognizably human (even recognizably American), themes are easily recognizable (loyalty, comradeship, bravery), and so on.

Less familiar to the general public are fictions with strange narrative *forms*. Movies and television doubtless avoid these because they might confuse the casual viewer. There does exist a wide range of experimental forms in narrative literature, however. Forms, of course, are simply *conventions* for telling stories that have become traditional over the centuries. A convention is a way of doing something because it works and has been done that way before. Still, new narrative conventions, like new dress fashions or automobile designs, continually arise. Old forms become outmoded and new ones replace or supplement them. For example, "happy endings" are out of favor (at least in serious fiction), as are surprise endings. Plots in which "nothing happens," on the other hand, are very fashionable.

Undermining Conventions

Throughout literary history, authors have delighted in tinkering with established narrative conventions. Recently, some have taken to tearing the seamless web of action and character of the realistic "well-made" story. They seek to expose the artificiality of fiction itself, to reveal the nuts and bolts that hold it together. Fiction is artificial in the sense that it is a product of artifice,

304

of labor, of conscious and deliberate human construction. In recent years, the dismantling of "well-made" fiction has been associated with an intellectual and artistic movement called *postmodernism*. Postmodernism challenges many traditions, especially the desirability or even possibility of artistic illusion. Postmodern plots, for example, do not "add up" the way conventional plots do. They deliberately question the unwritten "law" of causation. A traditional plot, remember, poses an initial situation that allows various events, but that gives rise to only a single one. That single event, in turn, eventuates in a single new situation, then a single new event, and so on. In one kind of postmodern fiction, however, a single situation might lead not to a single event but to two or more, and these might be mutually contradictory.

For example, consider the fiction described by Dr. Stephen Albert in Jorge Luis Borges's "The Garden of Forking Paths" (pp. 314–322). Dr. Albert, an expert on ancient Chinese literature, explains the structure of a Chinese novel, *The Garden of Forking Paths*,[1] written many centuries ago by the author Ts'ui Pên. This strange novel undermines the convention of single-event causality. In ordinary fiction a situation may suggest several different eventualities, but convention allows only one to materialize. In Ts'ui Pên's *The Garden of Forking Paths*, the situation, the node or bud of the narrative tree, gives rise not to a single branch, but to *all conceivable branches*. As Dr. Albert explains it:

> In all fiction, when a man is faced with alternatives he chooses one at the expense of the others. In the almost unfathomable Ts'ui Pên, he chooses—simultaneously—all of them.

Dr. Albert invents an example:

> Fang . . . has a secret. A stranger knocks at his door. Fang makes up his mind to kill him. Naturally there are various possible outcomes. Fang can kill the intruder, the intruder can kill Fang, both can be saved, both can die and so on and so on. In Ts'ui Pên's work, all the possible solutions occur, each one being the point of departure for other bifurcations.

In other words, in Ts'ui Pên's novel, *everything* that *can* happen *does* happen. This notion is so strange that we need another example to illustrate it. Let's go back to the first plot we discussed in chapter 2, the initial situation in Carson McCullers's "A Tree A Rock A Cloud." The boy enters the café. This situation gives rise to a single event—the old man addresses the boy and the boy listens to him. However, other events could have happened: the boy could have ignored the old man and simply drunk his coffee. Or he could have spoken only to Leo. Or he could have left the café. Or a mill hand could have beaten the old man up. Or lightning could have struck, setting fire to the café. And so on. The *normal* single-branch convention is indicated by the word *or*, but in Ts'ui Pên's narrative theory there is no *or*—only *and*. *All* these events

---

[1] I use italics for Ts'ui Pên's novel but quotation marks for Borges's short story.

would have occurred, plus every other conceivable consequence of the boy's presence in the café.

Borges's *own* story, however, is not of this order; its plot does not branch infinitely. Each event gives rise to one and only one new situation. The initial situation is that a Chinese teacher named Yu Tsun is spying for Germany in England during World War I. He must inform the head of German espionage that the British Army has massed artillery in the town of Albert in northern France. Because he has no direct way of communicating with Berlin, Yu Tsun must get the name "Albert" into the British headlines so that the German secret service, which constantly monitors the British press, will learn of the impending attack. Yu Tsun decides that the most sensational way to signal "Albert" is to murder someone by that name. The name "Albert," linked to that of "Yu Tsun," will signal the Allied buildup to the chief of German espionage, and the German army will be able to escape the artillery barrage. Ultimately, Yu Tsun will be captured by the British intelligence agent Captain Richard Madden and brought to justice. The discourse of Borges's short story turns out to be the confession that Yu Tsun has written in his prison cell as he awaits execution as a spy.

According to the phone book, the nearest person surnamed "Albert" lives about a half-hour train's ride away from Yu Tsun's room. This Albert, picked arbitrarily for his last name, is Dr. Stephen Albert, as chance would have it, an eminent scholar of Chinese literature. Indeed, Dr. Albert is the only man in the world who understands the structure of the awesome novel by Yu Tsun's ancestor Ts'ui Pên called *The Garden of Forking Paths*. Assuming that Yu Tsun is a visiting scholar who has come to discuss the novel, Dr. Albert welcomes him warmly. In the few minutes before his death, Dr. Albert explains that Ts'ui Pên's strange novel is really a meditation on the nature of time (and therefore of narrativity):

> . . . your [Yu Tsun's] ancestor did not think of time as absolute and uniform. He believed in an infinite series of times, in a dizzily growing, ever spreading network of diverging, converging and parallel times. This web of time — the strands of which approach one another, bifurcate, intersect or ignore each other through the centuries — embraces *every* possibility. We do not exist in most of them. In some you exist and not I, while in others I do, and you do not, and in yet others both of us exist. In this one, in which chance has favoured me, you have come to my gate. In another, you, crossing the garden, have found me dead. In yet another, I say these very same words, but am an error, a phantom.

However, Stephen Albert has not thought of still another possibility, the very one that is about to eventuate, namely, that in a few moments Yu Tsun will murder him for reasons of espionage.

Though Borges's short story has only a single-branching structure, overtones of Ts'ui Pên's mysterious multi-branching novel arise in Yu Tsun's consciousness. Yu Tsun feels strange emanations as he stands in Albert's garden:

> I felt within me and around me something invisible and intangible pullulating. It was not the pullulation of two divergent, parallel, and finally converging armies [the example from Ts'ui Pên's novel given by Albert], but an agitation more inaccessible, more intimate.

This "pullulation" — a word that means the "sending out of many shoots" — is Yu Tsun's sense of the multiple possibilities of his *own* situation. He is sensitized to these possibilities not only by Dr. Albert's explanation of *The Garden of Forking Paths*, but because he himself faces an extreme moment. He is about to commit a desperate act, which he knows will lead to his capture and execution. At such moments, one might well feel the absolute arbitrariness of any choice.

A strange, strange vision of the universe, isn't it? in which every situation leads to an infinity of consequences, creating worlds adjacent to ours but about which we know nothing. Yet is it so much stranger than the universe proposed by contemporary astronomy, with its incredible theories of antimatter, black holes, and the like? Postmodernist fictions like Borges's can raise the same kind of intriguing questions as those advanced by scientists and philosophers.

Questioning the Discourse

The postmodernist undermining of narrative tradition is not limited to plot conventions. Discourse, no less than story, may be questioned. For example, a narrator may interrogate or even mock her own narrative practices. This sort of mockery occurs as early as Miguel de Cervantes's *Don Quixote* (often called the first novel). In Nathaniel Hawthorne's short story "Wakefield" (pp. 457–462), the narrator makes a point of telling us how arbitrarily his story has been constructed. Though he claims to have read about Wakefield in "some old magazine or newspaper," the narrator remembers only the situation — a man absenting himself from his wife without apparent reason for twenty years. To illustrate this odd situation, which he remembers only vaguely, the narrator constructs a short story out of whole cloth, "writing it before our very eyes," so to speak. He assigns the hero an arbitrary name and contrives plot details to motivate the man's strange decision. "What sort of a man was Wakefield?" asks the narrator. "We are free to shape out our own ideas . . ." The narration challenges the simplistic assumption that fictions are the products of a narrator's actual experience, or somehow "just happened."

Fiction that raises questions about its own nature is often called *self-conscious*. In this usage, the word does not carry its ordinary sense. *Self-conscious* does not mean "embarrassed" or the like. Rather, the term refers to fiction that raises questions not only about the story told, but also about the act of telling it. The narrator of a self-conscious fiction asks questions more usually found in authors' workbooks or journals in literary criticism, or in textbooks like this one. It is as if the narrator purposely taunts us with the fact that the fiction is a created object, an object that required labor and involved decisions of a cold-blooded sort. Such a fiction does not wish to let us slide easily into the pleasant world of illusion, for it is precisely that illusion that is questioned.

A term sometimes used for this effect is *metafiction. Meta-* is a Greek prefix that means "after" or "beyond," sometimes with the implication of "changing." Thus *metacarpus* is that part of an arm "beyond" the carpus, or wrist. *Metamorphosis* means a change in form (*-morphe* means "form"). *Metaphysics* is a branch of philosophy that goes beyond physics.

A good example of metafiction is John Barth's "Lost in the Funhouse" (pp. 323–339). On its surface, this short story concerns the adventures of Ambrose, the thirteen-year-old protagonist, temporarily lost behind the walls of the funhouse of an Ocean City amusement park. Running parallel but "going beyond" Ambrose's adventures is a disquisition on the nature of fiction itself, on its history, on commonplaces of prose style and narrative composition (the use of description in characterization, for example), on metaphor, on punctuation, on the conventional alternation between scene and summary. The narrator relates these observations to his own success or failure in telling this very story. Generally he despairs about whether he is succeeding:

> The boys' father was tall and thin, balding, fair-complexioned. Assertions of that sort are not effective; the reader may acknowledge the proposition, but.

The first sentence is familiarly narrative-descriptive, but the second is metafictional. Notice how it is left incomplete.

Elsewhere, the narrator revises words but doesn't strike out the words they replace, as if he can't quite decide what he wants to say. One sentence reads "'I swear,' Magda said, in mock *in feigned* exasperation." The narrator also repeats phrases for no apparent reason:

> Many bathed in the surf . . . others paid to use a municipal pool and only sunbathed on the beach. We would do the latter. We would do the latter. We would do the latter.

He tries out different possible endings:

> One possible ending would be to have Ambrose come across another lost person in the dark. They'd match their wits together against the funhouse, struggle like Ulysses past obstacle after obstacle, help and encourage each other. Or a girl.

These and many other odd metafictional sentences intrude on the story without warning.

The "authorial" narrator of "Lost in the Funhouse" also speaks about himself. For example, he tries to calculate the number of acts of sexual intercourse — between 1632 when Lord Baltimore was granted the charter to the Maryland colony and the present — necessary for his birth in Maryland in the twentieth century. Ambrose is not the source of these general observations, but they are similar to the quirky meditations that filter through his consciousness — on sex, on war, on the behavior of his brother or Magda, on his parents and family. It is not hard to imagine that Ambrose will be a novelist when he grows up, or that, perhaps, the narrator *is* Ambrose grown up, even though the discourse is not presented in the first person.

Regardless of how we account for the elaborate metafictional commentary of "Lost in the Funhouse," it clearly intends to subvert the narrative, thereby forcing us to ask interesting questions about the whole enterprise of fiction and our eagerness to participate in it. We are made to reconsider our easy indulgence in fictional illusion and our tendency to ignore the hard work it took to create it. Strangely enough, however, the questions do not make the fictional Ambrose any less "real" or his problems any less poignant. So strong is our desire for fictional illusion that we seek to accommodate even blatantly metafictional elements to a more customary kind of reading.

Attacks on the Discourse by the Story

In "Lost in the Funhouse" the discourse undermines the story. The opposite effect can also occur, that is, the story can undermine the discourse. A very short story that does so is Julio Cortázar's "Continuity of Parks."

❖ JULIO CORTÁZAR*
Continuity of Parks**

He had begun to read the novel a few days before. He had put it down because of some urgent business conferences, opened it again on his way back to the estate by train; he permitted himself a slowly growing interest in the plot, in the characterization. That afternoon, after writing a letter giving his power of attorney and discussing a matter of joint ownership with the manager of his estate, he returned to the book in the tranquillity of his study which looked out upon the park with its oaks. Sprawled in his favorite armchair, its back toward the door—even the possibility of an intrusion would have irritated him, had he thought of it—he let his left hand caress repeatedly the green velvet upholstery and set to reading the final chapters. He remembered effortlessly the names and his mental image of the characters; the novel spread its glamour over him almost at once. He tasted the almost perverse pleasure of disengaging himself line by line from the things around him, and at the same time feeling his head rest comfortably on the green velvet of the chair with its high back, sensing that the cigarettes rested within reach of his hand, that beyond the great windows the air of afternoon danced under the oak trees in the park. Word by word, licked up by the

---

*Author biography can be found on page 340.
**Translated by Paul Blackburn.

sordid dilemma of the hero and heroine, letting himself be absorbed to the point where the images settled down and took on color and movement, he was witness to the final encounter in the mountain cabin. The woman arrived first, apprehensive; now the lover came in, his face cut by the backlash of a branch. Admirably, she stanched the blood with her kisses, but he rebuffed her caresses, he had not come to perform again the ceremonies of a secret passion, protected by a world of dry leaves and furtive paths through the forest. The dagger warmed itself against his chest, and underneath liberty pounded, hidden close. A lustful, panting dialogue raced down the pages like a rivulet of snakes, and one felt it had all been decided from eternity. Even to those caresses which writhed about the lover's body, as though wishing to keep him there, to dissuade him from it; they sketched abominably the frame of that other body it was necessary to destroy. Nothing had been forgotten: alibis, unforeseen hazards, possible mistakes. From this hour on, each instant had its use minutely assigned. The cold-blooded, twice-gone-over reexamination of the details was barely broken off so that a hand could caress a cheek. It was beginning to get dark.

Not looking at one another now, rigidly fixed upon the task which awaited them, they separated at the cabin door. She was to follow the trail that led north. On the path leading in the opposite direction, he turned for a moment to watch her running, her hair loosened and flying. He ran in turn, crouching among the trees and hedges until, in the yellowish fog of dusk, he could distinguish the avenue of trees which led up to the house. The dogs were not supposed to bark, they did not bark. The estate manager would not be there at this hour, and he was not there. He went up the three porch steps and entered. The woman's words reached him over the thudding of blood in his ears: first a blue chamber, then a hall, then a carpeted stairway. At the top, two doors. No one in the first room, no one in the second. The door of the salon, and then, the knife in hand, the light from the great windows, the high back of an armchair covered in green velvet, the head of the man in the chair reading a novel.

(1967)

This short story starts out conventionally enough, in what seems to be the familiar framing or embedding structure used in such short stories as Fyodor Dostoevsky's "Polzunkov" (pp. 430–440), Isaac Babel's "How It Was Done in Odessa" (pp. 75–81), and Mark Twain's "The Celebrated Jumping Frog of Calaveras County" (pp. 380–384). In "Continuity of Parks," the "outer" or "embedding" story is that of a wealthy executive deeply absorbed in reading a novel. His act of reading constitutes the discourse that frames the events of the inner, framed story, that of the novel he is reading, a "sordid dilemma" of adulterous lovers.

Like the executive, "sprawled in his favorite armchair . . . caress[ing] repeatedly the green velvet upholstery," we become engrossed in the inner story. We follow the couple's plot to destroy "that other body" (obviously the heroine's husband, who stands in the way of the adulterous couple's happiness); the hero's rejection of the heroine's kisses as he clutches the murder weapon to his chest; her departure to the north and his to the south through an avenue of trees to a house where he finds—guess what?—"the high back of an armchair covered in green velvet, the head of the man in the chair reading a novel."

The heroine's husband is none other than our executive reading the novel about the adulterous couple! But how can that be? The executive lives in the discourse and the lover lives in the story. "Continuity of Parks" forces us to accept a new convention: that a fictional character can leave his "natural" habitat, the story, and intrude into the world of the discourse that is framing his story. Conventional fiction's clear and sharp line between story and discourse is erased. The husband — who is only the narratee addressed by the novel — gets killed by the fictional protagonist of the book he reads. But if we accept that possibility, we tacitly adopt the postmodernist premise that all these conventions are merely arbitrary. Once again, we witness an assault on the very idea of narrative fiction. We may even find the "infraction" amusing, in the same way that we are amused by the Marx brothers's assaults on the conventional, stuffed-shirt characters in their movies.

Speaking of slapstick comedy, an example of this intentional blurring of boundaries between story and discourse occurs in a famous silent film, Buster Keaton's *Sherlock Holmes, Jr.* (1924). Buster Keaton plays a movie projectionist who gets so caught up in the movie he is projecting that he forgets that it's only a fiction. Angry at what the villain is doing to the heroine, he leaves the projection booth and jumps "into" the screen, trying to save her. However, his entry into the world of the fiction is not entirely successful. He is bewildered to find that the scene keeps changing to other movies — for example, from a city movie to a jungle movie. The narrative anomaly of *Sherlock Holmes, Jr.* is the mirror opposite of that of "Continuity of Parks." Instead of the embedded story invading the discourse, the discourse (in the person of Buster Keaton) invades the story, but unsuccessfully.

Filter at Odds with Itself

Many other examples of the postmodernist questioning of the conventions of fiction could be cited. Indeed, you probably remember some good metafictions yourself, especially if you watch MTV, an interesting medium for narrative experimentation. Let me end my own discussion with another literary example, again by Julio Cortázar, called "The Idol of the Cyclades" (pp. 340–345). The convention that this short story calls into question is the coherence of a character's filter.

The filter is that of Morand, a French archaeologist. The short story begins with Morand's reminiscence of digging on an island in the Greek Cyclades chain with his wife, Teresa, and an Argentinean friend named Somoza. Somoza discovers an ancient statue of a woman, dating from long before the Hellenic period. The three smuggle the statue out of Greece by bribing an official, who stipulates that they must keep it several years before selling it. Somoza hides the statue in a lonely house on the outskirts of Paris and spends his time obsessively trying to reproduce it. Afraid that Somoza has fallen in love with Teresa, Morand avoids him. Still, Morand goes to Somoza's hideaway one day when Somoza telephones him. He senses that Somoza, who can hardly articulate his thoughts, has gone crazy. Somoza points to a "castle in the air," describing "an arc which includes the roof and the statuette set on its thin column of marble." Against his better judgment, Morand cannot avoid seeing Somoza's fantastic vision. And despite his own earlier efforts to keep Teresa away from Somoza, he finds himself leaving a message for her to come to Somoza's house. Morand imagines (or actually sees?) more and more of Somoza's fantasy, including details of the idol's creation and the crude rites for propitiating her with the blood of victims hacked to death with a stone axe. Caressing the idol, Somoza intones a prayer in an incomprehensible language that Morand nevertheless comprehends, a prayer of

> the hunt in the caverns of smoke, of the number of deer in the pen, of the name which had to be spoken only afterwards, of the circle of blue grease, of the swing of the double rivers, of Pohk's childhood [presumably some hero of the time], of the procession to the eastern steps and the high ones in the accursed shadows.

As he listens to Somoza's weird re-creation of the primordial cult of the goddess Haghesa, Morand wants to warn Teresa to bring a psychiatrist, but it's too late. Somoza begins to speak of the need for a blood sacrifice for the idol. When Somoza strips and starts swinging a stone axe, Morand understands that he himself is to be the victim. Using judo, Morand saves himself by sinking the axe into Somoza's forehead. Part of Morand's mind continues to function rationally. He thinks about calling the police and arguing self-defense; he consults his watch; he decides to meet Teresa outside to spare her the sight of blood; and when he hears her taxi, he thinks "that Teresa was punctuality itself." However, Morand's *body* is acting quite at odds with his rational mind. His hands soak themselves in Somoza's blood and coat the idol with it. His nose sniffs the air. His body strips itself and waits with axe in hand for Teresa's arrival. Clearly Morand's bones, muscles, and nerves are possessed by the idol, becoming — as Somoza had become — the idol's executioner. Morand's wife will clearly be the next victim.

I have included this short story not for its morbid content but as an example of a certain kind of formal tour de force. What makes it technically interesting? It is the way in which it splits the filter, the protagonist's psyche. Even as the civilized remnants of Morand's consciousness try to stay rational, his body follows the instructions of the ancient cult. But his mind, too, is becoming possessed. His perception, for example, has been affected. Although he is still able to hear normal sounds, such as that of the arriving taxi, he is increasingly attuned to the double flutes from which the ancient disciples of Haghesa drank blood for inspiration and renewal.

To effect its strange theme, Cortázar's short story subverts the convention of the uniformity or homogeneity of a character's filter. It conveys how it feels to be possessed by an alien force — from the *inside*. Whereas a movie might show gross changes in Morand's appearance (hair on his hands and so on), the short story enables us to experience his transformation from sophisticated Parisian to primitive brute at a post within his own mind.

These four short stories provide only a small sample of the kind of technical innovation that appears in today's postmodern fiction. Such stories are not only exciting in themselves, but also illustrate the seemingly endless variety of narrative form. If you enjoy such experimentation with narrative technique, you might read other fiction by such modern masters as Alain Robbe-Grillet, Donald Barthelme, Italo Calvino, Nathalie Sarraute, Roald Dahl, Robert Coover, Raymond Carver, Ursula Le Guin, and many others.

❖ JORGE LUIS BORGES
The Garden of Forking Paths*

Jorge Luis Borges (1899–1986) was born to an aristocratic family and lived most of his life in Buenos Aires, Argentina. As a child he had access to the books of a grandmother, reading more English than Spanish literature. Borges's family went to Europe in 1914 and he attended a school in Switzerland where he read widely in Continental literature. As a man of means, he was able to set himself up as an author upon his return to Buenos Aires in 1921. He was originally more interested in poetry and literary and film criticism than in fiction. Always a bookish person, he ultimately became director of the National Library of Buenos Aires and professor of English and American Literature at the university. He also lectured at the University of Texas and was the Charles Eliot Norton Professor of Poetry at Harvard. Borges wrote only short fiction, usually of a fantastic or mysterious cast. Many of his stories have been translated into English in volumes such as *Labyrinths* (1962), *Ficciones* ("Fictions," 1962), *Dreamtigers* (1964), *Other Inquisitions* (1966), *The Aleph* (1970), *Extraordinary Tales* (1971), *Doctor Brodie's Report* (1972), *A Universal History of Infamy* (1972), and *Chronicles of Bustos Domecq* (1976). He published many poems and books of nonfiction, especially on literature and film.

To Victoria Ocampo

In his *A History of the World War* (page 212), Captain Liddell Hart reports that a planned offensive by thirteen British divisions, supported by fourteen hundred artillery pieces, against the German line at Serre-Montauban, scheduled for July 24, 1916, had to be postponed until the morning of the 29th. He comments that torrential rain caused this delay — which lacked any special significance.[1] The following deposition, dictated by, read over, and then signed by Dr. Yu Tsun, former teacher of English at the Tsingtao[2] *Hochschule*, casts unsuspected light upon this event. The first two pages are missing.

. . . and I hung up the phone. Immediately I recollected the voice that had spoken in German. It was that of Captain Richard Madden. Madden, in Viktor Runeberg's office, meant the end of all our work and — though this seemed a secondary matter, *or should have seemed so to me* — of our lives also. His being there meant that Runeberg had been arrested or murdered.** Before the sun set on this same day, I ran

---

*Translated by Helen Temple and Ruthven Todd.
[1] A reference to the Battle of the Somme, fought in France in 1916.
[2] A port and manufacturing city in China.
**A malicious and outlandish statement. In point of fact, Captain Richard Madden had been attacked by the Prussian spy Hans Rabener, alias Viktor Runeberg, who drew an automatic pistol when Madden appeared with orders for the spy's arrest. Madden, in self defence, had inflicted wounds of which the spy later died. — Note by the manuscript editor [of the original Borges work].

the same risk. Madden was implacable. Rather, to be more accurate, he was obliged to be implacable. An Irishman in the service of England, a man suspected of equivocal feelings if not of actual treachery, how could he fail to welcome and seize upon this extraordinary piece of luck: the discovery, capture and perhaps the deaths of two agents of Imperial Germany?

I went up to my bedroom. Absurd though the gesture was, I closed and locked the door. I threw myself down on my narrow iron bed, and waited on my back. The never changing rooftops filled the window, and the hazy six o'clock sun hung in the sky. It seemed incredible that this day, a day without warnings or omens, might be that of my implacable death. In despite of my dead father, in despite of having been a child in one of the symmetrical gardens of Hai Feng, was I to die now?

Then I reflected that all things happen, happen to one, precisely *now*. Century follows century, and things happen only in the present. There are countless men in the air, on land and at sea, and all that really happens happens to me. . . . The almost unbearable memory of Madden's long horse-face put an end to these wandering thoughts.

In the midst of my hatred and terror (now that it no longer matters to me to speak of terror, now that I have outwitted Richard Madden, now that my neck hankers for the hangman's noose), I knew that the fast-moving and doubtless happy soldier did not suspect that I possessed the Secret — the name of the exact site of the new British artillery park on the Ancre.[3] A bird streaked across the misty sky and, absently, I turned it into an airplane and then that airplane into many in the skies of France, shattering the artillery park under a rain of bombs. If only my mouth, before it should be silenced by a bullet, could shout this name in such a way that it could be heard in Germany. . . . My voice, my human voice, was weak. How could it reach the ear of the Chief? The ear of that sick and hateful man who knew nothing of Runeberg or of me except that we were in Staffordshire.[4] A man who, sitting in his arid Berlin office, leafed infinitely through newspapers, looking in vain for news from us. I said aloud, 'I must flee.'

I sat up on the bed, in senseless and perfect silence, as if Madden was already peering at me. Something — perhaps merely a desire to prove my total penury[5] to myself — made me empty out my pockets. I found just what I knew I was going to find. The American watch, the nickel-plated chain and the square coin, the key ring with the useless but compromising keys to Runeberg's office, the notebook, a letter which I decided to destroy at once (and which I did not destroy), a five shilling piece, two single shillings and some pennies, a red and blue pencil, a handkerchief — and a revolver with a single bullet. Absurdly I held it and weighed it in my hand, to give myself courage. Vaguely I thought that a pistol shot can be heard for a great distance.

In ten minutes I had developed my plan. The telephone directory gave me the name of the one person capable of passing on the information. He lived in a suburb of Fenton, less than half an hour away by train.

I am a timorous man. I can say it now, now that I have brought my incredibly

---

[3] A tributary of the Somme River.
[4] A county in the English midlands.
[5] Poverty.

risky plan to an end. It was not easy to bring about, and I know that its execution was terrible. I did not do it for Germany — no! Such a barbarous country is of no importance to me, particularly since it had degraded me by making me become a spy. Furthermore, I knew an Englishman — a modest man — who, for me, is as great as Goethe.[6] I did not speak with him for more than an hour, but during that time, he *was* Goethe.

I carried out my plan because I felt the Chief had some fear of those of my race, of those uncountable forebears whose culmination lies in me. I wished to prove to him that a yellow man could save his armies. Besides, I had to escape the Captain. His hands and voice could, at any moment, knock and beckon at my door.

Silently, I dressed, took leave of myself in the mirror, went down the stairs, sneaked a look at the quiet street, and went out. The station was not far from my house, but I thought it more prudent to take a cab. I told myself that I thus ran less chance of being recognized. The truth is that, in the deserted street, I felt infinitely visible and vulnerable. I recall that I told the driver to stop short of the main entrance. I got out with a painful and deliberate slowness.

I was going to the village of Ashgrove, but took a ticket for a station further on. The train would leave in a few minutes, at eight-fifty. I hurried, for the next would not go until half past nine. There was almost no one on the platform. I walked through the carriages. I remember some farmers, a woman dressed in mourning, a youth deep in Tacitus' *Annals*[7] and a wounded, happy soldier.

At last the train pulled out. A man I recognized ran furiously, but vainly, the length of the platform. It was Captain Richard Madden. Shattered, trembling, I huddled in the distant corner of the seat, as far as possible from the fearful window.

From utter terror I passed into a state of almost abject happiness. I told myself that the duel had already started and that I had won the first encounter by besting my adversary in his first attack — even if it was for only forty minutes — by an accident of fate. I argued that so small a victory prefigured a total victory. I argued that it was not so trivial, that were it not for the precious accident of the train schedule, I would be in prison or dead. I argued, with no less sophism,[8] that my timorous happiness was proof that I was man enough to bring this adventure to a successful conclusion. From my weakness I drew strength that never left me.

I foresee that man will resign himself each day to new abominations, that soon only soldiers and bandits will be left. To them I offer this advice: *Whosoever would undertake some atrocious enterprise should act as if it were already accomplished, should impose upon himself a future as irrevocable as the past.*

Thus I proceeded, while with the eyes of a man already dead, I contemplated the fluctuations of the day which would probably be my last, and watched the diffuse coming of night.

The train crept along gently, amid ash trees. It slowed down and stopped, almost in the middle of a field. No one called the name of a station. 'Ashgrove?' I asked some children on the platform. 'Ashgrove,' they replied. I got out.

---

[6](1749–1832) German poet, philosopher, and novelist.
[7]A detailed history of the Roman Empire from the death of Augustus to the reign of Nero.
[8]False argument.

A lamp lit the platform, but the children's faces remained in a shadow. One of them asked me: 'Are you going to Dr Stephen Albert's house?' Without waiting for my answer, another said: 'The house is a good distance away but you won't get lost if you take the road to the left and bear to the left at every crossroad.' I threw them a coin (my last), went down some stone steps and started along a deserted road. At a slight incline, the road ran downhill. It was a plain dirt way, and overhead the branches of trees intermingled, while a round moon hung low in the sky as if to keep me company.

For a moment I thought that Richard Madden might in some way have divined my desperate intent. At once I realized that this would be impossible. The advice about turning always to the left reminded me that such was the common formula for finding the central courtyard of certain labyrinths. I know something about labyrinths. Not for nothing am I the great-grandson of Ts'ui Pên. He was Governor of Yunnan[9] and gave up temporal power to write a novel with more characters than there are in the *Hung Lou Mêng*,[10] and to create a maze in which all men would lose themselves. He spent thirteen years on these oddly assorted tasks before he was assassinated by a stranger. His novel had no sense to it and nobody ever found his labyrinth.

Under the trees of England I meditated on this lost and perhaps mythical labyrinth. I imagined it untouched and perfect on the secret summit of some mountain; I imagined it drowned under rice paddies or beneath the sea; I imagined it infinite, made not only of eight-sided pavilions and of twisting paths but also of rivers, provinces and kingdoms. . . . I thought of a maze of mazes, of a sinuous, ever growing maze which would take in both past and future and would somehow involve the stars.

Lost in these imaginary illusions I forgot my destiny — that of the hunted. For an undetermined period of time I felt myself cut off from the world, an abstract spectator. The hazy and murmuring countryside, the moon, the decline of the evening, stirred within me. Going down the gently sloping road I could not feel fatigue. The evening was at once intimate and infinite.

The road kept descending and branching off, through meadows misty in the twilight. A high-pitched and almost syllabic music kept coming and going, moving with the breeze, blurred by the leaves and by distance.

I thought that a man might be an enemy of other men, of the differing moments of other men, but never an enemy of a country: not of fireflies, words, gardens, streams, or the West wind.

Meditating thus I arrived at a high, rusty iron gate. Through the railings I could see an avenue bordered with poplar trees and also a kind of summer house or pavilion. Two things dawned on me at once, the first trivial and the second almost incredible: the music came from the pavilion and that music was Chinese. That was why I had accepted it fully, without paying it any attention. I do not remember whether there was a bell, a push-button, or whether I attracted attention by clapping my hands. The stuttering sparks of the music kept on.

But from the end of the avenue, from the main house a lantern approached; a

---

[9]A province in southwest China.
[10]*The Dream of the Red Chamber*. Considered one of the greatest Chinese novels, it depicts the decline in the fortunes of a large, aristocratic family.

lantern which alternately, from moment to moment, was crisscrossed or put out by the trunks of the trees; a paper lantern shaped like a drum and coloured like the moon. A tall man carried it. I could not see his face for the light blinded me.

He opened the gate and spoke slowly in my language.

'I see that the worthy Hsi P'eng has troubled himself to see to relieving my solitude. No doubt you want to see the garden?'

Recognizing the name of one of our consuls, I replied, somewhat taken back. 'The garden?'

'The garden of forking paths.'

Something stirred in my memory and I said, with incomprehensible assurance:

'The garden of my ancestor, Ts'ui Pên.'

'Your ancestor? Your illustrious ancestor? Come in.'

The damp path zigzagged like those of my childhood. When we reached the house, we went into a library filled with books from both East and West. I recognized some large volumes bound in yellow silk — manuscripts of the Lost Encyclopedia which was edited by the Third Emperor of the Luminous Dynasty. They had never been printed. A phonograph record was spinning near a bronze phoenix.[11] I remember also a rose-glazed jar and yet another, older by many centuries, of that blue colour which our potters copied from the Persians. . . .

Stephen Albert was watching me with a smile on his face. He was, as I have said, remarkably tall. His face was deeply lined and he had grey eyes and a grey beard. There was about him something of the priest, and something of the sailor. Later, he told me he had been a missionary in Tientsin[12] before he 'had aspired to become a Sinologist.'[13]

We sat down, I upon a large, low divan, he with his back to the window and to a large circular clock. I calculated that my pursuer, Richard Madden, could not arrive in less than an hour. My irrevocable decision could wait.

'A strange destiny,' said Stephen Albert, 'that of Ts'ui Pên — Governor of his native province, learned in astronomy, in astrology and tireless in the interpretation of the canonical books, a chess player, a famous poet and a calligrapher. Yet he abandoned all to make a book and a labyrinth. He gave up all the pleasures of oppression, justice, of a well-stocked bed, of banquets, and even of erudition, and shut himself up in the Pavilion of the Limpid Sun for thirteen years. At his death, his heirs found only a mess of manuscripts. The family, as you doubtless know, wished to consign them to the fire, but the executor of the estate — a Taoist or a Buddhist monk[14] — insisted on their publication.'

'Those of the blood of Ts'ui Pên,' I replied, 'still curse the memory of that monk. Such a publication was madness. The book is a shapeless mass of contradictory rough drafts. I examined it once upon a time: the hero dies in the third chapter, while

---

[11]Mythical bird of great beauty fabled to live 500 or so years, to burn itself to death, and to rise from its ashes in the freshness of youth, and live through another life cycle.
[12]A port in northeastern China.
[13]A person who specializes in the study of Chinese language, literature, history, politics, customs, etc.
[14]China's two major religious orders.

in the fourth he is alive. As for that other enterprise of Ts'ui Pên . . . his Labyrinth. . . .'

'Here is the Labyrinth,' Albert said, pointing to a tall, laquered writing cabinet.

'An ivory labyrinth?' I exclaimed. 'A tiny labyrinth indeed . . . !'

'A symbolic labyrinth,' he corrected me. 'An invisible labyrinth of time. I, a barbarous Englishman, have been given the key to this transparent mystery. After more than a hundred years most of the details are irrecoverable, lost beyond all recall, but it isn't hard to imagine what must have happened. At one time, Ts'u Pên must have said: "I am going into seclusion to write a book," and at another, "I am retiring to construct a maze." Everyone assumed these were separate activities. No one realized that the book and the labyrinth were one and the same. The Pavilion of the Limpid Sun was set in the middle of an intricate garden. This may have suggested the idea of a physical maze.

'Ts'ui Pên died. In all the vast lands which once belonged to your family, no one could find the labyrinth. The novel's confusion suggested that *it* was the labyrinth. Two circumstances showed me the direct solution to the problem. First, the curious legend that Ts'ui Pên had proposed to create an infinite maze, second, a fragment of a letter which I discovered.'

Albert rose. For a few moments he turned his back to me. He opened the top drawer in the high black and gilded writing cabinet. He returned holding in his hand a piece of paper which had once been crimson but which had faded with the passage of time: it was rose coloured, tenuous, quadrangular. Ts'ui Pên's calligraphy was justly famous. Eagerly, but without understanding, I read the words which a man of my blood had written with a small brush: 'I leave to various future times, but not to all, my garden of forking paths.'

I handed back the sheet of paper in silence. Albert went on:

'Before I discovered this letter, I kept asking myself how a book could be infinite. I could not imagine any other than a cyclic volume, circular. A volume whose last page would be the same as the first and so have the possibility of continuing indefinitely. I recalled, too, the night in the middle of *The Thousand and One Nights*[15] when Queen Scheherezade, through a magical mistake on the part of her copyist, started to tell the story of *The Thousand and One Nights*, with the risk of again arriving at the night upon which she will relate it, and thus on to infinity. I also imagined a Platonic[16] hereditary work, passed on from father to son, to which each individual would add a new chapter or correct, with pious care, the work of his elders.

'These conjectures gave me amusement, but none seemed to have the remotest application to the contradictory chapters of Ts'ui Pên. At this point, I was sent from Oxford the manuscript you have just seen.

'Naturally, my attention was caught by the sentence, "I leave to various future times, but not to all, my garden of forking paths." I had no sooner read this, than I understood. *The Garden of Forking Paths* was the chaotic novel itself. The phrase "to various future times, but not to all" suggested the image of bifurcating in

---

[15]The tales told by Scheherezade to the sultan in order to prolong her life.
[16]Characteristic of the Greek philosopher Plato.

time, not in space. Rereading the whole work confirmed this theory. In all fiction, when a man is faced with alternatives he chooses one at the expense of the others. In the almost unfathomable Ts'ui Pên, he chooses — simultaneously — all of them. He thus *creates* various futures, various times which start others that will in their turn branch out and bifurcate in other times. This is the cause of the contradictions in the novel.

'Fang, let us say, has a secret. A stranger knocks at his door. Fang makes up his mind to kill him. Naturally there are various possible outcomes. Fang can kill the intruder, the intruder can kill Fang, both can be saved, both can die and so on and so on. In Ts'ui Pên's work, all the possible solutions occur, each one being the point of departure for other bifurcations. Sometimes the pathways of this labyrinth converge. For example, you come to this house; but in other possible pasts you are my enemy; in others my friend.

'If you will put up with my atrocious pronunciation, I would like to read you a few pages of your ancestor's work.'

His countenance, in the bright circle of lamplight, was certainly that of an ancient, but it shone with something unyielding, even immortal.

With slow precision, he read two versions of the same epic chapter. In the first, an army marches into battle over a desolate mountain pass. The bleak and sombre aspect of the rocky landscape made the soldiers feel that life itself was of little value, and so they won the battle easily. In the second, the same army passes through a palace where a banquet is in progress. The splendour of the feast remained a memory throughout the glorious battle, and so victory followed.

With proper veneration I listened to these old tales, although perhaps with less admiration for them in themselves than for the fact that they had been thought out by one of my own blood, and that a man of a distant empire had given them back to me, in the last stage of a desperate adventure, on a Western island. I remember the final words, repeated at the end of each version like a secret command: 'Thus the heroes fought, with tranquil heart and bloody sword. They were resigned to killing and dying.'

At that moment I felt within me and around me something invisible and intangible pullulating.[17] It was not the pullulation of two divergent, parallel, and finally converging armies, but an agitation more inaccessible, more intimate, prefigured by them in some way. Stephen Albert continued:

'I do not think that your illustrious ancestor toyed idly with variations. I do not find it believable that he would waste thirteen years labouring over a never ending experiment in rhetoric. In your country the novel is an inferior genre; in Ts'ui Pên's period, it was a despised one. Ts'ui Pên was a fine novelist but he was also a man of letters who, doubtless, considered himself more than a mere novelist. The testimony of his contemporaries attests to this, and certainly the known facts of his life confirm his leanings towards the metaphysical and the mystical. Philosophical conjectures take up the greater part of his novel. I know that of all problems, none disquieted him more, and none concerned him more than the profound one of time. Now then, this is the *only* problem that does not figure in the pages of *The Garden*. He does not even use the word which means *time*. How can these voluntary omissions be explained?'

---

[17]Breeding or creating rapidly.

I proposed various solutions, all of them inadequate. We discussed them. Finally Stephen Albert said: 'In a guessing game to which the answer is chess, which word is the only one prohibited?' I thought for a moment and then replied:

'The word is *chess*.'

'Precisely,' said Albert. '*The Garden of Forking Paths* is an enormous guessing game, or parable, in which the subject is time. The rules of the game forbid the use of the word itself. To eliminate a word completely, to refer to it by means of inept phrases and obvious paraphrases, is perhaps the best way of drawing attention to it. This, then, is the tortuous method of approach preferred by the oblique Ts'ui Pên in every meandering of his interminable novel. I have gone over hundreds of manuscripts, I have corrected errors introduced by careless copyists, I have worked out the plan from this chaos, I have restored, or believe I have restored, the original. I have translated the whole work. I can state categorically that not once has the word *time* been used in the whole book.

'The explanation is obvious. *The Garden of Forking Paths* is a picture, incomplete yet not false, of the universe such as Ts'ui Pên conceived it to be. Differing from Newton and Schopenhauer, your ancestor did not think of time as absolute and uniform. He believed in an infinite series of times, in a dizzily growing, ever spreading network of diverging, converging and parallel times. This web of time — the strands of which approach one another, bifurcate, intersect or ignore each other through the centuries — embraces *every* possibility. We do not exist in most of them. In some you exist and not I, while in others I do, and you do not, and in yet others both of us exist. In this one, in which chance has favoured me, you have come to my gate. In another, you, crossing the garden, have found me dead. In yet another, I say these very same words, but am an error, a phantom.'

'In all of them,' I enunciated, with a tremor in my voice. 'I deeply appreciate and am grateful to you for the restoration of Ts'ui Pên's garden.'

'Not in *all*,' he murmured with a smile. 'Time is forever dividing itself towards innumerable futures and in one of them I am your enemy.'

Once again I sensed the pullulation of which I have already spoken. It seemed to me that the dew-damp garden surrounding the house was infinitely saturated with invisible people. All were Albert and myself, secretive, busy and multiform in other dimensions of time. I lifted my eyes and the short nightmare disappeared. In the black and yellow garden there was only a single man, but this man was as strong as a statue and this man was walking up the path and he was Captain Richard Madden.

'The future exists now,' I replied. 'But I am your friend. Can I take another look at the letter?'

Albert rose from his seat. He stood up tall as he opened the top drawer of the high writing cabinet. For a moment his back was again turned to me. I had the revolver ready. I fired with the utmost care: Albert fell without a murmur, at once. I swear that his death was instantaneous, as if he had been struck by lightning.

What remains is unreal and unimportant. Madden broke in and arrested me. I have been condemned to hang. Abominably, I have yet triumphed! The secret name of the city to be attacked got through to Berlin. Yesterday it was bombed. I read the news in the same English newspapers which were trying to solve the riddle of the murder of the learned Sinologist Stephen Albert by the unknown Yu Tsun. The Chief, however, had already solved this mystery. He knew that my problem was to shout, with my feeble voice, above the tumult of war, the name of the city called Albert, and I had no other course open to me than to kill someone of that name. He does not know, for no one can, of my infinite penitence and sickness of the heart.

(1941)

QUESTIONS

1. How do the children at Ashgrove station know that Yu Tsun is going to Dr. Stephen Albert's house? Can you answer that question on both a realistic and a symbolic or fantastic level?

2. How many narrative frames does the reader pass through before reaching Ts'ui Pên's novel? How many narrators, scholars, and editors leave traces along the way? Are they all trustworthy? How do you know?

3. Do Ts'ui Pên's (and the narrator's) speculations on time have any scientific or philosophical validity?

4. Yu Tsun murders a man he doubtless admires in order to give information to a country he finds barbarous. What political conditions or ideological pressures might have led him to this act?

5. Is this short story an elaborate puzzle or something more? Does the story of Yu Tsun's espionage account for all the images and associations? What themes are suggested by the images and associations *not* accounted for by the ostensible story?

❖ JOHN BARTH
Lost in the Funhouse

John Barth (1930–) is a native of the Eastern Shore of the Chesa-
peake Bay in Maryland. He graduated from Johns Hopkins University
in Baltimore and returned there as writer-in-residence and professor of
English. He published his first novel, *The Floating Opera* in 1956. Later
novels are *The End of the Road* (1958), *The Sot-Weed Factor* (1960),
Giles Goat-Boy (1966), *Letters* (1979), *Sabbatical: A Romance* (1982),
Tidewater Tales (1987), and *Last Voyage of Somebody the Sailor*
(1991). "Lost in the Funhouse" is the title story of a short story collection (1968): the subtitle of this volume, *Fiction for Print, Tape, Live
Voice*, gives some sense of Barth's interest in fictional experimentation.
In 1972, Barth won the National Book Award for a collection of
novellas called *Chimera*. Barth also published a collection of nonfictional essays called *The Friday Book: Essays and Other Nonfiction*
(1984).

For whom is the funhouse fun? Perhaps for lovers. For Ambrose it is *a place of fear
and confusion*. He has come to the seashore with his family for the holiday, *the
occasion of their visit is Independence Day, the most important secular holiday of the
United States of America.* A single straight underline is the manuscript mark for italic
type, *which in turn* is the printed equivalent to oral emphasis of words and phrases as
well as the customary type for titles of complete works, not to mention. Italics are also
employed, in fiction stories especially, for "outside," intrusive, or artificial voices, such
as radio announcements, the texts of telegrams and newspaper articles, et cetera. They
should be used *sparingly*. If passages originally in roman type are italicized by
someone repeating them, its customary to acknowledge the fact. *Italics mine.*

   Ambrose was "at that awkward age." His voice came out high-pitched as a
child's if he let himself get carried away; to be on the safe side, therefore, he moved and
spoke with *deliberate calm* and *adult gravity*. Talking soberly of unimportant or
irrelevant matters and listening consciously to the sound of your own voice are useful
habits for maintaining control in this difficult interval. *En route* to Ocean City he sat in
the back seat of the family car with his brother Peter, age fifteen, and Magda G——,
age fourteen, a pretty girl and exquisite young lady, who lived not far from them on
B—— Street in the town of D——, Maryland. Initials, blanks, or both were often
substituted for proper names in nineteenth-century fiction to enhance the illusion of
reality. It is as if the author felt it necessary to delete the names for reasons of tact or
legal liability. Interestingly, as with other aspects of realism, it is an *illusion* that is
being enhanced, by purely artificial means. Is it likely, does it violate the principle of
verisimilitude, that a thirteen-year-old boy could make such a sophisticated observa-

323

tion? A girl of fourteen is *the psychological coeval*[1] of a boy of fifteen or sixteen; a thirteen-year-old boy, therefore, even one precocious in some other respects, might be three years *her emotional junior.*

Thrice a year—on Memorial, Independence, and Labor Days—the family visits Ocean City for the afternoon and evening. When Ambrose and Peter's father was their age, the excursion was made by train, as mentioned in the novel *The 42nd Parallel* by John Dos Passos. Many families from the same neighborhood used to travel together, with dependent relatives and often with Negro servants; schoolfuls of children swarmed through the railway cars; everyone shared everyone else's Maryland fried chicken, Virginia ham, deviled eggs, potato salad, beaten biscuits, iced tea. Nowadays (that is, in 19—, the year of our story) the journey is made by automobile —more comfortably and quickly though without the extra fun though without the *camaraderie* of a general excursion. It's all part of the deterioration of American life, their father declares; Uncle Karl supposes that when the boys take *their* families to Ocean City for the holidays they'll fly in Autogiros.[2] Their mother, sitting in the middle of the front seat like Magda in the second, only with her arms on the seat-back behind the men's shoulders, wouldn't want the good old days back again, the steaming trains and stuffy long dresses; on the other hand she can do without Autogiros, too, if she has to become a grandmother to fly in them.

Description of physical appearance and mannerisms is one of several standard methods of characterization used by writers of fiction. It is also important to "keep the senses operating"; when a detail from one of the five senses, say visual, is "crossed" with a detail from another, say auditory, the reader's imagination is oriented to the scene, perhaps unconsciously. This procedure may be compared to the way surveyors and navigators determine their positions by two or more compass bearings, a process known as triangulation. The brown hair on Ambrose's mother's forearms gleamed in the sun like. Though right-handed, she took her left arm from the seat-back to press the dashboard cigar lighter for Uncle Karl. When the glass bead in its handle glowed red, the lighter was ready for use. The smell of Uncle Karl's cigar smoke reminded one of. The fragrance of the ocean came strong to the picnic ground where they always stopped for lunch, two miles inland from Ocean City. Having to pause for a full hour almost within sound of the breakers was difficult for Peter and Ambrose when they were younger; even at their present age it was not easy to keep their anticipation, *stimulated by the briny spume,* from turning into short temper. The Irish author James Joyce, in his unusual novel entitled *Ulysses,* now available in this country, uses the adjectives *snot-green* and *scrotum-tightening* to describe the sea. Visual, auditory, tactile, olfactory, gustatory. Peter and Ambrose's father, while steering their black 1936 LaSalle sedan with one hand, could with the other remove the first cigarette from a white pack of Lucky Strikes and, more remarkably, light it with a match forefingered from its book and thumbed against the flint paper without being detached. The matchbook cover merely advertised U. S. War Bonds and Stamps. A fine metaphor, simile, or other figure of speech, in addition to its obvious "first-order" relevance to the thing it describes, will be seen upon reflection to have a second order of signifi-

---

[1] Equal.
[2] Early form of helicopter, but with conventional propeller.

cance: it may be drawn from the *milieu* of the action, for example, or be particularly appropriate to the sensibility of the narrator, even hinting to the reader things of which the narrator is unaware; or it may cast further and subtler lights upon the things it describes, sometimes ironically qualifying the more evident sense of the comparison.

To say that Ambrose's and Peter's mother was *pretty* is to accomplish nothing; the reader may acknowledge the proposition, but his imagination is not engaged. Besides, Magda was also pretty, yet in an altogether different way. Although she lived on B —— Street she had very good manners and did better than average in school. Her figure was very well developed for her age. Her right hand lay casually on the plush upholstery of the seat, very near Ambrose's left leg, on which his own hand rested. The space between their legs, between her right and his left leg, was out of the line of sight of anyone sitting on the other side of Magda, as well as anyone glancing into the rear-view mirror. Uncle Karl's face resembled Peter's—rather, vice versa. Both had dark hair and eyes, short husky statures, deep voices. Magda's left hand was probably in a similar position on her left side. The boys' father is difficult to describe; no particular feature of his appearance or manner stood out. He wore glasses and was principal of a T —— County grade school. Uncle Karl was a masonry contractor.

Although Peter must have known as well as Ambrose that the latter, because of his position in the car, would be the first to see the electrical towers of the power plant at V ——, the halfway point of their trip, he leaned forward and slightly toward the center of the car and pretended to be looking for them through the flat pinewoods and tuckahoe creeks[3] along the highway. For as long as the boys could remember, "looking for the Towers" had been a feature of the first half of their excursions to Ocean City, "looking for the standpipe" of the second. Though the game was childish, their mother preserved the tradition of rewarding the first to see the Towers with a candy-bar or piece of fruit. She insisted now that Magda play the game; the prize, she said, was "something hard to get nowadays." Ambrose decided not to join in; he sat far back in his seat. Magda, like Peter, leaned forward. Two sets of straps were discernible through the shoulders of her sun dress; the inside right one, a brassiere-strap, was fastened or shortened with a small safety pin. The right armpit of her dress, presumably the left as well, was damp with perspiration. The simple strategy for being first to espy the Towers, which Ambrose had understood by the age of four, was to sit on the right-hand side of the car. Whoever sat there, however, had also to put up with the worst of the sun, and so Ambrose, without mentioning the matter, chose sometimes the one and sometimes the other. Not impossibly Peter had never caught on to the trick, or thought that his brother hadn't simply because Ambrose on occasion preferred shade to a Baby Ruth or tangerine.

The shade-sun situation didn't apply to the front seat, owing to the windshield; if anything the driver got more sun, since the person on the passenger side not only was shaded below by the door and dashboard but might swing down his sunvisor all the way too.

"Is that them?" Magda asked. Ambrose's mother teased the boys for letting Magda win, insinuating that "somebody [had] a girlfriend." Peter and Ambrose's father reached a long thin arm across their mother to butt his cigarette in the

---

[3]Creeks bordered by a certain kind of leafy plant.

dashboard ashtray, under the lighter. The prize this time for seeing the Towers first was a banana. Their mother bestowed it after chiding their father for wasting a half-smoked cigarette when everything was so scarce. Magda, to take the prize, moved her hand from so near Ambrose's that he could have touched it as though accidentally. She offered to share the prize, things like that were so hard to find; but everyone insisted it was hers alone. Ambrose's mother sang an iambic trimeter couplet from a popular song, femininely rhymed:

> *"What's good is in the Army;*
> *What's left will never harm me."*

Uncle Karl tapped his cigar ash out the ventilator window; some particles were sucked by the slipstream back into the car through the rear window on the passenger side. Magda demonstrated her ability to hold a banana in one hand and peel it with her teeth. She still sat forward; Ambrose pushed his glasses back onto the bridge of his nose with his left hand, which he then negligently let fall to the seat cushion immediately behind her. He even permitted the single hair, gold, on the second joint of his thumb to brush the fabric of her skirt. Should she have sat back at that instant, his hand would have been caught under her.

Plush upholstery prickles uncomfortably through gabardine slacks in the July sun. The function of the *beginning* of a story is to introduce the principal characters, establish their initial relationships, set the scene for the main action, expose the background of the situation if necessary, plant motifs and foreshadowings where appropriate, and initiate the first complication or whatever of the "rising action." Actually, if one imagines a story called "The Funhouse," or "Lost in the Funhouse," the details of the drive to Ocean City don't seem especially relevant. The *beginning* should recount the events between Ambrose's first sight of the funhouse early in the afternoon and his entering it with Magda and Peter in the evening. The *middle* would narrate all relevant events from the time he goes in to the time he loses his way; middles have the double and contradictory function of delaying the climax while at the same time preparing the reader for it and fetching him to it. Then the *ending* would tell what Ambrose does while he's lost, how he finally finds his way out, and what everybody makes of the experience. So far there's been no real dialogue, very little sensory detail, and nothing in the way of a *theme*. And a long time has gone by already without anything happening; it makes a person wonder. We haven't even reached Ocean City yet: we will never get out of the funhouse.

The more closely an author identifies with the narrator, literally or meta-phorically, the less advisable it is, as a rule, to use the first-person narrative viewpoint. Once three years previously the young people *aforementioned* played Niggers and Masters in the backyard; when it was Ambrose's turn to be Master and theirs to be Niggers Peter had to go serve his evening papers; Ambrose was afraid to punish Magda alone, but she led him to the whitewashed Torture Chamber between the woodshed and the privy in the Slaves Quarters; there she knelt sweating among bamboo rakes and dusty Mason jars, pleadingly embraced his knees, and while bees droned in the lattice as if on an ordinary summer afternoon, purchased clemency at a surprising price set by herself. Doubtless she remembered nothing of this event; Ambrose on the other hand seemed unable to forget the least detail of his life. He even recalled how, standing beside himself with awed impersonality in the reeky heat, he'd stared the while at an empty cigar box in which Uncle Karl kept stone-cutting chisels: beneath the words *El Producto*, a laureled, loose-toga'd lady regarded the sea from a marble bench; beside her, forgotten or not yet turned to, was a five-stringed lyre. Her chin reposed on the back of her right hand; her left depended negligently from the bench-arm. The lower half of scene and lady was peeled away; the words EXAMINED BY —— were inked there into the wood. Nowadays cigar boxes are made of pasteboard. Ambrose wondered what Magda would have done, Ambrose wondered what Magda would do when she sat back on his hand as he resolved she should. Be angry. Make a teasing joke of it. Give no sign at all. For a long time she leaned forward, playing cowpoker with Peter against Uncle Karl and Mother and watching for the first sign of Ocean City. At nearly the same instant, picnic ground and Ocean City standpipe hove into view; an Amoco filling station on their side of the road cost Mother and Uncle Karl fifty cows and the game; Magda bounced back, clapping her right hand on Mother's right arm; Ambrose moved clear "in the nick of time."

At this rate our hero, at this rate our protagonist will remain in the funhouse forever. Narrative ordinarily consists of alternating dramatization and summarization. One symptom of nervous tension, paradoxically, is repeated and violent yawning; neither Peter nor Magda nor Uncle Karl nor Mother reacted in this manner. Although they were no longer small children, Peter and Ambrose were each given a dollar to spend on boardwalk amusements in addition to what money of their own they'd brought along. Magda too, though she protested she had ample spending money. The boys' mother made a little scene out of distributing the bills; she pretended that her sons and Magda were small children and cautioned them not to spend the sum too quickly or in one place. Magda promised with a merry laugh and, having both hands free, took the bill with her left. Peter laughed also and pledged in a falsetto to be a good boy. His imitation of a child was not clever. The boys' father was tall and thin, balding, fair-complexioned. Assertions of that sort are not effective; the reader may acknowledge the proposition, but. We should be much farther along than we are; something has gone wrong; not much of this preliminary rambling seems relevant. Yet everyone begins in the same place; how is it that most go along without difficulty but a few lose their way?

"Stay out from under the boardwalk," Uncle Karl growled from the side of his mouth. The boys' mother pushed his shoulder *in mock annoyance*. They were all standing before Fat May the Laughing Lady who advertised the funhouse. Larger than life, Fat May mechanically shook, rocked on her heels, slapped her thighs while recorded laughter — uproarious, female — came amplified from a hidden loudspeaker. It chuckled, wheezed, wept; tried in vain to catch its breath; tittered, groaned, exploded raucous and anew. You couldn't hear it without laughing yourself, no matter how you felt. Father came back from talking to a Coast-Guardsman on duty and reported that the surf was spoiled with crude oil from tankers recently torpedoed offshore. Lumps of it, difficult to remove, made tarry tidelines on the beach and stuck on swimmers. Many bathed in the surf nevertheless and came out speckled; others paid to use a municipal pool and only sunbathed on the beach. We would do the latter. We would do the latter. We would do the latter.

Under the boardwalk, matchbook covers, grainy other things. What is the story's theme? Ambrose is ill. He perspires in the dark passages; candied apples-on-a-stick, delicious-looking, disappointing to eat. Funhouses need men's and ladies' rooms at intervals. Others perhaps have also vomited in corners and corridors; may even have had bowel movements liable to be stepped in in the dark. The word *fuck* suggests suction and/or and/or flatulence. Mother and Father; grandmothers and grandfathers on both sides; great-grandmothers and great-grandfathers on four sides, et cetera. Count a generation as thirty years: in approximately the year when Lord Baltimore was granted charter to the province of Maryland by Charles I, five hundred twelve women — English, Welsh, Bavarian, Swiss — of every class and character, received into themselves the penises the intromittent organs of five hundred twelve men, ditto, in every circumstance and posture, to conceive the five hundred twelve ancestors of the two hundred fifty-six ancestors of the et cetera et cetera et cetera et cetera et cetera et cetera et cetera of the author, of the narrator, of this story, *Lost in the Funhouse*. In alleyways, ditches, canopy beds, pinewoods, bridal suites, ship's cabins, coach-and-fours, coaches-and-four, sultry toolsheds; on the cold sand under board-walks, littered with *El Producto* cigar butts, treasured with Lucky Strike cigarette stubs, Coca-Cola caps, gritty turds, cardboard lollipop sticks, matchbook covers warning that A Slip of the Lip Can Sink a Ship.[4] The shluppish whisper, continuous as seawash round the globe, tidelike falls and rises with the circuit of dawn and dusk.

Magda's teeth. She *was* left-handed. Perspiration. They've gone all the way, through, Magda and Peter, they've been waiting for hours with Mother and Uncle Karl while Father searches for his lost son; they draw french-fried potatoes from a paper cup and shake their heads. They've named the children they'll one day have and bring to Ocean City on holidays. Can spermatozoa properly be thought of as male animalcules when there are no female spermatozoa? They grope through hot, dark windings, past Love's Tunnel's fearsome obstacles. Some perhaps lose their way.

Peter suggested then and there that they do the funhouse; he had been through it before, so had Magda, Ambrose hadn't and suggested, his voice cracking on account of Fat May's laughter, that they swim first. All were chuckling, couldn't help it; Ambrose's father, Ambrose's and Peter's father came up grinning like a lunatic with two boxes of syrup-coated popcorn, one for Mother, one for Magda; the men were to help themselves. Ambrose walked on Magda's right; being by nature left-handed, she carried the box in her left hand. Up front the situation was reversed.

"What are you limping for?" Magda inquired of Ambrose. He supposed in a husky tone that his foot had gone to sleep in the car. Her teeth flashed. "Pins and needles?" It was the honeysuckle on the lattice of the former privy that drew the bees. Imagine being stung there. How long is this going to take?

The adults decided to forgo the pool; but Uncle Karl insisted they change into swimsuits and do the beach. "He wants to watch the pretty girls," Peter teased, and ducked behind Magda from Uncle Karl's pretended wrath. "You've got all the pretty girls you need right here," Magda declared, and Mother said: "Now that's the gospel truth." Magda scolded Peter, who reached over her shoulder to sneak some popcorn. "Your brother and father aren't getting any." Uncle Karl wondered if they were going to have fireworks that night, what with the shortages. It wasn't the shortages, Mr.

---

[4] A World War II slogan cautioning Americans about sharing information that might be of use to the enemy.

M—— replied; Ocean City had fireworks from pre-war. But it was too risky on account of the enemy submarines, some people thought.

"Don't seem like Fourth of July without fireworks," said Uncle Karl. The inverted tag in dialogue writing is still considered permissible with proper names or epithets, but sounds old-fashioned with personal pronouns. "We'll have 'em again soon enough," predicted the boys' father. Their mother declared she could do without fireworks: they reminded her too much of the real thing. Their father said all the more reason to shoot off a few now and again. Uncle Karl asked *rhetorically* who needed reminding, just look at people's hair and skin.

"The oil, yes," said Mrs. M——.

Ambrose had a pain in his stomach and so didn't swim but enjoyed watching the others. He and his father burned red easily. Magda's figure was exceedingly well developed for her age. She too declined to swim, and got mad, and became angry when Peter attempted to drag her into the pool. She always swam, he insisted; what did she mean not swim? Why did a person come to Ocean City?

"Maybe I want to lay here with Ambrose," Magda teased.

Nobody likes a pedant.

"Aha," said Mother. Peter grabbed Magda by one ankle and ordered Ambrose to grab the other. She squealed and rolled over on the beach blanket. Ambrose pretended to help hold her back. Her tan was darker than even Mother's and Peter's. "Help out, Uncle Karl!" Peter cried. Uncle Karl went to seize the other ankle. Inside the top of her swimsuit, however, you could see the line where the sunburn ended and, when she hunched her shoulders and squealed again, one nipple's auburn edge. Mother made them behave themselves. "*You* should certainly know," she said to Uncle Karl. Archly. "That when a lady says she doesn't feel like swimming, a gentleman doesn't ask questions." Uncle Karl said excuse *him*; Mother winked at Magda; Ambrose blushed; stupid Peter kept saying "Phooey on *feel like!*" and tugging at Magda's ankle; then even he got the point, and cannonballed with a holler into the pool.

"I swear," Magda said, in mock *in feigned* exasperation.

The diving would make a suitable literary symbol. To go off the high board you had to wait in a line along the poolside and up the ladder. Fellows tickled girls and goosed one another and shouted to the ones at the top to hurry up, or razzed them for bellyfloppers. Once on the springboard some took a great while posing or clowning or deciding on a dive or getting up their nerve; others ran right off. Especially among the younger fellows the idea was to strike the funniest pose or do the craziest stunt as you fell, a thing that got harder to do as you kept on and kept on. But whether you hollered *Geronimo!*[5] or *Sieg heil!*, held your nose or "rode a bicycle," pretended to be shot or did a perfect jacknife or changed your mind halfway down and ended up with nothing, it was over in two seconds, after all that wait. Spring, pose, splash. Spring, neat-o, splash. Spring, aw fooey, splash.

The grown-ups had gone on; Ambrose wanted to converse with Magda; she was remarkably well developed for her age; it was said that that came from rubbing with a turkish towel, and there were other theories. Ambrose could think of nothing to say except how good a diver Peter was, who was showing off for her benefit. You could

[5]An American paratrooper's battle cry, supposedly referring to the famous Indian chief.

pretty well tell by looking at their bathing suits and arm muscles how far along the different fellows were. Ambrose was glad he hadn't gone in swimming, the cold water shrank you up so. Magda pretended to be uninterested in the diving; she probably weighed as much as he did. If you knew your way around in the funhouse like your own bedroom, you could wait until a girl came along and then slip away without ever getting caught, even if her boyfriend was right with her. She'd think *he* did it! It would be better to be the boyfriend, and act outraged, and tear the funhouse apart.

Not act; *be.*

"He's a master diver," Ambrose said. In feigned admiration. "You really have to slave away at it to get that good." What would it matter anyhow if he asked her right out whether she remembered, even teased her with it as Peter would have?

There's no point in going farther; this isn't getting anybody anywhere; they haven't even come to the funhouse yet. Ambrose is off the track, in some new or old part of the place that's not supposed to be used; he strayed into it by some one-in-a-million chance, like the time the roller-coaster car left the tracks in the nineteen-teens against all the laws of physics and sailed over the boardwalk in the dark. And they can't locate him because they don't know where to look. Even the designer and operator have forgotten this other part, that winds around on itself like a whelk shell. That winds around the right part like the snakes on Mercury's caduceus.[6] Some people, perhaps, don't "hit their stride" until their twenties, when the growing-up business is over and women appreciate other things besides wisecracks and teasing and strutting. Peter didn't have one-tenth the imagination *he* had, not one-tenth. Peter did this naming-their-children thing as a joke, making up names like Aloysius and Murga-troyd, but Ambrose knew *exactly* how it would feel to be married and have children of your own, and be a loving husband and father, and go comfortably to work in the mornings and to bed with your wife at night, and wake up with her there. With a breeze coming through the sash and birds and mockingbirds singing in the Chinese-cigar trees. His eyes watered, there aren't enough ways to say that. He would be quite famous in his line of work. Whether Magda was his wife or not, one evening when he was wise-lined and gray at the temples he'd smile gravely, at a fashionable dinner party, and remind her of his youthful passion. The time they went with his family to Ocean City; the *erotic fantasies* he used to have about her. How long ago it seemed, and childish! Yet tender, too, *n'est-ce pas?*[7] Would she have imagined that the world-famous whatever remembered how many strings were on the lyre on the bench beside the girl on the label of the cigar box he'd stared at in the toolshed at age ten while she, age eleven. Even then he had felt *wise beyond his years;* he'd stroked her hair and said in his deepest voice and correctest English, as to a dear child: "I shall never forget this moment."

But though he had breathed heavily, groaned as if ecstatic, what he'd really felt throughout was an odd detachment, as though some one else were Master. Strive as he might to be transported, he heard his mind take notes upon the scene: *This is what they call* passion. *I am experiencing it.* Many of the digger machines were out of order in the penny arcades and could not be repaired or replaced for the duration. Moreover

---

[6]Symbolic staff carried by the god Mercury, with two entwined snakes crowned by a pair of wings.
[7]A rhetorical question meaning "Don't you agree?" (French).

the prizes, made now in USA, were less interesting than formerly, pasteboard items for the most part, and some of the machines wouldn't work on white pennies.[8] The gypsy fortune-teller machine might have provided a foreshadowing of the climax of this story if Ambrose had operated it. It was even dilapidateder than most: the silver coating was worn off the brown metal handles, the glass windows around the dummy were cracked and taped, her kerchiefs and silks long-faded. If a man lived by himself, he could take a department-store mannequin with flexible joints and modify her in certain ways. *However*: by the time he was that old he'd have a real woman. There was a machine that stamped your name around a white-metal coin with a star in the middle: A———. His son would be the second, and when the lad reached thirteen or so he would put a strong arm around his shoulder and tell him calmly: "It is perfectly normal. We have all been through it. It will not last forever." Nobody knew how to be what they were right. He'd smoke a pipe, teach his son how to fish and softcrab, assure him he needn't worry about himself. Magda would certainly give, Magda would certainly yield a great deal of milk, although guilty of occasional solecisms.[9] It don't taste so bad. Suppose the lights came on now!

The day wore on. You think you're yourself, but there are other persons in you. Ambrose gets hard when Ambrose doesn't want to, *and obversely*.[10] Ambrose watches them disagree; Ambrose watches him watch. In the funhouse mirror-room you can't see yourself go on forever, because no matter how you stand, your head gets in the way. Even if you had a glass periscope, the image of your eye would cover up the thing you really wanted to see. The police will come; there'll be a story in the papers. That must be where it happened. Unless he can find a surprise exit, an unofficial backdoor or escape hatch opening on an alley, say, and then stroll up to the family in front of the funhouse and ask where everybody's been; *he's* been out of the place for ages. That's just where it happened, in that last lighted room: Peter and Magda found the right exit; he found one that you weren't supposed to find and strayed off into the works somewhere. In a perfect funhouse you'd be able to go only one way, like the divers off the highboard; getting lost would be impossible; the doors and halls would work like minnow traps or the valves in veins.

On account of German U-boats,[11] Ocean City was "browned out": streetlights were shaded on the seaward side; shop-windows and boardwalk amusement places were kept dim, not to silhouette tankers and Liberty-ships[12] for torpedoing. In a short story about Ocean City, Maryland, during World War II, the author could make use of the image of sailors on leave in the penny arcades and shooting galleries, sighting through the crosshairs of toy machine guns at swastika'd subs, while out in the black Atlantic a U-boat skipper squints through his periscope at real ships outlined by the glow of penny arcades. After dinner the family strolled back to the amusement end of the boardwalk. The boys' father had burnt red as always and was masked with Noxzema, a minstrel in reverse. The grownups stood at the end of the boardwalk where the Hurricane of '33 had cut an inlet from the ocean to Assawoman Bay.

---

[8]Zinc-coated steel pennies minted in 1943, intended to conserve copper for the war effort.
[9]Substandard uses of language.
[10]Vice versa.
[11]Submarines.
[12]Mass-produced cargo ships.

"Pronounced with a long *o*," Uncle Karl reminded Magda with a wink. His shirt sleeves were rolled up; Mother punched his brown biceps with the arrowed heart on it and said his mind was naughty. Fat May's laugh came suddenly from the funhouse, as if she'd just got the joke; the family laughed too at the coincidence. Ambrose went under the boardwalk to search for out-of-town matchbook covers with the aid of his pocket flashlight; he looked out from the edge of the North American continent and wondered how far their laughter carried over the water. Spies in rubber rafts; survivors in lifeboats. If the joke had been beyond his understanding, he could have said: "*The laughter was over his head.*" And let the reader see the serious wordplay on second reading.

He turned the flashlight on and then off at once even before the woman whooped. He sprang away, heart athud, dropping the light. What had the man grunted? Perspiration drenched and chilled him by the time he scrambled up to the family. "See anything?" his father asked. His voice wouldn't come; he shrugged and violently brushed sand from his pants legs.

"Let's ride the old flying horses!" Magda cried. I'll never be an author. It's been forever already, everybody's gone home, Ocean City's deserted, the ghost-crabs are tickling across the beach and down the littered cold streets. And the empty halls of clapboard hotels and abandoned funhouses. A tidal wave; an enemy air raid; a monster-crab swelling like an island from the sea. *The inhabitants fled in terror.* Magda clung to his trouser leg; he alone knew the maze's secret. "He gave his life that we might live," said Uncle Karl with a scowl of pain, as he. The fellow's hands had been tattooed; the woman's legs, the woman's fat white legs had. *An astonishing coincidence.* He yearned to tell Peter. He wanted to throw up for excitement. They hadn't even chased him. He wished he were dead.

One possible ending would be to have Ambrose come across another lost person in the dark. They'd match their wits together against the funhouse, struggle like Ulysses[13] past obstacle after obstacle, help and encourage each other. Or a girl. By the time they found the exit they'd be closest friends, sweethearts if it were a girl; they'd know each other's inmost souls, be bound together *by the cement of shared adventure*; then they'd emerge into the light and it would turn out that his friend was a Negro. A blind girl. President Roosevelt's son. Ambrose's former archenemy.

Shortly after the mirror room he'd groped along a musty corridor, his heart already misgiving him at the absence of phosphorescent arrows and other signs. He'd found a crack of light — not a door, it turned out, but a seam between the plyboard wall panels — and squinting up to it, espied a small old man, *in appearance not unlike* the photographs at home of Ambrose's late grandfather, nodding upon a stool beneath a bare, speckled bulb. A crude panel of toggle- and knife-switches hung beside the open fuse box near his head; elsewhere in the little room were wooden levers and ropes belayed to boat cleats. At the time, Ambrose wasn't lost enough to rap or call; later he couldn't find that crack. Now it seemed to him that he'd possibly dozed off for a few minutes somewhere along the way; certainly he was exhausted from the afternoon's sunshine and the evening's problems; he couldn't be sure he hadn't dreamed part or all of the sight. Had an old black wall fan droned like bees and shimmied two flypaper

---

[13]Roman name of Odysseus, the hero of Homer's *Odyssey*.

streamers? Had the funhouse operator — gentle, somewhat sad and tired-appearing, in expression not unlike the photographs at home of Ambrose's late Uncle Konrad — murmured in his sleep? Is there really such a person as Ambrose, or is he a figment of the author's imagination? Was it Assawoman Bay or Sinepuxent? Are there other errors of fact in this fiction? Was there another sound besides the little slap slap of thigh on ham, like water sucking at the chine-boards of a skiff?

When you're lost, the smartest thing to do is stay put till you're found, hollering if necessary. But to holler guarantees humiliation as well as rescue; keeping silent permits some saving of face — you can act surprised at the fuss when your rescuers find you and swear you weren't lost, if they do. What's more you might find your own way yet, *however belatedly.*

"Don't tell me your foot's still asleep!" Magda exclaimed as the three young people walked from the inlet to the area set aside for ferris wheels, carrousels, and other carnival rides, they having decided in favor of the vast and ancient merry-go-round instead of the funhouse. What a sentence, everything was wrong from the outset. People don't know what to make of him, he doesn't know what to make of himself, he's only thirteen, *athletically and socially inept*, not astonishingly bright, but there are antennae; he has . . . some sort of receivers in his head; things speak to him, he understands more than he should, the world winks at him through its objects, grabs grinning at his coat. Everybody else is in on some secret he doesn't know; they've forgotten to tell him. Through simple *procrastination* his mother put off his baptism until this year. Everyone else had it done as a baby; he'd assumed the same of himself, as had his mother, so she claimed, until it was time for him to join Grace Methodist-Protestant and the oversight came out. He was mortified, but pitched sleepless through his private catechizing, intimidated by the ancient mysteries, a thirteen year old would never say that, resolved to experience conversion like St. Augustine.[14] When the water touched his brow and Adam's sin left him, he contrived by a strain like defecation to bring tears into his eyes — but felt nothing. There was some simple, radical difference about him; he hoped it was genius, feared it was madness, devoted himself to amiability and inconspicuousness. Alone on the seawall near his house he was seized by the terrifying transports he'd thought to find in toolshed, in Communion-cup. The grass was alive! The town, the river, himself, were not imaginary; time roared in his ears like wind; the world was *going on!* This part ought to be dramatized. The Irish author James Joyce once wrote. Ambrose M——— is going to scream.

There is no *texture of rendered sensory detail*, for one thing. The faded distorting mirrors beside Fat May; the impossibility of choosing a mount when one had but a single ride on the great carrousel; the *vertigo attendant on his recognition* that Ocean City was worn out, the place of fathers and grandfathers, straw-boatered men and parasoled ladies survived by their amusements. Money spent, the three paused at Peter's insistence beside Fat May to watch the girls get their skirts blown up. The object was to tease Magda, who said: "I swear, Peter M———, you've got a one-track mind! Amby and me aren't *interested* in such things." In the tumbling-barrel, too, just inside the Devil's-mouth entrance to the funhouse, the girls were upended and their

---

[14](354–430) Inspired by his reading of the writings of St. Ambrose (340?–397), he converted to Christianity in 386.

boyfriends and others could see up their dresses if they cared to. Which was the whole point, Ambrose realized. Of the entire funhouse! If you looked around, you noticed that almost all the people on the boardwalk were paired off into couples except the small children; in a way, that was the whole point of Ocean City! If you had X-ray eyes and could see everything going on at that instant under the boardwalk and in all the hotel rooms and cars and alleyways, you'd realize that all that normally *showed*, like restaurants and dance halls and clothing and test-your-strength machines, was merely preparation and intermission. Fat May screamed.

Because he watched the goings-on from the corner of his eye, it was Ambrose who spied the half-dollar on the boardwalk near the tumbling-barrel. Losers weepers. The first time he'd heard some people moving through a corridor not far away, just after he'd lost sight of the crack of light, he'd decided not to call to them, for fear they'd guess he was scared and poke fun; it sounded like roughnecks; he'd hoped they'd come by and he could follow in the dark without their knowing. Another time he'd heard just one person, unless he imagined it, bumping along as if on the other side of the plywood; perhaps Peter coming back for him, or Father, or Magda lost too. Or the owner and operator of the funhouse. He'd called out once, as though merrily: "Anybody know where the heck we are?" But the query was too stiff, his voice cracked, when the sounds stopped he was terrified: maybe it was a queer who waited for fellows to get lost, or a longhaired filthy monster that lived in some cranny of the funhouse. He stood rigid for hours it seemed like, scarcely respiring. His future was shockingly clear, in outline. He tried holding his breath to the point of unconsciousness. There ought to be a button you could push to end your life absolutely without pain; disappear in a flick, like turning out a light. He would push it instantly! He despised Uncle Karl. But he despised his father too, for not being what he was supposed to be. Perhaps his father hated *his* father, and so on, and his son would hate him, and so on. Instantly!

Naturally he didn't have nerve enough to ask Magda to go through the funhouse with him. With incredible nerve and to everyone's surprise he invited Magda, quietly and politely, to go through the funhouse with him. "I warn you, I've never been through it before," he added, *laughing easily*; "but I reckon we can manage somehow. The important thing to remember, after all, is that it's meant to be a *fun*house; that is, a place of amusement. If people really got lost or injured or too badly frightened in it, the owner'd go out of business. There'd even be lawsuits. No character in a work of fiction can make a speech this long without interruption or acknowledgment from the other characters."

Mother teased Uncle Karl: "Three's a crowd, I always heard." But actually Ambrose was relieved that Peter now had a quarter too. Nothing was what it looked like. Every instant, under the surface of the Atlantic Ocean, millions of living animals devoured one another. Pilots were falling in flames over Europe; women were being forcibly raped in the South Pacific. His father should have taken him aside and said: "There is a simple secret to getting through the funhouse, as simple as being first to see the Towers. Here it is. Peter does not know it; neither does your Uncle Karl. You and I are different. Not surprisingly, you've often wished you weren't. Don't think I haven't noticed how unhappy your childhood has been! But you'll understand, when I tell you, why it had to be kept secret until now. And you won't regret not being like your brother and your uncle. *On the contrary!*" If you knew all the stories behind all the people on the boardwalk, you'd see that *nothing* was what it looked like. Husbands and wives often hated each other; parents didn't necessarily love their children; et cetera. A child took things for granted because he had nothing to compare his life to and everybody acted as if things were as they should be. Therefore each saw himself as the hero of the story, when the truth might turn out to be that he's the villain, or the coward. And there wasn't one thing you could do about it!

Hunchbacks, fat ladies, fools — that no one chose what he was was unbearable. In the movies he'd meet a beautiful young girl in the funhouse; they'd have hairs-breadth escapes from real dangers; he'd do and say the right things; she also; in the end they'd be lovers; their dialogue lines would match up; he'd be perfectly at ease; she'd not only like him well enough, she'd think he was *marvelous;* she'd lie awake thinking about *him,* instead of vice versa — the way *his* face looked in different lights and how he stood and exactly what he'd said — and yet that would be only one small episode in his wonderful life, among many many others. Not a *turning point* at all. What had happened in the toolshed was nothing. He hated, he loathed his parents! One reason for not writing a lost-in-the-funhouse story is that either everybody's felt what Ambrose feels, in which case it goes without saying, or else no normal person feels such things, in which case Ambrose is a freak. "Is anything more tiresome, in fiction, than the problems of sensitive adolescents?" And it's all too long and rambling, as if the author. For all a person knows the first time through, the end could be just around any corner; perhaps, *not impossibly* it's been within reach any number of times. On the other hand he may be scarcely past the start, with everything yet to get through, an intolerable idea.

Fill in: His father's raised eyebrows when he announced his decision to do the funhouse with Magda. Ambrose understands now, but didn't then, that his father was wondering whether he knew what the funhouse was *for* — especially since he didn't object, as he should have, when Peter decided to come along too. The ticket-woman, witchlike, mortifying him when inadvertently he gave her his name-coin instead of the half-dollar, then unkindly calling Magda's attention to the birthmark on his temple: "Watch out for him, girlie, he's a marked man!" She wasn't even cruel, he understood, only vulgar and insensitive. Somewhere in the world there was a young woman with such splendid understanding that she'd see him entire, like a poem or story, and find his words so valuable after all that when he confessed his apprehensions she would explain why they were in fact the very things that made him precious to her . . . and to Western Civilization! There was no such girl, the simple truth being. Violent yawns as they approached the mouth. Whispered advice from an old-timer on a bench near the barrel: "Go crabwise and ye'll get an eyeful without upsetting!" Composure vanished at the first pitch: Peter hollered joyously, Magda tumbled, shrieked, clutched her skirt; Ambrose scrambled crabwise, tight-lipped with terror, was soon out, watched his dropped name-coin slide among the couples. Shamefaced he saw that to get through expeditiously was not the point; Peter feigned assistance in order to trip Magda up, shouted "I see Christmas!" when her legs went flying. The old man, his latest betrayer, cackled approval. A dim hall then of black-thread cobwebs and recorded gibber: he took Magda's elbow to steady her against revolving discs set in the slanted floor to throw your feet out from under, and explained to her in a calm, deep voice his theory that each phase of the funhouse was triggered either automatically, by a series of photoelectric devices, or else manually by operators stationed at peepholes. But he lost his voice thrice as the discs unbalanced him; Magda was anyhow squealing; but at one point she clutched him about the waist to keep from falling, and her right cheek pressed for a moment against his belt-buckle. Heroically he drew her up, it was his chance to clutch her close as if for support and say: "I love you." He even put an arm lightly about the small of her back before a sailor-and-girl pitched into them from behind, sorely treading his left big toe and knocking Magda asprawl with them. The sailor's girl was a string-haired hussy with a loud laugh and light blue drawers; Ambrose realized that he wouldn't have said "I love you" anyhow, and was smitten with self-contempt. How much better it would be to be that common sailor! A wiry little Seaman 3rd, the fellow squeezed a girl to each side and stumbled hilarious into the mirror room, closer to Magda in thirty seconds than Ambrose had got in thirteen years. She giggled at something the fellow said to Peter; she drew her hair from her eyes with a movement so womanly it struck Ambrose's heart; Peter's smacking her backside then seemed particularly coarse. But Magda made a pleased indignant face and cried, "All right for *you*, mister!" and pursued Peter into the maze without a backward glance. The sailor followed after, leisurely, drawing his girl against his hip; Ambrose understood not only that they were all so relieved to be rid of his burdensome company that they didn't even notice his absence, but that he himself shared their relief. Stepping from the treacherous passage at last into the mirror-maze, he saw once again, more clearly than ever, how readily he deceived himself into supposing he was a person. He even foresaw, wincing at his dreadful self-knowledge, that he would repeat the deception, at ever-rarer intervals, all his wretched life, so fearful were the alternatives. Fame, madness, suicide; perhaps all three. It's not believable that so young a boy could articulate that reflection, and in fiction the merely true must always yield to the plausible. Moreover, the symbolism is in places heavy-footed. Yet Ambrose M—— understood, as few adults do, that the famous loneliness of the great was no popular myth but a general truth — furthermore, that it was as much cause as effect.

   All the preceding except the last few sentences is exposition that should've been done earlier or interspersed with the present action instead of lumped together. No reader would put up with so much with such *prolixity*.[15] It's interesting that Ambrose's father, though presumably an intelligent man (as indicated by his role as grade-school principal), neither encouraged nor discouraged his sons at all in any way — as if he either didn't care about them or cared all right but didn't know how to act. If this fact should contribute to one of them's becoming a celebrated but wretchedly unhappy scientist, was it a good thing or not? He too might someday face the question; it would be useful to know whether it had tortured his father for years, for example, or never once crossed his mind.

   In the maze two important things happened. First, our hero found a name-coin someone else had lost or discarded: *AMBROSE*, suggestive of the famous light-ship[16] and of his late grandfather's favorite dessert,[17] which his mother used to prepare on special occasions out of coconut, oranges, grapes, and what else. Second, as he

---

[15]Wordiness.

[16]A ship that protected the entrance to New York harbor.

[17]Ambrosia.

wondered at the endless replication of his image in the mirrors, second, as he *lost himself in the reflection* that the necessity for an observer makes perfect observation impossible, better make him eighteen at least, yet that would render other things unlikely, he heard Peter and Magda chuckling somewhere together in the maze. "Here!" "No, here!" they shouted to each other; Peter said, "Where's Amby?" Magda murmured. "Amb?" Peter called. In a pleased, friendly voice. He didn't reply. The truth was, his brother was a *happy-go-lucky youngster* who'd've been better off with a regular brother of his own, but who seldom complained of his lot and was generally cordial. Ambrose's throat ached; there aren't enough different ways to say that. He stood quietly while the two young people giggled and thumped through the glittering maze, hurrah'd their discovery of its exit, cried out in joyful alarm at what next beset them. Then he set his mouth and followed after, as he supposed, took a wrong turn, strayed into the pass *wherein he lingers yet.*

The action of conventional dramatic narrative may be represented by a diagram called Freitag's Triangle[18]:

or more accurately by a variant of that diagram:

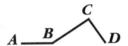

in which *AB* represents the exposition, *B* the introduction of conflict, *BC* the "rising action," complication, or development of the conflict, *C* the climax, or turn of the action, *CD* the dénouement, or resolution of the conflict. While there is no reason to regard this pattern as an absolute necessity, like many other conventions it became conventional because great numbers of people over many years learned by trial and error that it was effective; one ought not to forsake it, therefore, unless one wishes to forsake as well the effect of drama or has clear cause to feel that deliberate violation of the "normal" pattern can better can better effect that effect. This can't go on much longer; it can go on forever. He died telling stories to himself in the dark; years later, when that vast unsuspected area of the funhouse came to light, the first expedition found his skeleton in one of its labyrinthine corridors and mistook it for part of the entertainment. He died of starvation telling himself stories in the dark; but unbeknownst unbeknownst to him, an assistant operator of the funhouse, happening to overhear him, crouched just behind the plyboard partition and wrote down his every word. The operator's daughter, an exquisite young woman with a figure unusually well developed for her age, crouched just behind the partition and transcribed his every word. Though she had never laid eyes on him, she recognized that here was one of Western Culture's truly great imaginations, the eloquence of whose suffering would be an inspiration to unnumbered. And her heart was torn between her love for the

---

[18]Named after Gustav Freytag (1816–1895), a German critic who analyzed narrative conventions.

misfortunate young man (yes, she loved him, though she had never laid though she knew him only — but how well! — through his words, and the deep, calm voice in which he spoke them) between her love et cetera and her womanly intuition that only in suffering and isolation could he give voice et cetera. Lone dark dying. Quietly she kissed the rough plyboard, and a tear fell upon the page. Where she had written in shorthand *Where she had written in shorthand* Where she had written in shorthand *Where she* et cetera. A long time ago we should have passed the apex of Freitag's Triangle and made brief work of the *dénouement;* the plot doesn't rise by meaningful steps but winds upon itself, digresses, retreats, hesitates, sighs, collapses, expires. The climax of the story must be its protagonist's discovery of a way to get through the funhouse. But he has found none, may have ceased to search.

What relevance does the war have to the story? Should there be fireworks outside or not?

Ambrose wandered, languished, dozed. Now and then he fell into his habit of rehearsing to himself the unadventurous story of his life, narrated from the third-person point of view, from his earliest memory parenthesis of maple leaves stirring in the summer breath of tidewater Maryland end of parenthesis to the present moment. Its principal events, on this telling, would appear to have been *A, B, C,* and *D.*

He imagined himself years hence, successful, married, at ease in the world, the trials of his adolescence far behind him. He has come to the seashore with his family for the holiday: how Ocean City has changed! But at one seldom at one ill-frequented end of the boardwalk a few derelict amusements survive from times gone by: the great carrousel from the turn of the century, with its monstrous griffins and mechanical concert band; the roller coaster rumored since 1916 to have been condemned; the mechanical shooting gallery in which only the image of our enemies changed. His own son laughs with Fat May and wants to know what a funhouse is; Ambrose hugs the sturdy lad close and smiles around his pipestem at his wife.

The family's going home. Mother sits between Father and Uncle Karl, who teases him good-naturedly who chuckles over the fact that the comrade with whom he'd fought his way shoulder to shoulder through the funhouse had turned out to be a blind Negro girl — to their mutual discomfort, as they'd opened their souls. But such are the walls of custom, which even. Whose arm is where? How must it feel. He dreams of a funhouse vaster by far than any yet constructed; but by then they may be out of fashion, like steamboats and excursion trains. Already quaint and seedy: the draperied ladies on the frieze of the carrousel are his father's father's mooncheeked dreams; if he thinks of it more he will vomit his apple-on-a-stick.

He wonders: will he become a regular person? Something has gone wrong; his vaccination didn't take; at the Boy-Scout initiation campfire he only pretended to be deeply moved, as he pretends to this hour that it is not so bad after all in the funhouse, and that he has a little limp. How long will it last? He envisions a truly astonishing funhouse, incredibly complex yet utterly controlled from a great central switchboard like the console of a pipe organ. Nobody had enough imagination. He could design such a place himself, wiring and all, and he's only thirteen years old. He would be its operator: panel lights would show what was up in every cranny of its cunning of its multifarious vastness; a switch-flick would ease this fellow's way, complicate that's, to balance things out; if anyone seemed lost or frightened, all the operator had to do was.

He wishes he had never entered the funhouse. But he has. Then he wishes he were dead. But he's not. Therefore he will construct funhouses for others and be their secret operator — though he would rather be among the lovers for whom funhouses are designed.

(1967)

QUESTIONS

1. The implied author presents the framework of a conventional story among the metafictional fragments and interruptions. How much of that conventional story can you reconstruct? Is it more or less interesting than the text as printed? Why?

2. Because this short story has both narrative and essayistic passages, it might be said to have both a narrator and an essayist. How are the two related to one another? To the implied author? Are they both reliable?

3. Much of the short story is concerned with an adolescent's discoveries about sex. How is that theme related, if at all, to the concern with storytelling structures and techniques?

4. One way to become aware of the gender politics of a fiction is to imagine it with the sexes reversed: change Ambrose into a girl, Magda into a handsome boy, Peter into an older sister, Uncle Karl into Aunt Karla, and so on. How would the story be changed? What if you left the characters as is, but used Magda as the filter character?

5. Some critics argue that the funhouse is a metaphor for fiction. When you read the story, is your perspective closer to that of the "lovers for whom funhouses are designed" or that of the "secret operator"? Is there any fun in being the operator?

❖ JULIO CORTÁZAR
The Idol of the Cyclades*

Julio Cortázar (1914–1984) was born, of Argentinean parents, in Brussels but educated at Buenos Aires University. He taught French literature in Argentina, managed a publishing association, and did translating until the rightist dictatorship took over in the 1950s, when he moved to Paris. There he worked as a free-lance translator for UNESCO to supplement his literary royalties. He became increasingly anti-Peronist, to the point of writing a novel — A Manual for Manuel — which has been described as "a primer on the necessity of revolutionary action." Cortázar's fiction is as excitingly experimental as it is politically radical. Novels that have been translated into English include The Winners (1960), Hopscotch (1963), '62: A Model Kit (1968), A Manual for Manuel (1978), and A Certain Lucas (1984). His stories appear in such collections as Cronopias and Fumas (1962), All Fires the Fire (1966), End of the Game (1967), Blow-Up (1968, whose title story informed Antonioni's famous film of that name), A Change of Light (1980), and We Love Glenda So Much (1983). Cortázar also published important nonfiction, particularly on political subjects.

"It strikes me the same whether you listen to me or not," Somoza said. "That's how it is, and it seems only fair to me that you know that."

Morand was startled, as though he'd come back from very far off. He remembered that before he'd been drowsing in a half-dream, it had occurred to him that Somoza was going crazy.

"Forgive me, I was distracted for a moment," he said. "Will you concede that all this . . . Anyway, to get here and find you in the middle of . . ."

But that Somoza was going crazy, to take that for granted was too easy.

"That's right, there are no words for it," Somoza said. "At least in our words."

They looked at one another for a second, and Morand was the first to avert his eyes while Somoza's voice rose again in that impersonal tone typical of these explanations which, the next moment, went beyond all intelligibility. Morand chose not to look at him, but then fell again into a helpless contemplation of the small statue set upon the column, and it was like a return to that golden afternoon of cigar smoke and the smell of herbs when, incredibly, Somoza and he had dug her up out of the island. He remembered how Teresa, a few yards off stretched out on a boulder from which she was trying to make out the coastline of Paros, had whirled around hearing Somoza's cry, and after a second's hesitation had run toward them, forgetting that she had the upper half of her red bikini in her hand. She had leaned over the excavation out of which Somoza's hand sprang with the statuette almost unrecognizable under its moldiness and chalk deposits, until Morand, angry and laughing at the same moment, yelled at her to cover herself, and Teresa stood up staring at him as if she had not

*Translated by Paul Blackburn.

340

understood, suddenly turned her back on them and hid her breasts between her hands while Somoza handed the statuette up to Morand and jumped out of the pit. Nearly without transition Morand remembered the hours that followed, the night in the big camping tents on the banks of the rushing stream, Teresa's shadow walking in the moonlight under the olives, and it was as though Somoza's voice now, echoing monotonously in the almost-empty studio with its sculptures, would come to him again out of that night, making part of his memory, when Somoza had confusedly intimated his ridiculous hopes to him, and he, between two swallows of retsina,[1] had laughed happily and had accused him of being a phony archaeologist and an incurable poet.

"There are no words for it," Somoza had just said. "At least in our words."

In the great tent at the bottom of the Skyros valley, his hands had held the statuette up and caressed it so as to end by stripping it of its false clothes, time and oblivion (Teresa among the olives was still infuriated by Morand's reproach, by his stupid prejudices), and the night turned slowly while Somoza confided to him his senseless hope that someday he would be able to approach the statue by ways other than the hands and the eyes of science; meanwhile the wine and tobacco mixed into the conversation with the crickets and the waters of the stream until there was nothing left but a confused sense of not being able to understand one another. Later, when Somoza had gone back to his tent carrying the statuette with him, and Teresa got tired of being by herself and came back to lie down, Morand talked with her about Somoza's daydreams, and they asked one another with that amiable Parisian irony if everyone from the Río de la Plata had such a simple-minded imagination. Before going to sleep, they discussed what had taken place that afternoon, until, finally, Teresa accepted Morand's excuses, finally kissed him, and everything was as usual on the island, everywhere, it was he and she and the night overhead and the long oblivion.

"Anyone else know about it?" Morand asked.

"No. You and I. Seems to me that was right," Somoza said. "These last months, I've hardly stepped out of here. At first there was an old woman came to clean up the studio and wash my clothes for me, but she got on my nerves."

"It seems incredible that one could live like this in the suburbs of Paris. The silence . . . Listen, at least you have to go down to the town to do the shopping."

"Before, yes, I told you already. Now nothing's missing. Everything that's necessary's here."

Morand looked in the direction that Somoza's finger pointed, past the statuette and the reproductions abandoned on the shelves. He saw wood, whitewash, stone, hammers, dust, the shadow of trees against the windows. The finger seemed to indicate a corner of the studio where nothing was, hardly a dirty rag on the floor.

But these last two years very little had changed between them, there'd also been a far corner emptied of time, with a dirty rag which was like all they had not said to one another and which perhaps they should have said. The island expedition, a romantic and crazy idea conceived on a café terrace on the boulevard Saint-Michel, had ended as soon as they discovered the idol in the valley ruins. Perhaps the fear that they would be found out finished off the cheerfulness of the first few weeks, and the day came finally when Morand intercepted a glance of Somoza's while the three of them were going down to the beach, and that night he discussed it with Teresa and they decided to come back as early as possible, because they guessed that Somoza, and it seemed to them almost unfair, that he was beginning — so unexpectedly — to be falling for her. In Paris, they continued to see one another at great intervals, almost always for professional reasons, but Morand went to the appointments alone. Somoza asked after Teresa the first time, but afterward she seemed to be of no importance to him. Everything that they should have been saying weighed heavily between the two, perhaps the three of them. Morand agreed that Somoza should keep the statuette for a while. It would be impossible to sell it before a couple of years anyway; Marcos, the man who knew a colonel who was acquainted with an Athens customs official, had imposed the time-lapse as a condition of allowing himself to be bribed. Somoza took the statue to his apartment, and Morand saw it each time that they met. It was never suggested that sometimes Somoza visit Morand and his wife, like so many other things they did not mention any more and which at bottom were always Teresa. Somoza seemed to be completely occupied with his *idée fixe*,[2] and if once in a while he invited Morand to come back to his apartment for a cognac, there was nothing more to it than that. Nothing very extraordinary, after all Morand knew very well Somoza's tastes for certain marginal literatures, just as he was put off by Somoza's longing. The thing that surprised him most was the fanaticism of that hope which emerged during those hours of almost automatic confidences, and when he felt his own presence as highly unnecessary, the repeated caressing of the beautiful and expressionless statue's little body, repeating the spells in a monotone until it became tiresome, the same formulas of passage. As seen by Morand, Somoza's obsession was susceptible to analysis: in some sense, every archaeologist identifies himself with the past he explores and brings to light. From that point to believing that intimacy with one of those vestiges could alienate, alter time and space, open a fissure whereby one could comply with . . . Somoza never used that kind of vocabulary; what he said was always more or less than that, a haphazard language full of allusions and exorcisms moving from obstinate and irreducible levels. For that reason, then, he had begun to work clumsily on replicas of the statuette; Morand had managed to see the first of them even before Somoza had left Paris, and he listened with a friendly courtesy to those stiffheaded commonplaces re: the repetition of gesture and situation as a way of abrogation, Somoza's cocksureness that his obstinate approach would come to identify itself with the initial structure, with a superimposition which would be more than that because, as yet, there was no duality, just fusion, primordial contact (not his words, but Morand had to translate them in some way, later, when he reconstructed them for Teresa). Contact which, Somoza finally said, had been established forty-eight hours before, on the night of the summer solstice.

"All right," Morand admitted, lighting another cigarette, "but I'd be happy if you could explain to me why you're so sure that . . . okay, that you've gotten to the bottom of it."

"Explain? . . . don't you see it?"

He stretched out his hand once more toward a castle in the air, to a corner of the loft; it described an arc which included the roof and the statuette set on its thin column of marble, enveloped in the brilliant cone of light from the reflector. Incon-

---

[2]Obsession [French].

gruously enough, Morand remembered that Teresa had crossed the frontier, carrying the statuette hidden in the toy chest Marcos had made in a basement in Placca.

"It couldn't be that it wasn't going to happen," Somoza said almost childishly. "I was getting a little bit closer every replica I made. The form was becoming familiar to me. I want to say that . . . Ah, it would take days to explain it to you . . . and the absurd thing is that there everything comes in one . . . But when it's this . . ."

His hand waved about, came and went, marking out the *that* and the *this*.

"The truth of the matter is that you've managed to become a sculptor," Morand said, hearing himself speak and it sounding stupid. "The last two replicas are perfect. Whenever you get around to letting me keep the statue, I'll never know if you've given me the original or not."

"I'll never give her to you," Somoza said simply. "And don't think that I've forgotten that she belongs to both of us. But I'll never give her to you. The only thing I would have wished is that Teresa and you had stayed with me, had matched me. Yes, I would have liked it had you been with me the evening it came."

It was the first time in almost two years that Morand had heard him mention Teresa, as if until that moment she had been somehow dead for him, but his manner of naming Teresa was hopelessly antique, it was Greece that morning when they'd gone down to the beach. Poor Somoza. Still. Poor madman. But even more strange was to ask oneself why, at the last minute, before getting into the car after Somoza's telephone call, he had felt it necessary to call Teresa at her office to ask her to meet them later at the studio. He would have to ask her about it later, to know what Teresa had been thinking while she listened to his instructions on how to get to the solitary summerhouse on the hill. He'd have Teresa repeat exactly, word for word, what she'd heard him say. Silently Morand damned this mania for systems which made him reconstitute life as though he were restoring a Greek vase for the museum, glueing the tiniest particles with minute care, and Somoza's voice there, mixed with the coming and going gestures of his hands which also seemed to want to glue pieces of air, putting together a transparent vase, his hands which pointed out the statuette, obliging Morand to look once more against his will at that white lunar body, a kind of insect antedating all history, worked under inconceivable circumstances by someone inconceivably remote, thousands of years ago, even further back, the dizzying distances of the animal, of the leap, vegetal rites alternating with tides and syzygies and seasons of rut and humdrum ceremonies of propitiation, the expressionless face where only the line of the nose broke its blind mirror of insupportable tension, the breasts hardly visible, the triangle of the sex and the arms crossed over the belly, embracing it, the idol of beginnings, the primeval terror under the rites from time immemorial, the hatchet of stone from the immolations on the altars high on the hills. It was enough to make him believe that he also was turning into an imbecile, as if being an archaeologist were not sufficient.

"Please," said Morand, "couldn't you make some effort to explain to me even though you believe that none of it can be explained? The only thing I'm definitely sure of is that you've spent these months carving replicas, and that two nights ago . . ."

"It's so simple," Somoza said, "I've always felt that the flesh was still in contact with the other. But I had to retrace five thousand years of wrong roads. Curious that they themselves, the descendants of the Aegeans, were guilty of that mistake. But nothing's important now. *Look, it goes like this.*"

Close to the idol, he raised one hand and laid it gently over the breasts and the belly. The other caressed the neck, went up to the statue's absent mouth, and Morand heard Somoza speaking in a stifled and opaque voice, a little as if it were his hands or perhaps that nonexistent mouth, they that were speaking of the hunt in the caverns of smoke, of the number of deer in the pen, of the name which had to be spoken only afterwards, of the circle of blue grease, of the swing of the double rivers, of Pohk's childhood, of the procession to the eastern steps and the high ones in the accursed shadows. He wondered if, in one of Somoza's lapses of attention, he could manage to telephone and reach Teresa and warn her to bring Dr. Vernet with her. But Teresa would already have started and be on the way, and at the edge of the rocks where The Many was roaring, the master of the greens struck off the left horn of the handsomest buck and was handing it to the master of those who guarded the salt, to renew the pact with Haghesa.

"Listen, let me breathe," Morand said, rising and taking a step forward. "It's fabulous, and furthermore I have a terrible thirst. Let's drink something, I can go out and get a . . ."

"The whiskey is there," said Somoza, slowly removing his hands from the statue. "I shall not drink, I must fast before the sacrifice."

"Pity," Morand said, looking for the bottle. "I hate to drink alone. What sacrifice?"

He poured a whiskey up to the brim of the glass.

"That of the union, to use your words. Don't you hear them? The double flute, like the one on the statuette we saw in the Athens Museum. The sound of life on the left, and that of discord on the right. Discord is also life for Haghesa, but when the sacrifice is completed, the flutists cease to blow into the pipe on the right and one will hear only the piping of the new life that drinks the spilt blood. And the flutists will fill their mouths with blood and blow on the left pipe, and I shall anoint her face with blood, you see, like this, and the eyes shall appear and the mouth beneath the blood."

"Stop talking nonsense," Morand said, taking a good slug of the whiskey. "Blood would not go very well with our marble doll. Yeah, it's hot."

Somoza had taken off his smock with a leisurely and deliberate movement. When he saw that he was unbuttoning his trousers, Morand told himself that he had been wrong to let him get excited, in consenting to this explosion of his mania. Austere and brown, Somoza drew himself up erect and naked under the light of the reflector and seemed to lose himself in contemplation of a point in space. From a corner of his half-open mouth there fell a thread of spittle and Morand, setting the glass down quickly on the floor, figured that to get to the door he had to trick him in some way. He never found out where the stone hatchet had come from which was swinging in Somoza's hand. He understood.

"That was thoughtful," he said backing away slowly. "The pact with Haghesa, eh? And poor Morand's going to donate the blood, you're sure of that?"

Without looking at him, Somoza began to move toward him delineating an arc of a circle, as if he were following a precharted course.

"If you really want to kill me," Morand shouted at him, backing into the darkened area, "why this big scene? Both of us know perfectly well it's over Teresa. But what good's it going to do you, she's never loved you and she'll never love you!"

The naked body was already moving out of the circle illuminated by the reflector. Hidden in the shadows of the corner, Morand stepped on the wet rags on the floor and figured he couldn't go further back. He saw the hatchet lifted and he jumped as Nagashi had taught him at the gym in the place des Ternes. Somoza caught the toe-kick in the center of his thigh and the nishi hack on the left side of his neck. The hatchet came down on a diagonal, too far out, and Morand resiliently heaved back the torso which toppled against him, and caught the defenseless wrist. Somoza was still a muffled, dull yell when the cutting edge of the hatchet caught him in the center of his forehead.

Before turning to look at him, Morand vomited in the corner of the loft, all over the dirty rags. He felt emptied, and vomiting made him feel better. He picked the glass up off the floor and drank what was left of the whiskey, thinking Teresa was going to arrive any minute and that he had to do something, call the police, make some explanation. While he was dragging Somoza's body back into the full light of the reflector, he was thinking that it should not be difficult to show that he had acted in self-defense. Somoza's eccentricities, his seclusion from the world, his evident madness. Crouching down, he soaked his hands in the blood running from the face and scalp of the dead man, checking his wrist watch at the same time, twenty of eight. Teresa would not be long now, better to go out and wait for her in the garden or in the street, to spare her the sight of the idol with its face dripping with blood, the tiny red threads that glided past the neck, slipped around the breasts, joined in the delicate triangle of the sex, ran down the thighs. The hatchet was sunk deep into the skull of the sacrifice, and Morand pulled it out, holding it up between his sticky hands. He shoved the corpse a bit more with his foot, leaving it finally up next to the column, sniffed the air and went over to the door. Better open it so that Teresa could come in. Leaning the hatchet up against the door, he began to strip off his clothes, because it was getting hot and smelled stuffy, the caged herd. He was naked already when he heard the noise of the taxi pulling up and Teresa's voice dominating the sound of the flutes; he put the light out and waited, hatchet in hand, behind the door, licking the cutting edge of the hatchet lightly and thinking that Teresa was punctuality itself.

(1967)

QUESTIONS

1. "The Idol of the Cyclades" clearly turns on effects of suspense and surprise. Where and how are these introduced? How does the implied author prepare us for them?

2. Imagine the short story with Morand as a first-person narrator. How would that change affect the short story, especially the character's filter and the narrator's slant?

3. Even if you did not know that "Continuity of Parks" and "Idol of the

Cyclades" were by the same real author, might you guess so? How? Try to frame your answer in terms of the implied author.

4. Are "Continuity of Parks" and "Idol of the Cyclades" simply fictional experiments or do they convey some deeper themes? If so, what are they?

5. The short story ends as Morand's perceptual capacity has already been infected. Extend the short story by writing a few paragraphs that show the cognitive or higher intellectual centers of his brain being attacked. Try to preserve the flavor of the style of the original.

SUGGESTIONS FOR WRITING

1. An oral storyteller can talk directly to an audience and even incorporate the audience in the story. A writer can do neither of those things. Can you imagine an experiment in written fiction that might be equivalent to the experience of live audiences and narrators?

2. One of the common devices in experimental fiction is paradox: making two assertions that can't both be true. Are there any real-life situations best described through a paradox? If so, can this kind of experiment be an attempt at realism?

3. Recount a metafictional or experiential narrative that you have read or seen recently, for example, on MTV. Explain how it deviates from conventional narrative practice.

4. Metafictional devices often call attention to a story's frame. Sometimes there are multiple frames: storytellers telling stories about storytelling. Why would frames or other technical aspects of fiction be worth this kind of attention?

5. Read an experimental story such as "Kew Gardens" and then go back and reread a more traditional story. Did reading the experimental story make you more aware of the conventions and literary devices in the traditional narrative? Do you see any metafictional elements that you might not have been aware of before?

Further Reading

Me and Miss Mandible

Donald Barthelme (1931–1989) was raised in Houston, Texas. He wrote poetry and fiction in high school. At the University of Houston he edited the school newspaper and frequently contributed film reviews. He was the director of the Contemporary Arts Museum in Houston and then went to New York where he edited the journal *Location*. Later he returned to the University of Houston as Cullen Distinguished Professor of English. In a style that is at once surrealistic and comic, Barthelme wrote four novels—*Snow White* (1967), *The Dead Father* (1975), *Paradise* (1987), and a reworking of the Arthurian legend, *The King* (1990). He is even better known for his short stories, many of which first appeared in the *New Yorker*. Barthelme's short stories were printed or reprinted in *Come Back, Dr. Caligari* (1964, which contained "Me and Miss Mandible"), *Unspeakable Practices, Unnatural Acts* (1968), *City Life* (1970), *Sadness* (1972), *Amateurs* (1976), *Great Days* (1976), *Sixty Stories* (1981), *Overnight to Many Distant Cities* (1983), and *Forty Stories* (1987). He also wrote fiction for children: *The Slightly Irregular Fire Engine* (1971). Some of his nonfiction is included in a volume entitled *Guilty Pleasures* (1974).

13 September

Miss Mandible wants to make love to me but she hesitates because I am officially a child; I am, according to the records, according to the gradebook on her desk, according to the card index in the principal's office, eleven years old. There is a misconception here, one that I haven't quite managed to get cleared up yet. I am in fact thirty-five, I've been in the Army, I am six feet one, I have hair in the appropriate places, my voice is a baritone, I know very well what to do with Miss Mandible if she ever makes up her mind.

In the meantime we are studying common fractions. I could, of course, answer all the questions, or at least most of them (there are things I don't remember). But I prefer to sit in this too-small seat with the desktop cramping my thighs and examine the life around me. There are thirty-two in the class, which is launched every morning with the pledge of allegiance to the flag. My own allegiance, at the moment, is divided between Miss Mandible and Sue Ann Brownly, who sits across the aisle from me all day long and is, like Miss Mandible, a fool for love. Of the two I prefer, today, Sue Ann; although between eleven and eleven and a half (she refuses to reveal her exact age) she is clearly a woman, with a woman's disguised aggression and a woman's peculiar contradictions.

15 September

Happily our geography text, which contains maps of all the principal land-masses of the world, is large enough to conceal my clandestine journal-keeping, accomplished in an ordinary black composition book. Every day I must wait until Geography to put down such thoughts as I may have had during the morning about my situation and my fellows. I have tried writing at other times and it does not work. Either the teacher is walking up and down the aisles (during this period, luckily, she sticks close to the map rack in the front of the room) or Bobby Vanderbilt, who sits behind me, is punching me in the kidneys and wanting to know what I am doing. Vanderbilt, I have found out from certain desultory conversations on the playground, is hung up on sports cars, a veteran consumer of *Road & Track*. This explains the continual roaring sounds which seem to emanate from his desk; he is reproducing a record album called *Sounds of Sebring*.

19 September

Only I, at times (only at times), understand that somehow a mistake has been made, that I am in a place where I don't belong. It may be that Miss Mandible also knows this, at some level, but for reasons not fully understood by me she is going along with the game. When I was first assigned to this room I wanted to protest, the error seemed obvious, the stupidest principal could have seen it; but I have come to believe it was deliberate, that I have been betrayed again.

Now it seems to make little difference. This life-role is as interesting as my former life-role, which was that of a claims adjuster for the Great Northern Insurance Company, a position which compelled me to spend my time amid the debris of our civilization: rumpled fenders, roofless sheds, gutted warehouses, smashed arms and legs. After ten years of this one has a tendency to see the world as a vast junkyard, looking at a man and seeing only his (potentially) mangled parts, entering a house only to trace the path of the inevitable fire. Therefore when I was installed here, although I knew an error had been made, I countenanced it, I was shrewd; I was aware that there might well be some kind of advantage to be gained from what seemed a disaster. The role of The Adjuster teaches one much.

22 September

I am being solicited for the volleyball team. I decline, refusing to take unfair profit from my height.

23 September

Every morning the roll is called: Bestvina, Bokenfohr, Broan, Brownly, Cone, Coyle, Crecelius, Darin, Durbin, Geiger, Guiswite, Heckler, Jacobs, Kleinschmidt, Lay, Logan, Masei, Mitgang, Pfeilsticker. It is like the litany chanted in the dim miserable dawns of Texas by the cadre sergeant of our basic training company.

In the Army, too, I was ever so slightly awry. It took me a fantastically long time to realize what the others grasped almost at once: that much of what we were doing was absolutely pointless, to no purpose. I kept wondering why. Then something happened that proposed a new question. One day we were commanded to whitewash, from the ground to the topmost leaves, all of the trees in our training area. The corporal who relayed the order was nervous and apologetic. Later an off-duty captain sauntered by and watched us, white-splashed and totally weary, strung out among the freakish shapes we had created. He walked away swearing. I understood the principle (orders are orders), but I wondered: Who decides?

29 September

Sue Ann is a wonder. Yesterday she viciously kicked my ankle for not paying attention when she was attempting to pass me a note during History. It is swollen still. But Miss Mandible was watching me, there was nothing I could do. Oddly enough Sue Ann reminds me of the wife I had in my former role, while Miss Mandible seems to be a child. She watches me constantly, trying to keep sexual significance out of her look; I am afraid the other children have noticed. I have already heard, on that ghostly frequency that is the medium of classroom communication, the words *"Teacher's pet!"*

2 October

Sometimes I speculate on the exact nature of the conspiracy which brought me here. At times I believe it was instigated by my wife of former days, whose name was . . . I am only pretending to forget. I know her name very well, as well as I know the name of my former motor oil (Quaker State) or my old Army serial number (US 54109268). Her name was Brenda.

7 October

Today I tiptoed up to Miss Mandible's desk (when there was no one else in the room) and examined its surface. Miss Mandible is a clean-desk teacher, I discovered. There was nothing except her gradebook (the one in which I exist as a sixth-grader) and a text, which was open at a page headed *Making the Processes Meaningful.* I read: "Many pupils enjoy working fractions when they understand what they are doing. They have confidence in their ability to take the right steps and to obtain correct answers. However, to give the subject full social significance, it is necessary that many realistic situations requiring the processes be found. Many interesting and lifelike problems involving the use of fractions should be solved . . ."

8 October

I am not irritated by the feeling of having been through all this before. Things are done differently now. The children, moreover, are in some ways different from those who accompanied me on my first voyage through the elementary schools: *"They have confidence in their ability to take the right steps and to obtain correct answers."* This is surely true. When Bobby Vanderbilt, who sits behind me and has the great tactical advantage of being able to maneuver in my disproportionate shadow, wishes to bust a classmate in the mouth he first asks Miss Mandible to lower the blind, saying that the sun hurts his eyes. When she does so, *bip!* My generation would never have been able to con authority so easily.

13 October

I misread a clue. Do not misunderstand me: it was a tragedy only from the point of view of the authorities. I conceived that it was my duty to obtain satisfaction for the injured, for an elderly lady (not even one of our policyholders, but a claimant against Big Ben Transfer & Storage, Inc.) from the company. The settlement was

$165,000; the claim, I still believe, was just. But without my encouragement Mrs. Bichek would never have had the self-love to prize her injury so highly. The company paid, but its faith in me, in my efficacy in the role, was broken. Henry Goodykind, the district manager, expressed this thought in a few not altogether unsympathetic words, and told me at the same time that I was to have a new role. The next thing I knew I was here, at Horace Greeley Elementary, under the lubricious eye of Miss Mandible.

17 October

Today we are to have a fire drill. I know this because I am a Fire Marshal, not only for our room but for the entire right wing of the second floor. This distinction, which was awarded shortly after my arrival, is interpreted by some as another mark of my somewhat dubious relations with our teacher. My armband, which is red and decorated with white felt letters reading FIRE, sits on the little shelf under my desk, next to the brown paper bag containing the lunch I carefully make for myself each morning. One of the advantages of packing my own lunch (I have no one to pack it for me) is that I am able to fill it with things I enjoy. The peanut butter sandwiches that my mother made in my former existence, many years ago, have been banished in favor of ham and cheese. I have found that my diet has mysteriously adjusted to my new situation; I no longer drink, for instance, and when I smoke, it is in the boys' john, like everybody else. When school is out I hardly smoke at all. It is only in the matter of sex that I feel my own true age; this is apparently something that, once learned, can never be forgotten. I live in fear that Miss Mandible will one day keep me after school, and when we are alone, create a compromising situation. To avoid this I have become a model pupil: another reason for the pronounced dislike I have encountered in certain quarters. But I cannot deny that I am singed by those long glances from the vicinity of the chalkboard; Miss Mandible is in many ways, notably about the bust, a very tasty piece.

24 October

There are isolated challenges to my largeness, to my dimly realized position in the class as Gulliver. Most of my classmates are polite about this matter, as they would be if I had only one eye, or wasted, metal-wrapped legs. I am viewed as a mutation of some sort but essentially a peer. However Harry Broan, whose father has made himself rich manufacturing the Broan Bathroom Vent (with which Harry is frequently reproached; he is always being asked how things are in Ventsville), today inquired if I wanted to fight. An interested group of his followers had gathered to observe this suicidal undertaking. I replied that I didn't feel quite up to it, for which he was obviously grateful. We are now friends forever. He has given me to understand privately that he can get me all the bathroom vents I will ever need, at a ridiculously modest figure.

25 October

"*Many interesting and lifelike problems involving the use of fractions should be solved . . .*" The theorists fail to realize that everything that is either interesting or lifelike in the classroom proceeds from what they would probably call interpersonal relations: Sue Ann Brownly kicking me in the ankle. How lifelike, how womanlike, is her tender solicitude after the deed! Her pride in my newly acquired limp is transparent; everyone knows that she has set her mark upon me, that it is a victory in her unequal struggle with Miss Mandible for my great, overgrown heart. Even Miss Mandible knows, and counters in perhaps the only way she can, with sarcasm. "Are you wounded, Joseph?" Conflagrations smolder behind her eyelids, yearning for the Fire Marshal clouds her eyes. I mumble that I have bumped my leg.

30 October

I return again and again to the problem of my future.

4 November

The underground circulating library has brought me a copy of *Movie-TV Secrets*, the multicolor cover blazoned with the headline "Debbie's Date Insults Liz!" It is a gift from Frankie Randolph, a rather plain girl who until today has had not one word for me, passed on via Bobby Vanderbilt. I nod and smile over my shoulder in acknowledgment; Frankie hides her head under her desk. I have seen these magazines being passed around among the girls (sometimes one of the boys will condescend to inspect a particularly lurid cover). Miss Mandible confiscates them whenever she finds one. I leaf through *Movie-TV Secrets* and get an eyeful. "The exclusive picture on these pages isn't what it seems. We know how it looks and we know what the gossipers will do. So in the interests of a nice guy, we're publishing the facts first. Here's what really happened!" The picture shows a rising young movie idol in bed, pajama-ed and bleary-eyed, while an equally blowzy young woman looks startled beside him. I am happy to know that the picture is not really what it seems; it seems to be nothing less than divorce evidence.

What do these hipless eleven-year-olds think when they come across, in the same magazine, the full-page ad for Maurice de Paree, which features "Hip Helpers" or what appear to be padded rumps? ("A real undercover agent that adds appeal to those hips and derriere, both!") If they cannot decipher the language the illustrations leave nothing to the imagination. "Drive him frantic . . ." the copy continues. Perhaps this explains Bobby Vanderbilt's preoccupation with Lancias and Maseratis; it is a defense against being driven frantic.

Sue Ann has observed Frankie Randolph's overture, and catching my eye, she pulls from her satchel no less than seventeen of these magazines, thrusting them at me as if to prove that anything any of her rivals has to offer, she can top. I shuffle through them quickly, noting the broad editorial perspective:

"Debbie's Kids Are Crying"
"Eddie Asks Debbie: Will You . . . ?"
"The Nightmares Liz Has About Eddie!"
"The Things Debbie Can Tell About Eddie"
"The Private Life of Eddie and Liz"
"Debbie Gets Her Man Back?"
"A New Life for Liz"
"Love Is a Tricky Affair"
"Eddie's Taylor-Made Love Nest"
"How Liz Made a Man of Eddie"

"Are They Planning to Live Together?"
"Isn't It Time to Stop Kicking Debbie Around?"
"Debbie's Dilemma"
"Eddie Becomes a Father Again"
"Is Debbie Planning to Re-wed?"
"Can Liz Fulfill Herself?"
"Why Debbie Is Sick of Hollywood"

Who are these people, Debbie, Eddie, Liz, and how did they get themselves in such a terrible predicament? Sue Ann knows, I am sure; it is obvious that she has been studying their history as a guide to what she may expect when she is suddenly freed from this drab, flat classroom.

I am angry and I shove the magazines back at her with not even a whisper of thanks.

5 November

The sixth grade at Horace Greeley Elementary is a furnace of love, love, love. Today it is raining, but inside the air is heavy and tense with passion. Sue Ann is absent; I suspect that yesterday's exchange has driven her to her bed. Guilt hangs about me. She is not responsible, I know, for what she reads, for the models proposed to her by a venal publishing industry; I should not have been so harsh. Perhaps it is only the flu.

Nowhere have I encountered an atmosphere as charged with aborted sexuality as this. Miss Mandible is helpless; nothing goes right today. Amos Darin has been found drawing a dirty picture in the cloakroom. Sad and inaccurate, it was offered not as a sign of something else but as an act of love in itself. It has excited even those who have not seen it, even those who saw but understood only that it was dirty. The room buzzes with imperfectly comprehended titillation. Amos stands by the door, waiting to be taken to the principal's office. He wavers between fear and enjoyment of his temporary celebrity. From time to time Miss Mandible looks at me reproachfully, as if blaming me for the uproar. But I did not create this atmosphere, I am caught in it like all the others.

8 November

Everything is promised my classmates and me, most of all the future. We accept the outrageous assurances without blinking.

9 November

I have finally found the nerve to petition for a larger desk. At recess I can hardly walk; my legs do not wish to uncoil themselves. Miss Mandible says she will take it up with the custodian. She is worried about the excellence of my themes. Have I, she asks, been receiving help? For an instant I am on the brink of telling her my story. Something, however, warns me not to attempt it. Here I am safe, I have a place; I do not wish to entrust myself once more to the whimsy of authority. I resolve to make my themes less excellent in the future.

11 November

A ruined marriage, a ruined adjusting career, a grim interlude in the Army when I was almost not a person. This is the sum of my existence to date, a dismal total. Small wonder that re-education seemed my only hope. It is clear even to me that I need reworking in some fundamental way. How efficient is the society that provides thus for the salvage of its clinkers!

14 November

The distinction between children and adults, while probably useful for some purposes, is at bottom a specious one, I feel. There are only individual egos, crazy for love.

15 November

The custodian has informed Miss Mandible that our desks are all the correct size for sixth-graders, as specified by the Board of Estimate and furnished the schools by the Nu-Art Educational Supply Corporation of Englewood, California. He has pointed out that if the desk size is correct, then the pupil size must be incorrect. Miss Mandible, who has already arrived at this conclusion, refuses to press the matter further. I think I know why. An appeal to the administration might result in my removal from the class, in a transfer to some sort of setup for "exceptional children." This would be a disaster of the first magnitude. To sit in a room with child geniuses (or, more likely, children who are "retarded") would shrivel me in a week. Let my experience here be that of the common run, I say; let me be, please God, typical.

20 November

We read signs as promises. Miss Mandible understands by my great height, by my resonant vowels, that I will one day carry her off to bed. Sue Ann interprets these same signs to mean that I am unique among her male acquaintances, therefore most desirable, therefore her special property as is everything that is Most Desirable. If neither of these propositions works out then life has broken faith with them.

I myself, in my former existence, read the company motto ("Here to Help in Time of Need") as a description of the duty of the adjuster, drastically mislocating the company's deepest concerns. I believed that because I had obtained a wife who was made up of wife-signs (beauty, charm, softness, perfume, cookery) I had found love. Brenda, reading the same signs that have now misled Miss Mandible and Sue Ann Brownly, felt she had been promised that she would never be bored again. All of us, Miss Mandible, Sue Ann, myself, Brenda, Mr. Goodykind, still believe that the American flag betokens a kind of general righteousness.

But I say, looking about me in this incubator of future citizens, that signs are signs, and some of them are lies.

23 November

It may be that my experience as a child will save me after all. If only I can remain quietly in this classroom, making my notes while Napoleon plods through Russia in the droning voice of Harry Broan, reading aloud from our History text. All of the mysteries that perplexed me as an adult have their origins here. But Miss Mandible will not permit me to remain ungrown. Her hands rest on my shoulders too warmly, and for too long.

7 December

It is the pledges that this place makes to me, pledges that cannot be redeemed, that will confuse me later and make me feel I am not *getting anywhere*. Everything is presented as the result of some knowable process; if I wish to arrive at four I get there by way of two and two. If I wish to burn Moscow the route I must travel has already been marked out by another visitor. If, like Bobby Vanderbilt, I yearn for the wheel of the Lancia 2.4-liter coupé, I have only to go through the appropriate process, that is, get the money. And if it is money itself that I desire, I have only to make it. All of these goals are equally beautiful in the sight of the Board of Estimate; the proof is all around us, in the no-nonsense ugliness of this steel and glass building, in the straightline matter-of-factness with which Miss Mandible handles some of our less reputable wars. Who points out that arrangements sometimes slip, that errors are made, that signs are misread? *"They have confidence in their ability to take the right steps and to obtain correct answers."*

8 December

My enlightenment is proceeding wonderfully.

9 December

Disaster once again. Tomorrow I am to be sent to a doctor, for observation. Sue Ann Brownly caught Miss Mandible and me in the cloakroom, during recess, Miss Mandible's naked legs in a scissors around my waist. For a moment I thought Sue Ann was going to choke. She ran out of the room weeping, straight for the principal's office, certain now which of us was Debbie, which Eddie, which Liz. I am sorry to be the cause of her disillusionment, but I know that she will recover. Miss Mandible is ruined but fulfilled. Although she will be charged with contributing to the delinquency of a minor, she seems at peace; *her* promise has been kept. She knows now that everything she has been told about life, about America, is true.

I have tried to convince the school authorities that I am a minor only in a very special sense, that I am in fact mostly to blame — but it does no good. They are as dense as ever. My contemporaries are astounded that I present myself as anything other than an innocent victim. Like the Old Guard marching through the Russian drifts, the class marches to the conclusion that truth is punishment.

Bobby Vanderbilt has given me his copy of *Sounds of Sebring*, in farewell.

(1964)

❖ ANN BEATTIE
A Reasonable Man

Ann Beattie (1947–) was born and raised in the Washington, D.C., area. She studied at American University and the University of Connecticut, where she did graduate work. She has taught at Connecticut, Harvard, and Virginia. Beattie is a graphic reporter of the trials and tribulations of the generations of the sixties and seventies—their experiments with dope and sex, with dropping out, with communal living, and the like. As one critic puts it, she specializes in the "inconclusive." Her novels include *Chilly Scenes of Winter* (1976, which was made into a film of the same name), *Falling in Place* (1980), *Love Always* (1985), and *Picturing Will* (1989). Her many short stories, published in such magazines as *Atlantic Monthly* and *The New Yorker* appear in the collections *Distortions* (1976), *Secrets and Surprises* (1979, which contains "A Reasonable Man"), *The Burning House* (1982), *Where You'll Find Me* (1986), and *What Was Mine* (1991). She has also published a children's book, *Spectacles* (1985), and a collection of essays on art, *Alex Katz* (1987).

She is waiting for the telephone to ring. It has not rung for at least six days, which is most unusual. Usually there would be a wrong number, or some sort of salesman trying to sell something she had never considered buying or that she did not know existed. In fact, it might be more than six days. At first she may not have been conscious that the phone was not ringing. You don't notice something being absent for a day or two: a mislaid pen, clouds. It may well not have rung for quite some time.

She tells the man this at dinner, remarking on how unusual it is. The man likes to know exactly why she mentions things because he often cannot follow her. So she is in the habit, now, of mentioning something and commenting on it, explaining why she mentioned it at all. Of course, this is often more trouble than it's worth, so their dinners are sometimes silent from beginning to end. They are good dinners. She is competent in that area. A home economics major, she fixes dinners that are not only good to eat, but balanced and nutritious. They rarely have colds. They have never had a major illness. Tonight they eat cream of asparagus soup, a salad of beans and pears on chopped lettuce, broiled chicken with mushrooms, a glass of white wine and baked custard.

"For heaven's sake," the man says. "It might have rung when you were out getting groceries. If you had been downstairs, it might have rung and you wouldn't have heard it." He raises a single green bean to his lips. She smiles at him. He chews, swallows and smiles. Everything he says is logical. She follows perfectly. She does not believe that the phone rang when she was out buying groceries, and anyway, she bought groceries three days ago. She was not downstairs today, or yesterday. She frowns. Did she go down there yesterday? He lifts another piece of food to his mouth.

356

He notices that she is frowning. "You see that, don't you?" he says. Of course. She understands everything the man says.

The phone has not rung for seven days — assuming that it will not ring tonight. In a novel she is very fond of the main character tries to bring on her period by sleeping in white, on fresh bed sheets. She tries to think what she could do to make the phone ring. Perhaps make love to the man. That may be a little difficult, though, because he is still at a meeting and will be tired and hungry when he comes home. She will feed him and then seduce him. Another thing she might try, if this doesn't work, is showering.

The man comes home. He looks as though he has been in a windstorm. He confirms that it is very windy out. "Look," he says, pointing her toward the kitchen window. Leaves that they did not rake up during the winter blow across the yard. She is so glad! Usually her procrastination results in nothing good, but there are the leaves, blowing through the air and across the grass, which is already turning green.

"Didn't you go out today?" the man asks.

"No. I didn't go anywhere. I didn't have anywhere to go."

"But you went out yesterday, I presume."

"Yesterday?" (She is not a good liar.)

He nods again.

"I don't think I went out yesterday. No."

He sighs heavily. Seducing him will not be easy.

He brightens a bit at the table when she serves him marinated herring. He likes fish very much. The main course is beef stew, which he also seems to enjoy. They have oranges for dessert, coffee with milk.

"Tomorrow I guess you'll be going out to do some errands," he says. "Would you take my gray suit to the cleaners, please?"

"Certainly," she says. She will tell him that she forgot. That will work for one day. But the day after tomorrow she will have to go to the cleaners. That might not be so bad: the phone might ring tomorrow, and then the next day she would have no reason to wait home because the phone would have rung recently. She smiles.

"Aren't you going to answer me?" he says.

"I did answer. I said I would."

He looks at her blankly. His eyes are blank, but his mouth is a little tight.

"I didn't hear you," he says, with syrupy graciousness.

She thinks that she, too, might have a hearing problem. After dinner, alone in the kitchen, she puts down the dishtowel and goes to the phone, puts her ear against it. Shouldn't it hum like the refrigerator when it isn't ringing? There is always some slight noise, isn't there? She's had insomnia in the past and felt as though there were a war going on in the house, it was so noisy. The faint hum of electrical appliances, the glow in the little box in back of the television when it's not on. There must be something wrong with her hearing, or with the phone.

The next day she goes to the cleaners. There's a way to make the phone ring! Go out and leave it and surely it will ring in the empty house. She is not as happy as she might be about this, though, for the obvious reason that she will not have the satisfaction of hearing the phone. Driving home, she tries to remember the last phone conversation she had. She can't. It might have been with her neighbor, or with some salesman . . . a relative? If she kept a journal, she could check on this. Maybe now is the time to keep a journal. That way she could just flip back through the pages and check on details she has forgotten. She parks the car and goes into a drugstore and buys a blue tablet—actually it is called a theme book—and a special pen to write with: a black fountain pen, and a bottle of ink. She has to go back for the ink. She has never thought things through. At vacation time the man would stand at the front door saying, "Do you have beach shoes? Did you bring our toothbrushes? What about a hat for the sun? I know you brought suntan lotion, but what about Solarcaine?" She would run to her closet, to the bathroom, take down hatboxes, reopen her suitcase. "And Robby's raft—did you put that in the trunk?" Yes. She always thought a lot about Robby. He always had the correct clothes packed, his favorite toys included, comics to read in the car. She took very good care of Robby. She does not quite understand why he must live with his grandmother. Of all of them, she took the best care of Robby. She *does* understand why he is with the man's mother, but she does not like it, or want to accept it. She has been very honest with the man, has told him her feelings about this, and has not been converted to his way of thinking. She never did anything to Robby. He agrees with this. And she does not see why she can't have him. There they disagree. They disagree, and the man has not made love to her for months—as long as the disagreement has gone on.

She is so frustrated. Filling the pen is harder than she thought—to do it carefully, making sure not to spill the ink or put too much in. And what details, exactly, should she write down? What if she wanted to remember the times she went to the bathroom the day before? Should she include everything? It would take too long. And it would seem silly to write down the times she went to the bathroom. The journal is to make her feel better. What would be the point of flipping back through her journal and seeing things that would embarrass her? There are enough things that embarrass her around the house. All the bowls that the man likes so much are a tiny bit lopsided. He agrees with her there, but says no value should be placed on a perfect bowl. Once he became very excited and told her there was no such thing as perfection —it was all in the eye of the beholder. He went on to talk about molecules; fast, constantly moving molecules that exist in all things. She is afraid of the bowls now, and doesn't dust them. He wants her to dust them—to take pride in them. He talks and talks about the negative value of "perfection." He put the word in quotes. This, he explained, was because he, himself, did not think in those terms, but it was a convenient word. He left the note on the door one morning before leaving for work, and she found it when she went into the kitchen. She asked about it. It is established that they can ask about anything. Anything at all. And that the other has to answer. She would like to ask him if he has had the phone disconnected. She can ask, but she is frightened to.

The man's mother pays for her to take the crafts classes. In the summer, June through August, they spun the bowls (they could have made vases, plates, but she stuck with bowls); September through November they learned macramé, and for Christmas she gave all of it away—a useless tangle of knots. She had no plants to hang in them, and she did not want them hung on her walls. She likes plain walls. The one Seurat is enough. She likes to look at the walls and think. For the past four months they have been making silver jewelry. She is getting worse at things instead of better. Fatigue at having been at it so long, perhaps, or perhaps what she said to her teacher, which her teacher denied; that she is just too old, that her imagination is insufficient, that her touch is not delicate enough. She is used to handling large things: plates, vacuums. She has no feel for the delicate fibers of silver. Her teacher told her that she certainly *did*. He wears one of the rings she made — bought it from her and wears it to every class. She is flattered, although she has no way of knowing whether he is wearing it out of class. Like the garish orange pin Robby selected for her in the dime store, his gift to her for her birthday. He was four years old, and naturally the bright orange pin caught his eye. She wore it to the PTA meeting, on her coat, to show him how much she liked it. She took it off in the car and put it back on before coming in the house — just in case the baby-sitter had failed and he was still awake. Now, however, she would never consider taking off the pin. She wears it every day. It's as automatic as combing her hair. She's as used to seeing it on her blouse or dress as she is to waiting for the phone to ring.

The man says it is remarkable that they always have such good meals when she shops so seldom. She went out two days ago to the cleaners, and she showed him the stub, so he knows this, but he is still subtly criticizing her failure to go out every day. She gets tired of going out. She has to go to crafts classes Thursday, Friday and Saturday nights, and on Sunday she has to go to his mother's house. She says this to him by way of argument, but actually she *loves* to go to his mother's house. It is the best day of the week. She does not love, or even like, his mother, but she can be with Robby from afternoon until his bedtime. They can throw the ball back and forth on the front lawn (who cares if they spy on them through the window?), and she can brush his hair (she cuts it too short! Just a little longer. He's so beautiful that the short hair doesn't make him ugly, but he would be even more beautiful if it could grow an inch on the sides, on the top). He gives her pictures he has colored. He thinks that kindergarten should be more sophisticated and is a little embarrassed about the pictures, but he explains that he has to do what the teacher says. She nods. If he were older, she could explain that she *had* to make the bowls. He rebels by drawing sloppily, sometimes. "I didn't even try on that one," he says. She knows what he means. She says — as the man says to her about the bowls, as the crafts instructor says — that they are still beautiful. He likes that. He gives them all to her. There is not even one tacked up in his grandmother's kitchen. There are none on her walls, either, but she looks through the pile on the coffee table every day. She prefers the walls blank. When he comes with Grandma to visit, which hardly ever happens, she puts them up if she knows he's coming or points to the pile to show him that she has them close-by to examine. She never did anything to Robby, not one single thing. She argues and argues with the man about this. He goes to business meetings at night and comes home late. He does not fully enjoy the meals she prepares because he is so tired. This he denies. He says he does fully enjoy them. What can she say? How can you prove that someone is not savoring sweet-potato soufflé?

"How *do* you cook such delicious things when you shop so seldom?" he asks.

"I don't shop that infrequently," she says.

"Don't vegetables . . . I mean, aren't they very perishable?"

"No," she says. She smiles sweetly.

"You always have fresh vegetables, don't you?"

"Sometimes I buy them fresh and parboil them myself. Later I steam them."

"Ah," he says. He does not know exactly what she is talking about.

"Today I was out for a walk," she says. No way he can prove she wasn't.

"It's a late spring," he says. "But today it was very nice, actually."

They are having a civilized discussion. Perhaps she can lure him into bed. Perhaps if that works, the phone will also ring. Hasn't he noticed that it doesn't ring at night, that it hasn't for nights? That's unusual, too. She would ask what he makes of this, but talking about the phone makes him angry, and if he's angry, he'll never get into bed. She fingers her pin. He sees her do it. A mistake. It reminds him of Robby.

She sips her wine and thinks about their summer vacation — the one they already took. She can remember so little about the summer. She will not remember the spring if she doesn't get busy and write in her book. What, exactly, should she write? She thinks the book should contain feelings instead of just facts. Surely that would be less boring to do. Well, she was going to write something during the afternoon, but she was feeling blue, and worried — about the telephone — and it wouldn't cheer her up to go back and read about feeling blue and being worried. Her crafts teacher had given her a book of poetry to read: *Winter Trees* by Sylvia Plath. It was interesting. She was certainly interested in it, but it depressed her. She didn't go out of the house for days. Finally — she is glad she can remember clearly some details — he asked her to go to the cleaners and she went out. She did several errands that day. What was the weather like, though? Or does it really matter? She corrects herself: it does matter. It matters very much what season it is, whether the weather is typical or unusual. If you have something to say about the weather, you will always be able to make conversation with people, and communicating is very important. Even for yourself: you should know that you feel blue because the weather is cold or rainy, happy because it's a sunny day with high clouds. Tonight she feels blue. Probably it is cold out. She would ask, but she has already lied that she was out. It might have turned cold, however.

"I was out quite early," she says. "What was the weather like when you came home?"

"Ah," he says. "I called this morning."

She looks up at him, suddenly. He sees her surprise, knows she wasn't out.

"Just to say that I loved you," he says.

He smiles. It is not worth seducing him to make the phone ring. She will shower, wash her hair, stand there a long time, hoping, but she won't make love to the man. He is a rotten liar.

In the morning, when he is gone, she finds that she remembers her feelings of the night before exactly, and writes them down, at length, in the book.

On Friday night he no longer picks her up after crafts class. He has joined a stock club, and he has a meeting that night. The bus stop is only a block from where the class meets; it lets her off five minutes from where she lives. It is unnecessary for the man ever to pick her up. But he says that the streets are dangerous at night, and that she must be tired. She says that the bus ride refreshes her. She likes riding buses, looking at the people. There is good bus service. He smiles. But it is not necessary to ride them; and the streets are dangerous at night.

Tonight her instructor asks to speak to her when the class has ended. She has no interest in the thin silver filaments she is working with and says he can talk to her now. "No," he says. "Later is fine."

She remains when the others have left. The others are all younger than she, with one exception: a busty grandmother who is learning crafts hoping to ease her arthritis. The others are in their teens or early twenties. They have long hair and wear Earth shoes and are unfriendly. They are intense. Perhaps that's what it is. They don't talk because they're intense. They walk (so the ads for these shoes say) feeling clouds beneath them, their spines perfectly and comfortably straight, totally relaxed and enjoying their intensity. Their intensity results in delicate necklaces, highly glazed bowls — some with deer and trees, others with Mister Moon smiling. All but three are women.

When they have all left, he opens a door to a room at the back of the classroom. It opens into a tiny room, where there is a mattress on the floor, covered with a plaid blanket, two pairs of tennis shoes aligned with it, and a high narrow bookcase between the pipe and window. He wants to know what she thought of the Sylvia Plath book. She says that it depressed her. That seems to be the right response, the one that gets his head nodding — he always nods when he looks over her shoulder. He told her in November that he admired her wanting to perfect her bowls — her not moving on just to move on to something else. They nod at each other. In the classroom they whisper so as not to disturb anyone's intensity. It is strange now to speak to him in a normal tone of voice. When she sees her son, now, she also whispers. That annoys the man and his mother. What does she have to say to him that they can't all hear? They are noisy when they play, but when they are in the house — in his room, or when she is pouring him some juice from the refrigerator — she will kneel and whisper. A gentle sound, like deer in the woods. She made the bowl with the deer on it, gave it to the instructor because he was so delighted with it. He was very appreciative. He said that he meant for her to keep the book. But he would lend her another. Or two: *The Death Notebooks* and *A Vision*. The instructor puts his foot on the edge of the second shelf to get one of the books down from the top. She is afraid he will fall, stands closer to him, behind him, in case he does. She has a notion of softening his fall. He does not fall. He hands her the books. The instructor knows all about her, she is sure. The man's mother visited his studio before she suggested, firmly, that she enroll. The man's mother was charmed by the instructor. Imagine what she must have said to him about her. From the first, he was kind to her. When he gave her *Winter Trees*, he somehow got across the idea to her that many women felt enraged — sad and enraged. He said a few things to her that impressed her at the time. If only she had had the notebook then, she could have written them down, reread them.

He boils water in a pan for tea. She admires the blue jar he spoons the tea out of. He made it. Similarly, he admires her work. She sees that her bowl holds some oranges and bananas. She would like to ask what false or unfair things the man's mother said about her. That would cast a pall over things, though. The instructor would feel uncomfortable. It is not right to blurt out everything you feel like saying. People don't live like that in society. Talk about something neutral. Talk about the weather. She says to the instructor what the man always says to her: it is a late spring. She says more: she is keeping a journal. He asks again — the third time? — whether she writes poetry. She says, truthfully, that she does not. He shows her a box full of papers that he doodled on, wrote on, the semester he dropped out of Stanford. The doodles are very complex, heavily inked. The writing is sloppy, in big letters that were written with a heavy black pen. She understands from reading a little that he was unhappy when he dropped out of Stanford. He says that writing things down helps. Expressing yourself helps. Her attention drifts. When she concentrates again, he is saying the opposite: she must feel these classes are unpleasant, having been sentenced to them; all those books — he gestures to the bookcase — were written by unhappy people, and it's doubtful if writing them made them any happier. Not Sylvia Plath, certainly. He tells her that she should not feel obliged to act nicely, feel happy. He thumps his hand on the books he has just given her.

She tells him that the phone never rings anymore. She tells him that last, after the story about the summer vacation, how she and Robby set out to race through the surf, and Robby lagged behind, and she felt such incredible energy, she ran and ran. They got separated. She ran all the way to the end of the sand, to the rocks, and then back — walked back — and couldn't find Robby or the man anywhere. All the beach umbrellas looked the same, and so did the people. What exactly did Robby look like? Or the man? The man looked furious. He found her, came back for her in his slacks and shirt, having taken Robby back to the motel. His shoes were caked with wet sand, his face furious. She is not sure how to connect this to what she really wants to talk about, the inexplicably silent telephone.

(1979)

❖ AMBROSE BIERCE

An Occurrence at Owl Creek Bridge

Ambrose Bierce (1841–1914) was born in poverty in Ohio and had little formal education. At nineteen, during the Civil War, he enlisted in the Union Army, was twice wounded, and became an officer. A postwar job with the army took him to San Francisco where wide reading helped him acquire the education that he had not had as a child. He also began writing and publishing short pieces of fiction and nonfiction. He moved to England in 1872 where he became a well-known journalist and published three volumes of essays. Returning to San Francisco in 1876, he began to write fiction more seriously. His stories are collected in *Tales of Soldiers and Civilians* (1891, which includes "An Occurrence at Owl Creek Bridge") and *Can Such Things Be?* (1893). He also wrote verse, plays, and much nonfiction, most famously a mordant collection of aphorisms called *The Devil's Dictionary* (1906). His work was collected in twelve volumes in 1966. Bierce's strange disappearance in Mexico during the Pancho Villa revolution was the subject of a recent Hollywood movie, *Old Gringo*.

I

A man stood upon a railroad bridge in northern Alabama, looking down into the swift water twenty feet below. The man's hands were behind his back, the wrists bound with a cord. A rope closely encircled his neck. It was attached to a stout cross-timber above his head and the slack fell to the level of his knees. Some loose boards laid upon the sleepers supporting the metals of the railway supplied a footing for him and his executioners — two private soldiers of the Federal army, directed by a sergeant who in civil life may have been a deputy sheriff. At a short remove upon the same temporary platform was an officer in the uniform of his rank, armed. He was a captain. A sentinel at each end of the bridge stood with his rifle in the position known as "support," that is to say, vertical in front of the left shoulder, the hammer resting on the forearm thrown straight across the chest — a formal and unnatural position, enforcing an erect carriage of the body. It did not appear to be the duty of these two men to know what was occurring at the centre of the bridge; they merely blockaded the two ends of the foot planking that traversed it.

Beyond one of the sentinels nobody was in sight; the railroad ran straight away into a forest for a hundred yards, then, curving, was lost to view. Doubtless there was an outpost farther along. The other bank of the stream was open ground — a gentle acclivity topped with a stockade of vertical tree trunks, loop-holed for rifles, with a single embrasure through which protruded the muzzle of a brass cannon commanding the bridge Midway of the slope between bridge and fort were the spectators — a single company of infantry in line, at "parade rest," the butts of the rifles on the ground, the barrels inclining slightly backward against the right shoulder, the hands crossed upon the stock. A lieutenant stood at the right of the line, the point of his sword upon the ground, his left hand resting upon his right. Excepting the group of four at the center of the bridge, not a man moved. The company faced the bridge, staring stonily, motionless. The sentinels, facing the banks of the stream, might have been statues to adorn the bridge. The captain stood with folded arms, silent, observing the work of his subordinates, but making no sign. Death is a dignitary who when he comes announced is to be received with formal manifestations of respect, even by those most familiar with him. In the code of military etiquette silence and fixity are forms of deference.

The man who was engaged in being hanged was apparently about thirty-five years of age. He was a civilian, if one might judge from his habit, which was that of a planter. His features were good — a straight nose, firm mouth, broad forehead, from which his long, dark hair was combed straight back, falling behind his ears to the collar of his well-fitting frockcoat. He wore a mustache and pointed beard, but no whiskers; his eyes were large and dark gray, and had a kindly expression which one would hardly have expected in one whose neck was in the hemp. Evidently this was no vulgar assassin. The liberal military code makes provision for hanging many kinds of persons, and gentlemen are not excluded.

The preparations being complete, the two private soldiers stepped aside and each drew away the plank upon which he had been standing. The sergeant turned to the captain, saluted and placed himself immediately behind that officer, who in turn moved apart one pace. These movements left the condemned man and the sergeant standing on the two ends of the same plank, which spanned three of the cross-ties of the bridge. The end upon which the civilian stood almost, but not quite, reached a fourth. This plank had been held in place by the weight of the captain; it was now held by that of the sergeant. At a signal from the former the latter would step aside, the plank would tilt and the condemned man go down between two ties. The arrangement commended itself to his judgment as simple and effective. His face had not been covered nor his eyes bandaged. He looked a moment at his "unsteadfast footing," then let his gaze wander to the swirling water of the stream racing madly beneath his feet. A piece of dancing driftwood caught his attention and his eyes followed it down the current. How slowly it appeared to move! What a sluggish stream!

He closed his eyes in order to fix his last thoughts upon his wife and children. The water, touched to gold by the early sun, the brooding mists under the banks at some distance down the stream, the fort, the soldiers, the piece of drift — all had distracted him. And now he became conscious of a new disturbance. Striking through the thought of his dear ones was a sound which he could neither ignore nor understand, a sharp, distinct, metallic percussion like the stroke of a blacksmith's hammer upon the anvil; it had the same ringing quality. He wondered what it was, and whether immeasurably distant or near by — it seemed both. Its recurrence was regular, but as slow as the tolling of a death knell. He awaited each stroke with impatience and — he knew not why — apprehension. The intervals of silence grew progressively longer; the delays became maddening. With their greater infrequency the sounds increased in strength and sharpness. They hurt his ear like the thrust of a knife; he feared he would shriek. What he heard was the ticking of his watch.

He unclosed his eyes and saw again the water below him. "If I could free my hands," he thought, "I might throw off the noose and spring into the stream. By diving I could evade the bullets and, swimming vigorously, reach the bank, take to the woods and get away home. My home, thank God, is as yet outside their lines; my wife and little ones are still beyond the invader's farthest advance."

As these thoughts, which have here to be set down in words, were flashed into the doomed man's brain rather than evolved from it the captain nodded to the sergeant. The sergeant stepped aside.

II

Peyton Farquhar was a well-to-do planter, of an old and highly respected Alabama family. Being a slave owner and like other slave owners a politician he was naturally an original secessionist and ardently devoted to the Southern cause. Circumstances of an imperious nature, which it is unnecessary to relate here, had prevented him from taking service with the gallant army that had fought the disastrous campaigns ending with the fall of Corinth, and he chafed under the inglorious restraint, longing for the release of his energies, the larger life of the soldier, the opportunity for distinction. That opportunity, he felt, would come, as it comes to all in war time. Meanwhile he did what he could. No service was too humble for him to perform in aid of the South, no adventure too perilous for him to undertake if consistent with the character of a civilian who was at heart a soldier, and who in good faith and without too much qualification assented to at least a part of the frankly villainous dictum that all is fair in love and war.

One evening while Farquhar and his wife were sitting on a rustic bench near the entrance to his grounds, a gray-clad soldier rode up to the gate and asked for a drink of water. Mrs. Farquhar was only too happy to serve him with her own white hands. While she was fetching the water her husband approached the dusty horseman and inquired eagerly for news from the front.

"The Yanks are repairing the railroads," said the man, "and are getting ready for another advance. They have reached the Owl Creek bridge, put it in order and built a stockade on the north bank. The commandant has issued an order, which is posted everywhere, declaring that any civilian caught interfering with the railroad, its bridges, tunnels or trains will be summarily hanged. I saw the order."

"How far is it to the Owl Creek bridge?" Farquhar asked.

"About thirty miles."

"Is there no force on this side the creek?"

"Only a picket post half a mile out, on the railroad, and a single sentinel at this end of the bridge."

"Suppose a man—a civilian and student of hanging—should elude the picket post and perhaps get the better of the sentinel," said Farquhar, smiling, "what could he accomplish?"

The soldier reflected. "I was there a month ago," he replied. "I observed that the flood of last winter had lodged a great quantity of driftwood against the wooden pier at this end of the bridge. It is now dry and would burn like tow."

The lady had now brought the water, which the soldier drank. He thanked her ceremoniously, bowed to her husband and rode away. An hour later, after nightfall, he repassed the plantation, going northward in the direction from which he had come. He was a Federal scout.

III

As Peyton Farquhar fell straight downward through the bridge he lost consciousness and was as one already dead. From this state he was awakened — ages later, it seemed to him — by the pain of a sharp pressure upon his throat, followed by a sense of suffocation. Keen, poignant agonies seemed to shoot from his neck downward through every fibre of his body and limbs. These pains appeared to flash along well-defined lines of ramification and to beat with an inconceivably rapid periodicity. They seemed like streams of pulsating fire heating him to an intolerable temperature. As to his head, he was conscious of nothing but a feeling of fullness — of congestion. These sensations were unaccompanied by thought. The intellectual part of his nature was already effaced; he had power only to feel, and feeling was torment. He was conscious of motion. Encompassed in a luminous cloud, of which he was now merely the fiery heart, without material substance, he swung through unthinkable arcs of oscillation, like a vast pendulum. Then all at once, with terrible suddenness, the light about him shot upward with the noise of a loud plash; a frightful roaring was in his ears, and all was cold and dark. The power of thought was restored; he knew that the rope had broken and he had fallen into the stream. There was no additional strangulation; the noose about his neck was already suffocating him and kept the water from his lungs. To die of hanging at the bottom of a river! — the idea seemed to him ludicrous. He opened his eyes in the darkness and saw above him a gleam of light, but how distant, how inaccessible! He was still sinking, for the light became fainter and fainter until it was a mere glimmer. Then it began to grow and brighten, and he knew that he was rising toward the surface — knew it with reluctance, for he was now very comfortable. "To be hanged and drowned," he thought, "that is not so bad; but I do not wish to be shot. No; I will not be shot; that is not fair."

He was not conscious of an effort, but a sharp pain in his wrist apprised him that he was trying to free his hands. He gave the struggle his attention, as an idler might observe the feat of a juggler, without interest in the outcome. What splendid effort! — what magnificent, what superhuman strength! Ah, that was a fine endeavor! Bravo! The cord fell away; his arms parted and floated upward, the hands dimly seen on each side in the growing light. He watched them with a new interest as first one and then the other pounced upon the noose at his neck. They tore it away and thrust it fiercely aside, its undulations resembling those of a water-snake. "Put it back, put it back!" He thought he shouted these words to his hands, for the undoing of the noose had been succeeded by the direst pang that he had yet experienced. His neck ached horribly; his brain was on fire; his heart, which had been fluttering faintly, gave a great leap, trying to force itself out at his mouth. His whole body was racked and wrenched with an insupportable anguish! But his disobedient hands gave no heed to the command. They beat the water vigorously with quick, downward strokes, forcing him to the surface. He felt his head emerge; his eyes were blinded by the sunlight; his chest expanded convulsively, and with a supreme and crowning agony his lungs engulfed a great draught of air, which instantly he expelled in a shriek!

He was now in full possession of his physical senses. They were, indeed, preternaturally keen and alert. Something in the awful disturbance of his organic system had so exalted and refined them that they made record of things never before perceived. He felt the ripples upon his face and heard their separate sounds as they struck. He looked at the forest on the bank of the stream, saw the individual trees, the leaves and the veining of each leaf — saw the very insects upon them: the locusts, the brilliant-bodied flies, the gray spiders stretching their webs from twig to twig. He noted the prismatic colors in all the dewdrops upon a million blades of grass. The humming of the gnats that danced above the eddies of the stream, the beating of the dragonflies' wings, the strokes of the waterspiders' legs, like oars which had lifted their boat — all these made audible music. A fish slid along beneath his eyes and he heard the rush of its body parting the water.

He had come to the surface facing down the stream; in a moment the visible world seemed to wheel slowly round, himself the pivotal point, and he saw the bridge, the fort, the soldiers upon the bridge, the captain, the sergeant, the two privates, his executioners. They were in silhouette against the blue sky. They shouted and gesticulated, pointing at him. The captain had drawn his pistol, but did not fire; the others were unarmed. Their movements were grotesque and horrible, their forms gigantic.

Suddenly he heard a sharp report and something struck the water smartly within a few inches of his head, spattering his face with spray. He heard a second report, and saw one of the sentinels with his rifle at his shoulder, a light cloud of blue smoke rising from the muzzle. The man in the water saw the eye of the man on the bridge gazing into his own through the sights of the rifle. He observed that it was a gray eye and remembered having read that gray eyes were keenest, and that all famous marksmen had them. Nevertheless, this one had missed.

A counter-swirl had caught Farquhar and turned him half round; he was again looking into the forest on the bank opposite the fort. The sound of a clear, high voice in a monotonous singsong now rang out behind him and came across the water with a distinctness that pierced and subdued all other sounds, even the beating of the ripples in his ears. Although no soldier, he had frequented camps enough to know the dread significance of that deliberate, drawling, aspirated chant; the lieutenant on shore was taking a part in the morning's work. How coldly and pitilessly — with what an even, calm intonation, presaging, and enforcing tranquillity in the men — with what accurately measured intervals fell those cruel words:

"Attention, company! . . . Shoulder arms! . . . Ready! . . . Aim! . . . Fire!"

Farquhar dived — dived as deeply as he could. The water roared in his ears like the voice of Niagara, yet he heard the dulled thunder of the volley and, rising again toward the surface, met shining bits of metal, singularly flattened, oscillating slowly downward. Some of them touched him on the face and hands, then fell away, continuing their descent. One lodged between his collar and neck; it was uncomfortably warm and he snatched it out.

As he rose to the surface, gasping for breath, he saw that he had been a long time under water; he was perceptibly farther down stream — nearer to safety. The soldiers had almost finished reloading; the metal ramrods flashed all at once in the sunshine as they were drawn from the barrels, turned in the air, and thrust into their sockets. The two sentinels fired again, independently and ineffectually.

The hunted man saw all this over his shoulder; he was now swimming vigorously with the current. His brain was as energetic as his arms and legs; he thought with the rapidity of lightning.

"The officer," he reasoned, "will not make that martinet's error a second time. It is as easy to dodge a volley as a single shot. He has probably already given the command to fire at will. God help me, I cannot dodge them all!"

An appalling plash within two yards of him was followed by a loud, rushing sound, *diminuendo*, which seemed to travel back through the air to the fort and died in an explosion which stirred the very river to its deeps! A rising sheet of water curved over him, fell down upon him, blinded him, strangled him! The cannon had taken a hand in the game. As he shook his head free from the commotion of the smitten water he heard the deflected shot humming through the air ahead, and in an instant it was cracking and smashing the branches in the forest beyond.

"They will not do that again," he thought; "the next time they will use a charge of grape. I must keep my eye upon the gun; the smoke will apprise me — the report arrives too late; it lags behind the missile. That is a good gun."

Suddenly he felt himself whirled round and round — spinning like a top. The water, the banks, the forests, the now distant bridge, fort and men — all were commingled and blurred. Objects were represented by their colors only; circular horizontal streaks of color — that was all he saw. He had been caught in a vortex and was being whirled on with a velocity of advance and gyration that made him giddy and sick. In a few moments he was flung upon the gravel at the foot of the left bank of the stream — the southern bank — and behind a projecting point which concealed him from his enemies. The sudden arrest of his motion, the abrasion of one of his hands on the gravel, restored him, and he wept with delight. He dug his fingers into the sand, threw it over himself in handfuls and audibly blessed it. It looked like diamonds, rubies, emeralds; he could think of nothing beautiful which it did not resemble. The trees upon the bank were giant garden plants; he noted a definite order in their arrangement, inhaled the fragrance of their blooms. A strange, roseate light shone through the spaces among their trunks and the wind made in their branches the music of aeolian harps. He had no wish to perfect his escape — was content to remain in that enchanting spot until retaken.

A whiz and rattle of grapeshot among the branches high above his head roused him from his dream. The baffled cannoneer had fired him a random farewell. He sprang to his feet, rushed up the sloping bank, and plunged into the forest.

All that day he traveled, laying his course by the rounding sun. The forest seemed interminable; nowhere did he discover a break in it, not even a woodman's road. He had not known that he lived in so wild a region. There was something uncanny in the revelation.

By nightfall he was fatigued, footsore, famishing. The thought of his wife and children urged him on. At last he found a road which led him in what he knew to be the right direction. It was as wide and straight as a city street, yet it seemed untraveled. No fields bordered it, no dwelling anywhere. Not so much as the barking of a dog suggested human habitation. The black bodies of the trees formed a straight wall on both sides, terminating on the horizon in a point, like a diagram in a lesson in perspective. Overhead, as he looked up through this rift in the wood, shone great golden stars looking unfamiliar and grouped in strange constellations. He was sure they were arranged in some order which had a secret and malign significance. The wood on either side was full of singular noises, among which — once, twice, and again — he distinctly heard whispers in an unknown tongue.

His neck was in pain and lifting his hand to it he found it horribly swollen. He knew that it had a circle of black where the rope had bruised it. His eyes felt congested; he could no longer close them. His tongue was swollen with thirst; he relieved its fever by thrusting it forward from between his teeth into the cold air. How softly the turf had carpeted the untraveled avenue — he could no longer feel the roadway beneath his feet!

Doubtless, despite his suffering, he had fallen asleep while walking, for now he sees another scene — perhaps he has merely recovered from a delirium. He stands at the gate of his own home. All is as he left it, and all bright and beautiful in the morning sunshine. He must have traveled the entire night. As he pushes open the gate and passes up the wide white walk, he sees a flutter of female garments; his wife, looking fresh and cool and sweet, steps down from the veranda to meet him. At the bottom of the steps she stands waiting, with a smile of ineffable joy, an attitude of matchless grace and dignity. Ah, how beautiful she is! He springs forward with extended arms. As he is about to clasp her he feels a stunning blow upon the back of the neck; a blinding white light blazes all about him with a sound like the shock of a cannon — then all is darkness and silence!

Peyton Farquhar was dead; his body, with a broken neck, swung gently from side to side beneath the timbers of the Owl Creek bridge.

(1890)

❖ ELIZABETH BOWEN
Careless Talk

Elizabeth Bowen (1899–1973) was born in Dublin, Ireland, but educated at the London Council of Art. She settled with her husband in
Oxford, where she wrote several novels: *The Hotel* (1927), *The Last
September* (1929), *Friends and Relations* (1931), *To the North* (1933),
The House in Paris (1936), *The Heat of the Day* (1949), *The Little Girls*
(1963), and *Eva Trout* (1968). Bowen moved back to London and
became associated with the Bloomsbury Group, whose most renowned author was Virginia Woolf. She worked at a government job
in the British Ministry of Information during World War II, a job that
provided the experience for stories like "Careless Talk." Her best-
known novel is probably *The Death of the Heart* (1938). All her short
stories appear in the volume *The Collected Stories of Elizabeth Bowen*
(1975). Bowen also published four volumes of memoirs and travel
sketches.

'How good, how kind, *how* thoughtful!' said Mary Dash. 'I can't tell you what a
difference they will make! And you brought them like this all the way from Shepton
Mallet in the train?' She looked helpless. 'Where do you think I had better put them?
This table's going to be terribly small for four, and *think*, if one of Eric Farnham's
sweeping gesticulations . . .' She signalled a waiter. 'I want these put somewhere for
me till the end of lunch. *Carefully*,' she added. 'They are three eggs.' The waiter bowed
and took the parcel away. 'I do hope they will be all right,' said Mrs Dash, looking
suspiciously after him. 'But at least they'll be quieter with the hats, or something. I
expect you see how crowded everywhere is?'

Joanna looked round the restaurant and saw. The waiters had to melt to get
past the backs of the chairs; between the net-curtained windows, drowsy with August
rain, mirrors reflected heads in smoke and electric light and the glitter of buttons on
uniforms. Every European tongue struck its own note, with exclamatory English on
top of all. As fast as people went wading out people came wading in, and so many
greeted each other that Joanna might easily have felt out of it. She had not lunched in
London for four months and could not resist saying so to her friend.

'Honestly, you haven't deteriorated,' said Mary. Herself, she was looking
much as ever, with orchids pinned on to her last year's black. 'Then how lucky I
caught you just today! And I'm glad the others will be late. The only men one likes
now are always late. While it's still just you and me, there's so much to say. I don't
know what I've done without you, Joanna.' She fixed enraptured eyes on Joanna's face.
'For instance, can you tell me what's become of the Stones?'

'No, I'm afraid I can't. I . . .'

'And Edward and I were wondering if you could tell us about the Hickneys. I know they are somewhere in Dorset or Somerset. They're not by any chance anywhere near you? . . . Well, never mind. Tell me about yourself.'

But at this point Eric Farnham joined them. 'You don't know how sorry I am,' he said. 'I was kept. But you found the table all right. Well, Joanna, this couldn't be nicer, could it?'

'Isn't she looking radiant?' said Mary Dash. 'We have been having the most tremendous talk.'

Eric was now at the War Office, and Joanna, who had not seen him in uniform before, looked at him naïvely, twice. He reminded her of one of the pictures arrived at in that paper game when, by drawing on folded-over paper, you add to one kind of body an intriguingly wrong kind of head. He met her second look kindly through his shell-rimmed glasses. 'How do you think the war is going?' she said.

'Oh, we mustn't ask him things' said Mary quickly. 'He's doing most frightfully secret work.' But this was lost on Eric, who was consulting his wristwatch. 'As Ponsonby's later than I am,' he said, 'that probably means he'll be pretty late. Though God knows what they do at that Ministry. I propose not waiting for Ponsonby. First of all, what will you two drink?'

'Ponsonby?' Joanna said.

'No, I don't expect you'd know him. He's only been about lately,' said Mary. 'He's an expert; he's very interesting.'

'He could be,' said Eric. 'He was at one time. But he's not supposed to be interesting just now.' The drinks came; then they got together over the *cartes du jour*. Ponsonby did not arrive till just after the potted shrimps. 'This is dreadful,' he said. 'I do hope you'll forgive me. But things keep on happening, you know.' He nodded rapidly round to several tables, then dropped exhausted into his place. 'Eat?' he said. 'Oh, really, anything—shrimps. After that, whatever you're all doing.'

'Well, Mary's for grouse,' said Eric. Ponsonby, after an instant of concentration, said, 'In that case, grouse will do me fine.'

'Now you must talk to Joanna,' said Mary Dash. 'She's just brought me three eggs from the country and she's longing to know about everything.'

Ponsonby gave Joanna a keen, considering look. 'Is it true,' he said, 'that in the country there are no cigarettes at all?'

'I believe there are sometimes some. But I don't—'

'There are. Then that alters everything,' said Ponsonby. 'How lucky you are!'

'I got my hundred this morning,' said Eric, 'from my regular man. But those will have to last me to Saturday. I can't seem to cut down, somehow. Mary, have you cut down?'

'I've got my own, if that's what you mean,' said she. 'I just got twenty out of my hairdresser.' She raised her shilling-size portion of butter from its large bed of ice and spread it tenderly over her piece of toast. 'Now, what is your news?' she said. 'Not that I'm asking anything, of course.'

'I don't think anything's happened to me,' said Eric, 'or that anything else has happened that you wouldn't know about. When I say happened I mean *happened*, of course. I went out of London for one night; everywhere outside London seemed to me very full. I must say I was glad to be home again.' He unlocked his chair from the chair behind him, looked at the grouse on his plate, then took up his knife and fork.

'Eric,' said Mary, after a minute, 'the waiter's trying to tell you there's no more of that wine *en carafe*.'

'Bring it in a bottle then. I wonder how much longer—'

'Oh, my dear, so do *I*,' said Mary. 'One daren't think about that. Where we were dining last night they already had several numbers scratched off the wine list. Which reminds me. Edward sent you his love.'

'Oh, how *is* Edward?' Joanna said. 'What is he doing?'

'Well, I'm not strictly supposed to say. By the way, Eric, I asked Joanna, and she doesn't know where the Stones *or* the Hickneys are.'

'In the case of the Hickneys, I don't know that it matters.'

'Oh, don't be inhuman. You know you're not!'

'I must say,' said Eric, raising his voice firmly, 'I do like London now a lot of those people have gone. Not *you*, Joanna; we all miss you very much. Why don't you come back? You've no idea how nice it is.'

Joanna, colouring slightly, said, 'I've got no place left to come back to. Belmont Square—'

'Oh, my Lord, yes,' he said. 'I did hear about your house. I was so sorry. Completely? . . . Still, you don't want a house, you know. None of us live in houses. You could move in on someone. Sylvia has moved in on Mona—'

'That's not a good example,' said Mary quickly. 'Mona moved out almost at once and moved in on Isobel, but the worst of that is that now Isobel wants her husband back, and meanwhile Sylvia's taken up with a young man, so Mona can't move back to her own flat. But what would make it difficult for Joanna is having taken on all those hens. Haven't you?'

'Yes, and I have evacuees—'

'But we won't talk about those, will we?' said Mary quickly. 'Any more than you would want to hear about bombs. I think one great rule is never to bore each other. Eric, *what's* that you are saying to Ponsonby?'

Eric and Ponsonby had seized the occasion to exchange a few rapid remarks. They stopped immediately. 'It was quite boring,' Ponsonby explained.

'I don't believe you,' said Mary. 'These days everything's frightfully interesting. Joanna, you must be feeling completely dazed. Will everyone ask you things when you get home?'

'The worst of the country these days,' said Joanna, 'is everyone gets so wrapped up in their own affairs.'

'Still, surely they must want to know about us? I suppose London is too much the opposite,' said Mary. 'One lives in a perfect whirl of ideas. Ponsonby, who was that man I saw you with at the Meunière? I was certain I knew his face.'

'That was a chap called Odgers. Perhaps he reminded you of somebody else? We were talking shop. I think that's a nice place, don't you? I always think they do veal well. That reminds me, Eric. Was your friend the other evening a Pole, or what?'

'The fact is I hardly know him,' said Eric. 'I'm never quite sure of his name myself. He's a Pole all right, but Poles aren't really my thing. He was quite interesting, as a matter of fact; he had quite a line of his own on various things. Oh, well, it was nothing particular . . . No, I can't do you Poles, Mary. Warrington's really the man for Poles.'

'I know he is, but he keeps them all up his sleeve. You do know about Edward and the Free French? I hope it didn't matter my having told you that, but Edward took it for granted that you already knew.'

Ponsonby recoiled from his wristwatch. 'Good heavens,' he said, 'it *can't* be as late as this? If it is, there's someone waiting for me.'

'Look,' said Eric, 'I'll hurry on coffee.'

'You know,' Mary added anxiously, 'you really can't concentrate without your coffee. Though I know we mustn't be difficult. It's like this all the time,' she said to Joanna. 'Have *you* got to hurry, Eric?'

'I needn't exactly hurry. I just ought to keep an eye on the time.'

'I'll do that for you,' Mary said. 'I'd love to. You see you've hardly had a word with Joanna, and she's wanting so much to catch up with life. I tell you one thing that *is* worrying me: that waiter I gave Joanna's lovely eggs to hasn't been near this table again. Do you think I put temptation right in his way? Because, do you know, all the time we've been talking I've been thinking up a new omelette I want to make. One's mind gets like that these days,' she said to Joanna. 'One seems able to think of twenty things at one time. Eric, do you think you could flag the *maître d'hôtel*? I don't know how I'd feel if I lost three eggs.'

(1941)

❖ ITALO CALVINO
Big Fish, Little Fish*

Italo Calvino (1923–1985) was born in Santiago de Las Vegas, Cuba, but was raised in San Remo, Italy. He fought in the Italian Resistance from 1943 to 1945, and after the war he studied at the University of Turin. Calvino was much influenced by the Italian neorealist movement, in particular, the great novelist Cesare Pavese. But he turned from realism to the world of fantasy, arguing that the fable is "the irreplaceable scheme of all human stories." By "fable" he meant stories of knights encountering strange animals and enchantments in magical places. But his fables, though often featuring a child as protagonist, are really addressed to adults. Typically, Calvino's child-hero is enchanted by life, but his adventure highlights the absurdities of the adult world. Calvino's novels include *The Path to the Nest of Spiders* (1947), *The Cloven Viscount* (1952), *The Baron in the Trees* (1957), *The Nonexistent Knight* (1959), *Invisible Cities* (1972), *The Castle of Crossed Destinies* (1973), *If on a Night a Traveller . . .* (1979), and *Mr. Palomar* (1983). Calvino's short story collections include *Adam, One Afternoon* (1957), *Marcovaldo* (1963), *Cosmicomics* (1965), *t zero* (1967), *Difficult Loves* (1970, which includes "Big Fish, Little Fish"), *The Watcher* (1971), and *Under the Jaguar Sun* (1986). He also edited a collection of Italian folktales and wrote essays, mostly of literary criticism.

Zeffirino's father never wore a proper bathing suit. He would put on rolled-up shorts and an undershirt, a white duck cap on his head; and he never moved from the rocky shore. His passion was limpets, the flat mollusks that cling to the rocks until their terribly hard shell virtually becomes part of the rock itself. Zeffirino's father used a knife to prize them loose. Every Sunday, with his bespectacled stare, he passed in review, one by one, all the rocks along the point. He kept on until his little basket was full of limpets; some he ate as he collected them, sucking the moist, hard flesh as if from a spoon; the others he put in a basket. Every now and then he raised his eyes to glance, somewhat bewildered, over the smooth sea, and call, "Zeffirino! Where are you?"

Zeffirino spent whole afternoons in the water. The two of them went out to the point; his father would leave him there, then go off at once after his shellfish. Stubborn and motionless as they were, the limpets held no attraction for Zeffirino; it was the crabs, first and foremost, that interested him, then polyps, medusas, and so on, through all the varieties of fish. In the summer his pursuit became more difficult and ingenious; and by now there wasn't a boy his age who could handle a spear gun as well as he could. In the water, those stocky kids, all breath and muscle, are the best; and

---

*Translated by William Weaver

that's how Zeffirino was growing up. Seen on the shore, holding his father's hand, he looked like one of those kids with cropped hair and gaping mouth who have to be slapped to make them move. In the water, however, he outstripped them all; and, even better, underwater.

That day Zeffirino had managed to assemble a complete kit for underwater fishing. He had had the mask since the previous year, a present from his grandmother; a cousin whose feet were small had lent him her fins; he took the spear gun from his uncle's house without saying anything, but told his father it had been lent him, too. Actually, he was a careful boy, who knew how to use and take care of things, and he could be trusted if he borrowed something.

The sea was beautiful and clear. Zeffirino answered "Yes, Papà" to all the usual warnings, and went into the water. With the glass mask and the snorkel for breathing, with his legs ending like fish, and with that object in his hand — half gun and half spear and a little bit like a pitchfork, too — he no longer resembled a human being. Instead, once in the sea, though he darted off half submerged, you immediately recognized him as himself: from the kick he gave with the fins, from the way the gun jutted out beneath his arm, from his determination as he proceeded, his head at the surface of the water.

The sea bed was pebbles at first, then rocks, some of them bare and eroded, others bearded with thick, dark seaweed. From every cranny of the rocks, or among the tremulous beards swaying in the current, a big fish might suddenly appear; from behind the glass of the mask Zeffirino cast his eyes around, eagerly, intently.

A sea bed seems beautiful the first time, when you discover it; but, as with all things, the really beautiful part comes later, when you learn everything, stroke by stroke. You feel as if you were drinking them in, the aquatic trails: you go on and on and never want to stop. The glass of the mask is an enormous, single eye for swallowing colors and shadows. Now the dark ended, and he was beyond that sea of rock. On the sand of the bottom, fine wrinkles could be discerned, traced by the movement of the sea. The sun's rays penetrated all the way down, winking and flashing, and there was the glint of schools of hook-chasers, those tiny fish that swim in a very straight line, then suddenly, all of them together, make a sharp right turn.

A little puff of sand rose and it was the switching tail of a sea bream, there on the bottom. It wasn't even aware that the spear gun was aimed directly at it. Zeffirino was now swimming totally underwater; and the bream, after a few absent flicks of its striped sides, suddenly sped off at mid-depth. Among rocks bristling with sea urchins, the fish and the fisherman swam to an inlet with porous, almost bare rock. He can't get away from me here, Zeffirino thought; and at that moment the bream vanished. From nooks and hollows a stream of little air bubbles rose, then promptly ceased, to resume somewhere else. The sea anemones glowed, expectant. The bream peered from one lair, vanished into another, and promptly popped out from a distant gap. It skirted a spur of rock, headed downward. Zeffirino saw a patch of luminous green toward the bottom; the fish became lost in that light, and he dived after it.

He passed through a low arch at the foot of the cliff, and found the deep water and the sky above him again. Shadows of pale stone surrounded the bed, and out toward the open sea they descended, a half-submerged breakwater. With a twist of his hips and a thrust of the fins, Zeffirino surfaced to breathe. The snorkel surfaced, he blew out some drops that had infiltrated the mask; but the boy kept his head in the water. He had found the bream again: two bream, in fact! He was already taking aim when he saw a whole squadron of them proceeding calmly to the left, while another school glistened on the right. This was a place rich in fish, like an enclosed pond; and wherever Zeffirino looked he saw a flicker of sharp fins, the glint of scales; his joy and wonder were so great, he forgot to shoot even once.

The thing was not to be in a hurry, to study the best shots, and not to sow panic on all sides. Keeping his head down, Zeffirino moved toward the nearest rock; along its face, in the water, he saw a white hand swaying. The sea was motionless; on the taut and polished surface, concentric circles spread out, as if raindrops were falling. The boy raised his head and looked. Lying prone on the edge of the rock shelf, a fat woman in a bathing suit was taking the sun. And she was crying. Her tears ran down her cheeks one after another and dropped into the sea.

Zeffirino pushed his mask up on his forehead and said, "Excuse me."

The fat woman said, "Make yourself at home, kid." And she went on crying. "Fish as much as you like."

"This place is full of fish," he explained. "Did you see how many there are?"

The fat woman kept her head raised, her eyes staring straight ahead, filled with tears. "I didn't see anything. How could I? I can't stop crying."

As long as it was a matter of sea and fish, Zeffirino was the smartest; but in the presence of people, he resumed his gaping, stammering air. "I'm sorry, signora. . . ." He would have liked to get back to his bream, but a fat, crying woman was such an unusual sight that he stayed there, spellbound, gaping at her in spite of himself.

"I'm not a signora, kid," the fat woman said with her noble, somewhat nasal voice. "Call me 'signorina.' Signorina De Magistris. And what's your name?"

"Zeffirino."

"Well, fine, Zeffirino. How's the fishing — or the shooting? What do you call it?"

"I don't know what they call it. So far I haven't caught anything. But this is a good place."

"Be careful with that gun, though. I don't mean for my sake, poor me. I mean for you. Take care you don't hurt yourself."

Zeffirino assured her she needn't worry. He sat down on the rock beside her and watched her cry for a while. There were moments when it looked as if she might stop, and she sniffed with her reddened nose, raising and shaking her head. But meanwhile, at the corners of her eyes and under her lids, a bubble of tears seemed to swell until her eyes promptly brimmed over.

Zeffirino didn't know quite what to think. Seeing a lady cry was a thing that made your heart ache. But how could anyone be sad in this enclosure of sea crammed with every variety of fish to fill the heart with desire and joy? And how could you dive into that greenness and pursue fish when there was a grown-up person nearby dissolved in tears? At the same moment, in the same place, two yearnings existed, opposed and unreconcilable, but Zeffirino could neither conceive of them both together, nor surrender to the one or to the other.

"Signorina?" he asked.

"Yes?"

"Why are you crying?"

"Because I'm unlucky in love."

"Ah!"

"You can't understand; you're still a kid."

"You want to try swimming with my mask?"

"Thank you very much. Is it nice?"

"It's the nicest thing in the world."

Signorina De Magistris got up and fastened the straps of her suit at the back. Zeffirino gave her the mask and carefully explained how to put it on. She shook her head a little, half joking and half embarrassed, with the mask over her face; but behind it you could see her eyes, which didn't stop crying for a moment. She stepped into the water awkwardly, like a seal, and began paddling, holding her face down.

The gun under his arm, Zeffirino also went in swimming.

"When you see a fish, tell me," he shouted to the signorina. In the water he didn't fool around; and the privilege of coming out fishing with him was one he granted rarely.

But the signorina raised her head and shook it. The glass had clouded over and her features were no longer visible. She took off the mask. "I can't see anything," she said. "My tears make the glass cloud over. I can't. I'm sorry." And she stood there crying in the water.

"This is bad," Zeffirino said. He hadn't brought along a half of a potato, which you can rub on the glass to clear it again; but he did the best he could with some spit, then put the mask on himself. "Watch me," he said to the fat lady. And they proceeded together through that sea, he all fins, his head down, she swimming on her side, one arm extended and the other bent, her head bitterly erect and inconsolable.

She was a poor swimmer, Signorina De Magistris, always on her side, making clumsy, stabbing strokes. And beneath her, for yards, the fish raced through the sea, starfish and squid navigated, anemones yawned. Now Zeffirino's gaze saw landscapes approaching that would dazzle anyone. The water was deep, and the sandy bed was dotted with little stones among which skeins of seaweed swayed in the barely perceptible motion of the sea—though, observed from above, the rocks themselves seem to sway on the uniform expanse of sand, in the midst of the still water dense with seaweed.

All of a sudden, the signorina saw him disappear, head down, his behind surfacing for a moment, then the fins; and then his pale shadow was underwater, dropping toward the bottom. It was the moment when the bass realized the danger: the trident spear, already fired, caught him obliquely, and its central prong drove through his tail and transfixed him. The bass raised its prickly fins and lunged, slapping the water; the other prongs of the spear hadn't hooked him, and he still hoped to escape by sacrificing his tail. But all he achieved was to catch a fin on one of the other prongs; and so he was a goner. Zeffirino was already winding in the line, and the boy's pink and happy shadow fell above the fish.

The spear rose from the water with the bass impaled on it, then the boy's arm, then the masked head, with a gurgle of water from the snorkel. And Zeffirino bared his face: "Isn't he a beauty? Eh, signorina?" The bass was big, silvery and black. But the woman continued crying.

Zeffirino climbed up on the tip of a rock. With some effort, Signorina De

Magistris followed him. To keep the fish fresh, the boy picked a little natural basin, full of water. They crouched down beside it. Zeffirino gazed at the iridescent colors of the bass, stroked its scales, and invited the signorina to do the same.

"You see how beautiful he is? You see how prickly?" When it looked as if a shaft of interest was piercing the fat lady's gloom, he said, "I'll just go off for a moment to see if I can catch another." And, fully equipped, he dived in.

The woman stayed behind with the fish. And she discovered that never had a fish been more unhappy. Now she ran her fingers over its ring-shaped mouth, along its fins, its tail. She saw a thousand tiny holes in its handsome silver body: sea lice, minuscule parasites of fish, had long since taken possession of the bass and were gnawing their way into its flesh.

Unaware of this, Zeffirino was already emerging again with a gilded umbra on the spear; and he held it out to Signorina De Magistris. The two had already divided their tasks: the woman took the fish off the prongs and put it in the pool, and Zeffirino stuck his head back into the water to go catch something else. But each time he first looked to see if the signorina had stopped crying: if the sight of a bass or an umbra wouldn't make her stop, what could possibly console her?

Gilded streaks marked the sides of the umbra. Two fins, parallel, ran down its back. And in the space between these fins, the signorina saw a deep, narrow wound, antedating those of the spear gun. A gull's beak must have pecked the fish's back with such force it was hard to figure out why it hadn't killed the fish. She wondered how long the umbra had been swimming around bearing that pain.

Faster than Zeffirino's spear, down toward a school of tiny, hesitant spicara, the sea bream plunged. He barely had time to gulp down one of the little fish before the spear stuck in his throat. Zeffirino had never fired such a good shot.

"A champion fish!" he cried, taking off his mask. "I was following the little ones! He swallowed one, and then I . . ." And he described the scene, stammering with emotion. It was impossible to catch a bigger, more beautiful fish; Zeffirino would have liked the signorina finally to share his contentment. She looked at the fat, silvery body, the throat that had just swallowed the little greenish fish, only to be ripped by the teeth of the spear: such was life throughout the sea.

In addition, Zeffirino caught a little gray fish and a red fish, a yellow-striped bream, a plump gilthead, and a flat bogue; even a mustached, spiky gurnard. But in all of them, besides the wounds of the spear, Signorina De Magistris discovered the bites of the lice that had gnawed them, or the stain of some unknown affliction, or a hook stuck for ages in the throat. This inlet the boy had discovered, where all sorts of fish gathered, was perhaps a refuge for animals sentenced to a long agony, a marine lazaretto, an arena of desperate duels.

Now Zeffirino was venturing along the rocks: octopus! He had come upon a colony squatting at the foot of a boulder. On the spear one big purplish octopus now emerged, a liquid like watered ink dripping from its wounds; and a strange uneasiness overcame Signorina De Magistris. To keep the octopus they found a more secluded basin, and Zeffirino wanted never to leave it, to stay and admire the gray-pink skin that slowly changed hues. It was late, too, and the boy was beginning to get a bit of gooseflesh, his swim had lasted so long. But Zeffirino was hardly one to renounce a whole family of octopus, now discovered.

The signorina observed the octopus, its slimy flesh, the mouths of the suckers, the reddish and almost liquid eye. Alone among the whole catch, the polyp seemed to be without blemish or torment. The tentacles of an almost human pink, so limp and sinuous and full of secret armpits, prompted thoughts of health and life, and some lazy contractions caused them to twist still, with a slight opening of the suckers. In mid-air, the hand of Signorina De Magistris sketched a caress over the coils of the octopus; her fingers moved to imitate its contraction, closer and closer, and finally touched the coils lightly.

Evening was falling; a wave began to slap the sea. The tentacles vibrated in the air like whips, and suddenly, with all its strength, the octopus was clinging to the arm of Signorina De Magistris. Standing on the rock, as if fleeing from her own imprisoned arm, she let out a cry that sounded like: It's the octopus! The octopus is torturing me!

Zeffirino, who at that very moment had managed to flush a squid, stuck his head out of the water and saw the fat woman with the octopus, which stretched out one tentacle from her arm to catch her by the throat. He also heard the end of the scream: it was a high, constant scream, but — so it seemed to the boy — without tears.

A man armed with a knife rushed up and started aiming blows at the octopus's eye. He decapitated it almost with one stroke. This was Zeffirino's father, who had filled his basket with limpets and was searching along the rocks for his son. Hearing the cry, narrowing his bespectacled gaze, he had seen the woman and run to help her, with the blade he used for his limpets. The tentacles immediately relaxed; Signorina De Magistris fainted.

When she came to, she found the octopus cut into pieces, and Zeffirino and his father made her a present of it, so she could fry it. It was evening, and Zeffirino put on his shirt. His father, with precise gestures, explained to her the secret of a good octopus fry. Zeffirino looked at her and several times thought she was about to start up again; but no, not a single tear came from her.

(1970)

❖ SAMUEL L. CLEMENS

The Celebrated Jumping Frog of Calaveras County

Samuel Clemens (1835–1910), who wrote under the pen name Mark Twain, was born in Florida, Missouri, and raised in Hannibal, a town destined to immortality as the setting of his famous novels about Huckleberry Finn and Tom Sawyer. Clemens's formal education ended at thirteen when he started working for a local newspaper. He traveled the country as a typesetter and in the five years before the Civil War, apprenticed as a steamboat pilot — then a spectacular job — on the Mississippi River, an experience vividly recounted in his *Life on the Mississippi* (1883). "Mark Twain" in fact is a technical term in riverboat jargon. Like many other adventurous souls, Clemens went West, where he got a job on a newspaper in Nevada and began to write stories and occasional pieces — such as "The Celebrated Jumping Frog of Calaveras County." He published two books on his travels, *Innocents Abroad* (1869) and *Roughing It* (1871), and collaborated with Charles Dudley Warner on a novel called *The Gilded Age* (1873). *Tom Sawyer* appeared in 1876, *Huckleberry Finn* in 1884, *A Connecticut Yankee in King Arthur's Court* in 1889, and *Puddn'head Wilson* in 1894. He became wealthy from his writing and from his many performances as public speaker and joke-teller, but he made bad investments. Still, he was able to recuperate some of his losses and died reasonably well-off. His thinking became more pessimistic in his old age, an attitude reflected in novels like *The Mysterious Stranger* (1916).

In compliance with the request of a friend of mine, who wrote me from the East, I called on good-natured, garrulous old Simon Wheeler, and inquired after my friend's friend *Leonidas W. Smiley*, as requested to do, and I hereunto append the result. I have a lurking suspicion that *Leonidas W. Smiley* is a myth; that my friend never knew such a personage; that he only conjectured that, if I asked old Wheeler about him, it would remind him of his infamous *Jim* Smiley, and he would go to work and bore me nearly to death with some infernal reminiscence of him as long and tedious as it should be useless to me. If that was the design, it certainly succeeded.

I found Simon Wheeler dozing comfortably by the barroom stove of the old, dilapidated tavern in the ancient mining camp of Angel's, and I noticed that he was fat and bald-headed, and had an expression of winning gentleness and simplicity upon his tranquil countenance. He roused up and gave me good-day. I told him a friend of mine had commissioned me to make some inquiries about a cherished companion of his boyhood named *Leonidas W. Smiley — Rev. Leonidas W. Smiley —* a young minister of the Gospel, who he had heard was at one time a resident of Angel's Camp. I added that, if Mr. Wheeler could tell me anything about this Rev. Leonidas W. Smiley, I would feel under many obligations to him.

Simon Wheeler backed me into a corner and blockaded me there with his chair, and then sat me down and reeled off the monotonous narrative which follows this paragraph. He never smiled, he never frowned, he never changed his voice from the gentle-flowing key to which he turned the initial sentence, he never betrayed the slightest suspicion of enthusiasm; but all through the interminable narrative there ran a vein of impressive earnestness and sincerity, which showed me plainly that, so far from his imagining that there was anything ridiculous or funny about his story, he regarded it as a really important matter, and admired its two heroes as men of transcendent genius in *finesse*. To me, the spectacle of a man drifting serenely along through such a queer yarn without ever smiling, was exquisitely absurd. As I said before, I asked him to tell me what he knew of Rev. Leonidas W. Smiley, and he replied as follows. I let him go on in his own way, and never interrupted him once:

"There was a feller here once by the name of *Jim* Smiley, in the winter of '49—or may be it was the spring of '50—I don't recollect exactly, somehow, though what makes me think it was one or the other is because I remember the big flume wasn't finished when he first came to the camp; but any way, he was the curiosest man about always betting on any thing that turned up you ever see, if he could get any body to bet on the other side; and if he couldn't, he'd change sides. Any way that suited the other man would suit him—any way just so's he got a bet, *he* was satisfied. But still he was lucky, uncommon lucky; he most always come out winner. He was always ready and laying for a chance; there couldn't be no solitary thing mentioned but that feller'd offer to bet on it, and take any side you please, as I was just telling you. If there was a horserace, you'd find him flush, or you'd find him busted at the end of it; if there was a dog-fight, he'd bet on it; if there was a cat-fight, he'd bet on it; if there was a chicken-fight, he'd bet on it; why, if there was two birds setting on a fence, he would bet you which one would fly first; or if there was a camp-meeting, he would be there regular, to bet on Parson Walker, which he judged to be the best exhorter about there, and so he was, too, and a good man. If he even seen a straddlebug start to go anywheres, he would bet you how long it would take him to get wherever he was going to, and if you took him up, he would follow that straddlebug to Mexico but what he would find out where he was bound for and how long he was on the road. Lots of the boys here has seen that Smiley, and can tell you about him. Why, it never made no difference to *him*—he would bet on *any* thing—the dangdest feller. Parson Walker's wife laid very sick once, for a good while, and it seemed as if they warn't going to save her; but one morning he come in, and Smiley asked how she was, and he said she was considerable better—thank the Lord for his inf'nit mercy—and coming on so smart that, with the blessing of Prov'dence, she'd get well yet; and Smiley, before he thought, says, 'Well, I'll risk two-and-a-half that she won't, any way.'

"Thish-year Smiley had a mare—the boys called her the fifteen-minute nag, but that was only in fun, you know, because, of course, she was faster than that—and he used to win money on that horse, for all she was so slow and always had the asthma, or the distemper, or the consumption, or something of that kind. They used to give her two or three hundred yards start, and then pass her under way; but always at the

fag-end of the race she'd get excited and desperate-like, and come cavorting and
straddling up, and scattering her legs around limber, sometimes in the air, and
sometimes out to one side amongst the fences, and kicking up m-o-r-e dust,
and raising m-o-r-e racket with her coughing and sneezing and blowing her
nose — and always fetch up at the stand just about a neck ahead, as near as you could
cypher it down.

   "And he had a little small bull pup, that to look at him you'd think he wa'n't
worth a cent, but to set around and look ornery, and lay for a chance to steal
something. But as soon as money was up on him, he was a different dog; his underjaw'd
begin to stick out like the fo'castle of a steamboat, and his teeth would uncover, and
shine savage like the furnaces. And a dog might tackle him, and bullyrag him, and bite
him, and throw him over his shoulder two or three times, and Andrew Jackson —
which was the name of the pup — Andrew Jackson would never let on but what *he* was
satisfied, and hadn't expected nothing else — and the bets being doubled and doubled
on the other side all the time, till the money was all up; and then all of a sudden he
would grab that other dog jest by the j'int of his hind leg and freeze to it — not chaw,
you understand, but only jest grip and hang on till they throwed up the sponge, if it
was a year. Smiley always come out winner on that pup, till he harnessed a dog once
that didn't have no hind legs, because they'd been sawed off by a circular saw, and
when the thing had gone along far enough, and the money was all up, and he come to
make a snatch for his pet holt, he saw in a minute how he'd been imposed on, and how
the other dog had him in the door, so to speak, and he 'peared surprised, and then he
looked sorter discouraged-like, and didn't try no more to win the fight, and so he got
shucked out bad. He give Smiley a look, as much as to say his heart was broke, and it
was *his* fault, for putting up a dog that hadn't no hind legs for him to take holt of,
which was his main dependence in a fight, and then he limped off a piece and laid
down and died. It was a good pup, was that Andrew Jackson, and would have made a
name for hisself if he'd lived, for the stuff was in him, and he had genius — I know it,
because he hadn't had no opportunity to speak of, and it don't stand to reason that a
dog could make such a fight as he could under them circumstances, if he hadn't no
talent. It always makes me feel sorry when I think of that last fight of his'n, and the
way it turned out.

   "Well, thish-yer Smiley had rattarriers, and chicken cocks, and tomcats, and
all them kind of things, till you couldn't rest, and you couldn't fetch nothing for him to
bet on but he'd match you. He ketched a frog one day, and took him home, and said he
cal'klated to ederacate him; and so he never done nothing for three months but set in
his back yard and learn that frog to jump. And you bet he *did* learn him, too. He'd give
him a little punch behind, and the next minute you'd see that frog whirling in the air
like a doughnut — see him turn one summerset, or may be a couple, if he got a good
start, and come down flat footed and all right, like a cat. He got him up so in the
matter of catching flies, and kept him in practice so constant, that he'd had a fly every
time as far as he could see him. Smiley said all a frog wanted was education, and he
could do most anything — and I believe him. Why, I've seen him set Dan'l Webster
down here on this floor — Dan'l Webster was the name of the frog — and sing out,
'Flies, Dan'l, flies!' and quicker'n you could wink, he'd spring straight up, and snake a
fly off'n the counter there, and flop down on the floor again as solid as a gob of mud,
and fall to scratching the side of his head with his hind foot as indifferent as if he

hadn't no idea he'd been doin' any more'n any frog might do. You never see a frog so modest and straightfor'ard as he was, for all he was so gifted. And when it come to fair and square jumping on a dead level, he could get over more ground at one straddle than any animal of his breed you ever see. Jumping on a dead level was his strong suit, you understand; and when it come to that Smiley would ante up money on him as long as he had a red. Smiley was monstrous proud of his frog, and well he might be, for fellers that had traveled and been everywheres, all said he laid over any frog that ever *they* see.

"Well, Smiley kept the beast in a little lattice box, and he used to fetch him down town sometimes and lay for a bet. One day a feller — a stranger in the camp, he was — come across him with his box, and says:

"'What might it be that you've got in the box?'

"And Smiley says, sorter indifferent like, 'It might be a parrot, or it might be a canary, may be, but it ain't — it's only just a frog.'

"And the feller took it, and looked at it careful, and turned it round this way and that, and says, 'H'm — so 't is. Well, what's *he* good for?'

"'Well,' Smiley says, easy and carelessness, 'He's good enough for *one* thing, I should judge — he can outjump any frog in Calaveras county.'

"The feller took the box again, and took another long, particular look, and give it back to Smiley, and says, very deliberate, 'Well, I don't see no p'ints about that frog that's any better'n any other frog.'

"'May be you don't,' Smiley says. 'May be you understand frogs, and may be you don't understand 'em; may be you've had experience, and may be you an't only a amature, as it were. Anyways, I've got *my* opinion, and I'll risk forty dollars he can outjump any frog in Calaveras county.'

"And the feller studied a minute, and then says, kinder sad like, 'Well, I'm only a stranger here, and I an't got no frog, but if I had a frog, I'd bet you.'

"And then Smiley says, 'That's all right — that's all right — if you'll hold my box a minute, I'll go and get you a frog.' And so the feller took the box and put up his forty dollars along with Smiley's, and set down to wait.

"So he set there a good while thinking and thinking to hisself, and then he got the frog out and prized his mouth open and took a teaspoon and filled him full of quail shot — filled him pretty near up to his chin — and set him on the floor. Smiley he went to the swamp and slopped around in the mud for a long time, and finally he ketched a frog, and fetched him in, and give him to this feller, and says:

"'Now, if you're ready, set him alongside of Dan'l, with his fore-paws just even with Dan'l, and I'll give the word.' Then he says, 'One-two-three-jump!' and him and the feller touched up the frogs from behind, and the new frog hopped off, but Dan'l give a heave, and hysted up his shoulders — so — like a Frenchman, but it wa'n't no use — couldn't budge; he was planted as solid as an anvil, and he couldn't no more stir than if he was anchored out. Smiley was a good deal surprised, and he was disgusted too, but he didn't have no idea what the matter was, of course.

"The feller took the money and started away; and when he was going out of the door, he sorter jerked his thumb over his shoulders — this way — at Dan'l, and says again, very deliberate, 'Well, I don' see no p'ints about that frog that's any better'n any other frog.'

"Smiley he stood scratching his head and looking down at Dan'l a long time, and at last he says, 'I do wonder what in the nation that frog throw'd off for—I wonder if there ain't something the matter with him—he 'pears to look mighty baggy, somehow.' And he ketched Dan'l by the nap of the neck, and lifted him up and says, 'Why, blame my cats, if he don't weigh five pound!' and turned him upside down, and he belched out a double handful of shot. And then he see how it was, and he was the maddest man—he set the frog down and took out after that feller, but he never ketched him. And—"

[Here Simon Wheeler heard his name called from the front yard, and got up to see what was wanted.] And turning to me as he moved away, he said: "Just set where you are, stranger, and rest easy—I ain't going to be gone a second."

But, by your leave, I did not think that a continuation of the history of the enterprising vagabond *Jim* Smiley would be likely to afford me much information concerning the Rev. *Leonidas W.* Smiley, and so I started away.

At the door I met the sociable Wheeler returning, and he buttonholed me and recommenced:

"Well, thish-yer Smiley had a yaller one-eyed cow that didn't have no tail, only jest a short stump like a bannanner, and—"

"Oh! hang Smiley and his afflicted cow!" I muttered, good-naturedly, and bidding the old gentleman good-day, I departed.

(1865)

❖ COLETTE

The Hand

Colette (1873–1954) was born Sidonie-Gabrielle Colette in a small town in Burgundy. She married the Parisian author Henri Guthier-Villars at twenty and went to live in Paris. Her husband helped her write a series of short novels, the "Claudine" books (*Claudine at School*, etc.) which told of the adventures of a young girl growing up in the provinces. Unfortunately Villars not only "spiced" these books up, but signed them as his own. Colette divorced Villars and went on the stage to support herself. The novel that best conveys these experiences is *La Vagabonde* (1911). She married and divorced another man, and finally found the right husband in Maurice Godeket, who devoted his life to helping her career. Colette was an extremely prolific writer, publishing over fifty novels and many more short stories and pieces of nonfiction. Her most famous novels are *Chéri* (1920) and its sequel *The Last of Chéri* (1926). Her later novels include *The Cat* (1933), *Julie de Carneilhan* (1941), and *Gigi* (1944), which was made into a renowned musical and movie. Colette was also famous as a drama critic and fashion writer.

He had fallen asleep on his young wife's shoulder, and she proudly supported the weight of his head, with its fair hair, his sanguine-complexioned face and closed eyes. He had slipped his large arm beneath the slim, adolescent back and his strong hand lay flat on the sheet, beside the young woman's right elbow. She smiled as she looked at the man's hand emerging there, quite alone and far removed from its owner. Then she let her glance stray round the dimly lit bedroom. A conch-shaped lamp threw a subdued glow of periwinkle-blue over the bed. 'Too happy to sleep,' she thought.

Too excited also, and often surprised by her new state. For only two weeks she had taken part in the scandalous existence of a honeymoon couple, each of them relishing the pleasure of living with an unknown person they were in love with. To meet a good-looking, fair-haired young man, recently widowed, good at tennis and sailing, and marry him a month later: her conjugal romance fell little short of abduction. Whenever she lay awake beside her husband, like tonight, she would still keep her eyes closed for a long time, then open them and relish with astonishment the blue of the brand-new curtains, replacing the apricot-pink which had filtered with the morning light into the room where she had slept as a girl.

A shudder ran through the sleeping body lying beside her and she tightened her left arm round her husband's neck, with the delightful authority of weak creatures. He did not wake up.

'What long eyelashes he has,' she said to herself.

She silently praised also the full, graceful mouth, the brick-red skin and the forehead, neither noble nor lofty, but still free of wrinkles.

Her husband's right hand, beside her, also shuddered, and beneath the curve of her back she felt the right arm, on which her whole weight was resting, come to life.

'I'm heavy . . . I'd like to reach up and put the light out, but he's so fast asleep. . . .'

The arm tensed again, gently, and she arched her back to make herself lighter.

'It's as though I were lying on an animal,' she thought.

She turned her head slightly on the pillow and looked at the hand lying beside her.

'How big it is! It's really bigger than my whole head!'

The light which crept from under the edge of a blue crystal globe fell on to this hand and showed up the slightest reliefs in the skin, exaggerated the powerful, knotty knuckles and the veins which stood out because of the pressure on the arm. A few russet hairs, at the base of the fingers, all lay in the same direction, like ears of wheat in the wind, and the flat nails, whose ridges had not been smoothed out by the polisher, gleamed beneath their coat of pink varnish.

'I'll tell him not to put varnish on his nails,' thought the young wife. 'Varnish and carmine don't suit a hand so . . . a hand so . . .'

An electric shock ran through the hand and spared the young woman the trouble of thinking of an adjective. The thumb stiffened until it was horribly long and spatulate, and moved close up against the index finger. In this way the hand suddenly acquired an apelike appearance.

'Oh!' said the young woman quietly, as though faced with some minor indecency.

The horn of a passing car pierced the silence with a noise so shrill that it seemed luminous. The sleeper did not wake but the hand seemed offended and reared up, tensing itself like a crab and waiting for the fray. The piercing sound receded and the hand, gradually relaxing, let fall its claws, became a soft animal, bent double and shaken with faint jerks which looked like a death agony. The flat, cruel nail on the over-long thumb glistened. On the little finger there appeared a slight deviation which the young woman had never noticed, and the sprawling hand revealed its fleshy palm like a red belly.

'And I've kissed that hand! . . . How horrible! I can't ever have looked at it!'

The hand was disturbed by some bad dream, and seemed to respond to this sudden reaction, this disgust. It regrouped its forces, opened out wide, spread out its tendons, its nerves and its hairiness like a panoply of war. Then it slowly withdrew, grasped a piece of sheeting, dug down with its curving fingers and squeezed and squeezed with the methodical pleasure of a strangler. . . .

'Oh!' cried the young woman.

The hand disappeared, the large arm was freed of its burden and in one moment became a protective girdle, a warm bulwark against the terrors of night. But next morning, when the tray with frothing chocolate and toast was on the bed, she saw the hand again, russet and red, and the ghastly thumb crooked over the handle of a knife.

'Do you want this piece of toast, darling? I'm doing it for you.'

She shuddered and felt gooseflesh high up on her arms and down her back. 'Oh, no . . . no . . .'

Then she concealed her fear, controlled herself bravely and, beginning her life of duplicity, resignation, base and subtle diplomacy, she leant over and humbly kissed the monstrous hand.

(1924)

❖ JOSEPH CONRAD
The Secret Sharer

Joseph Conrad (1857–1924) was born Teodor Josef Konrad Korzen-
iowski in Ukraine of Polish parents. He immigrated to France and then
to England at twenty-one. Between 1874 and 1894 he spent much of
his life at sea, latterly as captain of his own ship. He knew no English
when he arrived in England, but, astonishingly, became one of the
great English writers of the twentieth century. A predominant theme
of his many novels and short stories is the fate of man alone and
confronted by the riddle of life. These confrontations usually occur in
exotic locations: the East Indies, Central Africa, South America, and, of
course, at sea. His famous early novels are *Almayer's Folly* (1895), *An
Outcast of the Islands* (1896), *The Nigger of the 'Narcissus'* (1898),
and *Lord Jim* (1900). During this period he also wrote brilliant long
short stories or "novellas" such as "Youth," "Heart of Darkness," and
"Typhoon" (1902). Later novels include *Nostromo* (1904), *The Secret
Agent* (1907), *Under Western Eyes* (1911), *Chance* (1914), *Victory*
(1915), and *The Rescue* (1920). *The Collected Works* appeared in
1926.

I

On my right hand there were lines of fishing stakes resembling a mysterious system
of half-submerged bamboo fences, incomprehensible in its division of the domain of
tropical fishes, and crazy of aspect as if abandoned forever by some nomad tribe of
fishermen now gone to the other end of the ocean; for there was no sign of human
habitation as far as the eye could reach. To the left a group of barren islets, suggesting
ruins of stone walls, towers, and blockhouses, had its foundations set in a blue sea that
itself looked solid, so still and stable did it lie below my feet; even the track of light
from the westering sun shone smoothly, without that animated glitter which tells of an
imperceptible ripple. And when I turned my head to take a parting glance at the tug
which had just left us anchored outside the bar, I saw the straight line of the flat shore
joined to the stable sea, edge to edge, with a perfect and unmarked closeness, in one
leveled floor half brown, half blue under the enormous dome of the sky. Corresponding
in their insignificance to the islets of the sea, two small clumps of trees, one on each
side of the only fault in the impeccable joint, marked the mouth of the river Meinam
we had just left on the first preparatory stage of our homeward journey; and, far back
on the inland level, a larger and loftier mass, the grove surrounding the great Paknam
pagoda, was the only thing on which the eye could rest from the vain task of exploring
the monotonous sweep of the horizon. Here and there gleams as of a few scattered
pieces of silver marked the windings of the great river; and on the nearest of them, just
within the bar, the tug steaming right into the land became lost to my sight, hull and
funnel and masts, as though the impassive earth had swallowed her up without an

effort, without a tremor. My eye followed the light cloud of her smoke, now here, now there, above the plain, according to the devious curves of the stream, but always fainter and farther away, till I lost it at last behind the miter-shaped hill of the great pagoda. And then I was left alone with my ship, anchored at the head of the Gulf of Siam.

She floated at the starting point of a long journey, very still in an immense stillness, the shadows of her spars flung far to the eastward by the setting sun. At that moment I was alone on her decks. There was not a sound in her—and around us nothing moved, nothing lived, not a canoe on the water, not a bird in the air, not a cloud in the sky. In this breathless pause at the threshold of a long passage we seemed to be measuring our fitness for a long and arduous enterprise, the appointed task of both our existences to be carried out, far from all human eyes, with only sky and sea for spectators and for judges.

There must have been some glare in the air to interfere with one's sight, because it was only just before the sun left us that my roaming eyes made out beyond the highest ridges of the principal islet of the group something which did away with the solemnity of perfect solitude. The tide of darkness flowed on swiftly; and with tropical suddenness a swarm of stars came out above the shadowy earth, while I lingered yet, my hand resting lightly on my ship's rail as if on the shoulder of a trusted friend. But, with all that multitude of celestial bodies staring down at one, the comfort of quiet communion with her was gone for good. And there were also disturbing sounds by this time—voices, footsteps forward; the steward flitted along the main-deck, a busily ministering spirit; a hand bell tinkled urgently under the poop deck. . . .

I found my two officers waiting for me near the supper table, in the lighted cuddy. We sat down at once, and as I helped the chief mate, I said:

"Are you aware that there is a ship anchored inside the islands? I saw her mastheads above the ridge as the sun went down."

He raised sharply his simple face, overcharged by a terrible growth of whisker, and emitted his usual ejaculations: "Bless my soul, sir! You don't say so!"

My second mate was a round-cheeked, silent young man, grave beyond his years, I thought; but as our eyes happened to meet I detected a slight quiver on his lips. I looked down at once. It was not my part to encourage sneering on board my ship. It must be said, too, that I knew very little of my officers. In consequence of certain events of no particular significance, except to myself, I had been appointed to the command only a fortnight before. Neither did I know much of the hands forward. All these people had been together for eighteen months or so, and my position was that of the only stranger on board. I mention this because it has some bearing on what is to follow. But what I felt most was my being a stranger to the ship; and if all the truth must be told, I was somewhat of a stranger to myself. The youngest man on board (barring the second mate), and untried as yet by a position of the fullest responsibility, I was willing to take the adequacy of the others for granted. They had simply to be equal to their tasks; but I wondered how far I should turn out faithful to that ideal conception of one's own personality every man sets up for himself secretly.

Meantime the chief mate, with an almost visible effect of collaboration on the part of his round eyes and frightful whiskers, was trying to evolve a theory of the anchored ship. His dominant trait was to take all things into earnest consideration. He was of a painstaking turn of mind. As he used to say, he "liked to account to himself" for practically everything that came in his way, down to a miserable scorpion he had found in his cabin a week before. The why and the wherefore of that scorpion — how it got on board and came to select his room rather than the pantry (which was a dark place and more what a scorpion would be partial to), and how on earth it managed to drown itself in the inkwell of his writing desk — had exercised him infinitely. The ship within the islands was much more easily accounted for; and just as we were about to rise from table he made his pronouncement. She was, he doubted not, a ship from home lately arrived. Probably she drew too much water to cross the bar except at the top of spring tides. Therefore she went into that natural harbor to wait for a few days in preference to remaining in an open roadstead.

"That's so," confirmed the second mate, suddenly, in his slightly hoarse voice. "She draws over twenty feet. She's the Liverpool ship *Sephora* with a cargo of coal. Hundred and twenty-three days from Cardiff."

We looked at him in surprise.

"The tugboat skipper told me when he came on board for your letters, sir," explained the young man. "He expects to take her up the river the day after tomorrow."

After thus overwhelming us with the extent of his information he slipped out of the cabin. The mate observed regretfully that he "could not account for that young fellow's whims." What prevented him telling us all about it at once, he wanted to know.

I detained him as he was making a move. For the last two days the crew had had plenty of hard work, and the night before they had very little sleep. I felt painfully that I — a stranger — was doing something unusual when I directed him to let all hands turn in without setting an anchor watch. I proposed to keep on deck myself till one o'clock or thereabouts. I would get the second mate to relieve me at that hour.

"He will turn out the cook and the steward at four," I concluded, "and then give you a call. Of course at the slightest sign of any sort of wind we'll have the hands up and make a start at once."

He concealed his astonishment. "Very well, sir." Outside the cuddy he put his head in the second mate's door to inform him of my unheard-of caprice to take a five hours' anchor watch on myself. I heard the other raise his voice incredulously —"What? The Captain himself?" Then a few more murmurs, a door closed, then another. A few moments later I went on deck.

My strangeness, which had made me sleepless, had prompted that unconventional arrangement, as if I had expected in those solitary hours of the night to get on terms with the ship of which I knew nothing, manned by men of whom I knew very little more. Fast alongside a wharf, littered like any ship in port with a tangle of unrelated things, invaded by unrelated shore people, I had hardly seen her yet properly. Now, as she lay cleared for sea, the stretch of her main-deck seemed to me very fine under the stars. Very fine, very roomy for her size, and very inviting. I descended the poop and paced the waist, my mind picturing to myself the coming passage through the Malay Archipelago, down the Indian Ocean, and up the Atlantic. All its phases were familiar enough to me, every characteristic, all the alternatives which were likely to face me on the high seas — everything! . . . except the novel responsibility of command. But I took heart from the reasonable thought that the ship was like other ships, the men like other men, and that the sea was not likely to keep any special surprises expressly for my discomfiture.

Arrived at that comforting conclusion, I bethought myself of a cigar and went below to get it. All was still down there. Everybody at the after end of the ship was sleeping profoundly. I came out again on the quarter-deck, agreeably at ease in my sleeping suit on that warm breathless night, barefooted, a glowing cigar in my teeth, and, going forward, I was met by the profound silence of the fore end of the ship. Only as I passed the door of the forecastle I heard a deep, quiet, trustful sigh of some sleeper inside. And suddenly I rejoiced in the great security of the sea as compared with the unrest of the land, in my choice of that untempted life presenting no disquieting problems, invested with an elementary moral beauty by the absolute straightforwardness of its appeal and by the singleness of its purpose.

The riding light in the forerigging burned with a clear, untroubled, as if symbolic, flame, confident and bright in the mysterious shades of the night. Passing on my way aft along the other side of the ship, I observed that the rope side ladder, put over, no doubt, for the master of the tug when he came to fetch away our letters, had not been hauled in as it should have been. I became annoyed at this, for exactitude in some small matters is the very soul of discipline. Then I reflected that I had myself peremptorily dismissed my officers from duty, and by my own act had prevented the anchor watch being formally set and things properly attended to. I asked myself whether it was wise ever to interfere with the established routine of duties even from the kindest of motives. My action might have made me appear eccentric. Goodness only knew how that absurdly whiskered mate would "account" for my conduct, and what the whole ship thought of that informality of their new captain. I was vexed with myself.

Not from compunction certainly, but, as it were mechanically, I proceeded to get the ladder in myself. Now a side ladder of that sort is a light affair and comes in easily, yet my vigorous tug, which should have brought it flying on board, merely recoiled upon my body in a totally unexpected jerk. What the devil! . . . I was so astounded by the immovableness of that ladder that I remained stockstill, trying to account for it to myself like that imbecile mate of mine. In the end, of course, I put my head over the rail.

The side of the ship made an opaque belt of shadow on the darkling glassy shimmer of the sea. But I saw at once something elongated and pale floating very close to the ladder. Before I could form a guess, a faint flash of phosphorescent light, which seemed to issue suddenly from the naked body of a man, flickered in the sleeping water with the elusive, silent play of summer lightning in a night sky. With a gasp I saw revealed to my stare a pair of feet, the long legs, a broad livid back immersed right up to the neck in a greenish cadaverous glow. One hand, awash, clutched the bottom rung of the ladder. He was complete but for the head. A headless corpse! The cigar dropped out of my gaping mouth with a tiny plop and a short hiss quite audible in the absolute stillness of all things under heaven. At that I suppose he raised up his face, a dimly pale oval in the shadow of the ship's side. But even then I could only barely make out down there the shape of his black-haired head. However, it was enough for the horrid, frost-bound sensation which had gripped me about the chest to pass off. The moment of vain exclamations was past, too. I only climbed on the spare spar and leaned over the rail as far as I could, to bring my eyes nearer to that mystery floating alongside.

As he hung by the ladder, like a resting swimmer, the sea lightning played about his limbs at every stir; and he appeared in it ghastly, silvery, fishlike. He remained as mute as a fish, too. He made no motion to get out of the water, either. It was inconceivable that he should not attempt to come on board, and strangely troubling to suspect that perhaps he did not want to. And my first words were prompted by just that troubled incertitude.

"What's the matter?" I asked in my ordinary tone, speaking down to the face upturned exactly under mine.

"Cramp," it answered, no louder. Then slightly anxious, "I say, no need to call anyone."

"I was not going to," I said.

"Are you alone on deck?"

"Yes."

I had somehow the impression that he was on the point of letting go the ladder to swim away beyond my ken — mysterious as he came. But, for the moment, this being appearing as if he had risen from the bottom of the sea (it was certainly the nearest land to the ship) wanted only to know the time. I told him. And he, down there, tentatively:

"I suppose your captain's turned in?"

"I am sure he isn't," I said.

He seemed to struggle with himself, for I heard something like the low, bitter murmur of doubt. "What's the good?" His next words came out with a hesitating effort.

"Look here, my man. Could you call him out quietly?"

I thought the time had come to declare myself.

"*I* am the captain."

I heard a "By Jove!" whispered at the level of the water. The phosphorescence flashed in the swirl of the water all about his limbs, his other hand seized the ladder.

"My name's Leggatt."

The voice was calm and resolute. A good voice. The self-possession of that man had somehow induced a corresponding state in myself. It was very quietly that I remarked:

"You must be a good swimmer."

"Yes. I've been in the water practically since nine o'clock. The question for me now is whether I am to let go this ladder and go on swimming till I sink from exhaustion, or — to come on board here."

I felt this was no mere formula of desperate speech, but a real alternative in the view of a strong soul. I should have gathered from this that he was young; indeed, it is only the young who are ever confronted by such clear issues. But at the time it was pure intuition on my part. A mysterious communication was established already between us two — in the face of that silent, darkened tropical sea. I was young, too; young enough to make no comment. The man in the water began suddenly to climb up the ladder, and I hastened away from the rail to fetch some clothes.

Before entering the cabin I stood still, listening in the lobby at the foot of the stairs. A faint snore came through the closed door of the chief mate's room. The second mate's door was on the hook, but the darkness in there was absolutely soundless. He, too, was young and could sleep like a stone. Remained the steward, but he was not likely to wake up before he was called. I got a sleeping suit out of my room and, coming back on deck, saw the naked man from the sea sitting on the main hatch, glimmering white in the darkness, his elbows on his knees and his head in his hands. In a moment he had concealed his damp body in a sleeping suit of the same gray-stripe pattern as the one I was wearing and followed me like my double on the poop. Together we moved right aft, barefooted, silent.

"What is it?" I asked in a deadened voice, taking the lighted lamp out of the binnacle, and raising it to his face.

"An ugly business."

He had rather regular features; a good mouth; light eyes under somewhat heavy, dark eyebrows; a smooth, square forehead; no growth on his cheeks; a small, brown mustache, and a well-shaped, round chin. His expression was concentrated, meditative, under the inspecting light of the lamp I held up to his face; such as a man thinking hard in solitude might wear. My sleeping suit was just right for his size. A well-knit young fellow of twenty-five at most. He caught his lower lip with the edge of white, even teeth.

"Yes," I said, replacing the lamp in the binnacle. The warm, heavy tropical night closed upon his head again.

"There's a ship over there," he murmured.

"Yes, I know. The *Sephora*. Did you know of us?"

"Hadn't the slightest idea. I am the mate of her—" He paused and corrected himself. "I should say I *was*."

"Aha! Something wrong?"

"Yes. Very wrong indeed. I've killed a man."

"What do you mean? Just now?"

"No, on the passage. Weeks ago. Thirty-nine south. When I say a man—"

"Fit of temper," I suggested, confidently.

The shadowy, dark head, like mine, seemed to nod imperceptibly above the ghostly gray of my sleeping suit. It was, in the night, as though I had been faced by my own reflection in the depths of a somber and immense mirror.

"A pretty thing to have to own up to for a Conway boy," murmured my double, distinctly.

"You're a Conway boy?"

"I am," he said, as if startled. Then, slowly . . . "Perhaps you too—"

It was so; but being a couple of years older I had left before he joined. After a quick interchange of dates a silence fell; and I thought suddenly of my absurd mate with his terrific whiskers and the "Bless my soul—you don't say so" type of intellect. My double gave me an inkling of his thoughts by saying: "My father's a parson in Norfolk. Do you see me before a judge and jury on that charge? For myself I can't see the necessity. There are fellows that an angel from heaven—— And I am not that. He was one of those creatures that are just simmering all the time with a silly sort of wickedness. Miserable devils that have no business to live at all. He wouldn't do his duty and wouldn't let anybody else do theirs. But what's the good of talking! You know well enough the sort of ill-conditioned snarling cur——"

He appealed to me as if our experiences had been as identical as our clothes. And I knew well enough the pestiferous danger of such a character where there are no means of legal repression. And I knew well enough also that my double there was no homicidal ruffian. I did not think of asking him for details, and he told me the story roughly in brusque, disconnected sentences. I needed no more. I saw it all going on as though I were myself inside that other sleeping suit.

"It happened while we were setting a reefed foresail, at dusk. Reefed foresail! You understand the sort of weather. The only sail we had left to keep the ship running; so you may guess what it had been like for days. Anxious sort of job, that. He gave me some of his cursed insolence at the sheet. I tell you I was overdone with this terrific weather that seemed to have no end to it. Terrific, I tell you—and a deep ship. I believe the fellow himself was half crazed with funk. It was no time for gentlemanly reproof, so I turned round and felled him like an ox. He up and at me. We closed just as an awful sea made for the ship. All hands saw it coming and took to the rigging, but I had him by the throat, and went on shaking him like a rat, the men above us yelling, 'Look out! look out!' Then a crash as if the sky had fallen on my head. They say that for over ten minutes hardly anything was to be seen of the ship—just the three masts and a bit of the forecastle head and of the poop all awash driving along in a smother of foam. It was a miracle that they found us, jammed together behind the forebitts. It's clear that I meant business, because I was holding him by the throat still when they picked us up. He was black in the face. It was too much for them. It seems they rushed us aft together, gripped as we were, screaming 'Murder!' like a lot of lunatics, and broke into the cuddy. And the ship running for her life, touch and go all the time, any minute her last in a sea fit to turn your hair gray only a-looking at it. I understand that the skipper, too, started raving like the rest of them. The man had been deprived of sleep for more than a week, and to have this sprung on him at the height of a furious gale nearly drove him out of his mind. I wonder they didn't fling me overboard after getting the carcass of their precious shipmate out of my fingers. They had rather a job to separate us, I've been told. A sufficiently fierce story to make an old judge and a respectable jury sit up a bit. The first thing I heard when I came to myself was the maddening howling of that endless gale, and on that the voice of the old man. He was hanging on to my bunk, staring into my face out of his sou'wester.

"'Mr. Leggatt, you have killed a man. You can act no longer as chief mate of this ship.'"

His care to subdue his voice made it sound monotonous. He rested a hand on the end of the skylight to steady himself with, and all that time did not stir a limb, so far as I could see. "Nice little tale for a quiet tea party," he concluded in the same tone.

One of my hands, too, rested on the end of the skylight; neither did I stir a limb, so far as I knew. We stood less than a foot from each other. It occurred to me that if old "Bless my soul—you don't say so" were to put his head up the companion and catch sight of us, he would think he was seeing double, or imagine himself come upon a scene of weird witchcraft; the strange captain having a quiet confabulation by the wheel with his own gray ghost. I became very much concerned to prevent anything of the sort. I heard the other's soothing undertone.

"My father's a parson in Norfolk," it said. Evidently he had forgotten he had told me this important fact before. Truly a nice little tale.

"You had better slip down into my stateroom now," I said, moving off stealthily. My double followed my movements; our bare feet made no sound; I let him in, closed the door with care, and, after giving a call to the second mate, returned on deck for my relief.

"Not much sign of any wind yet," I remarked when he approached.

"No, sir. Not much," he assented, sleepily, in his hoarse voice, with just enough deference, no more, and barely suppressing a yawn.

"Well, that's all you have to look out for. You have got your orders."

"Yes, sir."

I paced a turn or two on the poop and saw him take up his position face forward with his elbow in the ratlines of the mizzen rigging before I went below. The mate's faint snoring was still going on peacefully. The cuddy lamp was burning over the table on which stood a vase with flowers, a polite attention from the ship's provision merchant — the last flowers we should see for the next three months at the very least. Two bunches of bananas hung from the beam symmetrically, one on each side of the rudder casing. Everything was as before in the ship — except that two of her captain's sleeping suits were simultaneously in use, one motionless in the cuddy, the other keeping very still in the captain's stateroom.

It must be explained here that my cabin had the form of the capital letter L, the door being within the angle and opening into the short part of the letter. A couch was to the left, the bed place to the right; my writing desk and the chronometers' table faced the door. But anyone opening it, unless he stepped right inside, had no view of what I call the long (or vertical) part of the letter. It contained some lockers surmounted by a bookcase; and a few clothes, a thick jacket or two, caps, oilskin coat, and such like, hung on hooks. There was at the bottom of that part a door opening into my bathroom, which could be entered also directly from the saloon. But that way was never used.

The mysterious arrival had discovered the advantage of this particular shape. Entering my room, lighted strongly by a big bulkhead lamp swung on gimbals above my writing desk, I did not see him anywhere till he stepped out quietly from behind the coats hung in the recessed part.

"I heard somebody moving about, and went in there at once," he whispered.

I, too, spoke under my breath.

"Nobody is likely to come in here without knocking and getting permission."

He nodded. His face was thin and the sunburn faded, as though he had been ill. And no wonder. He had been, I heard presently, kept under arrest in his cabin for nearly seven weeks. But there was nothing sickly in his eyes or in his expression. He was not a bit like me, really; yet, as we stood leaning over my bed place, whispering side by side, with our dark heads together and our backs to the door, anybody bold enough to open it stealthily would have been treated to the uncanny sight of a double captain busy talking in whispers with his other self.

"But all this doesn't tell me how you came to hang on to our side ladder," I inquired, in the hardly audible murmurs we used, after he had told me something more of the proceedings on board the *Sephora* once the bad weather was over.

"When we sighted Java Head I had had time to think all those matters out several times over. I had six weeks of doing nothing else, and with only an hour or so every evening for a tramp on the quarter-deck."

He whispered, his arms folded on the side of my bed place, staring through the open port. And I could imagine perfectly the manner of this thinking out — a stubborn if not a steadfast operation; something of which I should have been perfectly incapable.

"I reckoned it would be dark before we closed with the land," he continued, so low that I had to strain my hearing near as we were to each other, shoulder touching shoulder almost. "So I asked to speak to the old man. He always seemed very sick when he came to see me — as if he could not look me in the face. You know, that foresail saved the ship. She was too deep to have run long under bare poles. And it was I that managed to set it for him. Anyway, he came. When I had him in my cabin — he stood by the door looking at me as if I had the halter round my neck already — I asked him right away to leave my cabin door unlocked at night while the ship was going through Sunda Straits. There would be the Java coast within two or three miles, off Angier Point. I wanted nothing more. I've had a prize for swimming my second year in the Conway."

"I can believe it," I breathed out.

"God only knows why they locked me in every night. To see some of their faces you'd have thought they were afraid I'd go about at night strangling people. Am I a murdering brute? Do I look it? By Jove! If I had been he wouldn't have trusted himself like that into my room. You'll say I might have chucked him aside and bolted out, there and then — it was dark already. Well, no. And for the same reason I wouldn't think of trying to smash the door. There would have been a rush to stop me at the noise, and I did not mean to get into a confounded scrimmage. Somebody else might have got killed — for I would not have broken out only to get chucked back, and I did not want any more of that work. He refused, looking more sick than ever. He was afraid of the men, and also of that old second mate of his who had been sailing with him for years — a gray-headed old humbug; and his steward, too, had been with him devil knows how long — seventeen years or more — a dogmatic sort of loafer who hated me like poison, just because I was the chief mate. No chief mate ever made more than one voyage in the *Sephora*, you know. Those two old chaps ran the ship. Devil only knows what the skipper wasn't afraid of (all his nerve went to pieces altogether in that hellish spell of bad weather we had) — of what the law would do to him — of his wife, perhaps. Oh, yes! she's on board. Though I don't think she would have meddled. She would have been only too glad to have me out of the ship in any way. The 'brand of Cain' business, don't you see. That's all right. I was ready enough to go off wandering on the face of the earth — and that was price enough to pay for an Abel of that sort. Anyhow, he wouldn't listen to me. 'This thing must take its course. I represent the law here.' He was shaking like a leaf. 'So you won't?' 'No!' 'Then I hope you will be able to sleep on that,' I said, and turned my back on him. 'I wonder that *you* can,' cries he, and locks the door.

"Well after that, I couldn't. Not very well. That was three weeks ago. We have had a slow passage through the Java Sea; drifted about Carimata for ten days. When we anchored here they thought, I suppose, it was all right. The nearest land (and that's five miles) is the ship's destination; the consul would soon set about catching me; and there would have been no object in bolting to these islets there. I don't suppose there's a drop of water on them. I don't know how it was, but tonight that steward, after bringing me my supper, went out to let me eat it, and left the door unlocked. And I ate it — all there was, too. After I had finished I strolled out on the quarter-deck. I don't know that I meant to do anything. A breath of fresh air was all I wanted, I believe. Then a sudden temptation came over me. I kicked off my slippers and was in the water before I had made up my mind fairly. Somebody heard the splash and they raised an awful hullabaloo. 'He's gone! Lower the boats! He's committed suicide! No, he's swimming.' Certainly I was swimming. It's not so easy for a swimmer like me to commit suicide by drowning. I landed on the nearest islet before the boat left the ship's side. I heard them pulling about in the dark, hailing, and so on, but after a bit they gave up. Everything quieted down and the anchorage became as still as death. I sat down on a stone and began to think. I felt certain they would start searching for me at daylight. There was no place to hide on those stony things — and if there had been, what would have been the good? But now I was clear of that ship, I was not going back. So after a while I took off all my clothes, tied them up in a bundle with a stone inside, and dropped them in the deep water on the outer side of that islet. That was suicide enough for me. Let them think what they liked, but I didn't mean to drown myself. I meant to swim till I sank — but that's not the same thing. I struck out for another of these little islands, and it was from that one that I first saw your riding light. Something to swim for. I went on easily, and on the way I came upon a flat rock a foot or two above water. In the daytime, I dare say, you might make it out with a glass from your poop. I scrambled up on it and rested myself for a bit. Then I made another start. That last spell must have been over a mile."

His whisper was getting fainter and fainter, and all the time he stared straight out through the porthole, in which there was not even a star to be seen. I had not interrupted him. There was something that made comment impossible in his narrative, or perhaps in himself; a sort of feeling, a quality, which I can't find a name for. And when he ceased, all I found was a futile whisper: "So you swam for our light?"

"Yes — straight for it. It was something to swim for. I couldn't see any stars low down because the coast was in the way, and I couldn't see the land, either. The water was like glass. One might have been swimming in a confounded thousand-feet deep cistern with no place for scrambling out anywhere; but what I didn't like was the notion of swimming round and round like a crazed bullock before I gave out; and as I didn't mean to go back . . . No. Do you see me being hauled back, stark naked, off one of these little islands by the scruff of the neck and fighting like a wild beast? Somebody would have got killed for certain, and I did not want any of that. So I went on. Then your ladder——"

"Why didn't you hail the ship?" I asked, a little louder.

He touched my shoulder lightly. Lazy footsteps came right over our heads and stopped. The second mate had crossed from the other side of the poop and might have been hanging over the rail for all we knew.

"He couldn't hear us talking — could he?" My double breathed into my very ear, anxiously.

His anxiety was in answer, a sufficient answer, to the question I had put to him. An answer containing all the difficulty of that situation. I closed the porthole quietly, to make sure. A louder word might have been overheard.

"Who's that?" he whispered then.

"My second mate. But I don't know much more of the fellow than you do."

And I told him a little about myself. I had been appointed to take charge while I least expected anything of the sort, not quite a fortnight ago. I didn't know either the ship or the people. Hadn't had the time in port to look about me or size anybody up. And as to the crew, all they knew was that I was appointed to take the ship home. For the rest, I was almost as much of a stranger on board as himself, I said. And at the moment I felt it most acutely. I felt that it would take very little to make me a suspect person in the eyes of the ship's company.

He had turned about meantime; and we, the two strangers in the ship, faced each other in identical attitudes.

"Your ladder——" he murmured, after a silence. "Who'd have thought of finding a ladder hanging over at night in a ship anchored out here! I felt just then a very unpleasant faintness. After the life I've been leading for nine weeks, anybody would have got out of condition. I wasn't capable of swimming round as far as your rudder chains. And, lo and behold! there was a ladder to get hold of. After I gripped it I said to myself, 'What's the good?' When I saw a man's head looking over I thought I would swim away presently and leave him shouting — in whatever language it was. I didn't mind being looked at. I—I liked it. And then you speaking to me so quietly — as if you had expected me — made me hold on a little longer. It had been a confounded lonely time — I don't mean while swimming. I was glad to talk a little to somebody that didn't belong to the *Sephora*. As to asking for the captain, that was a mere impulse. It could have been no use, with all the ship knowing about me and the other people pretty certain to be round here in the morning. I don't know — I wanted to be seen, to talk with somebody, before I went on. I don't know what I would have said. . . . 'Fine night, isn't it?' or something of the sort."

"Do you think they will be round here presently?" I asked with some incredulity.

"Quite likely," he said, faintly.

He looked extremely haggard all of a sudden. His head rolled on his shoulders.

"H'm. We shall see then. Meantime get into that bed," I whispered. "Want help? There."

It was a rather high bed place with a set of drawers underneath. This amazing swimmer really needed the lift I gave him by seizing his leg. He tumbled in, rolled over on his back, and flung one arm across his eyes. And then, with his face nearly hidden, he must have looked exactly as I used to look in that bed. I gazed upon my other self for a while before drawing across carefully the two green serge curtains which ran on a brass rod. I thought for a moment of pinning them together for greater safety, but I sat down on the couch, and once there I felt unwilling to rise and hunt for a pin. I would do it in a moment. I was extremely tired, in a peculiarly intimate way, by the strain of stealthiness, by the effort of whispering and the general secrecy of this excitement. It was three o'clock by now and I had been on my feet since nine, but I was not sleepy; I could not have gone to sleep. I sat there, fagged out, looking at the curtains, trying to clear my mind of the confused sensation of being in two places at once, and greatly bothered by an exasperating knocking in my head. It was a relief to discover suddenly that it was not in my head at all, but on the outside of the door. Before I could collect myself the words "Come in" were out of my mouth, and the steward entered with a tray, bringing in my morning coffee. I had slept, after all, and I was so frightened that I shouted, "This way! I am here, steward," as though he had been miles away. He put down the tray on the table next the couch and only then said, very quietly, "I can see you are here, sir." I felt him give me a keen look, but I dared not meet his eyes just then. He must have wondered why I had drawn the curtains of my bed before going to sleep on the couch. He went out, hooking the door open as usual.

I heard the crew washing decks above me. I knew I would have been told at once if there had been any wind. Calm, I thought, and I was doubly vexed. Indeed, I felt dual more than ever. The steward reappeared suddenly in the doorway. I jumped up from the couch so quickly that he gave a start.

"What do you want here?"

"Close your port, sir—they are washing decks."

"It is closed," I said, reddening.

"Very well, sir." But he did not move from the doorway and returned my stare in an extraordinary, equivocal manner for a time. Then his eyes wavered, all his expression changed, and in a voice unusually gentle, almost coaxingly:

"May I come in to take the empty cup away, sir?"

"Of course!" I turned my back on him while he popped in and out. Then I unhooked and closed the door and even pushed the bolt. This sort of thing could not go on very long. The cabin was as hot as an oven, too. I took a peep at my double, and discovered that he had not moved, his arm was still over his eyes; but his chest heaved; his hair was wet; his chin glistened with perspiration. I reached over him and opened the port.

"I must show myself on deck," I reflected.

Of course, theoretically, I could do what I liked, with no one to say nay to me within the whole circle of the horizon; but to lock my cabin door and take the key away I did not dare. Directly I put my head out of the companion I saw the group of my two officers, the second mate barefooted, the chief mate in long India-rubber boots, near the break of the poop, and the steward halfway down the poop ladder talking to them eagerly. He happened to catch sight of me and dived, the second ran down on the main-deck shouting some order or other, and the chief mate came to meet me, touching his cap.

There was a sort of curiosity in his eye that I did not like. I don't know whether the steward had told them that I was "queer" only, or downright drunk, but I know the man meant to have a good look at me. I watched him coming with a smile which, as he got into point-blank range, took effect and froze his very whiskers. I did not give him time to open his lips.

"Square the yards by lifts and braces before the hands go to breakfast."

It was the first particular order I had given on board that ship; and I stayed on deck to see it executed, too. I had felt the need of asserting myself without loss of time. That sneering young cub got taken down a peg or two on that occasion, and I also seized the opportunity of having a good look at the face of every foremast man as they filed past me to go to the after braces. At breakfast time, eating nothing myself, I presided with such frigid dignity that the two mates were only too glad to escape from the cabin as soon as decency permitted; and all the time the dual working of my mind distracted me almost to the point of insanity. I was constantly watching myself, my secret self, as dependent on my actions as my own personality, sleeping in that bed, behind that door which faced me as I sat at the head of the table. It was very much like being mad, only it was worse because one was aware of it.

I had to shake him for a solid minute, but when at last he opened his eyes it was in the full possession of his senses, with an inquiring look.

"All's well so far," I whispered. "Now you must vanish into the bathroom."

He did so, as noiseless as a ghost, and then I rang for the steward, and facing him boldly, directed him to tidy up my stateroom while I was having my bath — "and be quick about it." As my tone admitted of no excuses, he said, "Yes, sir," and ran off to fetch his dustpan and brushes. I took a bath and did most of my dressing, splashing, and whistling softly for the steward's edification, while the secret sharer of my life stood drawn up bolt upright in that little space, his face looking very sunken in daylight, his eyelids lowered under the stern, dark line of his eyebrows drawn together by a slight frown.

When I left him there to go back to my room the steward was finishing dusting. I sent for the mate and engaged him in some insignificant conversation. It was, as it were, trifling with the terrific character of his whiskers; but my object was to give him an opportunity for a good look at my cabin. And then I could at last shut, with a clear conscience, the door of my stateroom and get my double back into the recessed part. There was nothing else for it. He had to sit still on a small folding stool, half smothered by the heavy coats hanging there. We listened to the steward going into the bathroom out of the saloon, filling the water bottles there, scrubbing the bath, setting things to rights, whisk, bang, clatter — out again into the saloon — turn the key —click. Such was my scheme for keeping my second self invisible. Nothing better could be contrived under the circumstances. And there we sat; I at my writing desk ready to appear busy with some papers, he behind me out of sight of the door. It would not have been prudent to talk in daytime; and I could not have stood the excitement of that queer sense of whispering to myself. Now and then, glancing over my shoulder, I saw him far back there, sitting rigidly on the low stool, his bare feet close together, his arms folded, his head hanging on his breast — and perfectly still. Anybody would have taken him for me.

I was fascinated by it myself. Every moment I had to glance over my shoulder. I was looking at him when a voice outside the door said:

"Beg pardon, sir."

"Well!" . . . I kept my eyes on him, and so when the voice outside the door announced, "There's a ship's boat coming our way, sir," I saw him give a start — the first movement he had made for hours. But he did not raise his bowed head.

"All right. Get the ladder over."

I hesitated. Should I whisper something to him? But what? His immobility seemed to have been never disturbed. What could I tell him he did not know already? . . . Finally I went on deck.

II

The skipper of the *Sephora* had a thin red whisker all round his face, and the sort of complexion that goes with hair of that color; also the particular, rather smeary shade of blue in the eyes. He was not exactly a showy figure; his shoulders were high, his stature but middling — one leg slightly more bandy than the other. He shook hands, looking vaguely around. A spiritless tenacity was his main characteristic, I judged. I behaved with a politeness which seemed to disconcert him. Perhaps he was shy. He mumbled to me as if he were ashamed of what he was saying; gave his name (it was something like Archbold — but at this distance of years I hardly am sure), his ship's name, and a few other particulars of that sort, in the manner of a criminal making a reluctant and doleful confession. He had had terrible weather on the passage out — terrible — terrible — wife aboard, too.

By this time we were seated in the cabin and the steward brought in a tray with a bottle and glasses. "Thanks! No." Never took liquor. Would have some water, though. He drank two tumblerfuls. Terrible thirsty work. Ever since daylight had been exploring the islands round his ship.

"What was that for — fun?" I asked, with an appearance of polite interest.

"No!" He sighed. "Painful duty."

As he persisted in his mumbling and I wanted my double to hear every word, I hit upon the notion of informing him that I regretted to say I was hard of hearing.

"Such a young man, too!" he nodded, keeping his smeary blue, unintelligent eyes fastened upon me. "What was the cause of it — some disease?" he inquired, without the least sympathy and as if he thought that, if so, I'd got no more than I deserved.

"Yes; disease," I admitted in a cheerful tone which seemed to shock him. But my point was gained, because he had to raise his voice to give me his tale. It is not worth while to record that version. It was just over two months since all this had happened, and he had thought so much about it that he seemed completely muddled as to its bearings, but still immensely impressed.

"What would you think of such a thing happening on board your own ship? I've had the *Sephora* for these fifteen years. I am a well-known shipmaster."

He was densely distressed — and perhaps I should have sympathized with him if I had been able to detach my mental vision from the unsuspected sharer of my cabin as though he were my second self. There he was on the other side of the bulkhead, four or five feet from us, no more, as we sat in the saloon. I looked politely at Captain Archbold (if that was his name), but it was the other I saw, in a gray sleeping suit, seated on a low stool, his bare feet close together, his arms folded, and every word said between us falling into the ears of his dark head bowed on his chest.

"I have been at sea now, man and boy, for seven-and-thirty years, and I've never heard of such a thing happening in an English ship. And that it should be my ship. Wife on board, too."

I was hardly listening to him.

"Don't you think," I said, "that the heavy sea which, you told me, came aboard just then might have killed the man? I have seen the sheer weight of a sea kill a man very neatly, by simply breaking his neck."

"Good God!" he uttered, impressively, fixing his smeary blue eyes on me. "The sea! No man killed by the sea ever looked like that." He seemed positively scandalized at my suggestion. And as I gazed at him certainly not prepared for anything original on his part, he advanced his head close to mine and thrust his tongue out at me so suddenly that I couldn't help starting back.

After scoring over my calmness in this graphic way he nodded wisely. If I had seen the sight, he assured me, I would never forget it as long as I lived. The weather was too bad to give the corpse a proper sea burial. So next day at dawn they took it up on the poop, covering its face with a bit of bunting; he read a short prayer, and then, just as it was, in its oilskins and long boots, they launched it amongst those mountainous seas that seemed ready every moment to swallow up the ship herself and the terrified lives on board of her.

"That reefed foresail saved you," I threw in.

"Under God—it did," he exclaimed fervently. "It was by a special mercy, I firmly believe, that it stood some of those hurricane squalls."

"It was the setting of that sail which——" I began.

"God's own hand in it," he interrupted me. "Nothing less could have done it. I don't mind telling you that I hardly dared give the order. It seemed impossible that we could touch anything without losing it, and then our last hope would have been gone."

The terror of that gale was on him yet. I let him go on for a bit, then said, casually—as if returning to a minor subject:

"You were very anxious to give up your mate to the shore people, I believe?"

He was. To the law. His obscure tenacity on that point had in it something incomprehensible and a little awful; something, as it were, mystical, quite apart from his anxiety that he should not be suspected of "countenancing any doings of that sort." Seven-and-thirty virtuous years at sea, of which over twenty of immaculate command, and the last fifteen in the *Sephora*, seemed to have laid him under some pitiless obligation.

"And you know," he went on, groping shame-facedly amongst his feelings, "I did not engage that young fellow. His people had some interest with my owners. I was in a way forced to take him on. He looked very smart, very gentlemanly, and all that. But do you know—I never liked him, somehow. I am a plain man. You see, he wasn't exactly the sort for the chief mate of a ship like the *Sephora*."

I had become so connected in thoughts and impressions with the secret sharer of my cabin that I felt as if I, personally, were being given to understand that I, too, was not the sort that would have done for the chief mate of a ship like the *Sephora*. I had no doubt of it in my mind.

"Not at all the style of man. You understand," he insisted, superfluously, looking hard at me.

I smiled urbanely. He seemed at a loss for a while.

"I suppose I must report a suicide."

"Beg pardon?"

"Sui-cide! That's what I'll have to write to my owners directly I get in."

"Unless you manage to recover him before tomorrow," I assented, dispassionately. . . . "I mean, alive."

He mumbled something which I really did not catch, and I turned my ear to him in a puzzled manner. He fairly bawled:

"The land—I say, the mainland is at least seven miles off my anchorage."

"About that."

My lack of excitement, of curiosity, of surprise, of any sort of pronounced interest, began to arouse his distrust. But except for the felicitous pretense of deafness I had not tried to pretend anything. I had felt utterly incapable of playing the part of ignorance properly, and therefore was afraid to try. It is also certain that he had brought some ready-made suspicions with him, and that he viewed my politeness as a strange and unnatural phenomenon. And yet how else could I have received him? Not heartily! That was impossible for psychological reasons, which I need not state here. My only object was to keep off his inquiries. Surlily? Yes, but surliness might have provoked a point-blank question. From its novelty to him and from its nature, punctilious courtesy was the manner best calculated to restrain the man. But there was the danger of his breaking through my defense bluntly. I could not, I think, have met him by a direct lie, also for psychological (not moral) reasons. If he had only known how afraid I was of his putting my feeling of identity with the other to the test! But, strangely enough—(I thought of it only afterwards)—I believe that he was not a little disconcerted by the reverse side of that weird situation, by something in me that reminded him of the man he was seeking—suggested a mysterious similitude to the young fellow he had distrusted and disliked from the first.

However that might have been, the silence was not very prolonged. He took another oblique step.

"I reckon I had no more than a two-mile pull to your ship. Not a bit more."

"And quite enough, too, in this awful heat," I said.

Another pause full of mistrust followed. Necessity, they say, is mother of invention, but fear, too, is not barren of ingenious suggestions. And I was afraid he would ask me point-blank for news of my other self.

"Nice little saloon, isn't it?" I remarked, as if noticing for the first time the way his eyes roamed from one closed door to the other. "And very well fitted out, too. Here, for instance," I continued, reaching over the back of my seat negligently and flinging the door open, "is my bathroom."

He made an eager movement, but hardly gave it a glance. I got up, shut the door of the bathroom, and invited him to have a look round, as if I were very proud of my accommodation. He had to rise and be shown round, but he went through the business without any raptures whatever.

"And now we'll have a look at my stateroom," I declared, in a voice as loud as I dared to make it, crossing the cabin to the starboard side with purposely heavy steps.

He followed me in and gazed around. My intelligent double had vanished. I played my part.

"Very convenient—isn't it?"

"Very nice. Very comf . . ." He didn't finish and went out brusquely as if to escape from some unrighteous wiles of mine. But it was not to be. I had been too frightened not to feel vengeful; I felt I had him on the run, and I meant to keep him on the run. My polite insistence must have had something menacing in it, because he gave in suddenly. And I did not let him off a single item; mate's room, pantry, storerooms, the very sail locker which was also under the poop—he had to look into them all. When at last I showed him out on the quarter-deck he drew a long, spiritless sigh, and mumbled dismally that he must really be going back to his ship now. I desired my mate, who had joined us, to see to the captain's boat.

The man of whiskers gave a blast on the whistle which he used to wear hanging round his neck, and yelled, "*Sephora's* away!" My double down there in my cabin must have heard, and certainly could not feel more relieved than I. Four fellows came running out from somewhere forward and went over the side, while my own men, appearing on deck too, lined the rail. I escorted my visitor to the gangway ceremoniously, and nearly overdid it. He was a tenacious beast. On the very ladder he lingered, and in that unique, guiltily conscientious manner of sticking to the point:

"I say . . . you . . . you don't think that——"

I covered his voice loudly:

"Certainly not. . . . I am delighted. Good-by."

I had an idea of what he meant to say, and just saved myself by the privilege of defective hearing. He was too shaken generally to insist, but my mate, close witness of that parting, looked mystified and his face took on a thoughtful cast. As I did not want to appear as if I wished to avoid all communication with my officers, he had the opportunity to address me.

"Seems a very nice man. His boat's crew told our chaps a very extraordinary story, if what I am told by the steward is true. I suppose you had it from the captain, sir?"

"Yes. I had a story from the captain."

"A very horrible affair—isn't it, sir?"

"It is."

"Beats all these tales we hear about murders in Yankee ships."

"I don't think it beats them. I don't think it resembles them in the least."

"Bless my soul—you don't say so! But of course I've no acquaintance whatever with American ships, not I, so I couldn't go against your knowledge. It's horrible enough for me. . . . But the queerest part is that those fellows seemed to have some idea the man was hidden aboard here. They had really. Did you ever hear of such a thing?"

"Preposterous—isn't it?"

We were walking to and fro athwart the quarter-deck. No one of the crew forward could be seen (the day was Sunday), and the mate pursued:

"There was some little dispute about it. Our chaps took offense. 'As if we would harbor a thing like that,' they said. 'Wouldn't you like to look for him in our coal-hole?' Quite a tiff. But they made it up in the end. I suppose he did drown himself. Don't you, sir?"

"I don't suppose anything."

"You have no doubt in the matter, sir?"

"None whatever."

I left him suddenly. I felt I was producing a bad impression, but with my double down there it was most trying to be on deck. And it was almost as trying to be below. Altogether a nerve-trying situation. But on the whole I felt less torn in two when I was with him. There was no one in the whole ship whom I dared take into my confidence. Since the hands had got to know his story, it would have been impossible to pass him off for anyone else, and an accidental discovery was to be dreaded now more than ever. . . .

The steward being engaged in laying the table for dinner, we could talk only with our eyes when I first went down. Later in the afternoon we had a cautious try at whispering. The Sunday quietness of the ship was against us; the stillness of air and water around her was against us; the elements, the men were against us — everything was against us in our secret partnership; time itself — for this could not go on forever. The very trust in Providence was, I suppose, denied to his guilt. Shall I confess that this thought cast me down very much? And as to the chapter of accidents which counts for so much in the book of success, I could only hope that it was closed. For what favorable accident could be expected?

"Did you hear everything?" were my first words as soon as we took up our position side by side, leaning over my bed place.

He had. And the proof of it was his earnest whisper, "The man told you he hardly dared to give the order."

I understood the reference to be to that saving foresail.

"Yes. He was afraid of it being lost in the setting."

"I assure you he never gave the order. He may think he did, but he never gave it. He stood there with me on the break of the poop after the main topsail blew away, and whimpered about our last hope — positively whimpered about it and nothing else — and the night coming on! To hear one's skipper go on like that in such weather was enough to drive any fellow out of his mind. It worked me up into a sort of desperation. I just took it into my own hands and went away from him, boiling, and—— But what's the use telling you? *You* know! . . . Do you think that if I had not been pretty fierce with them I should have got the men to do anything? Not I! The bo's'n perhaps? Perhaps! It wasn't a heavy sea — it was a sea gone mad! I suppose the end of the world will be something like that; and a man may have the heart to see it coming once and be done with it — but to have to face it day after day——I don't blame anybody. I was precious little better than the rest. Only — I was an officer of that old coal wagon, anyhow——"

"I quite understand," I conveyed that sincere assurance into his ear. He was out of breath with whispering; I could hear him pant slightly. It was all very simple. The same strung-up force which had given twenty-four men a chance, at least, for their lives, had, in a sort of recoil, crushed an unworthy mutinous existence.

But I had no leisure to weigh the merits of the matter — footsteps in the saloon, a heavy knock. "There's enough wind to get under way with, sir." Here was the call of a new claim upon my thoughts and even upon my feelings.

"Turn the hands up," I cried through the door. "I'll be on deck directly."

I was going out to make the acquaintance of my ship. Before I left the cabin our eyes met — the eyes of the only two strangers on board. I pointed to the recessed part where the little campstool awaited him and laid my finger on my lips. He made a gesture — somewhat vague — a little mysterious, accompanied by a faint smile, as if of regret.

This is not the place to enlarge upon the sensations of a man who feels for the first time a ship move under his feet to his own independent word. In my case they were not unalloyed. I was not wholly alone with my command; for there was that stranger in my cabin. Or rather, I was not completely and wholly with her. Part of me was absent. That mental feeling of being in two places at once affected me physically as if the mood of secrecy had penetrated my very soul. Before an hour had elapsed since the ship had begun to move, having occasion to ask the mate (he stood by my side) to take a compass bearing of the pagoda, I caught myself reaching up to his ear in whispers. I say I caught myself, but enough had escaped to startle the man. I can't describe it otherwise than by saying that he shied. A grave, preoccupied manner, as though he were in possession of some perplexing intelligence, did not leave him henceforth. A little later I moved away from the rail to look at the compass with such a stealthy gait that the helmsman noticed it — and I could not help noticing the unusual roundness of his eyes. These are trifling instances, though it's to no commander's advantage to be suspected of ludicrous eccentricities. But I was also more seriously affected. There are to a seaman certain words, gestures, that should in given conditions come as naturally, as instinctively as the winking of a menaced eye. A certain order should spring on to his lips without thinking; a certain sign should get itself made, so to speak, without reflection. But all unconscious alertness had abandoned me. I had to make an effort of will to recall myself back (from the cabin) to the conditions of the moment. I felt that I was appearing an irresolute commander to those people who were watching me more or less critically.

And, besides, there were the scares. On the second day out, for instance, coming off the deck in the afternoon (I had straw slippers on my bare feet) I stopped at the open pantry door and spoke to the steward. He was doing something there with his back to me. At the sound of my voice he nearly jumped out of his skin, as the saying is, and incidentally broke a cup.

"What on earth's the matter with you?" I asked, astonished.

He was extremely confused. "Beg your pardon, sir. I made sure you were in your cabin."

"You see I wasn't."

"No, sir. I could have sworn I had heard you moving in there not a moment ago. It's most extraordinary . . . very sorry, sir."

I passed on with an inward shudder. I was so identified with my secret double that I did not even mention the fact in those scanty, fearful whispers we exchanged. I suppose he had made some slight noise of some kind or other. It would have been miraculous if he hadn't at one time or another. And yet, haggard as he appeared, he looked always perfectly self-controlled, more than calm — almost invulnerable. On my suggestion he remained almost entirely in the bathroom, which, upon the whole, was the safest place. There could be really no shadow of an excuse for anyone ever wanting to go in there, once the steward had done with it. It was a very tiny place. Sometimes he reclined on the floor, his legs bent, his head sustained on one elbow. At others I would find him on the campstool, sitting in his gray sleeping suit and with his cropped dark hair like a patient, unmoved convict. At night I would smuggle him into my bed place, and we would whisper together, with the regular footfalls of the officer of the watch passing and repassing over our heads. It was an infinitely miserable time. It was lucky that some tins of fine preserves were stowed in a locker in my stateroom; hard bread I could always get hold of; and so he lived on stewed chicken, *pâté de foie gras*, asparagus, cooked oysters, sardines — on all sorts of abominable sham delicacies out of tins. My early-morning coffee he always drank; and it was all I dared do for him in that respect.

Every day there was the horrible maneuvering to go through so that my room and then the bathroom should be done in the usual way. I came to hate the sight of the steward, to abhor the voice of that harmless man. I felt that it was he who would bring on the disaster of discovery. It hung like a sword over our heads.

The fourth day out, I think (we were then working down the east side of the Gulf of Siam, tack for tack, in light winds and smooth water) — the fourth day, I say, of this miserable juggling with the unavoidable, as we sat at our evening meal, that man, whose slightest movement I dreaded, after putting down the dishes ran up on deck busily. This could not be dangerous. Presently he came down again; and then it appeared that he had remembered a coat of mine which I had thrown over a rail to dry after having been wetted in a shower which had passed over the ship in the afternoon. Sitting stolidly at the head of the table I became terrified at the sight of the garment on his arm. Of course he made for my door. There was no time to lose.

"Steward," I thundered. My nerves were so shaken that I could not govern my voice and conceal my agitation. This was the sort of thing that made my terrifically whiskered mate tap his forehead with his forefinger. I had detected him using that gesture while talking on deck with a confidential air to the carpenter. It was too far to hear a word, but I had no doubt that this pantomime could only refer to the strange new captain.

"Yes, sir," the pale-faced steward turned resignedly to me. It was this maddening course of being shouted at, checked without rhyme or reason, arbitrarily chased out of my cabin, suddenly called into it, sent flying out of his pantry on incomprehensible errands, that accounted for the growing wretchedness of his expression.

"Where are you going with that coat?"

"To your room, sir."

"Is there another shower coming?"

"I'm sure I don't know, sir. Shall I go up again and see, sir?"

"No! never mind."

My object was attained, as of course my other self in there would have heard everything that passed. During this interlude my two officers never raised their eyes off their respective plates; but the lip of that confounded cub, the second mate, quivered visibly.

I expected the steward to hook my coat on and come out at once. He was very slow about it; but I dominated my nervousness sufficiently not to shout after him. Suddenly I became aware (it could be heard plainly enough) that the fellow for some reason or other was opening the door of the bathroom. It was the end. The place was literally not big enough to swing a cat in. My voice died in my throat and I went stony all over. I expected to hear a yell of surprise and terror, and made a movement, but had not the strength to get on my legs. Everything remained still. Had my second self taken the poor wretch by the throat? I don't know what I could have done next moment if I had not seen the steward come out of my room, close the door, and then stand quietly by the sideboard.

"Saved," I thought. "But, no! Lost! Gone! He was gone!"

I laid my knife and fork down and leaned back in my chair. My head swam. After a while, when sufficiently recovered to speak in a steady voice, I instructed my mate to put the ship round at eight o'clock himself.

"I won't come on deck," I went on. "I think I'll turn in, and unless the wind shifts I don't want to be disturbed before midnight. I feel a bit seedy."

"You did look middling bad a little while ago," the chief mate remarked without showing any great concern.

They both went out, and I stared at the steward clearing the table. There was nothing to be read on that wretched man's face. But why did he avoid my eyes, I asked myself. Then I thought I should like to hear the sound of his voice.

"Steward!"

"Sir!" Startled as usual.

"Where did you hang up that coat?"

"In the bathroom, sir." The usual anxious tone. "It's not quite dry yet, sir."

For some time longer I sat in the cuddy. Had my double vanished as he had come? But of his coming there was an explanation, whereas his disappearance would be inexplicable. . . . I went slowly into my dark room, shut the door, lighted the lamp, and for a time dared not turn round. When at last I did I saw him standing bolt-upright in the narrow recessed part. It would not be true to say I had a shock, but an irresistible doubt of his bodily existence flitted through my mind. Can it be, I asked myself, that he is not visible to other eyes than mine? It was like being haunted. Motionless, with a grave face, he raised his hands slightly at me in a gesture which meant clearly, "Heavens! what a narrow escape!" Narrow indeed. I think I had come creeping quietly as near insanity as any man who has not actually gone over the border. That gesture restrained me, so to speak.

The mate with the terrific whiskers was not putting the ship on the other tack. In the moment of profound silence which follows upon the hands going to their stations I heard on the poop his raised voice: "Hard alee!" and the distant shout of the order repeated on the main-deck. The sails, in that light breeze, made but a faint fluttering noise. It ceased. The ship was coming round slowly: I held my breath in the renewed stillness of expectation; one wouldn't have thought that there was a single living soul on her decks. A sudden brisk shout, "Mainsail haul!" broke the spell, and in the noisy cries and rush overhead of the men running away with the main brace we two, down in my cabin, came together in our usual position by the bed place.

He did not wait for my question. "I heard him fumbling here and just managed to squat myself down in the bath," he whispered to me. "The fellow only opened the door and put his arm in to hang the coat up. All the same——"

"I never thought of that," I whispered back, even more appalled than before at the closeness of the shave, and marveling at that something unyielding in his character which was carrying him through so finely. There was no agitation in his whisper. Whoever was being driven distracted, it was not he. He was sane. And the proof of his sanity was continued when he took up the whispering again.

"It would never do for me to come to life again."

It was something that a ghost might have said. But what he was alluding to was his old captain's reluctant admission of the theory of suicide. It would obviously serve his turn—if I had understood at all the view which seemed to govern the unalterable purpose of his action.

"You must maroon me as soon as ever you can get amongst these islands off the Cambodge shore," he went on.

"Maroon you! We are not living in a boy's adventure tale," I protested. His scornful whispering took me up.

"We aren't indeed! There's nothing of a boy's tale in this. But there's nothing else for it. I want no more. You don't suppose I am afraid of what can be done to me? Prison or gallows or whatever they may please. But you don't see me coming back to explain such things to an old fellow in a wig and twelve respectable tradesmen, do you? What can they know whether I am guilty or not—or of *what* I am guilty, either? That's my affair. What does the Bible say? 'Driven off the face of the earth.' Very well, I am off the face of the earth now. As I came at night so I shall go."

"Impossible!" I murmured. "You can't."

"Can't? . . . Not naked like a soul on the Day of Judgment. I shall freeze on to this sleeping suit. The Last Day is not yet—and . . . you have understood thoroughly. Didn't you?"

I felt suddenly ashamed of myself. I may say truly that I understood—and my hesitation in letting that man swim away from my ship's side had been a mere sham sentiment, a sort of cowardice.

"It can't be done now till next night," I breathed out. "The ship is on the off-shore tack and the wind may fail us."

"As long as I know that you understand," he whispered. "But of course you do. It's a great satisfaction to have got somebody to understand. You seem to have been there on purpose." And in the same whisper, as if we two whenever we talked had to say things to each other which were not fit for the world to hear, he added, "It's very wonderful."

We remained side by side talking in our secret way—but sometimes silent or just exchanging a whispered word or two at long intervals. And as usual he stared through the port. A breath of wind came now and again into our faces. The ship might have been moored in dock, so gently and on an even keel she slipped through the water, that did not murmur even at our passage, shadowy and silent like a phantom sea.

At midnight I went on deck, and to my mate's great surprise put the ship round on the other tack. His terrible whiskers flitted round me in silent criticism. I certainly should not have done it if it had been only a question of getting out of that sleepy gulf as quickly as possible. I believe he told the second mate, who relieved him, that it was a great want of judgment. The other only yawned. That intolerable cub shuffled about so sleepily and lolled against the rails in such a slack, improper fashion that I came down on him sharply.

"Aren't you properly awake yet?"

"Yes, sir! I am awake."

"Well, then, be good enough to hold yourself as if you were. And keep a lookout. If there's any current we'll be closing with some islands before daylight."

The east side of the gulf is fringed with islands, some solitary, others in groups. On the blue background of the high coast they seem to float on silvery patches of calm water, arid and gray, or dark green and rounded like clumps of evergreen bushes, with the larger ones, a mile or two long, showing the outlines of ridges, ribs of gray rock under the dank mantle of matted leafage. Unknown to trade, to travel, almost to geography, the manner of life they harbor is an unsolved secret. There must be villages — settlements of fishermen at least — on the largest of them, and some communication with the world is probably kept up by native craft. But all that forenoon, as we headed for them, fanned along by the faintest of breezes, I saw no sign of man or canoe in the field of the telescope I kept on pointing at the scattered group.

At noon I gave no orders for a change of course, and the mate's whiskers became much concerned and seemed to be offering themselves unduly to my notice. At last I said:

"I am going to stand right in. Quite in — as far as I can take her."

The stare of extreme surprise imparted an air of ferocity also to his eyes, and he looked truly terrific for a moment.

"We're not doing well in the middle of the gulf," I continued, casually. "I am going to look for the land breezes tonight."

"Bless my soul! Do you mean, sir, in the dark amongst the lot of all them islands and reefs and shoals?"

"Well — if there are any regular land breezes at all on this coast one must get close inshore to find them, mustn't one?"

"Bless my soul!" he exclaimed again under his breath. All that afternoon he wore a dreamy, contemplative appearance which in him was a mark of perplexity. After dinner I went into my stateroom as if I meant to take some rest. There we two bent our dark heads over a half-unrolled chart lying on my bed.

"There," I said. "It's got to be Koh-ring. I've been looking at it ever since sunrise. It has got two hills and a low point. It must be inhabited. And on the coast opposite there is what looks like the mouth of a biggish river — with some towns, no doubt, not far up. It's the best chance for you that I can see."

"Anything. Koh-ring let it be."

He looked thoughtfully at the chart as if surveying chances and distances from a lofty height — and following with his eyes his own figure wandering on the blank land of Cochin-China, and then passing off that piece of paper clean out of sight into uncharted regions. And it was as if the ship had two captains to plan her course for her. I had been so worried and restless running up and down that I had not had the patience to dress that day. I had remained in my sleeping suit, with straw slippers and a soft floppy hat. The closeness of the heat in the gulf had been most oppressive, and the crew were used to seeing me wandering in that airy attire.

"She will clear the south point as she heads now," I whispered into his ear. "Goodness only knows when, though, but certainly after dark. I'll edge her in to half a mile, as far as I may be able to judge in the dark——"

"Be careful," he murmured, warningly — and I realized suddenly that all my future, the only future for which I was fit, would perhaps go irretrievably to pieces in any mishap to my first command.

I could not stop a moment longer in the room. I motioned him to get out of sight and made my way on the poop. That unplayful cub had the watch. I walked up and down for a while thinking things out, then beckoned him over.

"Send a couple of hands to open the two quarter-deck ports," I said, mildly.

He actually had the impudence, or else so forgot himself in his wonder at such an incomprehensible order, as to repeat:

"Open the quarter-deck ports! What for, sir?"

"The only reason you need concern yourself about is because I tell you to do so. Have them open wide and fastened properly."

He reddened and went off, but I believe made some jeering remark to the carpenter as to the sensible practice of ventilating a ship's quarter-deck. I know he popped into the mate's cabin to impart the fact to him because the whiskers came on deck, as it were by chance, and stole glances at me from below — for signs of lunacy or drunkenness, I suppose.

A little before supper, feeling more restless than ever, I rejoined, for a moment, my second self. And to find him sitting so quietly was surprising, like something against nature, inhuman.

I developed my plan in a hurried whisper.

"I shall stand in as close as I dare and then put her round. I will presently find means to smuggle you out of here into the sail locker, which communicates with the lobby. But there is an opening, a sort of square for hauling the sails out, which gives straight on the quarter-deck and which is never closed in fine weather, so as to give air to the sails. When the ship's way is deadened in stays and all the hands are aft at the main braces you will have a clear road to slip out and get overboard through the open quarter-deck port. I've had them both fastened up. Use a rope's end to lower yourself into the water so as to avoid a splash — you know. It could be heard and cause some beastly complication."

He kept silent for a while, then whispered, "I understand."

"I won't be there to see you go," I began with an effort. "The rest . . . I only hope I have understood, too."

"You have. From first to last" — and for the first time there seemed to be a faltering, something strained in his whisper. He caught hold of my arm, but the ringing of the supper bell made me start. He didn't though; he only released his grip.

After supper I didn't come below again till well past eight o'clock. The faint, steady breeze was loaded with dew; and the wet, darkened sails held all there was of propelling power in it. The night, clear and starry, sparkled darkly, and the opaque, lightless patches shifting slowly against the low stars were the drifting islets. On the port bow there was a big one more distant and shadowily imposing by the great space of sky it eclipsed.

On opening the door I had a back view of my very own self looking at a chart. He had come out of the recess and was standing near the table.

"Quite dark enough," I whispered.

He stepped back and leaned against my bed with a level, quiet glance. I sat on the couch. We had nothing to say to each other. Over our heads the officer of the watch moved here and there. Then I heard him move quickly. I knew what that meant. He was making for the companion; and presently his voice was outside my door.

"We are drawing in pretty fast, sir. Land looks rather close."

"Very well," I answered. "I am coming on deck directly."

I waited till he was gone out of the cuddy, then rose. My double moved too. The time had come to exchange our last whispers, for neither of us was ever to hear each other's natural voice.

"Look here!" I opened a drawer and took out three sovereigns. "Take this anyhow. I've got six and I'd give you the lot, only I must keep a little money to buy some fruit and vegetables for the crew from native boats as we go through Sunda Straits."

He shook his head.

"Take it," I urged him, whispering desperately. "No one can tell what —— "

He smiled and slapped meaningly the only pocket of the sleeping jacket. It was not safe, certainly. But I produced a large old silk handkerchief of mine, and tying the three pieces of gold in a corner, pressed it on him. He was touched, I supposed, because he took it at last and tied it quickly round his waist under the jacket, on his bare skin.

Our eyes met; several seconds elapsed, till, our glances still mingled, I extended my hand and turned the lamp out. Then I passed through the cuddy, leaving the door of my room wide open. . . . "Steward!"

He was still lingering in the pantry in the greatness of his zeal, giving a rub-up to a plated cruet stand the last thing before going to bed. Being careful not to wake up the mate, whose room was opposite, I spoke in an undertone.

He looked round anxiously. "Sir!"

"Can you get me a little hot water from the galley?"

"I am afraid, sir, the galley fire's been out for some time now."

"Go and see."

He flew up the stairs.

"Now," I whispered, loudly, into the saloon — too loudly, perhaps, but I was afraid I couldn't make a sound. He was by my side in an instant — the double captain slipped past the stairs — through a tiny dark passage . . . a sliding door. We were in the sail locker, scrambling on our knees over the sails. A sudden thought struck me. I saw myself wandering barefooted, bareheaded, the sun beating on my dark poll. I snatched off my floppy hat and tried hurriedly in the dark to ram it on my other self. He dodged and fended off silently. I wonder what he thought had come to me before he understood and suddenly desisted. Our hands met gropingly, lingered united in a steady, motionless clasp for a second. . . . No word was breathed by either of us when they separated.

I was standing quietly by the pantry door when the steward returned.

"Sorry, sir. Kettle barely warm. Shall I light the spirit lamp?"

"Never mind."

I came out on deck slowly. It was now a matter of conscience to shave the land as close as possible — for now he must go overboard whenever the ship was put in stays. Must! There could be no going back for him. After a moment I walked over to leeward and my heart flew into my mouth at the nearness of the land on the bow. Under any other circumstances I would not have held on a minute longer. The second mate had followed me anxiously.

I looked on till I felt I could command my voice.

"She will weather," I said then in a quiet tone.

"Are you going to try that, sir?" he stammered out incredulously.

I took no notice of him and raised my tone just enough to be heard by the helmsman.

"Keep her good full."

"Good full, sir."

The wind fanned my cheek, the sails slept, the world was silent. The strain of watching the dark loom of the land grow bigger and denser was too much for me. I had shut my eyes — because the ship must go closer. She must! The stillness was intolerable. Were we standing still?

When I opened my eyes the second view started my heart with a thump. The black southern hill of Koh-ring seemed to hang right over the ship like a towering fragment of the ever-lasting night. On that enormous mass of blackness there was not a gleam to be seen, not a sound to be heard. It was gliding irresistibly towards us and yet seemed already within reach of the hand. I saw the vague figures of the watch grouped in the waist, gazing in awed silence.

"Are you going on, sir?" inquired an unsteady voice at my elbow.

I ignored it. I had to go on.

"Keep her full. Don't check her way. That won't do now," I said, warningly.

"I can't see the sails very well," the helmsman answered me, in strange, quavering tones.

Was she close enough? Already she was, I won't say in the shadow of the land, but in the very blackness of it, already swallowed up as it were, gone too close to be recalled, gone from me altogether.

"Give the mate a call," I said to the young man who stood at my elbow as still as death. "And turn all hands up."

My tone had a borrowed loudness reverberated from the height of the land. Several voices cried out together: "We are all on deck, sir."

Then stillness again, with the great shadow gliding closer, towering higher, without a light, without a sound. Such a hush had fallen on the ship that she might have been a bark of the dead floating in slowly under the very gate of Erebus.

"My God! Where are we?"

It was the mate moaning at my elbow. He was thunderstruck, and as it were deprived of the moral support of his whiskers. He clapped his hands and absolutely cried out, "Lost!"

"Be quiet," I said, sternly.

He lowered his tone, but I saw the shadowy gesture of his despair. "What are we doing here?"

"Looking for the land wind."

He made as if to tear his hair, and addressed me recklessly.

"She will never get out. You have done it, sir. I knew it'd end in something like this. She will never weather, and you are too close now to stay. She'll drift ashore before she's round. O my God!"

I caught his arm as he was raising it to batter his poor devoted head, and shook it violently.

"She's ashore already," he wailed, trying to tear himself away.

"Is she? . . . Keep good full there!"

"Good full, sir," cried the helmsman in a frightened, thin, childlike voice.

I hadn't let go the mate's arm and went on shaking it. "Ready about, do you hear? You go forward"—shake—"and stop there"—shake—"and hold your noise" —shake—"and see these head-sheets properly overhauled"—shake, shake—shake.

And all the time I dared not look towards the land lest my heart should fail me. I released my grip at last and he ran forward as if fleeing for dear life.

I wondered what my double there in the sail locker thought of this commotion. He was able to hear everything—and perhaps he was able to understand why, on my conscience, it had to be thus close—no less. My first order "Hard alee!" re-echoed ominously under the towering shadow of Koh-ring as if I had shouted in a mountain gorge. And then I watched the land intently. In that smooth water and light wind it was impossible to feel the ship coming-to. No! I could not feel her. And my second self was making now ready to ship out and lower himself overboard. Perhaps he was gone already . . . ?

The great black mass brooding over our very mastheads began to pivot away from the ship's side silently. And now I forgot the secret stranger ready to depart, and remembered only that I was a total stranger to the ship. I did not know her. Would she do it? How was she to be handled?

I swung the mainyard and waited helplessly. She was perhaps stopped, and her very fate hung in the balance, with the black mass of Koh-ring like the gate of the everlasting night towering over her taffrail. What would she do now? Had she way on her yet? I stepped to the side swiftly, and on the shadowy water I could see nothing except a faint phosphorescent flash revealing the glassy smoothness of the sleeping surface. It was impossible to tell—and I had not learned yet the feel of my ship. Was she moving? What I needed was something easily seen, a piece of paper, which I could throw overboard and watch. I had nothing on me. To run down for it I didn't dare. There was no time. All at once my strained, yearning stare distinguished a white object floating within a yard of the ship's side. White on the black water. A phosphorescent flash passed under it. What was that thing? . . . I recognized my own floppy hat. It must have fallen off his head . . . and he didn't bother. Now I had what I wanted— the saving mark for my eyes. But I hardly thought of my other self, now gone from the ship, to be hidden forever from all friendly faces, to be a fugitive and a vagabond on the earth, with no brand of the curse on his sane forehead to stay a slaying hand . . . too proud to explain.

And I watched the hat—the expression of my sudden pity for his mere flesh. It had been meant to save his homeless head from the dangers of the sun. And now—behold—it was saving the ship, by serving me for a mark to help out the ignorance of my strangeness. Ha! It was drifting forward, warning me just in time that the ship had gathered sternway.

"Shift the helm," I said in a low voice to the seaman standing still like a statue.

The man's eyes glistened wildly in the binnacle light as he jumped round to the other side and spun round the wheel.

I walked to the break of the poop. On the overshadowed deck all hands stood by the forebraces waiting for my order. The stars ahead seemed to be gliding from right to left. And all was so still in the world that I heard the quiet remark, "She's round," passed in a tone of intense relief between two seamen.

"Let go and haul."

The foreyards ran round with a great noise, amidst cheery cries. And now the frightful whiskers made themselves heard giving various orders. Already the ship was drawing ahead. And I was alone with her. Nothing! no one in the world should stand now between us, throwing a shadow on the way of silent knowledge and mute affection, the perfect communion of a seaman with his first command.

Walking to the taffrail, I was in time to make out, on the very edge of a darkness thrown by a towering black mass like the very gateway of Erebus — yes, I was in time to catch an evanescent glimpse of my white hat left behind to mark the spot where the secret sharer of my cabin and of my thoughts, as though he were my second self, had lowered himself into the water to take his punishment: a free man, a proud swimmer striking out for a new destiny.

(1910)

❖ STEPHEN CRANE
Moonlight on the Snow

Stephen Crane (1871–1900) was born in Newark, New Jersey. He attended Syracuse University for a term before becoming a newspaperman, a profession he continued until publication of his novels *Maggie: A Girl of the Streets* (1893) and *The Red Badge of Courage* (1895). The latter, about a soldier terrified by battle in the Civil War, made him famous. Thereafter he got work as a foreign correspondent, covering the Spanish-American War. He contracted tuberculosis and died at 28 in a sanatorium in Germany. Crane was among the first American writers dedicated to a clear-eyed, naturalistic presentation of how life was really lived, especially in the slums and under the pressures of war and natural disaster. His short stories were collected in *The Open Boat and Other Tales* (1898), *The Monster* (1899), *Whilomville Stories* (1900), and *Wounds in the Rain: War Stories* (1900). *The Complete Short Stories and Sketches of Stephen Crane* was published in 1963.

I

The town of Warpost had an evil name for three hundred miles in every direction. It radiated like the shine from some stupendous light. The citizens of the place had been for years grotesquely proud of their fame as a collection of hard-shooting gentlemen, who invariably "got" the men who came up against them. When a citizen went abroad in the land, he said, "I'm f'm Warpost." And it was as if he had said, "I am the devil himself."

But ultimately it became known to Warpost that the serene-browed angel of peace was in the vicinity. The angel was full of projects for taking comparatively useless bits of prairie, and sawing them up into town lots, and making chaste and beautiful maps of his handiwork, which shook the souls of people who had never been in the West. He commonly travelled here and there in a light waggon, from the tailboard of which he made orations, which soared into the empyrean regions of true hydrogen gas. Towns far and near listened to his voice, and followed him singing, until in all that territory you could not throw a stone at a jack-rabbit without hitting the site of a projected mammoth hotel, estimated cost, fifteen thousand dollars. The stern and lonely buttes were given titles like grim veterans awarded tawdry patents of nobility: Cedar Mountain, Red Cliffs, Look-out Peak. And from the East came both the sane and the insane with hope, with courage, with horded savings, with cold decks, with Bibles, with knives in boots, with humility and fear, with bland impudence. Most came with their own money; some came with money gained during a moment of inattention on the part of somebody in the East. And high in the air was the serene-browed angel of peace, with his endless gabble and his pretty maps. It was curious to walk out of an

416

evening to the edge of a vast silent sea of prairie, and to reflect that the angel had parcelled this infinity into building lots.

But no change had come to Warpost. Warpost sat with her reputation for bloodshed pressed proudly to her bosom, and saw her mean neighbours leap into being as cities. She saw drunken old reprobates selling acres of red-hot dust, and becoming wealthy men of affairs, who congratulated themselves on their shrewdness in holding land which, before the boom, they would have sold for enough to buy a treat all round in the Straight Flush Saloon — only, nobody would have given it.

Warpost saw dollars rolling into the coffers of a lot of contemptible men who couldn't shoot straight. She was amazed and indignant. She saw her standard of excellence, her creed, her reason for being great, all tumbling about her ears, and after the preliminary gasps she sat down to think it out.

The first man to voice a conclusion was Bob Hether, the popular barkeeper in Stevenson's Crystal Palace.

"It's this here gun-fighter business," he said, leaning on his bar, and, with the gentle, serious eyes of a child, surveying a group of prominent citizens who had come in to drink at the expense of Tom Larpent, a gambler. They solemnly nodded assent. They stood in silence, holding their glasses and thinking.

Larpent was chief factor in the life of the town. His gambling-house was the biggest institution in Warpost. Moreover, he had been educated somewhere, and his slow speech had a certain mordant quality which was apt to puzzle Warpost, and men heeded him for the reason that they were not always certain as to what he was saying.

"Yes, Bob," he drawled, "I think you are right. The value of human life has to be established before there can be theatres, waterworks, street-cars, women, and babies."

The other men were rather aghast at this cryptic speech, but somebody managed to snigger appreciatively, and the tension was eased.

Smith Hanham, who whirled roulette for Larpent, then gave his opinion.

"Well, when all this here coin is floatin' round, it 'pears to me we orter git our hooks on some of it. Them little tin-horns over at Crowdger's Corner are up to their necks in it, an' we ain't yit seen a centavo — not a centavetto. That ain't right. It's all well enough to sit round takin' money away from innercent cowpunchers s'long's ther's nothin' better; but when these here speculators come 'long flashin' rolls as big as water buckets, it's up to us to whirl in an' git some of it."

This became the view of the town, and, since the main stipulation was virtue, Warpost resolved to be virtuous. A great meeting was held, at which it was decreed that no man should kill another man, under penalty of being at once hanged by the populace. All the influential citizens were present, and asserted their determination to deal out a swift punishment which would take no note of an acquaintance or friendship with the guilty man. Bob Hether made a loud, long speech, in which he declared that he, for one, would help hang his "own brother," if his "own brother" transgressed this law which now, for the good of the community, must be for ever held sacred. Everybody was enthusiastic, save a few Mexicans, who did not quite understand; but as they were more than likely to be the victims of any affray in which they engaged, their silence was not considered ominous.

At half-past ten on the next morning Larpent shot and killed a man who had accused him of cheating at a game. Larpent had then taken a chair by the window.

II

Larpent grew tired of sitting in the chair by the window. He went to his bedroom, which opened off the gambling hall. On the table was a bottle of rye whisky, of a brand which he specially and secretly imported from the East. He took a long drink; he changed his coat, after laving his hands and brushing his hair. He sat down to read, his hand falling familiarly upon an old copy of Scott's "Fair Maid of Perth."

In time, he heard the slow trample of many men coming up the stairs. The sound certainly did not indicate haste; in fact, it declared all kinds of hesitation. The crowd poured into the gambling hall; there was low talk; a silence; more low talk. Ultimately somebody rapped diffidently on the door of the bedroom.

"Come in," said Larpent. The door swung back and disclosed Warpost, with a delegation of its best men in the front, and at the rear men who stood on their toes and craned their necks. There was no noise. Larpent looked up casually into the eyes of Bob Hether. "So you've come up to the scratch all right, eh, Bobbie?" he asked kindly. "I was wondering if you would weaken on the blood-curdling speech you made yesterday."

Hether first turned deadly pale, and then flushed beet-red. His six-shooter was in his hand, and it appeared for a moment as if his weak fingers would drop it to the floor.

"Oh, never mind," said Larpent in the same tone of kindly patronage. "The community must and shall hold this law for ever sacred, and your own brother lives in Connecticut, doesn't he?" He laid down his book and arose. He unbuckled his revolver belt and tossed it on the bed. A look of impatience had come suddenly upon his face. "Well, you don't want me to be master of ceremonies at my own hanging, do you? Why don't somebody say something or do something? You stand around like a lot of bottles. Where's your tree, for instance? You know there isn't a tree between here and the river. Damned little jack-rabbit town hasn't even got a tree for its hanging. Hello, Coats, you live in Crowdger's Corner, don't you? Well, you keep out of this thing, then. The Corner has had its boom, and this is a speculation in real estate which is the business solely of the citizens of Warpost."

The behaviour of the crowd became extraordinary. Men began to back away; eye did not meet eye; they were victims of an inexplicable influence, it was as if they had heard sinister laughter from a gloom.

"I know," said Larpent considerately, "that this isn't as if you were going to hang a comparative stranger. In a sense, this is an intimate affair. I know full well you could go out and jerk a comparative stranger into kingdom-come and make a sort of festal occasion of it. But when it comes to performing the same office for an old friend, even the ferocious Bobbie Hether stands around on one leg like a damned white-livered coward. In short, my milk-fed patriots, you seem fat-headed enough to believe that I am going to hang myself if you wait long enough; but unfortunately I am going to allow you to conduct your own real estate speculations. It seems to me there should be enough men here who understand the value of corner lots in a safe and godly town, and hence should be anxious to hurry this business."

The icy tones had ceased, and the crowd breathed a great sigh, as if it had been freed of a physical pain. But still no one seemed to know where to reach for the scruff of this weird situation. Finally there was some jostling on the outskirts of the crowd, and some men were seen to be pushing old Billie Simpson forward amid some protests. Simpson was on state occasions the voice of the town. Somewhere in his past he had been a Baptist preacher. He had fallen far, very far, and the only remnant of his former dignity was a fatal facility of speech when half drunk. Warpost used him on those state occasions when it became bitten with a desire to "do the thing up in style." So the citizens pushed the blear-eyed old ruffian forward until he stood hemming and hawing in front of Larpent. It was evident at once that he was brutally sober, and hence wholly unfitted for whatever task had been planned for him. A dozen times he croaked like a frog, meanwhile wiping the back of his hand rapidly across his mouth. At last he managed to stammer—

"Mister Larpent——"

In some indescribable manner, Larpent made his attitude of respectable attention to be grossly contemptuous and insulting.

"Yes, Mister Simpson?"

"Er—now—Mister Larpent," began the old man hoarsely, "we wanted to know——" Then obviously feeling that there was a detail which he had forgotten, he turned to the crowd and whispered, "Where is it?" Many men precipitately cleared themselves out of the way, and down this lane Larpent had an unobstructed view of the body of the man he had slain. Old Simpson again began to croak like a frog.

"Mister Larpent."

"Yes, Mister Simpson."

"Do you—er—do you—admit——"

"Oh, certainly," said the gambler, good-humouredly. "There can be no doubt of it, Mister Simpson, although, with your well-known ability to fog things, you may later possibly prove that you did it yourself. I shot him because he was too officious. Not quite enough men are shot on that account, Mister Simpson. As one fitted by nature to be consummately officious, I hope you will agree with me, Mister Simpson."

Men were plucking old Simpson by the sleeve, and giving him directions. One could hear him say, "What? Yes. All right. What? All right." In the end he turned hurriedly upon Larpent and blurted out—

"Well, I guess we're goin' to hang you."

Larpent bowed. "I had a suspicion that you would," he said, in a pleasant voice. "There has been an air of determination about the entire proceeding, Mister Simpson."

There was an awkward moment.

"Well—well—well, come ahead——"

Larpent courteously relieved a general embarrassment.

"Why, of course. We must be moving. Clergy first, Mister Simpson. I'll take my old friend, Bobbie Hether, on my right hand, and we'll march soberly to the business, thus lending a certain dignity to this outing of real estate speculators."

"Tom," quavered Bob Hether, "for Gawd sake, keep your mouth shut."

"He invokes the deity," remarked Larpent, placidly. "But no; my last few minutes I am resolved to devote to inquiries as to the welfare of my friends. Now, you, for instance, my dear Bobbie, present to-day the lamentable appearance of a rattlesnake that has been four times killed and then left in the sun to rot. It is the effect of friendship upon a highly delicate system. You suffer? It is cruel. Never mind; you will feel better presently."

III

Warpost had always risen superior to her lack of a tree by making use of a fixed wooden crane, which appeared over a second story window on the front of Pigrim's general store. This crane had a long tackle always ready for hoisting merchandise to the stores' loft. Larpent, coming in the midst of a slow moving throng, cocked a bright bird-like eye at this crane.

"Mm — yes," he said.

Men began to work frantically. They called each to each in voices strenuous but low. They were in a panic to have the thing finished. Larpent's cold ironical survey drove them mad, and it entered the minds of some that it would be felicitous to hang him before he could talk more. But he occupied the time in pleasant discourse.

"I see that Smith Hanham is not here. Perhaps some undue tenderness of sentiment keeps him away. Such feelings are entirely unnecessary. Don't you think so, Bobbie? Note the feverish industry with which the renegade parson works at the rope. You will never be hung, Simpson. You will be shot for fooling too near a petticoat which doesn't belong to you — the same old habit which got you flung out of the church, you red-eyed old satyr. Ah, the Cross Trail coach approaches. What a situation."

The crowd turned uneasily to follow his glance, and saw, truly enough, the dusty rickety old vehicle coming at the gallop of four lean horses. Ike Boston was driving the coach, and far away he had seen and defined the throng in front of Pigrim's store. First calling out excited information to his passengers, who were all inside, he began to lash his horses and yell. As a result, he rattled wildly up to the scene just as they were arranging the rope around Larpent's neck.

"Whoa," said he to his horses.

The inhabitants of Warpost peered at the windows of the coach, and saw therein six pale, horror-stricken faces. The men at the rope stood hesitating. Larpent smiled blandly. There was a silence. At last a broken voice cried from the coach —

"Driver! driver! What is it? What is it?"

Ike Boston spat between the wheel horses and mumbled that he s'posed anybody could see, less'n they were blind. The door of the coach opened, and out stepped a beautiful young lady. She was followed by two little girls, hand clasped in hand, and a white-haired old gentleman, with a venerable and peaceful face. And the rough West stood in naked immorality before the eyes of the gentle East. The leather-faced men of Warpost had never imagined such perfection of feminine charm, such radiance, and as the illumined eyes of the girl wandered doubtfully, fearfully, toward the man with the rope around his neck, a certain majority of practised ruffians tried to look as if they were having nothing to do with the proceedings.

"Oh," she said, in a low voice, "what are you going to do?"

At first none made reply, but ultimately a hero managed to break the harrowing stillness by stammering out, "Nothin'!" And then, as if aghast at his own prominence, he shied behind the shoulders of a big neighbour.

"Oh, I know," she said. "But it's wicked. Don't you see how wicked it is? Papa, do say something to them."

The clear, deliberate tones of Tom Larpent suddenly made every one stiffen. During the early part of the interruption he had seated himself upon the steps of Pigrim's store, in which position he had maintained a slightly bored air. He now was standing with the rope around his neck and bowing. He looked handsome and distinguished and — a devil, a devil as cold as moonlight upon the ice.

"You are quite right, miss. They are going to hang me; but I can give you my word that the affair is perfectly regular. I killed a man this morning, and you see these people here who look like a fine collection of premier scoundrels are really engaged in forcing a real estate boom. In short, they are speculators, land barons, and not the children of infamy, which you no doubt took them for at first."

"O-oh!" she said, and shuddered.

Her father now spoke haughtily. "What has this man done? Why do you hang him without a trial, even if you have fair proofs?"

The crowd had been afraid to speak to the young lady, but a dozen voices answered her father.

"Why, he admits it." "Didn't ye hear?" "There ain't no doubt about it." "No." "He *ses* he did."

The old man looked at the smiling gambler. "Do you admit that you committed murder?"

Larpent answered slowly. "For the first question in a temporary acquaintance that is a fairly strong beginning. Do you wish me to speak as man to man, or to one who has some kind of official authority to meddle in a thing that is none of his affair?"

"I — ah — I," stuttered the other. "Ah — man to man."

"Then," said Larpent, "I have to inform you that this morning, at about 10.30, a man was shot and killed in my gambling house. He was engaged in the exciting business of trying to grab some money, out of which he claimed I had swindled him. The details are not interesting."

The old gentleman waved his arm in a gesture of terror and despair, and tottered toward the coach; the young lady fainted; the two little girls wailed. Larpent sat on the steps with the rope around his neck.

IV

The chief function of Warpost was to prey upon the bands of cowboys who, when they were paid, rode gaily into town to look for sin. To this end there were in Warpost many thugs and thieves. There was treachery and obscenity and merciless greed in every direction. Even Mexico was levied upon to furnish a kind of ruffian which appears infrequently in the northern races. Warpost was not good; it was not tender; it was not chivalrous, but——

But——

There was a quality to the situation in front of Pigrim's store which made Warpost wish to stampede. There were the two children, their angelic faces turned toward the sky, weeping in the last anguish of fear; there was the beautiful form of the young lady prostrate in the dust of the road, with her trembling father bending over her; on the steps sat Larpent, waiting, with a derisive smile, while from time to time he turned his head in the rope to make a forked-tongued remark as to the character and bearing of some acquaintance. All the simplicity of a mere lynching was gone from this thing. Through some bewildering inner power of its own, it was carried out of the hands of its inaugurators, and was marching along like a great drama, and they were only spectators. To them it was ungovernable; they could do no more than stand on one foot and wonder.

Some were heartily ill of everything, and wished to run away. Some were so interested in the new aspect that they had forgotten why they had originally come to the front of Pigrim's store. These were the poets. A large practical class wished to establish at once the identity of the new-comers. Who were they? Where did they come from? Where were they going to? It was truthfully argued that they were the parson for the new church at Crowdger's Corner, with his family.

And a fourth class—a dark-browed, muttering class—wished to go at once to the root of all disturbance by killing Ike Boston for trundling up in his old omnibus, and dumping out upon their ordinary lynching party such a load of tears and inexperience and sentimental argument. In low tones they addressed vitriolic reproaches.

"But how'd I know?" he protested, almost with tears—"how'd I know the'd be all this here kick-up?"

But Larpent suddenly created a great stir. He stood up, and his face was inspired with new, strong resolution.

"Look here, boys," he said decisively, "you hang me to-morrow—or, anyhow, later on to-day. We can't keep frightening the young lady and these two poor babies out of their wits. Ease off on the rope, Simpson, you blackguard. Frightening women and children is your game, but I'm not going to stand it. Ike Boston, take your passengers on to Crowdger's Corner, and tell the young lady that, owing to her influence, the boys changed their minds about making me swing. Somebody lift the rope where it's caught under my ear, will you? Boys, when you want me, you'll find me in the Crystal Palace."

His tone was so authoritative that some obeyed him at once, involuntarily; but, as a matter of fact, his plan met with general approval. Warpost heaved a great sigh of relief. Why had nobody thought earlier of so easy a way out of all these here tears?

V

Larpent went to the Crystal Palace, where he took his comfort like a gentleman, conversing with his friends and drinking. At nightfall two men rode into town, flung their bridles over a convenient post, and clanked into the Crystal Palace. Warpost knew them in a glance. Talk ceased, and there was a watchful squaring aback.

The foremost was Jack Potter, a famous town marshal of Yellow Sky, but now the sheriff of the county. The other was Scratchy Wilson, once a no-less famous desperado. They were both two-handed men of terrific prowess and courage, but Warpost could hardly believe her eyes at view of this daring invasion. It was unprecedented.

Potter went straight to the bar, behind which frowned Bobbie Hether.

"You know a man by the name of Larpent?"

"Supposin' I do?" said Bobbie, sourly.

"Well, I want him. Is he in the saloon?"

"Maybe he is, an' maybe he isn't," said Bobbie.

Potter went back among the glinting eyes of the citizens.

"Gentlemen, I want a man named Larpent. Is he here?"

Warpost was sullen, but Larpent answered lazily for himself.

"Why, you must mean me. My name is Larpent. What do you want?"

"I've got a warrant for your arrest."

There was a movement all over the room as if a puff of wind had come. The swing of a hand would have brought on a murderous *mêlée*. But after an instant the rigidity was broken by Larpent's laughter.

"Why, you're sold, sheriff," he cried. "I've got a previous engagement. The boys are going to hang me to-night."

If Potter was surprised, he betrayed nothing.

"The boys won't hang you to-night, Larpent," he said calmly, "because I'm goin' to take you in to Yellow Sky."

Larpent was looking at the warrant. "Only grand larceny," he observed. "But still, you know, I've promised these people to appear at their performance."

"You're goin' in with me," said the impassive sheriff.

"You bet he is, sheriff," cried an enthusiastic voice; and it belonged to Bobbie Hether. The barkeeper moved down inside his rail, and, inspired like a prophet, he began a harangue to the citizens of Warpost. "Now, look here, boys, that's just what we want, ain't it? Here we were goin' to hang Tom Larpent jest for the reputation of the town, like. 'Long comes Sheriff Potter, the reg-u-lerly con-sti-tuted officer of the law, an' he says, 'No; the man's mine.' Now, we want to make the reputation of the town as a law-abidin' place; so what do we say to Sheriff Potter? We says, 'A-a-ll right, sheriff; you're reg'lar; we ain't; he's your man.' But supposin' we go to fighten over it; then what becomes of the reputation of the town which we was goin' to swing Tom Larpent for?"

The immediate opposition to these views came from a source which a stranger might have difficulty in imagining. Men's foreheads grew thick with lines of obstinacy and disapproval. They were perfectly willing to hang Larpent yesterday, to-day, or to-morrow as a detail in a set of circumstances at Warpost, but when some outsiders from the alien town of Yellow Sky came into the sacred precincts of Warpost, and proclaimed their intention of extracting a citizen for cause, any citizen for any cause, the stomach of Warpost was fed with a clan's blood, and her children gathered under one invisible banner, prepared to fight as few people in few ages were enabled to fight for their points of view. There was a guttural murmuring.

"No; hold on," screamed Bobbie, flinging up his hands. "He'll come clear all right. Tom," he appealed wildly to Larpent, "you never committed no —— —— low-down grand larceny?"

"No," said Larpent, coldly.

"But how was it? Can't you tell us how it was?"

Larpent answered with plain reluctance. He waved his hand to indicate that it was all of little consequence.

"Well, he was a tenderfoot, and he played poker with me, and he couldn't play quite good enough. But he thought he could; he could play extremely well, he thought. So he lost his money. I thought he'd squeal."

"Boys," begged Bobbie, "let the sheriff take him."

Some answered at once, "Yes." Others continued to mutter. The sheriff had held his hand because, like all quiet and honest men, he did not wish to perturb any progress toward a peaceful solution, but now he decided to take the scene by the nose and make it obey him.

"Gentlemen," he said formally, "this man is comin' with me. Larpent, get up and come along."

This might have been the beginning, but it was practically the end. The two opinions in the minds of Warpost fought in the air and, like a snow squall, discouraged all action. Amid general confusion Jack Potter and Scratchy Wilson moved to the door with their prisoner. The last thing seen by the men in the Crystal Palace was the bronze countenance of Jack Potter as he backed from the place.

A man, filled with belated thought, suddenly cried out—

"Well, they'll hang him for this here shootin' game anyhow."

Bobbie Hether looked disdain upon the speaker.

"Will they? An' where 'll they get their witnesses? From here, do y' think? No; not a single one. All he's up against is a case of grand larceny, and—even supposin' he done it—what in hell does grand larceny amount to?"

(1902)

❖ ISAK DINESEN

The Ring

Isak Dinesen was the pen name of Karen Blixen (1885–1962), a Danish baroness. She married in 1914 and went to Africa where she lived for seventeen years. Her autobiography of those times was published under the title *Out of Africa* (1937), recently made into a film. She actively helped the natives in her locale and was missed when she returned to Denmark. Her earliest short stories were collected in the volume *Seven Gothic Tales* (1934) and later ones under the title *Winter's Tales* (1942). She lived in Denmark under the Nazi occupation and wrote a novel, *The Angelic Avengers* (1946), under another pseudonym, Pierre Andrézel. Other short story collections are *Last Tales* (1957) and *Anecdotes of Destiny* (1958, which contains "The Ring"). Another of the stories in that volume, "Babette's Feast," has been made into a brilliant movie. Her posthumous stories are published under the title *Carnival* (1977). Some of Dinesen's essays were reprinted in the volume *Daguerreotypes* (1979).

On a summer morning a hundred and fifty years ago a young Danish squire and his wife went out for a walk on their land. They had been married a week. It had not been easy for them to get married, for the wife's family was higher in rank and wealthier than the husband's. But the two young people, now twenty-four and nineteen years old, had been set on their purpose for ten years; in the end her haughty parents had had to give in to them.

They were wonderfully happy. The stolen meetings and secret, tearful love letters were now things of the past. To God and man they were one; they could walk arm in arm in broad daylight and drive in the same carriage, and they would walk and drive so till the end of their days. Their distant paradise had descended to earth and had proved, surprisingly, to be filled with the things of everyday life: with jesting and railleries, with breakfasts and suppers, with dogs, haymaking and sheep. Sigismund, the young husband, had promised himself that from now there should be no stone in his bride's path, nor should any shadow fall across it. Lovisa, the wife, felt that now, every day and for the first time in her young life, she moved and breathed in perfect freedom because she could never have any secret from her husband.

To Lovisa—whom her husband called Lise—the rustic atmosphere of her new life was a matter of wonder and delight. Her husband's fear that the existence he could offer her might not be good enough for her filled her heart with laughter. It was not a long time since she had played with dolls; as now she dressed her own hair, looked over her linen press and arranged her flowers she again lived through an enchanting and cherished experience: one was doing everything gravely and solicitously, and all the time one knew one was playing.

It was a lovely July morning. Little woolly clouds drifted high up in the sky,

425

the air was full of sweet scents. Lise had on a white muslin frock and a large Italian straw hat. She and her husband took a path through the park; it wound on across the meadows, between small groves and groups of trees, to the sheep field. Sigismund was going to show his wife his sheep. For this reason she had not brought her small white dog, Bijou, with her, for he would yap at the lambs and frighten them, or he would annoy the sheep dogs. Sigismund prided himself on his sheep; he had studied sheep-breeding in Mecklenburg and England, and had brought back with him Cotswold rams by which to improve his Danish stock. While they walked he explained to Lise the great possibilities and difficulties of the plan.

She thought: "How clever he is, what a lot of things he knows!" and at the same time: "What an absurd person he is, with his sheep! What a baby he is! I am a hundred years older than he."

But when they arrived at the sheepfold the old sheepmaster Mathias met them with the sad news that one of the English lambs was dead and two were sick. Lise saw that her husband was grieved by the tidings; while he questioned Mathias on the matter she kept silent and only gently pressed his arm. A couple of boys were sent off to fetch the sick lambs, while the master and servant went into the details of the case. It took some time.

Lise began to gaze about her and to think of other things. Twice her own thoughts made her blush deeply and happily, like a red rose, then slowly her blush died away, and the two men were still talking about sheep. A little while after their conversation caught her attention. It had turned to a sheep thief.

This thief during the last months had broken into the sheepfolds of the neighborhood like a wolf, had killed and dragged away his prey like a wolf and like a wolf had left no trace after him. Three nights ago the shepherd and his son on an estate ten miles away had caught him in the act. The thief had killed the man and knocked the boy senseless, and had managed to escape. There were men sent out to all sides to catch him, but nobody had seen him.

Lise wanted to hear more about the horrible event, and for her benefit old Mathias went through it once more. There had been a long fight in the sheep house, in many places the earthen floor was soaked with blood. In the fight the thief's left arm was broken; all the same, he had climbed a tall fence with a lamb on his back. Mathias added that he would like to string up the murderer with these two hands of his, and Lise nodded her head at him gravely in approval. She remembered Red Ridinghood's wolf, and felt a pleasant little thrill running down her spine.

Sigismund had his own lambs in his mind, but he was too happy in himself to wish anything in the universe ill. After a minute he said: "Poor devil."

Lise said: "How can you pity such a terrible man? Indeed Grandmamma was right when she said that you were a revolutionary and a danger to society!" The thought of Grandmamma, and of the tears of past days, again turned her mind away from the gruesome tale she had just heard.

The boys brought the sick lambs and the men began to examine them carefully, lifting them up and trying to set them on their legs; they squeezed them here and there and made the little creatures whimper. Lise shrank from the show and her husband noticed her distress.

"You go home, my darling," he said, "this will take some time. But just walk ahead slowly, and I shall catch up with you."

So she was turned away by an impatient husband to whom his sheep meant more than his wife. If any experience could be sweeter than to be dragged out by him to look at those same sheep, it would be this. She dropped her large summer hat with its blue ribbons on the grass and told him to carry it back for her, for she wanted to feel the summer air on her forehead and in her hair. She walked on very slowly, as he had told her to do, for she wished to obey him in everything. As she walked she felt a great new happiness in being altogether alone, even without Bijou. She could not remember that she had ever before in all her life been altogether alone. The landscape around her was still, as if full of promise, and it was hers. Even the swallows cruising in the air were hers, for they belonged to him, and he was hers.

She followed the curving edge of the grove and after a minute or two found that she was out of sight to the men by the sheep house. What could now, she wondered, be sweeter than to walk along the path in the long flowering meadow grass, slowly, slowly, and to let her husband overtake her there? It would be sweeter still, she reflected, to steal into the grove and to be gone, to have vanished from the surface of the earth from him when, tired of the sheep and longing for her company, he should turn the bend of the path to catch up with her.

An idea struck her; she stood still to think it over.

A few days ago her husband had gone for a ride and she had not wanted to go with him, but had strolled about with Bijou in order to explore her domain. Bijou then, gamboling, had led her straight into the grove. As she had followed him, gently forcing her way into the shrubbery, she had suddenly come upon a glade in the midst of it, a narrow space like a small alcove with hangings of thick green and golden brocade, big enough to hold two or three people in it. She had felt at that moment that she had come into the very heart of her new home. If today she could find the spot again she would stand perfectly still there, hidden from all the world. Sigismund would look for her in all directions; he would be unable to understand what had become of her and for a minute, for a short minute — or, perhaps, if she was firm and cruel enough, for five — he would realize what a void, what an unendurably sad and horrible place the universe would be when she was no longer in it. She gravely scrutinized the grove to find the right entrance to her hiding-place, then went in.

She took great care to make no noise at all, therefore advanced exceedingly slowly. When a twig caught the flounces of her ample skirt she loosened it softly from the muslin, so as not to crack it. Once a branch took hold of one of her long golden curls; she stood still, with her arms lifted, to free it. A little way into the grove the soil became moist; her light steps no longer made any sound upon it. With one hand she held her small handkerchief to her lips, as if to emphasize the secretness of her course. She found the spot she sought and bent down to divide the foliage and make a door to her sylvan closet. At this the hem of her dress caught her foot and she stopped to loosen it. As she rose she looked into the face of a man who was already in the shelter.

He stood up erect, two steps off. He must have watched her as she made her way straight toward him.

She took him in in one single glance. His face was bruised and scratched, his hands and wrists stained with dark filth. He was dressed in rags, barefooted, with tatters wound round his naked ankles. His arms hung down to his sides, his right hand clasped the hilt of a knife. He was about her own age. The man and the woman looked at each other.

This meeting in the wood from beginning to end passed without a word; what happened could only be rendered by pantomime. To the two actors in the pantomime it was timeless; according to a clock it lasted four minutes.

She had never in her life been exposed to danger. It did not occur to her to sum up her position, or to work out the length of time it would take to call her husband or Mathias, whom at this moment she could hear shouting to his dogs. She beheld the man before her as she would have beheld a forest ghost: the apparition itself, not the sequels of it, changes the world to the human who faces it.

Although she did not take her eyes off the face before her she sensed that the alcove had been turned into a covert. On the ground a couple of sacks formed a couch; there were some gnawed bones by it. A fire must have been made here in the night, for there were cinders strewn on the forest floor.

After a while she realized that he was observing her just as she was observing him. He was no longer just run to earth and crouching for a spring, but he was wondering, trying to know. At that she seemed to see herself with the eyes of the wild animal at bay in his dark hiding-place: her silently approaching white figure, which might mean death.

He moved his right arm till it hung down straight before him between his legs. Without lifting the hand he bent the wrist and slowly raised the point of the knife till it pointed at her throat. The gesture was mad, unbelievable. He did not smile as he made it, but his nostrils distended, the corners of his mouth quivered a little. Then slowly he put the knife back in the sheath by his belt.

She had no object of value about her, only the wedding ring which her husband had set on her finger in church, a week ago. She drew it off, and in this movement dropped her handkerchief. She reached out her hand with the ring toward him. She did not bargain for her life. She was fearless by nature, and the horror with which he inspired her was not fear of what he might do to her. She commanded him, she besought him to vanish as he had come, to take a dreadful figure out of her life, so that it should never have been there. In the dumb movement her young form had the grave authoritativeness of a priestess conjuring down some monstrous being by a sacred sign.

He slowly reached out his hand to hers, his finger touched hers, and her hand was steady at the touch. But he did not take the ring. As she let it go it dropped to the ground as her handkerchief had done.

For a second the eyes of both followed it. It rolled a few inches toward him and stopped before his bare foot. In a hardly perceivable movement he kicked it away and again looked into her face. They remained like that, she knew not how long, but she felt that during that time something happened, things were changed.

He bent down and picked up her handkerchief. All the time gazing at her, he again drew his knife and wrapped the tiny bit of cambric round the blade. This was difficult for him to do because his left arm was broken. While he did it his face under the dirt and sun-tan slowly grew whiter till it was almost phosphorescent. Fumbling with both hands, he once more stuck the knife into the sheath. Either the sheath was too big and had never fitted the knife, or the blade was much worn — it went in. For two or three more seconds his gaze rested on her face; then he lifted his own face a little, the strange radiance still upon it, and closed his eyes.

The movement was definitive and unconditional. In this one motion he did what she had begged him to do: he vanished and was gone. She was free.

She took a step backward, the immovable, blind face before her, then bent as she had done to enter the hiding-place, and glided away as noiselessly as she had come. Once outside the grove she stood still and looked round for the meadow path, found it and began to walk home.

Her husband had not yet rounded the edge of the grove. Now he saw her and helloed to her gaily; he came up quickly and joined her.

The path here was so narrow that he kept half behind her and did not touch her. He began to explain to her what had been the matter with the lambs. She walked a step before him and thought: All is over.

After a while he noticed her silence, came up beside her to look at her face and asked, "What is the matter?"

She searched her mind for something to say, and at last said: "I have lost my ring."

"What ring?" he asked her.

She answered, "My wedding ring."

As she heard her own voice pronounce the words she conceived their meaning.

Her wedding ring. "With this ring" — dropped by one and kicked away by another — "with this ring I thee wed." With this lost ring she had wedded herself to something. To what? To poverty, persecution, total loneliness. To the sorrows and the sinfulness of this earth. "And what therefore God has joined together let man not put asunder."

"I will find you another ring," her husband said. "You and I are the same as we were on our wedding day; it will do as well. We are husband and wife today too, as much as yesterday, I suppose."

Her face was so still that he did not know if she had heard what he said. It touched him that she should take the loss of his ring so to heart. He took her hand and kissed it. It was cold, not quite the same hand as he had last kissed. He stopped to make her stop with him.

"Do you remember where you had the ring on last?" he asked.

"No," she answered.

"Have you any idea," he asked, "where you may have lost it?"

"No," she answered. "I have no idea at all."

(1958)

❖ FYODOR DOSTOEVSKY

Polzunkov*

Fyodor Dostoevsky (1821–1881) was born in Moscow and attended college in St. Petersburg. A man of nervous temperament (he suffered from epilepsy), Dostoevsky despised his engineering studies and the army into which they led him and began writing fiction. His early novels include *Poor Folk* (1846) and *The Double* (1846). He was arrested for sedition in 1849 and sentenced to death. At the last minute, his sentence was commuted to four years in exile in Siberia. His experiences in exile led to *Notes from the House of the Dead* (1862) and *Notes from Underground* (1864). His most famous novel *Crime and Punishment* (1866) follows the mental experience of a man who commits murder not out of passion but out of intellectual curiosity. Later novels include *The Idiot* (1869), *The Possessed* (or *The Devils*, 1871), and *The Brothers Karamazov* (1880). Among his shorter fiction are "White Nights" and "The Gambler." Dostoevsky was tormented by neurotic obsessions, which included compulsive gambling. He suffered terrible personal grief, losing his wife, a child, and his brother. He held extreme political and religious views, views that shifted from the radical left to the radical right. His struggle with ideology carries over into the struggles of his characters, who are some of the most interesting and complex in the history of fiction. Of all nineteenth-century writers he best captured the experience of the neurotic mind. (Freud, for instance, remarked that he learned much about human psychology from Dostoevsky.)

I began to scrutinize the man closely. Even in his exterior there was something so peculiar that it compelled one, however far away one's thoughts might be, to fix one's eyes upon him and go off into the most irrepressible roar of laughter. That is what happened to me. I must observe that the little man's eyes were so mobile, or perhaps he was so sensitive to the magnetism of every eye fixed upon him, that he almost by instinct guessed that he was being observed, turned at once to the observer and anxiously analysed his expression. His continual mobility, his turning and twisting, made him look strikingly like a dancing doll. It was strange! He seemed afraid of jeers, in spite of the fact that he was almost getting his living by being a buffoon for all the world, and exposed himself to every buffet in a moral sense and even in a physical one, judging from the company he was in. Voluntary buffoons are not even to be pitied. But I noticed at once that this strange creature, this ridiculous man, was by no means a buffoon by profession. There was still something gentlemanly in him. His very uneasiness, his continual apprehensiveness about himself, were actually a testimony in his favour. It seemed to me that his desire to be obliging was due more to kindness of

---

*Translated by Constance Garnett

heart than to mercenary considerations. He readily allowed them to laugh their loudest at him and in the most unseemly way, to his face, but at the same time — and I am ready to take my oath on it — his heart ached and was sore at the thought that his listeners were so caddishly brutal as to be capable of laughing, not at anything said or done, but at him, at his whole being, at his heart, at his head, at his appearance, at his whole body, flesh and blood. I am convinced that he felt at that moment all the foolishness of his position; but the protest died away in his heart at once, though it invariably sprang up again in the most heroic way. I am convinced that all this was due to nothing else but a kind heart, and not to fear of the inconvenience of being kicked out and being unable to borrow money from some one. This gentleman was for ever borrowing money, that is, he asked for alms in that form, when after playing the fool and entertaining them at his expense he felt in a certain sense entitled to borrow money from them. But, good heavens! what a business the borrowing was! And with what a countenance he asked for the loan! I could not have imagined that on such a small space as the wrinkled, angular face of that little man room could be found, at one and the same time, for so many different grimaces, for such strange, variously characteristic shades of feeling, such absolutely killing expressions. Everything was there — shame and an assumption of insolence, and vexation at the sudden flushing of his face, and anger and fear of failure, and entreaty to be forgiven for having dared to pester, and a sense of his own dignity, and a still greater sense of his own abjectness — all this passed over his face like lightning. For six whole years he had struggled along in God's world in this way, and so far had been unable to take up a fitting attitude at the interesting moment of borrowing money! I need not say that he never could grow callous and completely abject. His heart was too sensitive, too passionate! I will say more, indeed: in my opinion, he was one of the most honest and honourable men in the world, but with a little weakness: of being ready to do anything abject at any one's bidding, good-naturedly and disinterestedly, simply to oblige a fellow-creature. In short, he was what is called "a rag" in the fullest sense of the word. The most absurd thing was, that he was dressed like any one else, neither worse nor better, tidily, even with a certain elaborateness, and actually had pretentions to respectability and personal dignity. This external equality and internal inequality, his uneasiness about himself and at the same time his continual self-depreciation — all this was strikingly incongruous and provocative of laughter and pity. If he had been convinced in his heart (and in spite of his experience it did happen to him at moments to believe this) that his audience were the most good-natured people in the world, who were simply laughing at something amusing, and not at the sacrifice of his personal dignity, he would most readily have taken off his coat, put it on wrong side outwards, and have walked about the streets in that attire for the diversion of others and his own gratification. But equality he could never anyhow attain. Another trait: the queer fellow was proud, and even, by fits and starts, when it was not too risky, generous. It was worth seeing and hearing how he could sometimes, not sparing himself, consequently with pluck, almost with heroism, dispose of one of his patrons who had infuriated him to madness. But that was at moments . . . In short, he was a martyr in the fullest sense of the word, but the most useless and consequently the most comic martyr.

There was a general discussion going on among the guests. All at once I saw our queer friend jump upon his chair, and call out at the top of his voice, anxious for the exclusive attention of the company.

"Listen," the master of the house whispered to me. "He sometimes tells the most curious stories. . . . Does he interest you?"

I nodded and squeezed myself into the group. The sight of a well-dressed gentleman jumping upon his chair and shouting at the top of his voice did, in fact, draw the attention of all. Many who did not know the queer fellow looked at one another in perplexity, the others roared with laughter.

"I knew Fedosey Nikolaitch. I ought to know Fedosey Nikolaitch better than any one!" cried the queer fellow from his elevation. "Gentlemen, allow me to tell you something. I can tell you a good story about Fedosey Nikolaitch! I know a story — exquisite!"

"Tell it, Osip Mihalitch, tell it."

"Tell it."

"Listen."

"Listen, listen."

"I begin; but, gentlemen, this is a peculiar story. . . ."

"Very good, very good."

"It's a comic story."

"Very good, excellent, splendid. Get on!"

"It is an episode in the private life of your humble . . ."

"But why do you trouble yourself to announce that it's comic?"

"And even somewhat tragic!"

"Eh ? ? ? !"

"In short, the story which it will afford you all pleasure to hear me now relate, gentlemen — the story, in consequence of which I have come into company so interesting and profitable . . ."

"No puns!"

"This story."

"In short the story — make haste and finish the introduction. The story, which has its value," a fair-haired young man with moustaches pronounced in a husky voice, dropping his hand into his coat pocket and, as though by chance, pulling out a purse instead of his handkerchief.

"The story, my dear sirs, after which I should like to see many of you in my place. And, finally, the story, in consequence of which I have not married."

"Married! A wife! Polzunkov tried to get married!!"

"I confess I should like to see Madame Polzunkov."

"Allow me to inquire the name of the would-be Madame Polzunkov," piped a youth, making his way up to the storyteller.

"And so for the first chapter, gentlemen. It was just six years ago, in spring, the thirty-first of March — note the date, gentlemen — on the eve . . ."

"Of the first of April!" cried a young man with ringlets.

"You are extraordinarily quick at guessing. It was evening. Twilight was gathering over the district town of N., the moon was about to float out . . . every-thing in proper style, in fact. And so in the very late twilight I, too, floated out of my poor lodging on the sly — after taking leave of my restricted granny, now dead. Excuse me, gentlemen, for making use of such a fashionable expression, which I heard for the last time from Nikolay Nikolaitch. But my granny was indeed restricted: she was blind, dumb, deaf, stupid — everything you please. . . . I confess I was in a tremor, I was prepared for great deeds; my heart was beating like a kitten's when some bony hand clutches it by the scruff of the neck."

"Excuse me, Monsieur Polzunkov."

"What do you want?"

"Tell it more simply; don't over-exert yourself, please!"

"All right," said Osip Mihalitch, a little taken aback. "I went into the house of Fedosey Nikolaitch (the house that he had bought). Fedosey Nikolaitch, as you know, is not a mere colleague, but the full-blown head of a department. I was announced, and was at once shown into the study. I can see it now; the room was dark, almost dark, but candles were not brought. Behold, Fedosey Nikolaitch walks in. There he and I were left in the darkness. . . ."

"Whatever happened to you?" asked an officer.

"What do you suppose?" asked Polzunkov, turning promptly, with a convulsively working face, to the young man with ringlets. "Well, gentlemen, a strange circumstance occurred, though indeed there was nothing strange in it: it was what is called an everyday affair — I simply took out of my pocket a roll of paper . . . and he a roll of paper."

"Paper notes?"

"Paper notes; and we exchanged."

"I don't mind betting that there's a flavour of bribery about it," observed a respectably dressed, closely cropped young gentleman.

"Bribery!" Polzunkov caught him up.

"'Oh, may I be a Liberal,
Such as many I have seen!'

If you, too, when it is your lot to serve in the provinces, do not warm your hands at your country's hearth . . . For as an author said: 'Even the smoke of our native land is sweet to us.' She is our Mother, gentlemen, our Mother Russia; we are her babes, and so we suck her!"

There was a roar of laughter.

"Only would you believe it, gentlemen, I have never taken bribes?" said Polzunkov, looking round at the whole company distrustfully.

A prolonged burst of Homeric laughter drowned Polzunkov's words in guffaws.

"It really is so, gentlemen. . . ."

But here he stopped, still looking round at every one with a strange expression of face; perhaps — who knows? — at that moment the thought came into his mind that he was more honest than many of all that honourable company. . . . Anyway, the serious expression of his face did not pass away till the general merriment was quite over.

"And so," Polzunkov began again when all was still, "though I never did take bribes, yet that time I transgressed; I put in my pocket a bribe . . . from a bribe-taker . . . that is, there were certain papers in my hands which, if I had cared to send to a certain person, it would have gone ill with Fedosey Nikolaitch."

"So then he bought them from you?"

"He did."

"Did he give much?"

"He gave as much as many a man nowadays would sell his conscience for complete, with all its variations . . . if only he could get anything for it. But I felt as though I were scalded when I put the money in my pocket. I really don't understand what always comes over me, gentlemen — but I was more dead than alive, my lips twitched and my legs trembled; well, I was to blame, to blame, entirely to blame. I was utterly conscience-stricken; I was ready to beg Fedosey Nikolaitch's forgiveness."

"Well, what did he do — did he forgive you?"

"But I didn't ask his forgiveness . . . I only mean that that is how I felt. Then I have a sensitive heart, you know. I saw he was looking me straight in the face. 'Have you no fear of God, Osip Mihalitch?' said he. Well, what could I do? From a feeling of propriety I put my head on one side and I flung up my hands. 'In what way,' said I, 'have I no fear of God, Fedosey Nikolaitch?' But I just said that from a feeling of propriety . . . I was ready to sink into the earth. 'After being so long a friend of our family, after being, I may say, like a son — and who knows what Heaven had in store for us, Osip Mihalitch? — and all of a sudden to inform against me — to think of that now! . . . What am I to think of mankind after that, Osip Mihalitch?' Yes, gentlemen, he did read me a lecture! 'Come,' he said, 'you tell me what I am to think of mankind after that, Osip Mihalitch.' 'What is he to think?' I thought; and do you know, there was a lump in my throat, and my voice was quivering, and knowing my hateful weakness, I snatched up my hat. 'Where are you off to, Osip Mihalitch? Surely on the eve of such a day you cannot bear malice against me? What wrong have I done you? . . .' 'Fedosey Nikolaitch,' I said, 'Fedosey Nikolaitch . . .' In fact, I melted, gentlemen, I melted like a sugar-stick. And the roll of notes that was lying in my pocket, that, too, seemed screaming out: 'You ungrateful brigand, you accursed thief!' It seemed to weigh a hundredweight . . . (if only it had weighed a hundredweight!). . . . 'I see,' says Fedosey Nikolaitch, 'I see your penitence . . . you know to-morrow. . . .' 'St. Mary of Egypt's day. . . .' 'Well, don't weep,' said Fedosey Nikolaitch, 'that's enough: you've erred, and you are penitent! Come along! Maybe I may succeed in bringing you back again into the true path,' says he . . . 'maybe, my modest Penates' (yes, 'Penates,' I remember he used that expression, the rascal) 'will warm,' says he, 'your harden . . . I will not say hardened, but erring heart. . . .' He took me by the arm, gentlemen, and led me to his family circle. A cold shiver ran down my back; I shuddered! I thought with what eyes shall I present myself — you must know, gentlemen . . . eh, what shall I say? — a delicate position had arisen here."

"Not Madame Polzunkov?"

"Marya Fedosyevna, only she was not destined, you know, to bear the name you have given her; she did not attain that honour. Fedosey Nikolaitch was right, you see, when he said that I was almost looked upon as a son in the house; it had been so, indeed, six months before, when a certain retired junker called Mihailo Maximitch Dvigailov, was still living. But by God's will he died, and he put off settling his affairs till death settled his business for him."

"Ough!"

"Well, never mind, gentlemen, forgive me, it was a slip of the tongue. It's a bad pun, but it doesn't matter it's being bad—what happened was far worse, when I was left, so to say, with nothing in prospect but a bullet through the brain, for that junker, though he would not admit me into his house (he lived in grand style, for he had always known how to feather his nest), yet perhaps correctly he believed me to be his son."

"Aha!"

"Yes, that was how it was! So they began to cold-shoulder me at Fedosey Nikolaitch's. I noticed things, I kept quiet; but all at once, unluckily for me (or perhaps luckily!), a cavalry officer galloped into our little town like snow on our head. His business—buying horses for the army—was light and active, in cavalry style, but he settled himself solidly at Fedosey Nikolaitch's, as though he were laying siege to it! I approached the subject in a roundabout way, as my nasty habit is; I said one thing and another, asking him what I had done to be treated so, saying that I was almost like a son to him, and when might I expect him to behave more like a father. . . . Well, he began answering me. And when he begins to speak you are in for a regular epic in twelve cantos, and all you can do is to listen, lick your lips and throw up your hands in delight. And not a ha'p'orth of sense, at least there's no making out the sense. You stand puzzled like a fool—he put you in a fog, he twists about like an eel and wriggles away from you. It's a special gift, a real gift—it's enough to frighten people even if it is no concern of theirs. I tried one thing and another, and went hither and thither. I took the lady songs and presented her with sweets and thought of witty things to say to her. I tried sighing and groaning. 'My heart aches,' I said, 'it aches from love.' And I went in for tears and secret explanations. Man is foolish, you know. . . . I never reminded myself that I was thirty . . . not a bit of it! I tried all my arts. It was no go. It was a failure, and I gained nothing but jeers and gibes. I was indignant, I was choking with anger. I slunk off and would not set foot in the house. I thought and thought and made up my mind to denounce him. Well, of course, it was a shabby thing—I meant to give away a friend, I confess. I had heaps of material and splendid material—a grand case. It brought me fifteen hundred roubles when I changed it and my report on it for bank notes!"

"Ah, so that was the bribe!"

"Yes, sir, that was the bribe—and it was a bribe-taker who had to pay it—and I didn't do wrong, I can assure you! Well, now I will go on: he drew me, if you will kindly remember, more dead than alive into the room where they were having tea. They all met me, seeming as it were offended, that is, not exactly offended, but hurt—so hurt that it was simply. . . . They seemed shattered, absolutely shattered, and at the same time there was a look of becoming dignity on their faces, a gravity in their expression, something fatherly, parental . . . the prodigal son had come back to them—that's what it had come to! They made me sit down to tea, but there was no need to do that: I felt as though a samovar was toiling in my bosom and my feet were like ice. I was humbled, I was cowed. Marya Fominishna, his wife, addressed me familiarly from the first word.

"'How is it you have grown so thin, my boy?'

"'I've not been very well, Marya Fominishna,' I said. My wretched voice shook.

"And then quite suddenly — she must have been waiting for a chance to get a dig at me, the old snake — she said —

"'I suppose your conscience felt ill at ease, Osip Mihalitch, my dear! Our fatherly hospitality was a reproach to you! You have been punished for the tears I have shed.'

"Yes, upon my word, she really said that — she had the conscience to say it. Why, that was nothing to her, she was a terror! She did nothing but sit there and pour out tea. But if you were in the market, my darling, I thought you'd shout louder than any fishwife there. . . . That's the kind of woman she was. And then, to my undoing, the daughter, Marya Fedosyevna, came in, in all her innocence, a little pale and her eyes red as though she had been weeping. I was bowled over on the spot like a fool. But it turned out afterwards that the tears were a tribute to the cavalry officer. He had made tracks for home and taken his hook for good and all; for you know it was high time for him to be off — I may as well mention the fact here; not that his leave was up precisely, but you see. . . . It was only later that the loving parents grasped the position and had found out all that had happened. . . . What could they do? They hushed their trouble up — an addition to the family!

"Well, I could not help it — as soon as I looked at her I was done for; I stole a glance at my hat, I wanted to get up and make off. But there was no chance of that, they took away my hat . . . I must confess, I did think of getting off without it. 'Well!' I thought — but no, they latched the doors. There followed friendly jokes, winking, little airs and graces. I was overcome with embarrassment, said something stupid, talked nonsense, about love. My charmer sat down to the piano and with an air of wounded feeling sang the song about the hussar who leaned upon the sword — that finished me off!

"'Well,' said Fedosey Nikolaitch, 'all is forgotten, come to my arms!'

"I fell just as I was, with my face on his waistcoat.

"'My benefactor! You are a father to me!' said I. And I shed floods of hot tears. Lord, have mercy on us, what a to-do there was! He cried, his good lady cried, Mashenka cried . . . there was a flaxen-headed creature there, she cried too. . . . That wasn't enough: the younger children crept out of all the corners (the Lord had filled their quiver full) and they howled too . . . Such tears, such emotion, such joy! They found their prodigal, it was like a soldier's return to his home. Then followed refreshments, we played forfeits, and 'I have a pain' — 'Where is it? — 'In my heart' — 'Who gave it you?' My charmer blushed. The old man and I had some punch — they won me over and did for me completely.

"I returned to my grandmother with my head in a whirl. I was laughing all the way home; for full two hours I paced up and down our little room. I waked up my old granny and told her of my happiness.

"'But did he give you any money, the brigand?'

"'He did, granny, he did, my dear — luck has come to us all of a heap: we've only to open our hand and take it.'

"I waked up Sofron.

"'Sofron,' I said, 'take off my boots.'

"Sofron pulled off my boots.

"'Come, Sofron, congratulate me now, give me a kiss! I am going to get married, my lad, I am going to get married. You can get jolly drunk to-morrow, you can have a spree, my dear soul — your master is getting married.'

"My heart was full of jokes and laughter. I was beginning to drop off to sleep, but something made me get up again. I sat in thought: to-morrow is the first of April, a bright and playful day — what should I do? And I thought of something. Why, gentlemen, I got out of bed, lighted a candle, and sat down to the writing-table just as I was. I was in a fever of excitement, quite carried away — you know, gentlemen, what it is when a man is quite carried away? I wallowed joyfully in the mud, my dear friends. You see what I am like; they take something from you, and you give them something else as well and say, 'Take that, too.' They strike you on the cheek and in your joy you offer them your whole back. Then they try to lure you like a dog with a bun, and you embrace them with your foolish paws and fall to kissing them with all your heart and soul. Why, see what I am doing now, gentlemen! You are laughing and whispering — I see it! After I have told you all my story you will begin to turn me into ridicule, you will begin to attack me, but yet I go on talking and talking and talking! And who tells me to? Who drives me to do it? Who is standing behind my back whispering to me, 'Speak, speak and tell them'? And yet I do talk, I go on telling you, I try to please you as though you were my brothers, all my dearest friends. . . . Ech!"

The laughter which had sprung up by degrees on all sides completely drowned at last the voice of the speaker, who really seemed worked up into a sort of ecstasy. He paused, for several minutes his eyes strayed about the company, then suddenly, as though carried away by a whirlwind, he waved his hand, burst out laughing himself, as though he really found his position amusing, and fell to telling his story again.

"I scarcely slept all night, gentlemen. I was scribbling all night: you see, I thought of a trick. Ech, gentlemen, the very thought of it makes me ashamed. It wouldn't have been so bad if it all had been done at night — I might have been drunk, blundered, been silly and talked nonsense — but not a bit of it! I woke up in the morning as soon as it was light, I hadn't slept more than an hour or two, and was in the same mind. I dressed, I washed, I curled and pomaded my hair, put on my new dress coat and went straight off to spend the holiday with Fedosey Nikolaitch, and I kept the joke I had written in my hat. He met me again with open arms, and invited me again to his fatherly waistcoat. But I assumed an air of dignity. I had the joke I thought of the night before in my mind. I drew a step back.

"'No, Fedosey Nikolaitch, but will you please read this letter,' and I gave it him together with my daily report. And do you know what was in it? Why, 'for such and such reasons the aforesaid Osip Mihalitch asks to be discharged,' and under my petition I signed my full rank! Just think what a notion! Good Lord, it was the cleverest thing I could think of! As to-day was the first of April, I was pretending, for the sake of a joke, that my resentment was not over, that I had changed my mind in the night and was grumpy, and more offended than ever, as though to say, 'My dear benefactor, I don't want to know you nor your daughter either. I put the money in my pocket yesterday, so I am secure — so here's my petition for a transfer to be discharged. I don't care to serve under such a chief as Fedosey Nikolaitch. I want to go into a different office and then, maybe, I'll inform.' I pretended to be a regular scoundrel, I wanted to frighten them. And a nice way of frightening them, wasn't it? A pretty thing, gentlemen, wasn't it? You see, my heart had grown tender towards them since the day before, so I thought I would have a little joke at the family — I would tease the fatherly heart of Fedosey Nikolaitch.

"As soon as he took my letter and opened it, I saw his whole countenance change.

"'What's the meaning of this, Osip Mihalitch?'

"And like a little fool I said —

"'The first of April! Many happy returns of the day, Fedosey Nikolaitch!' just like a silly school-boy who hides behind his grandmother's arm-chair and then shouts 'oof' into her ear suddenly at the top of his voice, meaning to frighten her. Yes . . . yes, I feel quite ashamed to talk about it, gentlemen! No, I won't tell you."

"Nonsense! What happened then?"

"Nonsense, nonsense! Tell us! Yes, do," rose on all sides.

"There was an outcry and a hullabaloo, my dear friends! Such exclamations of surprise! And 'you mischievous fellow, you naughty man,' and what a fright I had given them — and all so sweet that I felt ashamed and wondered how such a holy place could be profaned by a sinner like me.

"'Well, my dear boy,' piped the mamma, 'you gave me such a fright that my legs are all of a tremble still, I can hardly stand on my feet! I ran to Masha as though I were crazy: "Mashenka," I said, "what will become of us! See how *your* friend has turned out!" and I was unjust to you, my dear boy. You must forgive an old woman like me, I was taken in! Well, I thought, when he got home last night, he got home late, he began thinking and perhaps he fancied that we sent for him on purpose, yesterday, that we wanted to get hold of him. I turned cold at the thought! Give over, Mashenka, don't go on winking at me — Osip Mihalitch isn't a stranger! I am your mother, I am not likely to say any harm! Thank God, I am not twenty, but turned forty-five.'

"Well, gentlemen, I almost flopped at her feet on the spot. Again there were tears, again there were kisses. Jokes began. Fedosey Nikolaitch, too, thought he would make April fools of us. He told us the fiery bird had flown up with a letter in her diamond beak! He tried to take us in, too — didn't we laugh? weren't we touched? Foo! I feel ashamed to talk about it.

"Well, my good friends, the end is not far off now. One day passed, two, three, a week; I was regularly engaged to her. I should think so! The wedding rings were ordered, the day was fixed, only they did not want to make it public for a time — they wanted to wait for the Inspector's visit to be over. I was all impatience for the Inspector's arrival — my happiness depended upon him. I was in a hurry to get his visit over. And in the excitement and rejoicing Fedosey Nikolaitch threw all the work upon me: writing up the accounts, making up the reports, checking the books, balancing the totals. I found things in terrible disorder — everything had been neglected, there were muddles and irregularities everywhere. Well, I thought, I must do my best for my father-in-law! And he was ailing all the time, he was taken ill, it appears; he seemed to get worse day by day. And, indeed, I grew as thin as a rake myself, I was afraid I would break down. However, I finished the work grandly. I got things straight for him in time.

"Suddenly they sent a messenger for me. I ran headlong — what could it be? I saw my Fedosey Nikolaitch, his head bandaged up in a vinegar compress, frowning, sighing, and moaning.

"'My dear boy, my son,' he said, 'if I die, to whom shall I leave you, my darlings?'

"His wife trailed in with all his children; Mashenka was in tears and I blubbered, too.

"'Oh no,' he said. 'God will be merciful, He will not visit my transgressions on you.'

"Then he dismissed them all, told me to shut the door after them, and we were left alone, tête-à-tête.

"'I have a favour to ask of you.'

"'What favour?'

"'Well, my dear boy, there is no rest for me even on my deathbed. I am in want.'

"'How so?' I positively flushed crimson, I could hardly speak.

"'Why I had to pay some of my own money into the Treasury. I grudge nothing for the public weal, my boy! I don't grudge my life. Don't you imagine any ill. I am sad to think that slanderers have blackened my name to you. . . . You were mistaken, my hair has gone white from grief. The Inspector is coming down upon us and Matveyev is seven thousand roubles short, and I shall have to answer for it. . . . Who else? It will be visited upon me, my boy: where were my eyes? And how can we get it from Matveyev? He has had trouble enough already: why should I bring the poor fellow to ruin?'

"'Holy saints!' I thought, 'what a just man! What a heart!'

"'And I don't want to take my daughter's money, which has been set aside for her dowry: that sum is sacred. I have money of my own, it's true, but I have lent it all to friends—how is one to collect it all in a minute?'

"I simply fell on my knees before him. 'My benefactor!' I cried, 'I've wronged you, I have injured you; it was slanderers who wrote against you; don't break my heart, take back your money!'

"He looked at me and there were tears in his eyes. 'That was just what I expected from you, my son. Get up! I forgave you at the time for the sake of my daughter's tears—now my heart forgives you freely! You have healed my wounds. I bless you for all time!'

"Well, when he blessed me, gentlemen, I scurried home as soon as I could. I got the money:

"'Here, father, here's the money. I've only spent fifty roubles.'

"'Well, that's all right,' he said. 'But now every trifle may count; the time is short, write a report dated some days ago that you were short of money and had taken fifty roubles on account. I'll tell the authorities you had it in advance.'

"Well, gentlemen, what do you think? I did write that report, too!"

"Well, what then? What happened? How did it end?"

"As soon as I had written the report, gentlemen, this is how it ended. The next day, in the early morning, an envelope with a government seal arrived. I looked at it and what had I got? The sack! That is, instructions to hand over my work, to deliver the accounts—and to go about my business!"

"How so?"

"That's just what I cried at the top of my voice, 'How so?' Gentlemen, there was a ringing in my ears. I thought there was no special reason for it — but no, the Inspector had arrived in the town. My heart sank. 'It's not for nothing,' I thought. And just as I was I rushed off to Fedosey Nikolaitch.

"'How is this?' I said.

"'What do you mean?' he said.

"'Why, I am dismissed.'

"'Dismissed? how?'

"'Why, look at this!'

"'Well, what of it?'

"'Why, but I didn't ask for it!'

"'Yes, you did — you sent in your papers on the first of — April.' (I had never taken that letter back!)

"'Fedosey Nikolaitch! I can't believe my ears, I can't believe my eyes! Is this you?

"'It is me, why?'

"'My God!'

"'I am sorry, sir. I am very sorry that you made up your mind to retire from the service so early. A young man ought to be in the service, and you've begun to be a little light-headed of late. And as for your character, set your mind at rest: I'll see to that! Your behaviour has always been so exemplary!'

"'But that was a little joke, Fedosey Nikolaitch! I didn't mean it, I just gave you the letter for your fatherly . . . that's all.'

"'That's all? A queer joke, sir! Does one jest with documents like that? Why, you are sometimes sent to Siberia for such jokes. Now, good-bye. I am busy. We have the Inspector here — the duties of the service before everything; you can kick up your heels, but we have to sit here at work. But I'll get you a character —— Oh, another thing: I've just bought a house from Matveyev. We are moving in in a day or two. So I expect I shall not have the pleasure of seeing you at our new residence. *Bon voyage!*'

"I ran home.

"'We are lost, granny!'

"She wailed, poor dear, and then I saw the page from Fedosey Nikolaitch's running up with a note and a bird-cage, and in the cage there was a starling. In the fullness of my heart I had given her the starling. And in the note there were the words: 'April 1st,' and nothing more. What do you think of that, gentlemen?"

"What happened then? What happened then?"

"What then! I met Fedosey Nikolaitch once, I meant to tell him to his face he was a scoundrel."

"Well?"

"But somehow I couldn't bring myself to it, gentlemen."

(1848)

❖ RALPH ELLISON
The Battle Royal

Ralph Ellison (1914–) was born in Oklahoma City. He studied music at Tuskegee Institute and then went to New York City, where he met Richard Wright. He got a position with the Federal Writers Project and in 1942 became editor of the *Negro Quarterly*. He published short stories and articles in magazines such as the *New Masses*. His only novel is *Invisible Man* (1952), which a *Book Week* poll named as "the most distinguished single work published in the last twenty years." In 1970, Ellison became the Albert Schweitzer Professor of Humanities at New York University. Ellison's short stories have not yet been collected. "The Battle Royal," originally published in a magazine, was revised to become the first chapter of *Invisible Man*. Some of Ellison's essays are collected in the volume *Shadow and Act* (1964) and more recently in *Going to the Territory* (1986).

It goes a long way back, some twenty years. All my life I had been looking for something, and everywhere I turned someone tried to tell me what it was. I accepted their answers too, though they were often in contradiction and even self-contradictory. I was naïve. I was looking for myself and asking everyone except myself questions which I, and only I, could answer. It took me a long time and much painful boomeranging of my expectations to achieve a realization everyone else appears to have been born with: That I am nobody but myself. But first I had to discover that I am an invisible man!

And yet I am no freak of nature, nor of history. I was in the cards, other things having been equal (or unequal) eighty-five years ago. I am not ashamed of my grandparents for having been slaves. I am only ashamed of myself for having at one time been ashamed. About eighty-five years ago they were told that they were free, united with others of our country in everything pertaining to the common good, and, in everything social, separate like the fingers of the hand. And they believed it. They exulted in it. They stayed in their place, worked hard, and brought up my father to do the same. But my grandfather is the one. He was an odd old guy, my grandfather, and I am told I take after him. It was he who caused the trouble. On his deathbed he called my father to him and said, "Son, after I'm gone I want you to keep up the good fight. I never told you, but our life is a war and I have been a traitor all my born days, a spy in the enemy's country ever since I give up my gun back in the Reconstruction. Live with your head in the lion's mouth. I want you to overcome 'em with yeses, undermine 'em with grins, agree 'em to death and destruction, let 'em swoller you till they vomit or bust wide open." They thought the old man had gone out of his mind. He had been the meekest of men. The younger children were rushed from the room, the shades drawn and the flame of the lamp turned so low that it sputtered on the wick like the old man's breathing. "Learn it to the younguns," he whispered fiercely; then he died.

But my folks were more alarmed over his last words than over his dying. It was as though he had not died at all, his words caused so much anxiety. I was warned emphatically to forget what he had said and, indeed, this is the first time it has been mentioned outside the family circle. It had a tremendous effect upon me, however. I could never be sure of what he meant. Grandfather had been a quiet old man who never made any trouble, yet on his deathbed he had called himself a traitor and a spy, and he had spoken of his meekness as a dangerous activity. It became a constant puzzle which lay unanswered in the back of my mind. And whenever things went well for me I remembered my grandfather and felt guilty and uncomfortable. It was as though I was carrying out his advice in spite of myself. And to make it worse, everyone loved me for it. I was praised by the most lily-white men of the town. I was considered an example of desirable conduct — just as my grandfather had been. And what puzzled me was that the old man had defined it as *treachery*. When I was praised for my conduct I felt a guilt that in some way I was doing something that was really against the wishes of the white folks, that if they had understood they would have desired me to act just the opposite, that I should have been sulky and mean, and that that really would have been what they wanted, even though they were fooled and thought they wanted me to act as I did. It made me afraid that some day they would look upon me as a traitor and I would be lost. Still I was more afraid to act any other way because they didn't like that at all. The old man's words were like a curse. On my graduation day I delivered an oration in which I showed that humility was the secret, indeed, the very essence of progress. (Not that I believed this — how could I, remembering my grandfather? — I only believed that it worked.) It was a great success. Everyone praised me and I was invited to give the speech at a gathering of the town's leading white citizens. It was a triumph for our whole community.

It was in the main ballroom of the leading hotel. When I got there I discovered that it was on the occasion of a smoker, and I was told that since I was to be there anyway I might as well take part in the battle royal to be fought by some of my schoolmates as part of the entertainment. The battle royal came first.

All of the town's big shots were there in their tuxedoes, wolfing down the buffet foods, drinking beer and whiskey and smoking black cigars. It was a large room with a high ceiling. Chairs were arranged in neat rows around three sides of a portable boxing ring. The fourth side was clear, revealing a gleaming space of polished floor. I had some misgivings over the battle royal, by the way. Not from a distaste for fighting, but because I didn't care too much for the other fellows who were to take part. They were tough guys who seemed to have no grandfather's curse worrying their minds. No one could mistake their toughness. And besides, I suspected that fighting a battle royal might detract from the dignity of my speech. In those pre-invisible days I visualized myself as a potential Booker T. Washington. But the other fellows didn't care too much for me either, and there were nine of them. I felt superior to them in my way, and I didn't like the manner in which we were all crowded together into the servants' elevator. Nor did they like my being there. In fact, as the warmly lighted floors flashed past the elevator we had words over the fact that I, by taking part in the fight, had knocked one of their friends out of a night's work.

We were led out of the elevator through a rococo hall into an anteroom and told to get into our fighting togs. Each of us was issued a pair of boxing gloves and ushered out into the big mirrored hall, which we entered looking cautiously about us and whispering, lest we might accidentally be heard above the noise of the room. It was foggy with cigar smoke. And already the whiskey was taking effect. I was shocked to see some of the most important men of the town quite tipsy. They were all there — bankers, lawyers, judges, doctors, fire chiefs, teachers, merchants. Even one of the more fashionable pastors. Something we could not see was going on up front. A clarinet was vibrating sensuously and the men were standing up and moving eagerly forward. We were a small tight group, clustered together, our bare upper bodies touching and shining with anticipatory sweat; while up front the big shots were becoming increasingly excited over something we still could not see. Suddenly I heard the school superintendent, who had told me to come, yell, "Bring up the shines, gentlemen! Bring up the little shines!"

We were rushed up to the front of the ballroom, where it smelled even more strongly of tobacco and whiskey. Then we were pushed into place. I almost wet my pants. A sea of faces, some hostile, some amused, ringed around us, and in the center, facing us, stood a magnificent blonde — stark naked. There was a dead silence. I felt a blast of cold air chill me. I tried to back away, but they were behind me and around me. Some of the boys stood with lowered heads trembling. I felt a wave of irrational guilt and fear. My teeth chattered, my skin turned to goose flesh, my knees knocked. Yet I was strongly attracted and looked in spite of myself. Had the price of looking been blindness, I would have looked. The hair was yellow like that of a circus kewpie doll, the face heavily powdered and rouged, as though to form an abstract mask, the eyes hollow and smeared a cool blue, the color of a baboon's butt. I felt a desire to spit upon her as my eyes brushed slowly over her body. Her breasts were firm and round as the domes of East Indian temples, and I stood so close as to see the fine skin texture and beads of pearly perspiration glistening like dew around the pink and erected buds of her nipples. I wanted at one and the same time to run from the room, to sink through the floor, or go to her and cover her from my eyes and the eyes of the others with my body; to feel the soft thighs, to caress her and destroy her, to love her and murder her, to hide from her, and yet to stroke where below the small American flag tattooed upon her belly her thighs formed a capital V. I had a notion that of all in the room she saw only me with her impersonal eyes.

And then she began to dance, a slow sensuous movement; the smoke of a hundred cigars clinging to her like the thinnest of veils. She seemed like a fair bird-girl girdled in veils calling to me from the angry surface of some gray and threatening sea. I was transported. Then I became aware of the clarinet playing and the big shots yelling at us. Some threatened us if we looked and others if we did not. On my right I saw one boy faint. And now a man grabbed a silver pitcher from a table and stepped close as he dashed ice water upon him and stood him up and forced two of us to support him as his head hung and moans issued from his thick bluish lips. Another boy began to plead to go home. He was the largest of the group, wearing dark red fighting trunks much too small to conceal the erection which projected from him as though in answer to the insinuating low-registered moaning of the clarinet. He tried to hide himself with his boxing gloves.

And all the while the blonde continued dancing, smiling faintly at the big shots who watched her with fascination, and faintly smiling at our fear. I noticed a certain merchant who followed her hungrily, his lips loose and drooling. He was a large man who wore diamond studs in a shirtfront which swelled with the ample paunch underneath, and each time the blonde swayed her undulating hips he ran his hand through the thin hair of his bald head and, with his arms upheld, his posture clumsy like that of an intoxicated panda, wound his belly in a slow and obscene grind. This creature was completely hypnotized. The music had quickened. As the dancer flung herself about with a detached expression on her face, the men began reaching out to touch her. I could see their beefy fingers sink into the soft flesh. Some of the others tried to stop them and she began to move around the floor in graceful circles, as they gave chase, slipping and sliding over the polished floor. It was mad. Chairs went crashing, drinks were spilt, as they ran laughing and howling after her. They caught her just as she reached a door, raised her from the floor, and tossed her as college boys are tossed at a hazing, and above her red, fixed-smiling lips I saw the terror and disgust in her eyes, almost like my own terror and that which I saw in some of the other boys. As I watched, they tossed her twice and her soft breasts seemed to flatten against the air and her legs flung wildly as she spun. Some of the more sober ones helped her to escape. And I started off the floor, heading for the anteroom with the rest of the boys.

Some were still crying and in hysteria. But as we tried to leave we were stopped and ordered to get into the ring. There was nothing to do but what we were told. All ten of us climbed under the ropes and allowed ourselves to be blindfolded with broad bands of white cloth. One of the men seemed to feel a bit sympathetic and tried to cheer us up as we stood with our backs against the ropes. Some of us tried to grin. "See that boy over there?" one of the men said. "I want you to run across at the bell and give it to him right in the belly. If you don't get him, I'm going to get you. I don't like his looks." Each of us was told the same. The blindfolds were put on. Yet even then I had been going over my speech. In my mind each word was as bright as flame. I felt the cloth pressed into place, and frowned so that it would be loosened when I relaxed.

But now I felt a sudden fit of blind terror. I was unused to darkness. It was as though I had suddenly found myself in a dark room filled with poisonous cotton-mouths. I could hear the bleary voices yelling insistently for the battle royal to begin.

"Get going in there!"

"Let me at the big nigger!"

I strained to pick up the school superintendent's voice, as though to squeeze some security out of that slightly more familiar sound.

"Let me at those black sonsabitches!" someone yelled.

"No, Jackson, no!" another voice yelled. "Here somebody, help me hold Jack."

"I want to get at that ginger-colored nigger. Tear him limb from limb," the first voice yelled.

I stood against the ropes trembling. For in those days I was what they called ginger-colored, and he sounded as though he might crunch me between his teeth like a crisp ginger cookie.

Quite a struggle was going on. Chairs were being kicked about and I could hear voices grunting as with a terrific effort. I wanted to see, to see more desperately than ever before. But the blindfold was as tight as a thick skin-puckering scab and when I raised my gloved hands to push the layers of white aside a voice yelled, "Oh, no you don't, black bastard! Leave that alone!"

"Ring the bell before Jackson kills him a coon!" someone boomed in the sudden silence. And I heard the bell clang and the sound of feet scuffling forward.

A glove smacked against my head. I pivoted, striking out stiffy as someone went past, and felt the jar ripple along the length of my arm to my shoulder. Then it seemed as though all nine of the boys had turned upon me at once. Blows pounded me from all sides while I struck out as best I could. So many blows landed upon me that I wondered if I were not the only blindfolded fighter in the ring, or if the man called Jackson hadn't succeeded in getting me after all.

Blindfolded, I could no longer control my motions. I had no dignity. I stumbled about like a baby or a drunken man. The smoke had become thicker and with each new blow it seemed to sear and further restrict my lungs. My saliva became like a hot bitter glue. A glove connected with my head, filling my mouth with warm blood. It was everywhere. I could not tell if the moisture I felt upon my body was sweat or blood. A blow landed hard against the nape of my neck. I felt myself going over my head hitting the floor. Streaks of blue light filled the black world behind the blindfold. I lay prone, pretending that I was knocked out, but felt myself seized by hands and yanked to my feet. "Get going, black boy! Mix it up!" My arms were like lead, my head smarting from blows. I managed to feel my way to the ropes and held on, trying to catch my breath. A glove landed in my midsection and I went over again, feeling as though the smoke had become a knife jabbed into my guts. Pushed this way and that by the legs milling around me, I finally pulled erect and discovered that I could see the black, sweat-washed forms weaving in the smoky-blue atmosphere like drunken dancers weaving to the rapid drum-like thuds of blows.

Everyone fought hysterically. It was complete anarchy. Everybody fought everybody else. No group fought together for long. Two, three, four, fought one, then turned to fight each other, were themselves attacked. Blows landed below the belt and in the kidney, with the gloves open as well as closed, and with my eye partly open now there was not so much terror. I moved carefully, avoiding blows, although not too many to attract attention, fighting from group to group. The boys groped about like blind, cautious crabs crouching to protect their mid-sections, their heads pulled in short against their shoulders, their arms stretched nervously before them, with their fists testing the smoke-filled air like the knobbed feelers of hypersensitive snails. In one corner I glimpsed a boy violently punching the air and heard him scream in pain as he smashed his hand against a ring post. For a second I saw him bent over holding his hand, then going down as a blow caught his unprotected head. I played one group against the other, slipping in and throwing a punch then stepping out of range while pushing the others into the melee to take the blows blindly aimed at me. The smoke was agonizing and there were no rounds, no bells at three minute intervals to relieve our exhaustion. The room spun round me, a swirl of lights, smoke, sweating bodies surrounded by tense white faces. I bled from both nose and mouth, the blood spattering upon my chest.

The men kept yelling, "Slug him, black boy! Knock his guts out!"

"Uppercut him! Kill him! Kill that big boy!"

Taking a fake fall, I saw a boy going down heavily beside me as though we were felled by a single blow, saw a sneaker-clad foot shoot into his groin as the two who had knocked him down stumbled upon him. I rolled out of range, feeling a twinge of nausea.

The harder we fought the more threatening the men became. And yet, I had begun to worry about my speech again. How would it go? Would they recognize my ability? What would they give me?

I was fighting automatically when suddenly I noticed that one after another of the boys was leaving the ring. I was surprised, filled with panic, as though I had been left alone with an unknown danger. Then I understood. The boys had arranged it among themselves. It was the custom for the two men left in the ring to slug it out for the winner's prize. I discovered this too late. When the bell sounded two men in tuxedoes leaped into the ring and removed the blindfold. I found myself facing Tatlock, the biggest of the gang. I felt sick at my stomach. Hardly had the bell stopped ringing in my ears than it clanged again and I saw him moving swiftly toward me. Thinking of nothing else to do I hit him smash on the nose. He kept coming, bringing the rank sharp violence of stale sweat. His face was a black blank of a face, only his eyes alive — with hate of me and aglow with a feverish terror from what had happened to us all. I became anxious. I wanted to deliver my speech and he came at me as though he meant to beat it out of me. I smashed him again and again, taking his blows as they came. Then on a sudden impulse I struck him lightly and as we clinched, I whispered, "Fake like I knocked you out, you can have the prize."

"I'll break your behind," he whispered hoarsely.

"For *them?*"

"For *me*, sonofabitch."

They were yelling for us to break it up and Tatlock spun me half around with a blow, and as a joggled camera sweeps in a reeling scene, I saw the howling red faces crouching tense beneath the cloud of blue-gray smoke. For a moment the world wavered, unraveled, flowed, then my head cleared and Tatlock bounced before me. That fluttering shadow before my eyes was his jabbing left hand. Then falling forward, my head against his damp shoulder, I whispered,

"I'll make it five dollars more."

"Go to hell!"

But his muscles relaxed a trifle beneath my pressure and I breathed, "Seven?"

"Give it to your ma," he said, ripping me beneath the heart.

And while I still held him I butted him and moved away. I felt myself bombarded with punches. I fought back with hopeless desperation. I wanted to deliver my speech more than anything else in the world, because I felt only these men could judge truly my ability, and now this stupid clown was ruining my chances. I began fighting carefully now, moving in to punch him and out again with my greater speed. A lucky blow to his chin and I had him going too — until I heard a loud voice yell, "I got my money on the big boy."

Hearing this, I almost dropped my guard. I was confused: Should I try to win against the voice out there? Would not this go against my speech, and was not this a moment for humility, for nonresistance? A blow to my head as I danced about sent my right eye popping like a jack-in-the-box and settled my dilemma. The room went red as I fell. It was a dream fall, my body languid and fastidious as to where to land, until the floor became impatient and smashed up to meet me. A moment later I came to. An hypnotic voice said FIVE emphatically. And I lay there, hazily watching a dark red spot of my own blood shaping itself into a butterfly, glistening and soaking into the soiled gray world of the canvas.

When the voice drawled TEN I was lifted up and dragged to a chair. I sat dazed. My eye pained and swelled with each throb of my pounding heart and I wondered if now I would be allowed to speak. I was wringing wet, my mouth still bleeding. We were grouped along the wall now. The other boys ignored me as they congratulated Tatlock and speculated as to how much they would be paid. One boy whimpered over his smashed hand. Looking up front, I saw attendants in white jackets rolling the portable ring away and placing a small square rug in the vacant space surrounded by chairs. Perhaps, I thought, I will stand on the rug to deliver my speech.

Then the M.C. called to us, "Come on up here boys and get your money."

We ran forward to where the men laughed and talked in their chairs, waiting. Everyone seemed friendly now.

"There it is on the rug," the man said. I saw the rug covered with coins of all dimensions and a few crumpled bills. But what excited me, scattered here and there, were the gold pieces.

"Boys, it's all yours," the man said. "You get all you grab."

"That's right, Sambo," a blond man said, winking at me confidentially.

I trembled with excitement, forgetting my pain. I would get the gold and the bills, I thought. I would use both hands. I would throw my body against the boys nearest me to block them from the gold.

"Get down around the rug now," the man commanded, "and don't anyone touch it until I give the signal."

"This ought to be good," I heard.

As told, we got around the square rug on our knees. Slowly the man raised his freckled hand as we followed it upward with our eyes.

I heard, "These niggers look like they're about to pray!"

Then, "Ready," the man said. "Go!"

I lunged for a yellow coin lying on the blue design of the carpet, touching it and sending a surprised shriek to join those rising around me. I tried frantically to remove my hand but could not let go. A hot, violent force tore through my body, shaking me like a wet rat. The rug was electrified. The hair bristled up on my head as I shook myself free. My muscles jumped, my nerves jangled, writhed. But I saw that this was not stopping the other boys. Laughing in fear and embarrassment, some were holding back and scooping up the coins knocked off by the painful contortions of the others. The men roared above us as we struggled.

"Pick it up, goddamnit, pick it up!" someone called like a bass-voiced parrot. "Go on, get it"

I crawled rapidly around the floor, picking up the coins, trying to avoid the coppers and to get greenbacks and the gold. Ignoring the shock by laughing, as I brushed the coins off quickly, I discovered that I could contain the electricity — a contradiction, but it works. Then the men began to push us onto the rug. Laughing embarrassedly, we struggled out of their hands and kept after the coins. We were all wet and slippery and hard to hold. Suddenly I saw a boy lifted into the air, glistening with sweat like a circus seal, and dropped, his wet back landing flush upon the charged rug, heard him yell and saw him literally dance upon his back, his elbows beating a frenzied tattoo upon the floor, his muscles twitching like the flesh of a horse stung by many flies. When he finally rolled off, his face was gray and no one stopped him when he ran from the floor amid booming laughter.

"Get the money," the M.C. called. "That's good hard American cash!"

And we snatched and grabbed, snatched and grabbed. I was careful not to come too close to the rug now, and when I felt the hot whiskey breath descend upon me like a cloud of foul air I reached out and grabbed the leg of a chair. It was occupied and I held on desperately.

"Leggo nigger! Leggo!"

The huge face wavered down to mine as he tried to push me free. But my body was slippery and he was too drunk. It was Mr. Colcord, who owned a chain of movie houses and "entertainment palaces." Each time he grabbed me I slipped out of his hands. It became a real struggle. I feared the rug more than I did the drunk, so I held on, surprising myself for a moment by trying to topple *him* upon the rug. It was such an enormous idea that I found myself actually carrying it out. I tried not to be obvious, yet when I grabbed his leg, trying to tumble him out of the chair, he raised up roaring with laughter, and looking at me with soberness dead in the eye, kicked me viciously in the chest. The chair leg flew out of my hand and I felt myself going and rolled. It was as though I had rolled through a bed of hot coals. It seemed a whole century would pass before I would roll free, a century in which I was seared through the deepest levels of my body to the fearful breath within me and the breath seared and heated to the point of explosion. It'll all be over in a flash, I thought as I rolled clear. It'll all be over in a flash.

But not yet, the men on the other side were waiting, red faces swollen as though from apoplexy as they bent forward in their chairs. Seeing their fingers coming toward me I rolled away as a fumbled football rolls off the receiver's fingertips, back into the coals. That time I luckily sent the rug sliding out of place and heard the coins ringing against the floor and the boys scuffling to pick them up and the M.C. calling, "All right, boys, that's all. Go get dressed and get your money."

I was limp as a dish rag. My back felt as though it had been beaten with wires.

When we had dressed the M.C. came in and gave us each five dollars, except Tatlock, who got ten for being last in the ring. Then he told us to leave. I was not to get a chance to deliver my speech, I thought. I was going out into the dim alley in despair when I was stopped and told to go back. I returned to the ballroom, where the men were pushing back their chairs and gathering in groups to talk.

The M.C. knocked on a table for quiet. "Gentlemen," he said, "we almost forgot an important part of the program. A most serious part, gentlemen. This boy was brought here to deliver a speech which he made at his graduation yesterday . . ."

"Bravo!"

"I'm told that he is the smartest boy we've got out there in Greenwood. I'm told that he knows more big words than a pocket-sized dictionary."

Much applause and laughter.

"So now, gentlemen, I want you to give him your attention."

There was still laughter as I faced them, my mouth dry, my eye throbbing. I began slowly, but evidently my throat was tense, because they began shouting, "Louder! Louder!"

"We of the younger generation extol the wisdom of that great leader and educator," I shouted, "who first spoke these flaming words of wisdom: 'A ship lost at sea for many days suddenly sighted a friendly vessel. From the mast of the unfortunate vessel was seen a signal: "Water, water; we die of thirst!" The answer from the friendly vessel came back: "Cast down your bucket where you are." The captain of the distressed vessel, at last heeding the injunction, cast down his bucket, and it came up full of fresh sparkling water from the mouth of the Amazon River.' And like him I say, and in his words, "To those of my race who depend upon bettering their condition in a foreign land, or who underestimate the importance of cultivating friendly relations with Southern white man, who is his next-door neighbor, I would say: "Cast down your bucket where you are" — cast it down in making friends in every manly way of the people of all races by whom we are surrounded. . . .'"

I spoke automatically and with such fervor that I did not realize that the men were still talking and laughing until my dry mouth, filling up with blood from the cut, almost strangled me. I coughed, wanting to stop and go to one of the tall brass, sand-filled spittoons to relieve myself, but a few of the men, especially the superintendent, were listening and I was afraid. So I gulped it down, blood, saliva and all, and continued. (What powers of endurance I had during those days! What enthusiasm! What a belief in the rightness of things!) I spoke even louder in spite of the pain. But still they talked and still they laughed, as though deaf with cotton in dirty ears. So I spoke with greater emotional emphasis. I closed my ears and swallowed blood until I was nauseated. The speech seemed a hundred times as long as before, but I could not leave out a single word. All had to be said, each memorized nuance considered, rendered. Nor was that all. Whenever I uttered a word of three or more syllables a group of voices would yell for me to repeat it. I used the phrase "social responsibility" and they yelled:

"What's that word you say, boy?"

"Social responsibility," I said.

"What?"

"Social . . ."

"Louder."

". . . responsibility."

"More!"

"Respon —"

"Repeat!"

"— sibility."

The room filled with the uproar of laughter until, no doubt, distracted by having to gulp down my blood, I made a mistake and yelled a phrase I had often seen denounced in newspaper editorials, heard debated in private

"Social . ."

"What?" they yelled.

". . . equality —"

The laughter hung smokelike in the sudden stillness. I opened my eyes, puzzled. Sounds of displeasure filled the room. The M.C. rushed forward. They shouted hostile phrases at me. But I did not understand.

A small dry mustached man in the front row blared out, "Say that slowly, son!"

"What sir?"

"What you just said!"

"Social responsibility, sir," I said.

"You weren't being smart, were you boy?" he said, not unkindly.

"No, sir!"

"You sure that about 'equality' was a mistake?"

"Oh, yes, sir," I said, "I was swallowing blood."

"Well, you had better speak more slowly so we can understand. We mean to do right by you, but you've got to know your place at all times. All right, now, go on with your speech."

I was afraid. I wanted to leave but I wanted also to speak and I was afraid they'd snatch me down.

"Thank you sir," I said, beginning where I had left off, and having them ignore me as before.

Yet when I finished there was a thunderous applause. I was surprised to see the superintendent come forth with a package wrapped in white tissue paper, and, gesturing for quiet, address the men.

"Gentlemen, you see that I did not overpraise this boy. He makes a good speech and some day he'll lead his people in the proper paths. And I don't have to tell you that this is important in these days and times. This is a good, smart boy, and so to encourage him in the right direction, in the name of the Board of Education I wish to present him a prize in the form of this . . ."

He paused, removing the tissue paper and revealing a gleaming calfskin brief case.

". . . . in the form of this first-class article from Shad Whitmore's shop."

"Boy," he said, addressing me, "take this prize and keep it well. Consider it a badge of office. Prize it. Keep developing as you are and some day it will be filled with important papers that will help shape the destiny of your people."

I was so moved that I could hardly express my thanks. A rope of bloody saliva forming a shape like an undiscovered continent drooled upon the leather and I wiped it quickly away. I felt an importance that I had never dreamed.

"Open it and see what's inside," I was told.

My fingers a-tremble, I complied, smelling the fresh leather and finding an official-looking document inside. It was a scholarship to the state college for Negroes. My eyes filled with tears and I ran awkwardly off the floor.

I was overjoyed; I did not even mind when I discovered that the gold pieces I had scrambled for were brass pocket tokens advertising a certain make of automobile.

When I reached home everyone was excited. Next day the neighbors came to congratulate me. I even felt safe from grandfather, whose death-bed curse usually spoiled my triumphs. I stood beneath his photograph with my brief case in hand and smiled triumphantly into his stolid black peasant's face. It was a face that fascinated me. The eyes seemed to follow everywhere I went.

That night I dreamed I was at a circus with him and that he refused to laugh at the clowns no matter what they did. Then later he told me to open my brief case and read what was inside and I did, finding an official envelope stamped with the state seal; and inside the envelope I found another and another, endlessly, and I thought I would fall of weariness. "Them's years," he said. "Now open that one." And I did and in it I found an engraved document containing a short message in letters of gold. "Read it," my grandfather said. "Out loud."

"To Whom it May Concern," I intoned. "Keep This Nigger-Boy Running."

I awoke with the old man's laughter ringing in my ears.

(It was a dream I was to remember and dream again for many years after. But at that time I had no insight into its meaning. First I had to attend college.)

(1947)

❖ GABRIEL GARCIA MÁRQUEZ
Monologue of Isabel
Watching It Rain in Macondo*

Gabriel Garcia Márquez (1928–) was born in Aracataca, a village in
Colombia. In 1947, he went to the university in the capital, Bogotá, but
the university closed when a civil war started. He moved to the
University of Cartagena, but became interested in journalism and
ended up abroad, first as foreign correspondent for *El Universal* and
then for the Cuban government news agency. Jobs as screenwriter,
editor, and advertising copywriter took him to New York and then to
Mexico City. All during these years he wrote fiction, much of which is
about village life in South America. Like Faulkner, he created an imaginary place, Macondo, and peopled it with a whole population of
characters. Garcia Márquez won the Nobel Prize for literature in 1982.
His novels include *Withering Leaves* (1955), *No One Writes to the
Colonel* (1961), *In Evil Hour* (1962), *One Hundred Years of Solitude*
(1967), *The Autumn of the Patriarch* (1975), *Chronicle of a Death
Foretold* (1981), *Love in the Time of Cholera* (1985), and *The General
in His Labyrinth* (1989). His translated short fiction has been collected
in *Big Mama's Funeral* (1962), *The Incredible and Sad Story of Innocent
Erendira and Her Heartless Grandmother* (1972), *Leaf Storm* (1972,
which includes "Monologue of Isabel"), *Collected Stories* (1984), and
Collected Novellas (1990).

Winter fell one Sunday when people were coming out of church. Saturday night had
been suffocating. But even on Sunday morning nobody thought it would rain. After
mass, before we women had time to find the catches on our parasols, a thick, dark wind
blew, which with one broad, round swirl swept away the dust and hard tinder of May.
Someone next to me said: "It's a water wind." And I knew it even before then. From
the moment we came out onto the church steps I felt shaken by a slimy feeling in my
stomach. The men ran to the nearby houses with one hand on their hats and a
handkerchief in the other, protecting themselves against the wind and the dust storm.
Then it rained. And the sky was a gray, jellyish substance that flapped its wings a hand
away from our heads.

During the rest of the morning my stepmother and I were sitting by the
railing, happy that the rain would revive the thirsty rosemary and nard in the
flowerpots after seven months of intense summer and scorching dust. At noon
the reverberation of the earth stopped and a smell of turned earth, of awakened and
renovated vegetation mingled with the cool and healthful odor of the rain in the
rosemary. My father said at lunchtime: "When it rains in May, it's a sign that there'll

---

*Translated by Gregory Rabassa

be good tides." Smiling, crossed by the luminous thread of the new season, my stepmother told me: "That's what I heard in the sermon." And my father smiled. And he ate with a good appetite and even let his food digest leisurely beside the railing, silent, his eyes closed, but not sleeping, as if to think that he was dreaming while awake.

It rained all afternoon in a single tone. In the uniform and peaceful intensity you could hear the water fall, the way it is when you travel all afternoon on a train. But without our noticing it, the rain was penetrating too deeply into our senses. Early Monday morning, when we closed the door to avoid the cutting, icy draft that blew in from the courtyard, our senses had been filled with rain. And on Monday morning they had overflowed. My stepmother and I went back to look at the garden. The harsh gray earth of May had been changed overnight into a dark, sticky substance like cheap soap. A trickle of water began to run off the flowerpots. "I think they had more than enough water during the night," my stepmother said. And I noticed that she had stopped smiling and that her joy of the previous day had changed during the night into a lax and tedious seriousness. "I think you're right," I said. "It would be better to have the Indians put them on the veranda until it stops raining." And that was what they did, while the rain grew like an immense tree over the other trees. My father occupied the same spot where he had been on Sunday afternoon, but he didn't talk about the rain. He said: "I must have slept poorly last night because I woke up with a stiff back." And he stayed there, sitting by the railing with his feet on a chair and his head turned toward the empty garden. Only at dusk, after he had turned down lunch, did he say: "It looks as if it will never clear." And I remembered the months of heat. I remembered August, those long and awesome siestas in which we dropped down to die under the weight of the hour, our clothes sticking to our bodies, hearing outside the insistent and dull buzzing of the hour that never passed. I saw the washed-down walls, the joints of the beams all puffed up by the water. I saw the small garden, empty for the first time, and the jasmine bush against the wall, faithful to the memory of my mother. I saw my father sitting in a rocker, his painful vertebrae resting on a pillow and his sad eyes lost in the labyrinth of the rain. I remembered the August nights in whose wondrous silence nothing could be heard except the millenary sound that the earth makes as it spins on its rusty, unoiled axis. Suddenly I felt overcome by an overwhelming sadness.

It rained all Monday, just like Sunday. But now it seemed to be raining in another way, because something different and bitter was going on in my heart. At dusk a voice beside my chair said: "This rain is a bore." Without turning to look, I recognized Martin's voice. I knew that he was speaking in the next chair, with the same cold and awesome expression that hadn't varied, not even after that gloomy December dawn when he started being my husband. Five months had passed since then. Now I was going to have a child. And Martin was there beside me saying that the rain bored him. "Not a bore," I said. "It seems terribly sad to me, with the empty garden and those poor trees that can't come in from the courtyard." Then I turned to look at him and Martin was no longer there. It was only a voice that was saying to me: "It doesn't look as if it will ever clear," and when I looked toward the voice I found only the empty chair.

On Tuesday morning we found a cow in the garden. It looked like a clay promontory in its hard and rebellious immobility, its hooves sunken in the mud and its head bent over. During the morning the Indians tried to drive it away with sticks and stones. But the cow stayed there, imperturbable in the garden, hard, inviolable, its hooves still sunken in the mud and its huge head humiliated by the rain. The Indians harassed it until my father's patient tolerance came to its defense. "Leave her alone," he said. "She'll leave the way she came."

At sundown on Tuesday the water tightened and hurt, like a shroud over the heart. The coolness of the first morning began to change into a hot and sticky humidity. The temperature was neither cold nor hot; it was the temperature of a fever chill. Feet sweated inside shoes. It was hard to say what was more disagreeable, bare skin or the contact of clothing on skin. All activity had ceased in the house. We sat on the veranda but we no longer watched the rain as we did on the first day. We no longer felt it falling. We no longer saw anything except the outline of the trees in the mist, with a sad and desolate sunset which left on your lips the same taste with which you awaken after having dreamed about a stranger. I knew that it was Tuesday and I remembered the twins of Saint Jerome, the blind girls who came to the house every week to sing us simple songs, saddened by the bitter and unprotected prodigy of their voices. Above the rain I heard the blind twins' little song and I imagined them at home, huddling, waiting for the rain to stop so they could go out and sing. The twins of Saint Jerome wouldn't come that day, I thought, nor would the beggar woman be on the veranda after siesta, asking, as on every Tuesday, for the eternal branch of lemon balm.

That day we lost track of meals. At siesta time my stepmother served a plate of tasteless soup and a piece of stale bread. But actually we hadn't eaten since sunset on Monday and I think that from then on we stopped thinking. We were paralyzed, drugged by the rain, given over to the collapse of nature with a peaceful and resigned attitude. Only the cow was moving in the afternoon. Suddenly a deep noise shook her insides and her hooves sank into the mud with greater force. Then she stood motionless for half an hour, as if she were already dead but could not fall down because the habit of being alive prevented her, the habit of remaining in one position in the rain, until the habit grew weaker than her body. Then she doubled her front legs (her dark and shiny haunches still raised in a last agonized effort) and sank her drooling snout into the mud, finally surrendering to the weight of her own matter in a silent, gradual, and dignified ceremony of total downfall. "She got that far," someone said behind me. And I turned to look and on the threshold I saw the Tuesday beggar woman who had come through the storm to ask for the branch of lemon balm.

Perhaps on Wednesday I might have grown accustomed to that overwhelming atmosphere if on going to the living room I hadn't found the table pushed against the wall, the furniture piled on top of it, and on the other side, on a parapet prepared during the night, trunks and boxes of household utensils. The spectacle produced a terrible feeling of emptiness in me. Something had happened during the night. The house was in disarray; the Guajiro Indians, shirtless and barefoot, with their pants rolled up to their knees, were carrying the furniture into the dining room. In the men's expression, in the very diligence with which they were working, one could see the cruelty of their frustrated rebellion, of their necessary and humiliating inferiority in the rain. I moved without direction, without will. I felt changed into a desolate meadow sown with algae and lichens, with soft, sticky toadstools, fertilized by the repugnant plants of dampness and shadows. I was in the living room contemplating the desert spectacle of the piled-up furniture when I heard my stepmother's voice warning me from her room that I might catch pneumonia. Only then did I realize that the water was up to my ankles, that the house was flooded, the floor covered by a thick surface of viscous, dead water.

On Wednesday noon it still hadn't finished dawning. And before three o'clock in the afternoon night had come on completely, ahead of time and sickly, with the same slow, monotonous, and pitiless rhythm of the rain in the courtyard. It was a premature dusk, soft and lugubrious, growing in the midst of the silence of the Guajiros, who were squatting on the chairs against the walls, defeated and impotent against the disturbance of nature. That was when news began to arrive from outside. No one brought it to the house. It simply arrived, precise, individualized, as if led by the liquid clay that ran through the streets and dragged household items along, things and more things, the leftovers of a remote catastrophe, rubbish and dead animals. Events that took place on Sunday, when the rain was still the announcement of a providential season, took two days to be known at our house. And on Wednesday the news arrived as if impelled by the very inner dynamism of the storm. It was learned then that the church was flooded and its collapse expected. Someone who had no reason to know said that night: "The train hasn't been able to cross the bridge since Monday. It seems that the river carried away the tracks." And it was learned that a sick woman had disappeared from her bed and had been found that afternoon floating in the courtyard.

Terrified, possessed by the fright and the deluge, I sat down in the rocker with my legs tucked up and my eyes fixed on the damp darkness full of hazy foreboding. My stepmother appeared in the doorway with the lamp held high and her head erect. She looked like a family ghost before whom I felt no fear whatever because I myself shared her supernatural condition. She came over to where I was. She still held her head high and the lamp in the air, and she splashed through the water on the veranda. "Now we have to pray," she said. And I noticed her dry and wrinkled face, as if she had just left her tomb or as if she had been made of some substance different from human matter. She was across from me with her rosary in her hand saying: "Now we have to pray. The water broke open the tombs and now the poor dead are floating in the cemetery."

I may have slept a little that night when I awoke with a start because of a sour and penetrating smell like that of decomposing bodies. I gave a strong shake to Martin, who was snoring beside me. "Don't you notice it?" I asked him. And he said: "What?" And I said: "The smell. It must be the dead people floating along the streets." I was terrified by that idea, but Martin turned to the wall and with a husky and sleepy voice said: "That's something you made up. Pregnant women are always imagining things."

At dawn on Thursday the smells stopped, the sense of distance was lost. The notion of time, upset since the day before, disappeared completely. Then there was no Thursday. What should have been Thursday was a physical, jellylike thing that could have been parted with the hands in order to look into Friday. There were no men or women there. My stepmother, my father, the Indians were adipose and improbable bodies that moved in the marsh of winter. My father said to me: "Don't move away from here until you're told what to do," and his voice was distant and indirect and didn't seem to be perceived by the ear but by touch, which was the only sense that remained active.

But my father didn't return: he got lost in the weather. So when night came I called my stepmother to tell her to accompany me to my bedroom. I had a peaceful and serene sleep, which lasted all though the night. On the following day the atmosphere was still the same, colorless, odorless, and without any temperature. As soon as I awoke I jumped into a chair and remained there without moving, because something told me that there was still a region of my consciousness that hadn't awakened completely. Then I heard the train whistle. The prolonged and sad whistle of the train fleeing the storm. *It must have cleared somewhere*, I thought, and a voice behind me seemed to answer my thought. "Where?" it said. "Who's there?" I asked looking. And I saw my stepmother with a long thin arm in the direction of the wall. "It's me," she said. And I asked her: "Can you hear it?" And she said yes, maybe it had cleared on the outskirts and they'd repaired the tracks. Then she gave me a tray with some steaming breakfast. It smelled of garlic sauce and boiled butter. It was a plate of soup. Disconcerted, I asked my stepmother what time it was. And she, calmly, with a voice that tasted of prostrated resignation, said: "It must be around two-thirty. The train isn't late after all this." I said: "Two-thirty! How could I have slept so long!" And she said: "You haven't slept very long. It can't be more than three o'clock." And I, trembling, feeling the plate slip through my fingers: "Two-thirty on Friday," I said. And she, monstrously tranquil: "Two-thirty on Thursday, child. *Still* two-thirty on Thursday."

I don't know how long I was sunken in that somnambulism where the senses lose their value. I only know that after many unaccountable hours I heard a voice in the next room. A voice that said: "Now you can roll the bed to this side." It was a tired voice, but not the voice of a sick person, rather that of a convalescent. Then I heard the sound of the bricks in the water. I remained rigid before I realized that I was in a horizontal position. Then I felt the immense emptiness. I felt the wavering and violent silence of the house, the incredible immobility that affected everything. And suddenly I felt my heart turned into a frozen stone. *I'm dead*, I thought. *My God, I'm dead.* I gave a jump in the bed. I shouted: "Ada! Ada!" Martin's unpleasant voice answered me from the other side. "They can't hear you, they're already outside by now." Only then did I realize that it had cleared and that all around us a silence stretched out, a tranquillity, a mysterious and deep beatitude, a perfect state which must have been very much like death. Then footsteps could be heard on the veranda. A clear and completely living voice was heard. Then a cool breeze shook the panel of the door, made a doorknob squeak, and a solid and monumental body, like a ripe fruit, fell deeply into the cistern in the courtyard. Something in the air revealed the presence of an invisible person who was smiling in the darkness. *Good Lord*, I thought then, confused by the mixup in time. *It wouldn't surprise me now if they were coming to call me to go to last Sunday's Mass.*

(1955)

❖ NATHANIEL HAWTHORNE

Wakefield

Nathaniel Hawthorne (1804–1864) was born in Salem, Massachusetts, and went to Bowdoin College in Maine. The son of a rich family, he was able to devote himself to literary studies immediately upon his graduation in 1825. Except for the novel *Fanshawe* (1828), Hawthorne's early writings were tales and sketches, often of an allegorical cast. He first collected these in *Twice-Told Tales* (1837). Hawthorne worked for a while at the Custom House in Boston, then married and rented the "Old Manse," a house built by Ralph Waldo Emerson's grandfather. The name of the house was immortalized in his second collection of short fiction called *Mosses from an Old Manse* (1846). He returned to Salem to become a surveyor at the Salem Custom House, a job that gave him much time for his writing. In 1850 he published his most famous novel, *The Scarlet Letter*, and his fame and fortune were immediately established. Thereafter he published the novels *The House of the Seven Gables* (1851) and *The Blithedale Romance* (1852). A final collection of stories appeared in 1852 under the title *The Snow-Image*. Hawthorne went to England in 1853 as a U.S. diplomat, resigned in 1857, but remained in Europe to write *The Marble Faun* (1860). He spent his last years back in Salem, where he died at the age of sixty.

In some old magazine or newspaper, I recollect a story, told as truth, of a man — let us call him Wakefield — who absented himself for a long time, from his wife. The fact, thus abstractedly stated, is not very uncommon, nor — without a proper distinction of circumstances — to be condemned either as naughty or nonsensical. Howbeit, this, though far from the most aggravated, is perhaps the strangest instance, on record, of marital delinquency; and, moreover, as remarkable a freak as may be found in the whole list of human oddities. The wedded couple lived in London. The man, under pretence of going a journey, took lodgings in the next street to his own house, and there, unheard of by his wife or friends, and without the shadow of a reason for such self-banishment, dwelt upwards of twenty years. During that period, he beheld his home every day, and frequently the forlorn Mrs. Wakefield. And after so great a gap in his matrimonial felicity — when his death was reckoned certain, his estate settled, his name dismissed from memory, and his wife, long, long ago, resigned to her autumnal widowhood — he entered the door one evening, quietly, as from a day's absence, and became a loving spouse till death.

This outline is all that I remember. But the incident, though of the purest originality, unexampled, and probably never to be repeated, is one, I think, which appeals to the general sympathies of mankind. We know, each for himself, that none of us would perpetrate such a folly, yet feel as if some other might. To my own contemplations, at least, it has often recurred, always exciting wonder, but with a sense that the story must be true, and a conception of its hero's character. Whenever any subject so forcibly affects the mind, time is well spent in thinking of it. If the reader choose, let him do his own meditation; or if he prefer to ramble with me through the twenty years of Wakefield's vagary, I bid him welcome; trusting that there will be a pervading spirit and a moral, even should we fail to find them, done up neatly, and condensed into the final sentence. Thought has always its efficacy, and every striking incident its moral.

What sort of a man was Wakefield? We are free to shape out our own idea, and call it by his name. He was now in the meridian of life; his matrimonial affections, never violent, were sobered into a calm, habitual sentiment; of all husbands, he was likely to be the most constant, because a certain sluggishness would keep his heart at rest, wherever it might be placed. He was intellectual, but not actively so; his mind occupied itself in long and lazy musings, that tended to no purpose, or had not vigor to attain it; his thoughts were seldom so energetic as to seize hold of words. Imagination, in the proper meaning of the term, made no part of Wakefield's gifts. With a cold, but not depraved nor wandering heart, and a mind never feverish with riotous thoughts, nor perplexed with originality, who could have anticipated, that our friend would entitle himself to a foremost place among the doers of eccentric deeds? Had his acquaintances been asked, who was the man in London, the surest to perform nothing to-day which should be remembered on the morrow, they would have thought of Wakefield. Only the wife of his bosom might have hesitated. She, without having analyzed his character, was partly aware of a quiet selfishness, that had rusted into his inactive mind — of a peculiar sort of vanity, the most uneasy attribute about him — of a disposition to craft, which had seldom produced more positive effects than the keeping of petty secrets, hardly worth revealing — and, lastly, of what she called a little strangeness, sometimes, in the good man. This latter quality is indefinable, and perhaps non-existent.

Let us now imagine Wakefield bidding adieu to his wife. It is the dusk of an October evening. His equipment is a drab great-coat, a hat covered with an oil-cloth, top-boots, an umbrella in one hand and a small portmanteau in the other. He has informed Mrs. Wakefield that he is to take the night-coach into the country. She would fain inquire the length of his journey, its object, and the probable time of his return; but, indulgent to his harmless love of mystery, interrogates him only by a look. He tells her not to expect him positively by the return coach, nor to be alarmed should he tarry three or four days; but, at all events, to look for him at supper on Friday evening. Wakefield himself, be it considered, has no suspicion of what is before him. He holds out his hand; she gives her own, and meets his parting kiss, in the matter-of-course way of a ten years' matrimony; and forth goes the middle-aged Mr. Wakefield, almost resolved to perplex his good lady by a whole week's absence. After the door has closed behind him, she perceives it thrust partly open, and a vision of her husband's face, through the aperture, smiling on her, and gone in a moment. For the time, this little incident is dismissed without a thought. But, long afterwards, when she has been more years a widow than a wife, that smile recurs, and flickers across all her reminiscences of Wakefield's visage. In her many musings, she surrounds the original smile with a multitude of fantasies, which make it strange and awful; as, for instance, if she imagines him in a coffin, that parting look is frozen on his pale features; or, if she dreams of him in Heaven, still his blessed spirit wears a quiet and crafty smile. Yet, for its sake, when all others have given him up for dead, she sometimes doubts whether she is a widow.

But, our business is with the husband. We must hurry after him, along the street, ere he lose his individuality, and melt into the great mass of London life. It would be vain searching for him there. Let us follow close at his heels, therefore, until, after several superfluous turns and doublings, we find him comfortably established by the fireside of a small apartment, previously bespoken. He is in the next street to his own, and at his journey's end. He can scarcely trust his good fortune, in having got thither unperceived — recollecting that, at one time, he was delayed by the throng, in the very focus of a lighted lantern; and, again, there were footsteps, that seemed to tread behind his own, distinct from the multitudinous tramp around him; and, anon, he heard a voice shouting afar, and fancied that it called his name. Doubtless, a dozen busy-bodies had been watching him, and told his wife the whole affair. Poor Wakefield! Little knowest thou thine own insignificance in this great world! No mortal eye but mine has traced thee. Go quietly to thy bed, foolish man; and, on the morrow, if thou wilt be wise, get thee home to good Mrs. Wakefield, and tell her the truth. Remove not thyself, even for a little week, from thy place in her chaste bosom. Were she, for a single moment, to deem thee dead, or lost, or lastingly divided from her, thou wouldst be woefully conscious of a change in thy true wife, forever after. It is perilous to make a chasm in human affections; not that they gape so long and wide — but so quickly close again!

Almost repenting of his frolic, or whatever it may be termed, Wakefield lies down betimes, and starting from his first nap, spreads forth his arms into the wide and solitary waste of the unaccustomed bed. 'No' — thinks he, gathering the bed clothes about him — 'I will not sleep alone another night.'

In the morning, he rises earlier than usual, and sets himself to consider what he really means to do. Such are his loose and rambling modes of thought, that he has taken this very singular step, with the consciousness of a purpose, indeed, but without being able to define it sufficiently for his own contemplation. The vagueness of the project, and the convulsive effort with which he plunges into the execution of it, are equally characteristic of a feeble-minded man. Wakefield sifts his ideas, however, as minutely as he may, and finds himself curious to know the progress of matters at home — how his exemplary wife will endure her widowhood, of a week; and, briefly, how the little sphere of creatures and circumstances, in which he was a central object, will be affected by his removal. A morbid vanity, therefore, lies nearest the bottom of the affair. But, how is he to attain his ends? Not, certainly, by keeping close in this comfortable lodging, where, though he slept and awoke in the next street to his home, he is as effectually abroad, as if the stage-coach had been whirling him away all night. Yet, should he reappear, the whole project is knocked in the head. His poor brains being hopelessly puzzled with this dilemma, he at length ventures out, partly resolving to cross the head of the street, and send one hasty glance towards his forsaken domicile. Habit — for he is a man of habits — takes him by the hand, and guides him, wholly unaware, to his own door, where, just at the critical moment, he is aroused by the scraping of his foot upon the step. Wakefield! whither are you going?

At that instant, his fate was turning on the pivot. Little dreaming of the doom to which his first backward step devotes him, he hurries away, breathless with agitation hitherto unfelt, and hardly dares turn his head, at the distant corner. Can it be, that nobody caught sight of him? Will not the whole household — the decent Mrs. Wakefield, the smart maid-servant, and the dirty little foot-boy — raise a huc-and cry, through London streets, in pursuit of their fugitive lord and master? Wonderful escape! He gathers courage to pause and look homeward, but is perplexed with a sense of change about the familiar edifice, such as affects us all, when, after a separation of months or years, we again see some hill or lake, or work of art, with which we were friends, of old. In ordinary cases, this indescribable impression is caused by the comparison and contrast between our imperfect reminiscences and the reality. In Wakefield, the magic of a single night has wrought a similar transformation, because, in that brief period, a great moral change has been effected. But this is a secret from himself. Before leaving the spot, he catches a far and momentary glimpse of his wife, passing athwart the front window, with her face turned towards the head of the street. The crafty nincompoop takes to his heels, scared with the idea, that, among a thousand such atoms of mortality, her eye must have detected him. Right glad is his heart, though his brain be somewhat dizzy, when he finds himself by the coal-fire of his lodgings.

So much for the commencement of this long whim-wham. After the initial conception, and the stirring up of the man's sluggish temperament to put it in practice, the whole matter evolves itself in a natural train. We may suppose him, as the result of deep deliberation, buying a new wig, of reddish hair, and selecting sundry garments, in a fashion unlike his customary suit of brown, from a Jew's old-clothes bag. It is accomplished. Wakefield is another man. The new system being now established, a retrograde movement to the old would be almost as difficult as the step that placed him in his unparalleled position. Furthermore, he is rendered obstinate by a sulkiness, occasionally incident to his temper, and brought on, at present, by the inadequate sensation which he conceives to have been produced in the bosom of Mrs. Wakefield. He will not go back until she be frightened half to death. Well, twice or thrice has she passed before his sight, each time with a heavier step, a paler cheek, and more anxious brow; and, in the third week of his non-appearance, he detects a portent of evil entering the house, in the guise of an apothecary. Next day, the knocker is muffled. Towards night-fall, comes the chariot of a physician, and deposits its big-wigged and solemn burthen at Wakefield's door, whence, after a quarter of an hour's visit, he emerges, perchance the herald of a funeral. Dear woman! Will she die? By this time, Wakefield is excited to something like energy of feeling, but still lingers away from his wife's bedside, pleading with his conscience, that she must not be disturbed at such a juncture. If aught else restrains him, he does not know it. In the course of a few weeks, she gradually recovers; the crisis is over; her heart is sad, perhaps, but quiet; and, let him return soon or late, it will never be feverish for him again. Such ideas glimmer through the mist of Wakefield's mind, and render him indistinctly conscious, that an almost impassable gulf divides his hired apartment from his former home. 'It is but in the next street!' he sometimes says. Fool! it is in another world. Hitherto, he has put off his return from one particular day to another; henceforward, he leaves the precise time undetermined. Not to-morrow — probably next week — pretty soon. Poor man!

The dead have nearly as much chance of re-visiting their earthly homes, as the self-banished Wakefield.

Would that I had a folio to write, instead of an article of a dozen pages! Then might I exemplify how an influence, beyond our control, lays its strong hand on every deed which we do, and weaves its consequences into an iron tissue of necessity. Wakefield is spell-bound. We must leave him, for ten years or so, to haunt around his house, without once crossing the threshold, and to be faithful to his wife, with all the affection of which his heart is capable, while he is slowly fading out of hers. Long since, it must be remarked, he has lost the perception of singularity in his conduct.

Now for a scene! Amid the throng of a London street, we distinguish a man, now waxing elderly, with few characteristics to attract careless observers, yet bearing, in his whole aspect, the hand-writing of no common fate, for such as have the skill to read it. He is meagre; his low and narrow forehead is deeply wrinkled; his eyes, small and lustreless, sometimes wander apprehensively about him, but oftener seem to look inward. He bends his head, but moves with an indescribable obliquity of gait, as if unwilling to display his full front to the world. Watch him, long enough to see what we have described, and you will allow, that circumstances—which often produce remarkable men from nature's ordinary handiwork—have produced one such here. Next, leaving him to sidle along the foot-walk, cast your eyes in the opposite direction, where a portly female, considerably in the wane of life, with a prayer-book in her hand, is proceeding to yonder church. She has the placid mien of settled widowhood. Her regrets have either died away, or have become so essential to her heart, that they would be poorly exchanged for joy. Just as the lean man and well conditioned woman are passing, a slight obstruction occurs, and brings these two figures directly in contact. Their hands touch; the pressure of the crowd forces her bosom against his shoulder; they stand, face to face, staring into each other's eyes. After a ten years' separation, thus Wakefield meets his wife!

The throng eddies away, and carries them asunder. The sober widow, resuming her former pace, proceeds to church, but pauses in the portal, and throws a perplexed glance along the street. She passes in, however, opening her prayer-book as she goes. And the man? With so wild a face, that busy and selfish London stands to gaze after him, he hurries to his lodgings, bolts the door, and throws himself upon the bed. The latent feelings of years break out; his feeble mind acquires a brief energy from their strength; all the miserable strangeness of his life is revealed to him at a glance; and he cries out, passionately—'Wakefield! Wakefield! You are mad!'

Perhaps he was so. The singularity of his situation must have so moulded him to itself, that, considered in regard to his fellow-creatures and the business of life, he could not be said to possess his right mind. He had contrived, or rather he had happened, to dissever himself from the world—to vanish—to give up his place and privileges with living men, without being admitted among the dead. The life of a hermit is nowise parallel to his. He was in the bustle of the city, as of old; but the crowd swept by, and saw him not; he was, we may figuratively say, always beside his wife, and at his hearth, yet must never feel the warmth of the one, nor the affection of the other. It was Wakefield's unprecedented fate, to retain his original share of human sympathies, and to be still involved in human interests, while he had lost his reciprocal influence on them. It would be a most curious speculation, to trace out the effect of such circumstances on his heart and intellect, separately, and in unison. Yet, changed as he was, he would seldom be conscious of it, but deem himself the same man as ever; glimpses of the truth, indeed, would come, but only for the moment; and still he would keep saying—'I shall soon go back!'—nor reflect, that he had been saying so for twenty years.

I conceive, also, that these twenty years would appear, in the retrospect, scarcely longer than the week to which Wakefield had at first limited his absence. He would look on the affair as no more than an interlude in the main business of his life. When, after a little while more, he should deem it time to re-enter his parlor, his wife would clap her hands for joy, on beholding the middle-aged Mr. Wakefield. Alas, what a mistake! Would Time but await the close of our favorite follies, we should be young men, all of us, and till Doom's Day.

One evening, in the twentieth year since he vanished, Wakefield is taking his customary walk towards the dwelling which he still calls his own. It is a gusty night of autumn, with frequent showers, that patter down upon the pavement, and are gone, before a man can put up his umbrella. Pausing near the house, Wakefield discerns, through the parlor-windows of the second floor, the red glow, and the glimmer and fitful flash, of a comfortable fire. On the ceiling, appears a grotesque shadow of good Mrs. Wakefield. The cap, the nose and chin, and the broad waist, form an admirable caricature, which dances, moreover, with the up-flickering and down-sinking blaze, almost too merrily for the shade of an elderly widow. At this instant, a shower chances to fall, and is driven, by the unmannerly gust, full into Wakefield's face and bosom. He is quite penetrated with its autumnal chill. Shall he stand, wet and shivering here, when his own hearth has a good fire to warm him, and his own wife will run to fetch the gray coat and small-clothes, which, doubtless, she has kept carefully in the closet of their bed-chamber? No! Wakefield is no such fool. He ascends the steps—heavily!—for twenty years have stiffened his legs, since he came down—but he knows it not. Stay, Wakefield! Would you go to the sole home that is left you? Then step into your grave! The door opens. As he passes in, we have a parting glimpse of his visage, and recognize the crafty smile, which was the precursor of the little joke, that he has ever since been playing off at his wife's expense. How unmercifully has he quizzed the poor woman! Well; a good night's rest to Wakefield!

This happy event—supposing it to be such—could only have occurred at an unpremeditated moment. We will not follow our friend across the threshold. He has left us much food for thought, a portion of which shall lend its wisdom to a moral; and be shaped into a figure. Amid the seeming confusion of our mysterious world, individuals are so nicely adjusted to a system, and systems to one another, and to a whole, that, by stepping aside for a moment, a man exposes himself to a fearful risk of losing his place forever. Like Wakefield, he may become, as it were, the Outcast of the Universe.

(1835)

In a Great Man's House

Ruth Prawer Jhabvala (1927–) was born in Germany of Polish and German parents. She received the M.A. degree at Queen Mary College, London, in 1951, married an Indian architect, and moved to New Delhi. The recipient of both Guggenheim and MacArthur fellowships, she now lives in New York. Her fiction is particularly deft in catching the emotional nuances of intercultural relations, especially between the West and India. Her novels include *To Whom She Will* (1955), *Amrita* (1956), *The Nature of Passion* (1956), *Esmond in India* (1958), *The Householder* (1960, made into a movie), *Get Ready for Battle* (1962), *Heat and Dust* (1975, made into a movie), *In Search of Love and Beauty* (1983), and *Three Continents* (1987). Among her collections of short stories are *Like Birds, Like Fishes* (1963), *A Stronger Climate: Nine Stories* (1968), *How I Became a Holy Mother* (1976, which contains "In a Great Man's House"), and *Out of India* (1986). She has worked actively as screenwriter and adaptor with director James Ivory and producer Ismael Merchant in a collaboration that has produced excellent adaptations of novels by Henry James and E. M. Forster: Her adaptation of *A Room with a View* won the Academy Award for best screenplay of 1987. She has also written several books of nonfiction about India.

The letter came in the morning, but when she told Khan Sahib about it, he said she couldn't go. There was no time for argument because someone had come to see him — a research scholar from abroad writing a thesis on Indian musical theory — so she was left to brood by herself. First she thought bad thoughts about Khan Sahib. Then she thought about the wedding. It was to take place in her home-town, in the old house where she had grown up and where her brother now lived with his family. She had a very clear vision of this house and the tree in its courtyard to which a swing was affixed. There was always a smell of tripe being cooked (her father had been very fond of it); a continuous sound of music, of tuning and singing and instrumental practice, came out of the many dark little rooms. Now these rooms would be packed with family members, flocking from all over the country to attend the wedding. They would all have a good time together. Only she was to be left here by herself in her silent, empty rooms — alone except for Khan Sahib and her thieving servants.

Later in the morning her sister Roxana, who of course had also had a letter, came to discuss plans. Roxana came with her eldest daughter and her youngest son and was very excited, looking forward to the journey and the wedding. She cried out when Hamida told her that Khan Sahib would not allow her to go.

Hamida said "It is the time of the big Music Conference. He says he needs me here." She added: "For what I don't know."

Roxana shook her head at such behaviour. Then she inclined it towards Khan Sahib's practice room from which she could hear the sound of voices. She asked, "Who is with him?" Her neck was craned forward, her earrings trembled, she wore the strained expression she always did when she was poking into someone else's business, especially Khan Sahib's.

"An American," Hamida replied with a shrug. "He has come to speak about something scholarly with him. Don't, Baba," she admonished Roxana's little boy who was smearing his fingers against the locked glass cabinet in which she kept precious things for show.

Roxana strained to listen to the voices, but when she could not make out anything, she began to shake her head again. She said "He must allow. He can't say no to you."

"Very big people will be coming for the Conference."

"But a niece's wedding! A brother's daughter!"

"They will all be coming to the house to visit Khan Sahib. Of course someone will have to be there for the cooking and other arrangements. Who can trust servants," she concluded with a sigh.

Roxana, who had no servants, puckered her mouth.

"Don't, Baba!" Hamida said again to the child who was doing dreadful damage with his sticky fingers to her polished panes.

"He wants to play," Roxana said. "He will need some new little silk clothes for the wedding. And this child also," she added, indicating her meek daughter sitting beside her. The girl did look rather shabby, but Hamida gave no encouragement. So then Roxana nudged her daughter and said "You must ask auntie nicely—nicely," and she leered to show her how. The girl was ashamed and lowered her eyes. Hamida was both ashamed and irritated. Her gold bangles jingled angrily as she unlocked her cabinet and took out the Japanese plastic doll Baba had been clamouring for. "Now sit quiet," she admonished him, and he did so.

Roxana leaned forward again with her greedy look of curiosity. Khan Sahib's visitor was leaving: they could hear Khan Sahib's loud hearty voice seeing him off from the front of the house. Then Khan Sahib returned into the house and walked through his practice room into the back room where the women sat. Roxana at once pulled her veil over her head and simpered. She always simpered in his presence: not only was he an elder brother-in-law but he was also the great man in the family.

Condescending and gracious, he did honour to both roles. He pinched the niece's cheek and swept Baba up into his arms. He laughed "Ha-ha!" at Baba who however was frightened of this uncle with the large moustache and loud voice. After laughing at him, Khan Sahib did not know what to do with him so he handed him over to Hamida who put him back on the floor.

"How is my brother?" he asked Roxana. He meant his brother-in-law—Roxana's husband—who was also a musician but in a very small way with a very small job in All India Radio.

"What shall I say: poor man," Roxana replied. It was her standard reply to Khan Sahib's queries on this subject. Her husband was a very humble, self-effacing man so it was up to her to be on the look-out on his behalf.

Hamida, who felt that all requests to Khan Sahib should come only through herself, did not wish to encourage this conversation. In any case, she now had things of her own to say: "They are leaving next week," she informed her husband. "They are going by train. The others will also be leaving from Bombay at the same time. Everyone is going of course. Sayyida has even postponed her operation."

Khan Sahib said to Roxana "Ask my brother to come and see me. There may be something for him at the Music Conference."

"God knows it is needed. There will be all sorts of expenses for the wedding. For myself it doesn't matter but at least these children should have some decent clothes to go to my brother's house."

"Well well," Khan Sahib reassured her. He looked at the niece with a twinkle: he had very fat cheeks and when he was good-humoured, as now, his eyes quite disappeared in them. But when he was not, then these same eyes looked large and rolled around. He told Hamida: "You had better take her to the shops. Some pretty little pink veils and blouses," he promised the girl and winked at her playfully. "She will look like a little flower." He had always longed for a daughter, and when he spoke to young girls, he was tender and loving.

"I can leave her with you now," Roxana said with a sigh of sacrifice.

"No, today I'm busy," Hamida said.

"See that you are a good girl," Roxana told the girl. "I don't want to hear any bad reports." She got up and adjusted her darned veil. "Come, Baba," she said. "Give that little doll back to auntie, it is hers."

Baba began to cry and Khan Sahib said "No no, it belongs to Baba, take it, child." But Hamida had already taken it away from him and swiftly locked it back into her cabinet. She also lost no time in ushering her sister out of the house. The girl followed them.

"When should I send him to you?" Roxana called back to Khan Sahib. He did not hear her because of Baba's loud cries; but Hamida said "I will send word."

"You can stay till tomorrow or even the day after if she needs you," Roxana told her daughter.

The girl had blushed furiously. She said "Auntie is busy."

Roxana ignored her and walked out with Baba in her arms. When the girl tried to follow, Hamida said "You can stay," though not very graciously. She didn't look at her again — she had no time, she had to hurry back to Khan Sahib. There was a lot left she had to say to him.

He was lying on his bed, resting. She said "I must go. What will people say? Everyone will think there has been some quarrel in the family."

"It is not possible." His eyes were shut and his stomach, rising like a dome above the bed, breathed up and down peacefully.

"But my own niece! My own brother's own daughter!"

"You are needed here."

She turned from him and began to tidy up his crowded dressing-table. Actually, it was very tidy already — she did it herself every morning — but she nervously moved a few phials and jars about while thinking out her next move. She could see him in the mirror. He looked like an immoveable mountain. What chance did she have against him? Her frail hands, loaded with rings, trembled. Then she began to tremble all over. She remembered similar scenes in the past — so many! so many! —

when she had desperately wanted something and he had lain like that, mountainously, on his bed.

He said "Massage my legs."

She was holding one of his phials of scent. She was overcome by the desire to fling it into the mirror — and then sweep all his scents and oils and hair-dyes off the table and throw them around and smash a lot of glass. Of course she didn't; she put the bottle down, though her hands trembled more than ever. Nowadays she always overcame these impulses. It had not been so in the past: then she had often been violent. Once she really had smashed all the bottles on his dressing-table. It had been a holocaust, and two servants had had to spend many hours cleaning and picking up the splinters. For weeks afterwards the room was saturated in flowery essences, and some of the stains had never come out. But what good had it done her? None. So nowadays she never threw things.

"The right leg," he said from the bed.

"I can't," she said.

"Tcha, you're useless."

She swung round from the mirror: "Then why do you want me here? If I'm useless why should I stay for your Conference!"

He continued to look peaceful. It was always that way: he was so confident, so relaxed in his superior strength. "Come here," he said. When she approached, he pointed at his right leg. She squatted by the side of his bed and began to massage him. But she really was no good at it. Even when she went to it with good will (which was not the case at present), her arms got tired very quickly. She also tended to become impatient quite soon.

"Harder, *harder*," he implored. "At least try."

Instead she left off. She remained on the floor and buried her head in his mattress. He didn't look at her but groped with his hands at her face; when he felt it wet, he clicked his tongue in exasperation. He said "What is the need for this? What is so bad?"

Everything, it seemed to her, was bad. Not only the fact that he wouldn't let her go to the wedding, but so many other things as well: her whole life. She buried her head deeper. She said "My son, my little boy." That was the worst of all, the point it seemed to her at which the sorrow of her life came to a head.

It had been the occasion of their worst quarrel (the time when she had broken all his bottles). Khan Sahib had insisted that the boy be sent away for education to an English-type boarding school in the hills. Hamida had fought him every inch of the way. She could not, would not be parted from Sajid. He was her only child, she could never have another. His birth had been very difficult: she had been in labour for two days and finally there had to be a Caesarian operation and both of them had nearly died. For his first few years Sajid had been very delicate, and she could not bear to let him out of her sight for a moment. She petted him, oiled him, dressed him in little silk shirts; she would not let him walk without shoes and socks and would not let him play with other children for fear of infection. But he grew into a robust boy who wanted to run out and play robust games. When she tried to stop him, he defied her and they had tremendous quarrels and she frequently lost her temper and beat him mercilessly.

"He will be coming home for his holiday soon," Khan Sahib said. "He will be here for two weeks."

"Two weeks! What is two weeks! When my heart aches for him — my arms are empty —"

"Go now," said Khan Sahib who had heard all this before.

"You want only one thing: to take everything you can away from me. To leave me with nothing. That is your only happiness and joy in life."

"Go go go," said Khan Sahib.

When she went into the other room, Hamida was surprised to see the girl sitting there. She had forgotten all about her. She was sitting very humbly on the edge of Hamida's grand overstuffed blue-and-silver brocade sofa. She was studying the photograph of Sajid, a beautiful colour-tinted studio portrait in a silver frame. When Hamida came in, she quickly replaced it on its little table as if she had done something wrong. And indeed Hamida picked it up again and inspected it for fingermarks and then wiped it carefully with the end of her veil.

"He is coming home soon for his holidays," she informed the girl.

"Then he will be there for the wedding?"

Hamida frowned. She said "It will be the time of the big Music Conference. His father will want him to be here." She spoke as if the wedding was very much inferior in importance and interest to the Music Conference.

"Look," she told the girl. She opened her work-basket and took out a fine lawn kurta which she was embroidering. "It is for him. Sajid." She spread it out with an air as if it were a great privilege for her niece to be allowed to look at it. And indeed the girl seemed to feel it to be so. She breathed "Oh!" in soft wonder. Hamida's work was truly exquisite; she was embroidering tiny bright flowers like stars intertwined with delicate leaves and branches.

"Can you do it?" Hamida questioned. "Is your mother teaching you?"

"She is not very good."

"No," Hamida said, smiling as she remembered Roxana's rough untidy work. "She never worked hard enough. Always impatient to be off somewhere and play. Without hard work no good results are achieved," she lectured the girl.

"Please teach me, auntie," the girl begged, looking up at Hamida with her sad childish eyes. Hamida was quite pleased, but she spoke sternly: "You have to sit for many hours and if I don't like your work I shall unpick it and you will have to start again from the beginning. Well, we shall see," she said as the girl looked willing and humble. Suddenly a thought struck her, and she leaned forward to regard her more closely: "Why are you so thin?" she demanded.

The girl's cheeks were wan — which was perhaps why her eyes looked so large. Her arms and wrists were as frail as the limbs of a bird. Hamida wondered whether she suffered from some hidden illness; next moment she wondered whether she got enough to eat. Oh that was a dreadful thought — that this child, her own sister's daughter, might not be getting sufficient food! Her father was poor, her mother was a bad manager and careless and thoughtless and not fit to run a household or look after children though she had so many.

Hamida began to question her niece closely. She asked how much milk was taken in the house every day; she asked about butter, biscuits, and fruit. The girl said oh yes, there was a lot of everything always, more than any of them could eat; but when she said it, she lowered her eyes away from her aunt like a person hiding something, and after a time she became quite silent and did not answer any more questions. What was she hiding? What was she covering up? Hamida became irritated with her and she spoke sharply now, but that only made the girl close up further.

The servant came in with a telegram. He gave it to Hamida who held it in one hand while the other flew to her beating heart. Wild thoughts — of Sajid, of accidents and hospitals — rushed around in her head. She went into the bedroom and woke up Khan Sahib. When she said telegram, he at once sat up with a start. His hands also trembled though he said that it was probably something to do with the Music Conference; he said that nowadays everything was done by telegram, modern people no longer wrote letters. She helped him put on his reading-glasses and then he slowly spelled out the telegram which continued to tremble in his hands.

But it was from Hamida's brother, asking her to start as soon as possible. Evidently they needed her help very urgently for the wedding preparations. Khan Sahib tossed the telegram into her lap and lay down to sleep again. Now he was cross to have been woken up. Hamida remained sitting on the edge of the bed. She was full of thoughts which she would have liked very much to share with him, but his huge back was turned to her forbiddingly.

She *had* to go. She could not not go. Her family needed her; she was always the most important person at these family occasions. They all ran around in a dither or sat and wrung their hands till she arrived and began to give orders. She was not the eldest in the family, but she was the one who had the most authority. Although quite tiny, she held herself very erect and her fine-cut features were usually severe. As Khan Sahib's wife, she was also the only one among them to hold an eminent position. The rest of them were as shabby and poor as Roxana and her husband. They were all musicians, but none of them was successful, and they eked out a living by playing at weddings and functions and taking in pupils and whatever else came their way.

"They really want me," she said to Khan Sahib's sleeping back. Let him pretend not to hear, but her heart was so full — she had to speak. "Not like you," she said. "For you what am I except a servant to keep your house clean and cook for your guests." She gave him a chance to reply, but of course she knew he wouldn't. "Just try and get your paid servants to do one half of the work that I do. All they are good for is to eat up your rice and lick up your butter, oh at that they are first-class maestros if I were not there to see and know everything. Well, you will find out when I have gone," she concluded.

To her surprise Khan Sahib stirred; he said "Gone where?"

Actually she had meant when I have gone from this earth, but now she took advantage of his mistake: "Gone to my brother's house for my niece's wedding, where else," she said promptly.

"You are not going."

"Who says no? Who is there that has the right to say no!" She shrieked on this last, but then remembered the girl in the next room. She lowered her voice — which however had the effect of making it more intense and passionate: "There is no work for me here. No place for me at all. Ever since you have snatched away my son from me, I have sat as a stranger in your house with no one to care whether I am alive or what has happened."

She was really moved by her own words but at the same time remained alert to sounds from the kitchen where the servant was up to God knew what mischief. There was no peace at all — not a moment for private thought or conversation — she had to be on the watch all the time. She got up from the bed and went into the kitchen. She looked at the servant suspiciously, then opened the refrigerator to see if he had been watering the milk. When she saw the jug full of milk, she remembered the underfed girl in the next room. She gave some orders to the servant and became very busy. She made milk-shake and fritters. She enjoyed doing it — she always enjoyed being in her kitchen which was very well equipped with modern gadgets. She loved having these things and did not allow anyone else to touch them but looked after them herself as if they were children.

The girl said she wasn't hungry. She said this several times, but when Hamida had coaxed and scolded her enough, she began to eat. It was a pleasure to watch her, she enjoyed everything so much. Hamida suddenly did an unexpected thing — she leaned forward and tenderly brushed a few strands of hair from the girl's forehead. The girl was surprised (Hamida was not usually demonstrative) and looked up from her plate with a shy, questioning glance.

"You are like my Sajid," Hamida said as if some explanation were called for. "He also — how he loved my fritters — how he licks and enjoys. Oh poor boy, God alone knows what rubbish they give him to eat in that school. English food," she said. "Boiled — in water."

She stuck out her tongue in distaste. It was one of her disappointments that Sajid did not complain more about the school food. Of course when he came home he did full justice to her cooking, but when she tried to draw him out on the subject of his school diet, he did not say what she desired to hear. He just shrugged and said it was okay. He always called it "grub". "The grub's okay," he said. She hated that word the way she hated all the English slang words which he used so abundantly, deliberately, knowing she could not understand them (she had little English). "Grub," she mimicked — and translated into Urdu: "Dog's vomit." He laughed. She would have liked to cry over his emaciated appearance, but the fact was he didn't look emaciated — his face was plump, and his cheeks full of colour.

Not like this poor girl. She looked at the child's thin neck, her narrow little shoulders; she sighed and said "You're seventeen now, you were born the year before father went." It was certainly time to arrange for her. Hamida thought wistfully how well she herself would be able to do so. She would make many contacts and look over many prospective families and choose the bridegroom very carefully. And then what a trousseau she would get together for her: what materials she would choose, what ornaments! There was nothing like that for a boy. Even now Sajid did her a big favour if he consented to wear one of the kurtas she embroidered for him. He preferred his school blazer and belt with Olympic buckle.

"I was married by seventeen," she told the girl. "So was Roxana, so were we all. Look at you — who will marry you — " She lifted the girl's forearm and held it up for show. The girl smiled, blushed, turned aside her face. Hamida began to question her again. "What does she give you in the morning? And then afterwards? And in between?" When the girl again became stubborn and silent, Hamida scolded her gently: "You can tell me. Don't I love you as much as she does, aren't you my own little daughter too, my precious jewel? Why hide anything from me?" She took the end of her veil and wiped a rim of milk from her niece's lips. She was deeply moved, so was the girl. They sat closer together, the niece leaned against her aunt shyly. "You must tell me everything," Hamida whispered.

"Last Friday—" the girl began.

"Yes?"

"They both cried." Her lip trembled but at Hamida's urging she went on bravely: "Baba had an upset stomach and she wanted to cook some special dish for him. But when she asked Papa for the money to buy a little more milk, he didn't have. So they both cried and we all cried too."

"And I!" Hamida cried with passion. "Perhaps I'm dead that my own family should sit and cry for a drop of milk!" Then she stopped short, frowning to recollect something; she said "She did come last Friday."

She remembered it clearly because she had got very cross with Roxana who had arrived in a motor-rickshaw for which Hamida had then had to pay. When Hamida had finished scolding, Roxana had asked her for a hundred rupees and then patiently listened to some more scolding. She cried a bit when Hamida finally said she could only have fifty, but when she left she was very cheerful again and knotted the fifty rupees into the end of her veil. Hamida had climbed on the roof to spy on her, and it was as she had suspected—when Roxana thought she was unobserved, she hailed another motor-rickshaw and went rattling off, with her veil fluttering in the wind. Hamida worried that the money might come untied; she almost had a vision of it happening and the notes flying away and Roxana not even noticing because she was enjoying her ride so much.

Khan Sahib was calling. He had woken up from his nap and required attendance. He informed Hamida that visitors were expected and that preparations would have to be made for their entertainment. When she asked when they were expected, he answered impatiently "Now, now." She made no comment or complaint. People were always coming to visit Khan Sahib. She took no interest in who they were but only in what and how much they would eat. She sent in platters of food and refilled them when they came out empty. She rarely bothered to peep into the room and did not try to overhear any of their conversation. Besides food, her only other concern was the clothes in which Khan Sahib would receive them.

She scanned his wardrobe now, the rows and rows of kurtas and shawls. He needed a lot of fine clothes always—for his concerts, receptions, functions, meetings with Ministers and other important people. It was her responsibility to have them made and keep them in order and decide what he was to wear on each occasion. But if he was not pleased with her choice, he would fling the clothes she had taken out for him across the room. Then she would have to take out others, and it was not unlikely that they too would meet with the same fate. Sometimes the floor was strewn with rejected clothes. Hamida did not care much. She let him curse and shout and throw things to his heart's content; afterwards she would call the servant to come in and clear up, while she herself sat in the kitchen and drank a cup of tea to relax herself.

But today his mood was good. He put up his arms like a child to allow her to change his kurta, and stretched out his legs so she could pull off his old churidars and fit on the new ones. He was in such a jolly mood that he even gave her a playful pinch while she was dressing him; when she pushed him away, he cackled and did it again. She pretended to be angry but did not really mind. Actually she was relieved that such childish amusements were all he required of her nowadays. It had not always been so. When they were younger, they had rarely managed to get through his toilette without her having to submit to a great deal more than only pinching. But now Khan Sahib was too heavy and fat to be able to indulge himself in this way.

She began to tell him about Roxana's family. She repeated what the girl had told her. "What is to become of them?" Hamida asked. She reproached him with not putting enough work in Roxana's husband's way. It was so easy for Khan Sahib — to arrange for him to accompany other musicians at concerts (Roxana's husband played the tabla) or help him to get students. Khan Sahib defended himself. He reminded her of the many occasions when he had arranged something for his brother-in-law who had then failed to turn up — either because he had forgotten or because he had become engrossed in some amusement.

Hamida had to admit "He is like that." She sighed, but Khan Sahib laughed: he was fond of his brother-in-law who in return adored, worshipped him. When Khan Sahib sang, his brother-in-law listened in ecstasy — really it was almost like a religious ecstasy, and tears of joy coursed down his face that God should allow human beings to reach so high.

"Brother too is the same," Hamida said. "How will they manage? The bridegroom's family will arrive and nothing will be done and we shall be disgraced. I *must* go."

Khan Sahib did not answer but stretched out one foot. She rubbed talcum powder into the heel to enable her to slip the leg of his tight churidars over it more easily.

"They are like children," she said. "Only enjoyment, enjoyment — of serious work they know nothing . . . Have you seen that poor child?" She jerked her head towards the room where the girl sat. "Seventeen years old, no word of any marriage, and thin as a dry thorn. Come here!" she called through the door. "In here! Your uncle wants to see you!"

The door opened very slowly. The girl slipped through and stood there, overcome. "Right in," Hamida ordered. The girl pressed herself against the wall. Hamida, anxious for her to make a good impression, was irritated to see her standing there trembling and blushing and looking down at her own feet. "Look up," Hamida said sharply. "Show your face."

"Aie-aie-aie," Khan Sahib said. He spoke to the girl as if she were some sweet little pet; he also made sounds with his lips as if coaxing a shy pet with a lump of sugar. "You must eat. Meat. Buttermilk. Rice pudding. Then you will become big and strong like Uncle." He was the only one to enjoy the joke. "Bring me these," he said, pointing to something on his dressing-table.

When the girl didn't know what he meant, Hamida became more irritated with her and cried out impatiently "His rings! His rings!"

"Gently, gently," said Khan Sahib. "Don't frighten the child. That's right," he said as the girl took up the rings and brought them to him. He spread out his hands for her. "Can you put them on? Do you know which one goes where? I'll teach you. The diamond — that's right — on this finger, this big big fat finger — that's very clever, oh very good — and the ruby here on this one — and now the other hand . . ."

He made it a game, and the girl smiled a bit as she fitted the massive rings on to his massive fingers. Hamida watched with pleasure. She loved the way Khan Sahib spoke to the child. He never spoke like that to his wife. His manner with her was always brusque, but with this girl he was infinitely gentle — as if she were a flower he was afraid of breaking, or one of those soft, soft notes that only he knew how to sing.

Later, when his guests had arrived and everything had been prepared and sent in to them where they reclined on carpets in the practice room, it was Hamida's turn to lie on the bed. She felt very tired and had a headache. Such sudden fits of exhaustion came over her frequently. She was physically a very frail, delicate lady. She lay with the curtains drawn and her eyes shut; her temples throbbed, so did her heart. Sounds of music and conversation came from the front of the house but here, in these back rooms where she lived, it was quite silent. Often at such times she felt very lonely and longed to have someone with her to whom she could say "Oh I'm so tired" or "My head is aching." But she was always alone. Even when Sajid was home from school, he usually stayed with the men in the front part of the house, or went out to play cricket with his friends; and when he did stay with her, he clattered about and made so much noise — he was an active, vigorous boy — that her rest was disturbed and she soon lost her temper with him and drove him away.

But today, when she opened her eyes, she saw the girl sitting beside her on the bed. Hamida said "My head is aching" and the girl breathed "Ah poor auntie" and these words, spoken with such gentle pity, passed over Hamida like a cooling sea-breeze on a scorching day. In a weak voice she requested the girl to rub her temples with eau-de-cologne. The girl obeyed so eagerly and performed this task with so much tenderness and love that Hamida's fatigue became a luxury. The noise from the practice room seemed to come from far away. Here there was no sound except from the fan turning overhead. The silence — the smell of the eau-de-cologne — the touch of the girl's fingers soothing her temples: these gave Hamida a sense of intimacy, of being close to another human being, that was quite new to her.

She put up her hand and touched the girl's cheek. She said "You don't look like your mother." Roxana, though she was scrawny now, had been a hefty girl. Also her skin had been rather coarse, whereas this girl's was smooth as a lotus petal. The girl's features too were much more delicate than Roxana's had ever been.

"Everyone says I look like — "

"Yes?"

"Oh no," the girl said blushing. "It's not true. You're much, much more beautiful."

Hamida was pleased, but she said depreciatingly "Nothing left now."

She sat up on the bed so that she could see herself in the mirror and the girl beside her. Their two faces were reflected in the heart-shaped glass surrounded by a frame carved with leaves and flowers; because it was dim in the room — the curtains were drawn — they looked like a faded portrait of long ago. It was true that there was a resemblance. If Hamida had had a daughter, she might have looked like this girl.

She fingered the girl's kameez. It was of coarse cotton and the pattern was also not very attractive. Hamida clicked her tongue: "Is this how you are going to attend the wedding?" But when she saw the girl shrinking into herself again, she went on: "Your mother is to blame. All right, she has no money but she has no taste either. This is not the colour to buy for a young girl. You should wear only pale blue, pink, lilac. Wait, I'll show you."

She opened her wardrobe. The shelves were as packed and as neatly arranged as Khan Sahib's. She pulled out many silk and satin garments and threw them on the bed. The girl looked on in wonder. Hamida ordered her to take off her clothes and laughed when she was shy. But she respected her modesty, the fact that she turned her back and crossed her little arms over her breasts: Hamida herself had also been very modest always. It was a matter of pride to her that not once in their married life had Khan Sahib seen her naked.

She made the girl try on many of her clothes. They all fitted perfectly — aunt and niece had the same childish body with surprisingly full breasts and hips. Hamida made her turn this way and that. She straightened a neckline here, a collar there, she turned up sleeves and plucked at hems, frowning to hide her enjoyment of all this activity. The girl however made no attempt to hide it — she looked in the mirror and laughed and how her eyes shone! But there was one thing missing still, and Hamida took out her keys and unlocked her safe. The girl cried out when the jewel boxes were opened and their contents revealed.

There were many heavy gold ornaments, but Hamida selected a light and dainty necklace and tiny star-shaped earrings to match. "Now look," she said, frowning more than ever and giving the girl a push towards the mirror. The girl looked; she gasped, she said "Oh auntie!" and then Hamida could frown no longer but she too laughed out loud and then she was kissing the girl, not once but many times, all over her face and on her neck.

At that moment Roxana came into the room. When she saw her daughter dressed up in her sister's clothes and jewels, she clapped her hands and exclaimed in joyful surprise. Hamida's good mood was gone in a flash, and the first thing she did was shut her jewel boxes and lock them back into her safe. The girl became very quiet and shy again and sat down in a corner and began to take off the earrings and necklace.

"No leave it!" her mother told her. "It looks pretty." She held up another kameez from among those on the bed. "How about this one? The colour would suit her very well."

"Why did you come?" Hamida asked.

"There has been a telegram. We have to start at once. Brother says our presence is urgently required. This lace veil is very nice. Try it on. Why are you shy? It is your own auntie."

Hamida began to fold all the clothes back again. She felt terribly sad, there was a weight on her heart. She asked "When are you leaving?"

"Tomorrow morning. Husband has gone to the station to buy the tickets. It may be difficult to get seats for all of us together, but let's see."

"You're *all* going?"

"Of course." She told the girl "You can pack up your old clothes in some paper that auntie will give you."

"Khan Sahib has called brother-in-law to come for the Music Conference."

"It is not possible. He has to attend my niece's wedding. And you?" she asked. "When are you leaving?"

Hamida didn't answer but was busy putting her clothes back into her wardrobe.

"He says no?" Roxana asked incredulously. Then she cried out in horror: "Hai! Hai!"

"Naturally, it is not possible for me to go," Hamida said. "Do you know what sort of people will be coming for this Conference? Have you any idea? All the biggest musicians in the country and many from abroad also will be travelling all the way to be present."

Roxana deftly snatched another kameez from among the pile Hamida was putting away. The girl meanwhile had unhooked the earrings and necklace and silently handed them to her aunt. Hamida could see Roxana in the mirror making frantic faces and gestures at the girl; she could also see that the girl refused to look at her mother but turned her back on her and began to take off Hamida's silk kameez.

Roxana said "Come quickly now — there is a lot to be done for the journey. You can keep that on," she said. "There is no time to change."

"Yes keep it on," Hamida said. The girl gave her aunt a swift look, then closed the kameez up again. She did not thank her but looked down at the ground.

Just as they were going, Hamida said "Leave her with me." She said it in a rush like a person who has flung all pride to the wind.

"She can come to you when we return," Roxana promised. "She can stay two-three days if you like . . . You want to stay with auntie, don't you? You love to be with her." She nudged the girl with her elbow, but the girl didn't say anything, didn't look up, and seemed in a hurry to leave.

When she was alone, Hamida lay down on the bed again. Khan Sahib seemed to be having a grand time with his visitors. She could hear them all shout and laugh. Whenever he spoke, everyone else fell silent to listen to him. When he told some anecdote, they all laughed as loud as they could to show their appreciation. He would be stretched out there like a king among them, one blue satin bolster behind his back, another under his elbow; his eyes would be twinkling, and from time to time he would give a twirl to his moustache. Of course he wouldn't have a moment's thought to spare for his wife alone by herself in the back room. He would also have completely forgotten about the wedding and her desire to go to it. What were her desires or other feelings to him?

She shut her eyes. She tried to recall the sensation of the girl's fingers soothing her headache, but she couldn't. The smell of the eau-de-cologne had also disappeared. All she could smell now was the thickly scented incense that came wafting out of the practice room. She found she was still holding the jewelry the girl had returned to her. She clutched it tightly so that it cut into her hand; the physical pain this gave her seemed to relieve the pressure on her heart. She raised the jewelry to her eyes, and a few tears dropped on it. She felt so sad, so abandoned to herself, without anyone's love or care.

Khan Sahib was singing a romantic song. Usually of course he sang only in the loftiest classical style, but occasionally, when in a relaxed mood, he liked to please people with something in a lighter vein. Although it was not his speciality — others devoted their whole lives to this genre — there was no one who could do it better than he. He drove people mad with joy. He was doing it now — she could hear their cries, their laughter, and it made him sing even more delicately as if he were testing them as to how much ecstasy they could bear. He sang: "Today by mistake I smiled — but then I remembered, and now where is that smile? Into what empty depths has it disappeared?" He wasn't Khan Sahib, he was a love-sick woman and he suffered, suffered as only a woman can. How did he know all that — how could he look so deep into a woman's feelings — a man like him with many coarse appetites? It was a wonder to Hamida again and again. She was propped on her elbow now, listening to him, and she was smiling: yes, truly smiling with joy. What things he could make her feel, that fat selfish husband of hers. He sang: "I sink in the ocean of sorrow. Have pity! Have pity! I drown."

(1976)

❖ FRANZ KAFKA
A Hunger Artist*

Franz Kafka (1883–1924) was born into a family of German-speaking
Jews in Prague, Czechoslovakia. He studied law at the German University in Prague and then worked for an insurance company until illness
forced him to quit in 1922. He died of tuberculosis at the age of
forty-one. In his lifetime, two of Kafka's novellas were published, *The
Metamorphosis* (1915) and *In the Penal Colony* (1919). But most of
Kafka's writing was published posthumously, due to the persistence
of his friend Max Brod. (Kafka destroyed a lot of his work and wanted
it all destroyed.) Three novels—none of them finished—saw the light
of day: *America* (begun in 1912, published in 1927), *The Trial* (begun
in 1914 and published in 1925), and *The Castle* (begun in 1922 and
published in 1927). Kafka's stories, parables, and other short fiction
appear in *The Great Wall of China* (1933), *A Franz Kafka Miscellany*
(1940), and most recently in *The Complete Stories* (1971). Kafka's
fiction anticipates with astonishing clarity the totalitarianism of the
thirties, the world of Hitler and Stalin, and captures uncannily the
sense of anonymity and alienation felt by the individual in the bureau-
cratic banality of a mass-culture world.

During these last decades the interest in professional fasting has markedly diminished. It used to pay very well to stage such great performances under one's own
management, but today that is quite impossible. We live in a different world now. At
one time the whole town took a lively interest in the hunger artist; from day to day of
his fast the excitement mounted; everybody wanted to see him at least once a day;
there were people who bought season tickets for the last few days and sat from morning
till night in front of his small barred cage; even in the nighttime there were visiting
hours, when the whole effect was heightened by torch flares; on fine days the cage was
set out in the open air, and then it was the children's special treat to see the hunger
artist; for their elders he was often just a joke that happened to be in fashion, but the
children stood open-mouthed, holding each other's hands for greater security, marveling at him as he sat there pallid in black tights, with his ribs sticking out so
prominently, not even on a seat but down among straw on the ground, sometimes
giving a courteous nod, answering questions with a constrained smile, or perhaps
stretching an arm through the bars so that one might feel how thin it was, and then
again withdrawing deep into himself, paying no attention to anyone or anything, not
even to the all-important striking of the clock that was the only piece of furniture in
his cage, but merely staring into vacancy with half-shut eyes, now and then taking a
sip from a tiny glass of water to moisten his lips.

---

*Translated by Willa and Edwin Muir

476

Besides casual onlookers there were also relays of permanent watchers selected by the public, usually butchers, strangely enough, and it was their task to watch the hunger artist day and night, three of them at a time, in case he should have some secret recourse to nourishment. This was nothing but a formality, instituted to reassure the masses, for the initiates knew well enough that during his fast the artist would never in any circumstances, not even under forcible compulsion, swallow the smallest morsel of food; the honor of his profession forbade it. Not every watcher, of course, was capable of understanding this, there were often groups of night watchers who were very lax in carrying out their duties and deliberately huddled together in a retired corner to play cards with great absorption, obviously intending to give the hunger artist the chance of a little refreshment, which they supposed he could draw from some private hoard. Nothing annoyed the artist more than such watchers; they made him miserable; they made his fast seem unendurable; sometimes he mastered his feebleness sufficiently to sing during their watch for as long as he could keep going, to show them how unjust their suspicions were. But that was of little use; they only wondered at his cleverness in being able to fill his mouth even while singing. Much more to his taste were the watchers who sat close up to the bars, who were not content with the dim night lighting of the hall but focused him in the full glare of the electric pocket torch given them by the impresario. The harsh light did not trouble him at all, in any case he could never sleep properly, and he could always drowse a little, whatever the light, at any hour, even when the hall was thronged with noisy onlookers. He was quite happy at the prospect of spending a sleepless night with such watchers; he was ready to exchange jokes with them, to tell them stories out of his nomadic life, anything at all to keep them awake and demonstrate to them again that he had no eatables in his cage and that he was fasting as not one of them could fast. But his happiest moment was when the morning came and an enormous breakfast was brought them, at his expense, on which they flung themselves with the keen appetite of healthy men after a weary night of wakefulness. Of course there were people who argued that this breakfast was an unfair attempt to bribe the watchers, but that was going rather too far, and when they were invited to take on a night's vigil without a breakfast, merely for the sake of the cause, they made themselves scarce, although they stuck stubbornly to their suspicions.

Such suspicions, anyhow, were a necessary accompaniment to the profession of fasting. No one could possibly watch the hunger artist continuously, day and night, and so no one could produce first-hand evidence that the fast had really been rigorous and continuous; only the artist himself could know that, he was therefore bound to be the sole completely satisfied spectator of his own fast. Yet for other reasons he was never satisfied; it was not perhaps mere fasting that had brought him to such skeleton thinness that many people had regretfully to keep away from his exhibitions, because the sight of him was too much for them, perhaps it was dissatisfaction with himself that had worn him down. For he alone knew, what no other initiate knew, how easy it was to fast. It was the easiest thing in the world. He made no secret of this, yet people did not believe him, at the best they set him down as modest, most of them, however, thought he was out for publicity or else was some kind of cheat who found it easy to fast because he had discovered a way of making it easy, and then had the impudence to admit the fact, more or less. He had to put up with all that, and in the course of time had got used to it, but his inner dissatisfaction always rankled, and never yet, after any term of fasting — this must be granted to his credit — had he left the cage of his own free will. The longest period of fasting was fixed by his impresario at forty days, beyond that term he was not allowed to go, not even in great cities, and there was good reason for it, too. Experience had proved that for about forty days the interest of the public could be stimulated by a steadily increasing pressure of advertisement, but after that the town began to lose interest, sympathetic support began notably to fall off; there were of course local variations as between one town and another or one country and another, but as a general rule forty days marked the limit. So on the fortieth day the flower-bedecked cage was opened, enthusiastic spectators filled the hall, a military band played, two doctors entered the cage to measure the results of the fast, which were announced through a megaphone, and finally two young ladies appeared, blissful at having been selected for the honor, to help the hunger artist down the few steps leading to a small table on which was spread a carefully chosen invalid repast. And at this very moment the artist always turned stubborn. True, he would entrust his bony arms to the outstretched helping hands of the ladies bending over him, but stand up he would not. Why stop fasting at this particular moment, after forty days of it? He had held out for a long time, an illimitably long time; why stop now, when he was in his best fasting form, or rather, not yet quite in his best fasting form? Why should he be cheated of the fame he would get for fasting longer, for being not only the record hunger artist of all time, which presumably he was already, but for beating his own record by a performance beyond human imagination, since he felt that there were no limits to his capacity for fasting? His public pretended to admire him so much, why should it have so little patience with him; if he could endure fasting longer, why shouldn't the public endure it? Besides, he was tired, he was comfortable sitting in the straw, and now he was supposed to lift himself to his full height and go down to a meal the very thought of which gave him a nausea that only the presence of the ladies kept him from betraying, and even that with an effort. And he looked up into the eyes of the ladies who were apparently so friendly and in reality so cruel, and shook his head, which felt too heavy on its strengthless neck. But then there happened yet again what always happened. The impresario came forward, without a word — for the band made speech impossible — lifted his arms in the air above the artist, as if inviting Heaven to look down upon its creature here in the straw, this suffering martyr, which indeed he was, although in quite another sense; grasped him round the emaciated waist, with exaggerated caution, so that the frail condition he was in might be appreciated; and committed him to the care of the blenching ladies, not without secretly giving him a shaking so that his legs and body tottered and swayed. The artist now submitted completely; his head lolled on his breast as if it had landed there by chance; his body was hollowed out; his legs in a spasm of self-preservation clung close to each other at the knees, yet scraped on the ground as if it were not really solid ground, as if they were only trying to find solid ground; and the whole weight of his body, a feather-weight after all, relapsed onto one of the ladies, who, looking round for help and panting a little — this post of honor was not at all what she had expected it to be — first stretched her neck as far as she could to keep her face at least free from contact with the artist, then finding this impossible, and her more fortunate companion not coming to her aid but merely holding extended on her own trembling hand the little bunch of knucklebones that was the artist's, to the great delight of the spectators burst into tears and had to be replaced by an attendant who had long been stationed in readiness. Then came the food, a little of which the impresario managed to get between the artist's lips, while he sat in a kind of half-fainting trance, to the accompaniment of cheerful patter designed to distract the public's attention from the artist's condition; after that, a toast was drunk to the public, supposedly prompted by a whisper from the artist in the impresario's ear; the band confirmed it with a mighty flourish, the spectators melted away, and no one had any cause to be dissatisfied with the proceedings, no one except the hunger artist himself, he only, as always.

So he lived for many years, with small regular intervals of recuperation, in visible glory, honored by the world, yet in spite of that troubled in spirit, and all the more troubled because no one would take his trouble seriously. What comfort could he possibly need? What more could he possibly wish for? And if some good-natured person, feeling sorry for him, tried to console him by pointing out that his melancholy was probably caused by fasting, it could happen, especially when he had been fasting for some time, that he reacted with an outburst of fury and to the general alarm began to shake the bars of his cage like a wild animal. Yet the impresario had a way of punishing these outbreaks which he rather enjoyed putting into operation. He would apologize publicly for the artist's behavior, which was only to be excused, he admitted, because of the irritability caused by fasting; a condition hardly to be understood by well-fed people; then by natural transition he went on to mention the artist's equally incomprehensible boast that he could fast for much longer than he was doing; he praised the high ambition, the good will, the great self-denial undoubtedly implicit in such a statement; and then quite simply countered it by bringing out photographs, which were also on sale to the public, showing the artist on the fortieth day of a fast lying in bed almost dead from exhaustion. This perversion of the truth, familiar to the artist though it was, always unnerved him afresh and proved too much for him. What was a consequence of the premature ending of his fast was here presented as the cause of it! To fight against this lack of understanding, against a whole world of non-under-standing, was impossible. Time and again in good faith he stood by the bars listening to the impresario, but as soon as the photographs appeared he always let go and sank with a groan back on to his straw, and the reassured public could once more come close and gaze at him.

A few years later when the witnesses of such scenes called them to mind, they often failed to understand themselves at all. For meanwhile the aforementioned change in public interest had set in; it seemed to happen almost overnight; there may have been profound causes for it, but who was going to bother about that; at any rate the pampered hunger artist suddenly found himself deserted one fine day by the amuse-ment seekers, who went streaming past him to other more favored attractions. For the last time the impresario hurried him over half Europe to discover whether the old interest might still survive here and there; all in vain; everywhere, as if by secret agreement, a positive revulsion from professional fasting was in evidence. Of course it could not really have sprung up so suddenly as all that, and many premonitory symptoms which had not been sufficiently remarked or suppressed during the rush and glitter of success now came retrospectively to mind, but it was now too late to take any countermeasures. Fasting would surely come into fashion again at some future date, yet that was no comfort for those living in the present. What, then, was the hunger artist to do? He had been applauded by thousands in his time and could hardly come down to showing himself in a street booth at village fairs, and as for adopting another profession, he was not only too old for that but too fanatically devoted to fasting. So he took leave of the impresario, his partner in an unparalleled career, and hired himself to a large circus; in order to spare his own feelings he avoided reading the conditions of his contract.

A large circus with its enormous traffic in replacing and recruiting men, animals and apparatus can always find a use for people at any time, even for a hunger artist, provided of course that he does not ask too much, and in this particular case anyhow it was not only the artist who was taken on but his famous and long-known name as well, indeed considering the peculiar nature of his performance, which was not impaired by advancing age, it could not be objected that here was an artist past his prime, no longer at the height of his professional skill, seeking a refuge in some quiet corner of a circus, on the contrary, the hunger artist averred that he could fast as well as ever, which was entirely credible, he even alleged that if he were allowed to fast as he liked, and this was at once promised him without more ado, he could astound the world by establishing a record never yet achieved, a statement which certainly provoked a smile among the other professionals, since it left out of account the change in public opinion, which the hunger artist in his zeal conveniently forgot.

He had not, however, actually lost his sense of the real situation and took it as a matter of course that he and his cage should be stationed, not in the middle of the ring as a main attraction, but outside, near the animal cages, on a site that was after all easily accessible. Large and gaily painted placards made a frame for the cage and announced what was to be seen inside it. When the public came thronging out in the intervals to see the animals, they could hardly avoid passing the hunger artist's cage and stopping there for a moment, perhaps they might even have stayed longer had not those pressing behind them in the narrow gangway, who did not understand why they should be held up on their way towards the excitements of the menagerie, made it impossible for anyone to stand gazing quietly for any length of time. And that was the reason why the hunger artist, who had of course been looking forward to these visiting hours as the main achievement of his life, began instead to shrink from them. At first he could hardly wait for the intervals; it was exhilarating to watch the crowds come streaming his way, until only too soon — not even the most obstinate self-deception, clung to almost consciously, could hold out against the fact — the conviction was borne in upon him that these people, most of them, to judge from their actions, again and again, without exception, were all on their way to the menagerie. And the first sight of them from the distance remained the best. For when they reached his cage he was at once deafened by the storm of shouting and abuse that arose from the two contending factions, which renewed themselves continuously, of those who wanted to stop and stare at him — he soon began to dislike them more than the others — not out of real interest but only out of obstinate self-assertiveness, and those who wanted to go straight on to the animals. When the first great rush was past, the stragglers came along, and these, whom nothing could have prevented from stopping to look at him as long as they had breath, raced past with long strides, hardly even glancing at him, in their haste to get to the menagerie in time. And all too rarely did it happen that he had a stroke of luck, when some father of a family fetched up before him with his children, pointed a finger at the hunger artist and explained at length what the phenomenon meant, telling stories of earlier years when he himself had watched similar but much more thrilling performances, and the children, still rather uncomprehending, since neither inside nor outside school had they been sufficiently prepared for this lesson — what did they care about fasting? — yet showed by the brightness of their intent eyes that new and better times might be coming. Perhaps, said the hunger artist to himself many a time, things would be a little better if his cage were set not quite so near the menagerie. That made it too easy for people to make their choice, to say nothing of what he suffered from the stench of the menagerie, the animals' restlessness by night, the carrying past of raw lumps of flesh for the beasts of prey, the roaring at feeding times, which depressed him continually. But he did not dare to lodge a complaint with the management; after all, he had the animals to thank for the troops of people who passed his cage, among whom there might always be one here and there to take an interest in him, and who could tell where they might seclude him if he called attention to his existence and thereby to the fact that, strictly speaking, he was only an impediment on the way to the menagerie.

A small impediment, to be sure, one that grew steadily less. People grew familiar with the strange idea that they could be expected, in times like these, to take an interest in a hunger artist, and with this familiarity the verdict went out against him. He might fast as much as he could, and he did so; but nothing could save him now, people passed him by. Just try to explain to anyone the art of fasting! Anyone who has no feeling for it cannot be made to understand it. The fine placards grew dirty and illegible, they were torn down; the little notice board telling the number of fast days achieved, which at first was changed carefully every day, had long stayed at the same figure, for after the first few weeks even this small task seemed pointless to the staff; and so the artist simply fasted on and on, as he had once dreamed of doing, and it was no trouble to him, just as he had always foretold, but no one counted the days, no one, not even the artist himself, knew what records he was already breaking, and his heart grew heavy. And when once in a time some leisurely passer-by stopped, made merry over the old figure on the board and spoke of swindling, that was in its way the stupidest lie ever invented by indifference and inborn malice, since it was not the hunger artist who was cheating, he was working honestly, but the world was cheating him of his reward.

Many more days went by, however, and that too came to an end. An overseer's eye fell on the cage one day and he asked the attendants why this perfectly good cage should be left standing there unused with dirty straw inside it; nobody knew, until one man, helped out by the notice board, remembered about the hunger artist. They poked into the straw with sticks and found him in it. "Are you still fasting?" asked the overseer, "when on earth do you mean to stop?" "Forgive me, everybody," whispered the hunger artist; only the overseer, who had his ear to the bars, understood him. "Of course," said the overseer, and tapped his forehead with a finger to let the attendants know what state the man was in, "we forgive you." "I always wanted you to admire my fasting," said the hunger artist. "We do admire it," said the overseer, affably. "But you shouldn't admire it," said the hunger artist. "Well then we don't admire it," said the overseer, "but why shouldn't we admire it?" "Because I have to fast, I can't help it," said the hunger artist. "What a fellow you are," said the overseer, "and why can't you help it?" "Because," said the hunger artist, lifting his head a little and speaking, with his lips pursed, as if for a kiss, right into the overseer's ear, so that no syllable might be lost, "because I couldn't find the food I liked. If I had found it, believe me, I should have made no fuss and stuffed myself like you or anyone else." These were his last words, but in his dimming eyes remained the firm though no longer proud persuasion that he was still continuing to fast.

"Well, clear this out now!" said the overseer, and they buried the hunger artist, straw and all. Into the cage they put a young panther. Even the most insensitive felt it refreshing to see this wild creature leaping around the cage that had so long been dreary. The panther was all right. The food he liked was brought him without hesitation by the attendants; he seemed not even to miss his freedom; his noble body, furnished almost to the bursting point with all that it needed, seemed to carry freedom around with it too; somewhere in his jaws it seemed to lurk; and the joy of life streamed with such ardent passion from his throat that for the onlookers it was not easy to stand the shock of it. But they braced themselves, crowded round the cage, and did not want ever to move away.

(1922)

❖ D.H. LAWRENCE
Two Blue Birds

D. H. [David Herbert] Lawrence (1885–1930) was born in Eastwood, a town in England's mining country, and studied for two years at Nottingham University. Upon graduation, he took a job as a school-teacher, but quit in 1912 when his first three novels—*The White Peacock* (1911), *The Trespasser* (1913), and especially *Sons and Lovers* (1913)—became popular successes. In 1914, Lawrence married a German noblewoman, Frieda von Richthofen Weekley. He published two other famous novels during World War I—*The Rainbow* (1915) and *Women in Love* (1916). Anti-German sentiment ran high during the war, so Lawrence and his wife left Britain in 1919 and lived in many places—Italy, Australia, Mexico, and Taos, New Mexico. His work is marked by a passionate anti-intellectualism, a belief in the supremacy of human instincts and the need to develop blood-ties with the earth and other human beings. His affinity for the "dark gods" shows up in his later fiction and nonfiction, in such novels as *Aaron's Rod* (1922), *Kangaroo* (1923), and *The Plumed Serpent* (1926). Under the influence of these beliefs he attacked conventional moral attitudes in *Lady Chatterly's Lover* (1928), a novel whose direct approach to sexuality scandalized England. Banned for many years, it only appeared in an unexpurgated edition in 1960. His short stories appeared in various collections over his lifetime: *The Prussian Officer* (1914), *England, My England* (1922), *The Ladybird* (1923), *The Woman Who Rode Away* (1928, which contains "Two Blue Birds"), and *The Lovely Lady* (1933). *The Complete Short Stories* appeared in 1960. Lawrence also wrote much nonfiction espousing his philosophy, criticizing literature, and describing his travels: *Sea and Sardinia* (1921), *Psychoanalysis and the Unconscious* (1921), *Studies in Classic American Literature* (1923), *Mornings in Mexico* (1927), *Pornography and Obscenity* (1929), *Apocalypse* (1931), and *Etruscan Places* (1932). He died of tuberculosis in France in 1930.

There was a woman who loved her husband, but she could not live with him. The husband, on his side, was sincerely attached to his wife, yet he could not live with her. They were both under forty, both handsome and both attractive. They had the most sincere regard for one another, and felt, in some odd way, eternally married to one another. They knew one another more intimately than they knew anybody else, they felt more known to one another than to any other person.

Yet they could not live together. Usually, they kept a thousand miles apart, geographically. But when he sat in the greyness of England, at the back of his mind, with a certain grim fidelity, he was aware of his wife, her strange yearning to be loyal and faithful, having her gallant affairs away in the sun, in the south. And she, as she drank her cocktail on the terrace over the sea, and turned her grey, sardonic eyes on the heavy dark face of her admirer, whom she really liked quite a lot, she was actually preoccupied with the clear-cut features of her handsome young husband, thinking of how he would be asking his secretary to do something for him, asking in that good-natured, confident voice of a man who knows that his request will be only too gladly fulfilled.

The secretary, of course, adored him. She was *very* competent, quite young, and quite good-looking. She adored him. But then all his servants always did, particularly his women-servants. His men-servants were likely to swindle him.

When a man has an adoring secretary, and you are the man's wife, what are you to do? Not that there was anything "wrong" — if you know what I mean! — between them. Nothing you could call adultery, to come down to brass tacks. No, no! They were just the young master and his secretary. He dictated to her, she slaved for him and adored him, and the whole thing went on wheels.

He didn't "adore" her. A man doesn't need to adore his secretary. But he depended on her. "I simply rely on Miss Wrexall." Whereas he could never rely on his wife. The one thing he knew finally about *her* was that she didn't intend to be relied on.

So they remained friends, in the awful unspoken intimacy of the once-married. Usually each year they went away together for a holiday, and, if they had not been man and wife, they would have found a great deal of fun and stimulation in one another. The fact that they were married, had been married for the last dozen years, and couldn't live together for the last three or four, spoilt them for one another. Each had a private feeling of bitterness about the other.

However, they were awfully kind. He was the soul of generosity, and held her in real, tender esteem, no matter how many gallant affairs she had. Her gallant affairs were part of her modern necessity. "After all, I've got to *live*. I can't turn into a pillar of salt in five minutes just because you and I can't live together! It takes years for a woman like me to turn into a pillar of salt. At least I hope so!"

"Quite!" he replied. "Quite! By all means put them in pickle, make pickled cucumbers of them, before you crystallize out. That's my advice."

He was like that: so awfully clever and enigmatic. She could more or less fathom the idea of the pickled cucumbers, but the "crystallizing out" — what did that signify?

And did he mean to suggest that he himself had been well pickled and that further immersion was for him unnecessary, would spoil his flavour? Was that what he meant? And herself, was she the brine and the vale of tears?

You never knew how catty a man was being, when he was really clever and enigmatic, withal a bit whimsical. He was adorably whimsical, with a twist of his flexible, vain mouth, that had a long upper lip, so fraught with vanity! But then a handsome, clear-cut, histrionic young man like that, how could he help being vain? The women made him so.

Ah, the women! How nice men would be if there were no other women!

And how nice the women would be if there were no other men! That's the best of a secretary. She may have a husband, but a husband is the mere shred of a man compared to a boss, a chief, a man who dictates to you and whose words you faithfully write down and then transcribe. Imagine a wife writing down anything her husband said to her! But a secretary! Every *and* and *but* of his she preserves for ever. What are candied violets in comparison!

Now it is all very well having gallant affairs under the southern sun, when you know there is a husband whom you adore dictating to a secretary whom you are too scornful to hate yet whom you rather despise, though you allow she has her good points, away north in the place you ought to regard as home. A gallant affair isn't much good when you've got a bit of grit in your eye. Or something at the back of your mind.

What's to be done? The husband, of course, did not send his wife away.

"You've got your secretary and your work," she said. "There's no room for me."

"There's a bedroom and a sitting-room exclusively for you," he replied. "And a garden and half a motor-car. But please yourself entirely. Do what gives you most pleasure."

"In that case," she said, "I'll just go south for the winter."

"Yes, do!" he said. "You always enjoy it."

"I always do," she replied.

They parted with a certain relentlessness that had a touch of wistful sentiment behind it. Off she went to her gallant affairs, that were like the curate's egg, palatable in parts. And he settled down to work. He said he hated working, but he never did anything else. Ten or eleven hours a day. That's what it is to be your own master!

So the winter wore away, and it was spring, when the swallows homeward fly, or northward, in this case. This winter, one of a series similar, had been rather hard to get through. The bit of grit in the gallant lady's eye had worked deeper in the more she blinked. Dark faces might be dark, and icy cocktails might lend a glow; she blinked her hardest to blink that bit of grit away, without success. Under the spicy balls of the mimosa she thought of that husband of hers in his library, and of that neat, competent but *common* little secretary of his, forever taking down what he said!

"How a man can *stand* it! How *she* can stand it, common little thing as she is, I don't know!" the wife cried to herself.

She meant this dictating business, this ten hours a day intercourse, *à deux*, with nothing but a pencil between them, and a flow of words.

What was to be done? Matters, instead of improving, had grown worse. The little secretary had brought her mother and sister into the establishment. The mother was a sort of cook-housekeeper, the sister was a sort of upper maid — she did the fine laundry, and looked after "his" clothes, and valeted him beautifully. It was really an excellent arrangement. The old mother was a splendid plain cook, the sister was all that could be desired as a valet de chambre, a fine laundress, an upper parlour-maid, and a table-waiter. And all economical to a degree. They knew his affairs by heart. His secretary flew to town when a creditor became dangerous, and she *always* smoothed over the financial crisis.

"He," of course, had debts, and he was working to pay them off. And if he had been a fairy prince who could call the ants to help him, he would not have been more wonderful than in securing this secretary and her family. They took hardly any wages. And they seemed to perform the miracle of loaves and fishes daily.

"She," of course, was the wife who loved her husband, but helped him into debt, and she still was an expensive item. Yet when she appeared at her "home," the secretarial family received her with most elaborate attentions and deference. The knight returning from the Crusades didn't create a greater stir. She felt like Queen Elizabeth at Kenilworth, a sovereign paying a visit to her faithful subjects. But perhaps there lurked always this hair in her soup! Won't they be glad to be rid of me again!

But they protested No! No! They had been waiting and hoping and praying she would come. They had been pining for her to be there, in charge: the mistress, "his" wife. Ah, "his" wife!

"His" wife! His halo was like a bucket over her head.

The cook-mother was "of the people," so it was the upper-maid daughter who came for orders.

"What will you order for tomorrow's lunch and dinner, Mrs. Gee?"

"Well, what do you usually have?"

"Oh, we want *you* to say."

"No, what do you *usually* have?"

"We don't have anything fixed. Mother goes out and chooses the best she can find, that is nice and fresh. But she thought you would tell her now what to get."

"Oh, I don't know! I'm not very good at that sort of thing. Ask her to go on just the same; I'm quite sure she knows best."

"Perhaps you'd like to suggest a sweet?"

"No, I don't care for sweets — and you know Mr. Gee doesn't. So don't make one for me."

Could anything be more impossible! They had the house spotless and running like a dream; how could an incompetent and extravagant wife dare to interfere, when she saw their amazing and almost inspired economy! But they ran the place on simply nothing!

Simply marvellous people! And the way they strewed palm-branches under her feet!

But that only made her feel ridiculous.

"Don't you think the family manage very well?" he asked her tentatively.

"Awfully well! Almost romantically well!" she replied. "But I suppose you're perfectly happy?"

"I'm perfectly comfortable," he replied.

"I can see you are," she replied. "Amazingly so! I never knew such comfort! Are you sure it isn't bad for you?"

She eyed him stealthily. He looked very well, and extremely handsome, in his histrionic way. He was shockingly well-dressed and valeted. And he had that air of easy *aplomb* and good humour which is so becoming to a man, and which he only acquires when he is cock of his own little walk, made much of by his own hens.

"No!" he said, taking his pipe from his mouth and smiling whimsically round at her. "Do I look as if it were bad for me?"

"No, you don't," she replied promptly: thinking, naturally, as a woman is supposed to think nowadays, of his health and comfort, the foundation, apparently, of all happiness.

Then, of course, away she went on the backwash.

"Perhaps for your work, though, it's not so good as it is for *you*," she said in a rather small voice. She knew he couldn't bear it if she mocked at his work for one moment. And he knew that rather small voice of hers.

"In what way?" he said, bristles rising.

"Oh, I don't know," she answered indifferently. "Perhaps it's not good for a man's work if he is too comfortable."

"I don't know about *that!*" he said, taking a dramatic turn round the library and drawing at his pipe. "Considering I work, actually, by the clock, for twelve hours a day, and for ten hours when it's a short day, I don't think you can say I am deteriorating from easy comfort."

"No, I suppose not," she admitted.

Yet she did think it, nevertheless. His comfortableness didn't consist so much in good food and a soft bed, as in having nobody, absolutely nobody and nothing, to contradict him. "I do like to think he's got nothing to aggravate him," the secretary had said to the wife.

"Nothing to aggravate him!" What a position for a man! Fostered by women who would let nothing "aggravate" him. If anything would aggravate his wounded vanity, this would!

So thought the wife. But what was to be done about it? In the silence of midnight she heard his voice in the distance, dictating away, like the voice of God to Samuel, alone and monotonous, and she imagined the little figure of the secretary busily scribbling shorthand. Then in the sunny hours of morning, while he was still in bed — he never rose till noon — from another distance came that sharp insect-noise of the typewriter, like some immense grasshopper chirping and rattling. It was the secretary, poor thing, typing out his notes.

That girl — she was only twenty-eight — really slaved herself to skin and bone. She was small and neat, but she was actually worn out. She did far more work than he did, for she had not only to take down all those words he uttered, she had to type them out, make three copies, while he was still resting.

"What on earth she gets out of it," thought the wife, "I don't know. She's simply worn to the bone, for a very poor salary, and he's never kissed her, and never will, if I know anything about him."

Whether his never kissing her — the secretary, that is — made it worse or better, the wife did not decide. He never kissed anybody. Whether she herself — the wife, that is — wanted to be kissed by him, even that she was not clear about. She rather thought she didn't.

What on earth did she want then? She was his wife. What on earth did she want of him?

She certainly didn't want to take him down in shorthand and type out again all those words. And she didn't really want him to kiss her; she knew him too well. Yes, she knew him too well. If you know a man too well, you don't want him to kiss you.

What then? What did she want? Why had she such an extraordinary hang-over about him? Just because she was his wife? Why did she rather "enjoy" other men — and she was relentless about enjoyment — without ever taking them seriously? And why must she take him so damn seriously, when she never really "enjoyed" him?

Of course she *had* had good times with him, in the past, before — ah! before a thousand things, all amounting really to nothing. But she enjoyed him no more. She never even enjoyed being with him. There was a silent, ceaseless tension between them, that never broke, even when they were a thousand miles apart.

Awful! That's what you call being married! What's to be done about it? Ridiculous, to know it all and not do anything about it!

She came back once more, and there she was, in her own house, a sort of super-guest, even to him. And the secretarial family devoting their lives to him.

Devoting their lives to him! But actually! Three women pouring out their lives for him day and night! And what did they get in return? Not one kiss! Very little money, because they knew all about his debts, and had made it their life-business to get them paid off! No expectations! Twelve hours' work a day! Comparative isolation, for he saw nobody!

And beyond that? Nothing! Perhaps a sense of uplift and importance because they saw his name and photograph in the newspapers sometimes. But would anybody believe that it was good enough?

Yet they adored it! They seemed to get a deep satisfaction out of it, like people with a mission. Extraordinary!

Well, if they did, let them. They were, of course, rather common, "of the people"; there might be a sort of glamour in it for them.

But it was bad for him. No doubt about it. His work was getting diffuse and poor in quality — and what wonder! his whole tone was going down — becoming commoner. Of course it was bad for him.

Being his wife, she felt she ought to do something to save him. But how could she? That perfectly devoted, marvellous secretarial family, how could she make an attack on them? Yet she'd love to sweep them into oblivion. Of course they were bad for him: ruining his work, ruining his reputation as a writer, ruining his life. Ruining him with their slavish service.

Of course she ought to make an onslaught on them! But how *could* she? Such devotion! And what had she herself to offer in their place? Certainly not slavish devotion to him, nor to his flow of words! Certainly not!

She imagined him stripped once more naked of secretary and secretarial family, and she shuddered. It was like throwing the naked baby in the dust-bin. Couldn't do that!

Yet something must be done. She felt it. She was almost tempted to get into debt for another thousand pounds and send in the bill, or have it sent in to him, as usual.

But no! Something more drastic!

Something more drastic, or perhaps more gentle. She wavered between the two. And wavering, she first did nothing, came to no decision, dragged vacantly on from day to day, waiting for sufficient energy to take her departure once more.

It was spring! What a fool she had been to come up in spring! And she was forty! What an idiot of a woman to go and be forty!

She went down the garden in the warm afternoon, when birds were whistling loudly from the cover, the sky being low and warm, and she had nothing to do. The garden was full of flowers: he loved them for their theatrical display. Lilac and snowball bushes, and laburnum and red may, tulips and anemones and coloured daisies. Lots of flowers! Borders of forget-me-nots! Bachelor's buttons! What absurd names flowers had! She would have called them blue dots and yellow blobs and white frills. Not so much sentiment, after all!

There is a certain nonsense, something showy and stagey, about spring, with its pushing leaves and chorus-girl flowers, unless you have something corresponding inside you. Which she hadn't.

Oh, heaven! Beyond the hedge she heard a voice, a steady rather theatrical voice. Oh, heaven! He was dictating to his secretary, in the garden. Good God, was there nowhere to get away from it!

She looked around: there was indeed plenty of escape. But what was the good of escaping? He would go on and on. She went quietly towards the hedge, and listened.

He was dictating a magazine article about the modern novel. "What the modern novel lacks is architecture." Good God! Architecture! He might just as well say: What the modern novel lacks is whalebone, or a teaspoon, or a tooth stopped.

Yet the secretary took it down, took it down, took it down! No, this could not go on! It was more than flesh and blood could bear.

She went quietly along the hedge, somewhat wolf-like in her prowl, a broad, strong woman in an expensive mustard-coloured silk jersey and cream-coloured pleated skirt. Her legs were long and shapely, and her shoes were expensive.

With a curious wolf-like stealth she turned the hedge and looked across at the small, shaded lawn where the daisies grew impertinently. "He" was reclining in a coloured hammock under the pink-flowering horsechestnut tree, dressed in white serge with a fine yellow-coloured linen shirt. His elegant hand dropped over the side of the hammock and beat a sort of vague rhythm to his words. At a little wicker table the little secretary, in a green knitted frock, bent her dark head over her note-book, and diligently made those awful shorthand marks. He was not difficult to take down, as he dictated slowly, and kept a sort of rhythm, beating time with his dangling hand.

"In every novel there must be one outstanding character with which we always sympathize—with *whom* we always sympathize—even though we recognize its—even when we are most aware of the human frailties——"

Every man his own hero, thought the wife grimly, forgetting that every woman is intensely her own heroine.

But what did startle her was a blue bird dashing about near the feet of the absorbed, shorthand-scribbling little secretary. At least it was a blue-tit, blue with grey and some yellow. But to the wife it seemed blue, that juicy spring day, in the translucent afternoon. The blue bird, fluttering round the pretty but rather *common* little feet of the little secretary.

The blue bird! The blue bird of happiness! Well, I'm blest, thought the wife. Well, I'm blest!

And as she was being blest, appeared another blue bird—that is, another blue-tit—and began to wrestle with the first blue-tit. A couple of blue birds of happiness, having a fight over it! Well, I'm blest!

She was more or less out of sight of the human preoccupied pair. But "he" was disturbed by the fighting blue birds, whose little feathers began to float loose.

"Get out!" he said to them mildly, waving a dark-yellow handkerchief at them. "Fight your little fight, and settle your private affairs, elsewhere, my dear little gentlemen."

The little secretary looked up quickly, for she had already begun to write it down. He smiled at her his twisted whimsical smile.

"No, don't take that down," he said affectionately. "Did you see those two tits laying into one another?"

"No!" said the little secretary, gazing brightly round, her eyes half-blinded with work.

But she saw the queer, powerful, elegant, wolf-like figure of the wife, behind her, and terror came into her eyes.

"I did!" said the wife, stepping forward with those curious, shapely, she-wolf legs of hers, under the very short skirt.

"Aren't they extraordinarily vicious little beasts?" said he.

"Extraordinarily!" she re-echoed, stooping and picking up a little breast-feather. "Extraordinarily! See how the feathers fly!"

And she got the feather on the tip of her finger, and looked at it. Then she looked at the secretary, then she looked at him. She had a queer, werewolf expression between her brows.

"I think," he began, "these are the loveliest afternoons, when there's no direct sun, but all the sounds and the colours and the scents are sort of dissolved, don't you know, in the air, and the whole thing is steeped, steeped in spring. It's like being on the inside; you know how I mean, like being inside the egg and just ready to chip the shell."

"Quite like that!" she assented without conviction.

There was a little pause. The secretary said nothing. They were waiting for the wife to depart again.

"I suppose," said the latter, "you're awfully busy, as usual?"

"Just about the same," he said, pursing his mouth deprecatingly.

Again the blank pause, in which he waited for her to go away again.

"I know I'm interrupting you," she said.

"As a matter of fact," he said, "I was just watching those two blue-tits."

"Pair of little demons!" said the wife, blowing away the yellow feather from her finger-tip.

"Absolutely!" he said.

"Well, I'd better go, and let you get on with your work," she said.

"No hurry!" he said, with benevolent nonchalance. "As a matter of fact, I don't think it's a great success, working out of doors."

"What made you try it?" said the wife. "You know you never could do it."

"Miss Wrexall suggested it might make a change. But I don't think it altogether helps, do you, Miss Wrexall?"

"I'm sorry," said the little secretary.

"Why should *you* be sorry?" said the wife, looking down at her as a wolf might look down half-benignly at a little black-and-tan mongrel. "You only suggested it for his good, I'm sure!"

"I thought the air might be good for him," the secretary admitted.

"Why do people like you never think about yourselves?" the wife asked.

The secretary looked her in the eye.

"I suppose we do, in a different way," she said.

"A *very* different way!" said the wife ironically. "Why don't you make *him* think about *you?*" she added slowly, with a sort of drawl. "On a soft spring afternoon like this, you ought to have him dictating poems to you, about the blue birds of happiness fluttering round your dainty little feet. I know *I* would, if I were his secretary."

There was a dead pause. The wife stood immobile and statuesque, in an attitude characteristic of her, half turning back to the little secretary, half averted. She half turned her back on everything.

The secretary looked at him.

"As a matter of fact," he said, "I was doing an article on the Future of the Novel."

"I know that," said the wife. "That's what's so awful! Why not something lively in the life of the novelist?"

There was a prolonged silence, in which he looked pained, and somewhat remote, statuesque. The little secretary hung her head. The wife sauntered slowly away.

"Just where were we, Miss Wrexall?" came the sound of his voice.

The little secretary started. She was feeling profoundly indignant. Their beautiful relationship, his and hers, to be so insulted!

But soon she was veering downstream on the flow of his words, too busy to have any feelings, except one of elation at being so busy.

Tea-time came; the sister brought out the tea-tray into the garden. And immediately, the wife appeared. She had changed, and was wearing a chicory-blue dress of fine cloth. The little secretary had gathered up her papers and was departing, on rather high heels.

"Don't go, Miss Wrexall," said the wife.

The little secretary stopped short, then hesitated.

"Mother will be expecting me," she said.

"Tell her you're not coming. And ask your sister to bring another cup. I want you to have tea with us."

Miss Wrexall looked at the man, who was reared on one elbow in the hammock, and was looking enigmatical, Hamletish.

He glanced at her quickly, then pursed his mouth in a boyish negligence.

"Yes, stay and have tea with us for once," he said. "I see strawberries, and I know you're the bird for them."

She glanced at him, smiled wanly, and hurried away to tell her mother. She even stayed long enough to slip on a silk dress.

"Why, how smart you are!" said the wife, when the little secretary reappeared on the lawn, in chicory-blue silk.

"Oh, don't look at my dress, compared to yours!" said Miss Wrexall. They were of the same colour, indeed!

"At least you earned yours, which is more than I did mine," said the wife, as she poured tea. "You like it strong?"

She looked with her heavy eyes at the smallish, birdy, blue-clad, overworked young woman, and her eyes seemed to speak many inexplicable dark volumes.

"Oh, as it comes, thank you," said Miss Wrexall, leaning nervously forward.

"It's coming pretty black, if you want to ruin your digestion," said the wife.

"Oh, I'll have some water in it, then."

"Better, I should say."

"How'd the work go — all right?" asked the wife, as they drank tea, and the two women looked at each other's blue dresses.

"Oh!" he said. "As well as you can expect. It was a piece of pure flummery. But it's what they want. Awful rot, wasn't it, Miss Wrexall?"

Miss Wrexall moved uneasily on her chair.

"It interested me," she said, "though not so much as the novel."

"The novel? Which novel?" said the wife. "Is there another new one?"

Miss Wrexall looked at him. Not for words would she give away any of his literary activities.

"Oh, I was just sketching out an idea to Miss Wrexall," he said.

"Tell us about it!" said the wife. "Miss Wrexall, *you* tell us what it's about."

She turned on her chair and fixed the little secretary.

"I'm afraid" — Miss Wrexall squirmed — "I haven't got it very clearly myself, yet."

"Oh, go along! Tell us what you *have* got then!"

Miss Wrexall sat dumb and very vexed. She felt she was being baited. She looked at the blue pleatings of her skirt.

"I'm afraid I can't," she said.

"Why are you afraid you can't? You're so *very* competent. I'm sure you've got it all at your finger-ends. I expect you write a good deal of Mr. Gee's books for him, really. He gives you the hint, and you fill it all in. Isn't that how you do it?" She spoke ironically, and as if she were teasing a child. And then she glanced down at the fine pleatings of her own blue skirt, very fine and expensive.

"Of course you're not speaking seriously?" said Miss Wrexall, rising on her mettle.

"Of course I am! I've suspected for a long time — at least, for some time — that you write a good deal of Mr. Gee's books for him, from his hints."

It was said in a tone of raillery, but it was cruel.

"I should be terribly flattered," said Miss Wrexall, straightening herself, "if I didn't know you were only trying to make me feel a fool."

"Make you feel a fool? My dear child! — why, nothing could be farther from me! You're twice as clever and a million times as competent as I am. Why, my dear child, I've the greatest admiration for you! I wouldn't do what you do, not for all the pearls in India. I *couldn't*, anyhow —— "

Miss Wrexall closed up and was silent.

"Do you mean to say my books read as if —— " he began, rearing up and speaking in a harrowed voice.

"I do!" said the wife. "*Just* as if Miss Wrexall had written them from your hints. I *honestly* thought she did — when you were too busy —— "

"How very clever of you!" he said.

"Very!" she cried. "Especially if I was wrong!"

"Which you were," he said.

"How very extraordinary!" she cried. "Well, I am once more mistaken!"

There was a complete pause.

It was broken by Miss Wrexall, who was nervously twisting her fingers.

"You want to spoil what there is between me and him, I can see that," she said bitterly.

"My dear, but what is there between you and him?" asked the wife.

"I was *happy* working with him, working for him! I was *happy* working for him!" cried Miss Wrexall, tears of indignant anger and chagrin in her eyes.

"My dear child!" cried the wife, with simulated excitement, "go *on* being happy working with him, go on being happy while you can! If it makes you happy, why then, enjoy it! Of course! Do you think I'd be so cruel as to want to take it away from you? — working with him? *I* can't do shorthand and typewriting and double-entrance book-keeping, or whatever it's called. I tell you, I'm utterly incompetent. I never earn anything. I'm the parasite on the British oak, like the mistletoe. The blue bird doesn't flutter round my feet. Perhaps they're too big and trampling."

She looked down at her expensive shoes.

"If I *did* have a word of criticism to offer," she said, turning to her husband, "it would be to you, Cameron, for taking so much from her and giving her nothing."

"But he gives me everything, everything!" cried Miss Wrexall. "He gives me everything!"

"What do you mean by everything?" said the wife, turning on her sternly.

Miss Wrexall pulled up short. There was a snap in the air and a change of currents.

"I mean nothing that *you* need begrudge me," said the little secretary rather haughtily. "I've never made myself cheap."

There was a blank pause.

"My God!" said the wife. "You don't call that being cheap? Why, I should say you got nothing out of him at all, you only give! And if you don't call that making yourself cheap — my God!"

"You see, we see things different," said the secretary.

"I should say we do! — *thank God!*" rejoined the wife.

"On whose behalf are you thanking God?" he asked sarcastically.

"Everybody's, I suppose! Yours, because you get everything for nothing, and Miss Wrexall's, because she seems to like it, and mine because I'm well out of it all."

"You *needn't* be out of it all," cried Miss Wrexall magnanimously, "if you didn't *put* yourself out of it all."

"Thank you, my dear, for your offer," said the wife, rising. "But I'm afraid no man can expect *two* blue birds of happiness to flutter round his feet, tearing out their little feathers!"

With which she walked away.

After a tense and desperate interim, Miss Wrexall cried:

"And *really*, need any woman be jealous of *me?*"

"Quite!" he said.

And that was all he did say.

(1927)

❖ KATHERINE MANSFIELD
Je Ne Parle Pas Français

Katherine Mansfield [Beauchamp] (1888–1923) was born near Wel-
lington, New Zealand, but educated in London at Queen's College.
She returned reluctantly to New Zealand for two years (1906–1908)
where she published her earliest stories. On a small family allowance,
she went back to England to launch a writing career. Her first collection of short stories was *In a German Pension* (1911). In 1912 she met
the English writer John Middleton Murry, whom she lived with and
married in 1918. Murry supported her writing and introduced her to
other English writers, like D. H. Lawrence. Her second book of stories,
Bliss, appeared in 1920, and her third and greatest, *The Garden Party*,
and fourth, *The Dove's Nest*, appeared in 1923. She died, tragically, of
tuberculosis at the age of thirty-four. All her short stories, including
those that appeared posthumously, have been published in *The Complete Stories of Katherine Mansfield* (1974). Mansfield's later stories
often turn on an "epiphany" (for a definition, see footnote 2, chapter
2, p. 22). She also wrote poetry. Mansfield's *Critical Writings* (1987),
Letters (1984), and *Journal* (1984) show a mind relentless in its pursuit
of artistic honesty.

I do not know why I have such a fancy for this little café. It's dirty and sad, sad. It's not
as if it had anything to distinguish it from a hundred others — it hasn't; or as if the
same strange types came here every day, whom one could watch from one's corner and
recognize and more or less (with a strong accent on the less) get the hang of.

But pray don't imagine that those brackets are a confession of my humility
before the mystery of the human soul. Not at all; I don't believe in the human soul. I
never have. I believe that people are like portmanteaux — packed with certain things,
started going, thrown about, tossed away, dumped down, lost and found, half emptied
suddenly, or squeezed fatter than ever, until finally the Ultimate Porter swings them
on to the Ultimate Train and away they rattle. . . .

Not but what these portmanteaux can be very fascinating. Oh, but very! I see
myself standing in front of them, don't you know, like a Customs official.

'Have you anything to declare? Any wines, spirits, cigars, perfumes, silks?'

And the moment of hesitation as to whether I am going to be fooled just
before I chalk that squiggle, and then the other moment of hesitation just after, as to
whether I have been, are perhaps the two most thrilling instants in life. Yes, they are,
to me.

But before I started that long and rather far-fetched and not frightfully
original digression, what I meant to say quite simply was that there are no portmanteaux to be examined here because the clientele of this café, ladies and gentlemen, does
not sit down. No, it stands at the counter, and it consists of a handful of workmen who

494

come up from the river, all powdered over with white flour, lime or something, and a few soldiers, bringing with them thin, dark girls with silver rings in their ears and market baskets on their arms.

Madame is thin and dark, too, with white cheeks and white hands. In certain lights she looks quite transparent, shining out of her black shawl with an extraordinary effect. When she is not serving she sits on a stool with her face turned, always, to the window. Her dark-ringed eyes search among and follow after the people passing, but not as if she was looking for somebody. Perhaps, fifteen years ago, she was; but now the pose has become a habit. You can tell from her air of fatigue and hopelessness that she must have given them up for the last ten years, at least. . . .

And then there is the waiter. Not pathetic — decidedly not comic. Never making one of those perfectly insignificant remarks which amaze you so coming from a waiter (as though the poor wretch were a sort of cross between a coffee-pot and a wine-bottle and not expected to hold so much as a drop of anything else). He is grey, flat-footed and withered, with long, brittle nails that set your nerves on edge while he scrapes up your two sous. When he is not smearing over the table or flicking at a dead fly or two, he stands with one hand on the back of a chair, in his far too long apron, and over his other arm the three-cornered dip of dirty napkin, waiting to be photographed in connection with some wretched murder. 'Interior of Café where Body was Found.' You've seen him hundreds of times.

Do you believe that every place has its hour of the day when it really does come alive? That's not exactly what I mean. It's more like this. There does seem to be a moment when you realize that, quite by accident, you happen to have come on to the stage at exactly the moment you were expected. Everything is arranged for you — waiting for you. Ah, master of the situation! You fill with important breath. And at the same time you smile, secretly, slyly, because Life seems to be opposed to granting you these entrances, seems indeed to be engaged in snatching them from you and making them impossible, keeping you in the wings until it is too late, in fact. . . . Just for once you've beaten the old hag.

I enjoyed one of these moments the first I ever came in here. That's why I keep coming back, I suppose. Revisiting the scene of my triumph, or the scene of the crime where I had the old bitch by the throat for once and did what I pleased with her.

Query: Why am I so bitter against Life? And why do I see her as a rag-picker on the American cinema, shuffling along wrapped in a filthy shawl with her old claws crooked over a stick?

Answer: The direct result of the American cinema acting upon a weak mind.

Anyhow, the 'short winter afternoon was drawing to a close,' as they say, and I was drifting along, either going home or not going home, when I found myself in here, walking over to this seat in the corner.

I hung up my English overcoat and grey felt hat on that same peg behind me, and after I had allowed the waiter time for at least twenty photographers to snap their fill of him, I ordered a coffee.

He poured me out a glass of the familiar, purplish stuff with a green wandering light playing over it, and shuffled off, and I sat pressing my hands against the glass because it was bitterly cold outside.

Suddenly I realized that, quite apart from myself, I was smiling. Slowly I raised my head and saw myself in the mirror opposite. Yes, there I sat, leaning on the table, smiling my deep, sly smile, the glass of coffee with its vague plume of steam before me and beside it the ring of white saucer with two pieces of sugar.

I opened my eyes very wide. There I had been for all eternity, as it were, and now at last I was coming to life. . . .

It was very quiet in the café. Outside, one could just see through the dusk that it had begun to snow. One could just see the shapes of horses and carts and people, soft and white, moving through the feathery air. The waiter disappeared and reappeared with an armful of straw. He strewed it over the floor from the door to the counter and round about the stove with humble, almost adoring gestures. One would not have been surprised if the door had opened and the Virgin Mary had come in, riding upon an ass, her meek hands folded over her big belly. . . .

That's rather nice, don't you think, that bit about the Virgin? It comes from the pen so gently; it has such a 'dying fall.' I thought so at the time and decided to make a note of it. One never knows when a little tag like that may come in useful to round off a paragraph. So, taking care to move as little as possible because the 'spell' was still unbroken (you know that?), I reached over to the next table for a writing-pad.

No paper or envelopes, of course. Only a morsel of pink blotting-paper, incredibly soft and limp and almost moist, like the tongue of a little dead kitten, which I've never felt.

I sat — but always underneath, in this state of expectation, rolling the little dead kitten's tongue round my finger and rolling the soft phrase round my mind while my eyes took in the girls' names and dirty jokes and drawings of bottles and cups that would not sit in the saucers, scattered over the writing-pad.

They are always the same, you know. The girls always have the same names, the cups never sit in the saucers; all the hearts are stuck and tied up with ribbons.

But then, quite suddenly, at the bottom of the page, written in green ink, I fell on to that stupid, stale little phrase: *Je ne parle pas français.*

There! it had come — the moment — the *geste!* And although I was so ready, it caught me, it tumbled me over; I was simply overwhelmed. And the physical feeling was so curious, so particular. It was as if all of me, except my head and arms, all of me that was under the table, had simply dissolved, melted, turned into water. Just my head remained and two sticks of arms pressing on to the table. But, ah! the agony of that moment! How can I describe it? I didn't think of anything. I didn't even cry out to myself. Just for one moment I was not. I was Agony, Agony, Agony.

Then it passed, and the very second after I was thinking: 'Good God! Am I capable of feeling as strongly as that? But I was absolutely unconscious! I hadn't a phrase to meet it with! I was overcome! I was swept off my feet! I didn't even try, in the dimmest way, to put it down!'

And up I puffed and puffed, blowing off finally with: 'After all I must be first-rate. No second-rate mind could have experienced such an intensity of feeling so . . . purely.'

The waiter has touched a spill at the red stove and lighted a bubble of gas under a spreading shade. It is no use looking out of the window, Madame; it is quite dark now. Your white hands hover over your dark shawl. They are like two birds that have come home to roost. They are restless, restless. . . . You tuck them, finally, under your warm little armpits.

Now the waiter has taken a long pole and clashed the curtains together. 'All gone,' as children say.

And besides, I've no patience with people who can't let go of things, who will follow after and cry out. When a thing's gone, it's gone. It's over and done with. Let it go then! Ignore it, and comfort yourself, if you do want comforting, with the thought that you never do recover the same thing that you lose. It's always a new thing. The moment it leaves you it's changed. Why, that's even true of a hat you chase after; and I don't mean superficially — I mean profoundly speaking . . . I have made it a rule of my life never to regret and never to look back. Regret is an appalling waste of energy, and no one who intends to be a writer can afford to indulge in it. You can't get it into shape; you can't build on it; it's only good for wallowing in. Looking back, of course, is equally fatal to Art. It's keeping yourself poor. Art can't and won't stand poverty.

Je ne parle pas français. Je ne parle pas français. All the while I wrote that last page my other self has been chasing up and down out in the dark there. It left me just when I began to analyse my grand moment, dashed off distracted, like a lost dog who thinks at last, at last, he hears the familiar step again.

'Mouse! Mouse! Where are you? Are you near? Is that you leaning from the high window and stretching out your arms for the wings of the shutters? Are you this soft bundle moving towards me through the feathery snow? Are you this little girl pressing through the swing-doors of the restaurant? Is that your dark shadow bending forward in the cab? Where are you? Where are you? Which way must I turn? Which way shall I run? And every moment I stand here hesitating you are farther away again. Mouse! Mouse!'

Now the poor dog has come back into the café, his tail between his legs, quite exhausted.

'It was a . . . false . . . alarm. She's nowhere . . . to . . . be seen.'

'Lie down then! Lie down! Lie down!'

My name is Raoul Duquette. I am twenty-six years old and a Parisian, a true Parisian. About my family — it really doesn't matter. I have no family; I don't want any. I never think about my childhood. I've forgotten it.

In fact, there's only one memory that stands out at all. That is rather interesting because it seems to me now so very significant as regards myself from the literary point of view. It is this.

When I was about ten our laundress was an African woman, very big, very dark, with a check handkerchief over her frizzy hair. When she came to our house she always took particular notice of me, and after the clothes had been taken out of the basket she would lift me up into it and give me a rock while I held tight to the handles and screamed for joy and fright. I was tiny for my age, and pale, with a lovely little half-open mouth — I feel sure of that.

One day when I was standing at the door, watching her go, she turned round and beckoned to me, nodding and smiling in a strange secret way. I never thought of not following. She took me into a little outhouse at the end of the passage, caught me up in her arms and began kissing me. Ah, those kisses! Especially those kisses inside my ears that nearly deafened me.

When she set me down she took from her pocket a little round fried cake covered with sugar, and I reeled along the passage back to our door.

As this performance was repeated once a week it is no wonder that I remember it so vividly. Besides, from that very first afternoon, my childhood was, to put it prettily, 'kissed away'. I became very languid, very caressing, and greedy beyond measure. And so quickened, so sharpened, I seemed to understand everybody and be able to do what I liked with everybody.

I suppose I was in a state of more or less physical excitement, and that was what appealed to them. For all Parisians are more than half — oh, well, enough of that. And enough of my childhood, too. Bury it under a laundry basket instead of a shower of roses and *passons outre*.

I date myself from the moment that I became the tenant of a small bachelor flat on the fifth floor of a tall, not too shabby house, in a street that might or might not be discreet. Very useful, that. . . . There I emerged, came out into the light and put out my two horns with a study and a bedroom and a kitchen on my back. And real furniture planted in the rooms. In the bedroom a wardrobe with a long glass, a big bed covered with a yellow puffed-up quilt, a bed-table with a marbled top and a toilet-set sprinkled with tiny apples. In my study — English writing-table with drawers, writing-chair with leather cushions, books, arm-chair, side-table with paper-knife and lamp on it and some nude studies on the walls. I didn't use the kitchen except to throw old papers into.

Ah, I can see myself that first evening, after the furniture men had gone and I'd managed to get rid of my atrocious old concierge — walking about on tiptoe, arranging and standing in front of the glass with my hands in my pockets and saying to that radiant vision: 'I am a young man who has his own flat. I write for two newspapers. I am going in for serious literature. I am starting a career. The book that I shall bring out will simply stagger the critics. I am going to write about things that have never been touched before. I am going to make a name for myself as a writer about the submerged world. But not as others have done before me. Oh, no! Very naïvely, with a sort of tender humour and from the inside, as though it were all quite simple, quite natural. I see my way quite perfectly. Nobody has ever done it as I shall do it because none of the others have lived my experiences. I'm rich — I'm rich.'

All the same I had no more money than I have now. It's extraordinary how one can live without money. . . . I have quantities of good clothes, silk underwear, two evening suits, four pairs of patent-leather boots with light uppers, all sorts of little things, like gloves and powder-boxes and a manicure-set, perfumes, very good soap, and nothing is paid for. If I find myself in need of right-down cash — well, there's always an African laundress and an outhouse, and I am very frank and *bon enfant* about plenty of sugar on the little fried cake afterwards. . . .

And here I should like to put something on record. Not from any strutting conceit, but rather with a mild sense of wonder. I've never yet made the first advances to any woman. It isn't as though I've known only one class of woman — not by any means. But from little prostitutes and kept women and elderly widows and shop-girls and wives of respectable men, and even advanced modern literary ladies at the most select dinners and soirées (I've been there), I've met invariably with not only the same readiness, but with the same positive invitation. It surprised me at first. I used to look across the table and think, 'Is that very distinguished young lady, discussing *le Kipling* with the gentleman with the brown beard, really pressing my foot?' And I was never really certain until I had pressed hers.

Curious, isn't it? I don't look at all like a maiden's dream. . . .

I am little and light with an olive skin, black eyes with long lashes, black silky hair cut short, tiny square teeth that show when I smile. My hands are supple and small. A woman in a bread-shop once said to me: 'You have the hands for making fine little pastries.' I confess, without my clothes I am rather charming. Plump, almost like a girl, with smooth shoulders, and I wear a thin gold bracelet above my left elbow.

But, wait! Isn't it strange I should have written all that about my body and so on? It's the result of my bad life, my submerged life. I am like a little woman in a café who has to introduce herself with a handful of photographs. 'Me in my chemise, coming out of an eggshell. . . . Me upside-down in a swing, with a frilly behind like a cauli-flower. . . .' You know the things.

If you think what I've written is merely superficial and impudent and cheap you're wrong. I'll admit it does sound so, but then it is not all. If it were, how could I have experienced what I did when I read that stale little phrase written in green ink, in the writing-pad? That proves there's more in me and that I really am important, doesn't it? Anything a fraction less than that moment of anguish I might have put on. But no! That was real.

'Waiter, a whisky.'

I hate whisky. Every time I take it into my mouth my stomach rises against it, and the stuff they keep here is sure to be particularly vile. I only ordered it because I am going to write about an Englishman. We French are incredibly old-fashioned and out-of-date still in some ways. I wonder I didn't ask him at the same time for a pair of tweed knickerbockers, a pipe, some long teeth and a set of ginger whiskers.

'Thanks, *mon vieux*. You haven't got perhaps a set of ginger whiskers?'

'No, monsieur,' he answers sadly. 'We don't sell American drinks.'

And having smeared a corne · of the table he goes back to have another couple of dozen taken by artificial light.

Ugh! The smell of it! And the sickly sensation when one's throat contracts.

'It's bad stuff to get drunk on,' says Dick Harmon, turning his little glass in his fingers and smiling his slow, dreaming smile. So he gets drunk on it slowly and dreamily and at a certain moment begins to sing very low, very low, about a man who walks up and down trying to find a place where he can get some dinner.

Ah! how I loved that song, and how I loved the way he sang it, slowly, slowly, in a dark, soft voice:

> There was a man
> Walked up and down
> To get a dinner in the town . . .

It seemed to hold, in its gravity and muffled measure, all those tall grey buildings, those fogs, those endless streets, those sharp shadows of policemen that mean England.

And then — the subject! The lean, starved creature walking up and down with every house barred against him because he had no 'home'. How extraordinarily English that is. . . . I remember that it ended where he did at last 'find a place' and ordered a little cake of fish, but when he asked for bread the waiter cried contemptuously, in a loud voice: 'We don't serve bread with one fishball.'

What more do you want? How profound those songs are! There is the whole psychology of a people; and how un-French — how un-French!

'Once more, Deeck, once more!' I would plead, clasping my hands and making a pretty mouth at him. He was perfectly content to sing it for ever.

There again. Even with Dick. It was he who made the first advances.

I met him at an evening party given by the editor of a new review. It was a very select, very fashionable affair. One or two of the older men were there and the ladies were extremely *comme il faut*. They sat on cubist sofas in full evening-dress and allowed us to hand them thimbles of cherry-brandy and to talk to them about their poetry. For, as far as I can remember, they were all poetesses.

It was impossible not to notice Dick. He was the only Englishman present, and instead of circulating gracefully round the room as we all did, he stayed in one place leaning against the wall, his hands in his pockets, that dreamy half-smile on his lips, and replying in excellent French in his low, soft voice to anybody who spoke to him.

'Who is he?'

'An Englishman. From London. A writer. And he is making a special study of modern French literature.'

That was enough for me. My little book, *False Coins*, had just been published. I was a young, serious writer who was making a special study of modern English literature.

But I really had not time to fling my line before he said, giving himself a soft shake, coming right out of the water after the bait, as it were: 'Won't you come and see me at my hotel? Come about five o'clock and we can have a talk before going out to dinner.'

'Enchanted!'

I was so deeply, deeply flattered that I had to leave him then and there to preen and preen myself before the cubist sofas. What a catch! An Englishman, reserved, serious, making a special study of French literature. . . .

That same night a copy of *False Coins* with a carefully cordial inscription was posted off, and a day or two later we did dine together and spent the evening talking.

Talking — but not only of literature. I discovered to my relief that it wasn't necessary to keep to the tendency of the modern novel, the need of a new form, or the reason why our young men appeared to be just missing it. Now and again, as if by accident, I threw in a card that seemed to have nothing to do with the game, just to see how he'd take it. But each time he gathered it into his hands with his dreamy look and smile unchanged. Perhaps he murmured: 'That's very curious.' But not as if it were curious at all.

That calm acceptance went to my head at last. It fascinated me. It led me on and on till I threw every card that I possessed at him and sat back and watched him arrange them in his hand.

'Very curious and interesting. . . .'

By that time we were both fairly drunk, and he began to sing his song very soft, very low, about the man who walked up and down seeking his dinner.

But I was quite breathless at the thought of what I had done. I had shown somebody both sides of my life. Told him everything as sincerely and truthfully as I could. Taken immense pains to explain things about my submerged life that really were disgusting and never could possibly see the light of literary day. On the whole I had made myself out far worse than I was — more boastful, more cynical, more calculating.

And there sat the man I had confided in, singing to himself and smiling. . . . It moved me so that real tears came into my eyes. I saw them glittering on my long silky lashes — so charming.

After that I took Dick about with me everywhere, and he came to my flat, and sat in the arm-chair, very indolent, playing with the paper-knife. I cannot think why his indolence and dreaminess always gave me the impression he had been to sea. And all his leisurely slow ways seemed to be allowing for the movement of the ship. This impression was so strong that often when we were together and he got up and left a little woman just when she did not expect him to get up and leave her, but quite the contrary, I would explain: 'He can't help it, Baby. He has to go back to his ship.' And I believed it far more than she did.

All the while we were together Dick never went with a woman. I sometimes wondered whether he wasn't completely innocent. Why didn't I ask him? Because I never did ask him anything about himself. But late one night he took out his pocket-book and a photograph dropped out of it. I picked it up and glanced at it before I gave it to him. It was of a woman. Not quite young. Dark, handsome, wild-looking, but so full in every line of a kind of haggard pride that even if Dick had not stretched out so quickly I wouldn't have looked longer.

'Out of my sight, you little perfumed fox-terrier of a Frenchman,' said she.

(In my very worst moments my nose reminds me of a fox-terrier's.)

'That is my Mother,' said Dick, putting up the pocket-book.

But if he had not been Dick I should have been tempted to cross myself, just for fun.

This is how we parted. As we stood outside his hotel one night waiting for the concierge to release the catch of the outer door, he said, looking up at the sky: 'I hope it will be fine to-morrow. I am leaving for England in the morning.'

'You're not serious.'

'Perfectly. I have to get back. I've some work to do that I can't manage here.'

'But — but have you made all your preparations?'

'Preparations?' He almost grinned. 'I've none to make.'

'But — *enfin*, Dick, England is not the other side of the boulevard.'

'It isn't much farther off,' said he. 'Only a few hours, you know.' The door cracked open.

'Ah, I wish I'd known at the beginning of the evening!' I felt hurt. I felt as a woman must feel when a man takes out his watch and remembers an appointment that cannot possibly concern her, except that its claim is the stronger. 'Why didn't you tell me?'

He put out his hand and stood, lightly swaying upon the step as though the whole hotel were his ship, and the anchor weighed.

'I forgot. Truly I did. But you'll write, won't you? Good night, old chap. I'll be over again one of these days.'

And then I stood on the shore alone, more like a little fox-terrier than ever. . . .

'But after all it was you who whistled to me, you who asked me to come! What a spectacle I've out wagging my tail and leaping round you, only to be left like this while the boat sails off in its slow, dreamy way. . . . Curse these English! No, this is too insolent altogether. Who do you imagine I am? A little paid guide to the night pleasures of Paris? . . . No, monsieur. I am a young writer, very serious, and extremely interested in modern English literature. And I have been insulted — insulted.'

Two days after came a long, charming letter from him, written in French that was a shade too French, but saying how he missed me and counted on our friendship, on keeping in touch.

I read it standing in front of the (unpaid-for) wardrobe mirror. It was early morning. I wore a blue kimono embroidered with white birds and my hair was still wet; it lay on my forehead, wet and gleaming.

'Portrait of Madame Butterfly,' said I, 'on hearing of the arrival of *ce cher Pinkerton.*'

According to the books I should have felt immensely relieved and delighted. '. . . Going over to the window he drew apart the curtains and looked out at the Paris trees, just breaking into buds and green. . . . Dick! Dick! My English friend!'

I didn't. I merely felt a little sick. Having been up for my first ride in an aeroplane I didn't want to go up again, just now.

That passed, and months after, in the winter, Dick wrote that he was coming back to Paris to stay indefinitely. Would I take rooms for him? He was bringing a woman friend with him.

Of course I would. Away the little fox-terrier flew. It happened most usefully, too; for I owed much money at the hotel where I took my meals, and two English people requiring rooms for an indefinite time was an excellent sum on account.

Perhaps I did rather wonder, as I stood in the larger of the two rooms with Madame, saying 'Admirable', what the woman friend would be like, but only vaguely. Either she would be very severe, flat back and front, or she would be tall, fair, dressed in mignonette green, name — Daisy, and smelling of rather sweetish lavender-water.

You see, by this time, according to my rule of not looking back, I had almost forgotten Dick. I even got the tune of his song about the unfortunate man a little bit wrong when I tried to hum it. . . .

I very nearly did not turn up at the station after all. I had arranged to, and had, in fact, dressed with particular care for the occasion. For I intended to take a new line with Dick this time. No more confidences and tears on eyelashes. No, thank you!

'Since you left Paris,' said I, knotting my black silver-spotted tie in the (also unpaid-for) mirror over the mantelpiece, 'I have been very successful, you know. I have two more books in preparation, and then I have written a serial story, *Wrong Doors*, which is just on the point of publication and will bring me in a lot of money. And then my little book of poems,' I cried, seizing the clothes-brush and brushing the velvet collar of my new indigoblue overcoat, 'my little book — *Left Umbrellas* — really did create,' and I laughed and waved the brush, 'an immense sensation!'

It was impossible not to believe this of the person who surveyed himself finally, from top to toe, drawing on his soft grey gloves. He was looking the part; he was the part.

That gave me an idea. I took out my note-book, and, still in full view, jotted down a note or two. . . . How can one look the part and not be the part? Or be the part and not look it? Isn't looking — being? Or being — looking? At any rate who is to say that it is not? . . .

This seemed to me extraordinarily profound at the time, and quite new. But I confess that something did whisper as, smiling, I put up the note-book: 'You — literary? you look as though you've taken down a bet on a racecourse!' But I didn't listen. I went out, shutting the door of the flat with a soft, quick pull so as not to warn the concierge of my departure, and ran down the stairs quick as a rabbit for the same reason.

But ah! the old spider. She was too quick for me. She let me run down the last little ladder of the web and then she pounced. 'One moment. One little moment, Monsieur,' she whispered, odiously confidential. 'Come in. Come in.' And she beckoned with a dripping soup-ladle. I went to the door, but that was not good enough. Right inside and the door shut before she would speak.

There are two ways of managing your concierge if you haven't any money. One is — to take the high hand, make her your enemy, bluster, refuse to discuss anything; the other is — to keep in with her, butter her up to the two knots of the black rag tying up her jaws, pretend to confide in her, and rely on her to arrange with the gas man and to put off the landlord.

I had tried the second. But both are equally detestable and unsuccessful. At any rate whichever you're trying is the worse, the impossible one.

It was the landlord this time. . . . Imitation of the landlord by the concierge threatening to toss me out. . . . Imitation of the concierge by the concierge taming the wild bull. . . . Imitation of the landlord rampant again, breathing in the concierge's face. I was the concierge. No, it was too nauseous. And all the while the black pot on the gas-ring bubbling away, stewing out the hearts and livers of every tenant in the place.

'Ah!' I cried, staring at the clock on the mantelpiece, and then, realizing that it didn't go, striking my forehead as though the idea had nothing to do with it. 'Madame, I have a very important appointment with the director of my newspaper at nine-thirty. Perhaps to-morrow I shall be able to give you . . .'

Out, out. And down the métro and squeezed into a full carriage. The more the better. Everybody was one bolster the more between me and the concierge. I was radiant.

'Ah! pardon, Monsieur!' said the tall charming creature in black with a big full bosom and a great bunch of violets dropping from it. As the train swayed it thrust the bouquet right into my eyes. 'Ah! pardon, Monsieur!'

But I looked up at her, smiling mischievously.

'There is nothing I love more, Madame, than flowers on a balcony.'

At the very moment of speaking I caught sight of the huge man in a fur-coat against whom my charmer was leaning. He poked his head over her shoulder and he went white to the nose; in fact his nose stood out a sort cheesegreen.

'What was that you said to my wife?'

Gare Saint-Lazare saved me. But you'll own that even as the author of *False Coins, Wrong Doors, Left Umbrellas*, and two in preparation, it was not too easy to go on my triumphant way.

At length, after countless trains had steamed into my mind, and countless Dick Harmons had come rolling towards me, the real train came. The little knot of us waiting at the barrier moved up close, craned forward, and broke into cries as though we were some kind of many-headed monster, and Paris behind us nothing but a great trap we had set to catch these sleepy innocents.

Into the trap they walked and were snatched and taken off to be devoured. Where was my prey?

'Good God!' My smile and my lifted hand fell together. For one terrible moment I thought this was the woman of the photograph, Dick's mother, walking towards me in Dick's coat and hat. In the effort — and you saw what an effort it was — to smile, his lips curled in just the same way and he made for me, haggard and wild and proud.

What had happened? What could have changed him like this? Should I mention it?

I waited for him and was even conscious of venturing a fox-terrier wag or two to see if he could possibly respond, in the way I said: 'Good evening. Dick! How are you, old chap? All right?'

'All right. All right.' He almost gasped. 'You've got the rooms?'

Twenty times, good God! I saw it all. Light broke on the dark waters and my sailor hadn't been drowned. I almost turned a somersault with amusement.

It was nervousness, of course. It was embarrassment. It was the famous English seriousness. What fun I was going to have! I could have hugged him.

'Yes, I've got the rooms,' I nearly shouted. 'But where is Madame?'

'She's been looking after the luggage,' he panted. 'Here she comes, now.'

Not this baby walking beside the old porter as though he were her nurse and had just lifted her out of her ugly perambulator while he trundled the boxes on it.

'And she's not Madame,' said Dick, drawling suddenly.

At that moment she caught sight of him and hailed him with her minute muff. She broke away from her nurse and ran up and said something very quick, in English; but he replied in French: 'Oh, very well. I'll manage.'

But before he turned to the porter he indicated me with a vague wave and muttered something. We were introduced. She held out her hand in that strange boyish way English-women do, and standing very straight in front of me with her chin raised and making—she too—the effort of her life to control her preposterous excitement, she said, wringing my hand (I'm sure she didn't know it was mine), *Je ne parle pas français.*

'But I'm sure you do,' I answered, so tender, so reassuring. I might have been a dentist about to draw her first little milk tooth.

'Of course she does.' Dick swerved back to us. 'Here, can't we get a cab or taxi or something? We don't want to stay in this cursed station all night. Do we?'

This was so rude that it took me a moment to recover; and he must have noticed, for he flung his arm round my shoulder in the old way, saying: 'Ah, forgive me, old chap. But we've had such a loathsome, hideous journey. We've taken years to come. Haven't we?' To her. But she did not answer.

She bent her head and began stroking her grey muff; she walked beside us stroking her grey muff all the way.

'Have I been wrong?' thought I. 'Is this simply a case of frenzied impatience on their part? Are they merely "in need of a bed," as we say? Have they been suffering agonies on the journey? Sitting, perhaps, very close and warm under the same travelling rug?' and so on and so on while the driver strapped on the boxes. That done . . .

'Look here, Dick. I go home by métro. Here is the address of your hotel. Everything is arranged. Come and see me as soon as you can.'

Upon my life I thought he was going to faint. He went white to the lips.

'But you're coming back with us,' he cried. 'I thought it was all settled. Of course you're coming back. You're not going to leave us.' No, I gave it up. It was too difficult, too English for me.

'Certainly, certainly. Delighted. I only thought, perhaps . . .'

'You must come!' said Dick to the little fox-terrier. And again he made that big awkward turn towards her.

'Get in, Mouse.'

And Mouse got in the black hole and sat stroking Mouse II and not saying a word.

Away we jolted and rattled like three little dice that life had decided to have a fling with.

I had insisted on taking the flap-seat facing them because I would not have missed for anything those occasional flashing glimpses I had as we broke through the white circles of lamp-light.

They revealed Dick, sitting far back in his corner, his coat-collar turned up, his hands thrust in his pockets, and his broad dark hat shading him as if it were a part of him—a sort of wing he hid under. They showed her, sitting up very straight, her lovely little face more like a drawing than a real face—every line was so full of meaning and so sharpcut against the swimming dark.

For Mouse was beautiful. She was exquisite, but so fragile and fine each time I looked at her it was as if for the first time. She came upon you with the same kind of shock that you feel when you have been drinking tea out of a thin innocent cup and suddenly, at the bottom, you see a tiny creature, half butterfly, half woman, bowing to you with her hands in her sleeves.

As far as I could make out she had dark hair and blue or black eyes. Her long lashes and the two little feathers traced above were most important.

She wore a long dark cloak such as one sees in old-fashioned pictures of Englishwomen abroad. Where her arms came out of it there was grey fur — fur round her neck, too, and her close-fitting cap was furry.

'Carrying out the mouse idea,' I decided.

Ah, but how intriguing it was — how intriguing! Their excitement came nearer and nearer to me, while I ran out to meet it, bathed in it, flung myself far out of my depth, until at last I was as hard put to it to keep control as they.

But what I wanted to do was to behave in the most extraordinary fashion — like a clown. To start singing, with large extravagant gestures, to point out of the window and cry: 'We are now passing, ladies and gentlemen, one of the sights for which *notre Paris* is justly famous,' to jump out of the taxi while it was going, climb over the roof and dive in by another door; to hang out of the window and look for the hotel through the wrong end of a broken telescope, which was also a peculiarly ear-splitting trumpet.

I watched myself do all this, you understand, and even managed to applaud in a private way by putting my gloved hands gently together, while I said to Mouse: 'And is this your first visit to Paris?'

'Yes, I've not been here before.'

'Ah, then you have a great deal to see.'

And I was just going to touch lightly upon the objects of interest and the museums when we wrenched to a stop.

Do you know — it's very absurd — but as I pushed open the door for them and followed up the stairs to the bureau on the landing I felt somehow that this hotel was mine.

There was a vase of flowers on the window-sill of the bureau and I even went so far as to re-arrange a bud or two and to stand off and note the effect while the manageress welcomed them. And when she turned to me and handed me the keys (the *garçon* was hauling up the boxes) and said: 'Monsieur Duquette will show you your rooms' — I had a longing to tap Dick on the arm with a key and say, very confidentially: 'Look here, old chap. As a friend of mine I'll be only too willing to make a slight reduction . . .'

Up and up we climbed. Round and round. Past an occasional pair of boots (why is it one never sees an attractive pair of boots outside a door?). Higher and higher.

'I'm afraid they're rather high up,' I murmured idiotically. 'But I chose them because . . .'

They so obviously did not care why I chose them that I went no further. They accepted everything. They did not expect anything to be different. This was just part of what they were going through — that was how I analysed it.

'Arrived at last.' I ran from one side of the passage to the other, turning on the lights, explaining.

'This one I thought for you, Dick. The other is larger and it has a little dressing-room in the alcove.'

My 'proprietary' eye noted the clean towels and covers, and the bed-linen embroidered in red cotton. I thought them rather charming rooms, sloping, full of angles, just the sort of rooms one would expect to find if one had not been to Paris before.

Dick dashed his hat down on the bed.

'Oughtn't I to help that chap with the boxes?' he asked — nobody.

'Yes, you ought,' replied Mouse, 'they're dreadfully heavy.'

And she turned to me with the first glimmer of a smile:

'Books, you know.' Oh, he darted such a strange look at her before he rushed out. And he not only helped, he must have torn the box off the *garçon's* back, for he staggered back, carrying one, dumped it down and then fetched in the other.

'That's yours, Dick,' said she.

'Well, you don't mind it standing here for the present, do you?' he asked, breathless, breathing hard (the box must have been tremendously heavy). He pulled out a handful of money. 'I suppose I ought to pay this chap.'

The *garçon*, standing by, seemed think so too.

'And will you require anything further, Monsieur?'

'No! No!' said Dick impatiently.

But at that Mouse stepped forward. She said, too deliberately, not looking at Dick, with her quaint clipped English accent: 'Yes, I'd like some tea. Tea for three.'

And suddenly she raised her muff as though her hands were clasped inside it, and she was telling the pale, sweaty *garçon* by that action that she was at the end of her resources, that she cried out to him to save her with 'Tea. Immediately!'

This seemed to me so amazingly in the picture, so exactly the gesture and cry that one would expect (though I couldn't have imagined it) to be wrung out of an Englishwoman faced with a great crisis, that I was almost tempted to hold up my hand and protest.

'No! No! Enough. Enough. Let us leave off there. At the word — tea. For really, really, you've filled your greediest subscriber so full that he will burst if he has to swallow another word.'

It even pulled Dick up. Like someone who has been unconscious for a long time he turned slowly to Mouse and slowly looked at her with his tired, haggard eyes, and murmured with the echo of his dreamy voice. 'Yes. That's a good idea.' And then: 'You must be tired, Mouse. Sit down.'

She sat down in a chair with lace tab on the arms; he leaned against the bed, and I established myself on a straight-backed chair, crossed my legs and brushed some imaginary dust off the knees of my trousers. (The Parisian at his ease.)

There came a tiny pause. Then he said: 'Won't you take off your coat, Mouse?'

'No, thanks. Not just now.'

Were they going to ask me? Or should I hold up my hand and call out in a baby voice: 'It's my turn to be asked.'

No, I shouldn't. They didn't ask me.

The pause became a silence. A real silence.

'. . . Come, my Parisian fox-terrier! Amuse these sad English! It's no wonder they are such a nation for dogs.'

But, after all — why should I? It was not my 'job', as they would say. Nevertheless, I made a vivacious little bound at Mouse.

'What a pity it is that you did not arrive by daylight. There is such a charming view from these two windows. You know, the hotel is on a corner and each window looks down an immensely long, straight street.'

'Yes,' said she.

'Not that that sounds very charming,' I laughed. 'But there is so much animation — so many absurd little boys' bicycles and people hanging out of windows and — oh, well, you'll see for yourself in the morning. . . . Very amusing. Very animated.'

'Oh, yes,' said she.

If the pale, sweaty *garçon* had not come in at that moment, carrying the tea-tray high on one hand as if the cups were cannon-balls and he a heavy weight-lifter on the cinema . . .

He managed to lower it on to a round table.

'Bring the table over here,' said Mouse. The waiter seemed to be the only person she cared to speak to. She took her hands out of her muff, drew off her gloves and flung back the old-fashioned cape.

'Do you take milk and sugar?'

'No milk, thank you, and no sugar.'

I went over for mine like a little gentleman. She poured out another cup.

'That's for Dick.'

And the faithful fox-terrier carried it across to him and laid it at his feet, as it were.

'Oh, thanks,' said Dick.

And then I went back to my chair and she sank back in hers.

But Dick was off again. He stared wildly at the cup of tea for a moment, glanced round him, put it down on the bed-table, caught up his hat and stammered at full gallop: 'Oh, by the way, do you mind posting a letter for me? I want to get it off by to-night's post. I must. It's very urgent. . . .' Feeling her eyes on him he flung: 'It's to my mother.' To me: 'I won't be long. I've got everything I want. But it must go off to-night. You don't mind? It . . . it won't take any time.'

'Of course I'll post it. Delighted.'

'Won't you drink your tea first?' suggested Mouse softly.

'. . . Tea? Tea? Yes, of course. Tea. . . . A cup of tea on the bed-table. . . .' In his racing dream he flashed the brightest, most charming smile at his little hostess.

'No, thanks. Not just now.'

And still hoping it would not be any trouble to me he went out of the room and closed the door, and we heard him cross the passage.

I scalded myself with mine in my hurry to take the cup back to the table and to say as I stood there: 'You must forgive me if I am impertinent . . . if I am too frank. But Dick hasn't tried to disguise it — has he? There is something the matter. Can I help?'

(Soft music. Mouse gets up, walks the stage for a moment or so before she returns to her chair and pours him out, oh, such a brimming, such a burning cup that the tears come into the friend's eyes while he sips — while he drains it to the bitter dregs. . . .)

I had time to do all this before she replied. First she looked in the tea-pot, filled it with hot water, and stirred it with a spoon.

'Yes, there is something the matter. No, I'm afraid you can't help, thank you.' Again I got that glimmer of a smile. 'I'm awfully sorry. It must be horrid for you.'

Horrid, indeed! Ah, why couldn't I tell her that it was months and months since I had been so entertained?

'But you are suffering,' I ventured softly, as though that was what I could not bear to see.

She didn't deny it. She nodded and bit her under-lip and I thought I saw her chin tremble.

'And there is really nothing I can do?' More softly still.

She shook her head, pushed back the table and jumped up.

'Oh, it will be all right soon,' she breathed, walking over to the dressing-table and standing with her back towards me. 'It will be all right. It can't go on like this.'

'But of course it can't,' I agreed, wondering whether it would look heartless if I lit a cigarette; I had a sudden longing to smoke.

In some way she saw my hand move to my breast-pocket, half draw out my cigarette-case and put it back again, for the next thing she said was: 'Matches . . . in . . . candlestick. I noticed them.'

And I heard from her voice that she was crying.

'Ah! thank you. Yes. Yes. I've found them.' I lighted my cigarette and walked up and down, smoking.

It was so quiet it might have been two o'clock in the morning. It was so quiet you heard the boards creak and pop as one does in a house in the country. I smoked the whole cigarette and stabbed the end into my saucer before Mouse turned round and came back to the table.

'Isn't Dick being rather a long time?'

'You are very tired. I expect you want to go to bed,' I said kindly. (And pray don't mind me if you do, said my mind.)

'But isn't he being a very long time?' she insisted.

I shrugged. 'He is, rather.'

Then I saw she looked at me strangely. She was listening.

'He's been gone ages,' she said, and she went with little light steps to the door, opened it, and crossed the passage into his room.

I waited. I listened too, now. I couldn't have borne to miss a word. She had left the door open. I stole across the room and looked after her. Dick's door was open, too. But — there wasn't a word to miss.

You know I had the mad idea that they were kissing in that quiet room — a long comfortable kiss. One of those kisses that not only puts one's grief to bed, but nurses it and warms it and tucks it up and keeps it fast enfolded until it is sleeping sound. Ah! how good that is.

It was over at last. I heard someone move and tiptoed away.

It was Mouse. She came back. She felt her way into the room carrying the letter for me. But it wasn't in an envelope; it was just a sheet of paper and she held it by the corner as though it was still wet.

Her head was bent so low — so tucked in her furry collar that I hadn't a notion — until she let the paper fall and almost fell herself on to the floor by the side of the bed, leaned her cheek against it, flung out her hands as though the last of her poor little weapons was gone and now she let herself be carried away, washed out into the deep water.

Flash! went my mind. Dick has shot himself, and then a succession of flashes while I rushed in, saw the body, head unharmed, small blue hole over temple, roused hotel, arranged funeral, attended funeral, closed cab, new morning-coat. . . .

I stooped down and picked up the paper and would you believe it — so ingrained is my Parisian sense of *comme il faut* — I murmured 'pardon' before I read it.

'Mouse, my little Mouse,

'It's no good. It's impossible. I can't see it through. Oh, I do love you. I do love you, Mouse, but I can't hurt her. People have been hurting her all her life. I simply dare not give her this final blow. You see, though she's stronger than both of us, she's so frail and proud. It would kill her — kill her, Mouse. And, oh God, I can't kill my mother! Not even for you. Not even for us. You do see that — don't you.

'It all seemed so possible when we talked and planned, but the very moment the train started it was all over. I felt her drag me back to her — calling. I can hear her now as I write. And she's alone and she doesn't know. A man would have to be a devil to tell her and I'm not a devil, Mouse. She mustn't know. Oh, Mouse, somewhere, somewhere in you don't you agree? It's all so unspeakably awful that I don't know if I want to go or not. Do I? Or is Mother just dragging me? I don't know. My head is too tired. Mouse, Mouse — what will you do? But I can't think of that, either. I dare not. I'd break down. And I must not break down. All I've got to do is — just to tell you this and go. I couldn't have gone off without telling you. You'd have been frightened. And you must not be frightened. You won't — will you? I can't bear — but no more of that. And don't write. I should not have the courage to answer your letters and the sight of your spidery handwriting . . .

'Forgive me. Don't love me any more. Yes. Love me. Love me. Dick.'

What do you think of that? Wasn't that a rare find? My relief at his not having shot himself was mixed with a wonderful sense of elation. I was even — more than even with my 'that's very curious and interesting' Englishman. . . .

She wept so strangely. With her eyes shut, with her face quite calm except for the quivering eyelids. The tears pearled down her cheeks and she let them fall.

But feeling my glance upon her she opened her eyes and saw me holding the letter.

'You've read it?'

Her voice was quite calm, but it was not her voice any more. It was like the voice you might imagine coming out of a tiny, cold sea-shell swept high and dry at last by the salt tide. . . .

I nodded, quite overcome, you understand, and laid the letter down.

'It's incredible! incredible!' I whispered.

At that she got up from the floor, walked over to the washstand, dipped her handkerchief into the jug and sponged her eyes, saying: 'Oh, no. It's not incredible at all.' And still pressing the wet ball to her eyes she came back to me, to her chair with the lace tabs, and sank into it.

'I knew all along, of course,' said the cold, salty little voice. 'From the very moment that we started. I felt it all through me, but I still went on hoping —' and here she took the handkerchief down and gave me a final glimmer — 'as one so stupidly does, you know.'

'As one does.'

Silence.

'But what will you do? You'll go back? You'll see him?'

That made her sit right up and stare across at me.

'What an extraordinary idea!' she said, more coldly than ever. 'Of course I shall not dream of seeing him. As for going back — that is quite out of the question. I can't go back.'

'But . . .'

'It's impossible. For one thing all my friends think I am married.'

I put out my hand. 'Ah, my poor little friend.'

But she shrank away. (False move.)

Of course there was one question that had been at the back of my mind all this time. I hated it.

'Have you any money?'

'Yes, I have twenty pounds — here,' and she put her hand on her breast. I bowed. It was a great deal more than I had expected.

'And what are your plans?'

Yes, I know. My question was the most clumsy, the most idiotic one I could have put. She had been so tame, so confiding, letting me, at any rate spiritually speaking, hold her tiny quivering body in one hand and stroke her furry head — and now, I'd thrown her away. Oh, I could have kicked myself.

She stood up. 'I have no plans. But — it's very late. You must go now, please.'

How could I get her back? I wanted her back. I swear I was not acting then.

'Do feel that I am your friend,' I cried. 'You will let me come to-morrow, early? You will let me look after you a little — take care of you a little? You'll use me just as you think fit?'

I succeeded. She came out of her hole . . . timid . . . but she came out.

'Yes, you're very kind. Yes. Do come to-morrow. I shall be glad. It makes things rather difficult because' — and again I clasped her boyish hand — '*je ne parle pas français*.'

Not until I was half-way down the boulevard did it come over me — the full force of it.

Why, they were suffering . . . those two . . . really suffering. I have seen two people suffer as I don't suppose I ever shall again. . . .

Of course you know what to expect. You anticipate, fully, what I am going to write. It wouldn't be me, otherwise.

I never went near the place again.

Yes, I still owe that considerable amount for lunches and dinners, but that's beside the mark. It's vulgar to mention it in the same breath with the fact that I never saw Mouse again.

Naturally, I intended to. Started out — got to the door — wrote and tore up letters — did all those things. But I simply could not make the final effort.

Even now I don't fully understand why. Of course I knew that I couldn't have kept it up. That had a great deal to do with it. But you would have thought, putting it at its lowest, curiosity couldn't have kept my fox-terrier nose away . . .

Je ne parle pas français. That was her swan-song for me.

But how she makes me break my rule. Oh, you've seen for yourself, but I could give you countless examples.

. . . Evenings, when I sit in some gloomy café, and an automatic piano starts playing a 'mouse' tune (there are dozens of tunes that evoke just her), I begin to dream things like . . .

A little house on the edge of the sea, somewhere far, far away. A girl outside in a frock rather like Red Indian women wear, hailing a light, barefoot boy who runs up from the beach.

'What have you got?'

'A fish,' I smile and give it to her.

. . . The same girl, the same boy, different costumes—sitting at an open window, eating fruit and leaning out and laughing.

'All the wild strawberries are for you, Mouse. I won't touch one.'

. . . A wet night. They are going home together under an umbrella. They stop on the door to press their wet cheeks together.

And so on and so on until some dirty old gallant comes up to my table and sits opposite and begins to grimace and yap. Until I hear myself saying: 'But I've got the little girl for you, *mon vieux*. So little . . . so tiny.' I kiss the tips of my fingers and lay them upon my heart. 'I give you my word of honour as a gentleman, a writer, serious, young, and extremely interested in modern English literature.'

I must go. I must go. I reach down my coat and hat. Madame knows me. 'You haven't dined yet?' she smiles.

'No, not yet, Madame.'

(1919)

❖ GUY DE MAUPASSANT
Love's Awakening

Guy de Maupassant (1850–1893) was born in the province of Normandy, France, and was educated by his mother and then in a seminary. He disliked his legal studies in Rouen and enlisted in the Franco-Prussian War of 1870–1871. Thereafter he worked for the government as a clerk. He came to associate with such famous writers as Edmond Goncourt, Emile Zola, Gustave Flaubert, and Alphonse Daudet. Catching the public eye with his first story "Ball of Fat," published in an anthology edited by Zola (1880), he produced an astonishing corpus of fiction in the thirteen years up to his death. Among his novels are *A Life* (1883), *Bel-Ami* (1885), *Mont-Oriol* (1887), *Pierre and Jean* (1988), *Stronger Than Death* (1889), and *Our Heart* (1890). But of more significance are over three hundred short stories, which can be found in the collections *Madame Tellier's Establishment* (1881), *Mademoiselle Fifi* (1882), *Tales and Novelettes* (1885), *Monsieur Parent* (1885), *Tales of Day and Night* (1885), *Madame Husson's Rosebush* (1888), and *Useless Beauty* (1890). *The Complete Short Stories of De Maupassant* was published in English in 1947. Though sometimes accused of cynicism, Maupassant could be better described as morally neutral. He presented life as he saw it, neither condemning evil nor praising good. He suffered an attack of insanity and died in an asylum at the age of forty-three.

No one was surprised at the marriage of Mr. Simon Lebrument and Miss Jeanne Cordier. Mr. Lebrument came to buy out the office of Mr. Papillon; he needed, it was understood, money with which to pay for it; and Miss Jeanne Cordier had three hundred thousand francs clear, in stocks and bonds.

Mr. Lebrument was a handsome bachelor, who had style, the style of a notary, a provincial style, but, after all, some style, which was a rare thing at Boutigny-le-Rebours.

Miss Cordier had grace and freshness, grace a little awkward and freshness a little mixed up; but she was nevertheless, a pretty girl, desirable and entertaining.

The wedding ceremonies turned Boutigny topsy-turvy. The married couple was much admired when they returned to the conjugal domicile to conceal their happiness, having resolved to make a little, simple journey to Paris, after they had spent a few days together.

It was charming, these few days together, as Mr. Lebrument knew how to manage his early relations with his wife with a delicacy, a directness, and sense of fitness that was remarkable. He took for his motto: "Everything comes to him who waits." He knew how to be patient and energetic at the same time. His success was rapid and complete.

At the end of four days Mrs. Lebrument adored her husband. She could not bear to be a moment away from him. He must be near her all day long, that she might caress his hands, his beard, his nose, etc. She would sit upon his knees and, taking him by the ears, would say: "Open your mouth and shut your eyes." He opened his mouth with confidence, shut his eyes halfway, and then would receive a very long, sweet kiss that made great shivers in his back. And in his turn, he never had enough caresses, enough lips, enough hands, enough of anything with which to enjoy his wife from morning until evening, and from evening until morning.

As soon as the first week had slipped away he said to his young companion:

"If you wish, we might leave for Paris Tuesday of next week. We shall be like lovers who are not married; go about to the theaters, the restaurants, the concert *cafés*, and everywhere, everywhere."

She jumped for joy. "Oh! yes, yes," she replied, "let us go as soon as possible."

"And, as we must not forget anything, you might ask your father to have your dowry ready; I will take it with me, and at the same time pay Mr. Papillon."

She answered: "I will speak to him about it tomorrow morning."

Then he seized her in his arms and began again the little tendernesses she loved so much, and had reveled in now for eight days.

The Tuesday following, the father-in-law and the mother-in-law accompanied their daughter and son-in-law to the station, whence they set out for the capital. The father-in-law remarked:

"I tell you it is imprudent to carry so much money in your pocketbook." And the young notary smiled.

"Do not be disturbed, father-in-law," he answered, "I am accustomed to these things. You know that in my profession it often happens that I have nearly a million about me. By carrying it with me, we escape a lot of formalities and delays, to say the least. Do not give yourself any uneasiness."

Then the trainman cried out, "All aboard!" and they hurried into a compartment where they found themselves with two old ladies.

Lebrument murmured in his wife's ear: "How annoying! Now I cannot smoke."

She answered in a low tone: "I am sorry too, but not on account of your cigar."

The engine puffed and started. The journey lasted an hour, during which they could not say anything of importance, because the two old ladies did not go to sleep.

When they were in the Saint-Lazare station, in Paris, Mr. Lebrument said to his wife:

"If you wish, my dear, we will first go and breakfast on the Boulevard, then return at our leisure to find our trunk and give it to the porter of some hotel."

She consented immediately: "Oh! yes," said she, "let us breakfast in some restaurant. Is it far from here?"

"Yes, rather far, but we will take an omnibus."

She was astonished: "Why not a cab?" she asked.

He groaned as he said smilingly: "And you are economical! A cab for five minutes' ride, at six sous per minute! You do not deprive yourself of anything!"

"That is true," said she, a little confused.

A large omnibus was passing, with three horses at a trot. Lebrument hailed it: "Conductor! Eh, conductor!"

The heavy carriage stopped. The young notary pushed his wife inside, saying hurriedly, in a low voice:

"You get in while I climb up on the outside to smoke at least a cigarette before breakfast."

She had not time for any answer. The conductor, who had seized her by the arm to aid her in mounting the steps, pushed her into the 'bus, where she landed, half-frightened, upon a seat, and in a sort of stupor watched the feet of her husband through the windows at the back, as he climbed to the top of the imperial.

There she remained immovable between a large gentleman who smelled of a pipe and an old woman who smelled of a dog. All the other travelers, in two mute lines — a grocer's boy, a workman, a sergeant of infantry, a gentleman with gold-rimmed spectacles and a silk cap with enormous visors, like gutters, and two ladies with an important, mincing air, which seemed to say: We are here, although we should be in a better place. Then there were two good sisters, a little girl in long hair, and an undertaker.

The assemblage had the appearance of a collection of caricatures in a freak museum, a series of expressions of the human countenance, like a row of grotesque puppets which one knocks down at a fair.

The jolts of the carriage made them toss their heads a little, and as they shook, the flesh of their cheeks trembled; and the disturbance of the rolling wheels gave them an idiotic or sleepy look.

The young woman remained inert: "Why did he not come with me?" she asked herself. A vague sadness oppressed her. He might, indeed, have deprived himself of his cigar!

The good sisters gave the signal to stop. They alighted, one after the other, leaving an odor of old and faded skirts.

Soon after they were gone another stopped the 'bus. A cook came in, red and out of breath. She sat down and placed her basket of provisions upon her knees. A strong odor of dishwater pervaded the omnibus.

"It is further than I thought," said the young woman to herself.

The undertaker got out and was replaced by a coachman who smelled of a stable. The girl in long hair was succeeded by an errand-boy who exhaled the perfume of his walks.

The notary's wife perceived all these things, ill at ease and so disheartened that she was ready to weep without knowing why.

Some others got out, still others came in. The omnibus went on through the interminable streets, stopped at the stations, and began its route again.

"How far it is!" said Jeanne. "Especially when one has nothing for diversion and cannot sleep!" She had not been so much fatigued for many days.

Little by little all the travelers got out. She remained alone, all alone. The conductor shouted:

"Vaugirard!"

As she blushed, he again repeated: "Vaugirard!"

She looked at him, not understanding that this must be addressed to her as all her neighbors had gone. For the third time the man said: "Vaugirard!"

Then she asked: "Where are we?"

He answered in a gruff voice: "We are at Vaugirard, Miss; I've told you twenty times already."

"Is it far from the Boulevard?" she asked.

"What Boulevard?"

"The Italian Boulevard."

"We passed that a long time ago."

"Ah! Will you be kind enough to tell my husband?"

"Your husband? Where is he?"

"On the outside."

"On the outside! It has been a long time since there was anybody there."

She made a terrified gesture. Then she said:

"How can it be? It is not possible. He got up there when I entered the omnibus. Look again; he must be there."

The conductor became rude: "Come, little one, this is talk enough. If there is one man lost, there are ten to be found. Scamper out, now! You will find another in the street."

The tears sprung to her eyes. She insisted: "But, sir, you are mistaken, I assure you that you are mistaken. He had a large pocketbook in his hand."

The employee began to laugh: "A large pocketbook? I remember. Yes, he got out at the Madeleine. That's right! He's left you behind! Ha! ha!"

The carriage was standing still. She got down and looked up, in spite of herself to the roof, with an instinctive movement of the eye. It was totally deserted.

Then she began to weep aloud, without thinking that anyone was looking at or listening to her. Finally she said:

"What is going to become of me?"

The inspector came up and inquired: "What's the matter?"

The conductor answered in a jocose fashion:

"This lady's husband has left her on the way."

The other replied: "Now, now, that is nothing. I am at your service." And he turned on his heels.

Then she began to walk ahead, too much frightened, too much excited to think even where she was going. Where was she going? What should she do? How could such an error have occurred? Such an act of carelessness, of disregard, of unheard-of distraction!

She had two francs in her pocket. To whom could she apply? Suddenly she remembered her cousin Barral, who was a clerk in the office of Naval Affairs.

She had just enough to hire a cab; she would go to him. And she met him just as he was starting for his office. Like Lebrument, he carried a large pocketbook under his arm.

She leaned out of the carriage and called: "Henry!"

He stopped, much surprised.

"Jeanne," said he, "here? — and alone? Where do you come from? What are you doing?"

She stammered, with her eyes full of tears: "My husband is lost somewhere —"

"Lost? where?"

"On the omnibus."

"On the omnibus! Oh!"

And she related to him the whole story, weeping much over the adventure. He listened reflectively, and then asked:

"This morning? And was his head perfectly clear?"

"Oh! yes! And he had my dowry."

"Your dowry? The whole of it?"

"Yes, the whole of it — in order to pay for his office."

"Well, my dear cousin, your husband, whoever he is, is probably watching the wheel — this minute."

She did not yet comprehend. She stammered: "My husband — you say —"

"I say that he has run off with your — your capital — and that's all about it."

She remained standing there, suffocated with grief, murmuring:

"Then he is — he is — is a wretch!"

Then, overcome with emotion, she fell on her cousin's shoulder, sobbing violently.

As people were stopping to look at them, he guided her gently into the entrance of his house, supporting her body. They mounted the steps, and as the maid came to open the door he ordered her:

"Sophie, run to the restaurant and bring breakfast for two persons. I shall not go to the office this morning."

                                                                    (1884)

Pictures of the Ice

Alice Munro (1931–) was born Alice Eric in Wingham, Ontario, Canada. She attended the University of Western Ontario from 1949 to 1951. Munro has not been attracted to the novel but to the short story, which, she feels, imparts "intense, but not connected, moments of experience." Most of her fiction concerns the lower classes living in the towns and farms of Western Ontario, an area which critics have begun to call "Alice Munro country." Her short stories are collected in *Lives of Girls and Women* (1972), *The Dance of the Happy Shades* (1973), *Something I've Been Meaning to Tell You* (1974), *The Beggar Maid: Stories of Flo and Rose* (1978), *The Moons of Jupiter* (1982), *The Progress of Love* (1986), and *Friend of My Youth* (1990, which contains "Pictures of the Ice").

Three weeks before he died — drowned in a boating accident in a lake whose name nobody had heard him mention — Austin Cobbett stood deep in the clasp of a three-way mirror in Crawford's Men's Wear, in Logan, looking at himself in a burgundy sports shirt and a pair of cream, brown, and burgundy plaid pants. Both permanent press.

"Listen to me," Jerry Crawford said to him. "With the darker shirt and the lighter pants you can't go wrong. It's youthful."

Austin cackled. "Did you ever hear that expression 'mutton dressed as lamb'?"

"Referred to ladies," Jerry said. "Anyway, it's all changed now. There's no old men's clothes, no old ladies' clothes anymore. Style applies to everybody."

When Austin got used to what he had on, Jerry was going to talk him into a neck scarf of complementary colors and a cream pullover. Austin needed all the cover-up he could get. Since his wife died, about a year ago, and they finally got a new minister at the United Church (Austin, who was over seventy, was officially retired but had been hanging on and filling in while they haggled over hiring a new man and what they would pay him), he had lost weight, his muscles had shrunk, he was getting the potbellied caved-in shape of an old man. His neck was corded and his nose lengthened and his cheeks drooping. He was a stringy old rooster — stringy but tough, and game enough to gear up for a second marriage.

"The pants are going to have to be taken in," Jerry said. "You can give us time for that, can't you? When's the happy happy day?"

Austin was going to be married in Hawaii, where his wife, his wife-to-be, lived. He named a date a couple of weeks ahead.

Phil Stadelman from the Toronto Dominion Bank came in then and did not recognize Austin from the back, though Austin was his own former minister. He'd never seen him in clothes like that.

518

Phil told his AIDS joke—Jerry couldn't stop him.

Why did the Newfie put condoms on his ears?

Because he didn't want to get hearing aids.

Then Austin turned around, and instead of saying, "Well, I don't know about you fellows, but I find it hard to think of AIDS as a laughing matter," or "I wonder what kind of jokes they tell in Newfoundland about the folks from Huron County," he said, "That's rich." He laughed.

That's rich. Then he asked Phil's opinion of his clothes.

"Do you think they're going to laugh when they see me coming in Hawaii?"

Karin heard about this when she went into the doughnut place to drink a cup of coffee after finishing her afternoon stint as a crossing guard. She sat at the counter and heard the men talking at a table behind her. She swung around on the stool and said, "Listen, I could have told you, he's changed. I see him every day and I could have told you."

Karin is a tall, thin woman with a rough skin and a hoarse voice and long blond hair dark for a couple of inches at the roots. She's letting it grow out dark and it's got to where she could cut it short, but she doesn't. She used to be a lanky blond girl, shy and pretty, riding around on the back of her husband's motorcycle. She has gone a little strange—not too much or she wouldn't be a crossing guard, even with Austin Cobbett's recommendation. She interrupts conversations. She never seems to wear anything but her jeans and an old navy-blue duffel coat. She has a hard and suspicious expression and she has a public grudge against her ex-husband. She will write things on his car, with her finger: *Fake Christian. Kiss arse Phony. Brent Duprey is a snake.* Nobody knows that she wrote *Lazarus Sucks*, because she went back (she does this at night) and rubbed it off with her sleeve. Why? It seemed dangerous, something that might get her into trouble—the trouble being of a vaguely supernatural kind, not a talk with the Chief of Police—and she has nothing against Lazarus in the Bible, only against Lazarus House, which is the place Brent runs, and where he lives now.

Karin lives where she and Brent lived together for the last few months—upstairs over the hardware store, at the back, a big room with an alcove (the baby's) and a kitchen at one end. She spends a lot of her time over at Austin's, cleaning out his house, getting everything ready for his departure to Hawaii. The house he lives in, still, is the old parsonage, on Pondicherry Street. The church has built the new minister a new house, quite nice, with a patio and a double garage—ministers' wives often work now; it's a big help if they can get jobs as nurses or teachers, and in that case you need two cars. The old parsonage is a grayish-white brick house with blue-painted trim on the veranda and the gables. It needs a lot of work. Insulating, sandblasting, new paint, new window frames, new tiles in the bathroom. Walking back to her own place at night, Karin sometimes occupies her mind thinking what she'd do to that place if it was hers and she had the money.

Austin shows her a picture of Sheila Brothers, the woman he is to marry. Actually, it's a picture of the three of them—Austin, his wife, and Sheila Brothers, in front of a log building and some pine trees. A Retreat, where he—they—first met Sheila. Austin has on his minister's black shirt and turned collar; he looks shifty, with his apologetic, ministerial smile. His wife is looking away from him, but the big bow of her flowered scarf flutters against his neck. Fluffy white hair, trim figure. Chic. Sheila Brothers — Mrs. Brothers, a widow — is looking straight ahead, and she is the only one who seems really cheerful. Short fair hair combed around her face in a businesslike way, brown slacks, white sweatshirt, with the fairly large bumps of her breasts and stomach plain to see, she meets the camera head-on and doesn't seem worried about what it will make of her.

"She looks happy," Karin says.

"Well. She didn't know she was going to marry me, at the time."

He shows her a postcard picture of the town where Sheila lives. The town where he will live in Hawaii. Also a photograph of her house. The town's main street has a row of palm trees down the middle, it has low white or pinkish buildings, lampposts with brimming flower baskets, and over all a sky of deep turquoise in which the town's name — a Hawaiian name there is no hope of pronouncing or remembering — is written in flowing letters like silk ribbon. The name floating in the sky looked as possible as anything else about it. As for the house, you could hardly make it out at all — just a bit of balcony among the red and pink and gold flowering trees and bushes. But there was the beach in front of it, the sand pure as cream and the jewel-bright waves breaking. Where Austin Cobbett would walk with friendly Sheila. No wonder he needed all new clothes.

What Austin wants Karin to do is clear everything out. Even his books, his old typewriter, the pictures of his wife and children. His son lives in Denver, his daughter in Montreal. He has written to them, he has talked to them on the phone, he has asked them to claim anything they want. His son wants the diningroom furniture, which a moving-truck will pick up next week. His daughter said she didn't want anything. (Karin think she's apt to reconsider; people always want *something*.) All the furniture, books, pictures, curtains, rugs, dishes, pots, and pans are to go to the Auction Barn. Austin's car will be auctioned as well, and his power mower and the snowblower his son gave him last Christmas. These will be sold after Austin leaves for Hawaii, and the money is to go to Lazarus House. Austin started Lazarus House when he was a minister. Only he didn't call it that; he called it Turnaround House. But now they have decided — Brent Duprey has decided — it would be better to have a name that is more religious, more Christian.

At first Austin was just going to give them all these things to use in or around the House. Then he thought that it would be showing more respect to give them the money, to let them spend it as they liked, buying things they liked, instead of using his wife's dishes and sitting on his wife's chintz sofa.

"What if they take the money and buy lottery tickets with it?" Karin asks him. "Don't you think it'll be a big temptation to them?"

"You don't get anywhere in life without temptations," Austin says, with his maddening little smile. "What if they won the lottery?"

"Brent Duprey is a snake."

Brent has taken over the whole control of Lazarus House, which Austin started. It was a place for people to stay who wanted to stop drinking or some other way of life they were in; now it's a born-again sort of place, with nightlong sessions of praying and singing and groaning and confessing. That's how Brent got hold of it — by becoming more religious than Austin. Austin got Brent to stop drinking; he pulled and pulled on Brent until he pulled him right out of the life he was leading and into a new life of running this House with money from the church, the government, and so on, and he made a big mistake, Austin did, in thinking he could hold Brent there. Brent once started on the holy road went shooting on past; he got past Austin's careful quiet kind of religion in no time and cut Austin out with the people in his own church who wanted a stricter, more ferocious kind of Christianity. Austin was shifted out of Lazarus House and the church at about the same time, and Brent bossed the new minister around without difficulty. And in spite of this, or because of it, Austin wants to give Lazarus House the money.

"Who's to say whether Brent's way isn't closer to God than mine is, after all?" he says.

Karin says just about anything to anybody now. She says to Austin, "Don't make me puke."

Austin says she must be sure to keep a record of her time, so she will be paid for all this work, and also, if there is anything here that she would particularly like, to tell him, so they can discuss it.

"Within reason," he says. "If you said you'd like the car or the snowblower, I guess I'd be obliged to say no, because that would be cheating the folks over at Lazarus House. How about the vacuum cleaner?"

Is that how he sees her — as somebody who's always thinking about cleaning houses? The vacuum cleaner is practically an antique, anyway.

"I bet I know what Brent said when you told him I was going to be in charge of all this," she says. "I bet he said, 'Are you going to get a lawyer to check up on her?' He did! Didn't he?"

Instead of answering that, Austin says, "Why would I trust a lawyer any more than I trust you?"

"Is that what you said to him?"

"I'm saying it to you. You either trust or you don't trust, in my opinion. When you decide you're going to trust, you have to start where you are."

Austin rarely mentions God. Nevertheless you feel the mention of God hovering on the edge of sentences like these, and it makes you so uneasy — Karin gets a crumbly feeling along her spine — that you wish he'd say it and get it over with.

Four years ago Karin and Brent were still married, and they hadn't had the baby yet or moved to their place above the hardware store. They were living in the old slaughterhouse. That was a cheap apartment building belonging to Morris Fordyce, but it really had at one time been a slaughterhouse. In wet weather Karin could smell pig, and always she smelled another smell that she thought was blood. Brent sniffed around the walls and got down and sniffed the floor, but he couldn't smell what she was smelling. How could he smell anything but the clouds of boozy breath that rose from his own gut? Brent was a drunk then, but not a sodden drunk. He played hockey on the O. T. (over thirty, old-timers) hockey team — he was quite a bit older than Karin — and he claimed that he had never played sober. He worked for Fordyce Construction for a while, and then he worked for the town, cutting up trees. He drank on the job when he could, and after work he drank at the Fish and Game Club or at the Green Haven Motel Bar, called the Greasy Heaven. One night he got a bulldozer going, which was sitting outside the Greasy Heaven, and he drove it across town to the Fish and Game Club. Of course he was caught, and charged with impaired driving of a bulldozer, a big joke all over town. Nobody who laughed at the joke came around to pay the fine. And Brent just kept getting wilder. Another night he took down the stairs that led to their apartment. He didn't bash the steps out in a fit of temper; he removed them thoughtfully and methodically, steps and uprights one by one, backing downstairs as he did so and leaving Karin cursing at the top. First she was laughing at him — she had had a few beers herself by that time — then, when she realized he was in earnest, and she was being marooned there, she started cursing. Coward neighbors peeped out of the doors behind him.

Brent came home the next afternoon and was amazed, or pretended to be. "What happened to the *steps?*" he yelled. He stomped around the hall, his lined, exhausted, excited face working, his blue eyes snapping, his smile innocent and conniving. "God damn that Morris! God-damn steps caved in. I'm going to sue the shit out of him. God damn *fuck!*" Karin was upstairs with nothing to eat but half a package of Rice Krispies with no milk, and a can of yellow beans. She had thought of phoning somebody to come with a ladder, but she was too mad and stubborn. If Brent wanted to starve her, she would show him. She would starve.

That time was really the beginning of the end, the change. Brent went around to see Morris Fordyce to beat him up and tell him about how he was going to have the shit sued out of him, and Morris talked to him in a reasonable, sobering way until Brent decided not to sue or beat up Morris but to commit suicide instead. Morris called Austin Cobbett then, because Austin had a reputation for knowing how to deal with people who were in a desperate way. Austin didn't talk Brent out of drinking then, or into the church, but he talked him out of suicide. Then, a couple of years later when the baby died, Austin was the only minister they knew to call. By the time he came to see them, to talk about the funeral, Brent had drunk everything in the house and gone out looking for more. Austin went after him and spent the next five days — with a brief time out for burying the baby — just staying with him on a bender. Then he spent the next week nursing him out of it, and the next month talking to him or sitting with him until Brent decided he would not drink anymore, he had been put in touch with God. Austin said that Brent meant by that that he had been put in touch with the fullness of his own life and the power of his innermost self. Brent said it was not for one minute himself; it was God.

Karin went to Austin's church with Brent for a while; she didn't mind that. She could see, though, that it wasn't going to be enough to hold Brent. She saw him bouncing up to sing the hymns, swinging his arms and clenching his fists, his whole body pried up. It was the same as he was after three or four beers when there was no way he could stop himself going for more. He was bursting. And soon enough he burst out of Austin's hold and took a good part of the church with him. A lot of people had wanted that loosening, more noise and praying and singing and not so much quiet persuading talking; they'd been wanting it for a long while.

None of it surprised her. It didn't surprise her that Brent learned to fill out papers and make the right impression and get government money; that he took over Turnaround House, which Austin had got him into, and kicked Austin out. He'd always been full of possibilities. It didn't really surprise her that he got as mad at her now for drinking one beer and smoking one cigarette as he used to do when she wanted to stop partying and go to bed at two o'clock. He said he was giving her a week to decide. No more drinking, no more smoking, Christ as her Saviour. One week. Karin said don't bother with the week. After Brent was gone, she quit smoking, she almost quit drinking, she also quit going to Austin's church. She gave up on nearly everything but a slow, smoldering grudge against Brent, which grew and grew. One day Austin stopped her on the street and she thought he was going to say some gentle, personal, condemning thing to her, for her grudge or her quitting church, but all he did was ask her to come and help him look after his wife, who was getting home from the hospital that week.

Austin is talking on the phone to his daughter in Montreal. Her name is Megan. She is around thirty, unmarried, a television producer.

"Life has a lot of surprises up its sleeve," Austin says. "You know this has nothing to do with your mother. This is a new life entirely. But I regret . . . No, no. I just mean there's more than one way to love God, and taking pleasure in the world is surely one of them. That's a revelation that's come on me rather late. Too late to be of any use to your mother. . . . No. Guilt is a sin and a seduction. I've said that to many a poor soul that liked to wallow in it. Regret's another matter. How could you get through a long life and escape it?"

I was right, Karin is thinking; Megan does want something. But after a little more talk — Austin says that he might take up golf, don't laugh, and that Sheila belongs to a play-reading club, he expects he'll be a star at that, after all his pulpit haranguing — the conversation comes to an end. Austin comes out to the kitchen — the phone is in the front hall; this is an old-fashioned house — and looks up at Karin, who is cleaning out the high cupboards.

"Parents and children, Karin," he says, sighing, sighing, looking humorous. "Oh, what a tangled web we weave, when first we — have children. Then they always want us to be the same, they want us to be parents — it shakes them up dreadfully if we should do anything they didn't think we'd do. Dreadfully."

"I guess she'll get used to it," Karin says, without much sympathy.

"Oh, she will, she will. Poor Megan."

Then he says he's going uptown to have his hair cut. He doesn't want to leave it any longer, because he always looks and feels so foolish with a fresh haircut. His mouth turns down as he smiles — first up, then down. That downward slide is what's noticeable on him everywhere — face slipping down into neck wattles, chest emptied out and mounded into that abrupt, queer little belly. The flow has left dry channels, deep lines. Yet Austin speaks — it's his perversity to speak — as if out of a body that is light and ready and a pleasure to carry around.

In a short time the phone rings again and Karin has to climb down and answer it.

"Karin? Is that you, Karin? It's Megan!"

"Your father's just gone up to get a haircut."

"Good. Good. I'm glad. It gives me a chance to talk to you. I've been hoping I'd get a chance to talk to you."

"Oh," says Karin.

"Karin. Now, listen. I know I'm behaving just the way adult children are supposed to behave in this situation. I don't like it. I don't like that in myself. But I can't help it. I'm suspicious. I wonder what's going on. Is he all right? What do you think of it? What do you think of this woman he's going to marry?"

"All I ever saw of her is her picture," Karin says.

"I am terribly busy right now and I can't just drop everything and come home and have a real heart-to-heart with him. Anyway, he's very difficult to talk to. He makes all the right noises, he seems so open, but in reality he's very closed. He's never been at all a personal kind of person, do you know what I mean? He's never done anything before for a *personal* kind of reason. He always did things *for* somebody. He always liked to find people who *needed* things done for them, a lot. Well, you know that. Even bringing you into the house, you know, to look after Mother — it wasn't exactly for Mother's sake or his sake he did that."

Karin can picture Megan — the long, dark, smooth hair, parted in the middle and combed over her shoulders, the heavily made-up eyes and tanned skin and pale-pink lipsticked mouth, the handsomely clothed plump body. Wouldn't her voice bring such looks to mind even if you'd never seen her? Such smoothness, such rich sincerity. A fine gloss on every word and little appreciative spaces in between. She talks as if listening to herself. A little too much that way, really. Could she be drunk?

"Let's face it, Karin. Mother was a snob." (Yes, she is drunk.) "Well, she had to have something. Dragged around from one dump to another, always doing good. Doing good wasn't her thing at all. So now, *now*, he gives it all up, he's off to the easy life. In Hawaii! Isn't it bizarre?"

"Bizarre." Karin has heard that word on television and heard people, mostly teen-agers, say it, and she knows it is not the church bazaar Megan's talking about. Nevertheless that's what the word makes her think of — the church bazaars that Megan's mother used to organize, always trying to give them some style and make things different. Striped umbrellas and a sidewalk café one year, Devonshire teas and a rose arbor the next. Then she thinks of Megan's mother on the chintz-covered sofa in the living room, weak and yellow after her chemotherapy, one of those padded, perky kerchiefs around her nearly bald head. Still, she could look up at Karin with a faint, formal surprise when Karin came into the room. "Was there something you wanted, Karin?" The thing that Karin was supposed to ask her, she would ask Karin.

Bizarre. Bazaar. Snob. When Megan got in that dig, Karin should have said, at least, "I know that." All she can think to say is "Megan. This is costing you money."

"Money, Karin! We're talking about my *father*. We're talking about whether my father is sane or whether he has flipped his *wig*, Karin!"

A day later a call from Denver. Don, Austin's son, is calling to tell his father that they better forget about the dining-room furniture, the cost of shipping it is too high. Austin agrees with him. The money could be better spent, he says. What's furniture? Then Austin is called upon to explain about the Auction Barn and what Karin is doing.

"Of course, of course, no trouble," Austin says. "They'll list everything they get and what it sold for. They can easily send a copy. They've got a computer, I understand. No longer the Dark Ages up here. . . .

"Yes," Austin says. "I hoped you'd see it that way about the money. It's a project close to my heart. And you and your sister are providing well for yourselves. I'm very fortunate in my children. . . .

"The Old Age Pension and my minister's pension," he says. "Whatever more could I want? And this lady, this lady, I can tell you, Sheila—she is not short of money, if I can put it that way. . . . " He laughs rather mischievously at something his son says.

After he hangs up, he says to Karin, "Well, my son is worried about my finances and my daughter is worried about my mental state. My mental-emotional state. The male and female way of looking at things. The male and female way of expressing their anxiety. Underneath it's the same thing. The old order changeth, yielding place to new."

Don wouldn't remember everything that was in the house, anyway. How could he? He was here the day of the funeral and his wife wasn't with him; she was too pregnant to come. He wouldn't have her to rely on. Men don't remember that sort of thing well. He just asked for the list so that it would look as if he were keeping track of everything and nobody'd better try to hoodwink him. Or hoodwink his father.

There were things Karin was going to get, and nobody need know where she had got them. Nobody came up to her place. A willow-pattern plate. The blue-and-gray flowered curtains. A little, fat jug of ruby-colored glass with a silver lid. A white damask cloth, a tablecloth, that she had ironed till it shone like a frosted snowfield, and the enormous napkins that went with it. The tablecloth alone weighed as much as a child, and the napkins would flop out of wineglasses like lilies—if you had wineglasses. Just as a start, she has already taken home six silver spoons in her coat pocket. She knows enough not to disturb the silver tea service or the good dishes. But some pink glass dishes for dessert, with long stems, have taken her eye. She can see her place transformed, with these things in it. More than that, she can feel the quiet and content they would extend to her. Sitting in a room so furnished, she wouldn't need to go out. She would never need to think of Brent, and ways to torment him. A person sitting in such a room could turn and floor anybody trying to intrude.

Was there something you wanted?

On Monday of Austin's last week—he was supposed to fly to Hawaii on Saturday—the first big storm of the winter began. The wind came in from the west, over the lake; there was driving snow all day and night. Monday and Tuesday the schools were closed, so Karin didn't have to work as a guard. But she couldn't stand staying indoors; she put on her duffel coat and wrapped her head and half her face in a wool scarf and plowed through the snow-filled streets to the parsonage.

The house is cold, the wind is coming in around the doors and windows. In the kitchen cupboard along the west wall, the dishes feel like ice. Austin is dressed but lying down on the living-room sofa, wrapped in various quilts and blankets. He is not reading or watching television or dozing, as far as she can tell—just staring. She makes him a cup of instant coffee.

"Do you think this'll stop by Saturday?" she says. She has the feeling that if he doesn't go Saturday, he just may not go at all. The whole thing could be called off, all plans could falter.

"It'll stop in due time," he says. "I'm not worried."

Karin's baby died in a snowstorm. In the afternoon, when Brent was drinking with his friend Rob and watching television, Karin said that the baby was sick and she needed money for a taxi to take him to the hospital. Brent told her to fuck off. He thought she was just trying to bother him. And partly she was—the baby had just thrown up once, and whimpered, and he didn't seem very hot. Then about suppertime, with Rob gone, Brent went to pick up the baby and play with him, forgetting that he was sick. "This baby's like a hot coal!" he yelled at Karin, and wanted to know why she hadn't got the doctor, why she hadn't taken the baby to the hospital. "You tell me why," said Karin, and they started to fight. "You said he didn't need to go," said Karin. "O.K., so he doesn't need to go." Brent called the taxi company, and the taxis weren't going out because of the storm, which up to then neither he nor Karin had noticed. He called the hospital and asked them what to do, and they said to get the fever down by wrapping the baby in wet towels. So they did that, and by midnight the storm had quieted down and the snowplows were out on the streets and they got the baby to the hospital. But he died. He probably would have died no matter what they'd done; he had meningitis. Even if he'd been a fussed-over precious little baby in a home where the father didn't get drunk and the mother and father didn't have fights, he might have died; he probably would have died, anyway.

Brent wanted it to be his fault, though. Sometimes he wanted it to be their fault. It was like sucking candy to him, that confession. Karin told him to shut up, she told him to *shut up*.

She said, "He would have died anyway."

When the storm is over, Tuesday afternoon, Karin puts on her coat and goes out and shovels the parsonage walk. The temperature seems to be dropping even lower; the sky is clear. Austin says they're going to go down to the lake to look at the ice. If there is a big storm like this fairly early in the year, the wind drives the waves up on the shore and they freeze there. Ice is everywhere, in unlikely formations. People go down and take pictures. The paper often prints the best of them. Austin wants to take some pictures, too. He says it'll be something to show people in Hawaii. So Karin shovels the car out, too, and off they go, Austin driving with great care. And nobody else is down there. It's too cold. Austin hangs on to Karin as they struggle along the boardwalk—or where the boardwalk must be, under the snow. Sheets of ice drop from the burdened branches of the willow trees to the ground, and the sun shines through them from the west; they're like walls of pearl. Ice is woven through the wire of the high fence to make it like a honeycomb. Waves have frozen as they hit the shore, making mounds and caves, a crazy landscape, out to the rim of the open water. And all the playground equipment, the children's swings and climbing bars, has been transformed by ice, hung with organ pipes or buried in what looks like half-carved statues, shapes of ice that might be people, animals, angels, monsters, left unfinished.

Karin is nervous when Austin stands alone to take pictures. He seems shaky to her—and what if he fell? He could break a leg, a hip. Old people break a hip and that's the end of them. Even taking off his gloves to work the camera seems risky. A frozen thumb might be enough to keep him here, make him miss his plane.

Back in the car, he does have to rub and blow on his hands. He lets her drive. If something dire happened to him, would Sheila Brothers come here, take over his care, settle into the parsonage, countermand his orders?

"This is strange weather," he says. "Up in northern Ontario it's balmy, even the little lakes are open, temperatures above freezing. And here we are in the grip of the ice and the wind straight off the Great Plains."

"It'll be all the same to you when you get to Hawaii," Karin says firmly. "Northern Ontario or the Great Plains or here, you'll be glad to be out of it. Doesn't she ever call you?"

"Who?" says Austin.

"*Her*. Mrs. Brothers."

"Oh, Sheila. She calls me late at night. The time's so much earlier, in Hawaii."

The phone rings with Karin alone in the house the morning before Austin is to leave. A man's voice, uncertain and sullen-sounding.

"He isn't here right now," Karin says. Austin has gone to the bank. "I could get him to call you when he comes in."

"Well, it's long distance," the man says. "It's Shaft Lake."

"Shaft Lake," repeats Karin, feeling around on the phone shelf for a pencil.

"We were just wondering. Like we were just checking. That we got the right time that he gets in. Somebody's got to drive down and meet him. So he gets in to Thunder Bay at three o'clock, is that right?"

Karin has stopped looking for a pencil. She finally says, "I guess that's right. As far as I know. If you called back around noon, he'd be here."

"I don't know for sure I can get to a phone around noon. I'm at the hotel here but then I got to go someplace else. I'd just as soon leave him the message. Somebody's going to meet him at the airport in Thunder Bay three o'clock tomorrow. O.K.?"

"O.K.," says Karin.

"You could tell him we got him a place to live, too."

"Oh. O.K."

"It's a trailer. He said he wouldn't mind living in a trailer. See, we haven't had any minister here in a long time."

"Oh," says Karin. "O.K. Yes. I'll tell him."

As soon as she has hung up, she finds Megan's number on the list above the phone, and dials it. It rings three or four times and then Megan's voice comes on, sounding brisker than the last time Karin heard it. Brisk but teasing.

"The lady of the house regrets that she cannot take your call at the moment, but if you would leave your name, message, and phone number she will try to get back to you as soon as possible."

Karin has already started to say she is sorry, but this is important, when she is interrupted by a beep, and realizes it's one of those machines. She starts again, speaking quickly but distinctly after a deep breath.

"I just wanted to tell you. I just wanted you to know. Your father is fine. He is in good health, and mentally he is fine and everything. So you don't have to worry. He is off to Hawaii tomorrow. I was just thinking about—I was just thinking about our conversation on the phone. So I thought I'd tell you, not to worry. This is Karin speaking."

And she just gets all that said in time, when she hears Austin at the door. Before he can ask or wonder what she's doing there in the hall, she fires a series of questions at him. Did he get to the bank? Did the cold make his chest hurt? When was it the Auction Barn truck was coming? When did the people from the Board want the parsonage keys? Was he going to phone Don and Megan before he left or after he got there, or what?

Yes. No. Monday for the truck. Tuesday for the keys, but no rush — if she wasn't finished, then Wednesday would be O.K. No more phone calls. He and his children have said all they need to say to each other. Once he's there, he will write them a letter. Write each of them a letter.

"After you're married?"

Yes. Well. Maybe sooner than that.

He has laid his coat across the bannister railing. Then she sees him put out a hand to steady himself, holding on to the railing. He pretends to be fiddling around with his coat.

"You O.K.?" she says. "You want a cup of coffee?"

For a moment he doesn't say anything. His eyes swim past her. How can anybody believe that this tottery old man, whose body looks to be shrivelling day by day, is on his way to marry a comforting widow and spend his days from now on walking on a sunny beach? It isn't in him to do such a thing, ever. He means to wear himself out, quick, quick, on people as thankless as possible, thankless as Brent. Meanwhile fooling all of them into thinking he's changed his spots. Otherwise, somebody might stop him going. Slipping out from under, fooling them, enjoying it.

But he really is after something in the coat. He brings out a pint of whiskey.

"Put a little of that in a glass for me," he says. "Never mind the coffee. Just a precaution. Against weakness. From the cold."

He is sitting on the steps when she brings him the whiskey. He drinks it shakily. He wags his head back and forth, as if trying to get it clear. He stands up. "Much better," he says. "Oh, very much better. Now, about those pictures of the ice, Karin. I was wondering, could you pick them up next week? If I left you the money? They're not ready yet."

Even though he's just in from the cold, he's white. Put a candle behind his face, it'd shine through as if he were wax or thin china.

"You'll have to leave me your address," she says. "Where to send them."

"Just hang on to them till I write you. That'd be best." So she has ended up with a whole roll of pictures of the ice, along with all those other things that she had her mind set on. The pictures show the sky bluer than it ever was, but the weaving in the fence, the shape of the organ pipes are not so plain to see. There needs to be a human figure, too, to show the size that things were. She should have taken the camera and captured Austin — who has vanished. He has vanished as completely as the ice, unless the body washes up in the spring. A thaw, a drowning, and they both disappear. Karin looks at these pictures of the pale, lumpy ice monstrosities, these pictures Austin took, so often that she gets the feeling that he is in them, after all. He's a blank in them, but bright.

She thinks now that he knew. Right at the last he knew that she'd caught on to him, she understood what he was up to. No matter how alone you are, and how tricky and determined, don't you need one person to know? She could be the one for him. Each of them knew what the other was up to, and didn't let on, and that was a link beyond the usual. Every time she thinks of it, she feels approved of—a most unexpected thing.

She puts one of the pictures in an envelope, and sends it to Megan. (She tore the list of addresses and phone numbers off the wall, just in case.) She sends another to Don. And another, stamped and addressed, across town, to Brent. She doesn't write anything on the pictures or enclose any note. She won't be bothering any of these people again. The fact is, it won't be long till she'll be leaving here.

She just wants to make them wonder.

(1990)

❖ EDNA O'BRIEN
The Favorite

Edna O'Brien (1936–) was born in Tuangraney, Ireland. Her education was at the Pharmaceutical College of Ireland, but she began to write professionally at a very young age. Her fiction is typically concerned with the repression of women. Many of her heroines have to cope with an inadequate male partner. Some critics have accused O'Brien of being defeatist about women's prospects, but others praise her realism and find in her work an implicit message that women must fight harder for their private and public rights. Her novels include *The Country Girls* (1960), *The Lonely Girl* (1962), *Girls in Their Married Bliss* (1964), *August Is a Wicked Month* (1965), *Casualties of Peace* (1966), *Zee and Company* (1970, which she also adapted into a screenplay), *Night* (1973), *Johnny I Hardly Knew You* (1977), *The High Road* (1988). Her short story anthologies include *The Love Object* (1968), *A Scandalous Woman* (1974), *Mrs. Reinhardt* (1978), *Seven Novels and Other Short Stories* (1978), *A Rose in the Heart* (1979), *A Fanatic Heart: Selected Short Stories of Edna O'Brien* (1984), and *Lantern Slides* (1990). She has written stage plays—*A Cheap Bunch of Nice Flowers* (1963), *A Pagan Place* (1973), *Virginia* (1981) —and screenplays—*The Girl with the Green Eyes* (1964), *Three into Two Won't Go* (1969)—as well as plays for television. Her nonfiction includes biography—*James and Nora: Portrait of Joyce's Marriage* (1981)—and travel sketches—*Mother Ireland* (1976), *Arabian Days* (1977).

She was the third child and in all sorts of ways lucky. For one thing, she was born on the Sabbath day, and consequently was reputed to be fair and wise and good and gay. They were able to tell her in later life that she was a model little baby, had no faults, had contracted no fevers except such harmless things as measles and mumps. The first time she went to be vaccinated the doctor was over in the swamp delivering a baby from a tinker woman in her late fifties; and the second time the doctor was inebriated, sitting in his basket chair saying things were bad, odious bad, because he had just been disappointed in a promotion that he was expecting. Instead he gave her a little gift, an egg under a green wire mesh, which when squeezed revealed a small canary-colored chick. She played and played with it. She kept it at night in a nest made of chaff from the bottom layer of a box of chocolates. When they gave her turpentine for the tapeworms it was not like medicine at all but on a loaf of sugar like a treat, and having sucked the ugly taste away she used to let the little cube dissolve in her mouth, and savor it, slowly, slowly. The first day she was put on a bicycle, she managed to stay up, to steer it down the length of the flag and around the corner, and only then did she jump off and let the bicycle tumble into the privet hedge, but by then they were clapping and saying bravo, bravo.

At school she did not distinguish herself, was not over-brainy like her elder sister or fanciful like her younger sister, always came in the middle a few marks above a pass. But at the cookery class she shone. She was given charge of the fire, so that she was the first to taste a little of the boxty, or a little of the bubbling jam from the tart, or some of the steamed pudding, or whatever. She had a pink bicycle, named after a witch, by the time she was ten, and soon after a blue basket for it, and later a crocheted cover for the saddle. People gave her things — her father gave her a foal so that she had a little investment while still in her puberty. If a neighbor wanted eggs, or cooking apples, or pears for bottling, they would ask her, rather than one of her sisters, and she would convey the message to her mother and deliver these things, and receive a little money or a little gift as a reward. Then she never went out without bringing something back, a small packet of biscuits, two or three mushrooms, an item of news, something. Her pet name was Whitey, because of her blonde hair, and whenever her father came in from the fields and while he would still be taking off his boots, he would say "Where's Whitey?" And then upon seeing her, because she often hid behind the scullery door, sheltering behind an old trench coat or ducked down behind one of the sacks of flour, he would spot her and say "There's my girl"; and oftener than not tell her how her foal was doing. Her rosary beads, white mother-of-pearl, had been blessed at Lourdes, and she had a special little filigree box to hold them in. Watching her pray in chapel, watching the beads slip slowly through her fingers, the dressmaker noted that they were a perfect match and a complement to her pearled teeth. If the umbrella happened to turn inside out Tess knew exactly what to do to get it right again and her mother had no qualms about lending her the one brown umbrella with the Lalique handle.

The day she went away to school everyone cried, her mother broke down and, quoting from a prayer, said life truly was a vale of tears. She had oodles of presents — silk hankies, georgette hankies, lawn hankies, hanky sachets, bottles of perfume, perfume sprays, scented stationery — more than she could fit. She hid them, or rather she placed them in the wooden cupboard where her summer clothes and her various toilet articles were neatly placed, and no one was allowed to touch them until she came back for her hols. Soon the cupboard developed a beautiful smell from stationery, the opened tin of talc, and the perfume spray into which a drop of hair oil had been put in order to try its puffing powers. Her autograph book was there too and was full of loving inscriptions to her and promises of friendship for life. Except for the one wicked inscription —

> Thirty two degrees is freezing point,
> What's squeezing point? Anon.

The convent was forty miles from home, in the western part of Connaught, and there was no bus service to it. She excelled herself there, was diligent, devout, the last to leave the chapel, and in no time at all tipped by the elder girls as future prefect. No dandruff on the collar of her coat, no monkeying about with nail varnish, no muck on her shoes. After their daily walk she made a point of using the foot-scraper, and as the head nun said was an example to all the Bolshies. She was one of the few girls who, when she tied her hair back with a velvet ribbon, was not asked to remove it or did not have it confiscated. She had two best friends who vied agonizingly for her love, and then two or three stooges — youngsters whom she took under her wing and who did things for her: shined her shoes, dressed her bed, put a fresh supply of water in the ewer every evening, and left little love letters under her pillow. The two girls who loved her could not do enough for her, and there wasn't a day that she didn't receive an illicit bar of chocolate or a slice of cake, and to her delight the skeleton of a leaf, which was like a beautiful gauze brooch, and which she cherished.

During the Christmas holidays, togged out as she was in a new blue suit and blue suede court shoes, she acquired her first boyfriend, an owner of a mill, a dark-haired handsome athlete, and a great catch. In fact she stole him from a namesake of hers, at a dance, and as a result she got called "Pinch me." She no longer liked the name Whitey — it was babyish. She wore her hair in very tight curls, oodles of curls, and with her court shoes wore nutmeg-colored stockings. His gift to her was a pair of fur-backed gauntlet gloves, and they arrived by post in a very long box that looked as if it might have contained a big fish. The family grouped around while she opened the parcel and then the exclamations were myriad. Along with being fur-backed they were lined with fur, of gray-and-white squirrel, fur that was soft as a little puppy, while the gloves themselves were long and sleek and were laid out of the tissue paper for all to see, but none to touch. The workman marveled at them and wondered what their raw materials were, what animals. She wore them when she went for her evening fashion parade. She set out for her walk always while it was still light, because in that way she was able to elicit the admiration of friends and neighbors. The routine was that she visited various houses, was treated to tea and cake, then later to ciderette, and so numerous were the calls she had to make that often she would not get back till midnight and then would have to be escorted by one or other of the ladies of the house. On those midnight walks their accents grew very grand and their plans very lyrical as they discussed men and trousseaux and holidays abroad. There was a certain gloom in the house during her absence, and the moment they heard the latch being lifted, the family jumped up and were jostling each other to greet her and to hear the news. She was the first to tell them of the plans for a new cinema-*cum*-dance hall, and of a rumor that the doctor was going blind and had seen stars in the dispensary, earth stars as opposed to sky stars. When her romance ended — the athlete went back to his former love — she thought of returning the gloves, but decided against it, and realized anyhow that he had gone back to the other girl simply because he had been threatened with a breach of promise. Asked about it she used to say "Poor Tom" and no more, so that she could not even be accused of having a sharp tongue.

On her eighteenth birthday she received a beautiful ring from her mother. The base was white gold, the mount a black enamel paste with a little diamond in the center. It had been her mother's single treasure, an heirloom that had been removed solemnly from the dead finger of a deceased aunt in Chicago. She was said to resemble this aunt in her beauty, in her gaiety, what with her high cheekbones, her blonde tresses, and her gauntness. The aunt had in fact taken strychnine, and had poisoned herself, because of a broken heart, the result of a wronged love affair with a Swede. Whenever strychnine was brought into the house they would look at it, mesmerized by its blue-white flakiness, thinking of their aunt, its potency, and the mystery of her being dead. But her sisters were much more intrigued by such morbidities than she was.

After the spell in the convent Tess went directly to the City of Dublin and commenced on a secretarial course. At first she lived in a hostel, loved taking walks at night, going window-shopping, loved the new machine she was learning to type on, and was told by the teacher that she would have made a good pianist. Soon she passed the necessary examinations, applied for various posts, and became secretary to a most important man in an overseas company. With her first wages she bought a tablecloth for her mother and sent it by registered post. Her bicycle was sent to her by train, and in the office where she worked the other girls used to beg her to let them take a spin around the enclosure at their lunch break.

There was a pool of girls, about thirty in all, and then some men who held slightly higher positions. Tess was the darling of them all. In the summer months they would fetch her bunches of roses, or bunches of lilac, or bunches of Canterbury bells, and very often a little punnet of strawberries or currants from their gardens. Many of them lived on the outskirts of the city, and along with being given treats Tess used to be invited out on Sundays.

She would go to Dollymount and walk barefoot over the silver sands and see the sea in all its splendor; she would go to Howth Head and see the sea from an opposite direction and count the buoys in the ocean. She would go to Killiney and be told it was a Little Naples. She would go out as far as Glendalough and hear the story of St. Kevin tempted as he was by a voluptuous woman, and hear of his restraint. She would partake of boiled mutton for lunch, queen cakes for tea, and late on Sunday evenings she would be found coming home on the last train, her body jogging with it, tired but contented like most of the other passengers.

It was on one of these journeys that she met Luke, and the very approach was like everything else that fitted into her charmed life. He was a commentator on a train, an especially exciting train, comprising a journey in which visitors were told about the beauty spots, the historical significance of places, and the numerous legends attached to each hill and each dale. He listened to her talk to an old woman who was sitting opposite. The talk centered on begonias, because the woman was carrying a big bunch of them and they were a very dark, arresting shade of red. They were as deep as if made of some sumptuous cloth. When the woman alighted and he closed the door, he asked most politely if he could have a word with Tess. Could he make a recording of her voice, since it was like a lark, and would be a wonderful addition to his train entertainment? As a reward she would be given a day trip to Killarney, be treated to a four-course lunch on board, and be able to see those famous lakes and the granite mountains. He walked her home to her digs, stood outside with her under the big linden tree, and said the usual charming things, how that she was sparkling, that she was a rose, that together they would go to Howth Head, together they would go to Dollymount and run over the sands, together at night they would go on that corkscrew road and look down at all the little twinkling lights that constituted the enviable residences of Little Naples. He got to know the things she liked—coconut creams, ham paste, and gin and lime. He would devise little picnics for her, bringing small jars of paste, biscuits sandwiched together, and the gin and lime in a washed-out blue magnesia bottle. When it transpired that he was a married man, she ended it as neatly as it had begun, and the only sign that her flatmates saw was that she took no supper and spent one whole day and one whole night in bed, eyes shut but not asleep. Her younger sister, who shared the bed with her, kept wanting to say consoling things, but was afraid to intrude, and the following morning when Tess was dressing herself she announced that from then on she intended to go without sugar and sweet things.

When she met the young country excise officer she saw at once that they were made for one another. They exchanged a few remarks about songs, their hobbies, and the parts of Dublin they liked the best. Her father was raging. He forbade it. He kicked her in the backside and told her he would not hear of it. Her father said there wasn't a man in the thirty-two counties of Ireland worthy of her and she said "Yes, Dad," but still went off in the evenings to meet the man with the curly black hair. She used to wait at the entrance to the pitch where he and the lads played football. Afterwards he'd walk towards her and they'd link and go off, apparently mindless of the whistles and insinuations that were thrown at them. They were in complete contrast, with her blonde hair and his black, but they walked as if they were one. As time went by, her father was asking the young man for tips for the horses, then for secret information as to the amount people received for their pensions, and then a request if perhaps the government could be cajoled into giving him a loan to buy fertilizer for his land. The young man did everything he could to help, and was really instated into the family when he helped to save hay in all his spare hours.

They were engaged within a month, and Tess changed the black enamel ring to the third finger of her right hand. Her engagement ring was a blue sapphire and there was much conjecture about its price.

For the wedding she had a bouquet of lily of the valley, plus a matching cloth tiara, and a dress made of baby-blue tulle. At the breakfast afterwards, during the well-wishing speeches you could hear a pin drop, so awed were the guests. Her former boss said her name may be Tess but his name for her was Sunshine, and her uncle spoke of a little present she had given him while still impecunious and a tot — a brown scapular — which he pulled out from behind his striped shirt and dangled for all to see. Her father said she was one of the more favorite members of the family, causing her sisters to snigger, because she was in fact *the* favorite. She owned two yearlings and her younger sister thought it would be funny if they stalked into the big room, galloping like mad, and made havoc of the dishes and the cut glasses and the big three-tiered cake on its ridiculous frilled stand. Tess herself made a little speech and from the far end of the table a young man began to hum "Lilli Marlene." As she had always predicted, her going-away suit was a sax-blue box jacket and pleated skirt, with a very pale blue blouse that could be tied at the neck with a soft knot. Two of the waitresses, who had got very drunk and had fallen under the table, caught her by the ankle as she went by and mourned over what lay in store for her. Tess laughed it off.

Two of her four births were quite difficult, but her husband was nearby to hold her hand. His cousin, a doctor, did the delivery, the nurses were all pie, and Tess was congratulated upon her real courage. She did not care for breast feeding and her husband fully understood. They had a nurse for the babies, and built on an extra little wing to their house so that the nursery life could be in one place and the grown-up life in another. As well as his earnings her husband had an income from his family, who owned a big sawmill and were said to be rolling in money. He was overgenerous and Tess used to say they'd die paupers.

In the evening, when all his work was done and his bit of gardening completed, he would stretch in front of the fire, give her a beck, say "Come here," and put her sitting in his lap. Then they would admire the wallpaper, or the coal scuttle, or one of the many precious items in the china cabinet that had been wedding presents to her. Eventually he would coax her to get up and make him a sandwich. Her sandwiches were wonderful. If people called unexpectedly she would always disappear into the kitchen and come back with a salver of them. She said it must have been something in her hands, because all she did was use up any bit of cold meat, add a pinch of salt and a tomato or something to moisten it all, and "Bob's your uncle." But she was proud of it, and proud that so many people called, especially new people who had come to take up temporary jobs—doctors curates, bank clerks, and schoolteachers.

Theirs was an old Georgian house at the top of the market town and it was called The Blue Shutters because the previous owners had had jalousies put in. It was a big Georgian house but they got it reasonably because the owners, two spinsters, had taken a shine to her husband and used to tease each other over him and write him little billets-doux. Then Tess had gone to auctions, and was wizard at bidding and getting bargains, so that all the rooms were soon filled with heavy dark-brown mahogany pieces and with overmantels and ornaments and jugs for artificial flowers. The spinsters had sent to France for all the bedroom wallpaper and so it happened that one bedroom seemed prettier than another. The house faced south so they got the best aspect of the sun, and likewise the garden was a model of construction and tillage. Flowers, fruits, and vegetables grew side by side, and the back wall had a series of pear trees grafted along it, so that from her kitchen window as she was peeling or chopping or ironing, Tess could see the blossom, then the fruits forming, then the big dun pears with irregular holes in them where the wasps had been scooping the flesh out. She had a maid to help her and a big tall boy, a bit soft in the head, to dig the garden. They had loganberries, raspberries, various currant bushes; they made jam in the seasons and bottled fruits in the autumn. Her parents came by hired car the first Sunday of every month, and when asked, Tess could honestly say "Can't complain" about any aspect of life.

They threw card parties, for the men, at Christmas, and though she never played Tess went from table to table—they fitted up little card tables—looking at the players' hands and making obscure but meaningful remarks such as "Not bad, Nicko," or "That'll shake 'em." Then, at midnight, she served supper—cold meats, stuffing, sausage rolls, along with pots of tea so as to liven them up. Her father would sing the made-up song about the horse doctor, old and blind, who so loved the cards that he put up his own Arab pony and lost, and had to drag the trap home by the shafts, where his complaining wife, Dilly, met him at the top of the drive. The song brought to mind the old days and all the various card games—the tense situations where men at the very last minute made or lost their all, where tables were turned upside down because of treachery. Tess would then pass tumblers of hot punch around, and in no time they would be clearing the dishes from the arbutus table, in order to start again. Her children would come in, in their pajamas, to say good night, and sometimes would sing a hymn, usually "Silent Night," and might be asked by one of the men if Santa Claus was up the chimney. Then she would dismiss them, stoke up the fire, and sit happily surrounded by all the squabbling men. One of the younger players might say to her husband what a lucky man he was, and Tess would smile, smile, while not appearing to hear. The prizes were white turkeys, which would be hanging by their feet in the pantry, white and fluffy and unblemished except for the spot of blood around the throat where their necks had been wrung, joyously wrung by the idiot. One year her husband won, and Tess did the sporting thing — she raffled all the names, but omitted his.

The card games, the Bishop's visit, and whenever their mammy went away to have a new baby constituted the epochs of the children's lives. They were wild as hares, got lost for hours on end, fell off their bicycles, or were off up the country watching a cow calf or a cat having kittens. They would bring home the kittens in cardboard boxes, and make pets of them, and paint them, and put bows in their hair, and eventually those selfsame kittens would have to be drowned or put in a sack and left in the middle of nowhere. Tess was not an animal-lover. All dogs, and they were all mongrels, were called Biddy, regardless of their sex, and invariably died of the same thing, which was distemper.

There were never less than six or seven at table, sometimes a visiting child, and then again one of theirs would be missing or on vacation. Tess had the habit of calling them by the wrong names, as if all their names were in her head jumbled together and it did not matter too much which was which. She always took an afternoon nap, and then the children would have to go on tiptoe, or go down the garden, or play out in the street, and someone, her favorite son, would be appointed to wake her at four.

He wrote poems for her, and left them on her dressing bureau, and she would show them to visitors and say weren't they "arch." She preferred her sons. She was rarely alone with any of them, because at night they read or did their homework or listened to the gramophone in their various "dens." Naturally she provided birthday parties and as the years went on they received Holy Communion and were confirmed, and the sitting room was full of framed, sometimes colored, photographs of them, to commemorate the occasion. She would take turns as to whom to have a set on, one child or another, sometimes even her husband. Then she would draw attention to what they were wearing and laugh at them and ask them to go and change or to please go and wash. Her word was law.

Her daughters did not resemble her, were not nearly so pretty. Her sons did have her coloring, so it was said. Not one of them was studious. Her daughters, especially her eldest daughter, Nora, got moodier each year, and refused to eat anything except steaks and bananas. Tess said the child's father was to blame. Whenever they went to the city to shop, they quarreled because Nora chose dark, rather forlorn clothes, and Tess would say it was no way for a young person to dress. Nora referred to her mother as The Duchess. It was a joke but not a welcome one.

It seemed no length at all till the eldest was due to go away to school, and Tess was studying prospectuses, buying uniforms, sewing on name-tapes, and packing them off. If a child cried or sniveled, she would say "Tis well for ye." Equally when a tinker, or a horde of tinkers, passed by the door she would say "Sure they're happier than you or I," and close the shutters in the front room to discourage them from rapping on the window, a thing they did when the doorbell was not immediately answered. If they persisted she sent the maid out with coppers and to tell them to scoot. Meanwhile she would have her hands to her ears, saying the noise of the bell was driving her insane. Occasionally she suffered from sinus.

The first little lasting cloud to appear in Tess's life was when she turned forty and began to put on weight. She was soon having to have her dresses out, and took to wearing smocks. Her husband said he had no objection. But had he? One night when he came home she got a distinct smell of cheap carnation scent from his lapel. No, he had not been to the barber's, he had not been anywhere. He couldn't account for it and neither could she. Another occasion he couldn't exactly say what had detained him. She had rung the office, to be told by the new awkward secretary that she was having a whale of a time, and that the boss had gone ages ago and was probably boozing. Yet an hour went by, and he had not appeared. His dinner had dried up and Tess had taken it in and out of the oven various times. He came in with a bit of grass between his teeth, chewing it. The pupils of his eyes were big and jet black.

The cat was out of the bag when, the following Sunday, a girl ran up to him in the church ground and offered him a peppermint sweet. They were two new girls from another area who had come to open a boutique, and were "man mad." They wore red a lot, were conspicuous miles off; and along with being identical in appearance, had the same ingratiating voices. One of them — and she could not tell which — had the gall to ring Tess up and invite her husband to the Mass that they were having offered in their new premises. Tess wrote it down on the "messages" pad and didn't refer to it when he came in. He attended the Mass the next evening, and as he admitted to her during their big reconciliation when he almost crushed her ribs, his heart was cut in two when he stood up for the Gospel. He had never deceived her before and would never again. After the Gospel he made a show of himself by leaving and came home with his head down and just sat in the front room smoking and staring at her, and now and then asking to be forgiven.

His next gift to her was the biggest gift of all — a mink stole. She wore it to dress dances and used to say to the ladies who admired it that it was much warmer than wool. Then she would hit it, or toss it onto a chair, implying that it meant nothing to her. But at home it was kept in a plastic bag on the top of the wardrobe, where no child could reach it when playing charades or improvising fancy dress. When her husband began to follow the hunt, she would drive him to the meet, get out of the car, wrap the stole around her neck, and accept a sherry or a hot bouillon and chat with one of the lords or ladies he was getting acquainted with. They lost friends and made friends. Even the girls from the boutique tried to worm their way into her life, by asking her to play badminton, but Tess declined and gave them a small donation towards a cup. She would make joking references to them how their prices were diabolical, or that they would be left on the shelf and find no husband. He made no comment, as if they were complete strangers to him.

One September after another, a child went off to boarding school, and as time went on the house began to grow quiet, and there were no piles of dirty clothing in the big rush basket on the landing; her husband would take his time about coming home in the evenings, and she would read a book, or try to read a book, and register the clock striking each quarter, and wish that people would call to tell her that she was pretty, or to eat some of her legendary sandwiches, or to give her the little items of news. No such luck. People went to the houses of younger couples as they had once flocked to hers, and her husband, though up to no monkey business, was no longer quite the same, did not surprise her with little half-pound boxes of chocolates, did not whistle when she came down the stairs dressed to go out. He was busy with his various commitments, had meetings two or three evenings a week, and on Sundays followed the hunt.

She had time on her hands, time to pluck her eyebrows, time to brood. The children wrote letters, mostly about the food or the harsh conditions in their school or some little surprise such as being given a toffee apple for a feast. She found her daughter's old diary and was a little shocked when she read "Mammy is as usual smarmy, but Daddy does not see through her." She could not say that it was then, no more than it was the moment when she smelled the cheap perfume on his lapel, nor the nausea when she read the disgusting magazine article about sex; it was not any of these events and yet they foreshadowed it.

One night her husband was sound asleep and for no reason she remembered one of her children, her favorite child, who had taken a fit because he had seen a man, a horned devil, in black, inside the windowpane. She herself had not seen it but she remembered her son's agitation and how she had not been able to quieten him. It was beyond her. Her husband was beside her, warm, his face almost beefy, and she had no idea what he thought, either sleeping or waking. Her children, her friends, her younger sister, who had grown odd and become attached to nature, all these people seemed to vibrate with more life, more urgency, even more desperation concerning the things they did. She felt odd, lonely, she felt afraid. Perhaps the shade of her dear dead aunt was at last coming to disquiet her. It was all in order—the same dinner each day of the week, the same night set aside for brief and unrenewing intercourse, the same grocery order on Saturday, the same humoring of the maid on Monday morning after the dance, the same the same the same.

It was as if she had just stepped onto ice.

"Oh Jesus," she uttered aloud. "Is this how it is when one begins to be unhappy?" She hadn't slept for four nights, not since the new plant had been installed in the factory. The noise and the incessancy of it followed her around the house all day and followed her to bed at night. She cursed machinery. In her mind were the various outlandish solutions such as asking the foreman to stop it, such as stuffing her ears with little plugs of cotton wool, such as moving to a bungalow outside the town, such as. She closed her eyes tight so that all of her sensibilities were like two burning coals crammed into her little head, and she knew then that the smugness that had always been hers was something about to be taken away. She was shorn.

Her husband heard her laughing. She had just smashed a hand mirror and was gloating over the seven years' bad luck in store. He did not know what to say. He had seen trouble coming.

"What is it?" he said softly.

"What is it," she said, and her voice was like slivers as she went on laughing at what she had just done. She stole out of bed, crept across the room, and in the chill, lifting the fawn curtain, stared ahead at the blankness within the windowpane.

(1974)

❖ FRANK O'CONNOR

The Drunkard

Frank O'Connor (1903–1966) is the pen name of Michael John O'Donovan, born of poor parents in Cork, Ireland. He left school at fourteen to earn his keep, did odd jobs for a while, and in 1922 to 1923 fought with the Irish Republican Army against the British. He was captured and put in prison until 1924. He was employed as a librarian in various Irish towns. He wrote two novels, *The Saint and Mary Kate* (1932) and *Dutch Interior* (1940), but he is most famous as a writer of short stories. After his literary reputation was established, O'Connor taught and lectured at Harvard, Northwestern, and Stanford. His short stories appear in *Guests of the Nations* (1931), *Bones of Contentions* (1936), *Crab Apple Jelly* (1944), *Traveller's Samples* (1951, which contains "The Drunkard"), *The Stories of Frank O'Connor* (1952), *More Stories, by Frank O'Connor* (1954), *Domestic Relations* (1957), *Collection Two* (1964), and the posthumous *Collection Three* (1969). *Collected Stories* appeared in 1982. O'Connor also wrote plays, travel sketches, autobiography, and works of literary history, such as *The Backward Look: A Survey of Irish Literature* (1967), and literary criticism, most importantly a study of the short story called *The Lonely Voice* (1963).

It was a terrible blow to Father when Mr. Dooley on the terrace died. Mr. Dooley was a commercial traveller with two sons in the Dominicans and a car of his own, so socially he was miles ahead of us, but he had no false pride. Mr. Dooley was an intellectual, and, like all intellectuals the thing he loved best was conversation, and in his own limited way Father was a well-read man and could appreciate an intelligent talker. Mr. Dooley was remarkably intelligent. Between business acquaintances and clerical contacts, there was very little he didn't know about what went on in town, and evening after evening he crossed the road to our gate to explain to Father the news behind the news. He had a low, palavering voice and a knowing smile, and Father would listen in astonishment, giving him a conversational lead now and again, and then stump triumphantly in to Mother with his face aglow and ask: "Do you know what Mr. Dooley is after telling me?" Ever since, when somebody has given me some bit of information off the record I have found myself on the point of asking: "Was it Mr. Dooley told you that?"

Till I actually saw him laid out in his brown shroud with the rosary beads entwined between his waxy fingers I did not take the report of his death seriously. Even then I felt there must be a catch and that some summer evening Mr. Dooley must reappear at our gate to give us the lowdown on the next world. But Father was very upset, partly because Mr. Dooley was about one age with himself, a thing that always gives a distinctly personal turn to another man's demise; partly because now he would have no one to tell him what dirty work was behind the latest scene at the Corporation. You could count on your fingers the number of men in Blarney Lane who read the papers as Mr. Dooley did, and none of these would have overlooked the fact that Father was only a labouring man. Even Sullivan, the carpenter, a mere nobody, thought he was a cut above Father. It was certainly a solemn event.

"Half past two to the Curragh," Father said meditatively, putting down the paper.

"But you're not thinking of going to the funeral?" Mother asked in alarm.

" 'Twould be expected," Father said, scenting opposition. "I wouldn't give it to say to them."

"I think," said Mother with suppressed emotion, "it will be as much as anyone will expect if you go to the chapel with him."

("Going to the chapel," of course, was one thing, because the body was removed after work, but going to a funeral meant the loss of a half-day's pay.)

"The people hardly know us," she added.

"God between us and all harm," Father replied with dignity, "we'd be glad if it was our own turn."

To give Father his due, he was always ready to lose a half day for the sake of an old neighbour. It wasn't so much that he liked funerals as that he was a conscientious man who did as he would be done by; and nothing could have consoled him so much for the prospect of his own death as the assurance of a worthy funeral. And, to give Mother her due, it wasn't the half-day's pay she begrudged, badly as we could afford it.

Drink, you see, was Father's great weakness. He could keep steady for months, even for years, at a stretch, and while he did he was as good as gold. He was first up in the morning and brought the mother a cup of tea in bed, stayed at home in the evenings and read the paper; saved money and bought himself a new blue serge suit and bowler hat. He laughed at the folly of men who, week in week out, left their hard-earned money with the publicans; and sometimes, to pass an idle hour, he took pencil and paper and calculated precisely how much he saved each week through being a teetotaller. Being a natural optimist he sometimes continued this calculation through the whole span of his prospective existence and the total was breathtaking. He would die worth hundreds.

If I had only known it, this was a bad sign; a sign he was becoming stuffed up with spiritual pride and imagining himself better than his neighbours. Sooner or later, the spiritual pride grew till it called for some form of celebration. Then he took a drink — not whisky, of course; nothing like that — just a glass of some harmless drink like lager beer. That was the end of Father. By the time he had taken the first he already realized that he had made a fool of himself, took a second to forget it and a third to forget that he couldn't forget, and at last came home reeling drunk. From this on it was "The Drunkard's Progress," as in the moral prints. Next day he stayed in from work with a sick head while Mother went off to make his excuses at the works, and inside a fortnight he was poor and savage and despondent again. Once he began he drank steadily through everything down to the kitchen clock. Mother and I knew all the phases and dreaded all the dangers. Funerals were one.

"I have to go to Dunphy's to do a half-day's work," said Mother in distress. "Who's to look after Larry?"

"I'll look after Larry," Father said graciously. "The little walk will do him good."

There was no more to be said, though we all knew I didn't need anyone to look after me, and that I could quite well have stayed at home and looked after Sonny, but I was being attached to the party to act as a brake on Father. As a brake I had never achieved anything, but Mother still had great faith in me.

Next day, when I got home from school, Father was there before me and made a cup of tea for both of us. He was very good at tea, but too heavy in the hand for anything else; the way he cut bread was shocking. Afterwards, we went down the hill to the church, Father wearing his best blue serge and a bowler cocked to one side of his head with the least suggestion of the master. To his great joy he discovered Peter Crowley among the mourners. Peter was another danger signal, as I knew well from certain experiences after Mass on Sunday morning: a mean man, as Mother said, who only went to funerals for the free drinks he could get at them. It turned out that he hadn't even known Mr. Dooley! But Father had a sort of contemptuous regard for him as one of the foolish people who wasted their good money in public-houses when they could be saving it. Very little of his own money Peter Crowley wasted!

It was an excellent funeral from Father's point of view. He had it all well studied before we set off after the hearse in the afternoon sunlight.

"Five carriages!" he exclaimed. "Five carriages and sixteen covered cars!" There's one alderman, two councillors and 'tis unknown how many priests. I didn't see a funeral like this from the road since Willie Mack, the publican, died.

"Ah, he was well liked," said Crowley in his husky voice.

"My goodness, don't I know that?" snapped Father. "Wasn't the man my best friend? Two nights before he died — only two nights — he was over telling me the goings-on about the housing contract. Them fellows in the Corporation are night and day robbers. But even I never imagined he was as well connected as that."

Father was stepping out like a boy, pleased with everything: the other mourners, and the fine houses along Sunday's Well. I knew the danger signals were there in full force: a sunny day, a fine funeral, and a distinguished company of clerics and public men were bringing out all the natural vanity and flightiness of Father's character. It was with something like genuine pleasure that he saw his old friend lowered into the grave; with the sense of having performed a duty and the pleasant awareness that however much he would miss poor Mr. Dooley in the long summer evenings, it was he and not poor Mr. Dooley who would do the missing.

"We'll be making tracks before they break up," he whispered to Crowley as the gravediggers tossed in the first shovelfuls of clay, and away he went, hopping like a goat from grassy hump to hump. The drivers, who were probably in the same state as himself, though without months of abstinence to put an edge on it, looked up hopefully.

"Are they nearly finished, Mick?" bawled one.

"All over now bar the last prayers," trumpeted Father in the tone of one who brings news of great rejoicing.

The carriages passed us in a lather of dust several hundred yards from the public-house, and Father, whose feet gave him trouble in hot weather, quickened his pace, looking nervously over his shoulder for any sign of the main body of mourners crossing the hill. In a crowd like that a man might be kept waiting.

When we did reach the pub the carriages were drawn up outside, and solemn men in black ties were cautiously bringing out consolation to mysterious females whose hands reached out modestly from behind the drawn blinds of the coaches. Inside the pub there were only the drivers and a couple of shawly women. I felt if I was to act as a brake at all, this was the time, so I pulled Father by the coattails.

"Dadda, can't we go home now?" I asked.

"Two minutes now," he said, beaming affectionately. "Just a bottle of lemonade and we'll go home."

This was a bribe, and I knew it, but I was always a child of weak character. Father ordered lemonade and two pints. I was thirsty and swallowed my drink at once. But that wasn't Father's way. He had long months of abstinence behind him and an eternity of pleasure before. He took out his pipe, blew through it, filled it, and then lit it with loud pops, his eyes bulging above it. After that he deliberately turned his back on the pint, leaned one elbow on the counter in the attitude of a man who did not know there was a pint behind him, and deliberately brushed the tobacco from his palms. He had settled down for the evening. He was steadily working through all the important funerals he had ever attended. The carriages departed and the minor mourners drifted in till the pub was half full.

"Dadda," I said, pulling his coat again, "can't we go home now?"

"Ah, your mother won't be in for a long time yet," he said benevolently enough. "Run out in the road and play, can't you?"

It struck me as very cool, the way grown-ups assumed that you could play all by yourself on a strange road. I began to get bored as I had so often been bored before. I knew Father was quite capable of lingering there till nightfall. I knew I might have to bring him home, blind drunk, down Blarney Lane, with all the old women at their doors, saying: "Mick Delaney is on it again." I knew that my mother would be half crazy with anxiety; that next day Father wouldn't go out to work; and before the end of the week she would be running down to the pawn with the clock under her shawl. I could never get over the lonesomeness of the kitchen without a clock.

I was still thirsty. I found if I stood on tiptoe I could just reach Father's glass, and the idea occurred to me that it would be interesting to know what the contents were like. He had his back to it and wouldn't notice. I took down the glass and sipped cautiously. It was a terrible disappointment. I was astonished that he could even drink such stuff. It looked as if he had never tried lemonade.

I should have advised him about lemonade but he was holding forth himself in great style. I heard him say that bands were a great addition to a funeral. He put his arms in the position of someone holding a rifle in reverse and hummed a few bars of Chopin's Funeral March. Crowley nodded reverently. I took a longer drink and began to see that porter might have its advantages. I felt pleasantly elevated and philosophic. Father hummed a few bars of the Dead March in *Saul*. It was a nice pub and a very fine funeral, and I felt sure that poor Mr. Dooley in Heaven must be highly gratified. At the same time I thought they might have given him a band. As Father said, bands were a great addition.

But the wonderful thing about porter was the way it made you stand aside, or rather aloft like a cherub rolling on a cloud, and watch yourself with your legs crossed, leaning against a bar counter, not worrying about trifles but thinking deep, serious, grown-up thoughts about life and death. Looking at yourself like that, you couldn't help thinking after a while how funny you looked, and suddenly you got embarrassed and wanted to giggle. But by the time I had finished the pint, that phase too had passed; I found it hard to put back the glass, the counter seemed to have grown so high. Melancholia was supervening again.

"Well," Father said reverently, reaching behind him for his drink, "God rest the poor man's soul, wherever he is!" He stopped, looked first at the glass, and then at the people round him. "Hello," he said in a fairly good-humoured tone, as if he were just prepared to consider it a joke, even if it was in bad taste, "who was at this?"

There was silence for a moment while the publican and the old women looked first at Father and then at his glass.

"There was no one at it, my good man," one of the women said with an offended air. "Is it robbers you think we are?"

"Ah, there's no one here would do a thing like that, Mick," said the publican in a shocked tone.

"Well, someone did it," said Father, his smile beginning to wear off.

"If they did, they were them that were nearer it," said the woman darkly, giving me a dirty look; and at the same moment the truth began to dawn on Father. I suppose I must have looked a bit starry-eyed. He bent and shook me.

"Are you all right, Larry?" he asked in alarm.

Peter Crowley looked down at me and grinned.

"Could you beat that?" he exclaimed in a husky voice.

I could, and without difficulty. I started to get sick. Father jumped back in holy terror that I might spoil his good suit, and hastily opened the back door.

"Run! run! run!" he shouted.

I saw the sunlit wall outside with the ivy overhanging it, and ran. The intention was good but the performance was exaggerated, because I lurched right into the wall, hurting it badly, as it seemed to me. Being always very polite, I said "Pardon" before the second bout came on me. Father, still concerned for his suit, came up behind and cautiously held me while I got sick.

"That's a good boy!" he said encouragingly. "You'll be grand when you get that up."

Begor, I was not grand! Grand was the last thing I was. I gave one unmerciful wail out of me as he steered me back to the pub and put me sitting on the bench near the shawlies. They drew themselves up with an offended air, still sore at the suggestion that they had drunk his pint.

"God help us!" moaned one, looking pityingly at me, "isn't it the likes of them would be fathers?"

"Mick," said the publican in alarm, spraying sawdust on my tracks, "that child isn't supposed to be in here at all. You'd better take him home quick in case a bobby would see him."

"Merciful God!" whimpered Father, raising his eyes to heaven and clapping his hands silently as he only did when distraught, "what misfortune was on me? Or what will his mother say? . . . If women might stop at home and look after their children themselves!" he added in a snarl for the benefit of the shawlies. "Are them carriages all gone, Bill?"

"The carriages are finished long ago, Mick," replied the publican.

"I'll take him home," Father said despairingly. . . . "I'll never bring you out again," he threatened me. "Here," he added, giving me the clean handkerchief from his breast pocket, "put that over your eye."

The blood on the handkerchief was the first indication I got that I was cut, and instantly my temple began to throb and I set up another howl.

"Whisht, whisht, whisht!" Father said testily, steering me out the door. "One'd think you were killed. That's nothing. We'll wash it when we get home."

"Steady now, old scout!" Crowley said, taking the other side of me. "You'll be all right in a minute."

I never met two men who knew less about the effects of drink. The first breath of fresh air and the warmth of the sun made me groggier than ever and I pitched and rolled between wind and tide till Father started to whimper again.

"God Almighty, and the whole road out! What misfortune was on me didn't stop at my work! Can't you walk straight?"

I couldn't. I saw plain enough that, coaxed by the sunlight, every woman old and young in Blarney Lane was leaning over her half-door or sitting on her doorstep. They all stopped gabbling to gape at the strange spectacle of two sober, middle-aged men bringing home a drunken small boy with a cut over his eye. Father, torn between the shamefast desire to get me home as quick as he could, and the neighbourly need to explain that it wasn't his fault, finally halted outside Mrs. Roche's. There was a gang of old women outside a door at the opposite side of the road. I didn't like the look of them from the first. They seemed altogether too interested in me. I leaned against the wall of Mrs. Roche's cottage with my hands in my trousers pockets, thinking mournfully of poor Mr. Dooley in his cold grave on the Curragh, who would never walk down the road again, and, with great feeling. I began to sing a favourite song of Father's.

Though lost to Mononia and cold in the grave
He returns to Kincora no more.

"Wisha, the poor child!" Mrs. Roche said. "Haven't he a lovely voice, God bless him!"

That was what I thought myself, so I was the more surprised when Father said "Whisht!" and raised a threatening finger at me. He didn't seem to realize the appropriateness of the song, so I sang louder than ever.

"Whisht, I tell you!" he snapped, and then tried to work up a smile for Mrs. Roche's benefit. "We're nearly home now. I'll carry you the rest of the way."

But, drunk and all as I was, I knew better than to be carried home ignominiously like that.

"Now," I said severely, "can't you leave me alone? I can walk all right. 'Tis only my head. All I want is a rest."

"But you can rest at home in bed," he said viciously, trying to pick me up, and I knew by the flush on his face that he was very vexed.

"Ah, Jasus," I said crossly, "what do I want to go home for? Why the hell can't you leave me alone?"

For some reason the gang of old women at the other side of the road thought this very funny. They nearly split their sides over it. A gassy fury began to expand in me at the thought that a fellow couldn't have a drop taken without the whole neighbourhood coming out to make game of him.

"Who are ye laughing at?" I shouted, clenching my fists at them. "I'll make ye laugh at the other side of yeer faces if ye don't let me pass."

They seemed to think this funnier still; I had never seen such ill-mannered people.

"Go away, ye bloody bitches!" I said.

"Whisht, whisht, whisht, I tell you!" snarled Father, abandoning all pretence of amusement and dragging me along behind him by the hand. I was maddened by the women's shrieks of laughter. I was maddened by Father's bullying. I tried to dig in my heels but he was too powerful for me, and I could only see the women by looking back over my shoulder.

"Take care or I'll come back and show ye!" I shouted. "I'll teach ye to let decent people pass. Fitter for ye to stop at home and wash yeer dirty faces."

" 'Twill be all over the road," whimpered Father. "Never again, never again, not if I lived to be a thousand!"

To this day I don't know whether he was forswearing me or the drink. By way of a song suitable to my heroic mood I bawled "The Boys of Wexford," as he dragged me in home. Crowley, knowing he was not safe, made off and Father undressed me and put me to bed. I couldn't sleep because of the whirling in my head. It was very unpleasant, and I got sick again. Father came in with a wet cloth and mopped up after me. I lay in a fever, listening to him chopping sticks to start a fire. After that I heard him lay the table.

Suddenly the front door banged open and Mother stormed in with Sonny in her arms, not her usual gentle, timid self, but a wild, raging woman. It was clear that she had heard it all from the neighbours.

"Mick Delaney," she cried hysterically, "what did you do to my son?"

"Whisht, woman, whisht, whisht!" he hissed, dancing from one foot to the other. "Do you want the whole road to hear?"

"Ah," she said with a horrifying laugh, "the road knows all about it by this time. The road knows the way you filled your unfortunate innocent child with drink to make sport for you and that other rotten, filthy brute."

"But I gave him no drink," he shouted, aghast at the horrifying interpretation the neighbours had chosen to give his misfortune. "He took it while my back was turned. What the hell do you think I am?"

"Ah," she replied bitterly, "everyone knows what you are now. God forgive you, wasting our hard-earned few ha'pence on drink, and bringing up your child to be a drunken corner-boy like yourself."

Then she swept into the bedroom and threw herself on her knees by the bed. She moaned when she saw the gash over my eye. In the kitchen Sonny set up a loud bawl on his own, and a moment later Father appeared in the bedroom door with his cap over his eyes, wearing an expression of the most intense self-pity.

"That's a nice way to talk to me after all I went through," he whined. "That's a nice accusation, that I was drinking. Not one drop of drink crossed my lips the whole day. How could it when he drank it all? I'm the one that ought to be pitied, with my day ruined on me, and I after being made a show for the whole road."

But next morning, when he got up and went out quietly to work with his dinner-basket, Mother threw herself on me in the bed and kissed me. It seemed it was all my doing, and I was being given a holiday till my eye got better.

"My brave little man!" she said with her eyes shining. "It was God did it you were there. You were his guardian angel."

(1951)

❖ GRACE PALEY
The Long-Distance Runner

Grace Paley (1922–) was born in New York City and educated at Hunter College. She has taught at Syracuse University and Sarah Lawrence College, but is very much a New York City writer. Asked about her politics, she describes herself as "Anarchist, if that's politics." Her fiction consists entirely of short stories, which can be found in the collections *The Little Disturbances of Man: Stories of Women and Men at Love* (1959), *Enormous Changes at the Last Minute* (1974, which contains "The Long Distance Runner"), and *Later the Same Day* (1985). The critic Michael Wood has said of Paley's stories that they create "a whole small country of damaged, fragile, haunted citizens."

One day, before or after forty-two, I became a long-distance runner. Though I was stout and in many ways inadequate to this desire, I wanted to go far and fast, not as fast as bicycles and trains, not as far as Taipei, Hingwen, places like that, islands of the slant-eyed cunt, as sailors in bus stations say when speaking of travel, but round and round the county from the sea side to the bridges, along the old neighborhood streets a couple of times, before old age and urban renewal ended them and me.

I tried the country first, Connecticut, which being wooded is always full of buds in spring. All creation is secret, isn't that true? So I trained in the wide-zoned suburban hills where I wasn't known. I ran all spring in and out of dogwood bloom, then laurel.

People sometimes stopped and asked me why I ran, a lady in silk shorts halfway down over her fat thighs. In training, I replied and rested only to answer if closely questioned. I wore a white sleeveless undershirt as well, with excellent support, not to attract the attention of old men and prudish children.

Then summer came, my legs seemed strong. I kissed the kids goodbye. They were quite old by then. It was near the time for parting anyway. I told Mrs. Raftery to look in now and then and give them some of that rotten Celtic supper she makes.

I told them they could take off any time they wanted to. Go lead your private life, I said. Only leave me out of it.

A word to the wise . . . said Richard.

You're depressed Faith, Mrs. Raftery said. Your boy friend Jack, the one you think's so hotsy-totsy, hasn't called and you're as gloomy as a tick on Sunday.

Cut the folkshit with me, Raftery, I muttered. Her eyes filled with tears because that's who she is: folkshit from bunion to topknot. That's how she got liked by me, loved, invented and endured.

When I walked out the door they were all reclining before the television set, Richard, Tonto and Mrs. Raftery, gazing at the news. Which proved with moving pictures that there *had* been a voyage to the moon and Africa and South America hid in a furious whorl of clouds.

547

I said, Goodbye. They said, Yeah, O.K., sure.

If that's how it is, forget it, I hollered and took the Independent subway to Brighton Beach.

At Brighton Beach I stopped at the Salty Breezes Locker Room to change my clothes. Twenty-five years ago my father invested $500 in its future. In fact he still clears about $3.50 a year, which goes directly (by law) to the Children of Judea to cover their deficit.

No one paid too much attention when I started to run, easy and light on my feet. I ran on the boardwalk first, past my mother's leafleting station—between a soft-ice-cream stand and a degenerated dune. There she had been assigned by her comrades to halt the tides of cruel American enterprise with simple socialist sense.

I wanted to stop and admire the long beach. I wanted to stop in order to think admiringly about New York. There aren't many rotting cities so tan and sandy and speckled with citizens at their salty edges. But I had already spent a lot of life lying down or standing and staring. I had decided to run.

After about a mile and a half I left the boardwalk and began to trot into the old neighborhood. I was running well. My breath was long and deep. I was thinking pridefully about my form.

Suddenly I was surrounded by about three hundred blacks.

Who you?

Who that?

Look at her! Just look! When you seen a fatter ass?

Poor thing. She ain't right. Leave her, you boys, you bad boys.

I used to live here, I said.

Oh yes, they said, in the white old days. That time too bad to last.

But we loved it here. We never went to Flatbush Avenue or Times Square. We loved our block.

Tough black titty.

I liked your speech, I said. Metaphor and all.

Right on. We get that from talking.

Yes my people also had a way of speech. And don't forget the Irish. The gift of gab.

Who they? said a small boy.

Cops.

Nowadays, I suggested, there's more than Irish on the police force.

You right, said two ladies. More more, much much more. They's French Chinamen Russkies Congoleans. Oh missee, you too right.

I lived in that house, I said. That apartment house. All my life. Till I got married.

Now that *is* nice. Live in one place. My mother live that way in South Carolina. One place. Her daddy farmed. She said. They ate. No matter winter war bad times. Roosevelt. Something! Ain't that wonderful! And it weren't cold! Big trees!

That apartment. I looked up and pointed. There. The third floor.

They all looked up. So what! You blubrous devil! said a dark young man. He wore horn-rimmed glasses and had that intelligent look that City College boys used to have when I was eighteen and first looked at them.

He seemed to lead them in contempt and anger, even the littlest ones who moved toward me with dramatic stealth singing, Devil, Oh Devil. I don't think the little kids had bad feeling because they poked a finger into me, then laughed.

Still I thought it might be wise to keep my head. So I jumped right in with some facts. I said, How many flowers' names do you know? Wild flowers, I mean. My people only knew two. That's what they say now anyway. Rich or poor, they only had two flowers' names. Rose and violet.

Daisy, said one boy immediately.

Weed, said another. That *is* a flower, I thought. But everyone else got the joke.

Saxifrage, lupine, said a lady. Viper's bugloss, said a small Girl Scout in medium green with a dark green sash. She held up a *Handbook of Wild Flowers*.

How many you know, fat mama? a boy asked warmly. He wasn't against my being a mother or fat. I turned all my attention to him.

Oh sonny, I said, I'm way ahead of my people. I know in yellows alone: common cinquefoil, trout lily, yellow adder's-tongue, swamp buttercup and common buttercup, golden sorrel, yellow or hop clover, devil's-paintbrush, evening primrose, black-eyed Susan, golden aster, also the yellow pickerelweed growing down by the water if not in the water, and dandelions of course. I've seen all these myself. Seen them.

You could see China from the boardwalk, a boy said. When it's nice.

I know more flowers than countries. Mostly young people these days have traveled in many countries.

Not me. I ain't been nowhere.

Not me either, said about seventeen boys.

I'm not allowed, said a little girl. There's drunken junkies.

But *I! I!* cried out a tall black youth, very handsome and well dressed. I am an African. My father came from the high stolen plains. *I* have been everywhere. I was in Moscow six months, learning machinery. I was in France, learning French. I was in Italy, observing the peculiar Renaissance and the people's sweetness. I was in England, where I studied the common law and the urban blight. I was at the Conference of Dark Youth in Cuba to understand our passion. I am now here. Here am I to become an engineer and return to my people, around the Cape of Good Hope in a Norwegian sailing vessel. In this way I will learn the fine old art of sailing in case the engines of the new society of my old inland country should fail.

We had an extraordinary amount of silence after that. Then one old lady in a black dress and high white lace collar said to another old lady dressed exactly the same way, Glad tidings when someone got brains in the head not fish juice. Amen, said a few.

Whyn't you go up to Mrs. Luddy living in your house, you lady, huh? The Girl Scout asked this.

Why she just groove to see you, said some sarcastic snickerer.

She got palpitations. Her man, he give it to her.

That ain't all, he a natural gift-giver.

I'll take you, said the Girl Scout. My name is Cynthia. I'm in Troop 355, Brooklyn.

I'm not dressed, I said, looking at my lumpy knees.

You shouldn't wear no undershirt like that without no runnin number or no team writ on it. It look like a undershirt.

Cynthia! Don't take her up there, said an important boy. Her head strange. Don't you take her. Hear?

Lawrence, she said softly, you tell me once more what to do I'll wrap you round that lamppost.

Git! she said, powerfully addressing *me.*

In this way I was led into the hallway of the whole house of my childhood.

The first door I saw was still marked in flaky gold, 1A. That's where the janitor lived, I said. He was a Negro.

How come like that? Cynthia made an astonished face. How come the janitor was a black man?

Oh Cynthia, I said. Then I turned to the opposite door, first floor front, 1B. I remembered. Now, here, this was Mrs. Goreditsky, very very fat lady. All her children died at birth. Born, then one, two, three. Dead. Five children, then Mr. Goreditsky said, I'm bad luck on you Tessie and he went away. He sent $15 a week for seven years. Then no one heard.

I know her, poor thing, said Cynthia. The city come for her summer before last. The way they knew it, it smelled. They wropped her up in a canvas. They couldn't get through the front door. It scraped off a piece of her. My uncle Ronald had to help them, but he got disgusted.

Only two years ago. She was still here! Wasn't she scared?

So we all, said Cynthia. White ain't everything.

Who lived up here, she asked, 2B? Right now, my best friend Nancy Rosalind lives here. She got two brothers, and her sister married and got a baby. She very light-skinned. Not her mother. We got all colors amongst us.

Your best friend? That's funny. Because it was *my* best friend. Right in that apartment. Joanna Rosen.

What become of her? Cynthia asked. She got a running shirt too?

Come on, Cynthia, if you really want to know, I'll tell you. She married this man, Marvin Steirs.

Who's he?

I recollected his achievements. Well, he's the president of a big corporation, JoMar Plastics. This corporation owns a steel company, a radio station, a new Xerox-type machine that lets you do twenty-five different pages at once. This corporation has a foundation, The JoMar Fund for Research in Conservation. Capitalism is like that, I added, in order to be politically useful.

How come you know? You go over their house a lot?

No. I happened to read all about them on the financial page, just last week. It made me think: a different life. That's all.

Different spokes for different folks, said Cynthia.

I sat down on the cool marble steps and remembered Joanna's cousin Ziggie. He was older than we were. He wrote a poem which told us we were lovely flowers and our legs were petals, which nature would force open no matter how many times we said no.

Then I had several other interior thoughts that I couldn't share with a child, the kind that give your face a blank or melancholy look.

Now you're not interested, said Cynthia. Now you're not gonna say a thing. Who lived here, 2A? Who? Two men lives here now. Women coming and women going. My mother says, Danger sign: Stay away, my darling, stay away.

I don't remember, Cynthia. I really don't.

You got it. What'd you come for, anyways?

Then I tried. 2A. 2A. Was it the twins? I felt a strong obligation as though remembering was in charge of the *existence* of the past. This is not so.

Cynthia, I said, I don't want to go any further. I don't even want to remember.

Come on, she said, tugging at my shorts, don't you want to see Mrs. Luddy, the one lives in your old house? That be fun, no?

No. No, I don't want to see Mrs. Luddy.

Now you shouldn't pay no attention to those boys downstairs. She will like you. I mean, she is kind. She don't like most white people, but she might like you.

No Cynthia, it's not that, but I don't want to see my father and mother's house now.

I didn't know what to say. I said, Because my mother's dead. This was a lie, because my mother lives in her own room with my father in the Children of Judea. With her hand over her socialist heart, she reads the paper every morning after breakfast. Then she says sadly to my father, Every day the same. Dying . . . dying, dying from killing.

My mother's dead Cynthia. I can't go in there.

Oh . . . oh, the poor thing, she said, looking into my eyes. Oh, if my mother died, I don't know what I'd do. Even if I was old as you. I could kill myself. Tears filled her eyes and started down her cheeks. If my mother died, what would I do? She is my protector, she won't let the pushers get me. She hold me tight. She gonna hide me in the cedar box if my Uncle Rudford comes try to get me back. She *can't* die, my mother.

Cynthia — honey — she won't die. She's young. I put my arm out to comfort her. You could come live with me, I said. I got two boys, they're nearly grown up. I missed it, not having a girl.

What? What you mean now, live with you and boys. She pulled away and ran for the stairs. Stay away from me, honky lady. I know them white boys. They just gonna try and jostle my black womanhood. My mother told me about that, keep you white honky devil boys to your devil self, you just leave me be you old bitch you. Somebody help me, she started to scream, you hear. Somebody help. She gonna take me away.

She flattened herself to the wall, trembling. I was too frightened by her fear of me to say, honey, I wouldn't hurt you, it's me. I heard her helpers, the voices of large boys crying, We coming, we coming, hold your head up, we coming. I ran past her fear to the stairs and up them two at a time. I came to my old own door. I knocked like the landlord, loud and terrible.

Mama not home, a child's voice said. No, no, I said. It's me! a lady! Someone's chasing me, let me in. Mama not home, I ain't allowed to open up for nobody.

It's me! I cried out in terror. Mama! Mama! let me in!

The door opened. A slim woman whose age I couldn't invent looked at me. She said, Get in and shut that door tight. She took a hard pinching hold on my upper arm. Then she bolted the door herself. Them hustlers after you. They make me pink. Hide this white lady now, Donald. Stick her under your bed, you got a high bed.

Oh that's O.K. I'm fine now, I said. I felt safe and at home.

You in my house, she said. You do as I say. For two cents, I throw you out.

I squatted under a small kid's pissy mattress. Then I heard the knock. It was tentative and respectful. My mama don't allow me to open. Donald! someone called. Donald!

Oh no, he said. Can't do it. She gonna wear me out. You know her. She already tore up my ass this morning once. Ain't *gonna* open up.

I lived there for about three weeks with Mrs. Luddy and Donald and three little baby girls nearly the same age. I told her a joke about Irish twins. Ain't Irish, she said.

Nearly every morning the babies woke us at about 6:45. We gave them all a bottle and went back to sleep till 8:00. I made coffee and she changed diapers. Then it really stank for a while. At this time I usually said, Well listen, thanks really, but I've got to go I guess. I guess I'm going. She'd usually say, Well, guess again. *I* guess you ain't. Or if she was feeling disgusted she'd say, Go on now! Get! You wanna go, I guess by now I have snorted enough white lady stink to choke a horse. Go on!

I'd get to the door and then I'd hear voices. I'm ashamed to say I'd become fearful. Despite my wide geographical love of mankind, I would be attacked by local fears.

There was a sentimental truth that lay beside all that going and not going. It *was* my house where I'd lived long ago my family life. There was a tile on the bathroom floor that I myself had broken, dropping a hammer on the toe of my brother Charles as he stood dreamily shaving, his prick halfway up his undershorts. Astonishment and knowledge first seized me right there. The kitchen was the same. The table was the enameled table common to our class, easy to clean, with wooden undercorners for indigent and old cockroaches that couldn't make it to the kitchen sink. (However, it was not the same table, because I have inherited that one, chips and all.)

The living room was something like ours, only we had less plastic. There may have been less plastic in the world at that time. Also, my mother had set beautiful cushions everywhere, on beds and chairs. It was the way she expressed herself, artistically, to embroider at night or take strips of flowered cotton and sew them across ordinary white or blue muslin in the most delicate designs, the way women have always used materials that live and die in hunks and tatters to say: This is my place.

Mrs. Luddy said, Uh huh!

Of course, I said, men don't have that outlet. That's how come they run around so much.

Till they drunk enough to lay down, she said.

Yes, I said, on a large scale you can see it in the world. First they make something, then they murder it. Then they write a book about how interesting it is.

You got something there, she said. Sometimes she said, Girl, you don't know *nothing*.

We often sat at the window looking out and down. Little tufts of breeze grew on that windowsill. The blazing afternoon was around the corner and up the block.

You say men, she said. Is that men? she asked. What you call — a Man?

Four flights below us, leaning on the stoop, were about a dozen people and around them devastation. Just a minute, I said. I had seen devastation on my way, running, gotten some of the pebbles of it in my running shoe and the dust of it in my eyes. I had thought with the indignant courtesy of a citizen, This is a disgrace to the City of New York which I love and am running through.

But now, from the commanding heights of home, I saw it clearly. The tenement in which Jack my old and present friend had come to gloomy manhood has been destroyed, first by fire, then by demolition (which is a swinging ball of steel that cracks bedrooms and kitchens). Because of this work, we could see several blocks wide and a block and a half long. Crazy Eddy's house still stood, famous 1510 gutted, with black window frames, no glass, open laths. The stubbornness of the supporting beams! Some persons or families still lived on the lowest floors. In the lots between, a couple of old sofas lay on their fat faces, their springs sticking up into the air. Just as in wartime a half-dozen ailanthus trees had already found their first quarter inch of earth and begun a living attack on the dead yards. At night, I knew animals roamed the place, squalling and howling, furious New York dogs and street cats and mighty rats. You would think you were in Bear Mountain Park, the terror of venturing forth.

Someone ought to clean that up, I said.

Mrs. Luddy said, Who you got in mind? Mrs. Kennedy? —

Donald made a stern face. He said, That just what I gonna do when I get big. Gonna get the Sanitary Man in and show it to him. You see that, you big guinea you, you clean it up right now! Then he stamped his feet and fierced his eyes.

Mrs. Luddy said, Come here, you little nigger. She kissed the top of his head and gave him a whack on the backside all at one time.

Well, said Donald, encouraged, look out there now you all! Go on I say, look! Though we had already seen, to please him we looked. On the stoop men and boys lounged, leaned, hopped about, stood on one leg, then another, took their socks off, and scratched their toes, talked, sat on their haunches, heads down, dozing.

Donald said, Look at them. They ain't got self-respect. They got Afros *on* their heads, but they don't know they black *in* their heads.

I thought he ought to learn to be more sympathetic. I said, There are reasons that people are that way.

Yes, ma'am, said Donald.

Anyway, how come you never go down and play with the other kids, how come you're up here so much?

My mama don't like me do that. Some of them is bad. Bad. I might become a dope addict. I got to stay clear.

You just a dope, that's a fact, said Mrs. Luddy.

He ought to be with kids his age more, I think.

He see them in school, miss. Don't trouble your head about it if you don't mind.

Actually, Mrs. Luddy didn't go down into the street either. Donald did all the shopping. She let the welfare investigator in, the meterman came into the kitchen to read the meter. I saw him from the back room, where I hid. She did pick up her check. She cashed it. She returned to wash the babies, change their diapers, wash clothes, iron, feed people, and then in free half hours she sat by that window. She was waiting.

I believed she was watching and waiting for a particular man. I wanted to discuss this with her, talk lovingly like sisters. But before I could freely say, Forget about that son of a bitch, he's a pig, I did have to offer a few solid facts about myself, my kids, about fathers, husbands, passers-by, evening companions, and the life of my father and mother in this room by this exact afternoon window.

I told her for instance, that in my worst times I had given myself one extremely simple physical pleasure. This was cream cheese for breakfast. In fact, I insisted on it, sometimes depriving the children of very important articles and foods.

Girl, you don't know nothing, she said.

Then for a little while she talked gently as one does to a person who is innocent and insane and incorruptible because of stupidity. She had had two such special pleasures for hard times she said. The first, men, but they turned rotten, white women had ruined the best, give them the idea their dicks made of solid gold. The second pleasure she had tried was wine. She said, I do like wine. You *has* to have something just for yourself by yourself. Then she said, But you can't raise a decent boy when you liquor-dazed every night.

White or black, I said, returning to men, they did think they were bringing a rare gift, whereas it was just sex, which is common like bread, though essential.

Oh, you can do without, she said. There's folks does without.

I told her Donald deserved the best. I loved him. If he had flaws, I hardly noticed them. It's one of my beliefs that children do not have flaws, even the worst do not.

Donald was brilliant — like my boys except that he had an easier disposition. For this reason I decided, almost the second moment of my residence in that household, to bring him up to reading level at once. I told him we would work with books and newspapers. He went immediately to his neighborhood library and brought some hard books to amuse me. *Black Folktales* by Julius Lester and *The Pushcart War*, which is about another neighborhood but relevant.

Donald always agreed with me when we talked about reading and writing. In fact, when I mentioned poetry, he told me he knew all about it, that David Henderson, a known black poet, had visited his second-grade class. So Donald was, as it turned out, well ahead of my nosy tongue. He was usually very busy shopping. He also had to spend a lot of time making faces to force the little serious baby girls into laughter. But if the subject came up, he could take *the* poem right out of the air into which language and event had just gone.

An example: That morning, his mother had said, Whew, I just got too much piss and diapers and wash. I wanna just sit down by that window and rest myself. He wrote a poem:

Just got too much pissy diapers
and wash and wash

> just wanna sit down by that window
> and look out
>   ain't nothing there.

Donald, I said, you are plain brilliant. I'm never going to forget you. For God's sakes don't you forget me.

You fool with him too much, said Mrs. Luddy. He already don't even remember his grandma, you never gonna meet someone like her, a curse never come past her lips.

I do remember, Mama, I remember. She lying in bed, right there. A man standing in the door. She say, Esdras, I put a curse on you head. You worsen tomorrow. How come she said like that?

Gomorrah, I believe Gomorrah, she said. She know the Bible inside out.

Did she live with you?

No. No, she visiting. She come up to see us all, her children, how we doing. She come up to see sights. Then she lay down and died. She was old.

I remained quiet because of the death of mothers. Mrs. Luddy looked at me thoughtfully, then she said:

My mama had stories to tell, she raised me on. *Her* mama was a little thing, no sense. Stand in the door of the cabin all day, sucking her thumb. It was slave times. One day a young field boy come storming along. He knock on the door of the first cabin hollering, Sister, come out, it's freedom. She come out. She say, Yeah? When? He say, Now! It's freedom now! Then he knock at the next door and say, Sister! It's freedom! Now! From one cabin he run to the next cabin, crying out, Sister, it's freedom now!

Oh I remember that story, said Donald. Freedom now! Freedom now! He jumped up and down.

You don't remember nothing boy. Go on, get Eloise, she want to get into the good times.

Eloise was two but undersized. We got her like that, said Donald. Mrs. Luddy let me buy her ice cream and green vegetables. She was waiting for kale and chard, but it was too early. The kale liked cold. You not about to be here November, she said. No, no. I turned away, lonesomeness touching me and sang our Eloise song:

> Eloise loves the bees
> the bees they buzz
> like Eloise does.

Then Eloise crawled all over the splintery floor, buzzing wildly.

Oh you crazy baby, said Donald, buzz buzz buzz.

Mrs. Luddy sat down by the window.

You all make a lot of noise, she said sadly. You just right on noisy.

The next morning Mrs. Luddy woke me up.

Time to go, she said.

What?

Home.

What? I said.

Well, don't you think your little spoiled boys crying for you? Where's Mama? They standing in the window. Time to go lady. This ain't Free Vacation Farm. Time we was by ourself a little.

Oh Ma, said Donald, she ain't a lot of trouble. Go on, get Eloise, she hollering. And button up your lip.

She didn't offer me coffee. She looked at me strictly all the time. I tried to look strictly back, but I failed because I loved the sight of her.

Donald was teary, but I didn't dare turn my face to him, until the parting minute at the door. Even then, I kissed the top of his head a little too forcefully and said, Well, I'll see you.

On the front stoop there were about half a dozen mid-morning family people and kids arguing about who had dumped garbage out of which window. They were very disgusted with one another.

Two young men in handsome dashikis stood in counsel and agreement at the street corner. They divided a comment. How come white womens got rotten teeth? And look so old? A young woman waiting at the light said, Hush . . .

I walked past them and didn't begin my run till the road opened up somewhere along Ocean Parkway. I was a little stiff because my way of life had used only small movements, an occasional stretch to put a knife or teapot out of reach of the babies. I ran about ten, fifteen blocks. Then my second wind came, which is classical, famous among runners, it's the beginning of flying.

In the three weeks I'd been off the street, jogging had become popular. It seemed that I was only one person doing her thing, which happened like most American eccentric acts to be the most "in" thing I could have done. In fact, two young men ran alongside of me for nearly a mile. They ran silently beside me and turned off at Avenue H. A gentleman with a mustache, running poorly in the opposite direction, waved. He called out, Hi, senora.

Near home I ran through our park, where I had aired my children on weekends and late-summer afternoons. I stopped at the northeast playground, where I met a dozen young mothers intelligently handling their little ones. In order to prepare them, meaning no harm, I said, In fifteen years, you girls will be like me, wrong in everything.

At home it was Saturday morning. Jack had returned looking as grim as ever, but he'd brought cash and a vacuum cleaner. While the coffee perked, he showed Richard how to use it. They were playing tick tack toe on the dusty wall.

Richard said, Well! Look who's here! Hi!

Any news? I asked.

Letter from Daddy, he said. From the lake and water country in Chile. He says it's like Minnesota.

He's never been to Minnesota, I said. Where's Anthony?

Here I am, said Tonto, appearing. But I'm leaving.

Oh yes, I said. Of course. Every Saturday he hurries through breakfast or misses it. He goes to visit his friends in institutions. These are well-known places like Bellevue, Hillside, Rockland State, Central Islip, Manhattan. These visits take him all day and sometimes half the night.

I found some chocolate-chip cookies in the pantry. Take them, Tonto, I said. I remember nearly all his friends as little boys and girls always hopping, skipping, jumping and cookie-eating. He was annoyed. He said, No! Chocolate cookies is what the commissaries are full of. How about money?

Jack dropped the vacuum cleaner. He said, No! They have parents for that.

I said, Here, five dollars for cigarettes, one dollar each.

Cigarettes! said Jack. Goddamnit! Black lungs and death! Cancer! Emphysema! He stomped out of the kitchen, breathing. He took the bike from the back room and started for Central Park, which has been closed to cars but opened to bicycle riders. When he'd been gone about ten minutes, Anthony said, It's really open only on Sundays.

Why didn't you say so? Why can't you be decent to him? I asked. It's important to me.

Oh Faith, he said, patting me on the head because he'd grown so tall, all that air. It's good for his lungs. And his muscles! He'll be back soon.

You should ride too, I said. You don't want to get mushy in your legs. You should go swimming once a week.

I'm too busy, he said. I have to see my friends.

Then Richard, who had been vacuuming under his bed, came into the kitchen. You still here, Tonto?

Going going gone, said Anthony, don't bat your eye.

Now listen, Richard said, here's a note. It's for Judy, if you get as far as Rockland. Don't forget it. Don't open it. Don't read it. I know he'll read it.

Anthony smiled and slammed the door.

Did I lose weight? I asked. Yes, said Richard. You look O.K. You never look too bad. But where were you? I got sick of Raftery's boiled potatoes. Where were you, Faith?

Well! I said. Well! I stayed a few weeks in my old apartment, where Grandpa and Grandma and me and Hope and Charlie lived, when we were little. I took you there long ago. Not so far from the ocean where Grandma made us very healthy with sun and air.

What are you talking about? said Richard. Cut the baby talk.

Anthony came home earlier than expected that evening because some people were in shock therapy and someone else had run away. He listened to me for a while. Then he said, I don't know what she's talking about either.

Neither did Jack, despite the understanding often produced by love after absence. He said, Tell me again. He was in a good mood. He said, You can even tell it to me twice.

I repeated the story. They all said, What?

Because it isn't usually so simple. Have you known it to happen much nowadays? A woman inside the steamy energy of middle age runs and runs. She finds the houses and streets where her childhood happened. She lives in them. She learns as though she was still a child what in the world is coming next.

(1974)

❖ EDGAR ALLAN POE*
The Cask of Amontillado

The thousand injuries of Fortunato I had borne as I best could; but when he ventured upon insult, I vowed revenge. You, who so well know the nature of my soul, will not suppose, however, that I gave utterance to a threat. *At length* I would be avenged; this was a point definitively settled — but the very definitiveness with which it was resolved precluded the idea of risk. I must not only punish, but punish with impunity. A wrong is unredressed when retribution overtakes its redresser. It is equally unredressed when the avenger fails to make himself felt as such to him who has done the wrong.

It must be understood that neither by word nor deed had I given Fortunato cause to doubt my good will. I continued, as was my wont, to smile in his face, and he did not perceive that my smile *now* was at the thought of his immolation.

He had a weak point — this Fortunato — although in other regards he was a man to be respected and even feared. He prided himself on his connoisseurship in wine. Few Italians have the true virtuoso spirit. For the most part their enthusiasm is adopted to suit the time and opportunity — to practise imposture upon the British and Austrian *millionaires*. In painting and gemmary Fortunato, like his countrymen, was a quack — but in the matter of old wines he was sincere. In this respect I did not differ from him materially; I was skilful in the Italian vintages myself, and bought largely whenever I could.

It was about dusk, one evening during the supreme madness of the carnival season, that I encountered my friend. He accosted me with excessive warmth, for he had been drinking much. The man wore motley. He had on a tight-fitting parti-striped dress, and his head was surmounted by the conical cap and bells. I was so pleased to see him that I thought I should never have done wringing his hand.

I said to him — "My dear Fortunato, you are luckily met. How remarkably well you are looking to-day! But I have received a pipe of what passes for Amontillado, and I have my doubts."

"How?" said he. "Amontillado? A pipe? Impossible! And in the middle of the carnival! '

"I have my doubts," I replied; "and I was silly enough to pay the full Amontillado price without consulting you in the matter. You were not to be found, and I was fearful of losing a bargain."

"Amontillado!"

"I have my doubts."

"Amontillado!"

"And I must satisfy them."

"Amontillado!"

---

*Author biography can be found on page 226.

"As you are engaged, I am on my way to Luchesi. If any one has a critical turn, it is he. He will tell me—"

"Luchesi cannot tell Amontillado from Sherry."

"And yet some fools will have it that his taste is a match for your own."

"Come, let us go."

"Whither?"

"To your vaults."

"My friend, no; I will not impose upon your good nature. I perceive you have an engagement. Luchesi—"

"I have no engagement;—come."

"My friend, no. It is not the engagement, but the severe cold with which I perceive you are afflicted. The vaults are insufferably damp. They are encrusted with nitre."

"Let us go, nevertheless. The cold is merely nothing. Amontillado! You have been imposed upon. And as for Luchesi, he cannot distinguish Sherry from Amontillado."

Thus speaking, Fortunato possessed himself of my arm. Putting on a mask of black silk, and drawing a *roquelaire* closely about my person, I suffered him to hurry me to my palazzo.

There were no attendants at home; they had absconded to make merry in honor of the time. I had told them that I should not return until the morning, and had given them explicit orders not to stir from the house. These orders were sufficient, I well knew, to insure their immediate disappearance, one and all, as soon as my back was turned.

I took from their sconces two flambeaux, and giving one to Fortunato, bowed him through several suites of rooms to the archway that led into the vaults. I passed down a long and winding staircase, requesting him to be cautious as he followed. We came at length to the foot of the descent, and stood together on the damp ground of the catacombs of the Montresors.

The gait of my friend was unsteady, and the bells upon his cap jingled as he strode.

"The pipe," said he.

"It is farther on," said I; "but observe the white web-work which gleams from these cavern walls."

He turned towards me, and looked into my eyes with two filmy orbs that distilled the rheum of intoxication.

"Nitre?" he asked, at length.

"Nitre," I replied. "How long have you had that cough?"

"Ugh! ugh! ugh!—ugh! ugh! ugh!—ugh! ugh! ugh!—ugh! ugh! ugh!—ugh! ugh! ugh!"

My poor friend found it impossible to reply for many minutes.

"It is nothing," he said, at last.

"Come," I said, with decision, "we will go back; your health is precious. You are rich, respected, admired, beloved; you are happy, as once I was. You are a man to be missed. For me it is no matter. We will go back; you will be ill, and I cannot be responsible. Besides, there is Luchesi—"

"Enough," he said; "the cough is a mere nothing; it will not kill me. I shall not die of a cough."

"True — true," I replied; "and, indeed, I had no intention of alarming you unnecessarily — but you should use all proper caution. A draught of this Medoc will defend us from the damps."

Here I knocked off the neck of a bottle which I drew from a long row of its fellows that lay upon the mould.

"Drink," I said, presenting him the wine.

He raised it to his lips with a leer. He paused and nodded to me familiarly, while his bells jingled.

"I drink," he said, "to the buried that repose around us."

"And I to your long life."

He again took my arm, and we proceeded.

"These vaults," he said, "are extensive."

"The Montresors," I replied, "were a great and numerous family."

"I forget your arms."

"A huge human foot d'or, in a field azure; the foot crushes a serpent rampant whose fangs are imbedded in the heel."

"And the motto?"

"*Nemo me impune lacessit.*"

"Good!" he said.

The wine sparkled in his eyes and the bells jingled. My own fancy grew warm with the Medoc. We had passed through walls of piled bones, with casks and puncheons intermingling, into the inmost recesses of the catacombs. I paused again, and this time I made bold to seize Fortunato by an arm above the elbow.

"The nitre!" I said; "see, it increases. It hangs like moss upon the vaults. We are below the river's bed. The drops of moisture trickle among the bones. Come, we will go back ere it is too late. Your cough — "

"It is nothing," he said; "let us go on. But first, another draught of the Medoc."

I broke and reached him a flaçon of De Grâve. He emptied it at a breath. His eyes flashed with a fierce light. He laughed and threw the bottle upwards with a gesticulation I did not understand.

I looked at him in surprise. He repeated the movement — a grotesque one.

"You do not comprehend?" he said.

"Not I," I replied.

"Then you are not of the brotherhood."

"How?"

"You are not of the masons."

"Yes, yes," I said, "yes, yes."

"You? Impossible! A mason?"

"A mason," I replied.

"A sign," he said.

"It is this," I answered, producing a trowel from beneath the folds of my *roquelaire.*

"You jest," he exclaimed, recoiling a few paces. "But let us proceed to the Amontillado."

"Be it so," I said, replacing the tool beneath the cloak, and again offering him my arm. He leaned upon it heavily. We continued our route in search of the Amontillado. We passed through a range of low arches, descended, passed on, and descending again, arrived at a deep crypt, in which the foulness of the air caused our flambeaux rather to glow than flame.

At the most remote end of the crypt there appeared another less spacious. Its walls had been lined with human remains, piled to the vault overhead, in the fashion of the great catacombs of Paris. Three sides of this interior crypt were still ornamented in this manner. From the fourth the bones had been thrown down, and lay promiscuously upon the earth, forming at one point a mound of some size. Within the wall thus exposed by the displacing of the bones, we perceived a still interior recess, in depth about four feet, in width three, in height six or seven. It seemed to have been constructed for no especial use within itself, but formed merely the interval between two of the colossal supports of the roof of the catacombs, and was backed by one of their circumscribing walls of solid granite.

It was in vain that Fortunato, uplifting his dull torch, endeavored to pry into the depth of the recess. Its termination the feeble light did not enable us to see.

"Proceed," I said; "herein is the Amontillado. As for Luchesi — "

"He is an ignoramus," interrupted my friend, as he stepped unsteadily forward, while I followed immediately at his heels. In an instant he had reached the extremity of the niche, and finding his progress arrested by the rock, stood stupidly bewildered. A moment more and I had fettered him to the granite. In its surface were two iron staples, distant from each other about two feet, horizontally. From one of these depended a short chain, from the other a padlock. Throwing the links about his waist, it was but the work of a few seconds to secure it. He was too much astounded to resist. Withdrawing the key I stepped back from the recess.

"Pass your hand," I said, "over the wall; you cannot help feeling the nitre. Indeed it is *very* damp. Once more let me *implore* you to return. No? Then I must positively leave you. But I must first render you all the little attentions in my power."

"The Amontillado!" ejaculated my friend, not yet recovered from his astonishment.

"True," I replied; "the Amontillado."

As I said these words I busied myself among the pile of bones of which I have before spoken. Throwing them aside, I soon uncovered a quantity of building stone and mortar. With these materials and with the aid of my trowel, I began vigorously to wall up the entrance of the niche.

I had scarcely laid the first tier of the masonry when I discovered that the intoxication of Fortunato had in a great measure worn off. The earliest indication I had of this was a low moaning cry from the depth of the recess. It was *not* the cry of a drunken man. There was then a long and obstinate silence. I laid the second tier, and the third, and the fourth; and then I heard the furious vibrations of the chain. The noise lasted for several minutes, during which, that I might hearken to it with the more satisfaction, I ceased my labors and sat down upon the bones. When at last the clanking subsided, I resumed the trowel, and finished without interruption the fifth, the sixth, and the seventh tier. The wall was now nearly upon a level with my breast. I again paused, and holding the flambeaux over the mason-work, threw a few feeble rays upon the figure within.

A succession of loud and shrill screams, bursting suddenly from the throat of the chained form, seemed to thrust me violently back. For a brief moment I hesitated —I trembled. Unsheathing my rapier, I began to grope with it about the recess: but the thought of an instant reassured me. I placed my hand upon the solid fabric of the catacombs, and felt satisfied. I reapproached the wall. I replied to the yells of him who clamored. I re-echoed—I aided—I surpassed them in volume and in strength. I did this, and the clamorer grew still.

It was now midnight, and my task was drawing to a close. I had completed the eighth, the ninth, and the tenth tier. I had finished a portion of the last and the eleventh; there remained but a single stone to be fitted and plastered in. I struggled with its weight; I placed it partially in its destined position. But now there came from out the niche a low laugh that erected the hairs upon my head. It was succeeded by a sad voice, which I had difficulty in recognising as that of the noble Fortunato. The voice said—

"Ha! ha! ha!—he! he!—a very good joke indeed—an excellent jest. We will have many a rich laugh about it at the palazzo—he! he! he!—over our wine—he! he! he!"

"The Amontillado!" I said.

"He! he! he!—he! he! he!—yes, the Amontillado. But is it not getting late? Will not they be awaiting us at the palazzo, the Lady Fortunato and the rest? Let us be gone."

"Yes," I said, "let us be gone."

"*For the love of God, Montresor!*"

"Yes," I said, "for the love of God!"

But to these words I hearkened in vain for a reply. I grew impatient. I called aloud—

"Fortunato!"

No answer. I called again—

"Fortunato!"

No answer still. I thrust a torch through the remaining aperture and let it fall within. There came forth in return only a jingling of the bells. My heart grew sick—on account of the dampness of the catacombs. I hastened to make an end of my labor. I forced the last stone into its position; I plastered it up. Against the new masonry I re-erected the old rampart of bones. For the half of a century no mortal has disturbed them. *In páce requiescat!*

(1846)

❖ KATHERINE ANNE PORTER
The Jilting of
Granny Weatherall

Katherine Anne Porter (1890–1980) was born in Indian Creek, Texas, and educated in private schools. She married at sixteen and got divorced at nineteen. She worked as a newspaper reporter in Fort Worth and Denver and then went to New York to do free-lance writing. She spent much of the twenties in Mexico, sending back cultural articles to influential American magazines. She also started writing fiction. A collection of short stories entitled *Flowering Judas* (1930, which includes "The Jilting of Granny Weatherall") won her national acclaim and a Guggenheim Fellowship, which allowed her to go to Europe. There she wrote two collections of stories and novellas —*Hacienda* (1934) and *Noon Wine* (1937). She returned to America in 1937 and published a collection of three novellas called *Pale Horse, Pale Rider* (1939). In 1944 she published another collection called *The Leaning Tower*. During the fifties she lectured at Stanford and the University of Michigan and worked on a long allegorical novel based on a voyage she took from Vera Cruz to Bremerhaven in the twenties. The novel, *Ship of Fools*, finally appeared in 1962 and was made into a film in 1965. *The Collected Stories of Katherine Anne Porter* was published in 1965 and won the National Book Award. *The Collected Essays and Occasional Writings of Katherine Anne Porter* appeared in 1970.

She flicked her wrist neatly out of Doctor Harry's pudgy careful fingers and pulled the sheet up to her chin. The brat ought to be in knee breeches. Doctoring around the country with spectacles on his nose! "Get along now, take your schoolbooks and go. There's nothing wrong with me."

Doctor Harry spread a warm paw like a cushion on her forehead where the forked green vein danced and made her eyelids twitch. "Now, now, be a good girl, and we'll have you up in no time."

"That's no way to speak to a woman nearly eighty years old just because she's down. I'd have you respect your elders, young man."

"Well, Missy, excuse me." Doctor Harry patted her cheek. "But I've got to warn you, haven't I? You're a marvel, but you must be careful or you're going to be good and sorry."

"Don't tell me what I'm going to be. I'm on my feet now, morally speaking. It's Cornelia. I had to go to bed to get rid of her."

Her bones felt loose, and floated around in her skin, and Doctor Harry floated like a balloon around the foot of the bed. He floated and pulled down his waistcoat and swung his glasses on a cord. "Well, stay where you are, it certainly can't hurt you."

"Get along and doctor your sick," said Granny Weatherall. "Leave a well woman alone. I'll call for you when I want you. . . . Where were you forty years ago when I pulled through milk-leg and double pneumonia? You weren't even born. Don't let Cornelia lead you on," she shouted, because Doctor Harry appeared to float up to the ceiling and out. "I pay my own bills, and I don't throw my money away on nonsense!"

She meant to wave good-by, but it was too much trouble. Her eyes closed of themselves, it was like a dark curtain drawn around the bed. The pillow rose and floated under her, pleasant as a hammock in a light wind. She listened to the leaves rustling outside the window. No, somebody was swishing newspapers: no, Cornelia and Doctor Harry were whispering together. She leaped broad awake, thinking they whispered in her ear.

"She was never like this, *never* like this!" "Well, what can we expect?" "Yes, eighty years old. . . ."

Well, and what if she was? She still had ears. It was like Cornelia to whisper around doors. She always kept things secret in such a public way. She was always being tactful and kind. Cornelia was dutiful; that was the trouble with her. Dutiful and good: "So good and dutiful," said Granny, "that I'd like to spank her." She saw herself spanking Cornelia and making a fine job of it.

"What'd you say, Mother?"

Granny felt her face tying up in hard knots.

"Can't a body think, I'd like to know?"

"I thought you might want something."

"I do. I want a lot of things. First off, go away and don't whisper."

She lay and drowsed, hoping in her sleep that the children would keep out and let her rest a minute. It had been a long day. Not that she was tired. It was always pleasant to snatch a minute now and then. There was always so much to be done, let me see: tomorrow.

Tomorrow was far away and there was nothing to trouble about. Things were finished somehow when the time came; thank God there was always a little margin over for peace: then a person could spread out the plan of life and tuck in the edges orderly. It was good to have everything clean and folded away, with the hair brushes and tonic bottles sitting straight on the white embroidered linen: the day started without fuss and the pantry shelves laid out with rows of jelly glasses and brown jugs and white stone-china jars with blue whirligigs and words painted on them: coffee, tea, sugar, ginger, cinnamon, allspice: and the bronze clock with the lion on top nicely dusted off. The dust that lion could collected in twenty-four hours! The box in the attic with all those letters tied up, well, she'd have to go through that tomorrow. All those letters—George's letters and John's letters and her letters to them both—lying around for the children to find afterwards made her uneasy. Yes, that would be tomorrow's business. No use to let them know how silly she had been once.

While she was rummaging around she found death in her mind and it felt clammy and unfamiliar. She had spent so much time preparing for death there was no need for bringing it up again. Let it take care of itself now. When she was sixty she had felt very old, finished, and went around making farewell trips to see her children and grandchildren, with a secret in her mind: This is the very last of your mother, children!

Then she made her will and came down with a long fever. That was all just a notion like a lot of other things, but it was lucky too, for she had once for all got over the idea of dying for a long time. Now she couldn't be worried. She hoped she had better sense now. Her father had lived to be one hundred and two years old and had drunk a noggin of strong hot toddy on his last birthday. He told the reporters it was his daily habit, and he owed his long life to that. He had made quite a scandal and was very pleased about it. She believed she'd just plague Cornelia a little.

"Cornelia! Cornelia!" No footsteps, but a sudden hand on her cheek. "Bless you, where have you been?"

"Here, mother."

"Well, Cornelia, I want a noggin of hot toddy."

"Are you cold, darling?"

"I'm chilly, Cornelia. Lying in bed stops the circulation. I must have told you that a thousand times."

Well, she could just hear Cornelia telling her husband that Mother was getting a little childish and they'd have to humor her. The thing that most annoyed her was that Cornelia thought she was deaf, dumb, and blind. Little hasty glances and tiny gestures tossed around her and over her head saying, "Don't cross her, let her have her way, she's eighty years old," and she sitting there as if she lived in a thin glass cage. Sometimes Granny almost made up her mind to pack up and move back to her own house where nobody could remind her every minute that she was old. Wait, wait, Cornelia, till your own children whisper behind your back!

In her day she had kept a better house and had got more work done. She wasn't too old yet for Lydia to be driving eighty miles for advice when one of the children jumped the track, and Jimmy still dropped in and talked things over: "Now, Mammy, you've a good business head, I want to know what you think of this? . . ." Old. Cornelia couldn't change the furniture around without asking. Little things, little things! They had been so sweet when they were little. Granny wished the old days were back again with the children young and everything to be done over. It had been a hard pull, but not too much for her. When she thought of all the food she had cooked, and all the clothes she had cut and sewed, and all the gardens she had made — well, the children showed it. There they were, made out of her, and they couldn't get away from that. Sometimes she wanted to see John again and point to them and say, Well, I didn't do so badly, did I? But that would have to wait. That was for tomorrow. She used to think of him as a man, but now all the children were older than their father, and he would be a child beside her if she saw him now. It seemed strange and there was something wrong with the idea. Why, he couldn't possibly recognize her. She had fenced in a hundred acres once, digging the post holes herself and clamping the wires with just a negro boy to help. That changed a woman. John would be looking for a young woman with the peaked Spanish comb in her hair and the painted fan. Digging post holes changed a woman. Riding country roads in the winter when women had their babies was another thing: sitting up nights with sick horses and sick negroes and sick children and hardly ever losing one. John, I hardly ever lost one of them! John would see that in a minute, that would be something he could understand, she wouldn't have to explain anything!

It made her feel like rolling up her sleeves and putting the whole place to rights again. No matter if Cornelia was determined to be everywhere at once, there were a great many things left undone on this place. She would start tomorrow and do them. It was good to be strong enough for everything, even if all you made melted and changed and slipped under your hands, so that by the time you finished you almost forgot what you were working for. What was it I set out to do? she asked herself intently, but she could not remember. A fog rose over the valley, she saw it marching across the creek swallowing the trees and moving up the hill like an army of ghosts. Soon it would be at the near edge of the orchard, and then it was time to go in and light the lamps. Come in, children, don't stay out in the night air.

Lighting the lamps had been beautiful. The children huddled up to her and breathed like little calves waiting at the bars in the twilight. Their eyes followed the match and watched the flame rise and settle in a blue curve, then they moved away from her. The lamp was lit, they didn't have to be scared and hang on to mother any more. Never, never, never more. God, for all my life I thank Thee. Without Thee, my God, I could never have done it. Hail, Mary, full of grace.

I want you to pick all the fruit this year and see that nothing is wasted. There's always someone who can use it. Don't let good things rot for want of using. You waste life when you waste good food. Don't let things get lost. It's bitter to lose things. Now, don't let me get to thinking, not when I am tired and taking a little nap before supper. . . .

The pillow rose about her shoulders and pressed against her heart and the memory was being squeezed out of it: oh, push down the pillow, somebody: it would smother her if she tried to hold it. Such a fresh breeze blowing and such a green day with no threats in it. But he had not come, just the same. What does a woman do when she has put on the white veil and set out the white cake for a man and he doesn't come? She tried to remember. No, I swear he never harmed me but in that. He never harmed me but in that . . . and what if he did? There was the day, the day, but a whirl of dark smoke rose and covered it, crept up and over into the bright field where everything was planted so carefully in orderly rows. That was hell, she knew hell when she saw it. For sixty years she had prayed against remembering him and against losing her soul in the deep pit of hell, and now the two things were mingled in one and the thought of him was a smoky cloud from hell that moved and crept in her head when she had just got rid of Doctor Harry and was trying to rest a minute. Wounded vanity, Ellen, said a sharp voice in the top of her mind. Don't let your wounded vanity get the upper hand of you. Plenty of girls get jilted. You were jilted, weren't you? Then stand up to it. Her eyelids wavered and let in streamers of blue-gray light like tissue paper over her eyes. She must get up and pull the shades down or she'd never sleep. She was in bed again and the shades were not down. How could that happen? Better turn over, hide from the light, sleeping in the light gave you nightmares. "Mother, how do you feel now?" and a stinging wetness on her forehead. But I don't like having my face washed in cold water!

Hapsy? George? Lydia? Jimmy? No, Cornelia, and her features were swollen and full of little puddles. "They're coming, darling, they'll all be here soon." Go wash your face, child, you look funny.

Instead of obeying, Cornelia knelt down and put her head on the pillow. She seemed to be talking but there was no sound. "Well, are you tongue-tied? Whose birthday is it? Are you going to give a party?"

Cornelia's mouth moved urgently in strange shapes. "Don't do that, you bother me, daughter."

"Oh, no, Mother. Oh, no. . . ."

Nonsense. It was strange about children. They disputed your every word. "No what, Cornelia?"

"Here's Doctor Harry."

"I won't see that boy again. He just left five minutes ago."

"That was this morning, Mother. It's night now. Here's the nurse."

"This is Doctor Harry, Mrs. Weatherall. I never saw you look so young and happy!"

"Ah, I'll never be young again—but I'd be happy if they'd let me lie in peace and get rested."

She thought she spoke up loudly, but no one answered. A warm weight on her forehead, a warm bracelet on her wrist, and a breeze went on whispering, trying to tell her something. A shuffle of leaves in the everlasting hand of God, He blew on them and they danced and rattled. "Mother, don't mind, we're going to give you a little hypodermic." "Look here, daughter, how do ants get in this bed? I saw sugar ants yesterday." Did you send for Hapsy too?

It was Hapsy she really wanted. She had to go a long way back through a great many rooms to find Hapsy standing with a baby on her arm. She seemed to herself to be Hapsy also, and the baby on Hapsy's arm was Hapsy and himself and herself, all at once, and there was no surprise in the meeting. Then Hapsy melted from within and turned flimsy as gray gauze and the baby was a gauzy shadow, and Hapsy came up close and said, "I thought you'd never come," and looked at her very searchingly and said, "You haven't changed a bit!" They leaned forward to kiss, when Cornelia began whispering from a long way off, "Oh, is there anything you want to tell me? Is there anything I can do for you?"

Yes, she had changed her mind after sixty years and she would like to see George. I want you to find George. Find him and be sure to tell him I forgot him. I want him to know I had my husband just the same and my children and my house like any other woman. A good house too and a good husband that I loved and fine children out of him. Better than I hoped for even. Tell him I was given back everything he took away and more. Oh, no, oh, God, no, there was something else besides the house and the man and the children. Oh, surely they were not all? What was it? Something not given back. . . . Her breath crowded down under her ribs and grew into a monstrous frightening shape with cutting edges; it bored up into her head, and the agony was unbelievable: Yes, John, get the Doctor now, no more talk, my time has come.

When this one was born it should be the last. The last. It should have been born first, for it was the one she had truly wanted. Everything came in good time. Nothing left out, left over. She was strong, in three days she would be as well as ever. Better. A woman needed milk in her to have her full health.

"Mother, do you hear me?"

"I've been telling you—"

"Mother, Father Connolly's here."

"I went to Holy Communion only last week. Tell him I'm not so sinful as all that."

"Father just wants to speak to you."

He could speak as much as he pleased. It was like him to drop in and inquire about her soul as if it were a teething baby, and then stay on for a cup of tea and a round of cards and gossip. He always had a funny story of some sort, usually about an Irishman who made his little mistakes and confessed them, and the point lay in some absurd thing he would blurt out in the confessional showing his struggles between native piety and original sin. Granny felt easy about her soul. Cornelia, where are your manners? Give Father Connolly a chair. She had her secret comfortable understanding with a few favorite saints who cleared a straight road to God for her. All as surely signed and sealed as the papers for the new Forty Acres. Forever . . . heirs and assigns forever. Since the day the wedding cake was not cut, but thrown out and wasted. The whole bottom dropped out of the world, and there she was blind and sweating with nothing under her feet and the walls falling away. His hand had caught her under the breast, she had not fallen, there was the freshly polished floor with the green rug on it, just as before. He had cursed like a sailor's parrot and said, "I'll kill him for you." Don't lay a hand on him, for my sake leave something to God. "Now, Ellen, you must believe what I tell you. . . ."

So there was nothing, nothing to worry about any more, except sometimes in the night one of the children screamed in a nightmare, and they both hustled out shaking and hunting for the matches and calling, "There, wait a minute, here we are!" John, get the doctor now, Hapsy's time has come. But there was Hapsy standing by the bed in a white cap. "Cornelia, tell Hapsy to take off her cap. I can't see her plain."

Her eyes opened very wide and the room stood out like a picture she had seen somewhere. Dark colors with the shadows rising towards the ceiling in long angles. The tall black dresser gleamed with nothing on it but John's picture, enlarged from a little one, with John's eyes very black when they should have been blue. You never saw him, so how do you know how he looked? But the man insisted the copy was perfect, it was very rich and handsome. For a picture, yes, but it's not my husband. The table by the bed had a linen cover and a candle and a crucifix. The light was blue from Cornelia's silk lampshades. No sort of light at all, just frippery. You had to live forty years with kerosene lamps to appreciate honest electricity. She felt very strong and she saw Doctor Harry with a rosy nimbus around him.

"You look like a saint, Doctor Harry, and I vow that's as near as you'll ever come to it."

"She's saying something."

"I heard you, Cornelia. What's all this carrying-on?"

"Father Connolly's saying—?

Cornelia's voice staggered and bumped like a cart in a bad road. It rounded corners and turned back again and arrived nowhere. Granny stepped up in the cart very lightly and reached for the reins, but a man sat beside her and she knew him by his hands, driving the cart. She did not look in his face, for she knew without seeing, but looked instead down the road where the trees leaned over and bowed to each other and a thousand birds were singing a Mass. She felt like singing too, but she put her hand in the bosom of her dress and pulled out a rosary, and Father Connolly murmured Latin in a very solemn voice and tickled her feet. My God, will you stop that nonsense? I'm a married woman. What if he did run away and leave me to face the priest by myself? I found another a whole world better. I wouldn't have exchanged my husband for anybody except St. Michael himself, and you may tell him that for me with a thank you in the bargain.

Light flashed on her closed eyelids, and a deep roaring shook her. Cornelia, is that lightning? I hear thunder. There's going to be a storm. Close all the windows. Call the children in. . . . "Mother, here we are, all of us." "Is that you, Hapsy?" "Oh, no, I'm Lydia. We drove as fast as we could." Their faces drifted above her, drifted away. The rosary fell out of her hands and Lydia put it back. Jimmy tried to help, their hands fumbled together, and Granny closed two fingers around Jimmy's thumb. Beads wouldn't do, it must be something alive. She was so amazed her thoughts ran round and round. So, my dear Lord, this is my death and I wasn't even thinking about it. My children have come to see me die. But I can't, it's not time. Oh, I always hated surprises. I wanted to give Cornelia the amethyst set — Cornelia, you're to have the amethyst set, but Hapsy's to wear it when she wants, and, Doctor Harry, do shut up. Nobody sent for you. Oh, my dear Lord, do wait a minute. I meant to do something about the Forty Acres, Jimmy doesn't need it and Lydia will later on, with that worthless husband of hers. I meant to finish the altar cloth and send six bottles of wine to Sister Borgia for her dyspepsia. I want to send six bottles of wine to Sister Borgia, Father Connolly, now don't let me forget.

Cornelia's voice made short turns and tilted over and crashed. "Oh, Mother, oh, Mother, oh, Mother. . . ."

"I'm not going, Cornelia. I'm taken by surprise. I can't go."

You'll see Hapsy again. What about her? "I thought you'd never come." Granny made a long journey outward, looking for Hapsy. What if I don't find her? What then? Her heart sank down and down, there was no bottom to death, she couldn't come to the end of it. The blue light from Cornelia's lampshade drew into a tiny point in the center of her brain, it flickered and winked like an eye, quietly it fluttered and dwindled. Granny lay curled down within herself, amazed and watchful, staring at the point of light that was herself; her body was now only a deeper mass of shadow in an endless darkness and this darkness would curl around the light and swallow it up. God, give a sign!

For the second time there was no sign. Again no bridegroom and the priest in the house. She could not remember any other sorrow because this grief wiped them all away. Oh, no, there's nothing more cruel than this — I'll never forgive it. She stretched herself with a deep breath and blew out the light.

(1930)

❖ AMY TAN
Jing-Mei Woo: Two Kinds

Amy Tan (1952–) was born in Oakland, California, to Chinese immigrants who arrived in America just two years before. She studied
linguistics at the University of California at Berkeley, then became a
consultant to programs for disabled children. She now devotes all her
time to writing. Her first book was collection of short stories, *The Joy
Luck Club* (1989), about Chinese emigrant mothers and their Chinese-
American daughters. Her second book is the novel *The Kitchen God's
Wife* (1991).

My mother believed you could be anything you wanted to be in America. You could
open a restaurant. You could work for the government and get good retirement. You
could buy a house with almost no money down. You could become rich. You could
become instantly famous.

"Of course you can be prodigy, too," my mother told me when I was nine.
"You can be best anything. What does Auntie Lindo know? Her daughter, she is only
best tricky."

America was where all my mother's hopes lay. She had come here in 1949
after losing everything in China: her mother and father, her family home, her first
husband, and two daughters, twin baby girls. But she never looked back with regret.
There were so many ways for things to get better.

We didn't immediately pick the right kind of prodigy. At first my mother
thought I could be a Chinese Shirley Temple. We'd watch Shirley's old movies on TV
as though they were training films. My mother would poke my arm and say, "*Ni
kan*" — You watch. And I would see Shirley tapping her feet, or singing a sailor song,
or pursing her lips into a very round O while saying, "Oh my goodness."

"*Ni kan*," said my mother as Shirley's eyes flooded with tears. "You already
know how. Don't need talent for crying!"

Soon after my mother got this idea about Shirley Temple, she took me to a
beauty training school in the Mission district and put me in the hands of a student who
could barely hold the scissors without shaking. Instead of getting big fat curls, I
emerged with an uneven mass of crinkly black fuzz. My mother dragged me off to the
bathroom and tried to wet down my hair.

"You look like Negro Chinese," she lamented, as if I had done this on
purpose.

The instructor of the beauty training school had to lop off these soggy clumps
to make my hair even again. "Peter Pan is very popular these days," the instructor
assured my mother. I now had hair the length of a boy's, with straight-across bangs
that hung at a slant two inches above my eyebrows. I liked the haircut and it made me
actually look forward to my future fame.

In fact, in the beginning, I was just as excited as my mother, maybe even more

570

so. I pictured this prodigy part of me as many different images, trying each one on for size. I was a dainty ballerina girl standing by the curtains, waiting to hear the right music that would send me floating on my tiptoes. I was like the Christ child lifted out of the straw manger, crying with holy indignity. I was Cinderella stepping from her pumpkin carriage with sparkly cartoon music filling the air.

In all of my imaginings, I was filled with a sense that I would soon become *perfect*. My mother and father would adore me. I would be beyond reproach. I would never feel the need to sulk for anything.

But sometimes the prodigy in me became impatient. "If you don't hurry up and get me out of here, I'm disappearing for good," it warned. "And then you'll always be nothing."

Every night after dinner, my mother and I would sit at the Formica kitchen table. She would present new tests, taking her examples from stories of amazing children she had read in *Ripley's Believe It or Not*, or *Good Housekeeping, Reader's Digest*, and a dozen other magazines she kept in a pile in our bathroom. My mother got these magazines from people whose houses she cleaned. And since she cleaned many houses each week, we had a great assortment. She would look through them all, searching for stories about remarkable children.

The first night she brought out a story about a three-year-old boy who knew the capitals of all the states and even most of the European countries. A teacher was quoted as saying the little boy could also pronounce the names of the foreign cities correctly.

"What's the capital of Finland?" my mother asked me, looking at the magazine story.

All I knew was the capital of California, because Sacramento was the name of the street we lived on in Chinatown. "Nairobi!" I guessed, saying the most foreign word I could think of. She checked to see if that was possibly one way to pronounce "Helsinki" before showing me the answer.

The tests got harder — multiplying numbers in my head, finding the queen of hearts in a deck of cards, trying to stand on my head without using my hands, predicting the daily temperatures in Los Angeles, New York, and London.

One night I had to look at a page from the Bible for three minutes and then report everything I could remember. "Now Jehoshaphat had riches and honor in abundance and . . . that's all I remember, Ma," I said.

And after seeing my mother's disappointed face one again, something inside of me began to die. I hated the tests, the raised hopes and failed expectations. Before going to bed that night, I looked in the mirror above the bathroom sink and when I saw only my face staring back — and that it would always be this ordinary face — I began to cry. Such a sad, ugly girl! I made high-pitched noises like a crazed animal, trying to scratch out the face in the mirror.

And then I saw what seemed to be the prodigy side of me — because I had never seen that face before. I looked at my reflection, blinking so I could see more clearly. The girl staring back at me was angry, powerful. This girl and I were the same. I had new thoughts, willful thoughts, or rather thoughts filled with lots of won'ts. I won't let her change me, I promised myself. I won't be what I'm not.

So now on nights when my mother presented her tests, I performed listlessly, my head propped on one arm. I pretended to be bored. And I was. I got so bored I started counting the bellows of the foghorns out on the bay while my mother drilled me in other areas. The sound was comforting and reminded me of the cow jumping over the moon. And the next day, I played a game with myself, seeing if my mother would give up on me before eight bellows. After a while I usually counted only one, maybe two bellows at most. At last she was beginning to give up hope.

Two or three months had gone by without any mention of my being a prodigy again. And then one day my mother was watching *The Ed Sullivan Show* on TV. The TV was old and the sound kept shorting out. Every time my mother got halfway up from the sofa to adjust the set, the sound would go back on and Ed would be talking. As soon as she sat down, Ed would go silent again. She got up, the TV broke into loud piano music. She sat down. Silence. Up and down, back and forth, quiet and loud. It was like a stiff embraceless dance between her and the TV set. Finally she stood by the set with her hand on the sound dial.

She seemed entranced by the music, a little frenzied piano piece with this mesmerizing quality, sort of quick passages and then teasing lilting ones before it returned to the quick playful parts.

"*Ni kan*," my mother said, calling me over with hurried hand gestures, "Look here."

I could see why my mother was fascinated by the music. It was being pounded out by a little Chinese girl, about nine years old, with a Peter Pan haircut. The girl had the sauciness of a Shirley Temple. She was proudly modest like a proper Chinese child. And she also did this fancy sweep of a curtsy, so that the fluffy skirt of her white dress cascaded slowly to the floor like the petals of a large carnation.

In spite of these warning signs, I wasn't worried. Our family had no piano and we couldn't afford to buy one, let alone reams of sheet music and piano lessons. So I could be generous in my comments when my mother bad-mouthed the little girl on TV.

"Play note right, but doesn't sound good! No singing sound," complained my mother.

"What are you picking on her for?" I said carelessly. "She's pretty good. Maybe she's not the best, but she's trying hard." I knew almost immediately I would be sorry I said that.

"Just like you," she said. "Not the best. Because you not trying." She gave a little huff as she let go of the sound dial and sat down on the sofa.

The little Chinese girl sat down also to play an encore of "Anitra's Dance" by Grieg. I remember the song, because later on I had to learn how to play it.

Three days after watching *The Ed Sullivan Show*, my mother told me what my schedule would be for piano lessons and piano practice. She had talked to Mr. Chong, who lived on the first floor of our apartment building. Mr. Chong was a retired piano teacher and my mother had traded housecleaning services for weekly lessons and a piano for me to practice on every day, two hours a day, from four until six.

When my mother told me this, I felt as though I had been sent to hell. I whined and then kicked my foot a little when I couldn't stand it anymore.

"Why don't you like me the way I am? I'm *not* a genius! I can't play the piano. And even if I could, I wouldn't go on TV if you paid me a million dollars!" I cried.

My mother slapped me. "Who ask you be genius?" she shouted. "Only ask you be your best. For you sake. You think I want you be genius? Hnnh! What for! Who ask you!"

"So ungrateful," I heard her mutter in Chinese. "If she had as much talent as she has temper, she would be famous now."

Mr. Chong, whom I secretly nicknamed Old Chong, was very strange, always tapping his fingers to the silent music of an invisible orchestra. He looked ancient in my eyes. He had lost most of the hair on top of his head and he wore thick glasses and had eyes that always looked tired and sleepy. But he must have been younger than I thought, since he lived with his mother and was not yet married.

I met Old Lady Chong once and that was enough. She had this peculiar smell like a baby that had done something in its pants. And her fingers felt like a dead person's, like an old peach I once found in the back of the refrigerator; the skin just slid off the meat when I picked it up.

I soon found out why Old Chong had retired from teaching piano. He was deaf. "Like Beethoven!" he shouted to me. "We're both listening only in our head!" And he would start to conduct his frantic silent sonatas.

Our lessons went like this. He would open the book and point to different things, explaining their purpose: "Key! Treble! Bass! No sharps or flats! So this is C major! Listen now and play after me!"

And then he would play the C scale a few times, a simple chord, and then, as if inspired by an old, unreachable itch, he gradually added more notes and running trills and a pounding bass until the music was really something quite grand.

I would play after him, the simple scale, the simple chord, and then I just played some nonsense that sounded like a cat running up and down on top of garbage cans. Old Chong smiled and applauded and then said, "Very good! But now you must learn to keep time!"

So that's how I discovered that Old Chong's eyes were too slow to keep up with the wrong notes I was playing. He went through the motions in half-time. To help me keep rhythm, he stood behind me, pushing down on my right shoulder for every beat. He balanced pennies on top of my wrists so I would keep them still as I slowly played scales and arpeggios. He had me curve my hand around an apple and keep that shape when playing chords. He marched stiffly to show me how to make each finger dance up and down, staccato like an obedient little soldier.

He taught me all these things, and that was how I also learned I could be lazy and get away with mistakes, lots of mistakes. If I hit the wrong notes because I hadn't practiced enough, I never corrected myself. I just kept playing in rhythm. And Old Chong kept conducting his own private reverie.

So maybe I never really gave myself a fair chance. I did pick up the basics pretty quickly, and I might have become a good pianist at that young age. But I was so determined not to try, not to be anybody different that I learned to play only the most ear-splitting preludes, the most discordant hymns.

Over the next year, I practiced like this, dutifully in my own way. And then one day I heard my mother and her friend Lindo Jong both talking in a loud bragging tone of voice so others could hear. It was after church, and I was leaning against the brick wall wearing a dress with stiff white petticoats. Auntie Lindo's daughter, Waverly, who was about my age, was standing farther down the wall about five feet away. We had grown up together and shared all the closeness of two sisters squabbling over crayons and dolls. In other words, for the most part, we hated each other. I thought she was snotty. Waverly Jong had gained a certain amount of fame as "Chinatown's Littlest Chinese Chess Champion."

"She bring home too many trophy," lamented Auntie Lindo that Sunday. "All day she play chess. All day I have no time do nothing but dust off her winnings." She threw a scolding look at Waverly, who pretended not to see her.

"You lucky you don't have this problem," said Auntie Lindo with a sigh to my mother.

And my mother squared her shoulders and bragged: "Our problem worser than yours. If we ask Jing-mei wash dish, she hear nothing but music. It's like you can't stop this natural talent."

And right then, I was determined to put a stop to her foolish pride.

A few weeks later, Old Chong and my mother conspired to have me play in a talent show which would be held in the church hall. By then, my parents had saved up enough to buy me a secondhand piano, a black Wurlitzer spinet with a scarred bench. It was the showpiece of our living room.

For the talent show, I was to play a piece called "Pleading Child" from Schumann's *Scenes from Childhood*. It was a simple, moody piece that sounded more difficult than it was. I was supposed to memorize the whole thing, playing the repeat parts twice to make the piece sound longer. But I dawdled over it, playing a few bars and then cheating, looking up to see what notes followed. I never really listened to what I was playing. I daydreamed about being somewhere else, about being someone else.

The part I liked to practice best was the fancy curtsy: right foot out, touch the rose on the carpet with a pointed foot, sweep to the side, left leg bends, look up and smile.

My parents invited all the couples from the Joy Luck Club to witness my debut. Auntie Lindo and Uncle Tin were there. Waverly and her two older brothers had also come. The first two rows were filled with children both younger and older than I was. The littlest ones got to go first. They recited simple nursery rhymes, squawked out tunes on miniature violins, twirled Hula Hoops, pranced in pink ballet tutus, and when they bowed or curtsied, the audience would sigh in unison, "Awww," and then clap enthusiastically.

When my turn came, I was very confident. I remember my childish excitement. It was as if I knew, without a doubt, that the prodigy side of me really did exist. I had no fear whatsoever, no nervousness. I remember thinking to myself, This is it! This is it! I looked out over the audience, at my mother's blank face, my father's yawn, Auntie Lindo's stiff-lipped smile, Waverly's sulky expression. I had on a white dress layered with sheets of lace, and a pink bow in my Peter Pan haircut. As I sat down I envisioned people jumping to their feet and Ed Sullivan rushing up to introduce me to everyone on TV.

And I started to play. It was so beautiful. I was so caught up in how lovely I looked that at first I didn't worry how I would sound. So it was a surprise to me when I hit the first wrong note and I realized something didn't sound quite right. And then I hit another and another followed that. A chill started at the top of my head and began to trickle down. Yet I couldn't stop playing, as though my hands were bewitched. I kept thinking my fingers would adjust themselves back, like a train switching to the right track. I played this strange jumble through two repeats, the sour notes staying with me all the way to the end.

When I stood up, I discovered my legs were shaking. Maybe I had just been nervous and the audience, like Old Chong, had seen me go through the right motions and had not heard anything wrong at all. I swept my right foot out, went down on my knee, looked up and smiled. The room was quiet, except for Old Chong, who was beaming and shouting, "Bravo! Bravo! Well done!" But then I saw my mother's face, her stricken face. The audience clapped weakly, and as I walked back to my chair, with my whole face quivering as I tried not to cry, I heard a little boy whisper loudly to his mother, "That was awful," and the mother whispered back, "Well, she certainly tried."

And now I realized how many people were in the audience, the whole world it seemed. I was aware of eyes burning into my back. I felt the shame of my mother and father as they sat stiffly throughout the rest of the show.

We could have escaped during intermission. Pride and some strange sense of honor must have anchored my parents to their chairs. And so we watched it all: the eighteen-year-old boy with a fake mustache who did a magic show and juggled flaming hoops while riding a unicycle. The breasted girl with white makeup who sang from *Madama Butterfly* and got honorable mention. And the eleven-year-old boy who won first prize playing a tricky violin song that sounded like a busy bee.

After the show, the Hsus, the Jongs, and the St. Clairs from the Joy Luck Club came up to my mother and father.

"Lots of talented kids," Aunti Lindo said vaguely, smiling broadly.

"That was somethin' else," said my father, and I wondered if he was referring to me in a humorous way, or whether he even remembered what I had done.

Waverly looked at me and shrugged her shoulders. "You aren't a genius like me," she said matter-of-factly. And if I hadn't felt so bad, I would have pulled her braids and punched her stomach.

But my mother's expression was what devastated me: a quiet, blank look that said she had lost everything. I felt the same way, and it seemed as if everybody were now coming up, like gawkers at the scene of an accident, to see what parts were actually missing. When we got on the bus to go home, my father was humming the busy-bee tune and my mother was silent. I kept thinking she wanted to wait until we got home before shouting at me. But when my father unlocked the door to our apartment, my mother walked in and then went to the back, into the bedroom. No accusations. No blame. And in a way, I felt disappointed. I had been waiting for her to start shouting, so I could shout back and cry and blame her for all my misery.

I assumed my talent-show fiasco meant I never had to play the piano again. But two days later, after school, my mother came out of the kitchen and saw me watching TV.

"Four clock," she reminded me as if it were any other day. I was stunned, as though she were asking me to go through the talent-show torture again. I wedged myself more tightly in front of the TV.

"Turn off TV," she called from the kitchen five minutes later.

I didn't budge. And then I decided. I didn't have to do what my mother said anymore. I wasn't her slave. This wasn't China. I had listened to her before and look what happened. She was the stupid one.

She came out from the kitchen and stood in the arched entryway of the living room. "Four clock," she said once again, louder.

"I'm not going to play anymore," I said nonchalantly. "Why should I? I'm not a genius."

She walked over and stood in front of the TV. I saw her chest was heaving up and down in an angry way.

"No!" I said, and I now felt stronger, as if my true self had finally emerged. So this was what had been inside me all along.

"No! I won't!" I screamed.

She yanked me by the arm, pulled me off the floor, snapped off the TV. She was frighteningly strong, half pulling, half carrying me toward the piano as I kicked the throw rugs under my feet. She lifted me up and onto the hard bench. I was sobbing by now, looking at her bitterly. Her chest was heaving even more and her mouth was open, smiling crazily as if she were pleased I was crying.

"You want me to be someone that I'm not!" I sobbed. "I'll never be the kind of daughter you want me to be!"

"Only two kinds of daughters," she shouted in Chinese. "Those who are obedient and those who follow their own mind! Only one kind of daughter can live in this house. Obedient daughter!"

"Then I wish I wasn't your daughter. I wish you weren't my mother," I shouted. As I said these things I got scared. It felt like worms and toads and slimy things crawling out of my chest, but it also felt good, as if this awful side of me had surfaced, at last.

"Too late change this," said my mother shrilly.

And I could sense her anger rising to its breaking point. I wanted to see it spill over. And that's when I remembered the babies she had lost in China, the ones we never talked about. "Then I wish I'd never been born!" I shouted. "I wish I were dead! Like them."

It was as if I had said the magic words. Alakazam! — and her face went blank, her mouth closed, her arms went slack, and she backed out of the room, stunned, as if she were blowing away like a small brown leaf, thin, brittle, lifeless.

It was not the only disappointment my mother felt in me. In the years that followed, I failed her so many times, each time asserting my own will, my right to fall short of expectations. I didn't get straight As. I didn't become class president. I didn't get into Stanford. I dropped out of college.

For unlike my mother, I did not believe I could be anything I wanted to be. I could only be me.

And for all those years, we never talked about the disaster at the recital or my terrible accusations afterward at the piano bench. All that remained unchecked, like a betrayal that was now unspeakable. So I never found a way to ask her why she had hoped for something so large that failure was inevitable.

And even worse, I never asked her what frightened me the most: Why had she given up hope?

For after our struggle at the piano, she never mentioned my playing again. The lessons stopped. The lid to the piano was closed, shutting out the dust, my misery, and her dreams.

So she surprised me. A few years ago, she offered to give me the piano, for my thirtieth birthday. I had not played in all those years. I saw the offer as a sign of forgiveness, a tremendous burden removed.

"Are you sure?" I asked shyly. "I mean, won't you and Dad miss it?"

"No, this your piano," she said firmly. "Always your piano. You only one can play."

"Well, I probably can't play anymore," I said. "It's been years."

"You pick up fast," said my mother, as if she knew this was certain. "You have natural talent. You could been genius if you want to."

"No I couldn't."

"You just not trying," said my mother. And she was neither angry nor sad. She said it as if to announce a fact that could never be disproved. "Take it," she said.

But I didn't at first. It was enough that she had offered it to me. And after that, every time I saw it in my parents' living room, standing in front of the bay windows, it made me feel proud, as if it were a shiny trophy I had won back.

Last week I sent a tuner over to my parents' apartment and had the piano reconditioned, for purely sentimental reasons. My mother had died a few months before and I had been getting things in order for my father, a little bit at a time. I put the jewelry in special silk pouches. The sweaters she had knitted in yellow, pink, bright orange — all the colors I hated — I put those in moth-proof boxes. I found some old Chinese silk dresses, the kind with little slits up the sides. I rubbed the old silk against my skin, then wrapped them in tissue and decided to take them home with me.

After I had the piano tuned, I opened the lid and touched the keys. It sounded even richer than I remembered. Really, it was a very good piano. Inside the bench were the same exercise notes with handwritten scales, the same secondhand music books with their covers held together with yellow tape.

I opened up the Schumann book to the dark little piece I had played at the recital. It was on the left-hand side of the page, "Pleading Child." It looked more difficult than I remembered. I played a few bars, surprised at how easily the notes came back to me.

And for the first time, or so it seemed, I noticed the piece on the right-hand side. It was called "Perfectly Contended." I tried to play this one as well. It had a lighter melody but the same flowing rhythm and turned out to be quite easy. "Pleading Child" was shorter but slower; "Perfectly Contended" was longer, but faster. And after I played them both a few times, I realized they were two halves of the same song.

(1989)

❖ LEO TOLSTOY
Three Deaths
A Tale

Leo Tolstoy (1828–1910) was born a nobleman in Yasnaya Polyana, Russia. An orphan, he was raised by an aunt. He studied law at the University of Kazan from 1845 through 1847. After managing the family estates for a few years, he entered the army in 1851 and fought as an officer in the Crimean War. During his service he wrote sketches of army life and three novels, *Childhood* (1852), *Boyhood* (1854), and *Youth* (1857). In 1855 he published a collection of short stories based on his experiences in the Caucasus called *Sevastopol Stories*. Thereafter he made two trips to Europe, but disliked what he saw and returned home to his estates. He published "Three Deaths" and *Family Happiness* in 1859 and another novel about life in the Caucasus, *Cossacks*, in 1862. From 1861 to 1876 he farmed his land and taught the children of his serfs in a school that he built for them. As he grew older his thoughts turned more and more to charity, and ultimately he was no less famous as a humanitarian than as a novelist. He published his greatest novels, the mighty *War and Peace*, in 1869, and *Anna Karenina*, in 1877. Thereafter he underwent a spiritual crisis, dissociating himself from conventional society and advocating his own brand of Christianity. He attracted many disciples, some of whom were arrested by the government. But Tolstoy himself was never interfered with. Fiction reflecting the attitudes of his later years include *The Death of Ivan Ilych* (1886), *Master and Man* (1895), and *Resurrection* (1899). He also published nonfiction explaining his personal philosophy: *What Men Live By* (1881), *My Confession* (1882), *What I Believe* (1884), and *The Kingdom of God Is Within You* (1893). Tolstoy's entire works were translated into English by Louis and Aylmer Maude in twenty-one volumes (1929–1937).

Chapter 1

It was autumn.

Along the highway came two equipages at a brisk pace. In the first carriage sat two women. One was a lady, thin and pale; the other, her maid, with a brilliant red complexion, and plump. Her short, dry locks escaped from under a faded cap; her red hand, in a torn glove, put them back with a jerk. Her full bosom, incased in a tapestry shawl, breathed of health; her keen black eyes now gazed through the window at the fields hurrying by them, now rested on her mistress, now peered solicitously into the corners of the coach.

Before the maid's face swung the lady's bonnet on the rack; on her knees lay a

578

puppy; her feet were raised by packages lying on the floor, and could almost be heard drumming upon them above the noise of the creaking of the springs and the rattling of the windows.

The lady, with her hands resting in her lap and her eyes shut, feebly swayed on the cushions which supported her back, and, slightly frowning, tried to suppress her cough.

She wore a white nightcap, and a blue neckerchief twisted around her delicate pale neck. A straight line, disappearing under the cap, parted her perfectly smooth blond hair, which was pomaded; and there was a dry, deathly appearance about the whiteness of the skin, in this wide parting. The withered and rather sallow skin was loosely drawn over her delicate and pretty features, and there was a hectic flush on the cheeks and cheekbones. Her lips were dry and restless, her thin eyelashes had lost their curve, and a cloth traveling capote made straight folds over her sunken chest. Although her eyes were closed, her face gave the impression of weariness, irascibility, and habitual suffering.

The lackey, leaning back, was napping on the coach-box. The *yamshchik*, or hired driver, shouting in a clear voice, urged on his four powerful and sweaty horses, occasionally looking back at the other driver, who was shouting just behind them in an open barouche. The tires of the wheels in their even and rapid course, left wide parallel tracks on the limy mud of the highway.

The sky was gray and cold, a moist mist was falling over the fields and the road. It was suffocating in the carriage, and smelt of eau-de-Cologne and dust. The invalid learned back her head, and slowly opened her eyes. Her great eyes were brilliant, and of a beautiful dark color.

"Again!" said she, nervously, pushing away with her beautiful attenuated hand the end of her maid's cloak, which occasionally hit against her leg. Her mouth contracted painfully.

Matriosha raised her cloak in both hands, lifting herself up on her strong legs, and then sat down again, farther away. Her fresh face was suffused with a brilliant scarlet.

The invalid's beautiful dark eyes eagerly followed the maid's motions; and then with both hands she took hold of the seat, and did her best to raise herself a little higher, but her strength was not sufficient.

Again her mouth became contracted, and her whole face took on an expression of unavailing, angry irony.

"If you would only help me . . . ah! It's not necessary. I can do it myself. Only have the goodness not to put those pillows behind me. . . . On the whole, you had better not touch them, if you don't understand!"

The lady closed her eyes, and then again, quickly raising the lids, gazed at her maid.

Matriosha looked at her, and gnawed her red lower lip. A heavy sigh escaped from the sick woman's breast; but the sigh was not ended, but was merged in a fit of coughing. She scowled, and turned her face away, clutching her chest with both hands. When the coughing fit was over, she once more shut her eyes, and continued to sit motionless. The coach and the barouche rolled into a village. Matriosha drew her fat hand from under her shawl, and made the sign of the cross.

"What is this?" demanded the lady.

"A post-station, madame."

"Why did you cross yourself, I should like to know?"

"The church, madame."

The invalid lady looked out of the window, and began slowly to cross herself, gazing with all her eyes at the great village church, in front of which her carriage was now passing.

The two vehicles came to a stop together at the post-house. The sick woman's husband and the doctor dismounted from the barouche, and came to the coach.

"How are you feeling?" asked the doctor, taking her pulse.

"Well, my dear, aren't you fatigued?" asked the husband, in French. "Wouldn't you like to get out?"

Matriosha, gathering up the bundles, squeezed herself into the corner, so as not to interfere with the conversation.

"No matter, it's all the same thing," replied the invalid. "I will not get out."

The husband, after standing there a little, went into the post-house. Matriosha, jumping from the coach, tiptoed across the muddy road into the inclosure.

"If I am miserable, there is no reason why the rest of you should not have breakfast," said the sick woman, smiling faintly to the doctor, who was standing by her window.

"It makes no difference to them how I am," she remarked to herself as the doctor, turning from her with slow step, started to run up the steps of the station-house. "They are well, and it's all the same to them. O my God!"

"How now, Edouard Ivanovitch?" said the husband, as he met the doctor, and rubbing his hands with a gay smile. "I have ordered my traveling-case brought; what do you say to that?"

"That's worth while," replied the doctor.

"Well, now, how about *her?*" asked the husband, with a sigh, lowering his voice and raising her brows.

"I have told you that she cannot reach Moscow, much less Italy, especially in such weather."

"What is to be done, then? Oh! my God! my God!"

The husband covered his eyes with his hand. . . . "Give it here," he added, addressing his man, who came bringing the traveling-case.

"You'll have to stop somewhere on the route," replied the doctor, shrugging his shoulders.

"But tell me, what can I do?" rejoining the husband. "I have employed every argument to keep her from going; I have spoken to her of our means, and of our children whom we should have to leave behind, and of my business. She would not hear a word. She has made her plans for living abroad, as if she were well. But if I should tell her what her real condition is, it would kill her."

"Well, she is a dead woman now; you may as well know it, Vasili Dmitritch. A person cannot live without lungs, and there is no way of making lungs grow again. It is melancholy, it is hard, but what is to be done about it? It is my business and yours to make her last days as easy as possible. The confessor is the person needed here."

"Oh, my God! Now just perceive how I am situated, in speaking to her of her last will. Let come whatever may, yet I cannot speak of that. And yet you know how good she is."

"Try at least to persuade her to wait until the roads are frozen," said the doctor, shaking his head significantly; "something might happen during the journey."

"Aksiusha, oh, Aksiusha!" cried the superintendent's daughter, throwing a cloak over her head, and tiptoeing down the muddy back steps. "Come along. Let us have a look at the Shirkinskaya lady; they say she's got lung trouble, and they're taking her abroad. I never saw how any one looked in consumption."

Aksiusha jumped down from the door-sill; and the two girls, hand in hand, hurried out of the gates. Shortening their steps, they walked by the coach, and stared in at the lowered window. The invalid bent her head toward them; but, when she saw their inquisitiveness, she frowned and turned away.

"Oh, de-e-ar!" said the superintendent's daughter, vigorously shaking her head. . . . "How wonderfully pretty she used to be, and how she has changed! It is terrible! Did you see? Did you see, Aksiusha?"

"Yes, and how thin she is!" assented Aksiusha. "Let us go by and look again; we'll make believe go to the well. Did you see, she turned away from us; still I got a good view of her. Isn't it too bad, Masha?"

"Yes, but what terrible mud!" replied Masha, and both of them started to run back within the gates.

"It's evident that I have become a fright," thought the sick woman. . . . . "But we must hurry, hurry, and get abroad, and there I shall soon get well."

"Well, and how are you, my dear?" inquired the husband, coming to the coach with still a morsel of something in his mouth.

"Always one and the same question," thought the sick woman, "and he's even eating!"

"It's no consequence," she murmured, between her teeth.

"Do you know, my dear, I am afraid that this journey in such weather will only make you worse. Edouard Ivanovitch says the same thing. Hadn't we better turn back?"

She maintained an angry silence.

"Maybe the weather will improve, the roads will become good, and that would be better for you; then at least we could start all together."

"Pardon me. If I had not listened to you so long, I should at this moment be at Berlin and have entirely recovered."

"What's to be done, my angel? it was impossible, as you know. But now if you would wait a month, you would be ever so much better; I could finish up my business, and we could take the children with us." . . . .

"The children are well, and I am not."

"But just see here, my love, if in this weather you should grow worse on the road. . . . At least we should be at home."

"What is the use being at home? . . . *Die* at home?" replied the invalid, peevishly.

But the word *die* evidently startled her, and she turned on her husband a supplicating and inquiring look. He dropped his eyes, and said nothing.

The sick woman's mouth suddenly contracted in a childish fashion, and the tears sprang to her eyes. Her husband covered his face with his handkerchief, and silently turned from the coach.

"No, I will go," cried the invalid; and, lifting her eyes to the sky, she clasped her hands, and began to whisper incoherent words. "My God! why must it be?" she said, and the tears flowed more violently.

She prayed long and fervently, but still there was just the same sense of constriction and pain in her chest, just the same gray melancholy in the sky and the fields and the road; just the same autumnal mist, neither thicker nor more tenuous, but ever the same in its monotony, falling on the muddy highway, on the roofs, on the carriage, and on the sheepskin coats of the drivers, who were talking in strong, gay voices, as they were oiling and adjusting the carriage.

Chapter II

The coach was ready, but the driver loitered. He had gone into the drivers' room. In the izba it was warm, close, dark, and suffocating, smelling of human occupation, of cooking bread, of cabbage, and of sheepskin garments.

Several drivers were in the room; the cook was engaged near the oven, on top of which lay a sick man wrapped up in his sheepskins.

"Uncle Khveodor! hey! Uncle Khveodor," called a young man, the driver, in a tulup, and with his knout in his belt, coming into the room, and addressing the sick man.

"What do you want, rattlepate? What are you calling to Fyedka for?" asked one of the drivers. "There's your carriage waiting for you."

"I want to borrow his boots. Mine are worn out," replied the young fellow, tossing back his curls and straightening his mittens in his belt. "Why? is he asleep? Say, Uncle Khveodor!" he insisted, going to the oven.

"What is it?" a weak voice was heard saying, and an emaciated face was lifted up from the oven.

A broad, gaunt hand, bloodless and covered with hairs, pulled up his overcoat over the dirty shirt that covered his bony shoulder. "Give me something to drink, brother; what is it you want?"

The young fellow handed him a small dish of water.

"I say, Fyedya," said he, hesitating, "I reckon you won't want your new boots now; let me have them? Probably you won't need them any more."

The sick man, dropping his weary head down to the lacquered bowl, and dipping this thin, hanging mustache in the brown water, drank feebly and eagerly.

His tangled beard was unclean; his sunken, clouded eyes were with difficulty raised to the young man's face. When he had finished drinking, he tried to raise his hand to wipe his wet lips, but his strength failed him, and he wiped them on the sleeve of his overcoat. Silently, and breathing with difficulty through his nose, be looked straight into the young man's eyes, and tried to collect his strength.

"Maybe you have promised them to some one else?" said the young driver. "If that's so, all right. The worst of it is, it is wet outside, and I have to go out to my work, and so I said to myself, 'I reckon I'll ask Fyedka for his boots; I reckon he won't be needing them.' But maybe you will need them, — just say."

Something began to bubble up and rumble in the sick man's chest; he bent over, and began to strangle, with a cough that rattled in his throat.

"Now I should like to know where he would need them?" unexpectedly snapped out the cook, angrily addressing the whole hovel. "This is the second month that he has not crept down from the oven. Just see how he is all broken up! and you can hear how it must hurt him inside. Where would he need boots? They would not think of burying him in new ones! And it was time long ago, God pardon me the sin of saying so. Just see how he chokes! He ought to be taken from this room to another, or somewhere. They say there's hospitals in the city; but what's you going to do? he takes up the whole room, and that's too much. There isn't any room at all. And yet you are expected to keep neat."

"Hey! Seryoha, come along, take your place, the people are waiting," cried the head man of the station, coming to the door.

Seryoha started to go without waiting for his reply, but the sick man during his cough intimated by his eyes that he was going to speak.

"You take the boots, Seryoha," said he, conquering the cough, and getting his breath a little. "Only do you hear, buy me a stone when I am dead," he added hoarsely.

"Thank you, uncle; then I will take them, and as for the stone, — yei-yei! — I will buy you one."

"There, children, you are witnesses," the sick man was able to articulate, and then once more he bent over and began to choke.

"All right, we have heard," said one of the drivers. "But run, Seryoha, or else the starosta will be after you again. You know Lady Shirkinskaya is sick."

Seryoha quickly pulled off his ragged, unwieldy boots, and flung them under the bench. Uncle Feodor's new ones fitted his feet exactly, and the young driver could not keep his eyes off them as he went to the carriage.

"Ek! what splendid boots! Here's some grease," called another driver with the grease-pot in his hand, as Seryoha mounted to his box and gathered up the reins. "Get them for nothing?"

"So you're jealous, are you?" cried Seryoha, lifting up and tucking around his legs the tails of his overcoat. "Off with you, my darlings," he cried to the horses, cracking his knout; and the coach and barouche, with their occupants, trunks, and other belongings, were hidden in the thick autumnal mist, and rapidly whirled away over the wet road.

The sick driver remained on the oven in the stifling hovel, and, not being able to throw off the phlegm, by a supreme effort turned over on the other side, and stopped coughing.

Till evening there was a continual coming and going, and eating of meals in the room, and the sick man was not noticed. Before night came on, the cook climbed up on the oven, and got the sheepskin coat from the farther side of his legs.

"Don't be angry with me, Nastasya," exclaimed the sick man. "I shall soon leave your room."

"All right, all right, it's of no consequence," muttered the woman. "But what is the matter with you, uncle? Tell me."

"All my inwards are gnawed out. God knows what it is!"

"And I don't doubt your gullet hurts you when you cough so!"

"It hurts me all over. My death is at hand, that's what it is. Okh! okh! okh!" groaned the sick man.

"Now cover up your legs this way," said Nastasya, comfortably arranging the overcoat so that it would cover him, and then getting down from the oven.

During the night the room was faintly lighted by a single taper. Nastasya and a dozen drivers were sleeping, snoring loudly, on the floor and the benches. Only the sick man feebly hawked and coughed, and tossed on the oven.

In the morning no sound was heard from him.

"I saw something wonderful in my sleep," said the cook, as she stretched herself in the early twilight the next morning. "I seemed to see Uncle Khveodor get down from the oven, and go out to cut wood. 'Look here,' says he, 'I'm going to help you, Nastya;' and I says to him, 'How can you split wood?' but he seizes the hatchet, and begins to cut so fast, so fast that nothing but chips fly. 'Why,' says I, 'haven't you been sick?' — 'No,' says he, 'I am well,' and he kind of lifted up the ax, and I was scared; and I screamed and woke up. He can't be dead, can he? — Uncle Khveodor! hey, uncle!"

Feodor did not move.

"Now he can't be dead, can he? Go and see," said one of the drivers, who had just waked up.

The emaciated hand, covered with reddish hair, that hung down from the oven, was cold and pale.

"Go tell the superintendent; it seems he is dead," said the driver.

Feodor had no relatives. He was a stranger. On the next day they buried him in the new burying-ground behind the grove; and Nastasya for many days had to tell everybody of the vision which she had seen, and how she had been the first to discover that Uncle Feodor was dead.

Chapter III

Spring had come.

Along the wet streets of the city swift streamlets ran purling between heaps of dung-covered ice; bright were the colors of people's dresses and the tones of their voices, as they hurried along. In the walled gardens, the buds on the trees were burgeoning, and the fresh breeze swayed their branches with a soft gentle murmur. Everywhere transparent drops were forming and falling. . . . .

The sparrows chattered incoherently, and fluttered about on their little wings. On the sunny side, on the walls, houses, and trees, all was full of life and brilliancy. The sky, and the earth, and the heart of man overflowed with youth and joy.

In front of a great seignorial mansion, in one of the principal streets, fresh straw had been laid down; in the house lay that same moribund invalid whom we saw hastening abroad.

Near the closed doors of her room stood the sick lady's husband, and a lady well along in years. On a divan sat the confessor, with cast-down eyes, holding something wrapped up under his stole. In one corner, in a Voltaire easy-chair, reclined an old lady, the sick woman's mother, weeping violently.

Near her stood the maid, holding a clean handkerchief, ready for the old lady's use when she should ask for it. Another maid was rubbing the old lady's temples, and blowing on her gray head underneath her cap.

"Well, Christ be with you, my dear," said the husband to the elderly lady who was standing with him near the door: "she has such confidence in you; you know how to talk with her; go and speak with her a little while, my darling, please go!"

He was about to open the door for her; but his cousin held him back, putting her handkerchief several times to her eyes, and shaking her head.

"There, now she will not see that I have been weeping," said she, and, opening the door herself, went to the invalid.

The husband was in the greatest excitement, and seemed quite beside himself. He started to go over to the old mother, but, after taking a few steps, he turned around, walked the length of the room, and approached the priest.

The priest looked at him, raised his brows toward heaven, and sighed. The thick gray beard also was lifted and fell again.

"My God! my God!" said the husband.

"What can you do?" exclaimed the confessor, sighing and again lifting up his brows and beard, and letting them drop.

"And the old mother there!" exclaimed the husband, almost in despair. "She will not be able to endure it. You see, she loved her so, she loved her so, that she . . . . I don't know. You might try, father, to calm her a little, and persuade her to go away."

The confessor arose and went over to the old lady.

"It is true, no one can appreciate a mother's heart," said he, "but God is compassionate."

The old lady's face was suddenly convulsed, and a hysterical sob shook her frame.

"God is compassionate," repeated the priest, when she had grown a little calmer. "I will tell you, in my parish there was a sick man, and much worse than Marya Dmitrievna, and he, though he was only a shopkeeper, was cured in a very short time, by means of herbs. And this very same shopkeeper is now in Moscow. I have told Vasili Dmitrievitch about him; it might be tried, you know. At all events, it would satisfy the invalid. With God, all things are possible."

"No, she won't get well," persisted the old lady. "Why should God have taken her, and not me?"

And again the hysterical sobbing overcame her, so violently that she fainted away.

The invalid's husband hid his face in his hands, and rushed from the room.

In the corridor the first person whom he met was a six-year-old boy, who was chasing his little sister with all his might and main.

"Do you bid me take the children to their mamasha?" inquired the nurse.

"No, she does not like to see them. They distract her."

The lad stopped for a moment, and, after looking eagerly into his father's face, he cut a dido with his leg, and with merry shouts ran on.

"I'm playing she's a horse, papasha," cried the little fellow, pointing to his sister.

Meantime, in the next room, the cousin had taken her seat near the sick woman, and was skilfully bringing the conversation by degrees round so as to prepare her for the thought of death. The doctor stood by the window, mixing some draught.

The invalid, in a white capote, all surrounded by cushions, was sitting up in bed, and gazed silent at her cousin.

"Ah, my dear!" she exclaimed, unexpectedly interrupting her, "don't try to prepare me; don't treat me like a little child! I am a Christian woman. I know all about it. I know that I have not long to live; I know that if my husband had heeded me sooner, I should have been in Italy, and possibly, yes probably, should have been well by this time. They all told him so. But what is to be done? it's as God saw fit. We all of us have sinned, I know that; but I hope in the mercy of God, that all will be pardoned, ought to be pardoned. I am trying to sound my own heart. I also have committed many sins, my love. But how much I have suffered in atonement! I have tried to bear my sufferings patiently." . . . .

"Then shall I have the confessor come in, my love? It will be all the easier for you, after you have been absolved," said the cousin.

The sick woman dropped her head in token of assent. "O God! pardon me, a sinner," she whispered.

The cousin went out, and beckoned to the confessor. "She is an angel," she said to the husband, with tears in her eyes. The husband wept. The priest went into the sick-room; the old lady still remained unconscious, and in the room beyond all was perfectly quiet. At the end of five minutes the confessor came out, and, taking off his stole, arranged his hair.

"Thanks be to the Lord, she is calmer now," said he. "She wishes to see you."

The cousin and the husband went to the sick-room. The invalid, gently weeping, was gazing at the images.

"I congratulate you, my love," said the husband.

"Thank you. How well I feel now! what ineffable joy I experience!" said the sick woman, and a faint smile played over her thin lips. "How merciful God is! Is He not? He is merciful and omnipotent!"

And again with an eager prayer she turned her tearful eyes toward the holy images.

Then suddenly something seemed to occur to her mind. She beckoned to her husband.

"You are never willing to do what I desire," said she, in a weak and querulous voice.

The husband, stretching his neck, listened to her submissively.

"What is it, my love?"

"How many times I have told you that these doctors don't know anything! There are simple women doctors; they make cures. That's what the good father said. . . . A shopkeeper . . . . send for him." . . . .

"For whom, my love?"

"Good heavens! you can never understand me." And the dying woman frowned, and closed her eyes.

The doctor came to her, and took her hand. Her pulse was evidently growing feebler and feebler. He made a sign to the husband. The sick woman remarked this gesture, and looked around in fright. The cousin turned away to hide her tears.

"Don't weep, don't torment yourselves on my account," said the invalid. "That takes away from me my last comfort."

"You are an angel!" exclaimed the cousin, kissing her hand.

"No, kiss me here. They only kiss the hands of those who are dead. My God! my God!"

That same evening the sick woman was a corpse, and the corpse in the coffin lay in the parlor of the great mansion. In the immense room, the doors of which were closed, sat the clerk, and with a monotonous voice read the Psalms of David through his nose.

The bright glare from the wax candles in the lofty silver candelabra fell on the white brow of the dead, on the heavy waxen hands, on the stiff folds of the cerement which brought out into awful relief the knees and the feet.

The clerk, not varying his tones, continued to read on steadily, and in the silence of the chamber of death his words rang out and died away. Occasionally from distant rooms came the voice of children and their romping.

"Thou hidest they face, they are troubled; thou takest away their breath, they die and return to their dust.

"Thou sendest forth thy Spirit, they are created; and thou renewest the face of the earth.

"The glory of the Lord shall endure forever." . . . .

The face of the dead was stern and majestic. But there was no motion either on the pure cold brow, or the firmly closed lips. She was all attention! But did she perhaps now understand these majestic words?

Chapter IV

At the end of a month, over the grave of the dead a stone chapel was erected. Over the driver's there was as yet no stone, and only the fresh green grass sprouted over the mound which served as the sole record of the past existence of a man.

"It will be a sin and a shame, Seryoha," said the cook at the station-house one day, "if you don't buy a gravestone for Khveodor. You kept saying, 'It's winter, winter,' but now why don't you keep your word? I heard it all. He was already come back once to ask why you don't do it; if you don't buy him one, he will come again, he will choke you."

"Well, now, have I denied it?" urged Seryoha. "I am going to buy him a stone, as I said I would. I can get one for a ruble and a half. I have not forgotten about it; I'll have to get it. As soon as I happen to be in town, then I'll buy him one."

"You ought at least to put up a cross, that's what you ought to do," said an old driver. "It isn't right at all. You're wearing those boots now."

"Yes. But where could I get him a cross? You wouldn't want to make one out of an old piece of stick, would you?"

"What is that you say? Make one out of an old piece of stick? No; take your ax, go out to the wood a little earlier than usual, and you can hew him out one. Take a little ash tree, and you can make one. You can have a covered cross. If you go then, you won't have to give the watchman a little drink of vodka. One doesn't want to give vodka for every trifle. Now, yesterday I broke my axletree, and I go and hew out a new one of green wood. No one said a word."

Early the next morning, almost before dawn, Seryoha took his ax, and went to the wood.

Over all things hung a cold, dead veil of falling mist, as yet untouched by the rays of the sun.

The east gradually grew brighter, reflecting its pale light over the vault of heaven still covered by light clouds. Not a single grass-blade below, not a single leaf on the topmost branches of the tree-top, waved. Only from time to time could be heard the sounds of fluttering wings in the thicket, or a rustling on the ground broke in on the silence of the forest.

Suddenly a strange sound, foreign to this nature, resounded and died away at the edge of the forest. Again the noise sounded, and was monotonously repeated again and again, at the foot of one of the ancient, immovable trees. A tree-top began to shake in an extraordinary manner; the juicy leaves whispered something; and the warbler, sitting on one of the branches, flew off a couple of times with a shrill cry, and, wagging its tail, finally perched on another tree.

The ax rang more and more frequently; the white chips, full of sap, were scattered upon the dewy grass, and a slight cracking was heard beneath the blows.

The tree trembled with all its body, leaned over, and quickly straightened itself, shuddering with fear on its base.

For an instant all was still, then once more the tree bent over; a crash was heard in its trunk; and, tearing the thicket, and dragging down the branches, it plunged toward the damp earth.

The noise of the ax and of footsteps ceased.

The warbler uttered a cry, and flew higher. The branch which she grazed with her wings shook for an instant, and then came to rest like all the others with their foliage.

The trees, more joyously than ever, extended their motionless branches over the new space that had been made in their midst.

The first sunbeams, breaking through the cloud, gleamed in the sky, and shone along the earth and heavens.

The mist, in billows, began to float along the hollows; the dew, gleaming, played on the green foliage; translucent white clouds hurried along their azure path.

The birds hopped about in the thicket, and, as if beside themselves, voiced their happiness; the juicy leaves joyfully and contentedly whispered on the tree-tops; and the branches of the living trees slowly and majestically waved over the dead and fallen tree.

(1859)

❖ KURT VONNEGUT, JR.
Harrison Bergeron

Kurt Vonnegut, Jr. (1922–) was born in Indianapolis. He spent a year at Cornell University and then joined the army. He was captured by the Germans in 1944 and sent to Dresden, where, as a prison-laborer in a slaughterhouse, he underwent the horrendous Allied bombing that destroyed the city in February 1945 (and inspired his novel *Slaughterhouse-Five*). After the war he studied anthropology at the University of Chicago and then worked for General Electric until 1950, when he set up as a full-time writer. The humor and satire of Vonnegut's science fiction and other writing covers a deeply serious inquiry into American values. Vonnegut worries about man's inability either to conquer or to save the environment. His novels include *Player Piano* (1952), *The Sirens of Titan* (1959), *Mother Night* (1961), *Cat's Cradle* (1963), *God Bless You, Mr. Rosewater or Pearls Before Swine* (1966), *Slaughterhouse-Five, or The Children's Crusade: A Duty-Dance with Death* (1969), *Breakfast of Champions or Good-Bye Blue Monday* (1973), *Slapstick, or Lonesome No More* (1976), *Jailbird* (1979), *Deadeye Dick* (1982), *Galapagos* (1985), and *Bluebeard* (1987). His short story collections are *Canary in a Cat House* (1961) and *Welcome to the Monkey House* (1968, which includes "Harrison Bergeron"). He has also written plays for stage and television. A miscellany of Vonnegut's nonfiction appeared under the title *Palm Sunday: An Autobiographical Collage* (1981).

The year was 2081, and everybody was finally equal. They weren't only equal before God and the law. They were equal every which way. Nobody was smarter than anybody else. Nobody was better looking than anybody else. Nobody was stronger or quicker than anybody else. All this equality was due to the 211th, 212th, and 213th Amendments to the Constitution, and to the unceasing vigilance of agents of the United States Handicapper General.

Some things about living still weren't quite right, though. April, for instance, still drove people crazy by not being springtime. And it was in that clammy month that the H-G men took George and Hazel Bergeron's fourteen-year-old son, Harrison, away.

It was tragic, all right, but George and Hazel couldn't think about it very hard. Hazel had a perfectly average intelligence, which meant she couldn't think about anything except in short bursts. And George, while his intelligence was way above normal, had a little mental handicap radio in his ear. He was required by law to wear it at all times. It was tuned to a government transmitter. Every twenty seconds or so, the transmitter would send out some sharp noise to keep people like George from taking unfair advantage of their brains.

George and Hazel were watching television. There were tears on Hazel's cheeks, but she'd forgotten for the moment what they were about.

On the television screen were ballerinas.

A buzzer sounded in George's head. His thoughts fled in panic, like bandits from a burglar alarm.

"That was a really pretty dance, that dance they just did," said Hazel.

"Huh?" said George.

"That dance — it was nice," said Hazel.

"Yup," said George. He tried to think a little about the ballerinas. They weren't really very good — no better than anybody else would have been, anyway. They were burdened with sashweights and bags of birdshot, and their faces were masked, so that no one, seeing a free and graceful gesture or a pretty face, would feel like something the cat drug in. George was toying with the vague notion that maybe dancers shouldn't be handicapped. But he didn't get very far with it before another noise in his ear radio scattered his thoughts.

George winced. So did two out of the eight ballerinas.

Hazel saw him wince. Having no mental handicap herself, she had to ask George what the latest sound had been.

"Sounded like somebody hitting a milk bottle with a ball peen hammer," said George.

"I'd think it would be real interesting, hearing all the different sounds," said Hazel, a little envious. "All the things they think up."

"Um," said George.

"Only, if I was Handicapper General, you know what I would do?" said Hazel. Hazel, as a matter of fact, bore a strong resemblance to the Handicapper General, a woman named Diana Moon Glampers. "If I was Diana Moon Glampers," said Hazel, "I'd have chimes on Sunday — just chimes. Kind of in honor of religion."

"I could think, if it was just chimes," said George.

"Well — maybe make 'em real loud," said Hazel. "I think I'd make a good Handicapper General."

"Good as anybody else," said George.

"Who knows better'n I do what normal is?" said Hazel.

"Right," said George. He began to think glimmeringly about his abnormal son who was now in jail, about Harrison, but a twenty-one-gun salute in his head stopped that.

"Boy!" said Hazel, "that was a doozy, wasn't it?"

It was such a doozy that George was white and trembling, and tears stood on the rims of his red eyes. Two of the eight ballerinas had collapsed to the studio floor, were holding their temples.

"All of a sudden you look so tired," said Hazel. "Why don't you stretch out on the sofa, so's you can rest your handicap bag on the pillows, honeybunch." She was referring to the forty-seven pounds of birdshot in a canvas bag, which was padlocked around George's neck. "Go on and rest the bag for a little while," she said. "I don't care if you're not equal to me for a while."

George weighed the bag with his hands. "I don't mind it," he said. "I don't notice it any more. It's just a part of me."

"You been so tired lately — kind of wore out," said Hazel. "If there was just some way we could make a little hole in the bottom of the bag, and just take out a few of them lead balls. Just a few."

"Two years in prison and two thousand dollars fine for every ball I took out," said George. "I don't call that a bargain."

"If you could just take a few out when you came home from work," said Hazel. "I mean — you don't compete with anybody around here. You just set around."

"If I tried to get away with it," said George, "then other people'd get away with it — and pretty soon we'd be right back to the dark ages again, with everybody competing against everybody else. You wouldn't like that, would you?"

"I'd hate it," said Hazel.

"There you are," said George. "The minute people start cheating on laws, what do you think happens to society?"

If Hazel hadn't been able to come up with an answer to this question, George couldn't have supplied one. A siren was going off in his head.

"Reckon it'd fall all apart," said Hazel.

"What would?" said George blankly.

"Society," said Hazel uncertainly. "Wasn't that what you just said?"

"Who knows?" said George.

The television program was suddenly interrupted for a news bulletin. It wasn't clear at first as to what the bulletin was about, since the announcer, like all announcers, had a serious speech impediment. For about half a minute, and in state of high excitement, the announcer tried to say, "Ladies and gentlemen — "

He finally gave up, handed the bulletin to a ballerina to read.

"That's all right — " Hazel said of the announcer, "he tried. That's the big thing. He tried to do the best he could with what God gave him. He should get a nice raise for trying so hard."

"Ladies and gentlemen — " said the ballerina, reading the bulletin. She must have been extraordinarily beautiful because the mask she wore was hideous. And it was easy to see that she was the strongest and most graceful of all the dancers, for her handicap bags were as big as those worn by two-hundred-pound men.

And she had to apologize at once for her voice, which was a very unfair voice for a woman to use. Her voice was a warm, luminous, timeless melody. "Excuse me — " she said, and she began again, making her voice absolutely uncompetitive.

"Harrison Bergeron, age fourteen," she said in a grackle squawk, "has just escaped from jail, where he was held on suspicion of plotting to overthrow the government. He is a genius and an athlete, is under-handicapped, and should be regarded as extremely dangerous."

A police photograph of Harrison Bergeron was flashed on the screen-upside down, then sideways, upside down again, then right side up. The picture showed the full length of Harrison against a background calibrated in feet and inches. He was exactly seven feet tall.

The rest of Harrison's appearance was Halloween and hardware. Nobody had ever born heavier handicaps. He had outgrown hindrances faster than the H-G men could think them up. Instead of a little ear radio for a mental handicap, he wore a tremendous pair of earphones, and spectacles with thick wavy lenses. The spectacles were intended to make him not only half blind, but to give him whanging headaches besides.

Scrap metal was hung all over him. Ordinarily, there was a certain symmetry, a military neatness to the handicaps issued to strong people, but Harrison looked like a walking junkyard. In the race of life, Harrison carried three hundred pounds.

And to offset his good looks, the H-G men required that he wear at all times a red rubber ball for a nose, keep his eyebrows shaved off, and cover his even white teeth with black caps at snaggle-tooth random.

"If you see this boy," said the ballerina, "do not — I repeat, do not — try to reason with him."

There was the shriek of a door being torn from its hinges.

Screams and barking cries of consternation came from the television set. The photograph of Harrison Bergeron on the screen jumped again and again, as though dancing to the tune of an earthquake.

George Bergeron correctly identified the earthquake, and well he might have — for many was the time his own home had danced to the same crashing tune. "My God — " said George, "that must be Harrison!"

The realization was blasted from his mind instantly by the sound of an automobile collision in his head.

When George could open his eyes again, the photograph of Harrison was gone. A living, breathing Harrison filled the screen.

Clanking, clownish, and huge, Harrison stood in the center of the studio. The knob of the uprooted studio door was still in his hand. Ballerinas, technicians, musicians, and announcers cowered on their knees before him, expecting to die.

"I am the Emperor!" cried Harrison. "Do you hear? I am the Emperor! Everybody must do what I say at once!" He stamped his foot and the studio shook.

"Even as I stand here — " he bellowed, "crippled, hobbled, sickened — I am a greater ruler than any man who ever lived! Now watch me become what I *can* become!"

Harrison tore the straps of his handicap harness like wet tissue paper, tore straps guaranteed to support five thousand pounds.

Harrison's scrap-iron handicaps crashed to the floor.

Harrison thrust his thumbs under the bar of the padlock that secured his head harness. The bar snapped like celery. Harrison smashed his headphones and spectacles against the wall.

He flung away his rubber-ball nose, revealed a man that would have awed Thor, the god of thunder.

"I shall now select my Empress!" he said, looking down on the cowering people. "Let the first woman who dares rise to her feet claim her mate and her throne!"

A moment passed, and then a ballerina arose, swaying like a willow.

Harrison plucked the mental handicap from her ear, snapped off her physical handicaps with marvelous delicacy. Last of all, he removed her mask.

She was blindingly beautiful.

"Now — " said Harrison, taking her hand, "shall we show the people the meaning of the word dance? Music!" he commanded.

The musicians scrambled back into their chairs, and Harrison stripped them of their handicaps, too. "Play your best," he told them, "and I'll make you barons and dukes and earls."

The music began. It was normal at first—cheap, silly, false. But Harrison snatched two musicians from their chairs, waved them like batons as he sang the music as he wanted it played. He slammed them back into their chairs.

The music began again and was much improved.

Harrison and his Empress merely listened to the music for a while—listened gravely, as though synchronizing their heartbeats with it.

They shifted their weights to their toes.

Harrison placed his big hands on the girl's tiny waist, letting her sense the weightlessness that would soon be hers.

And then, in an explosion of joy and grace, into the air they sprang!

Not only were the laws of the land abandoned, but the law of gravity and the laws of motion as well.

They reeled, whirled, swiveled, flounced, capered, gamboled, and spun.

They leaped like deer on the moon.

The studio ceiling was thirty feet high, but each leap brought dancers nearer to it.

It became their obvious intention to kiss the ceiling.

They kissed it.

And then, neutralizing gravity with love and pure will, they remained suspended in air inches below the ceiling, and they kissed each other for a long, long time.

It was then that Diana Moon Glampers, the Handicapper General, came into the studio with a double-barreled ten-gauge shotgun. She fired twice, and the Emperor and the Empress were dead before they hit the floor.

Diana Moon Glampers loaded the gun again. She aimed it at the musicians and told them they had ten seconds to get their handicaps back on.

It as then that the Bergerons' television tube burned out.

Hazel turned to comment about the blackout to George. But George had gone out into the kitchen for a can of beer.

George came back in with the beer, paused while a handicap signal shook him up. And then he sat down again. "You been crying?" he said to Hazel.

"Yup," she said.

"What about?" he said.

"I forget," she said. "Something real sad on television."

"What was it?" he said.

"It's all kind of mixed up in my mind," said Hazel.

"Forget sad things," said George.

"I always do," said Hazel.

"That's my girl," said George. He winced. There was a sound of a rivetting gun in his head.

"Gee—I could tell that one was a doozy," said Hazel.

"You can say that again," said George.

"Gee—" said Hazel, "I could tell that one was a doozy."

(1961)

❖ EUDORA WELTY
Why I Live at the P.O.

Eudora Welty (1909–) was born in Jackson, Mississippi, and went to Jackson State College for Women and the University of Wisconsin, from which she graduated in 1929. After a year studying advertising in New York, she returned home and worked for newspapers and a radio station. Employment with the Works Progress Administration enabled her to do photography at a professional level (her photographs were exhibited in New York in 1936), but she returned to Jackson (where she has lived ever since) and started writing fiction. Her many short stories have appeared in the collections *A Curtain of Green* (1941), *The Wide Net* (1943), *The Golden Apples* (1949), *Selected Stories* (1954), *The Bride of Inisfallen* (1955), *Thirteen Stories* (1965), and *The Collected Stories of Eudora Welty* (1980). Though her forte is the short story, she has also written five novels: *The Robber Bridegroom* (1942), *Delta Wedding* (1946), *The Ponder Heart* (1954), *Losing Battles* (1970), and *The Optimist's Daughter* (1972, for which she won the Pulitzer Prize in literature). She has also published poetry and children's fiction. Her nonfiction includes literary criticism and commentary on Mississippi during the Great Depression.

I was getting along fine with Mama, Papa-Daddy and Uncle Rondo until my sister Stella-Rondo just separated from her husband and came back home again. Mr. Whitaker! Of course I went with Mr. Whitaker first, when he first appeared here in China Grove, taking "Pose Yourself" photos, and Stella-Rondo broke us up. Told him I was one-sided. Bigger on one side than the other, which is a deliberate, calculated falsehood: I'm the same. Stella-Rondo is exactly twelve months to this day younger than I am and for that reason she's spoiled.

She's always had anything in the world she wanted and then she'd throw it away. Papa-Daddy gave her this gorgeous Add-a-Pearl necklace when she was eight years old and she threw it away playing baseball when she was nine, with only two pearls.

So as soon as she got married and moved away from home the first thing she did was separate! From Mr. Whitaker! This photographer with the popeyes she said she trusted. Came home from one of those towns up in Illinois and to our complete surprise brought this child of two.

Mama said she like to made her drop dead for a second. "Here you had this marvelous blonde child and never so much as wrote your mother a word about it," says Mama. "I'm thoroughly ashamed of you." But of course she wasn't.

Stella-Rondo just calmly takes off this *hat*, I wish you could see it. She says "Why, Mama, Shirley-T.'s adopted, I can prove it."

"How?" says Mama, but all I says was, "H'm!" There I was over the hot stove,

594

trying to stretch two chickens over five people and a completely unexpected child into the bargain, without one moment's notice.

"What do you mean — 'H'm!'?" says Stella-Rondo, and Mama say, "I heard that, Sister."

I said that oh, I didn't mean a thing, only that whoever Shirley-T. was, she was the spit-image of Papa-Daddy if he'd cut off his beard, which of course he'd never do in the world. Papa-Daddy's Mama's papa and sulks.

Stella-Rondo got furious! She said, "Sister, I don't need to tell you you got a lot of nerve and always did have and I'll thank you to make no future reference to my adopted child whatsoever."

"Very well," I said. "Very well, very well. Of course I noticed at once she looks like Mr. Whitaker's side too. That frown. She looks like a cross between Mr. Whitaker and Papa-Daddy."

"Well, all I can say is she isn't."

"She looks exactly like Shirley Temple to me," says Mama, but Shirley-T. just ran away from her.

So the first thing Stella-Rondo did at the table was turn Papa-Daddy against me.

"Papa-Daddy," she says. He was trying to cut up his meat. "Papa-Daddy!" I was taken completely by surprise. Papa-Daddy is about a million years old and's got this long-long beard. "Papa-Daddy, Sister says she fails to understand why you don't cut off your beard."

So Papa-Daddy l-a-y-s down his knife and fork! He's real rich. Mama say he is, he says he isn't. So he says, "Have I heard correctly? You don't understand why I don't cut off my beard?"

"Why," I say, "Papa-Daddy, of course I understand, I did not say any such of a thing, the idea!"

He says, "Hussy!"

I says, "Papa-Daddy, you know I wouldn't any more want you to cut off your beard than the man in the moon. It was the farthest thing from my mind! Stella-Rondo sat there and made that up while she was eating breast of chicken."

But he says, "So the postmistress fails to understand why I don't cut off my beard. Which job I got you through my influence with the government. 'Bird's nest' — is that what you call it?"

Not that it isn't the next to smallest P.O. in the entire state of Mississippi.

I says, "Oh, Papa-Daddy," I says, "I didn't say any such of a thing, I never dreamed it was a bird's nest, I have always been grateful though this is the next to smallest P.O. in the state of Mississippi, and I do not enjoy being referred to as a hussy by my own grandfather."

But Stella-Rondo says, "Yes, you did say it too. Anybody in the world could of heard you, that had ears."

"Stop right there," says Mama, looking at me.

So I pulled my napkin straight back through the napkin ring and left the table.

As soon as I was out of the room Mama says, "Call her back, or she'll starve to death," but Papa-Daddy says, "This is the beard I started growing on the Coast when I was fifteen years old." He would of gone on till nightfall if Shirley-T. hadn't lost the Milky Way she ate in Cairo.

So Papa-Daddy says, "I am going out and lie in the hammock, and you can all sit here and remember my words: I'll never cut off my beard as long as I live, even one inch, and I don't appreciate it in you at all." Passed right by me in the hall and went straight out and got in the hammock.

It would be a holiday. I wasn't five minutes before Uncle Rondo suddenly appeared in the hall in one of Stella-Rondo's flesh-colored kimonos, all cut on the bias, like something Mr. Whitaker probably thought was gorgeous.

"Uncle Rondo!" I says. "I didn't know who that was! Where are you going?"

"Sister," he says, "get out of my way, I'm poisoned."

"If you're poisoned stay away from Papa-Daddy," I says. "Keep out of the hammock. Papa-Daddy will certainly beat you on the head if you come within forty miles of him. He thinks I deliberately said he ought to cut off his beard after he got me the P.O., and I've told him and told him and told him, and he acts like he just don't hear me. Papa-Daddy must of gone stone deaf."

"He picked a fine day to do it then," says Uncle Rondo, and before you could say "Jack Robinson" flew out in the yard.

What he'd really done, he'd drunk another bottle of that prescription. He does it every single Fourth of July as sure as shooting, and it's horribly expensive. Then he falls over in the hammock and snores. So he insisted on zigzagging right on out to the hammock, looking like a half-wit.

Papa-Daddy woke up with this horrible yell and right there without moving an inch he tried to turn Uncle Rondo against me. I heard every word he said. Oh, he told Uncle Rondo I didn't learn to read till I was eight years old and he didn't see how in the world I ever got the mail put up at the P.O., much less read it all, and he said if Uncle Rondo could only fathom the lengths he had gone to get me that job! And he said on the other hand he thought Stella-Rondo had a brilliant mind and deserved credit for getting out of town. All the time he was just lying there swinging as pretty as you please and looping out his beard, and poor Uncle Rondo was *pleading* with him to slow down the hammock, it was making him as dizzy as a witch to watch it. But that's what Papa-Daddy likes about a hammock. So Uncle Rondo was too dizzy to get turned against me for the time being. He's Mama's only brother and is a good case of a one-track mind. Ask anybody. A certified pharmacist.

Just then I heard Stella-Rondo raising the upstairs window. While she was married she got this peculiar idea that it's cooler with the windows shut and locked. So she has to raise the window before she can make a soul hear her outdoors.

So she raises the window and say, "*Oh!*" You would have thought she was mortally wounded.

Uncle Rondo and Papa-Daddy didn't even look up, but kept right on with what they were doing. I had to laugh.

I flew up the stairs and threw the door open! I says, "What in the wide world's the matter, Stella-Rondo? You mortally wounded?"

"No," she says, "I am not mortally wounded but I wish you would do me the favor of looking out that window there and telling me what you see."

So I shade my eyes and look out the window.

"I see the front yard," I says.

"Don't you see any human beings?" she says.

"I see Uncle Rondo trying to run Papa-Daddy out of the hammock," I says. "Nothing more. Naturally, it's so suffocating-hot in the house, with all the windows shut and locked, everybody who cares to stay in their right mind will have to go out and get in the hammock before the Fourth of July is over."

"Don't you notice anything different about Uncle Rondo?" asks Stella-Rondo.

"Why, no, except he's got on some terrible-looking flesh-colored contraption I wouldn't be found dead in, is all I can see," I says.

"Never mind, you won't be found dead in it, because it happens to be part of my trousseau, and Mr. Whitaker took several dozen photographs of me in it," says Stella-Rondo. "What on earth could Uncle Rondo *mean* by wearing part of my trousseau out in the broad open daylight without saying so much as 'Kiss my foot,' *knowing* I only got home this morning after my separation and hung my negligee up on the bathroom door, just as nervous as I could be?"

"I'm sure I don't know, and what do you expect me to do about it?" I says. "Jump out the window?"

"No, I expect nothing of the kind. I simply declare that Uncle Rondo looks like a fool in it, that's all," she says. "It makes me sick to my stomach."

"Well, he looks as good as he can," I says. "As good as anybody in reason could." I stood up for Uncle Rondo, please remember. And I said to Stella-Rondo, "I think I would do well not to criticize so freely if I were you and came home with a two-year-old child I had never said a word about, and no explanation whatever about my separation."

"I asked you the instant I entered this house not to refer one more time to my adopted child, and you gave me your word of honor you would not," was all Stella-Rondo would say, and started pulling out every one of her eyebrows with some cheap Kress tweezers.

So I merely slammed the door behind me and went down and made some green-tomato pickle. Somebody had to do it. Of course Mama had turned both the niggers loose; she always said no earthly power could hold one anyway on the Fourth of July, so she wouldn't even try. It turned out that Jaypan fell in the lake and came within a very narrow limit of drowning.

So Mama trots in. Lifts up the lid and says, "H'm! Not very good for your Uncle Rondo in his precarious condition, I must say. Or poor little adopted Shirley-T. Shame on you!"

That made me tired. I says. "Well, Stella-Rondo had better thank her lucky stars it was her instead of me came trotting in with that very peculiar-looking child. Now if it had been me that trotted in from Illinois and brought a peculiar-looking child of two, I shudder to think of the reception I'd of got, much less controlled the diet of an entire family."

"But you must remember, Sister, that you were never married to Mr. Whitaker in the first place and didn't go up to Illinois to live," says Mama, shaking a spoon in my face. "If you had I would of been just as overjoyed to see you and your little adopted girl as I was to see Stella-Rondo, when you wound up with your separation and came on back home."

"You would not," I says.

"Don't contradict me, I would," says Mama.

But I said she couldn't convince me though she talked till she was blue in the face. Then I said, "Besides, you know as well as I do that that child is not adopted."

"She most certainly is adopted," says Mama, stiff as a poker.

I says, "Why, Mama, Stella-Rondo had her just as sure as anything in this world, and just too stuck up to admit it."

"Why, Sister," said Mama. "Here I thought we were going to have a pleasant Fourth of July, and you start right out not believing a word your own baby sister tells you!"

"Just like Cousin Annie Flow. Went to her grave denying the facts of life," I remind Mama.

"I told you if you ever mentioned Annie Flo's name I'd slap your face," says Mama, and slaps my face.

"All right, you wait and see," I says.

"I," says Mama, "*I* prefer to take my children's word for anything when it's humanly possible." You ought to see Mama, she weighs two hundred pounds and has real tiny feet.

Just then something perfectly horrible occurred to me.

"Mama," I says, "can that child talk?" I simply had to whisper! "Mama, I wonder if that child can be — you know — in any way? Do you realize," I says, "that she hasn't spoken one single, solitary word to a human being up to this minute? This is the way she looks," I says, and I looked like this.

Well, Mama and I just stood there and stared at each other. It was horrible!

"I remember well that Joe Whitaker frequently drank like a fish," says Mama. "I believed to my soul he drank *chemicals*." And without another word she marches to the foot of the stairs and calls Stella-Rondo.

"Stella-Rondo? O-o-o-o-o! Stella-Rondo!"

"What?" says Stella-Rondo from upstairs. Not even the grace to get up off the bed.

"Can that child of yours talk?" asks Mama.

Stella-Rondo says, "Can she what?"

"Talk! Talk!" says Mama. "Burdyburdyburdyburdy!"

So Stella-Rondo yells back, "Who says she can't talk?"

"Sister says so," says Mama.

"You didn't have to tell me, I know whose word of honor don't mean a thing in this house," says Stella-Rondo.

And in a minute the loudest Yankee voice I ever heard in my life yells out "OE'm Pop-OE the Sailor-r-r-r Ma-a-an!" and then somebody jumps up and down in the upstairs hall. In another second the house would of fallen down.

"Not only talks, she can tap-dance!" calls Stella-Rondo, "Which is more than some people I won't name can do."

"Why, the little precious darling thing!" Mama says, so surprised. "Just as smart as she can be!" Starts talking baby talk right there. Then she turns on me, "Sister, you ought to be thoroughly ashamed! Run upstairs this instant and apologize to Stella-Rondo and Shirley-T."

"Apologize for what?" I says. "I merely wondered if the child was normal, that's all. Now that she's proved she is, why, I have nothing further to say."

But Mama just turned on her heel and flew out, furious. She ran right upstairs and hugged the baby. She believed it was adopted. Stella-Rondo hadn't done a thing but turn her against me from upstairs while I stood there helpless over the hot stove. So that made Mama, Papa-Daddy and the baby all on Stella-Rondo's side.

Next, Uncle Rondo.

I must say that Uncle Rondo has been marvelous to me at various times in the past and I was completely unprepared to be made to jump out of my skin, the way it turned out. Once Stella-Rondo did something perfectly horrible to him — broke a chain letter from Flanders Field — and he took the radio back he had given her and gave it to me. Stella-Rondo was furious! For six months we all had to call her Stella instead of Stella-Rondo, or she wouldn't answer. I always thought Uncle Rondo had all the brains of the entire family. Another time he sent me to Mammoth Cave, with all expenses paid.

But this would be the day he was drinking that prescription, the Fourth of July.

So at supper Stella-Rondo speaks up and says she thinks Uncle Rondo ought to try to eat a little something. So finally Uncle Rondo said he would try a little cold biscuits and ketchup, but that was all. So *she* brought it to him.

"Do you think it wise to disport with ketchup in Stella-Rondo's flesh-colored kimono?" I says. Trying to be considerate! If Stella-Rondo couldn't watch out for her trousseau, somebody had to.

"Any objections?" asks Uncle Rondo, just about to pour out all the ketchup.

"Don't mind what she says, Uncle Rondo," says Stella-Rondo. "Sister has been devoting this solid afternoon to sneering out my bedroom window at the way you look."

"What's that?" says Uncle Rondo. Uncle Rondo has got the most terrible temper in the world. Anything is liable to make him tear the house down if it comes at the wrong time.

So Stella-Rondo says, "Sister says, 'Uncle Rondo certainly does look like a fool in that pink kimono!'"

Do you remember who it was really said that?

Uncle Rondo spills out all the ketchup and jumps out of his chair and tears off the kimono and throws it down on the dirty floor and puts his foot on it. It had to be sent all the way to Jackson to the cleaners and re-pleated.

"So that's your opinion of your Uncle Rondo, is it?" he says. "I look like a fool, do I? Well, that's the last straw. A whole day in this house with nothing to do, and then to hear you come out with a remark like that behind my back!"

"I didn't say any such of a thing, Uncle Rondo," I says, "and I'm not saying who did, either. Why, I think you look all right. Just try to take care of yourself and not talk and eat at the same time," I says. "I think you better go lie down."

"Lie down my foot," says Uncle Rondo. I ought to of known by that he was fixing to do something perfectly horrible.

So he didn't do anything that night in the precarious state he was in — just played Casino with Mama and Stella-Rondo and Shirley-T. and gave Shirley-T. a nickel with a head on both sides. It tickled her nearly to death, and she called him "Papa." But at 6:30 A.M. the next morning, he threw a whole five-cent package of some unsold one-inch firecrackers from the store as hard as he could into my bedroom and they every one went off. Not one bad one in the string. Anybody else, there'd be one that wouldn't go off.

Well, I'm just terribly susceptible to noise of any kind, the doctor has always told me I was the most sensitive person he had ever seen in his whole life, and I was simply prostrated. I couldn't eat! People tell me they heard it as far as the cemetery, and old Aunt Jep Patterson, that had been holding her own so good, thought it was Judgment Day and she was going to meet her whole family. It's usually so quiet here.

And I'll tell you it didn't take me any longer than a minute to make up my mind what to do. There I was with the whole entire house on Stella-Rondo's side and turned against me. If I have anything at all I have pride.

So I just decided I'd go straight down to the P.O. There's plenty of room there in the back, I says to myself.

Well! I made no bones about letting the family catch on to what I was up to. I didn't try to conceal it.

The first thing they knew, I marched in where they were all playing Old Maid and pulled the electric oscillating fan out by the plug, and everything got real hot. Next I snatched the pillow I'd done the needlepoint on right off the davenport from behind Papa-Daddy. He went "Ugh!" I beat Stella-Rondo up the stairs and finally found my charm bracelet in her bureau drawer under of a picture of Nelson Eddy.

"So that's the way the land lies," says Uncle Rondo. There he was, piecing on the ham. "Well, Sister, I'll be glad to donate my army cot if you got any place to set it up, providing you'll leave right this minute and let me get some peace." Uncle Rondo was in France.

"Thank you kindly for the cot and 'peace' is hardly the word I would select if I had to resort to firecrackers at 6:30 A.M. in a young girl's bedroom," I says back to him. "And as to where I intend to go, you seem to forget my position as postmistress of China Grove, Mississippi," I says. "I've always got the P.O."

Well, that made them all sit up and take notice.

I went out front and starting digging up some four-o'clocks to plant around the P.O.

"Ah-ah-ah!" says Mama, raising the window. "Those happen to be my four-o'clocks. Everything planted in that star is mine. I've never known you to make anything grow in your life."

"Very well," I says. "But I take the fern. Even you, Mama, can't stand there and deny that I'm the one watered that fern. And I happen to know where I can send in a box top and get a packet of one thousand mixed seeds, no two the same kind, free."

"Oh, where?" Mama wants to know.

But I says, "Too late. You 'tend to your house, and I'll 'tend to mine. You hear things like that all the time if you know how to listen to the radio. Perfectly marvelous offers. Get anything you want free."

So I hope to tell you I marched in and got that radio, and they could of all bit a nail in two, especially Stella-Rondo, that it used to belong to, and she well knew she couldn't get it back, I'd sue for it like a shot. And I very politely took the sewing-machine motor I helped pay the most on to give Mama for Christmas back in 1929, and a good big calendar, with the first-aid remedies on it. The thermometer and the Hawaiian ukulele certainly were rightfully mine, and I stood on the step-ladder and got all my watermelon-rind preserves and every fruit and vegetable I'd put up, every jar. Then I began to pull the tacks out of the bluebird wall vases on the archway to the dining room.

"Who told you you could have those, Miss Priss?" says Mama, fanning as hard as she could.

"I bought 'em and I'll keep track of 'em," I says. "I'll tack 'em up one on each side the post-office window, and you can see 'em when you come to ask me for your mail, if you're so dead to see 'em."

"Not I! I'll never darken the door to that post office again if I live to be a hundred," Mama says. "Ungrateful child! After all the money we spent on you at the Normal."

"Me either," says Stella-Rondo. "You can just let my mail lie there and *rot*, for all I care. I'll never come and relieve you of a single, solitary piece."

"I should worry," I says. "And who you think's going to sit down and write you all those big fat letters and postcards, by the way? Mr. Whitaker? Just because he was the only man ever dropped down in China Grove and you got him — unfairly — is he going to sit down and write you a lengthy correspondence after you come home giving no rhyme nor reason whatsoever for your separation and no explanation for the presence of that child? I may not have your brilliant mind, but I fail to see it."

So Mama says, "Sister, I've told you a thousand times that Stella-Rondo simply got homesick, and this child is far too big to be hers," and she says, "Now, why don't you all just sit down and play Casino?"

Then Shirley-T. sticks out her tongue at me in this perfectly horrible way. She has no more manners than the man in the moon. I told her she was going to cross her eyes like that some day and they'd stick.

"It's too late to stop me now," I says. "You should have tried that yesterday. I'm going to the P.O. and the only way you can possibly see me is to visit me there."

So Papa-Daddy says, "You'll never catch me setting foot in that post office, even if I should take a notion into my head to write a letter some place." He says, "I won't have you reachin' out of that little old window with a pair of shears and cuttin' off any beard of mine. I'm too smart for you!"

"We all are," says Stella-Rondo.

But I said, "If you're so smart, where's Mr. Whitaker?"

So then Uncle Rondo says, "I'll thank you from now on to stop reading all the orders I get on postcards and telling everybody in China Grove what you think is the matter with them," but I says, "I draw my own conclusions and will continue in the future to draw them." I says, "If people want to write their inmost secrets on penny postcards, there's nothing in the wide world you can do about it, Uncle Rondo."

"And if you think we'll ever *write* another postcard you're sadly mistaken," says Mama.

"Cutting off your nose to spite your face then," I says. "But if you're all determined to have no more to do with the U.S. mail, think of this: What will Stella-Rondo do now, if she wants to tell Mr. Whitaker to come after her?"

"Wah!" says Stella-Rondo. I knew she'd cry. She had a conniption fit right there in the kitchen.

"It will be interesting to see how long she holds out," I says. "And now—I am leaving."

"Good-bye," says Uncle Rondo.

"Oh, I declare," says Mama, "to think that a family of mine should quarrel on the Fourth of July, or the day after, over Stella-Rondo leaving old Mr. Whitaker and having the sweetest little adopted child! It looks like we'd all be glad!"

"Wah!" says Stella-Rondo, and has a fresh conniption fit.

"*He* left *her*—you mark my words," I says. "That Mr. Whitaker. I know Mr. Whitaker. After all, I knew him first. I said from the beginning he'd up and leave her. I foretold every single thing that's happened."

"Where did he go?" asks Mama.

"Probably to the North Pole, if he knows what's good for him," I says.

But Stella-Rondo just bawled and wouldn't say another word. She flew to her room and slammed the door.

"Now look what you've gone and done, Sister," says Mama. "You go apologize."

"I haven't got time, I'm leaving," I says.

"Well, what are you waiting around for?" asks Uncle Rondo.

So I just picked up the kitchen clock and marched off, without saying "Kiss my foot" or anything, and never did tell Stella-Rondo good-bye.

There was a nigger girl going along on a little wagon right in front.

"Nigger girl," I says, "come help me haul these things down the hill, I'm going to live in the post office."

Took her nine trips in her express wagon. Uncle Rondo came out on the porch and threw her a nickel.

And that's the last I've laid eyes on any of my family or my family laid eyes on me for five solid days and nights. Stella-Rondo may be telling the most horrible tales in the world about Mr. Whitaker, but I haven't heard them. As I tell everybody, I draw my own conclusions.

But oh, I like it here. It's ideal, as I've been saying. You see, I've got everything cater-cornered, the way I like. Hear the radio? All the war news. Radio, sewing machine, bookends, ironing board and that great big piano lamp—peace, that's what I like. Butter-bean vines planted all along the front where the strings are.

Of course, there's not much mail. My family are naturally the main people in China Grove, and if they prefer to vanish from the face of the earth, for all the mail they get or the mail they write, why, I'm not going to open my mouth. Some of the folks here in town are taking up for me and some turned against me. I know which is which. There are always people who quit buying stamps just to get on the right side of Papa-Daddy.

But here I am, and here I'll stay. I want the world to know I'm happy.

And if Stella-Rondo should come to me this minute, on bended knees, and *attempt* to explain the incidents of her life with Mr. Whitaker, I'd simply put my fingers in both my ears and refuse to listen.

(1941)

How to Write about Fiction

There are many reasons to write about fiction. One is to find out what you think about a fiction you have just read. The act of writing can make you aware of unconscious reactions and give shape to vague responses. Another reason is to communicate your ideas about it to other readers. A third reason is to argue with critics, who are simply other readers who have written down their own reactions and interpretations. Essentially, these reasons all come down to one principle: to read actively, rather than simply letting the fiction wash over you and disappear like a wave, you have to meet it on its own ground, which is to say, in writing. You must write to challenge the fiction, ask it questions, listen for its answers.

Writing about a fiction is a way of engaging it in a dialogue. You usually cannot talk with the author, who may be dead or a thousand miles away or have forgotten why she wrote what and as she did. However, you can communicate with the fiction, with its sources, and with critical articles that have appeared in reaction to it. These are all written texts. Your best way of joining in the conversation is to produce a text of your own.

Your response to a fiction may take almost any written form. You might find yourself writing a philosophical treatise, a poem, a legal brief for one of the characters, a screenplay, or a new short story. You might even want to copy the fiction (or part of it) word for word, so that you reproduce the outward motions of the writer's creative experience. In this case, the text you produce may be of little value, but the process can be worthwhile, because you are forced to think about why the writer chose this word rather than that or inserted a flashback instead of proceeding straight through from beginning to end.

One of the most commonly generated and useful sorts of texts is a reading diary, in which you record as quickly as possible any part of your reading experience. In such a diary you write down whatever occurs to you as you read; for instance, you might describe the way you gradually come to understand the fiction's action and themes, you might respond emotionally to characters and events, you might follow up a train of thought stimulated by the fiction, you might jot down memorable phrases or unknown words, or you might examine connections to other fictions or to your own life.

Each of these responses has an appropriate audience: yourself, a publisher, other readers of the story, the author himself as you imagine him. If, however, your audience is your instructor, who will be reading your text with the idea of assigning a grade, your choice of forms is likely to be limited to the standard critical essay. Whether produced as an assignment in an introductory literature class or for publication in a professional journal like *PMLA* or *New Literary History*, a critical essay usually succeeds best if it conforms to certain general guidelines. Some of these guidelines are purely conventional, but others assist your readers in following your ideas and in relating those ideas to the body of existing critical texts. Unless your instructor tells you otherwise —and an increasing number of literature teachers are broadening their ideas of appropriate and acceptable student writing—you can assume that some version of the critical essay is expected.

But what are the guidelines for this kind of critical writing, and how are you supposed to learn them? Published critical texts are written for an audience of other critics, scholars, and interested readers of literature. Their writers assume a certain level of knowledge about authors and periods and genres. They also assume a critical vocabulary: in dealing with short stories, for instance, they do not feel the need to define *plot, protagonist, flashback*, and the like, unless they wish to *re*define these terms for some reason. They also probably assume that their audience is familiar with the most commonly used critical approaches, such as structural analysis or psychoanalytic criticism, and with critics associated with such approaches.

Even if your primary audience is your instructor, you are usually better off writing as if for the larger critical audience, as if you were aiming at being published in a scholarly journal or literary magazine. When you have this kind of audience in mind, first provide information such as the title, author, and date of the story you are dealing with, and then explain what critical question you are addressing. Even if your instructor assigned both the text and the question, she will probably be more impressed if you treat the assignment as if it were the product of your own careful reading and deep pondering.

Writing to a general critical audience may help you make some of the distinctions that are hard for the beginning critic. For instance, the line between merely retelling a plot and analyzing it is a very fine one. But if you think of yourself as reminding literate readers of key plot details rather than filling them in on the whole story, you are less likely to waste their time. Likewise, if you remember that your readers' primary interest is in gaining insight into the fiction rather than in getting to know you, it might be easier to distinguish between useful observations culled from your reading experience and accidental associations that the fiction may have set off in your mind. If a fishing story by Ernest Hemingway reminds you of the time you hooked the big steelhead, that information may be either a useful key to the fiction or a boring irrelevancy, depending on how clearly you anticipate the audience's needs. Try to understand how the fiction triggered your memories and ask yourself whether it would be likely to have the same impact on a nonfishing reader. The problem here is not in writing from your own experience — which is always essential — but rather in keeping track of the subject at hand. Focus on the experience you share with your reader, which is the fiction itself.

The best way to get to know the standard critical format is to read good critics. Whatever sort of criticism you wish to write — whether you want to explain something obscure in a fiction, to analyze its structure, to compare it with another fiction, or to reassess the author's importance — you can benefit from the examples of such writers as Randall Jarrell, F.O. Matthiessen, Joanna Russ, Robert Scholes, or Jane Tompkins, to name a few of the more readable critics. Find a critic who makes you interested in the literature, who explains points clearly, and who opens up new ways of reading, and try to figure out what that critic is doing.

A few of the general guidelines can be simplified into *dos* and *don'ts*. Remember that these are rules of thumb, rather than infallible prescriptions.

Don't set yourself impossible tasks. You are unlikely to write a successful essay if you begin with too broad a question, such as "How does irony work in fiction?" or a question that demands unavailable knowledge, such as "What did Jane Austen have in mind when she created the character of Emma Woodhouse?" A professional scholar with a large library and a few years of uninterrupted work time might be able to produce a book that partially answers the first question. Nobody can answer the second, although we are all free to speculate.

Don't set yourself trivial tasks, either. Why bother to prove something that no one would ever disagree with? The narrator of Poe's "The Tell-Tale Heart" is probably crazy. True, but you are not going to get much credit for proving it in an essay.

Between the trivial and the cosmic lies a category of questions that are both manageable and interesting. The questions that follow each selection in the first part of this book are intended to illustrate some of that middle ground. When you look at them, don't just think of answers, but try to follow the reasoning that led to the question itself and see if you can use it to generate questions of your own. Sometimes a question in this book or on a classroom assignment will seem needlessly complicated or obscure or elementary until you come across a fiction that is opened up by just such a question. Then again, the question may simply be a bad one (despite the author's or instructor's best efforts). If so, figure out why, and try to figure out a better approach. One mark of a good question is that it leads you to new discoveries about the fiction. Another mark is that you will be able to find evidence but not obvious and conclusive proof. What constitutes evidence for an essay on fiction? That leads us to our list of dos for the student writer.

Do go to the text. Paraphrase, summarize, and above all quote freely in support of every major point you want to make. Quoting well is an art. Not everyone can find the perfect passage to demonstrate Wharton's style or Hemingway's ethic or Dinesen's use of symbols. Nor can you simply quote big blocks of text and hope that the evidence is somewhere in there, even if you have been careful to state the point as clearly as possible. As a general rule, the shorter the quotation, the more likely the reader will agree that it is an example of what you are talking about. If you are discussing word choice, quote single words. If you are examining the way a writer presents character through speech, quote a brief dialogue or a small group of short speeches that are the most revealing examples. You won't be able to select the best quotation unless you have several to choose from. Find several times as many examples as you need, and then pick the one that sums up all the rest.

When you quote, give the reader clear guidance on how you are interpreting the passage. Make sure that you have stated the point that the quotation is going to illustrate. Then introduce your quotations so that they flow smoothly from your argument. Finally, follow them up. Don't be afraid of repeating yourself, as long as you do so in different language or from a different perspective. Tell readers how the quotation they have just read illustrates your point. Out of a larger quotation, go back and point out individual words and phrases that are especially revealing or effective (or ineffective, if you want to criticize the fiction). To repeat, your first and most important source of information is the fiction itself, so use it fully.

Do make use of outside sources where they are appropriate and available. For some classroom exercises, you are required to extract as much meaning as possible from the text alone without even a title or author's name to guide you, but that is an exceptional situation. Usually you have access to the author's name, dates, gender, nationality, and sometimes, as in this anthology, a brief biography and critical introduction. This sort of information always influences our judgments and interpretations. When you know a story was written by Nathaniel Hawthorne you snap to attention. If you've read a lot of Hawthorne you may expect to have to cope with ambiguity, irony, and symbolism. Even if you haven't read anything else by him, you probably recognize him as a major author, somebody with a well-established reputation, whose stories are likely to look more seriously at the human condition than does the average supermarket best-seller.

You can also go beyond the obvious clues of author's identity and dates. No amount of biographical or historical information will tell you for sure what a writer meant in a particular fiction. However, biographical information can sometimes establish what it was *possible* for the writer to have meant. Could Jules Verne have been referring to actual submarines when he wrote *Twenty Thousand Leagues Under the Sea?* Was Stephen Crane drawing on personal experience of battle in *The Red Badge of Courage?* (Yes, on the first question, and no, on the second.) In answering these questions, you can eliminate possible misreadings of the texts themselves and sometimes hit on interesting and supportable readings that would not otherwise have occurred to you. Texts are not produced in isolation: they are constructed out of the language, the events, the characters, the storytelling conventions available to the writer. You don't read them in isolation either. Whether or not you are aware of it, you are always drawing on your knowledge of society, character, literature, and language in trying to make sense out of the words. It doesn't hurt to try to match *your* knowledge as closely as possible with the author's (or what you can reconstruct of it).

Once you master these dos and don'ts, you can write many kinds of essays about fictions. Writing about fiction can be categorized as *explication, interpretation, analysis, evaluation,* or *poetics.* An individual essay may be a mixture of more than one of these modes. You can try your hand at any of them, although the last two require a broad background in reading if your claims are to have much weight.

Explication is explaining. You explain how the story proceeds, what sorts of information it presents either outright or through implication, how the characters and events and objects are related, what specific contributions are made by individual words and sentences — in short, what everything means and how it means it. A full explication may be longer than the fiction it explicates. It is possible to find book-length explications of brief short stories. However, you can also choose to explicate a part of a story, such as a single plot episode, a single character's involvement, or a particular image.

Interpretation differs from explication in that it introduces information from the world outside the fiction. When you discuss the psychology of a particular character, you are interpreting the fictional person in terms of the psychology of real human beings. A Freudian interpretation applies the psychological theories developed by Sigmund Freud; a Jungian interpretation borrows from Carl Jung; presumably you could apply any credible model of the psyche to any fictional character to gain insight into the character's actions and motivations. Other sorts of interpretations are historical, sociological, religious, ethical, Marxist, or feminist. Each of these involves a meeting between the literary text and some system of thought. But good interpretations are not a matter of testing the author's claims against the truths of, say, the discipline of sociology. Instead, you read the fiction with the theory in mind, remaining open to any new insights it may provide.

Analysis is breaking something down into its constituent parts to find out more about its structure and function. What are the parts of a short story? Most of this book is about ways of analyzing fiction. Various chapters identify story elements like plot, character, setting, and theme, and discourse elements like narrator, narratee, filter, and slant. These are not just terms but tools that have proven useful for investigating many kinds of fiction.

Many levels of analysis are possible, because stories have larger and smaller levels of structure. One thing worth remembering is that what you are really analyzing is not the text itself, which is a matter of shapes on a page, but your experience of it. The text is made of letters, words, and sentences, but the story you experience contains places, events, and people. It isn't possible to slip a person into a book like a flower pressed between the pages. Yet we feel we know great characters; we can reconstruct their motives and predict their actions. We can love them or hate them. We rarely love or hate sentences. It might be useful to think of the text as something like a musical score. When you read, you perform the score, and turn the printed letters — mere abstract symbols — into something moving and meaningful.

So there are really three things you need to analyze: the text itself, the experience it generates, and the relationship between those two things. You read a series of words; you (re)construct a plot. Analysis involves looking at the verbal structures and the narrative structure, and at the way the former can direct us to the latter.

Evaluation means deciding how good or bad the story is — and how the story is good or bad. It is more than a recommendation to read this story, or not to read that one. To evaluate any story, you must set up criteria. What should a story do? or more precisely, What should this kind of story do? Different kinds of stories have different criteria for evaluation. A good mystery must provide readers with sufficient evidence to solve the mystery and yet puzzle them enough so that they don't quite solve it until the end. A good love story doesn't have to do anything of the sort. It makes no sense to say that *Romeo and Juliet* is a bad play because we aren't given enough clues to solve the murder. We know who killed whom; what we care about is the consequence to the lovers.

So evaluation also involves classification. You have to decide what form of story the author intended to write: to use a technical term, what *genre*. Then you can evaluate according to what you know about the standards appropriate to that genre. You could also argue that one genre is intrinsically more important or more capable of complexity than another, but that is a much more difficult claim to prove. To make significant comparisons among genres, you probably have to move beyond evaluation and into the realm of poetics.

Poetics is the study of how literary forms work, rather than the study of individual texts. The poetics of storytelling, called narratology, is an attempt to explain what narrative is capable of and how it operates. The terms we use in analyzing a particular story, such as *plot* or *filter*, arose out of narratology. A curious thing about poetics is that when you engage in it, you don't particularly care whether there are examples of a particular possibility. Can there be a plot without characters? Can a writer use two filters simultaneously? Poetics tries to answer such questions by looking at the form itself and the language from which it is made. Sometimes an example comes to mind: Samuel Beckett (perhaps) wrote a characterless narrative. Such a text would help validate the poetic theory. However, even if no example of a characterless plot exists, that doesn't necessarily mean it's impossible. Someone might write one someday, especially if for no other reason than to show it was possible. (You might try your hand at doing a paragraph or two of such a story, by way of experiment.)

All these ways of writing about literature — explication, interpretation, analysis, evaluation, poetics — are interrelated. You may find yourself needing to discuss a category first and then using it to explain something in a story. In that case, you are doing both poetics and explication. Most evaluation involves at least a little analysis to provide supporting evidence. Analysis can lead you into new and sometimes unexpected interpretations. Whatever approach you take, it is a good idea to base it on what struck you most strongly when you read the fiction. If you hated the fiction, you need to come to terms with that hatred before you can explicate or analyze or evaluate. If you were moved to tears, see if you can discover what started those tears rolling. If you were simply bored, try to figure out why other people value the fiction. Maybe you weren't giving the story a fair reading because you were tired or in a hurry. Or maybe you really did your best, but there is something in the story or its genre that makes it difficult for the kind of reader you are: conservative or liberal, Easterner or Midwesterner, Baptist or Buddhist. If so, there is no obligation to make yourself into a different person to meet the demands of the story. Like a scientist, you should report negative results as well as positive, and do your best to understand both. You won't be able to discover any truths about a story, let alone write about them effectively, if they are not your own truths.

Because the fiction as experienced is partly a product of the reader's imagination, skills, and experiences, it is never exactly the same story twice. Even your own rereading includes the memory of the first time through; hence the story is changed by that much. The overall contours may be the same, but the details, the emphases, and the effects continually alter. Nothing you write will ever be the final word on the story. On the other hand, no story will ever be fully exhausted so long as new readers are there to venture into it and to send back explorers' reports.

A Student Paper

Here is an example of a student paper, written by Cindy Tobisman, on Mary McCarthy's "C.Y.E." Cindy developed her paper through three stages — diary entries, a first draft, and a final version.

As she read through the short story for the first time, Cindy noted her reactions in her reading diary (see pp. 603–604).

Cindy's Diary Entries

filter is altered during the telling--she has become what she hates--she inflicted the torture on herself.
Intelligent, reads significance into everything, recalls minute details--i.e., how sash is worn

three phases, yesterday on subway, flashback to convent up-bringing, and present day--incorporates parts one and two--she is the combination of an adult and her convent experience

Merging of identities of the two (or one) Marys in the story. Her name is Mary, "Why is it that I have always been Mary?"

confessional style--tells her most embarrassing details--washing her ears out because she thinks CYE stands for "Clean Your Ears," exposes secret thoughts. It seems like she does this

because she has gained a distance from the events in the story--
she has matured to the point of not being affected by the
memories. At end, it is revealed that she can speak about the
events because she is no longer the person that she was--she
identifies with the other Mary (friend or Elinor). This shift is
subtle, how does McCarthy achieve this effect?

She has the memories of one person (Mary as a convent child),
but the wit and power over language of another (Mary of Mary
and Elinor). She becomes the novelist and can thus recreate the
reality, manipulate it, and filter it.

causation is the underlying theme in CYE--the implied author/
narrator's personality is defined through her relations to a
string of seemingly random events--her personality gives the
events of the story cohesiveness--a street sign has significance,
a sash, an acronym
Detective story--especially unconnected events find their
nexus in the implied author's personality--like a mystery, it is
the causality which ties the seemingly divergent events to-
gether--and only when the character filter/narrator explains
the causality do we gain a context through which we may view
and evaluate the events of her present and past. Ironically
though, it is this same filter through which we find coherence
for the events, that ultimately casts doubt on the integrity of
her character at the end by failing to reconcile her past
"mousy" self with her current personality. Instead, she turns
on her past self and in rejecting it, aligns herself with a different Mary, the one who tormented her.
Slightly unreliable narration--because the only characterization offered to the implied reader is that imparted by the character filter herself, and that is somewhat contradictory--dis-
crepancy between the early Mary and the later Mary. Who is
she? Also unreliable because we know that she lies--about "SI"
to postconvent friends.

CHARACTERIZATION
Story is told through the filter of M's mind
Char filter is the narrator in CYE
Very complex character--many implied traits--we know implicitly what sort of mental transition must have gone on for her
to have alienated herself from her childhood self-image--she
was sensitive and ambitious, despite her efforts to shed the
vulnerability that resulted from this combination, she is still
susceptible--she has a hard time looking at the sign "CYE BER-
NARD" at first--she wants to bury her "weak" traits

internal narrator, mental access, inner view, but very controlled by her

Characterize her filter: Religious overtones (". . . Lest anyone suspect that I am crucified there on that building, hanging exposed in black script lettering . . .")

Time, setting, pacing: Begins as "I sat frozen in my seat, staring at the picture of Miss Subways, February 1943." All a remembrance of her past. Between yesterday and the telling of the story. The narration covers a huge portion of time, but the telling is brief, only around ten or fifteen minutes. It recalls a string of instances leading up to the end. The end of the story is in sinc with "current" actions. The implied author/narrator has reached a point of convergence.

No true flashbacks--she always calls attention to her current adult perspective/filter--she is not reliving the past in the form of a flashback, she is merely recalling and retelling the past in detail and with adult embellishment. Past events are always in past tense

STRUCTURE
Use of "you" vs. use of "I" when describing her childhood. She identifies with the present, as seen by her use of "I," but when she talks about herself in the past, she uses "you"
"To be the butt of this kind of joke was a singularly painful experience, for you were never in a position to turn the tables, to join in the laughter at your own expense, because you could not possibly pretend to know what the joke was. Actually, as I see now, it was the intimacy of the two girls that set the standard: from the vantage point of their private world, anything outside seemed strange and ludicrous." And yet, the implied author does try to join in laughing at the joke--she internalizes the joke, calls herself CYE and seeks to play it off. "I chose what was actually the more shameful part. I accepted the nickname, made a sort of joke of it, used it brazenly myself on the telephone . . ."

Description, at service of the narrative

Not a lot of dialogue--internal dialogue and recalled dialogue only

STORY TIME AND PACING
(end)
She still cannot work out the riddle--it is estranged from her, like her old self. She is alienated from the significance of the letters/abbreviation "C.Y.E."--in this piece, there are a lot of allusions to significance, but none arises. There is a hint at symmetry and structure, but it never yields understanding--like the initials C.Y.E., the reader of this piece cannot really understand the meaning of the memories recorded by the implied author. And, we are led to believe, neither can she. She sees the pattern--"It is nearly enough to convince me that life is a system of recurrent pairs, the poison and the antidote being eternally packaged together by some considerate heavenly druggist."--The two Marys are the poison and the antidote--Mary, the implied author as a child, is a shy, over-intense student who takes herself seriously. Mary, the implied author as narrator, is witty, expressive and confident in her ability to recall events from her convent days and to impose mature, adult perspective on her earlier recollections. The second Mary is much more similar to the Mary of Mary and Elinor--she presents an enigmatic system of signifiers, CYE, or the story itself, but the only cohesiveness is implicit in the Mary who gives the nickname or tells the story. In order to understand the mentality behind the nickname, the implied author as an adult must become like the Mary who gave her the name. After she gains some control, she becomes the one who is in charge of meaning--she decides that CYE stands for "Clever Young Egg," but it is too late. In gaining perspective on her childhood, she has lost the ability to empathize with that child that she once was. As she herself says, "The past is manipulated to serve the interests of the present."

What struck Cindy first was the difference between the filter of the character, the young schoolgirl, and the slant of the adult woman who narrates the story, particularly the contrast between the shyness and painful sensitivity of the first and the confidence and accomplishment of the second. At this diary stage, Cindy, writing hastily, is a bit unclear about her technical terms ("filter," for example, is probably the wrong word for whatever Cindy meant by "filter is altered during the telling"). Still, the diary already shows a rough grasp of the short story's technique.

Cindy went on to note the time differences, distinguishing the present moment of the discourse (though she has not yet labelled "discourse" as such) from the past moment of the story, the period of the protagonist's life in the convent. Cindy also noted the disparity in duration between story and discourse: "The narration [this word is also incorrectly used: Cindy means *story*] covers a huge portion of time, but the telling is brief, only around ten or fifteen minutes.''

By her third paragraph, Cindy has realized that the short story displays two different personalities lodged in what is biologically the same person. She quotes an important line: "Why is it that I have always been Mary?" It is only later, after my reaction to her first draft, that Cindy would recognize that her argument needs to distinguish, clearly and consistently, between *three* individuals: The shy young Mary in the convent tormented by the initials "C.Y.E.," the confident adult Mary reminiscing about the past and rejecting her shy former self, and a composite Mary — the sum total of girl and woman. In her revisions, Cindy would assign three separate labels to these different Marys, namely, "the character," "the narrator," and "Mary C.Y.E.," the composite. These terms, used consistently, give crucial clarity to her final version. But at the diary stage Cindy was still a bit unclear about how to name — and therefore how to separate — these entities (for example, she referred, confusingly, to the "implied author/narrator" and to the "character filter/narrator," and wrote "Char filter is the narrator in CYE"). Cindy needed to check her terms more carefully, and she would do so in her draft and final version.

Cindy keenly observed that both the heroine and one of her tormentors are named "Mary." Since literally thousands of names were available for these two characters, Cindy concluded that the double use of the name Mary was not accidental. This led her ultimately to a major point — that the adult Mary changes from loser to winner by adopting the kind of "wit and power" she observed in her tormentor, Mary Heinrichs.

Cindy also felt a need to explain how "seemingly random events" of the protagonist's present and past experience were ostensibly brought together to explain her development (though in her paper she would come to conclude that the composite "Mary C.Y.E." is not an integrated personality). Cindy made another interesting observation: Despite the radical change in the protagonist's personality, the narrator still thinks in Christian terms, even if only metaphorically ("Lest anyone suspect that I am crucified there on that building, hanging exposed in black script lettering . . .").

Cindy's sharp eye also caught an important diversity in the narrator's use of pronouns. The narrator consistently refers to her present self as "I" but sometimes speaks of — or rather *to* — her former schoolgirl self as "you" ("To be the butt of this kind of joke was a singularly painful experience, for you were never in a position to turn the tables . . ."). Cindy would use this difference to good effect in her paper to emphasize how much the adult narrator feels alienated from her younger self.

In her final diary entry, Cindy decided that the short story really presents two puzzles: (1) the "real" meaning of C.Y.E. (that is, the meaning it had for its inventors, Mary Heinrichs and Elinor Henehan), and (2) the final meaning of the narrator's evolved personality. We can see Cindy struggling to find the best prose to express the analogy she draws between these two riddles. She was also struck by the powerful antithesis of "poison" and "antidote" and began to work out the full implications of the metaphor. These would be well formulated by the final version of her paper.

Cindy's First Draft

Mary McCarthy's short story, "C.Y.E." presents the implied reader with a sort of detective story. In the short story, seemingly unconnected events find their nexus *Confusing:* in the narrator's personality. Like a <u>mystery</u>, a street *"mystery"* *Sort this* sign, an acronym, and a convent are all imbued with *is not* *term out:* significance as the <u>character filter/narrator</u> reveals her *part of* *the* thought process. It is the internal causality which *series;* *narrator's* *and* *relocate.* *point of* lends the story its coherence ~~that~~ also reveals the narra- *view* tor's implied personality traits. Only after the <u>character</u> *wrong.* *should* <u>filter</u> explains the causality does the implied reader *term* *be called* *she* *"slant"* gain a context through which <u>~~they~~</u> may view the events *number* of Mary's past and present. *disagreement*

I ~~Ironically?~~ ʌit is this same filter through which we find coherence for the story's events, that ultimately casts doubt on the integrity of the filter at the end of the story by failing to reconcile her past "mousy" self with her current adult personality. Instead, Mary, the successful writer/narrator, turns on her past self and in rejecting it, aligns herself with her childhood tormentors (one of which is ironically named Mary). The process by which this discrepancy between the early Mary *arises* and the later Mary ~~arose~~ and ʌthe effects of this gap on the personality of the <u>character filter</u>ʌ? imbues the story *wrong* *a* *term* with ʌdual level**s** of significance. *wrong* *New* ⌐The <u>character filter/narrator's</u> style is confessional. She *term* *¶* tells the most embarrassing details of her childhood in the convent. There, she was dubbed "CYE" by the two *wrong* class clowns, Mary and Elinor. Throughout the story, *term* the <u>character filter</u> details the lengths which she

reached in the quest to rid herself of this dreaded nickname. As a child, the narrator, thinking that the acro-   *character?*
nym stood for "Clean Your Ears," tried to wash her ears
out. Despite her efforts and sleepless nights, she remained unable to decipher the significance of the letters "C.Y.E." The story details the relevance and reso-   *wrong*
nant implications of this affliction.   *word*

Use "discourse" instead   The structure of the story begins with yesterday on
the subway, and ends with the present day. During the
interim period, the implied narrator recalls ~~the~~ events
from her childhood. However, there are no true flashbacks. The narrator keeps a firm grasp on her adult
Use "slant" instead perspective. She uses "you" when she describes her
childhood self and "I" when she characterizes her
present personality. For instance, she narrates,

> To be the butt of this kind of joke was a singularly
> painful experience, for you were never in a position
> to turn the tables, to join in the laughter at your own
> expense, because you could not possibly pretend to
> know what the joke was. Actually, as I see now, it
> was the intimacy of the two girls that set the stan-
> dard: from the vantage point of their private world,
> anything outside seemed strange and ludicrous.

The short story itself details the process by which the
narrator achieves a resolution of a problem that has
been bothering her since her childhood, problematical
though this resolution might be. As a professional
writer, Mary has gained control over her affliction. She
is the master of words, of naming and of description.
Using this power, she decides that "C.Y.E." stood for
"Clever Young Egg."

However, although she is now free from the torment

imparted by the nickname, the narrator still cannot
work out the riddle of what "C.Y.E." really meant; it is
estranged from her, like her old self. She remains alienated from the significance of the ~~letters~~/abbreviation
"C.Y.E." This alienation from meaning is mirrored in
the structure of the implied author's story. Although
there are allusions and hints at a stable sense of the
character filter's personality, no clear characterization
arises. For instance, the character filter characterizes
her childhood self as sensitive and ambitious. As a result, she turned the nickname into an affliction. However, by the end of the story, she demonstrates quite a
different self. She writes, seeing her sensitive and ambitious self from the outside,

"abbre-
viation"
is
enough

Don't
you
mean
"narrator"?

> As for the pale, plain girl in the front of the study
> hall, her, too, I can no longer reach. I see her creeping
> down the corridor with a little knot of her class-
> mates. "Hello, Cye," I say with a touch of disdain for
> her rawness, her guileless ambition . . . I hate her,
> for she is my natural victim, and it is I who have
> given her the name, the shameful, inscrutable name
> that she will never, sleepless in her bed at night, be
> able to puzzle out."

Thus, though the story seems to be resolved when the
writer Mary reinterprets her childhood nickname in a
positive light, we are shown that this resolution is
problematical. In order to achieve this resolution, Mary
the mousy student has changed her identity to Mary
the class clown. The character filter has the memories
of one person and the wit and power over language of
another. This transition makes the character filter's
true character somewhat unreachable. Like the initials
C.Y.E., the implied reader of this piece cannot really

Unclear
whether
you mean
Mary
Heinrichs or
"Mary C.Y.E."

wrong
term --
you mean
the composite
"Mary C.Y.E."

sentence
is unclear

come to

[^] understand the meaning of the memories recorded by

the narrator. And, we are led to believe, neither can ~~she~~. *the narrator*

She sees the pattern, but cannot quite understand the

meaning for it. She writes,

> It is nearly enough to convince me that life is a sys-
> tem of recurrent pairs, the poison and the antidote
> being eternally packaged together by some consider-
> ate heavenly druggist.

In the context of the story, the two Marys are the poi-

son and the antidote; Mary, the implied author as a

child, is a shy, over-intense student who takes herself

too seriously, while Mary, the implied author as narra-

tor, is witty, expressive and confident in her ability to

recall events from her convent days and to impose a

mature, adult perspective on her earlier recollections.

The second Mary is much more similar to the Mary of

Mary and Elinor. She presents an enigmatic system of ⎱ *sentence*

signifiers, the initials "C.Y.E.," *and* ~~or~~ the story itself, but ⎰ *is*

the only cohesiveness is implicit in the Mary who <u>gives</u> *unclear*

<u>the nickname or tells the story</u>. In order to understand

the mentality behind the nickname, the implied author

as an adult, must become like the Mary who gave her

the name.

Thus, although the character filter has gained some

control over the nickname by becoming the one who is

in charge of its meaning, it is too late. In gaining per-

spective on her childhood, she has lost the ability to

empathize with that child that she once was. As she

herself says, "The past is manipulated to serve the in-

terests of the present."

In composing her draft, Cindy's first decision concerned her audience. She decided that the audience to address was her instructor — namely me. As stated previously (see p. 604), this is the usual situation in college classrooms. Since I obviously knew the short story well, she felt no need to explain things that an audience unfamiliar with the short story would need to be told. (But your own instructor may wish you to compose a paper with such an audience in mind; that kind of paper would read like a book review. If you are not certain who your audience is supposed to be, be sure to ask. It is very difficult to write convincingly without a clear sense of audience.)

The overall structure of Cindy's paper is well conceived, even in her draft. The first paragraph starts out by examining the short story's design, which is similar to a puzzle whose pieces will ostensibly cohere once assembled. But the second paragraph hints that the narrator is only partly successful in fitting the puzzle pieces together into a cohesive whole. The rest of Cindy's paper develops that "hint" further, arguing that the short story leaves us with a sense of a gap in the protagonist's personality. Summarizing the story in paragraph three, and the structure of the discourse in paragraph four, Cindy marshals the evidence for her argument in her long fifth paragraph. She argues that we must read past the narrator's confident view of her own development and recognize that she has purchased her present success at the price of rejecting her former self. To the extent that that rejection leaves her without a past, so to speak, she is less well-integrated (has less integrity than) a person who accepts his past as continuous and homogeneous with his present. Cindy feels that Mary C.Y.E. has lost something of herself, has become something of a riddle; hence Cindy's final title "Mary 'C.Y.E.': The Indeterminate Personality." The final paragraph offers an impressively chosen quotation to demonstrate the adult Mary C.Y.E.'s own intuition that she has manipulated the past to suit her present personality.

When I read Cindy's draft, I realized that she had chosen a point of departure about "C.Y.E." somewhat different from my own (see pp. 140–141). She is less willing than I to accept the adult narrator's self-satisfaction with her present state of mind as the true state of affairs. Since literary texts are generally open to a variety of interpretations, a conscientious instructor will welcome any reading of a short story as long it is well argued, and I found Cindy's interpretation well argued indeed. So I wrote the following in a summary note at the end of her draft:

> I find your point both interesting and well argued. My only problem is some confusion about how to name the various entities entailed in the short story. It strikes me that you're really dealing with three entities which are *not* combined. Hence I would avoid the use of the slash mark to show combination, as in "character filter/narrator." I think such phrases are both unwieldy and misleading. Try to find some other term for the composite figure of the character and narrator. By your reasoning this figure would necessarily be unintegrated to the extent that the narrator rejects her former self.

Cindy read my comments and made some vital changes in her paper,

clarifying the distinction between the three Marys and reorganizing her terminology to achieve consistency. I have underlined the important changes.

Cindy's Final Version

MARY "C.Y.E.": THE INDETERMINATE PERSONALITY
by Cindy Tobisman

Mary McCarthy's short story, "C.Y.E.," presents the
implied reader with a sort of detective story. In the
short story, seemingly unconnected events find their
nexus in the narrator's personality. A store sign, an
acronym, and a saint are all imbued with significance as
the narrator reveals her thought process. It is the internal causality which lends the story its coherence that
also reveals the narrator's implied personality traits.
Only after the narrator explains the causality does the
narratee gain a context through which *he* ~~they~~ may view
the events of Mary's past and present.

add "and slant"

It is this same filter through which we find coherence for the story's events, ~~that~~ ultimately casts doubt
on the integrity of the filter ~~at the end of the story~~ by
failing to reconcile her past "mousy" self with her current adult personality. Instead, Mary, the successful
writer/narrator, turns on her past self and in rejecting
it, aligns herself with her childhood tormenters (one of
whom ~~which~~ is ironically named Mary). By the end of the
story, the two personalities, Mary (the childhood character ~~filter~~) and Mary (the adult narrator), have become
integrated, albeit not well, into a single entity (Mary
"C.Y.E."). The process by which this discrepancy between the early Mary (the character ~~filter~~) and the later
Mary (the narrator) arose and the effects of this gap on

Insert: "but the short story as a whole"

phrase is redundant

add "whom I will call"

the personality of Mary "C.Y.E." imbues the story with a dual level of significance.

The narrator's style is confessional. She tells the most embarrassing details of her childhood in the convent. There, she was dubbed "CYE" by the two class clowns, Mary *Heinrichs* and Elinor *Halahan*. Throughout the story, the narrator details the lengths which she reached in the quest to rid herself of this dreaded nickname. As a child, the ~~narrator~~ *character*, thinking that the acronym stood for "Clean Your Ears," tried to wash her ears out. Despite her efforts and sleepless nights, she remained unable to decipher the significance of the letters "C.Y.E." The story details the relevance and resonant implications of this nickname.

The discourse of the story begins with yesterday on the subway, and ends with the present day. During the interim period, the implied narrator recalls events from her childhood. However, there are no true flashbacks. The narrator keeps a firm grasp on her adult slant. She uses "you" when she describes her childhood self and "I" when she characterizes her present personality. For instance, she narrates,

> To be the butt of this kind of joke was a singularly painful experience, for you were never in a position to turn the tables, to join in the laughter at your own expense, because you could not possibly pretend to know what the joke was. Actually, as I see now, it was the intimacy of the two girls that set the standard: from the vantage point of their private world, anything outside seemed strange and ludicrous.

The short story itself details the process by which the narrator achieves a resolution of a problem that has been bothering her since her childhood, problematical though this resolution might be. As a professional writer, the narrator has gained control over her affliction. She is the master of words, of naming and of description. Using this power, she decides that "C.Y.E." stood for "Clever Young Egg."

However, although she is now free from the torment imparted by the nickname, the narrator is still baffled by the real meaning of the nickname "C.Y.E.". She remains alienated from the significance of the abbreviation. This alienation from meaning is mirrored in the structure of the narrator's story. Although there are allusions and hints at a stable sense of Mary "C.Y.E.'s" personality, no clear characterization of this combination of Mary (the childhood character filter) and Mary (the adult narrator) arises. For instance, the narrator characterizes her childhood self as sensitive and vulnerable. As a result, she turned the nickname into an affliction. However, by the end of the story, she demonstrates quite a different self. She writes, seeing her sensitive and ambitious self from the outside,

> As for the pale, plain girl in the front of the study hall, her, too, I can no longer reach. I see her creeping down the corridor with a little knot of her classmates. "Hello, Cye," I say with a touch of disdain for her rawness, her guileless ambition . . . I hate her, for she is my natural victim, and it is I who have given her the name, the shameful, inscrutable name that she will never, sleepless in her bed at night, be able to puzzle out.

Thus, though the story seems to be resolved when the narrator reinterprets her childhood nickname in a positive light, we are shown that this resolution is problematical. In order to achieve this resolution, Mary the mousy student has aligned herself with Mary *Heinrichs,* the class clown. The adult Mary "C.Y.E." has the memories of one person and the wit and power over language of another. This transition makes Mary "C.Y.E.'s" true character somewhat unreachable. <u>The narratee of this piece can no more come to understand the meaning of the memories recorded by the narrator than to understand the significance of the initials,</u> "C.Y.E." And, we are led to believe, neither can the narrator. She sees the pattern, but cannot quite understand the meaning *of* it. She writes,

> It is nearly enough to convince me that life is a system of recurrent pairs, the poison and the antidote being eternally packaged together by some considerate heavenly druggist.

In the context of the story, the character filter Mary is the poison and the narrator is the antidote; Mary, as a child, was a shy, over-intense student who took herself too seriously, while Mary, as the narrator, is witty, expressive and confident in her ability to recall events from her convent days and to impose a mature, adult perspective on her earlier recollections. The adult Mary is much more similar to Mary *Heinrichs*.

Thus, although the composite, Mary "C.Y.E.," has gained some control over the nickname by becoming the one who is in charge of its meaning, it is too late. In gaining perspective on her childhood, she has lost the ability to empathize with that child that she once was. As she herself says, "The past is manipulated to serve the interests of the present."

Note, first of all, that confusingly used phrases like "character filter" and "character filter/narrator" have been replaced throughout by three more precise terms. These are established clearly in a sentence which Cindy added to her second paragraph: "By the end of the story, the two personalities, Mary (the childhood character) and Mary (the adult narrator), have become integrated, albeit not well, into a single entity (Mary 'C.Y.E.')." Since the third name was invented by Cindy, I suggested that she acknowledge the fact, thereby clearly indicating the main thrust of her interpretation. Other terms that she changed to make her argument clearer are "discourse" for "structure" and "slant" for "adult perspective."

Perhaps Cindy's most impressive stylistic improvement was recasting the sentence in paragraph five which draws the analogy between the riddle of C.Y.E. and that of Mary's unintegrated personality. The original confusion of

> Like the initials C.Y.E., the implied reader of this piece cannot really understand the meaning of the memories recorded by the narrator.

was changed to this perspicuous and even elegant sentence:

> The narratee of this piece can no more come to understand the meaning of the memories recorded by the narrator than to understand the significance of the initials, "C.Y.E."

Though I offered a few stylistic suggestions in the margins of the final version, my summary comment praised Cindy both on her original reading of the story and on her effective argument to support that reading.

Other Approaches

Cindy elected to write about an alternative reading, but there are many other approaches that would lead to a good paper on "C.Y.E." The way to begin is simple: Ask yourself honestly what your reaction to a given short story is. As suggested in "How to Write about Short Stories," that reaction may take many forms. You may wish to praise or criticize, or half-praise and half-criticize. You may wish to relate the experiences of the characters to your own (for example, how *you've* changed, gained confidence, as a result of schoolmates' attitudes toward you). You may wish to write an account of how you came — or didn't come — to terms with the short story because you could or could not accept its basic premise (that Mary is or is not a coherent personality, for example). You may wish to reconstruct your struggle to understand the short story's intention and your sense of success or failure in doing so. You may wish to analyze some important technical feature — the handling of time, for example, or the use or non-use of narrator's commentary. You may wish to compare the short story's ideology with your own, or to compare and contrast the ideologies (or some other feature) of two short stories (compare "C.Y.E.," for example, with James Joyce's "A Little Cloud" as studies in success and failure).

Whatever you do, make sure that you argue some single, clearly stated *point* about the short story, and let that point direct the organization of your paper. (Cindy's point, remember, is that the composite "Mary C.Y.E." is not a well-integrated personality, no matter how successful she may be as a writer, that her evolution remains no less problematic than the original meaning of "C.Y.E.") In a short paper (under 10 pages) don't try to make more than one point; it is better to work out the ramifications of that point than to shift to other points. Leave the grand analyses to the critics who have the time and experience to write whole books on a given novel or short story.

Glossary

Cross-references to related terms are signaled by quotation marks.

agent (in the narrative): one who performs or experiences story-events (the agent need not be human); see "character" below.

allegory: a narrative whose characters and events represent meanings outside the fiction, whether abstract qualities or ideas (Virtue, Sloth) or historical figures (Queen Elizabeth in Spenser's *Faerie Queene*).

antagonist: the character opposed to the protagonist (or "hero") of a narrative.

argument: a kind of text whose purpose is to persuade its addressee to take an action or position favored by the author.

atmosphere: the mood or aura that suffuses a narrative. It is invoked by the actions and feelings of the characters, but most particularly by the setting (e.g., the gloomy setting of Charles Dickens's *Great Expectations*).

authorial narrator: a narrator who acknowledges *being* the narrator, making much of his or her own presence in the discourse, but who did not participate in the story-events.

branching of story-events: the fundamental pattern of story; a given situation provokes our anticipation of the possibility of a variety of events, but in traditional narrative, only one event actually materializes.

causation: the property of traditional plots that requires that event B not only follow event A, but also be its consequence.

character: an agent who has one or more discernible traits, or qualities of personality.

character-I: in a first-person narration in which a (former) character tells his or her own story (see "internal narrator"), "character-I" refers to that person as character back in the story (as opposed to the "narrator-I" who speaks now in the discourse).

character-narrator: that kind of first-person narrator who had been a character back in the story (as opposed to "authorial narrator").

characterization: the process by which traits are assigned to characters.

closure: the satisfactory winding-up of a narrative, giving the reader the sense that everything demanded by the plot has in fact occurred and that narrative movement has come to rest. Traditional fictions signal closure with landmark events—a wedding, a death—but many modern fictions end on an uneventful note, as if to say "That's the way things are."

context (in narrative): whatever precedes and follows a given narrative feature — an event, character, prop, theme — and thus helps the reader interpret it.

description: a kind of text that renders the properties of things — typically, though not necessarily, objects visible to or imaginable by the senses.

dialogue: speech between characters. (Interior dialogue — or monologue — refers to speech within a character's own mind.)

direct naming of traits: that kind of characterization in which the narrator or some other character directly assigns a trait-name ("lazy," "brilliant") to a character.

direct quotation: the exact words used by a character in thinking or speaking, usually (though not necessarily) set off with quotation marks. In direct quotation, the character refers to herself by means of the pronoun "I" and uses a verb tense contemporary with the action. (See example under "indirect quotation.")

discourse: the means by which the story is communicated, that is, told or shown by a narrator.

discourse-time: the period of time that the discourse lasts, that is, the time it takes the narrator to "tell" or "show" the story. Thus, a three-page short story has a discourse-time that is one-third as long as that of a nine-page story, even though the story-time of the first may be longer than that of the second.

duration: the time relation between story and discourse with respect to how long each *lasts*. (See "scene," "summary," "pause," and "ellipsis.")

dynamic character: a character whose traits change during the course of the narrative.

ellipsis: one of the four durational relationships between story and discourse. In ellipsis, story-time continues but is not reported by the discourse. Ellipsis depends on the reader's capacity to infer the unmentioned events that may or may not be significant to the plot.

epiphany: "an intuitive grasp of reality achieved in a quick flash of recognition in which something, usually simple and commonplace, is seen in a new light" [C. Hugh Holman and William Harmon, *A Handbook to Literature*, 6th ed. (New York: Macmillan, 1992), p. 174].

event: a happening, the fundamental unit of story and of plot.

fable: an argument presented in the form of a narrative. The main point of the argument is usually called the "moral." The characters of fables are often animals whose conventional traits make them easily understood as allegorical representations of a strand of the argument. The fox, for example, is used as the essence of wiliness.

fallible: capable of failing. This term describes the "filter" of a character whose attitude toward the events and situations and others characters of the plot is clearly misguided.

fiction: (1) any text that makes no claims to truth (this meaning of the noun corresponds to the adjective "fictitious"); (2) a narrative that is a fiction [in sense (1)].

filter: the perspective or point of view of a character — the way the character perceives and conceives of the events and other characters in the story.

flashback: one of the possible time-order relations between story and discourse. In flashback, the event is told or shown out of order, that is, the narrator mentions it before mentioning other events that actually occurred earlier in the story.

flat character: a character who has only a single or very few traits.

frame-narrative: a narrative that contains another narrative inside (the frame-narrative of *Scheharazade* concerns the heroine's attempt to save her life by telling the sultan a different tale every night). A frame-narrative constitutes the discourse with respect to its *framed* story.

free quotation: a quotation of a character's thought or speech that is *not* marked by a "tag" such as "he said" or "she thought."

genre: a French term meaning "literary kind" or "type"; for example, tragedy, epic, lyric, novella, Western, and detective novel are different genres.

hero/heroine: the character whose fate means the most to the reader, that is, the character with whom the reader tends most to identify.

identification: the process by which the reader puts himself or herself in a character's place.

ideology: a comprehensive system of beliefs and ideas about the nature of things (e.g., Puritanism or Nazism). Adherents of an ideology may be unconscious that they follow it. What they believe and how they believe it seems simply common sense.

impersonal narration: narration whose narrator did not participate in the events of the story-world and who tells or shows the story from a vantage point outside that world.

implied author: the creator presupposed by the narrative itself. The implied author is the source of our sense of the fiction's underlying values and beliefs—its ideology. The values of the narrator usually correspond to those of the implied author, but in "unreliable narration" they do not.

implied reader: the reader presupposed by the narrative itself. For example, a narrative condemning racial discrimination implies a reader who believes in equality among the races.

indirect quotation: the citation of a character's speech or thought but with third-person self-reference and previous-tense verb forms, usually without quotation marks (thus "He wondered if he would see Jane" is the indirectly quoted form of "He wondered 'Will I see Jane?'").

inner view: the narrator's access to the character's consciousness.

inquit: the Latin word for the "tag" of indirect quotation: "He replied" and "she wondered " are inquits.

intention: the "point" toward which the narrative is directed.

internal narrator: a narrator who previously participated in the plot as one of the characters. He or she may have been either the protagonist or a secondary character, or "witness-narrator."

inverted narrative order: an order in which the discourse presents the story in an order different from that followed by the story-events themselves. "Flashback" is an example.

ironist: the maker of an irony.

irony: (1) situational or "irony of fate": an odd coincidence, that is, where events seem to conspire against expectations; (2) verbal irony: the underlying intention of a remark is quite different from, perhaps even the opposite of, its literal meaning. Verbal irony in narrative is the source of two important structures: the "fallible filter" and the "unreliable narration" (q.v.).

limited filter: the narrator's power to enter characters' minds is limited to a single (or a few) characters. (Contrast with "omniscience.")

metafiction: a fiction that raises questions about its own structure and therefore, implicitly or explicitly, about the basic conventions of narrative.

moral: the "thesis" of a fable.

motivation: the reasons, whether presented explicitly or implicitly, for a character's behavior.

myth: a narrative that explains nature in terms of supernatural events and characters. Myths are used by cultures to explain how and why things are as they are.

narratee: the audience to whom the narrator addresses the narrative. Narratees may be named and active personages (see Tillie Olsen's "I Stand Here Ironing" (pp. 122–127) and Isaac Babel's "How It Was Done in Odessa" (pp. 75–81), but often they are only implicit. In the latter case, there is little to distinguish them from implied readers.

narrative: a kind of text composed of events, characters, and settings. Unlike the text-types argument and description, narrative possesses a double time order —the time of the events narrated and the time that it takes to narrate those events.

narrative exposition: the presentation of events affecting the story that occurred *before* the story proper begins.

narrator: the agent who communicates—by "telling" or "showing"—the story.

narrator-I: in first-person or internal narration in which a (former) character tells his or her own story, narrator-I is the term referring to the character in his or her capacity as narrator, telling or showing the story "now," in the discourse.

omniscience: the power of a narrator to enter *any* character's mind at will.

order: the time relation between story and discourse that concerns its sequential aspect. In *normal* order, the sequence of the telling of the events corresponds exactly to the sequence in which the events occurred in the story. In "inverted narrative order"—for example, "flashback"—there is a disparity.

parable: an argument cast in the form of a narrative. (See "fable.")

paraphrase: generally, putting someone's statement into other words; in narrative, the term refers specifically to the narrator's putting the character's speeches or thoughts into the narrator's own words. (See "report.")

pause: one of the four durational relationships between story and discourse. The story stops for a moment as the narrator describes or comments on events, characters, themes, or anything that concerns him or her. When the story-events resume, no "story-time" has elapsed.

personal narration: narration in which the narrator seems to have a recognizable personality.

plot: the connected series of events that constitutes the story. In traditional plots, the basis of connection is "causation."

point: the consequence of the story, the reason that it gets told. Point is not the same thing as "theme." "Point" concerns only the fiction, whereas "theme" goes beyond the fiction, implying something about the real world.

props: objects in the setting.

protagonist: the leading character of a narrative.

real author: the historical person who actually wrote the fiction.

report: an account of a character's thoughts cast in the narrator's diction. (See "paraphrase.")

round character: a character who has many traits, some of which may even be mutually contradictory. (Hamlet is perhaps literature's "roundest" character).

scene: one of the four durational relationships between story and discourse. The telling or showing of the story-event lasts approximately as long as the event lasts.

self-conscious fiction: fiction that raises questions about its own mode of existence, about the very conventions of narrative and fictionality.

setting: the space in which the story-events occur. Setting consists of background and "props."

showing: narrating the events in such a way as to make them seem to be "just happening by themselves."

slant: the perspective or angle — moral, intellectual, emotional — from which the narrator presents the story. For example, a narrator may be very sympathetic or very indifferent to the fate of the characters.

static character: a character who does not change over the course of the story.

story: that part of the narrative that is told or shown. It is constituted by the whole set of events, characters, and settings.

story-time: the time it takes for the story-events to occur.

subserve: a term used to explain how one text-type, such as description, can contribute to the ends of another text-type, such as narrative.

summary: one of the four durational relationships between story and discourse. In summary, discourse statements are much shorter than the events that they narrate; for example, "the war lasted for thirty years."

surprise: the effect on the reader when event B seems totally unprepared for by event A.

surprise ending: a twist ending, in which the last event is totally, and usually ironically, unexpected.

suspense: a particularly intense kind of narrative curiosity, often because one of the possible outcomes of the present situation endangers the character with whom the reader identifies.

symbol: "something that is itself and also stands for something else . . . [as] a flag is a piece of colored cloth that stands for country" [C. Hugh Holman and William Harmon, *A Handbook to Literature*, 6th ed. (New York: Macmillan, 1992), p. 466].

tag: a phrase such as "he said" or "she thought" that marks a given phrase as a quotation of a character's speech or thought.

target of irony: the person or thing ironized.

telling: narration in which the voice of a narrator seems clearly audible (as opposed to "showing").

text: a piece of writing or other communication that is self-contained and has "closure."

theme: a real-world concept or idea that, in narrative fiction, is communicated by means of fictional events, characters, and settings.

thesis: an assertion or argument about the real world that, in narrative fiction, is communicated by means of fictional events and characters.

trait: a physical, psychological, or moral quality of a character.

unreliable narration: a narration that seems suspicious or otherwise at odds with what really happened in the story as the reader infers it. Insofar as a narrator is unreliable, he or she is ironized by the implied author.

verisimilitude: truth-seeming or the semblance of truth (as opposed to literal truth).

witness-narrator: an internal I-narrator who is not the protagonist.

Acknowledgments

Ama Ata Aidoo, "Certain Winds from the South." © by Ama Ata Aidoo 1970. The story was first published in "Black Orpheus." Reprinted by kind permission of the author and of Shelley Power Literary Agency Ltd.

Margaret Atwood, "The Sin Eater," from DANCING GIRLS. Copyright © 1977, 1982 by O. W. Toad, Ltd. Reprinted by permission of Simon & Schuster, Inc.

Isaac Babel, "How It Was Done in Odessa." Reprinted by permission of S. G. Phillips, Inc. from THE COLLECTED STORIES OF ISAAC BABEL. Copyright © 1955 by S. G. Phillips, Inc.

James Baldwin, "The Rockpile," from GOING TO MEET THE MAN by James Baldwin. Copyright 1948, 1951, 1957, 1958, 1960. Used by permission of Doubleday, a division of Bantam Doubleday Dell Publishing Group, Inc.

John Barth, "Lost in the Funhouse," copyright © 1967 by The Atlantic Monthly Company, from LOST IN THE FUNHOUSE by John Barth. Used by permission of Doubleday, a division of Bantam Doubleday Dell Publishing Group, Inc.

Donald Barthelme, "Me and Miss Mandible," from SIXTY STORIES. Copyright 1981 by Donald Barthelme, reprinted with the permission of Wylie, Aitken & Stone, Inc.

Ann Beattie, "A Reasonable Man." From SECRETS AND SURPRISES by Ann Beattie. Copyright © 1976, 1977, 1978 by Ann Beattie. Reprinted by permission of Random House, Inc.

Jorge Luis Borges, "The Garden of Forking Paths," translated by Helen Temple and Ruthven Todd from FICCIONES. Copyright © 1962 by Grove Press, Inc.; Renewed © 1990 by Grove Weidenfeld. Used by permission of Grove Press, Inc.

Elizabeth Bowen, "Careless Talk." From THE COLLECTED STORIES OF ELIZABETH BOWEN by Elizabeth Bowen. Copyright © 1981 by Curtis Brown Ltd., Literary Executors of the Estate of Elizabeth Bowen. Reprinted by permission of Alfred A. Knopf, Inc.

Italo Calvino, "Big Fish, Little Fish" from *Difficult Loves* by Italo Calvino; copyright 1949 by Giulio Einaudi editore, Torino; copyright © 1958 by Giulio Einaudi editore s.p.a., Torino; English translation copyright © 1984 by Harcourt Brace Jovanovich, Inc.; reprinted by permission of Harcourt Brace Jovanovich, Inc.

Albert Camus, "The Guest." From EXILE AND THE KINGDOM by Albert Camus, trans., J. O'Brien. Copyright © 1957, 1958 by Alfred A. Knopf, Inc. Reprinted by permission of the publisher.

Anton Chekhov, "The Darling." From THE DARLING AND OTHER STORIES by Anton Chekhov, translated from the Russian by Constance Garnett (New York: Macmillan, 1916).

Colette, "The Hand" from THE COLLECTED STORIES by Colette, edited by Robert Phelps. Translation copyright © 1957, 1966, 1983 by Farrar, Straus and Giroux, Inc. Reprinted by permission of Farrar, Straus and Giroux, Inc.

Julio Cortázar, "Continuity of Parks." From END OF THE GAME AND OTHER STORIES by Julio Cortázar. Copyright © 1967 by Random House, Inc. Reprinted by permission of Pantheon Books, a division of Random House, Inc.

Julio Cortázar, "Idols of the Cyclades." From END OF THE GAME AND OTHER STORIES by Julio Cortázar. Copyright © 1967 by Random House, Inc. Reprinted by permission of Pantheon Books, a division of Random House, Inc.

Isak Dinesen, "The Ring." From ANECDOTES of DESTINY by Isak Dinesen. Copyright © 1958 by Isak Dinesen. Reprinted by permission of Random House, Inc.

Fyodor Doestoevsky, "Polzunkov." From WHITE NIGHTS AND OTHER STORIES by Fyodor Doestoevsky, translated from the Russian by Constance Garnett (New York: Macmillan, 1918).

Ralph Ellison, "The Battle Royal." From INVISIBLE MAN by Ralph Ellison. Copyright © 1948 by Ralph Ellison. Reprinted by permission of Random House, Inc.

William Faulkner, "Delta Autumn." From UNCOLLECTED STORIES OF WILLIAM FAULKNER by William Faulkner. Copyright © 1942 by William Faulkner. Reprinted by permission of Random House, Inc.

Gabriel Garcia Márquez, "Monologue of Isabel Watching It Rain in Macondo" from COLLECTED STORIES by Gabriel Garcia Márquez.

by permission of The Putnam Publishing Group from THE JOY LUCK CLUB by Amy Tan. Copyright © 1989 by Amy Tan.

Kurt Vonnegut, "Harrison Bergeron" by Kurt Vonnegut, from WELCOME TO THE MONKEY HOUSE by Kurt Vonnegut, Jr. Copyright © 1961 by Kurt Vonnegut Jr. Used by permission of Dell Books, a division of Bantam Doubleday Dell Publishing Group, Inc.

Alice Walker, "The Flowers" from *In Love & Trouble: Stories of Black Women*, copyright © 1973 by Alice Walker, reprinted by permission of Harcourt Brace Jovanovich, Inc.

Eudora Welty, "Why I Live at the P.O." from *A Curtain of Green and Other Stories*, copyright 1941 and renewed 1969 by Eudora Welty, reprinted by permission of Harcourt Brace Jovanovich, Inc.

Edith Wharton, "Roman Fever," from ROMAN FEVER AND OTHER STORIES. Reprinted with permission of Charles Scribner's Sons, an imprint of Macmillan Publishing Company, from ROMAN FEVER AND OTHER STORIES by Edith Wharton. Copyright 1934 Liberty Magazine, renewed © 1962 William R. Tyler.

Virginia Woolf, "Kew Gardens" from *A Haunted House and Other Stories*, copyright 1944 and renewed 1972 by Harcourt Brace Jovanovich, Inc., reprinted by permission of the publisher.

Index

637